LETTERS OF JAMES JOYCE

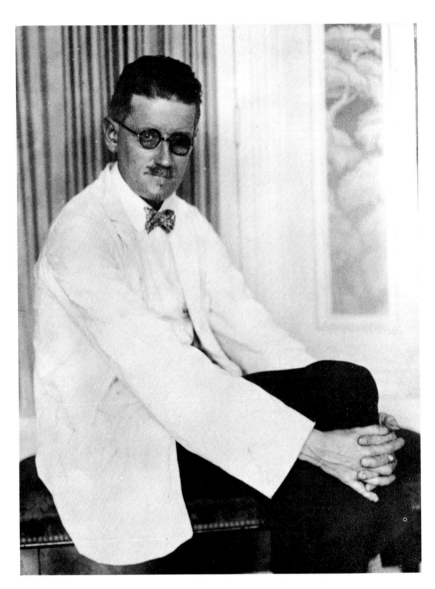

James Joyce in 1930. *Photograph by Ruth Asch.*

Letters of
JAMES
JOYCE

Volumes II *and* III

---

edited by RICHARD ELLMANN

VOLUME III

New York · THE VIKING PRESS

First published in 1966 by The Viking Press, Inc.
625 Madison Avenue, New York, N.Y. 10022

Library of Congress catalog card number: 57-5129
Printed in U.S.A. by Vail-Ballou Press, Inc.

CONTENTS

Contents xi

ILLUSTRATIONS

Frontispiece

James Joyce in 1930. *Photograph by Ruth Asch. Courtesy of Mrs Adaline Glasheen.*

Following page 96

Following page 192

18. Joyce photographed by Sylvia Beach on Bloomsday, 1925.
19. Joyce at Scheveningen, 1927.
20. Nora Joyce, 1920s.
21. Lucia Joyce with two other dancers.
22. Samuel Beckett in Paris, 1928. *Courtesy of S. Beckett.*
23. Drawing of Joyce by Wyndham Lewis, 1921. *Courtesy of the late Harriet Shaw Weaver.*
24. Portrait of Joyce by Patrick Tuohy, 1924.
25. Drawing of Joyce by Brancusi, 1929.
26. Drawing of Joyce by his daughter, Lucia, about 1930.
27. Scott Fitzgerald's sketch of a dinner party with Joyce, 1928.
28. Joyce with Stuart and Moune Gilbert.
29. The Joyces and Lucia with the Gilberts in Strasbourg, 1928. *Courtesy of Stuart Gilbert.*
30. The '*Déjeuner* Ulysse' at Hotel Léopold, Les Vaux-de-Cernay, 27 June 1929.

Following page 224

31. Joyce with the tenor John Sullivan.
32. Helen Kastor Joyce. *Courtesy of David Fleischman.*
33. David Fleischman, Helen Joyce's son by her first marriage.
34. Helen Fleischman, George, Nora, and James Joyce, Paul Ruggiero, and Frau Borach in Zurich, May 1930. *Courtesy of Paul Ruggiero.*
35. Joyce, Paul Léon, and C. P. Curran in Paris. *Courtesy of Mme Lucie Léon.*
36. Lucie Léon, about 1930. *Courtesy of Mme Léon.*
37. Paul Léon. *Courtesy of Mme Léon.*
38. A recent photograph of Mrs Maria Jolas. *Courtesy of Mrs Jolas.*
39. Maria and Eugene Jolas with their children and a governess, 1932. *Courtesy of Mrs Jolas.*
40. B. W. Huebsch, in a late photograph.
41. Joyce and Philippe Soupault.
42. Joyce with Augustus John, 1930.
43. The Joyces with their solicitor on their marriage day, London, 4 July 1931.
44. Joyce and his wife, 1930s.

Following page 480

45. James Joyce in the late 1930s. *Photograph by David Fleischman.*
46. Nora Joyce on the same afternoon. *Photograph by David Fleischman.*
47. Stephen Joyce.
48. Helen, Stephen, George, and James Joyce.
49. A series of views of Joyce with members of his family, from a home movie. *Courtesy of Robert Kastor.*
50. Herbert Gorman with Nora and James Joyce, 1930s.
51. Throwaway about the pleasure steamer *John Joyce.*
52. Nora Joyce with two friends at Beaugency. *Courtesy of Mme Lucie Léon.*
53. Daniel Brody, Joyce's publisher in Switzerland, with Hermann Broch.
54. Joyce with Carola Giedion-Welcker, Lucerne, 1935.
55. Joyce's funeral in Zurich. *Courtesy of Ferry Radax.*
56. Joyce's grave in the Fluntern Cemetery, Zurich. *Courtesy of Daniel Brody.*
57. Nora Joyce's grave. *Courtesy of Fritz Senn.*
58. Death mask of Joyce.

PHOTOGRAPHIC CREDITS: In addition to the individuals acknowledged above, thanks are due to the following for photographs and documents reproduced in this volume: *Cornell University Library* 9; *Lockwood Memorial Library, University of Buffalo*, 1, 6, 7, 11, 16, 18, 20, 21, 24, 25, 26, 28, 30, 31, 41, 42, 43, 44, 48; *Princeton University Library (Sylvia Beach Collection)*, 10, 19, 40; *Southern Illinois University Library*, 47, 50. *Jack Oppenheim* copied the photograph for 8.

Part IV

PARIS

1920-39

Paris (1920-39)

To live in Pola had been embarrassing for Joyce, to live in Rome irritating, to live in Trieste quaint but inconvenient. After those cities Zurich had been at least safe and unavoidable. To live in Paris came for a time suspiciously close to being pleasant. A pervasive enthusiasm for artistic change predisposed many Frenchmen to welcome him. Then too, the city was full of expatriates and visitors, some of them happily Irish, and most of them also ready to be attracted by original endeavour. Joyce complained outwardly, but inwardly approved his new situation. Though he shunned public life, there was some satisfaction in knowing that he was a point of civic interest, to be gestured at or whispered about as he stepped elegantly down the street. He sheltered himself behind silence on literary matters, a silence that became formidable, and behind a porous candour about his personal problems of money, children, and health. So he rebuffed with the one and absorbed with the other.

Thanks to Ezra Pound and to Pound's friends, Joyce found an audience ready for him. There was immediate talk of translating his books, of producing *Exiles* on the French stage, of writing articles about him. One admirer lent him a flat free of charge for the summer and early fall, another gave him an extra bed and a writing table, a third furnished a warm overcoat. Secretly encouraged, Joyce applied himself to both his literary task of finishing *Ulysses* and his practical one of having it published under suitable auspices. All attempts to find a publisher in England or the United States proved unavailing, but his meeting with Sylvia Beach on 11 July 1920, three days after his arrival in Paris, led ultimately to a solution. Miss Beach, an American woman, timidly offered, in April 1921, to publish *Ulysses* herself under the imprint of her Paris bookshop, Shakespeare and Company. Joyce at once consented.

Miss Beach was aided by her friend Adrienne Monnier, whose bookshop, the Maison des Amis des Livres, was on the rue de l'Odéon across from her own. They waged a literary campaign for Joyce which lasted for more than a year before *Ulysses* was in print. They enlisted the support of virtually everyone who ventured into their street, particularly of Valery Larbaud, whose reputation as a writer, translator, and critic of taste and talent was already secure. Larbaud gave a public lecture on *Ulysses* at Mlle Monnier's bookshop on 7 December 1921, two months before publication, and his knowledgeable endorsement encouraged a flow of advance subscriptions to Shakespeare and Company.

Ulysses appeared at last on Joyce's fortieth birthday, 2 February 1922. He was greatly agitated by the event and determined that publication in Paris should not retard the acceptance of his book in England and the United States. At first he suspected a boycott by reviewers; when articles began to appear, he followed them with nervous passion, thanked the critics by letter, thought up devices to keep the book before the public, coaxed his friends and badgered acquaintances into helping it. The greatness of *Ulysses* would have established itself, but Joyce felt compelled to accelerate its recognition whenever, wherever he could.

During this period his home life remained unsettled. After leaving the flat which had been loaned to him until November, 1920, he allowed himself to drift without conviction from one makeshift arrangement to another, as if reluctant to commit himself to anything permanent. Nora Joyce's temper was frayed by this haphazard life, and she felt too little interest in *Ulysses* to read it. Against her husband's wishes she took her children to see her family in Galway on 1 April 1922. This visit turned out to be ill-timed, for the Irish Civil War flamed up in the west of Ireland; they had to leave at once and return to Paris. The effect of this incident was to make Joyce even more dependent upon his wife's adherence than in the past, and he was gratified when she concessively agreed to read some of *Ulysses* a few months later. His relations with Nora were often tense during the rest of his life, but she never again seriously considered leaving him. The couple went so far as to be legally married in London on 4 July 1931, though this ceremony was chiefly to secure his family in their rights to his property.

The subject of the book that was to follow *Ulysses* had probably begun to grow in Joyce's mind before *Ulysses* was finished, since one of the first things he did was to sort out unused notes left from the earlier book. On 10 March 1923, a month after he had done this, he began to write *Finnegans Wake*. The title was confided to his wife and to no one else; it referred both to the hod carrier of the ballad, who was miraculously resurrected by the whisky at his wake, and to the tough, vegetable recurrence of human life and misbehaviour. The book was to combine the affirmation of life, which he had always defined as the central function of literature, with the scepticism about particular living beings which had always been natural to him. It was to be alternately lyrical and combative or satirical, and always comic. To avoid and transcend a 'goahead plot', it was to be based upon a theory of cyclical recurrence which insisted on the typical character of every particular, whether person or incident.

Joyce must have known from the start that his new book would not be easy to read, for he intended it to be a night view of man's life, as *Ulysses* had been a day view. He would use the techniques of the dream, since in dreams all ages become one, attempts at concealment fail to convince, social and conventional barriers disappear. 'Wideawake language' and 'cutandry' grammar would not serve him; to represent night accurately Joyce thought he must descend to the makinghouse of language below the conscious choice of settled words. He determined upon the pun, often multilingual, as a linguistic mixture which could suggest the nighttime merging of the particular and the typical, of the struggle for expression and the forms of speech. As in his other books, the immediate focus would be on a family as the basic human group, and the flux of history would coalesce momentarily in the lives of the Earwicker family at Chapelizod near Dublin.

The composition of *Finnegans Wake* was harassed by two major impediments. The first was Joyce's eye trouble, which began again on his arrival in Paris. He suffered from a painful inflammation of the iris, and his vision was blurred by the formation of successive cataracts. The result was that he submitted to a series of ten operations in addition to the one he had already undergone in Zurich. These took place on 3, 15?, and 28 April 1923, 10 June 1924, 29 November 1924, 15? April 1925, 8 December 1925, 12 December 1925, June 1926, and 15 May 1930. The last of these, the only one performed by Professor Alfred Vogt of Zurich, proved fairly successful; but Joyce continued to have severe eye attacks and was never free of anxiety on the score of possible future operations.

The second major trouble was the response of his friends to *Finnegans Wake*. Some parts of the book came into existence easily and were published in preliminary form in magazines: in Ford Madox Ford's *transatlantic review* (April 1924), T. S. Eliot's *Criterion* (July 1925), Adrienne Monnier's *Navire d'argent* (October 1925), Ernest Walsh's *This Quarter* (Autumn–Winter 1925–1926), and then in Eugene and Maria Jolas's *transition* (April 1927—April–May 1938). As the first of these appeared, Joyce's friends waited indulgently for the clarity to come. But when the book gave evidence of being written throughout in 'no language', they exchanged questioning looks and slowly began to express their doubts to Joyce himself. His brother denounced the 'drivelling rigmarole' as early as 1924, Ezra Pound wrote on 1 November 1926 that he could make nothing of the new work, Miss Weaver wondered on 4 February 1927 if he were not wasting his genius, Wyndham Lewis published an attack on all Joyce's writings later in this year.

Joyce was not so indifferent as might be supposed; he wrote hurt letters asking for encouragement and, with more vigour, sought new supporters. He worked into his fable, 'The Ondt and the Gracehoper,' afterwards pp. 414–19 of *Finnegans Wake*, a defence of his book against Lewis; he sampled Pound's judgment in other literary matters in order to point out several obvious lapses of taste; he instructed Miss Weaver both by letter and personally in his method and purpose; he published, on 7 July 1927, *Pomes Penyeach*, a collection of his later verse, as evidence that he could be grammatically sane if he chose. In May 1929 a group of his friends, marshalled by him, published a defence of his book entitled, with mock modesty that was like pretentiousness, *Our Exagmination round his Factification for Incamination of Work in Progress*. In July of this year he formally proposed to James Stephens, his fellow Dubliner, that Stephens complete the book for him, but Stephens conceived the tactful reply that, though he was willing to try, he was sure Joyce would finish it himself. He added that *Anna Livia Plurabelle*, which had been published in book form in 1928, was 'the greatest prose ever written by a man'.

The result of these tearings and mendings was a realignment of Joyce's acquaintance. His relationship with Miss Weaver was the least strained; but that with Pound became merely polite, and that with Lewis was now mutually distrustful. Even Sylvia Beach seems to have secretly flagged in her literary loyalty. A group of new friends, readier for innovation, offered a more unqualified allegiance; these were Eugene and Maria Jolas, Paul and Lucy Léon, Stuart and Moune Gilbert, Samuel Beckett, Louis Gillet, Nino Frank, and others for short periods.

In a mood of self-commiseration, Joyce fled his own affairs to embrace the cause of an Irish-French opera singer, John Sullivan, whose immense tenor voice astounded him and whose failure to secure engagements worthy of his talent seemed a parallel of his own plight. He was convinced that established cliques were working against Sullivan as against himself, and threw himself fanatically into securing Sullivan adequate recognition. This campaign began in November 1929, and did not taper off until after 1931. It gradually became clear to Joyce, as it was already to Sullivan, that the voice was losing some of its quality, but Joyce obstinately continued to work up interest in his friend.

He was recalled from his 'Sullivanizing' of the early 'thirties by some unexpected incidents in his family. The first was the marriage of his son George, on 10 December 1931, to Helen Kastor Fleischman. Next came his father's death in Dublin on 29 December 1931, a great grief which however was lightened somewhat for Joyce by the birth of his grandson, Stephen James Joyce, on 15 February 1932. But the principal family trouble came from his daughter, Lucia, who in 1932 showed signs of the schizophrenia which had presumably begun during her girlhood, but had been dismissed by her parents as childish eccentricity. The next seven years of Joyce's life were pervaded by a frantic and unhappily futile effort to cure her by every means known to medicine as well as by simples of his own devising. He felt in some sense responsible for her condition, and refused to accept any diagnosis which did not promise hope. It seemed to him that her mind was like his own, and he tried to find evidence in her writing and in her drawing of unrecognised talent. Lucia spent long and short periods in sanitariums and mental hospitals, between which she would return to stay with her parents until some incident occurred which made it necessary she be sent away again. Joyce found doctors to give her glandular treatments, others to inject sea water, others to try psychotherapy; he sent her on visits to friends in Switzerland, England, and even Ireland. The last in 1935 was disastrous: she grew worse rather than better. He placed her next in the care of Miss Weaver and a nurse in England, with a doctor attempting a new cure; when this failed, he brought her to France, where she stayed with Mrs Jolas; ultimately even Joyce conceded she must be put into a *maison de santé* near Paris. There he continued to visit her, he wrote letters to her, he refused to give up hope that she was getting better. Some of his friends felt he was too zealous in her behalf, but his family feeling had always been intense and now found full and open expression.

During the nineteen-thirties Joyce moved forward by fits and starts with *Finnegans Wake*. The outlines of the book were clear to him, but the interconnections had to be worded, the new linguistic medium had to be consistent and of one piece, and a few chapters were still to be written. At last after sixteen years he completed the book in 1938, and it was published on 4 May 1939.

The response to *Finnegans Wake* discontented him, and when war was declared in September he saw it as a force which might push his book into oblivion. A fresher anxiety was for Lucia, who had to be moved with the other occupants of her *maison de santé* to safer quarters at Pornichet near La Baule. Joyce and his wife made sure of her transfer by going there in September 1939. They returned to Paris in October, to find that George's wife had suffered a breakdown. They felt compelled to take charge of Stephen Joyce by sending him to Mrs Jolas's Ecole Bilingue, which had been moved from Neuilly to a village near Vichy called Saint-Gérand-le-Puy in what was later Unoccupied France. Joyce and his wife decided to follow their grandson there. After nineteen years in Paris they left the city and reached S. Gérand on 24 December 1939. Their affairs were in dismal confusion.

To Stanislaus Joyce (Postcard)   MS. Cornell

12 July 1920   *rue de l'Université 9, Paris*

Dear Stannie: MSS came today and sent them on. Am anxious to know
if you have safely the envelope left on the credenza with documents.
French translation of novel begins in *L'Action*[1] 1 August. Book publication when serial finished. Lugné Poe,[2] manager *Odéon* now of *L'Oeuvre*
considering *Exiles* for production. Translator and publisher for this
also found.[3] Admirer of mine has placed 3 room flat, furnished, at my
disposal for three months.[4] Address: rue de l'Assomption, 5, I, Passy,
Paris. Please let me know about documents. Stopped in Venice two
days. Last moment met D. casually. He promised to call at hotel and
wire Gattorno Milan for rooms but never turned up after. Linati
had rooms ready but the damned post delayed his letter. However we
found them. No stop in Switzerland but stayed night in Dijon. Saluti
a tutti. Ask Frank if he wants French assignats of the revolution
period.   JIM

To Alessandro Francini Bruni (Postcard)   MS. Francini

19 July 1920   *rue de l'Assomption 5, I, Passy, Paris*

Caro Francini: Grazie della lettera. Sto all'indirizzo qui sotto. Un
ammiratrice (che traduce attualmente il mio romanzo, la 1ᵃ puntata
uscirà in agosto) ha posto a mia disposizione gratis un quartiere
ammobiliato di 3 stanze. È possibile che la commedia sarà rappresentata
al Théâtre de l'Oeuvre. Lugné Poë la legge. La vita è caretta ma la
metà di Trieste almeno. Giorgio probabilmente entrerà per 3 mesi in un

---

[1] This publication, arranged by the editor of *L'Action*, Florent Fels, never came
about.

[2] Aurélien-Marie Lugné-Poë (1869–1940), French actor and play producer, founded
the Théâtre de l'Oeuvre in Paris in 1893.

[3] Jenny Serruys (later Mrs William Aspenwall Bradley) (b. 1886 in Belgium) had
agreed to translate *Exiles*. A literary agent in Paris, she met Joyce through Ezra
Pound.

[4] Mme Ludmila Bloch-Savitsky (1881–1957), who translated *A Portrait of the Artist*
into French as *Dedalus*, lent Joyce the flat he describes, at rue de l'Assomption 5. He
stayed there from 15 July to 1 November 1920.

ufficio—non tanto per lucro quanto per non annoiarsi troppo. Circe
progredisce di nuovo. Tanti saluti a te ed alla tua famiglia

JAMES JOYCE[1]

From EZRA POUND to JENNY SERRUYS   MS. Bradley

Postmark 20 July 1920   *3 Rue de Beaune*

Chère et Delicieuse, Yes, I know he is a great author; in fact the best
prose author we have, since James (Henry) and Hardy.

But still, and for Christ's sake, get him a bed for his too large son to
sleep on and some (if possible) bedding.

This prayer after a day's hell hunting visas—and I also a respectable
author whose soul—such as it is—vale et me ama—should not be
dragged down to a question of sheets and trucklebeds for the errors
J.J.'s his misspent premalthusian youth Benedictions,   E.P.

To JENNY SERRUYS   MS. Bradley

22 July 1920   *rue de l'Assomption 5, I, Passy, Paris*

Madame Je vous envoie ci-inclus quelques extraits des critiques de
mon roman et de la pièce aussi bien que l'histoire (en forme de lettre
publique) du livre de nouvelles. Mr Pound est parti hier matin et je l'ai
prié de vous envoyer directement de Londres un exemplaire du
'Portrait'.

Je vous remercie de votre interêt bienveillant et vous prie d'agréer
l'assurance de ma parfaite consideration.   JAMES JOYCE[2]

---

[1] (Translation)

'Dear Francini: Thank you for your letter. I am staying at the address given below.
A female admirer of mine (who is at the moment translating my novel, the first instalment of which will appear in August), has placed at my disposal without charge a
furnished 3-room flat. It is possible that the comedy will be produced at the Théâtre de
l'Oeuvre. Lugné-Poë is reading it. Living is expensive but only half as high as Trieste,
at least. Giorgio is probably going into an office for 3 months not so much for the
money as to avoid getting too bored. Circe is making progress once more. My best
wishes to you and your family.   James Joyce'

[2] (Translation)

'Madame I send you herewith several extracts from reviews of my novel and of the
play [*Exiles*] as well as the history (in the form of a public letter) ['A Curious History']
of the book of stories. Mr Pound left yesterday morning and I asked him to send you
directly from London a copy of *A Portrait*.

I thank you for your benevolent interest and offer my compliments.   James Joyce'

To STANISLAUS JOYCE with a note   MS. Cornell
to FRANTISEK SCHAUREK

25 July 1920   *rue de l'Assomption 5, I, Passy, Paris*

Dear Stannie,   MSS of Ulysses arrived safely and I sent them on.
Odyssey very much in the air here. Anatole France is writing *Le
Cyclope*,[1] G. Fauré the musician an opera *Penelope*.[2] Giraudoux has
written Elpenor (Paddy Dignam).[3] Guillaume Apollinaire *Les Mamelles
de Tirésias*.[4] I hope during the week to have definite news about
translations of novel and play. First chapter of former nearly finished.
The translator, a Madame Bloch, put this flat at my disposal, free, for
three months. She has two. Pound wanted to get the Duchess of
Marlborough[5] to apply for the position vacated by Mrs M.[6] but her
bloody old father W K Vanderbilt[7] died here in the next street to us the
day before yesterday, very inconsiderately, I think. It is not impossible
that Giorgio will get some kind of temporary work to keep him from
yawning in the office of the brother-in-law of my other translator (of the
play) Mlle. Jeanne Serruys. Lugné Poe is to give his decision next
Friday about putting it on at L'Oeuvre. Called to Burberry's here who
are laying in autumn and winter stocks.[8]

As regards the revolver university,[9] perhaps the place is closed, in
which then there is 850 or 1000 lire there for me. I forget which. Anyway give Francini 100 of it and ask Frank to have made out a cheque
(not crossed to me on their Paris bankers for the equivalent of the rest
in French franks—which please send on to me registered and express.
I enclose a letter for him. If you get this on Wednesday, say, you might
call to school and see Benedetti. The best time is between 12.30 and 2 so
that if the place is closed for repairs you can get the cash or, if not,
arrange to get it on Saturday and Frank can prepare the cheque on
Friday.

[1] Anatole France (1844–1924) never finished this satire, which he planned late in life.
[2] Gabriel Urbain Fauré (1835–1924), French composer and organist, had written an
opera, *Pénélope*, in 1913. It was based on a poem by René Fauchois.
[3] Jean Giraudoux (1882–1944), *Elpénor* (Paris, 1919).
[4] Guillaume Apollinaire (1880–1918), *Les Mamelles de Tirésias*, was first produced on
14 June 1917.
[5] The Duchess of Marlborough (1877–1921), née Consuelo Vanderbilt, was known for
her patronage of the arts.
[6] Edith Rockefeller McCormick.
[7] William Kissam Vanderbilt (1849–1920), the millionaire financier, died on 22 July.
[8] Stanislaus Joyce, when his brother was leaving Trieste, gave him some money to
send him a Burberry coat. He never received it.
[9] A pun on the Scuola Revoltella di Commercio, which was in process of becoming a
university.

We read about the troubles in Trieste. Those in Ireland are still worse. I regretted to observe the barometric depression to which you allude.[1] The perusal of my innocent pages is the only dispeller of illusions which repays the money invested. Madam Circe advances regally towards her completion after which I hope to join a tennis club.[2]

Jim

Caro Frank: Vuoi farmi il piacere di far prepare [sic] uno chèque su Parigi (*non sbarrato*) per l'importo in franchi francesi equivalente a 750 lire italiane. Stannie ti rimetterà il denaro che deve incassare alla scuola per me. Grazie d'anticipo.

Tempo bellissimo qui ed un quartiere ammobiliato gratis. Siamo vicini al bosco di Bologna d'una parte ed alla Senna dell'altra. Spero che Eileen si sia rimessa della sua indisposizione. Salutamela—nonche le bambine.

Non posso scrivere con questa vanga di penna. Fammi sapere se vuoi degli *assignats* del periodo della rivoluzione francese. Saluti cordiali

Jim[3]

To Claud W. Sykes (Postcard)   MS. Yale

29 July 1920   *rue de l'Assomption 5, I, Passy, Paris*

Dear Mr Sykes: Please write here and send back *Oxen of the Sun* when read. I remain here with my family for 2 or 3 months to write *Circe*. I wrote you 2 days ago to Manchester. Your card of 16 reached me here today Sincerely yours   James Joyce

---

[1] Stanislaus Joyce had written his brother on 6 July 1920 to apologize for not being 'in a very sociable mood during your stay here'. (MS. Private)

[2] Joyce was at this time wearing a pair of tennis shoes.

[3] (Translation)

'Dear Frank: Would you do me the favour of having a cheque made out on Paris (not crossed) for the sum in French francs equivalent to 750 Italian lire. Stannie will remit you the money which he is to collect at the school for me. Thanks in advance.

Lovely weather here and a furnished flat for nothing. We are close by the Bois de Boulogne on one side and the Seine on the other. I hope Eileen has recovered from her indisposition. Greet her for me—and the children too.

I can't write with this spade of a pen. Let me know if you would like some *assignats* of the period of the French Revolution. Cordial greetings   Jim'

To EZRA POUND   MS. Yale

31 July 1920   *rue de l'Assomption 5, I, Passy, Paris*

Dear Pound: Messrs Box and Cox,[1] interviewed by you, sent me three days ago with a much-ado-about-nothing letter a crossed cheque (£10) drawn by Box on Cox which, as I foresaw, no bank in Paris would touch with a 40 foot pole. Finally Miss Beach[2] put it into her account and paid me the money—470 frs. A series of articles ought to appear in the press, possibly by cable also to U.S.A. e.g.: Joyce gets Large Haul. Prompt Pinker Saves Desperate Dedalus. Glut of Greenbacks for Poet in Poverty. The enclosed letter from Huebsch is, I think, dubious; and his £25 on account of royalties on *Ulysses* seems to me a very remote possibility. He will probably remit £9.19.0 royalties to date, and Pinker will write asking me to send him a P.O. for 1/- due by me to him in excess of advance.

26 was Lucia's birthday: 27 Giorgio's. Not having received any money I was sitting gloomily silent on the latter day when Mr Rodker arrived. Hearing my story Mrs Rodker[3] and he very kindly invited this whole vagabond family out to dinner which was providential. Goll,[4] whom I knew in Zurich, called. He wants books for a modern anthology and talked of buying German rights of *Portrait* for 7-francs sometime, if possible, perhaps. I heard no more about the bed so I wrote to Bradley[5] but had no answer. I heard and saw no more of the many lucky mortals who made my acquaintance here. I suspect that the pleasure my exhilarating company gave them will last for the rest of their natural existences. Except Vanderpyl.[6] He says that Fels[7] is hopelessly in debt, *Action* doomed to disappear etc. but Mrs Bloch has already done the first chapter.

[1] James B. Pinker is meant. The allusion is to *Box and Cox* (1867), the operetta by F. Burnand and Sir Arthur Sullivan, and to the farce of the same name (1847) by J. M. Morton.

[2] Sylvia Beach (1887–1962), the famous bookseller and publisher of *Ulysses*, met Joyce at the house of André Spire on 11 July 1920. She had opened her bookshop, Shakespeare and Company, at 8 rue Dupuytren in November 1919, then moved during the summer of 1921 to 12 rue de l'Odéon.

[3] Mrs John Rodker (b. 1909) was a daughter of Mme Ludmila Bloch-Savitsky.

[4] Ivan Goll (1891–1950), French poet. He lived in Switzerland during the first World War, and met Joyce during that time.

[5] William Aspenwall Bradley (1878–1939), an American writer, editor, and translator. As a publisher's representative in Paris, Bradley was able to bring some of the best French writers to American notice. He married Jenny Serruys in November 1921.

[6] Fritz Vanderpyl, Belgian poet, novelist, and critic, was born in the Hague in 1876. He has lived in Paris since 1899, and from 1919 to 1940 was art critic of the *Petit Parisien*. His novel, *Marsden Stanton à Paris* (Paris, 1916), aroused much interest among younger writers in England when it appeared.

[7] See II, p. 450, n. 4. Unless specified as here, page references are to Volume III.

As regards the information concerning the intelligent government official (who should go with Pinker as secretary to the Nith Office when Rumbold is made king of Neland) I believe the instigation came direct from the consul in Zurich, Mr Percy Bennett, at present in Panama. As no one has taken any steps to remind him that he is a public servant he can sleep peacefully. The typescript could not have seemed suspicious except *Sirens* which was published long after the armistice.[1] And as for said government official if he has no money to give let me never hear of him again in this life or the next. Sincerely yours   JAMES JOYCE

P.S. of Quinn. Nothing. Rien. Nichts. E poi nulla.

To JENNY SERRUYS   MS. Bradley

5 August 1920   *rue de l'Assomption 5, I, Passy, Paris*

Chere Madame: Je vous remercie de votre aide bienveillant[2] et regrette que mes conditions actuelles m'ont obligé à vous importuner à mon égard [?] à un temps si critique. J'espère que la santé de votre mère soit maintenant rétablie à tel point de ne vous créer plus d'inquiétude.

Vous m'avez fait aussi un grand plaisir en me prêtant le livre[3] de M. Giraudoux que je vais lire avec beaucoup d'interêt.

En attendant le plaisir de vous revoir je vous prie d'agréer, chère madame, avec mes remerciements renouvelés, l'assurance de ma parfaite considération.   JAMES JOYCE[4]

[1] Pound had heard that British government censors had been suspicious, during the war, that the manuscript of *Ulysses* was an enemy cipher.

[2] Mlle Serruys had lent Joyce a portable bed, and promised him some more sheets and probably a table in a few days' time.

[3] Evidently *Elpénor*.

[4] (Translation)
'Dear Madame: I thank you for your benevolent help and regret that my present situation has obliged me to inconvenience you with my concerns at such a troubled moment. I hope that your mother's health has now improved to the point where it no longer gives you cause for concern.

You have also given me great pleasure in lending me M. Giraudoux's book which I shall read with much interest.

Awaiting the pleasure of seeing you again, I beg you to accept, dear madame, with my renewed thanks, the assurance of my esteem.   James Joyce'

From T. S. ELIOT[1]   MS. Buffalo

11 August 1920   *18 Crawford Mansions, Crawford Street, W.1*

Dear Mr. Joyce, Ezra Pound has given me a package[2] for you. I shall be
in Paris Sunday the 15th and shall be leaving on Monday. I shall be at
the Hotel de l'Élysée, 3 rue de Beaune, where Pound was. *I hope you can
dine with me that evening. Please*
Can you meet me there about 6.30, or up to 7? You can take the parcel
and I should very much like to meet you, at last.

    You won't have time to answer. But please come. Sincerely yours
                                               T. S. ELIOT

To HENRY DAVRAY[3]

11 August 1920   *rue de l'Assomption 5, I, Passy, Paris*

Cher Monsieur Davray: Je suis ici depuis quelque temps et compte y
rester plusieurs mois pour écrire les derniers chapitres de mon nouveau
livre *Ulysse*. En attendant Mme Ludmila Savitsky (une des collabora-
teurs de votre revue Anglo-française—elle a publié des vers et une
étude sur la poésie du M. Aldington) a traduit en français mon roman
A Portrait of the Artist as a Young Man. On pense à l'offrir en premier
lieu au *Mercure de France* en publication mensuelle (ou bi-mensuelle?)
et tant Mme Savitsky que les autres écrivains qui sont au courant du
projet croient que quelques paroles de votre part à M. Valette[4]
pourraient faire tourner le bilan en mon faveur. Ayant lu et critiqué le
livre vous-même vous pouvez parler en connaissance de cause. Ce serait
du reste la troisième traduction en six mois—les autres étant la
suédoise et l'espagnole.[5] Je vous serai vraiment reconnaissant si
moyennant votre présentation le *Mercure* ouvrira les portes pour
abriter l'artiste irlandais, jeune homme.

    Agréez, cher Monsieur Davray, l'assurance de ma parfaite considéra-
tion   JAMES JOYCE[6]

[1] Eliot, who had heard a good deal about Joyce from Ezra Pound, was travelling to
Paris with Wyndham Lewis. The meeting with Joyce is described in Wyndham Lewis,
Blasting and Bombardiering (London, 1937), pp. 272–94.
    [2] Eliot did not know the contents of the package, which proved to be a pair of second-
hand shoes, sent by Pound to save Joyce from the indignity of wearing tennis shoes.
    [3] From a photostatic copy.   [4] Jacques Vallette, editor of the *Mercure de France*.
    [5] For the Swedish translation, see above, II, p. 459, n. 1; the Spanish translation, by
'Alfonso Donado' (a pseudonym of Dámaso Alonso) was not published until 1926 in
Madrid. See pp. 129–32.
    [6] (Translation)
    'Dear M. Davray: I have been here for some time and plan to remain here for
several months in order to write the last chapters of my new book *Ulysses*. Meanwhile
Mme Ludmila Savitsky (one of the contributors to your Anglo-French review—she

To Harriet Shaw Weaver   MS. British Museum

16 August 1920   *rue de l'Assomption 5, I, Passy, Paris*

Dear Miss Weaver: Many thanks for the copy of *Dublin Review*. I read the article[1] with special interest. It is curious that it was not sent on to me by the presscutting agency when it appeared. In fact I have not received anything from them for quite a long time so that perhaps I am already forgotten. I should like to know what is the decision of the printer you alluded to as Mr Rodker, to whom I spoke here, suggested another plan. He would like to read the episodes *Nausikaa* and *Oxen of the Sun* in order to estimate their length. Could you perhaps let him have them for a few days? As regards Mr Huebsch I understand that he is coming to London. His behaviour towards me lately has not been satisfactory and his attitude with regard to the book seems to me dubious. I am altogether too tired to enter into any controversy with him or anyone else about it. The final adventure *Circe* is giving me in all ways a great deal of worry. I have written the greater part of it four or five times. I am glad Ulysses had only twelve adventures. Circe [sic] herself had less trouble weaving her web than I have with her episode.

I have been asked by a Mr Vanderpyl to have a copy of my novel sent to Mr Pierre Mille, 12 Quai de Bourbon, Paris IV[e], a writer and literary critic of *Le Temps*. I daresay you have been troubled enough with requests of this kind already. Two chapters are translated and there is talk of its appearing in the *Mercure de France*. There is also talk of *Exiles* being produced in French and Italian. I have not yet received the third act of the Italian version. I understand that the Spanish and Swedish translations are coming out soon. I hope that I shall soon have definite news to send you as I dislike talk that leads nowhere.

Mr Pound introduced me to a number of people here on whom I created anything but a good impression. He did his best to work up a

has published some poems and a study of the poetry of M. Aldington) has translated into French my novel *A Portrait of the Artist as a Young Man*. We are thinking of offering it first to the *Mercure de France* for monthly (or bi-monthly?) publication and Mme Savitsky as well as the other writers who are acquainted with the project believe that a few words from you to M. Valette would turn the scales in my favour. Having read and criticized the book yourself, you can speak with a clear knowledge of the matter. This would be, by the way, the third translation in six months—the others being in Swedish and Spanish. I shall really be grateful to you if by means of your introduction the *Mercure* opens its doors to shelter the Irish artist as a young man.

Please accept, my dear M. Davray, the assurance of my deepest esteem.

James Joyce'

[1] C.C.M., 'Some Recent Books,' *Dublin Review* CLXVI.332 (January–February–March 1920) 135–38, discussing *A Portrait*, describes it as Flaubertian and a work of genius, but also finds it an extraordinary personal record of 'so sick a soul'.

reputation for my books here but whether he will be as moderately successful as he was in London remains to be seen.

Do you mean[1] that the *Oxen of the Sun* episode resembles *Hades* because the nine circles of development (enclosed between the head-piece and tailpiece of opposite chaos)[2] seem to you to be peopled by extinct beings? With kind regards sincerely yours   JAMES JOYCE

To STANISLAUS JOYCE (Postcard)   MS. Cornell

[*27 August 1920*][3]   *Paris*

The Right Heart in the Wrong Place

Of spinach and gammon
Bull's full to the crupper,
White lice and black famine
Are the mayor of Cork's[4] supper
But the pride of old Ireland
Must be damnably humbled
If a Joyce is found cleaning
The boots of a Rumbold

S.O.S.

To CLAUD W. SYKES (Postcard)   MS. Yale

[*27 August 1920*]   [*Paris*]

The Right Man in the Wrong Place

(Air: My heart's in the highlands)
The pig's in the barley,
The fat's in the fire:
Old Europe can hardly
Find twopence to buy her.

---

[1] Miss Weaver had written Joyce on 30 June 1920, about the *Oxen of the Sun*, 'I think this episode might also have been called Hades for the reading of it is like being taken the rounds of hell.' In answer to his question about her meaning, she replied, on 25 August 1920, 'I must ask you once more not to pay the slightest attention to any foolish remark I may make—which really I must give up making—if I can.' (MS. Private).

[2] In *Ulysses* Stephen Dedalus twice refers to 'the void' upon which human life is founded. P. 266 (207).

[3] The date is given on a typed copy at S. Illinois (Croessmann).

[4] Joyce was stirred by the hunger strike of Terence MacSwiney (1880–1920), Lord Mayor of Cork, in Brixton Jail. MacSwiney was arrested on 12 August 1920 for having a British cipher and other revolutionary goods in his possession. He said at his trial four days later, 'I wish to state that I will put a limit to any term of imprisonment you may impose. I have taken no food since Thursday. Whatever your government may do I shall be free, alive or dead, within a month.' He was sentenced to two years in prison. His hunger strike lasted for 73 days and ended in his death on 25 October 1920.

Jack Spratt's in his office,
Puffed, powdered and curled:
Rumbold's[1] in Warsaw—
All's right with the world.

For your next production of *Pippa Passes*   J.J.

To STANISLAUS JOYCE   MS. Cornell

Postmark 29 August 1920   *rue de l'Assomption 5, Passy, Paris*

Dear Stannie: I had a letter yesterday from Miss Weaver, saying that
she has made me a further gift of £2000 (two thousand). Will send you
particulars later. Will you ask Frank to telephone to those sons of
bitches at the Adriatica[2] (the man's name is Bruna) who have bungled
the sending of my case of books which I gave them on the 30 June? I am
much inconvenienced by their cursed mumchanciness. Giorgio has
been offered a position here in an American Trust Agency which would
develop into a secretaryship and travellership for same. The salary
would be about 200 frs (French) a month to begin with. Lucia has
become Napoleon-mad, a fact you may inform Sordina of.[3] Quinn sent
3500 francs. Huebsch is crying off *Ulysses*. Miss Weaver writes nobody
will print it. So it will be printed, it seems, in Paris and bear Mr John
Rodker's imprint as English printer. Eliot, Wyndham Lewis, Rodker
and their wives keep moving between London, Paris and the country.
Dinners and lunches are the order of the day.[4] An admirer of mine, an
American officer,[5] presents me with an army overcoat. Budgen was here
a week, gone to London. Also Mrs Sykes: and her husband is coming.
What about *Little Reviews* etc?

I enclose cutting of Lord French's latest speech—delivered in Dublin.
He has left Ireland which, being an Irishman, he refuses to annihilate.[6]
Sir Horace Rumbold, has been unanimously chosen as First Emperor of

[1] Sir Horace Rumbold became British Ambassador to Warsaw in 1919.
[2] The Società Adriatica di Spedizione, headed by Leopoldo Popper, father of Amalia
(see II, p. 262).
[3] See II, p. 300, n. 6.
[4] Wyndham Lewis describes in *Blasting and Bombardiering* how Joyce insisted upon
paying for all the meals, cabs, and tips during the meetings that they and Eliot had in
Paris.
[5] William Aspenwall Bradley.
[6] John Denton Pinkstone, 1st Earl of Ypres, Lord French (1852–1925), field marshal,
was appointed Lord-Lieutenant of Ireland in 1918, a post which he held until 30 April
1921 after the passage of the Government of Ireland Act. He took part in an All-Ireland
conference on 24 August 1920, and the *Irish Times* of the following day quotes him as
having proposed a resolution, 'That this Conference records its conviction that the policy
of the Government in Ireland is inevitably leading to civil war, and it is of paramount
importance that immediate steps be taken to secure peace in Ireland.' His speech was a
forceful statement of the same position.

Ireland. Please hang the Union Jack out of the scullery window at the exact instant when he ascends his ancestral throne of alabaster.[1] If a man named Buckley calls, asking to see His Majesty, he is on no account to be admitted.[2] By Order   JAMES

(Heb. Vat. Terg. Ex. Lut. Hosp. Litt. Angl. Pon. Max.)[3]

P.S. Ask Frank to ask that Hungarian in his bank the Magyar for Mr e.g. *Mr* Joseph Smith[4]

To CLAUD W. SYKES (Postcard)   MS. Yale

31 August 1920   *rue de l'Assomption 5, Passy, Paris*

Dear Mr Sykes: Called twice to Dramatic Authors' Society. Mr Ballou is away still on holidays but I shall see someone named Leclerc on Tuesday who is said to have the affair in hand.[5] Sincerely yours

JAMES JOYCE

P.S. *Dubliners* arrived all right. Thanks.

To NATALIE CLIFFORD BARNEY[6]   MS. Bradley

6 September 1920   *rue de l'Assomption 5, I, Passy, Paris*

Dear Miss Barney: As I hear that you are leaving town on the 9th for some time I shall deem it a great favour if you can let me know before you go whether there is any reply either from Mr Poe or from Mr Valette. I have a letter for the manager of the *Vieux Columbier*[7] but do not wish to present it. The translator has finished the first chapter of my novel which is ready for publication in any review that will take it.

With many thanks for your kind intervention Sincerely yours

JAMES JOYCE

[1] Joyce is alluding to the imagery of the *Circe* episode of *Ulysses*, where Bloom is crowned 'emperor president and king chairman'. The 'thrones of alabaster' are identified as water-closets in the *Cyclops* episode, p. 422 (325).

[2] See p. 87, n. 3,

[3] Hebraeus Vaticanus Tergestis Exul Lutetiae Hospes Litterarum Anglicarum Pontifex Maximus, or Vatican Jew, Exile from Trieste, Guest of Paris, High Priest of English Letters.

[4] This would be Smith *úr*. Joyce was trying to represent Bloom's Hungarian grandfather.

[5] Sykes was arranging to have the English Players produce a play, *Le Voile du bonheur*.

[6] Natalie Clifford Barney (b. 1877 in Dayton, Ohio) maintained one of the better known literary salons in Paris from 1910. She was the author of *Mes Aventures de l'esprit* (Paris, 1929), *Pensées d'une Amazone* (Paris, 1920), and other books. Paul Valéry was for many years one of her most regular guests.

[7] Jacques Copeau (1878–1949), French playwright, actor, manager, and producer, founded the Théâtre du Vieux Colombier in 1913.

To ALESSANDRO FRANCINI BRUNI   MS. S. Illinois (Croessmann)

[? *8 September 1920*]   *rue de l'Assomption 5, Parigi, XVI*

Caro Francini: Un maledetto contrattempo intralcia il mio lavoro. La cassa di libri (peso ca. 40 chili, quadrata, segni 'J.J. 38'[1] spedita da Trieste, 29.vi.920, dalla Società Adriatica (A. Bruna), Piazza delle Poste) non si trova più! Ti prego passa dai miei verso le 13.30 quando troverai tutt'e due in casa. Domanda se sanno qualcosa. Se non forse tu potresti da parte tua—tuo padre non è o non era impiegato alla ferrovia. Da parte mia il Ministero degli Esteri (francese) dove c'è un segretario che ammira i miei scritti farà il possibile per rintracciarla lungo le linee francesi. Ma certo l'incaglio dev'essere in quel bel paese dove l'ano suona.[2] Puoi immaginarti il mio stato d'anima [sic] dopo sette anni di lavoro e quale. Tutti s'aspettano la chiusa delle avventure. Ho già scritto l'episodio di *Circe* un sei volte. Credo sia la cosa più forte ch'io abbia scritto malgrado la mia espulsione in circostanze note alla dea che mi protegge.

Ti mando alcuni giornali. Mio fratello può averli per un giorno ma non più, prego, perchè diventano stantii. Passali al Benco. Spedii diversa roba al Buttana. Non so se ne fece uso o no.

Avrai inteso del mio nuovo colpo di fortuna? Cosa c'è col tuo libretto?

Dunque, caro Franzin,[3] te prego, dai domanda a lori se i sa andove ze sta roba parchè mi go mandasto da un zerto sior Driatiko che ze proprio rente alla posta granda sta cassa el mi ga dito che i sui omini i la mandaria cul[4] caro e che iera pulido proprio ma esso i me dise che qualchedun le ga menà in condoto e ga messo sora non so che cossa o che i ga sbregà cul fero cossa so mi, ma sior Driatico ga firmato mona de ostia[5] che lu ga zercà così e colà in ogni buso cul lume e no ze gnanca rimasta la spusa, arra.

Una streta de man del tuo

JACOMO DEL OIO
sudito botanico

P.S. Cassa no iera ciavada[6] con ciave ma iera soltanto roba de ciodi che

---

[1] Joyce's initials and age.

[2] Joyce, amused by the Italian nationalism of Triestines who had lived so long under Austrian rule, parodies here the familiar identification of Italy as '[il] bel Paese là dove'l sì suona' ('The beautiful land where the *sì* rings out') (*Inferno*, XXXIII, l. 80).

[3] From this point Joyce writes in a corrupt Triestine dialect, the kind a Triestine would use in mimicking the way a Slovene speaks the dialect. So Adriatica becomes Driatika, the Triestine 'un italian' becomes 'un taliano,' and articles are omitted before nouns.

[4] A blend of 'col' ('with the') and 'cul' ('arse').

[5] A blasphemous vulgarism, for which 'son of a bitch' is a weak equivalent.

[6] A play on 'fucked' and 'locked'.

go comperasto da un taliano che se ciama el sior Greinitz Neffen[1] cul
sara do letere e trentoto che go copià drio l'Aufgabe de mio fio che
studia per ritmetico.   J. J.[2]

To JOHN RODKER   MS. John H. Thompson

13 September 1920   *rue de l'Assomption 5, Passy, Paris*

Dear Mr Rodker: Many thanks indeed for the copy of *Hymns*[3] so
kindly sent me with the friendly signature. I have read your verses with

[1] A mocking reference to the Italian nationalism of Triestines with un-Italian names.
Greinitz Neffen (Nephews) was a tool and hardware firm with its main office in Graz,
Austria. Its Triestine branch had just been taken over by an Italian corporation following
the first World War.

[2] (Translation)
'Dear Francini: A damned mishap is holding up my work. The case of books
(weight c. 40 kilos, square, stamped "J.J. 38" sent from Trieste, 29 June 1920, from
the Società Adriatica (A. Bruna), Piazza delle Poste) is not to be found! Please drop in
on my relatives about 1:30 p.m. when you will find both at home. Ask if they know
anything. If not perhaps you could yourself [do something]—is not or was not your
father a railway employee. For my part, the Ministry of Foreign Affairs (French)
where there is a secretary who admires my writings will do what is possible to trace
them along the French railways. But certainly the hitch must be in that beautiful
country where the arse is sounded. But imagine my state of mind after seven years of
work, and what work. Everyone is waiting for the end of the adventures. I have
already written the *Circe* episode some six times. I think it is the strongest thing I have
written in spite of my expulsion in circumstances known to the goddess who protects
me.
     I am sending you some newspapers. My brother can have them for a day but no
longer please since they get stale. Pass them on to Benco. I sent several things to
Buttana. I don't know if he made use of them or not.
     Have you heard of my new stroke of luck? What about your libretto?
     So, dear Franzin, come on and please ask them if they know where this stuff is
because I sent it through a certain Mister Driatiko who is near the main post office and
he told me that his men would send it by cart and everything would have gone all right
but now they say that someone took it to the lavatory and put I don't know what on it
or that they have torn it up with an iron or what do I know, but Mister Driatico signed
himself son of a bitch that he has searched up and down in every hole with a light and
not even the stink of it is left, arrah.
     A handshake from Giacomo of the Oil, botanic subject.
     P.S. The box was not locked with a key but only nailed with nails I bought from an
Italian who is named Mr Greinitz Neffen with only two letters and thirty-eight that I
copied from the homework of my son who is studying to be an arithmetician.   J.J.'
[3] John Rodker, *Hymns* (London, 1920). The poem on p. 21, 'Hymn of Hymns,' began
as follows:

> God damn Cosmoses—
> Eternities, infinities
> and all that galley.
>
> God damn
> white mushroomy flaccid
> and smelling of old clothes
> Man!
> whether Homeric
> or after
> Dostoievsky. . . .

much pleasure. A Mr Ivan Goll who is making an anthology of modern
poets had the bad idea of coming to me for information. I gave him your
name among others. A Milanese international review *Poesia* would
publish, I am sure, some of your verses, for example, those on pp 20–21.
If you consider it worthwhile doing so perhaps you could send me a
typed copy of a poem. They published lately some verses by Mr Pound
and by me.

I have not received that copy of *The Oxen of the Sun* but perhaps you
have read part of the *Nausikaa* episode. The best plan is to ask Miss
Weaver to let you see these two episodes so that you may judge of their
length.

Please excuse me for my delay in acknowledging receipt of your book
but I have been rather worried.

With renewed thanks and kind regards from me to Mrs Rodker and
yourself Sincerely yours   J<small>AMES</small> J<small>OYCE</small>

To S<small>TANISLAUS</small> J<small>OYCE</small>   MS. Cornell

14 September 1920   *rue de l'Assomption 5, Passy, Paris*

Dear Stannie: Have you written to me? I got no letter. Don't write 5,
I on address as some letters went astray. Simply 5. Concierges in Paris
deliver all letters within the house.

What in hell's name am I to do about my case of books? Did anybody
go or phone there. Please let me hear by return. Curse their bloody
bumbling bawling lousy good for nothing blatant souls! I expected they
would do what they could to upset me and any plans I had. Have
written *Circe* about five times. It allows me about four or five hours
sleep every night. The case of books was fetched on 30 June. It was
marked J.J. 38, weighed about 40–50 chilos. Sender: Bruna[,] Adriatica,
Piazza della Piave.

Miss Weaver writes that she would prefer, instead of making over the
£2000 to me in the form of War Loans, to pass me the money direct so
that I may apply it if and as I think fit (the capital, i.e., or part of it)
during 'my best, most creative years'. So that I expect we will open a
credit in some bank for the amount in my name. More anon.

The M.S. I sent to Quinn from Trieste on 10 June never reached him
(by his letter of 17 August) while that sent from Paris 6 weeks later did.
Isn't that enough to drive anyone wild! He sent however 3500 francs on
the second batch, and will send more if other parcel arrives. I suppose I
have to write it out all over again! Curse them again! He will give

20,000 lire for the entire MS of *Ulysses* but wants the end of it and the corrected proofs.

A scheme is proposed for a separate special edition of U. to be printed (1000 copies) here for U.K. and U.S.A. at 200 lire a copy by which I am calculated to get about 80,000 independent of the other ordinary edition. I foresee that my Triestine friends will buy up all this edition.

Giorgio has been offered a position at 500 fs (French) a month in the office of an Indian merchant here (similar to Ralli Bros). I give him coaching every night in English, French, German and Italian correspondence—all jumbled together—as I asked the principal to keep the job open for 3 weeks. I hope he is not overestimating my son's abilities. This is not the other post I wrote of. In any case if he likes it it would be a good opening as this is their first European branch and he would have to travel with the principal in Spain Italy and Germany.

I enclose a few cuttings from Irish papers. With most of your remarks I agree. Please contradict the following reports at present in circulation about me whenever they present themselves.

That I was sent to Ireland 8 years ago by the Austrian F.O. (report of Maunsel and Co)

That I made money during the war as a Brit. gov. spy (report of friends and relatives in Dublin)

That *Ulysses* was a prearranged pro-German code (report of Brit. war censor subsequently scouted by literary experts! This came to light last week)

That I was a Sinn Fein emissary in Switzerland and the English Players a blind (report of one of the English actors of my company, paid by me)

That I am addicted to cocaine, morphia etc (report of Triestines)

That I founded in Zurich the dadaist movement which is now exciting Paris (report of Irish press last week)

That I am a violent bolshevik propagandist (report of yourself for purposes of discussion)

That I am the cavalier servente of the Duch— of M—, Mme M— R— M—.; a prince— de X—, Mrs T–n–t A— and the Dowager Empress of Ch–na.

Write about those books please   JIM

P.S.

I see Trieste is in riot. Keep out of the way of both their lousy projectiles.

I enclose 3 stamps I found [in] my purse

To John Rodker   MS. John H. Thompson
29 September 1920 Michaelmas   *rue de l'Assomption 5, Paris XVI*

Dear Mr Rodker: The case of books papers etc which I sent on from
Trieste to enable me to write seems to be lost. I sent it on 29 June last.
Have you any spare copies of the *Little Review* containing my novel?
I should be glad to have them even temporarily as my copies were in the
case. To add to this, I have received notice to quit this flat (if one can
call it so) within a few weeks.

Thanks for your kind words about the *Oxen of the Sun* episode. My
New York publisher Mr Huebsch is in Paris and I shall speak to him of
your suggestion.

Kindest regards to Mrs Rodker and yourself from us all Sincerely
yours   JAMES JOYCE

P.S. Has no number of the *Little Review* appeared since May–June?

To Jenny Serruys   MS. Bradley
[7 October? 1920]   *rue de l'Assomption 5, Paris XVI*

Chère Madame: Je vous envoie ci-inclus deux lettres qui me sont
parvenues avec la même poste. Je viens de voir M. Copeau.[1] Il m'a dit
que son plan pour la saison 1920–21 est déjà complet et qu'il regrette de
ne pas avoir su de ma pièce au mois de juillet quand je suis arrivè ici. Je
vous écrirai de nouveau après mon entretien avec M. Poe. Peutêtre
pourriez-vous me renvoyer les lettres avec un mot pour me dire s'il y a
quelque chose de nouveau au sujet de mes livres égarés—digne troupeau
d'un pasteur egaré lui-même.

Agréez, chère Madame, mes civilités très empressées   JAMES JOYCE[2]

To Claud W. Sykes   MS. Yale
11 October 1920   *[Paris]*

Dear Mr Sykes: I sent back typescript of *Le Voile du Bonheur*[3] today
and am writing by this post to Mr Ballou (?). I hope it will be a success.

[1] See p. 18.
[2] (Translation)
    'Dear Madame: I send herewith two letters which arrived by the same post. I have
just seen M. Copeau. He told me that his repertory for the 1920–21 season is already
complete and that he regrets not having known of my play in the month of July when I
arrived here. I will write you again after my interview with M. Poe. Would you be
good enough to send back the letters with a line to tell me if there is anything new about
my strayed books—a flock worthy of a strayed master.
    Please accept my warm regards   James Joyce'
[3] See p. 18, n. 5.

Circe progresses. Am very busy flat hunting. *Exiles* is already translated and will be produced by M. Lugné-Poe, and Mme Suzanne Després[1] in December or January. Best wishes for your season Sincerely yours

JAMES JOYCE

To ANDRÉ SUARÈS[2] (Written on Joyce's visiting card) MS. Stanford

[*20 October 1920*][3]   *rue de l'Assomption 5, Passy, Paris*

Mr James Joyce[4] présente ses civilités a M. Suarès en le priant de vouloir bien excuser le façon de les présenter. Se trouvant dans une position très critique (il lui faut déménager entre trois où quatre jours avec sa famille—4 personnes en tous) il se permet de démander à un collègue d'art dont il admire l'œuvre litteraire s'il connait par hasard quelqu'un, artiste ou autre, qui doit s'absenter temporairement de Paris ou quelque autre occasion pour trouver un appartement quelconque. Dans le cas contraire il se voit déjà obligé à quitter Paris pour une autre—recherche de l'absolu. Il demande infiniment pardon de M. Suarès de cette manière de le remercier de l'interêt bienveillant à ses ecrits dont M. Suarès lui a parlé mais—*il tempo non è più galantuomo*[5]

To JENNY SERRUYS   MS. Bradley

20 October 1920   *rue de l'Assomption 5, Paris XVI*

Chère Madame: Je suis allé vous voir chez vous l'autre jour mais, ayant entendu que Mme votre mère venait d'être opérée, je ne voulais pas vous ennuyer dans les circonstances pareilles. J'espère que l'opération a réussi et que ses souffrances sont soulagées en conséquence.

Si je vous dérange maintenant c'est que je viens de recevoir un 'pneu' de M. Poe (ci-inclus). J'ai parlé avec lui samedi huit jours. Il me

---

[1] Suzanne Després (b. 1875), French actress, wife of Lugné-Poë.

[2] André Suarès (1866–1948), French man of letters, author of books on music, literature, and other subjects.

[3] A note by Suarès attached to Joyce's visiting card gives this date.

[4] These three words are printed on the card.

[5] (Translation)

'Mr James Joyce presents his compliments to M. Suarès and asks him to excuse the manner of presenting them. Finding himself in a very critical position (he must move in two or three days' time with his family—four persons in all), he ventures to ask his colleague in art whose literary work he admires if he happens to know anybody, artist or not, who has to be temporarily out of Paris, or any other possibility of finding a flat anywhere. In default of that he sees himself already obliged to leave Paris for another—search for the absolute. He asks a thousand pardons of M. Suarès for this mode of thanking him for the benevolent interest in his writings about which M. Suarès spoke to him but—time is not a gentleman any more.'

montra son 'mot à mot' et me pria de l'examiner. Ma pièce, selon lui, ne lui porterait point d'argent mais, malgré ça, il pense à la faire jouer. Deux jours après j'ai reçu un 'pneu' de lui, me priant de lui rendre le 'mot à mot' qu'il n'avait pas le droit de me prêter! Ce que je fis. Par retour de courrier une autre lettre (ci-incluse). Je lui répondis en disant que, comme la pièce ne lui semblait pas une affaire, je me fiais de lui comme astute et comme homme d'affaires. A noter qu'il veut aussi carte blanche pour la révision scenique du texte. Je lui écris aussi que j'étais sous l'impression que c'était vous qui feriez la traduction. Maintenant, je viens de recevoir cet autre 'pneu' que je vous remets.

Mon roman est trop long pour les *Ecrits Nouveaux*—comme la barbe de Polonius. M. Rodker me parla de le faire publier en forme de livre mais Mme Savitsky, qui faisait la traduction, n'a pas continué. Elle était partie de Paris pour Clamart Paris pour la Bretagne. Revenue à Paris elle repartit pour Cannes. Elle est malade, je crois. La pièce ne peut pas être publiée dans les *Ecrits Nouveaux* parceque—j'ai oublié la raison. Le *Mercure* n'a pas donné aucun signe de vie.

Quant à moi je dois quitter cet appartement samedi ou dimanche. Je n'ai rien trouvé, et je serai peutêtre obligé de quitter Paris avec ma famille. En ce cas je vous renverrai les effets avant de partir. Quoiqu'au moment d'écrire je n'ai pas la moindre idée où je peux aller.

Je vous envoie la présente par mon fils. J'espère qu'il vous trouvera. Il ne parle pas le français mais l'anglais, l'italien et l'allemand.

Agréez, Madame, l'assurance de ma parfaite consideration et pardonnez-moi, je vous prie, de vous avoir écrit quand j'aurais dû me taire.   James Joyce[1]

[1] (Translation)

'Dear Madame: I went to see you the other day but, when I heard that Madame your mother had just been operated, I did not wish to disturb you in such circumstances. I hope the operation was successful and that her sufferings have been alleviated as a result of it.

If I trouble you now it is because I have just received a 'pneu' from M. Poe (enclosed). I talked with him a week ago Saturday. He showed me his literal translation and asked me to examine it. My play, according to him, would not make any money but in spite of that he thinks of staging it. Two days later I received a 'pneu' from him, asking me to return him the translation which he had no right to lend me! Which I did. By return of post another letter (enclosed). I replied by saying that, as the play did not seem to him to be good business, I trusted him as astute and as a good businessman. Note that he wants carte blanche too for the scenic revision of the text. I wrote him also that I was under the impression that you were the one who was making the translation. Now I have just received this other 'pneu' which I send you.

My novel is too long for *Ecrits Nouveaux*—like the beard of Polonius. M. Rodker spoke to me of having it published in the form of a book but Mme Savitsky, who was making the translation, hasn't gone on with it. She left Paris for Clamart Paris for Brittany. Once back in Paris she was off again for Cannes. She is ill, I think. The play cannot be published in the *Ecrits Nouveaux* because—I have forgotten why. The *Mercure* has given no sign of life.

To STANISLAUS JOYCE   MS. Cornell

28 October 1920   *rue de l'Assomption 5, Paris XVI*

Dear Stannie: A few lines in haste. The Bank of England dividend
warrants relative to the additional £2000, forwarded by you, have
arrived. Besides this, however, Miss Weaver sent me a week ago
through her solicitors an extra gift of £200 in the form of a cheque
'thinking it may be useful at present'. *Exiles* is translated and accepted
by the Théâtre de l'Oeuvre. It will be produced by Lugné Poe and
Suzanne Desprès in December. Please give or send enclosed 100 lire to
Silvestri—if he is in Trieste—and get from him the lightning sketch he
made of me. I shall send him more later. Keep it[,] also unframed sketch
of his daughter in your room till my return or somewhere where the
mice won't eat the paint off. The whoreson Adriatica managed to
deliver my case of books here last night. There was no difficulty on the
part of the French douane. Some of *Dubliners* translated will appear in
a Swiss review:[1] and I suppose the *Portrait* is finished by now. Don't put
the door number after the house number when writing here. It bothers
the Paris postman who is obliging but not over bright. Qu'est ce que
c'est ce petit machin-là ?[2]   JIM

P.S. Silvestri—Androna del Porto, 4 (?)

To CARLO LINATI (Postcard)   MS. Yale

3 November 1920   *rue de l'Université 9, Parigi VII*

Caro Signor Linati: Grazie della cartolina. Sono tornato qui di nuovo
non avendo trovato un appartamento. *Gli Esuli* sono già tradotti in
francese ed accettati dal Théâtre de l'Oeuvre. Lugne-Poe e Suzanna
Desprée li interpreteranno in dicembre. Adesso scrivo la versione finale
di *Circe*. Ho dovuto aspettare l'arrivo della mia cassa di libri che mise la

---

As for me I must leave this flat Saturday or Sunday. I have found nothing, and I
may be forced to leave Paris with my family. In that event I will return your belongings before I leave. Though at the moment I write this I haven't the least notion where
I could go.

I send you this by my son. I hope he will find you. He does not speak French but
English, Italian and German.

Please accept my compliments, Madame, and forgive me, if you will, for having
written to you when I should have kept silent.   James Joyce'

[1] The only one of the stories of *Dubliners* published in a Swiss review was 'Un Incident
régrettable' ('A Painful Case') in *Revue de Genève* (Geneva) I.21 (March 1922) 359–69. It
was translated by Yva Fernandez, who was one of three translators of the entire book,
Gens de Dublin (Paris, 1926).

[2] 'What is that little thingamajig there?'

bellezza di 4 mesi fra qui e Trieste. Causa l'ultimo episodio (Nausikaa) la polizia americana mossa dalla figlia del procuratore di stato a Nuova York, ha sequestrato la rivista. La prima udienza ebbe luogo al 22 u. d. Si prepara un putiferio appena finito il maladetto libro sarà pubblicato prima in un'edizione speciale di 1000 esemplari a 250 lire l'uno, 500 per l'America e 500 per l'Europa. Saluti cordiali

JAMES JOYCE[1]

To EZRA POUND   TS. Yale

5 November 1920   *rue de l'Université 9, Paris VII*

Dear Pound: I am exhausted. An entire month of flathunting, out every morning and back at night, in taxis, buses, trams, trains, lifts, agencies, newspaper offices. I spent about 500 francs I am sure and found nothing so we are here again. I used to carry different parts of the *Circe* episode about with me. Very pleasant indeed. Also the case of books I had sent on from Trieste went astray. I had to write and wire and interview numerous people. I feared it was lost. At last it arrived after four months of its odyssey.

I ought to have written to Mr Quinn before but did not know what address to give. I thought of leaving Paris altogether. I shall write to him tomorrow. I am too tired today as we have just moved in here. I like the landlord here and his wife. They are very agreeable people but it is terribly dear. I have the room you engaged when we came. *Si torna all'antico.*[2] For today perhaps you can write or transmit to Mr Quinn as follows.

I knew nothing of the affair till yesterday when Mr Thayer of the *Dial* wrote to me offering two cents a word or more in exceptional case and saying that he was sorry about the *Little Review*.[3] This explained

---

[1] (Translation)
   'Dear Mr Linati: Thanks for the postcard. I am back here again, having failed to find a flat. *Exiles* is translated into French and accepted by the Théâtre de l'Oeuvre. Lugné Poe and Suzanne Desprès will present it in December. I am now writing the final version of *Circe*. I had to wait for my case of books to come. It took a good four months between here and Trieste. Due to the last episode (Nausikaa) the American police, roused by the daughter of the attorney-general of the state of New York, confiscated the review. The first hearing took place on the 22nd ult. There will be a stink as soon as the damned book is published, in a special edition to start with, of 1000 copies selling at 250 Lire each, 500 for America and 500 for Europe. Cordial greetings   James Joyce'
[2] 'One returns to the old.' A variant of Giuseppe Verdi's famous advice in a letter to Francesco Florino, 5 January 1871, '*Tornate all' antico e sarà un progresso.*'
[3] In September 1920 John S. Sumner (1876–1957?), the secretary of the New York Society for the Prevention of Vice, lodged an official complaint against the July–August 1920 number of the *Little Review*, which contained the second half of the *Nausicaa*

nothing and I had heard nothing from Miss Anderson, Miss Heap or Mr Rodker. In fact Mr Rodker at my suggestion had arranged, I thought, for the publication of *The Oxen of the Sun* episode in one entire number as I expected them to finish *Circe* in *November* but it will be delayed till December. The typescript was sent on by you from Sirmione on 9 June. The MS is in Mr Quinn's possession now and Mr Huebsch, against my wish, brought to New York a third copy in type. The last number of the L.R. I saw was the July–August number with the close of the *Nausikaa* episode. Has no number appeared since then or has *The Oxen of the Sun* episode been published wholly or in part? Is the *Little Review* closed?

Mr Quinn states that in his view there is one chance in nine of the official he names agreeing to his proposal.[1] In that case it seems to me that my intervention is useless. He also states that some arrangement has been made for a private edition to be published by Mr Huebsch for which I am to receive 2500 $. This is very pleasant news but before anything is concluded I must take advantage of the offer Mr Quinn made me lately of his legal services. . . .

The picture of Mr Quinn trying to teach the attorneygeneral (if that be his title) to spell my name is rather amusing. I suppose Mr Quinn pronounces it as I myself pronounce it. The result would possibly have been more successful if, in his *plaidoirie* with that functionary, he had alluded to me as 'Mustard Joyhorse'. Very sincerely yours

JAMES JOYCE

To JENNY SERRUYS   MS. Bradley

5 November 1920   *rue de l'Université 9, Paris VII*

Chère Madame: N'ayant pas trouvé un appartement nous voilà dans une maison meublée. Selon vos instructions je vous ai renvoyé le lit, le matelas et la table. *Si* je trouve un appartement peutêtre pourrais-je les ravoir. Je vous enverrai les draps quand ils reviendront de la blanchisseuse. Me permettez-vous de garder encore un peu les deux couvertures

---

episode. After a preliminary hearing in a police court on 22 October, the case was transferred to the Court of Special Sessions, where it was heard before three judges on 14 and 21 February 1921. Margaret Anderson and Jane Heap were fined fifty dollars each, with the understanding that the publication of *Ulysses* in the magazine would cease. John Quinn conducted their defence.

[1] Quinn endeavoured to persuade the Attorney-General of the United States not to prosecute *Ulysses* if it were published in book form.

qui me soulagent un peu dans mes moments—ou plutôt—heures, de 'scepticisme'

Avec bien des remerciements je vous prie, chère madame, d'agréer l'assurance de ma parfaite considération.   James Joyce[1]

To John Rodker   MS. John H. Thompson

10 November 1920   *rue de l'Université 9, Paris VII*

Dear Mr Rodker: As I could not find any flat in Paris we are staying in this *maison meublée.* My case of books has at last arrived. Could you send me the *Little Review* for September and October 1919? Has any number appeared since the July–August number of this year?[2] I mean has any part of *Oxen of the Sun* been published? I have received letters from New York concerning a prosecution. Have you received any letters from the New York editor? I should like to know before I reply.

Kind regards from us all to Mrs Rodker and yourself Sincerely yours
James Joyce

To Harriet Shaw Weaver   MS. British Museum

16 November 1920   *rue de l'Université 9, Paris VII*

Dear Miss Weaver: I am writing to Mr Quinn in the way I outlined in my letter to you and am glad that you agree with my view. May I trouble you to send me a copy of my novel which I need in order to present it to the actor who says that he is going to produce *Exiles*? Europe will soon be full of complimentary copies presented by me, or rather by you, to persons who perhaps will never read them. I enclose a notice of *Ulysses* from the New York *Dial*[3] which the editor of the review forwarded me. With many kind regards sincerely yours
James Joyce

---

[1] (Translation)
'Dear Madame: Not having found a flat, here we are in furnished rooms. In accordance with your instructions I have sent back to you the bed, the mattress, and the table. *If* I find a flat perhaps I might have them back. I will send you the sheets when they come back from the laundress. Will you allow me to keep for a while yet these two blankets which comfort me a little in my moments—or rather—hours, of "scepticism"
With many thanks I send you, dear madame, my compliments.   James Joyce'

[2] The *Little Review* number of September–December 1920 contained the first fourth of the *Oxen of the Sun* episode.

[3] Evelyn Scott, 'A Contemporary of the Future,' *Dial* (New York LXIX.7 (October 1920) 353–67.

To FRANK BUDGEN (Postcard)   MS. Yale

[*? November 1920*]   *rue de l'Université 9, Paris VII*

Dear Budgen: Couldn't find a flat in all Paris and here we are in a
private hotel. Damnably dear but I must finish *Circe*. Am making the
final draft. How are you? Everyone here coughing his or her guts up.
Have you been working? Your account in [of?] London is very nice—
like Sargent's.[1] I have not heard from him lately. I enclose 5 francs. Can
you please through any newsagent procure for me a copy of *News of
World* and *Reynold's News* for 29 May and 5 June of this year? There is
hell in New York about *Nausikaa*. Review seized and editor committed
for trial at next session, bailed out by Quinn. Quinn and Pound want
me to withdraw the book from the review so as to safeguard the private
edition, but it is as broad as it is long. Have you met Pound? Write me
a line or two. Sincerely yours   JAMES JOYCE

P.S. Did you see that Fleiner's[2] friend Spitteler[3] got the Nobel prize?

To JOHN QUINN[4]   TS. N.Y. Public Library (Manuscript)

24 November 1920   *rue de l'Université 9, Paris VII*

Dear Mr Quinn: I cabled you a few days ago as follows:

   Scotts: Scott's code, American edition.
   Tettoja: I have not received the telegram you mention.
   Moledura: You will receive a letter on this subject in a few days
             giving information and my own views pretty fully.
   Geizhund: I think a little delay will not be disadvantageous.

I presume you now have my letter. So far as I can learn from the
English editor[5] of it, the *Little Review* seems to have suspended
publication. He knows nothing of any number later than the July–
August and we are now almost in December.

Apart from what I wrote already concerning the publication by
Huebsch, I have two other things to add. The first is: proofs. I began
Ulysses in 1914 and shall finish it, I suppose, in 1921. This is, I think,
the twentieth address at which I have written it—and the coldest. The
complete notes fill a small valise, but in the course of continual

---

[1] Louis Augustus Sargent (1881–1965), English painter and a close friend of Budgen's.

[2] Fritz Fleiner (1867–1937), professor of law in the University of Zurich from 1915–36,
and Rector from 1932 to 1934. He wrote many books on legal subjects. Joyce had met
him through Budgen.

[3] Carl Friedrich Georg Spitteler (1845–1924), Swiss novelist and poet, was awarded the
Nobel Prize for Literature in 1919.

[4] From a typed copy.   [5] Ezra Pound.

changings very often it was not possible to sort them for the final time before the publication of certain instalments. The insertions (chiefly verbal or phrases, rarely passages) must be put in for the book publication. Before leaving Trieste I did this sorting for all episodes up to and including *Circe*. The episodes which have the heaviest burden of addenda are *Lotus-eaters*, *Lestrygonians*, *Nausikaa* and *Cyclops*. Therefore I must stipulate to have three sendings of proofs (preferably a widemargined one must be pulled), namely:

(1) A galley-page proof of all the book up to and including *Circe*.

(2) A similar proof of the three chapters of the *Nostos*

(3) A complete proof of the book in page form.

The second point is: that if Huebsch decides to print it and the copies are subscribed, an advance (and a substantial advance) of royalties be paid over by him at once.

I hope to finish the *Circe* episode before Christmas. *Eumeus*, being already drafted, I could send on in January. The printing of the book could be put in hand at once when the contract is signed. I must have a few months' leisure after January to write the *Ithaca* and *Penelope* episodes which, however, have been sketched since 1916 and are very short in comparison with the *Circe* episode. With kind regards Sincerely yours   JAMES JOYCE

To MME YASUSHI TANAKA[1]   MS. Tanaka

24 November 1920   *rue de l'Université 9, Paris VII*

Dear Madame: In reply to your letter I shall call on you on Sunday afternoon as it seems that that is the most convenient time for you. Sincerely yours   JAMES JOYCE

To MME YASUSHI TANAKA   MS. Tanaka

29 November 1920   *rue de l'Université 9, Paris VII*

Dear Mrs Tanaka: As promised I send you the notices but may I ask you to return them when read as I have no others. If you will drop a line to:

Mr Fritz Vanderpyl
Rue Gay Lussac 13
Paris VI

[1] Mme Yasushi Tanaka (Louise Gebhart Cann), an American who had come to Paris with her Japanese husband in 1920. Pound suggested to her that she might do an article about Joyce's work, and she had written to him to arrange a meeting. Her article appeared in the *Pacific Review*.

saying that you are writing the article on me, I am sure he will let you have the copy of *Egoist* (15 January 1913) which I lent him some time ago. It contains the whole story of Dubliners. Sincerely yours

James Joyce

To John McCormack   MS. McCormack

8 December 1920   *Boulevard Raspail 5, Paris*

Dear MacCormack: In the general confusion the other afternoon I had not an opportunity to tell you how delighted we were by your singing, especially the aria from *Don Giovanni*. I have lived in Italy practically ever since we last met but no Italian lyrical tenor that I know (Bonci[1] possibly excepted) could do such a feat of breathing and phrasing—to say nothing of the beauty of tone in which, I am glad to see, Roscommon can leave the peninsula a fair distance behind. We are all going to hear you again next Tuesday and I am sure you will have another big success.

Di nuovo tanti mirallegri ed una stretta di mano cordialissima.[2] Sincerely yours   James Joyce

To John Rodker (Postcard)   MS. S. Illinois (Croessmann)

Postmark 9 December 1920   *Boulevard Raspail 5, Paris VII*

Dear Mr Rodker: The above is our new address. I have had an attack in the eyes and was obliged to take a place which I can heat, no matter at what cost, but now I am much better. I hear that the L.R. is still in existence. If you have received the number containing *Oxen of the Sun*, could you send me two copies, please? I hope to finish *Circe* (the eighth draft) by Christmas Sincerely yours   James Joyce

To Ezra Pound   MS. Omar Pound

12 December 1920   *Boulevard Raspail 5, Paris VII*

Dear Pound: I am all right again except for bad fits of neuralgia.[3] This flat is frightfully dear but so was the hotel and there I had no ease in the cold sitting writing about tiresome Bloom with Mrs Pound's shawl

[1] Alessandro Bonci (b. 1870), Italian tenor.
[2] 'Again many congratulations and a very cordial handshake.'
[3] Joyce suffered an eye attack in November and early December 1920.

round my head and Miss Serruys' two blankets round the rest of my body. Only for the gasstove in this flat I should be down with a full-blasted attack of the eyes. I must get over the winter some way and so I have asked Miss Serruys and Bradley to get me some lessons[1]—a job I must take up again unless the hope in your letter is realized. That letter was rather a puzzle to me. Am I right in assuming that it is from Miss Anderson[2] to you? I have heard nothing of Mr Wallace of New York but I had a letter from a Mr Wallace[3] of Paris (who seems to be anything but a millionaire) he told me that a Dr Joseph Collins[4] of New York had charged him to give £2 each to Giorgio and Lucia for Xmas— which was very kind of Dr Collins (unknown to me) but I take it this is only a coincidence of names. How the deuce can I take direct action in the matter if, as Mr XYZ who writes to Miss M.C.A.[5] [says], the matter is to be 'unknown'. I must wait, mustn't I? A letter from the editor of N. Y. Evening Post sent on 1 September to an early Zurich address has reached me asking for contributions. Quinn's secretary replied to my cable saying the trial is fixed for tomorrow and suggesting I cable instructions to withdraw but, apart from what I said already, the remaining episode *Oxen of the Sun* is already published as Miss M.C.A. (if it be she) states that a special triple number appears on 25 November. My idea therefore that the review had gone out of existence after the July number seems to be right. Is its revival now with 96 pages due to Mr Wallace and Mr Dorrance?[6] How difficult it is to be informed correctly? In any case I shall wait to see effect of the new number and result of the trial after which I shall send on the Circe episode, now nearing completion, and wait to see what they do with it.

I hope you [are] not suffering from neuralgia. It is a most boring thing. Of course there is no news here. I understand that Lugné Poe intends to do an adaptation of *Exiles*. A Mrs Yasushi Tanaka, introduced by you, is doing an article on *Ulysses* for the *Pacific Review*, published by the University of Washington. No news of the novel or of

[1] Although Joyce several times threatened to give lessons in Paris, he in fact never did so.

[2] Margaret Anderson.

[3] Richard Wallace (1870?–1927), an American book illustrator who was also in the advertising business. He and his wife Lillian became good friends of the Joyces in Paris.

[4] Dr Joseph Collins (1866–1950), physician and writer. In his *Psychological Studies of Life and Letters* (New York, 1923), he devotes the second chapter (pp. 35–60) to 'Ireland's Latest Literary Antinomian: James Joyce'. Collins had heard of Joyce's financial need, the acuteness of which Joyce did not keep secret, and asked Wallace and another friend in Paris, Myron C. Nutting, to call on the indigent author, relieve any emergency and arrange a meeting when Collins should come to Paris.

[5] Margaret Anderson.

[6] Probably John Gordon Dorrance (b. 1870), editor of an anthology of American poetry in 1927.

Budry,[1] Fontanas &c or of Mrs Bloch. I do not even know where she is. Mrs Pound may remember that once in conversation with her I expressed a doubt as to whether Mrs Bloch had read the book. I have no news from Trieste either. They are a very friendly lot, I must say.

Now I have a nice little incipient neuralgia so will end this.

Kind regards from us all Sincerely yours   JAMES JOYCE

PS. The American ambassador's name is Wallace,[2] I find.

To JOHN McCORMACK   MS. McCormack

17 December 1920   *Boulevard Raspail 5, Paris VII*

Dear MacCormack: I send you the books promised, the novel for you, *Dubliners* for your brother but shall be obliged if he will return the latter when read as it is out of print. I shall enclose a review of *Ulysses* if I can find it which is doubtful. My wife wishes me to say that if your daughter finds any afternoon too boresome Lucia (who finds every afternoon boresome, I am afraid) would gladly keep her company. My telephone number is Saxe: 34-33. Sincerely yours   JAMES JOYCE

To EZRA POUND (Christmas card)   MS. Omar Pound

20 December 1920   *[Paris]*

Bis Dat Qui Cito Dat[3]

Yanks who hae wi' Wallace read,
Yanks whom Joyce has often bled,
Welcome to the hard plank bed,
    And bolschevistic flea.
Who for Bloom and Inisfail
Longs to pine in Sing Sing jail,
Picking oakum without bail,
    Let him publish me.

Best Xmas greetings to Mrs Pound and yourself from us all (see other side).[4] *Circe* finished this morning at last. Will revise, type and forward soon. No news *re* above.   JAMES JOYCE

[signed also by GEORGE, LUCIA, and NORA JOYCE]

[1] Paul Budry, French writer and translator.
[2] Hugh Campbell Wallace (1863-1931), United States Ambassador to France, 1919-21.
[3] 'He gives twice who gives quickly.'
[4] The other side was a Christmas picture of a man, two women, and a child labouring along a road towards a bridge. Joyce had put the initials of the four members of his family below the figures and had written underneath, 'The Joyce family Robinson.'

To G. Molyneux Palmer   MS. National Library
Postmark 20 December 1920   *Boulevard Raspail 5, Paris VII*

Dear Mr Palmer: I have spoken of your settings of my verses to my friend Mr John MacCormack, the tenor, who is here at present. If they have not been printed could you manage to send him in a very clear MS copy three of them, *At that hour when all things have repose, Gentle lady do not sing* and *It was out by Donnycarney*, keyed up to tenor pitch. His address is:

> Claridge's Hotel
> 74 Avenue des Champs Elysées
> Paris

but it would be well to send the songs very soon as he leaves shortly for the riviera.

I never heard how Mr Milner's[1] concerts went as I left Zurich abruptly. I returned to Trieste for some time and am now here finishing my book Ulysses for publication. *Exiles*, my play, will be given here in January by Lugné Poe (Théâtre de l'Oeuvre).

I shall be glad to hear from you and to know that your delicate music is meeting at last with the appreciation which it deserves. Sincerely yours   James Joyce

To Frank Budgen   MS. Yale
[*?20 December 1920*]   *Boulevard Raspail 5, Paris VII*

It seems we can't spend Xmas together. All good wishes from us all. Thanks for yours. Finished *Circe* this morning. Sincerely yours
                James Joyce, George, Lucia, Nora Joyce

To Ernest A. Boyd   MS. Colby College
30 December 1920   *Boulevard Raspail 5, Paris VII*

Dear Sir: M. LaMallide, editor of *La Vie des Peuples* (a copy of which I send you for your guidance) asked me to obtain for him from a good source three articles on the following subjects.

1) The Irish novel today
2) The Irish theatre today
3) The Irish economic question

He wishes to publish these articles at once in successive issues of his

[1] Augustus Milner, an Irishman by birth, was the leading baritone of the Municipal Theatre in Zurich. Just before leaving Zurich in 1919 Joyce arranged for Milner to give a concert of Irish music at the Tonhalle. But the plan fell through.

review. I have taken the liberty of forwarding the request to you as the recognized historian of the Irish literary movement in the hope that your engagements may allow you to accede to it. The articles should be in English and typed. They will be translated here. I do not know the scale of remuneration but, the franc being low and Paris review scales being low also, it will not be considerable. It might therefore repay you to forward your articles at the same time to Mr Ezra Pound, London editor of *The Dial*, for simultaneous publication in New York. The rates of *The Dial* are $5 a page for prose and $10 for verse.

Possibly you will be able to find a competent person among your acquaintances for the economic article. This, I understand, in view of the general tone of the review should be expository and not polemical. Sincerely yours   JAMES JOYCE

To G. MOLYNEUX PALMER   MS. National Library

16 January 1921   *Boulevard Raspail 5, Paris VII*

Dear Mr Palmer: The above is my address but you had better write it large and clear, the numeral in Arabic figure not as on your card in Roman as Paris postmen are champions of stupidity. I may mention that I have not received any songs from you since I wrote. Did you send them to me or to MacCormack? In any case send the second lot on to me and I shall redirect them. I hope you have copies and I shall do my best to have them published for you. It is a shame that they are not published already. I am very curious to hear the two additions—and to sing them. With kind regards sincerely yours   JAMES JOYCE

From JACQUES NATANSON[1] to JENNY SERRUYS   MS. Private

2 February 1921   *Théâtre de 'L'Oeuvre' 55 rue de Clichy, Paris 9*

Mademoiselle, Je viens de voir M. Lugné-Poe qui s'occupe précisément d' 'Exiles'. La pièce passera très prochainement. En tout cas elle sera jouée avant la fin de la saison. Dès que je serai définitivement fixé, je vous préviendrai.

Croyez, Mademoiselle, à mes sentiments respectueux

JACQUES NATANSON[2]

---

[1] Jacques Natanson (b. 1901), French dramatist. His plays were produced by Lugné-Poë at the Théâtre de l'Oeuvre after the first World War.

[2] (Translation)
'Mademoiselle, I have just seen M. Lugné-Poë who is now busy with *Exiles*. The play will go on very soon. In any case it will be given before the end of the season. The moment I know when for sure I will inform you. Yours sincerely

Jacques Natanson'

To JENNY SERRUYS   MS. Bradley

3 February 1921   *Boulevard Raspail 5*

Chère Madame: Je regrette d'avoir été trop tard ce matin pour vous trouver. Comme j'ai dit à votre sécretaire je me permettrai de revenir demain matin (vendredi) vers où après 11 heures. J'espère que vos engagements vous permettront de me recevoir à cette heure.

Agréez, chère Madame, mes civilités empressées.   JAMES JOYCE[1]

To JENNY SERRUYS   MS. Bradley

6 February 1921   *Boulevard Raspail 5, Paris VII*

Chère Madame: Monsieur Charpentier[2] m'a reçu d'une manière extrêmement gentille. Il m'a avancé la troisième partie de ce que je cherchais et m'a promis de faire de son mieux pour pouvoir me procurer le reste entre un delai de 8–10 jours c' à d samedi ou lundi prochain. D'abord il n'a pas voulu même accepter un ordre de paiement de ma part mais naturellement j'ai insisté. Avec ce qu'il m'a donné et le réserve que j'avais j'ai pu avec mon immense soulagement me débarrasser des plusieurs soucis. Si le reste arrive de la même façon alors je pourrai probablement travailler jusqu'à la fin de mon livre, fini lequel je ne souleverai pas la moindre objection si l'on m'expulse comme 'undesirable alien,' qui ne fait qu'ennuyer prodigieusement les gens qui ont commis l'imprudence de me connaître. Pourtant si vous avez l'occasion de rencontrer M. Charpentier il serait convenable peutêtre de lui dire quelque chose pas trop défavorable de mon être ou biens afin d'assurer le bon résultat définitif.

Avec mes meilleurs remerciements et mes salutations très respectueuses, Votre bien devoué   JAMES JOYCE[3]

[1] (Translation)
'Dear Madame: I am sorry to have been too late this morning to find you in. As I told your secretary I shall take the liberty of returning tomorrow morning (Friday) at about 11 o'clock or just after. I hope your engagements will permit you to receive me at that time.
Accept, dear Madame, my sincere greetings,   James Joyce'
[2] Clément Charpentier, later a Deputy, was a wealthy friend of Jenny Serruys.
[3] (Translation)
'Dear Madame: Monsieur Charpentier received me in a very courteous way. He advanced me a third of what I requested and promised to do his best to try to obtain the rest in eight or ten days' time, that is, on Saturday or the Monday following. At first he did not even want to accept a written promise to pay from me but of course I insisted. With what he gave me and what I had I have been able to my great relief to be rid of some of my worries. If the rest arrives in the same way then I shall probably be able to bring my book to the end, having finished which I shall raise not the slightest

To DANIEL HUMMEL   MS. Hummel

14 February 1921   *Boulevard Raspail 5, Paris VII,*
                                               Tél. Saxe 34–33

Sehr geehrter Herr Hummel: Sowohl Sie als Herr Ublinger müssen
mich entschuldigen wegen meines langen Schweigens. Denken Sie mal
der verfluchte Kapitel *Kirke* ist noch nicht zu Ende und im schönen
Mittel der Arbeit der Vater meiner Daktylo—ein berühmter Pariser
Arzt—hat einen Herzschlag bekommen. Ich schreibe jede Nacht bis 2,
3, sogar 5 Uhr. Hoffentlich werde ich in einer besseren Lage nächste
Woche sein. Dazu kommen auch die unvermeidlichen Sorgen aber, Gott
sei Dank, wir leben noch. Schreiben Sie mir eine Zeile ob es Ihnen beide
gut gehe and ich hoffe sehr Sie wiederzusehen binnem Kurzem.

Ist diese Ihre Adresse? Ich habe zwei Hausnummern auf diese Bogen
geschrieben.

Sargent war hier, war aber kränklich und ist schon verreist. Deswegen
und auch wegen der Sprachschwierigkeiten habe ich keine Rendezvous
arrangirt.

Freundliche Grüsse an Frau und Herrn Ublinger und an Sie selbst

JAMES JOYCE[1]

To CARLO LINATI (Postcard)   MS. Yale

18 February 1921   *Boulevard Raspail 5, Parigi VII*

Caro signor Linati: C'è qualcosa di nuovo riguardo la pubblicazione o
la produzione degli 'Esuli'? Lavoro come un ergastolano—fino alle 3 o 4
ogni mattina. Ho terminato *Circe* ed *Eumeo*. Restano i due ultimi

objection if they expel me as an 'undesirable alien,' an act which will only annoy
prodigiously the people who have committed the imprudence of making my acquaintance. But if you happen to meet M. Charpentier it would perhaps be possible to
tell him something not too unfavourable about me and my activities to assure a good
final result.

With my best thanks and very respectful greetings, Your devoted   James Joyce'
[1] (Translation)

'Dear Mr Hummel: Both you and Mr Ublinger must excuse me for my long silence.
Just imagine, the cursed chapter *Circe* is not finished yet and right in the middle of the
work my typist's father—a famous Paris doctor—has had a heart attack. I write
every night until 2, 3, even 5 o'clock. I hope I shall be in a better situation next week.
There are the inevitable worries besides but, thank God, we are still alive. Drop me a
line to tell me if you are both all right and I look forward to seeing you again before
long.

Is this your address? I wrote two house numbers on to this sheet.

Sargent was here, but he was ailing and has already left. This and the linguistic
difficulties are the reasons why I didn't arrange any meetings.

Kind regards to Mrs and Mr Ublinger and to yourself   James Joyce'

episodi *Itaca* e *Penelope* che mi danno parecchio filo da torcere. Non potrò essere a Milano prima di maggio. Il nostro incontro—tante volte rimandato—avrà luogo, spero, in una stagione più propizia di questa. Ha sentito del processo di *Ulisse* a N.Y.? Saluti cordiali

JAMES JOYCE[1]

To VALERY LARBAUD[2]   MS. Bib. Municipale, Vichy

23 February 1921   *Boulevard Raspail 5, Paris VII,*
                                                    Tél: Saxe 34–33

Cher Monsieur: Voilà la photographie que vous désirez mais il faut la coller encore. Je vous remercie vivement des paroles amicales et encourageantes que Mlle Beach m'a transmises. Si vous avez fini de lire *Ulysse* je vous prie de me renvoyer les numéros de la 'L.R.' au plus tôt possible car il y a des autres qui voudraient lire l'ouvrage. Si vous désirez je peux vous les redonner dans une quinzaine de jours. Salutations cordiales   JAMES JOYCE[3]

To HARRIET SHAW WEAVER   MS. British Museum

1 March 1921   *Boulevard Raspail 5, Paris VII*

Dear Miss Weaver: ... I have at least one item of news which is not bad. A few days ago I received a most enthusiastic letter from Mr Valery Larbaud the French translator of Samuel Butler and also a novelist saying that he is 'raving mad' over *Ulysses* which, he is kind

---

[1] (Translation)
'Dear Mr Linati: Is there anything new about the publication or production of *Exiles*? I'm working like a convict until 3 or 4 in the morning. I finished *Circe* and *Eumeus*. The two last episodes that are left, *Ithaca* and *Penelope*, are also giving me a hard time. I can't be in Milan before May. Our meeting—so often postponed—will, I hope, take place in a more propitious season than this. Do you know about the trial of *Ulysses* in New York? Cordial greetings   James Joyce'
[2] Valery Larbaud (1881–1957), the French novelist, poet, and critic, met Joyce on Christmas Eve 1920 at the instigation of Sylvia Beach and Adrienne Monnier. Larbaud had translated Coleridge, Landor, and Samuel Butler, and besides English knew Italian and Spanish well. He was the most respected critic of foreign literature in Paris. When he expressed interest in *Ulysses*, Joyce lent him the *Little Review* numbers and the typescript of the unpublished part of the *Oxen of the Sun* episode. On 22 February 1921 Larbaud wrote Miss Beach that since he had read Whitman at the age of eighteen, he had never been so enthusiastic about any book. Mr Bloom is 'as immortal as Falstaff'.
[3] (Translation)
'Dear Sir: Here is the photograph that you wanted but it needs to be mounted. I thank you warmly for the friendly and encouraging words which Miss Beach conveyed to me. If you have finished reading *Ulysses*, be so good as to send back the issues of the "L. R." as soon as possible because there are others who would like to read the work. If you wish I could give them back to you again in two weeks. With kind regards   James Joyce'

enough to say, is as 'great and comprehensive and human as Rabelais'. He says that he has been unable to write or sleep since he read it and he proposes to translate some pages of it with an article in the *Nouvelle Revue Française*. I hope he will not change his mind. With kind regard sincerely yours   JAMES JOYCE

To HARRIET SHAW WEAVER (Postcard)   MS. British Museum

9 April 1921   [*Paris*]

Dear Miss Weaver: Last night at 6 o'clock Mrs Harrison, to whom the final scenes of *Circe* had been passed on for typing after the accident to Dr Livisier,[1] called on me in a state of great agitation and told me that her husband, employed in the British Embassy here, had found the MS, read it and then torn it up and burned it. I tried to get the facts from her but it was very difficult. She told me he had burned only part and that the rest was 'hidden'. I begged her to come home and bring me the rest. She left, promising to return in an hour. I waited till 10.30 but she did not return nor did she write or telephone today till now (11.30 a.m.). I suspect she has concealed some of the facts. As I am very tired please excuse this brief note. Sincerely yours   JAMES JOYCE

P.S. I withdrew *Ulysses* by cable an hour after receipt of your letter.[2]

To JOHN QUINN[3]   TS. N.Y. Public Library (Manuscript)

19 April 1921   *Boulevard Raspail 5, Paris VII*

Dear Mr Quinn: I understand that the typescript of *Ulysses* is on its way back, as I instructed. The publication of *Ulysses* (complete) was arranged here in a couple of days.[4] You will receive a prospectus in a week or so. It appears in October.

I hope you received the MS of *Circe* and *Eumeus*. As a curiosity I threw in also the 8th draft of the former.

---

[1] That is, the heart attack of the typist's father. See p. 38.

[2] B. W. Huebsch had been unable to evolve a satisfactory way of publishing *Ulysses* without alterations in the United States, especially after the *Little Review* trial.

[3] From a typed copy.

[4] Joyce, when the prospects of American publication collapsed, told Sylvia Beach of his difficulties. She courageously proposed that he allow her to publish the book in Paris, and he accepted at once. The plan was for a first edition of a thousand copies, to be sold in advance by subscription as far as possible. A four-page prospectus was mailed to several hundred people.

Unfortunately, a bad thing has happened. The husband of one of my many typists (an employee of the British Embassy here, named Harrison) found some of the MS on her table, read it, tore it up and burnt it. Hysterical scenes followed, I believe, in the house and in the street. What I am concerned with is that there is now a lacuna of several pages in the typescript, which has already gone to the printer, and I must write it in. Unfortunately, I had sent you the MS a few days before (the MS burnt was a copy of my MS made by Miss Beach). I need about six or seven pages back again for a day or so and will return them registered. Mrs S. W. Beach[1] sails for Europe on 4 May and could bring them. May I ask you to lend them to me? Here is the nearest clue I can give you to the passage: It begins about p. 60 or so, where Bloom leaves the brothel; there is a scene on the steps and then a hue and cry in the street and the beginning of the quarrel with the soldiers.[2] Six or seven pages after Bloom's exit (which you will find at a glance by the long catalogue of the persons in pursuit) will suffice.

In great haste and with regards and best thanks for your advocacy, Sincerely yours   JAMES JOYCE

To HARRIET SHAW WEAVER   MS. British Museum

23 April 1921   *Boulevard Raspail 5, Paris VII*

Dear Miss Weaver: . . . I saw Mr Pound. He has read *Circe* and *Eumeus* about which he appears to be very excited. He told me he had sent or was sending them to you. I am glad they are gone out of my house. I suppose you have now received Miss Beach's letter.[3] I do not think it is necessary to say anything about Mr Aldington's article[4] (I am writing to him in any case to thank him for it) except that it ought to attract some attention to the book. While I consider his article quite fair (though somewhat irrelevant to my mind) perhaps it would be well to pass on to Mr Eliot when you have read them the two episodes Mr Pound sent and also the typescript of *Oxen of the Sun* which I could send if you approve. I mention this because he told me it was arranged

[1] Sylvia Beach's mother.   [2] *Ulysses*, pp. 684–92 (585–90).
[3] Sylvia Beach wrote asking Miss Weaver for names of people in England who might subscribe to *Ulysses*.
[4] Richard Aldington, 'The Influence of Mr. James Joyce,' *English Review* (London) 32 (April 1921) 333–41. Aldington thought *Ulysses* 'remarkable' but too disparaging of humanity, and a bad influence on other writers.

that Mr Aldington was to write an article and he to reply to it.[1] In that case he ought to see the book in its present (penultimate) stage.

I heard just now that the *Little Review*, a monthly which came out every five or six months lately, has suddenly become a weekly or fortnightly publication. I have not been able to see Mr Pound, from whom the rumour originated, but I shall let you know more tomorrow.

Needless to say I agree in advance to anything you propose about the English edition. With many thanks and kindest regards sincerely yours

JAMES JOYCE

To FRANK BUDGEN   MS. Yale

[*31 May 1921*]   *Boulevard Raspail 5, Paris VII*

Dear Budgen: I leave this address in a few days. Write to me *pro tem*,

c/o Shakespeare & Co
rue Dupuytren, 8,
Paris VI

The position would be in the Cunard or Ellerman line.[2] Get into touch at once with Wyndham Lewis whom I saw off last night. He knows Lady Cunard who did also a lot for me.[3] Then Robert McAlmon, an American poet and admirer of *Ulysses*, is a son-in-law of Sir John Ellerman.[4] He went off with Lewis and they will do all they can. Don't lose time.

Had several uproarious allnight sittings (and dancings) with Lewis as he will perhaps tell you. I like him.

Giorgio leaves with Hummel and Magli[5] for Zurich on Friday for a month.

O this moving job!
Merda!   J.J.
Lewis's address, I think, is

2 Alma Studios
Stratford Road,
London, W.8.

---

[1] T. S. Eliot, 'Ulysses, Order, and Myth,' *Dial* (New York) LXXV.5 (November 1923) 480–83.
[2] Joyce was trying to place Budgen, a former sailor, in a secure position.
[3] See II, p. 380.
[4] Sir John Ellerman (1862–1933), English shipping magnate. See p. 48, n. 1.
[5] Rudolf Maeglin (b. 1892), Swiss artist. In 1921 he and Joyce attended a Paris exhibition of Picasso's work.

To Valery Larbaud   MS. Bib. Municipale, Vichy

5 June 1921   *rue du Cardinal Lemoine 71, Paris V*

Cher Larbaud: Nous voilà donc installés chez vous[1] depuis deux jours et déjà, après le sacré démenagement, je commence à m'y trouver si bien que l'épisode d'*Ithaque* procède rapidement. Un endroit plus favorable on ne pourrait penser pour la fin tranquille d'un libre si tumultueux. J'ai laissé *Circe* et les pourceaux, truies, boudins, andouilles, grognements etc là-bas au boulevard Raspail. Ma femme et Lucie sont enchantées. Elles me prient d'ajouter leur noms en vous disant encore une fois notre gratitude.

Pas de réponse de la part de Gallimard. Et je crois que Poe ne donnera pas la pièce. J'attends les premières épreuves d'*Ulysse* au 10 courant. Lucie veut savoir le nom de la petite farce dont vous m'avez parlé.

Comment allez-vous? Si la carte postale que vous m'avez envoyé est typique du pays je me promets déjà un sejour là quand le livre sera fini. C'était si touchant que j'ai dû penser à notre ballade mélancolique irlandaise 'I saw from the beach'.[2] Elle semble avoir toutes les colonies allemandes dans ses caleçons.[3]

Peutêtre de temps à autre vous trouverez là-bas sur la plage ou dans votre demeure ou qui sait où une trace quelconque de mon héros (dans le 25ᵉ livre de l'Odysée, brulé par l'ambassadeur britannique à Athènes on parle de son sejour à Σόραμος)[4] je vous prie de m'en parler. Spéciale-ment à qui regarde la fin.

L'astre devant votre fenêtre me conseille de finir parce qu'il commence à devenir sombre. Bien cordialement votre   James Joyce[5]

---

[1] Larbaud, who planned to travel until autumn, offered Joyce rent-free his small but handsome flat for the summer months. Joyce moved in on 3 June, and remained until 1 October 1921.

[2] One of Thomas Moore's *Melodies*.   [3] Probably an allusion to German tourists.

[4] A Hellenized form of Shoreham Beach, Sussex.

[5] (Translation)

'Dear Larbaud: Here we are in your flat since two days ago and already, after the damned move, I begin to feel so comfortable that the episode of *Ithaca* is progressing rapidly. A more favourable place for the peaceful ending to such a tumultuous book could not be imagined. I have left *Circe* and the pigs, sows, chitterlings, grunts etc. on Boulevard Raspail. My wife and Lucia are delighted. They ask that I add their names in telling you once again of our gratitude.

No answer from Gallimard. And I suppose Poe will not give the play. I expect the first proofs of *Ulysses* on the tenth inst. Lucia would like to know the name of the little farce you mentioned to her.

How are you? If the postcard you sent me is typical of the country I promise myself a trip there when the book is finished. It was so touching that I could not help thinking of our melancholy Irish ballad, 'I saw from the beach.' She seems to have all the German colonies in her drawers.

To Claud W. Sykes (Postcard)   MS. Yale

6 June 1921   *rue Cardinal Lemoine 71, Paris V*

Dear Mr Sykes: Above is my new address. Did you return the typescript. A copy arrived about a week ago but my family opened the wrapper so I don't know if it is yours or Eliot's. This is Valery Larbaud's flat in a charming little quarter situated in a kind of park. Giorgio went to Zurich on Thursday for a month's holiday.

Kind regards to Mrs Sykes and yourself from us both Sincerely yours
                                                         James Joyce

To Alessandro Francini Bruni   MS. S. Illinois (Croessmann)

7 June 1921   *71 rue du Cardinal Lemoine, V^e, Parigi*

Caro Francini: Suppongo che quell'articolo nell'*E.N.*[1] sia opera tua. Grazie. La chiusa è bella. Eccomi di nuovo sloggiato (e Silvestri che vuol mandarmi una tela sua dove ha la testa? Avessi una casa mia ben volentieri ci metterei i suoi quadri nonchè certi ammenicoli lasciati costì)—il quinto sloggio in 11 mesi. Il quartiere Boulevard Raspail mi costava la bellezza di 2000 lire al mese. Questo invece non mi costa niente. Il romanziere francese Valery Larbaud è fuori della grazia di Dio causa il mio *Ulisse* che proclama la più vasta ed umana opera scritta in Europa dopo Rabelais. Prescindendo da questo (del quale giudicherà l'avvenire) ha saputo corroborare il suo parere coi fatti. Avendo avuto qualche sentore dei miei grovigli fece arredare di nuovo il suo appartamento e me lo mise a disposizione per i mesi estivi. È quaclhe cosa d'incredibile. Dietro il Panthéon a 10 minuti dal Lussemburgo una specie di piccolo parco, al quale si accede attraverso due cancelli, silenzio assoluto, grandi alberi, uccelli (non di quei che intendi tu, veh!)[2] pare di essere a 100 chilometri da Parigi. Il mobiglio è delizioso. Egli ed il primo attore del teatro *Vieux Colombier* hanno ideato una specie d'ammobiliamento fantastico eppure comodissimo. È possibile ch'io valga qualche cosa? Chi l'avrebbe detto dopo la mia ultima esperienza a Trieste? Larbaud dice che il solo episodio di *Circe*

Perhaps from time to time you will find on the beach or in your lodgings or who knows where some trace of my hero (in the 25th book of the Odyssey, burned by the British Ambassador to Athens, his stay in Σόραμος is spoken of) please tell me about it. Especially in what concerns the end.

The star before your window advises me to finish this because it is beginning to get dark. Very cordially yours   James Joyce'

[1] *Era Nuova*, a Triestine daily newspaper which was published between 1919 and 1923.
[2] 'Uccello' in Italian means not only 'bird', but also, vulgarly, 'penis.'

basterebbe per fare la rinomanza di uno scrittore francese per la vita.
Ma o! ed a! ed ahime! ed oibo! che libro! L'episodio d'*Itaca* adesso
tutto geometria, algebra e matematica e dopo *Penelope* finalmente!
Potessi tuffare la mia testa in un mare di ghiaccio! È già sotto i torchi il
libro ed aspetto le prime bozze domani l'altro. Sarà pubblicato però
appena in ottobre o novembre. Trattandosi di tre edizioni costose
bisogna evitare i refusi. I colori della legatura (scelti da me) saranno
lettere bianche in campo azzurro—la bandiera greca quantunque
realmente d'origine bavarese ed importata colla dinastia. Eppure in
certo qual modo simboleggiano bene il mito—le isole bianche sparse nel
mare.

Quanto al lato materiale credo se l'edizione va bene (le sottoscrizioni
vengono ogni giorno—oggi 3 dall'Australia) riceverò qualcosa fra
100.000 e 150.000. Ma non è questo che mi preoccupa. Nessuna somma
potrà mai pagarmi il lavoro e lo sciupìo . . Si potrebbe scrivere
qualcosa di veramente comico sui sottoscriventi di questo mio libraccio
—un figlio o nipote di Bela Kun, il ministro della guerra britannico
Winston Churchill, un vescovo anglicano ed un capo del movimento
rivoluzionario irlandese.[1] Son diventato un monumento—anzi ves-
pasiano![2]

Giorgio è a Zurigo per le sue vacanze. Ordinerò il libro di Papini[3] ma
non prometto di leggerlo per il momento. Salutami Benco e Silvestri
pittore-speditore.

Bien d'amitiés à Madame et à Daniele[4] . . . Una stretta di mano

JAMES JOYCE[5]

[1] Probably Desmond Fitzgerald. See p. 61.
[2] A 'Vespasian' is a urinal, so named in honour of the Roman emperor who taxed them.
[3] Giovanni Papini (1881–1956), Italian writer. The book was probably his *Storia di Cristo* (1921).
[4] Francini's son. The ellipsis following is Joyce's.
[5] (Translation)
'Dear Francini: I suppose this article in the *Era Nuova* is your work. Thank you.
The close is fine. Here I am, forced to move again (and Silvestri, who wants to send me
one of his paintings, where does he abide? If I had a house of my own I should be very
glad to put his pictures there, as well as some knick-knacks left behind)—my fifth
move in eleven months. The flat on the Boulevard Raspail cost me a good 2000 lire a
month. But this one costs me nothing. The French novelist Valery Larbaud is beside
himself on account of my *Ulysses* which he proclaims the vastest and most human
work written in Europe since Rabelais. Apart from that (which the future will settle) he has
known how to corroborate his opinion with deeds. Having had some indication of my
mix-up he had his flat redecorated and put it at my disposition for the summer months.
It is unbelievable. Behind the Pantheon, ten minutes from the Luxembourg, a kind of
little park, with access through two barred gates, absolute silence, great trees, birds
(not, mind you, the sort you're thinking of!), like being a hundred kilometers from
Paris. The furnishings are tasteful. He and the principal actor of the Vieux Colombier
theatre have designed a kind of furniture which is fantastical but very comfortable. Is
it possible that I am worth something? Who would have said so after my last experience
in Trieste? Larbaud says that a single episode, *Circe*, would suffice to make the fame

To VALERY LARBAUD (Postcard)   MS. Bib. Municipale, Vichy

21 June 1921   [*Paris*]

Cher Larbaud: Les premières épreuves sont arrivées et je travaille à droite et à gauche avec les corrections et avec *Ithaque*. M. Jean de Bosschère vint me voir. Il va en Angleterre et désire vous voir. J'ai commis l'imprudence de lui donner votre adresse?? Una stretta di mano

JAMES JOYCE[1]

To FRANK BUDGEN   MS. Yale

[*Late June 1921*]   *71 rue du Cardinal Lemoine, V^e, Paris*

Dear Budgen: Have you seen Lewis? If nothing has come out of the Lady Cunard suggestion the Ellerman line is still open. The friend I spoke of is here. Write to me. *Ithaca* is giving me fearful trouble. Corrected the first batch of proofs today up to Stephen on the strand[2] which I read out to you on a memorable night in Zurich (Universitäts-strasse 29) with mirthful comments.[3] Hummel and Giorgio left for Zurich on the 4th. In the words of the Cyclops narrator the curse of my deaf and dumb arse light sideways on Bloom and all his blooms and blossoms. I'll break the back of *Ithaca* tomorrow so 'elp me fucking Chroist. Write by return   J J

of a French writer for life. But oh! and ah! and alas! and ugh! what a book! The episode of *Ithaca* now is all geometry, algebra, and mathematics, and then finally *Penelope*! I'd like to dip my head in a sea of ice! The book is already in press and I expect the first proofs day after tomorrow. It will be published only in October or November. Three expensive editions being involved, misprints have to be avoided. The colours of the binding (chosen by me) will be white letters on a blue field—the Greek flag though really of Bavarian origin and imported with the dynasty. Yet in a special way they symbolize the myth well—the white islands scattered over the sea.

On the material side I think if the edition goes well (subscriptions come every day—three today from Australia) I will receive between 100,000 and 150,000 [lire]. But that is not what concerns me. No sum of money could compensate me for my toil and trouble . . Something really comic could be written about the subscribers to my tome—a son or nephew of Bela Kun, the British Minister of War Winston Churchill, an Anglican bishop and a leader of the Irish revolutionary movement. I have become a monument—no, a Vespasian.

Giorgio is in Zurich for his holidays. I will order Papini's book but I don't promise to read it for the moment. Greet Benco and Silvestri the painter-shipper.

Good wishes to your wife and to Daniele . . . A handshake   James Joyce'

[1] (Translation)

'Dear Larbaud: The first proofs have arrived and I am working right and left on the corrections and on *Ithaca*. M. Jean de Bosschère came to see me. He is going to England and wants to see you. I have been so indiscreet as to give him your address?? A cordial handshake   James Joyce'

[2] The *Proteus* episode.

[3] Described in the second chapter of Budgen's book, *James Joyce and the Making of 'Ulysses'*.

P.S. There is an article about me in *Today*[1] but I haven't seen it, the rlwy strike (for which *YOU*[2] are responsible) seems to have disorganised the parcels bloody post again. (English undefiled!)

To Ezra Pound   MS. Cornell

[12 August 1921]   *[Paris]*

Dear Pound: Here are the songs.[3] There are, I think, eight others. The composer's address is:

> Glencormac
> Bray
> Co Wicklow (Ireland)

I signed the contract yesterday with *La Sirène*.[4] The manager, Mr Fénéon,[5] who by the way lunches today with Quinn an old friend of his, it seems, wants as much publicity as possible attracted to the book and seems disappointed at the Germain–Dugard bungle[6] as he thought the thing was arranged. The latter enthusiast (il faut que je publie ça au mois de septembre![7] etc) has been pursued by another telegram and his description has been given to the police   J.J.

To Carlo Linati (Postcard)   MS. Yale

Postmark 14 August 1921   *rue Cardinal Lemoine 71, Parigi V*

Caro Linati: Cosa c'è cogli 'Esuli' e con Lei. Spero che sta bene. Ero malato 6 settimane di nuovo cogli occhi. Mi scriva un paio di righe. Vorrei anche aver il *Convegno* coll'articolo di Rodker sulla letteratura inglese. Saluti cordiali   James Joyce[8]

---

[1] The leading article, probably by Holbrook Jackson, in *To-Day* (London) VIII. 46 (June 1921) [133]–34.

[2] Budgen was a onetime socialist.

[3] Evidently the settings of Joyce's poems by G. Molyneux Palmer.

[4] Editions de la Sirène published *Dedalus; Portrait de l'artiste jeune par lui-même* in March 1924.

[5] Félix Fénéon. His letters to Joyce about the edition are at Buffalo.

[6] Probably a plan to publish the book first in a review.

[7] 'I must publish that during the month of September!'

[8] (Translation)
'Dear Linati: What is new with *Exiles* and with you? I hope you are well. I have had eye trouble again for six weeks. Write me a line or two. I would also like to have *Convegno* with the article by Rodker on English literature. Cordial greetings   James Joyce'

To Robert McAlmon[1]   MS. Brigham Young University

3 September 1921   *71 rue du Cardinal Lemoine, V^e*

Dear MacAlmon [sic]: Thanks for your friendly letter. I hope you got mine with the I.O.U.[2] Since that collapse I have knocked off about 10 hours a day, work 6 and go walking. I feel much better so. I send back your proof and the letter. Send on a few more stories, the ones the English printer boggled at. This one is all right but I'd like to see more. So is the letter. I hope it is published somewhere. By the way the proof has many misprints[.] I didn't correct them as I thought you might have sent me a second copy. Proof is very tricky.

I sent on that lot of *Penelope* to Budgen but he hasn't written yet about it. If you see him please ask him to send it back. I have now written in a great lot of balderdash all over the damn book and the first half is practically as it will appear. I shall give Molly another 2000 word spin, correct a few more episodes and write all over them and then begin to put the spectral penultimate *Ithaca* into shape. Meanwhile walking along the Seine I look for some secluded spot where I may 'catch a hold of Bloom and throw him in the bloody sea' (pron. 'say').

How did you get on with Budgen and what news is there of Miss Weaver and others. Rodker is here but is going away again. I can take charge of that typewriter if you like but perhaps you want it or haven't you a portable one? Miss Beach and Miss Monnier are in the south, so is Nutting.

If you ever find anything relating to what I am doing throw it into an envelope and perhaps it will go into the stew.

No more subscriptions for *Ulysses*. Only 4 or 5 last month.

Whatever you send to France send by registered *letter* post (I mean your proofs, for example) as parcel post goes through the customs and takes a devil of a time. Kind regards and good luck Sincerely yours

                                                    James Joyce

---

[1] Robert McAlmon (1896–1956), American short story writer and poet, and publisher in the early 1920s of Contact Editions. On 14 February 1921 he married Winifred Ellerman, better known under her *nom de plume* of Bryher, in New York City. He lived principally in Paris until 1940, when he returned to the United States. His reminiscences of Joyce and other writers are contained in *Being Geniuses Together* (London, 1938).

[2] McAlmon, heavily financed by his father-in-law, advanced sums of money to Joyce who generally repaid them later, although McAlmon did not care.

To Harriet Shaw Weaver   MS. British Museum

9 September 1921   *71 rue du Cardinal Lemoine, V^e*

Dear Miss Weaver: Incredible though it may seem I have a new eye attack threatening me. I seem exhausted but am working as much as I dare. You have my authorisation to make any arrangements you wish with Mr Mathews and Mr Richards.[1] I wrote to the latter two or three years ago on the subject of *Verbannte* and enclose my contract (on which I paid 1000 frs Swiss) with Mr Rascher. Neither he nor any other publisher ever sends any royalties so that there is practically nothing for Mr Pinker to administer (the private edition of *Ulysses* being my own affair and risk) though he is nominally my agent and, if Mr Richards desires, the agreement can be made through him. I hope that it will be made without trouble and that nobody, except you, will write to me on that or any other subject. I am far too nervous from illness and overwork to attend to business of any kind. Sincerely yours

James Joyce

To Valery Larbaud   MS. Bib. Municipale, Vichy

[24 September 1921] Saturday   *[Paris]*

Dear Larbaud: I am nearly dead with work and eyes. Sent *Penelope* to the printers so that you may have it to read when you come here. All will be ready for you on the 2 October. The *Ithaca* episode I shall put in order in October. When does your article appear in N.R.F.? A man called for the chair but not about the mirror. You will scarcely recognise parts of *Ulysses* I have worked so much on them. Una stretta di mano   James Joyce

From Reverend Charles Doyle, S.J.   MS. Buffalo

3 October 1921   *Belvedere College Dublin*

Dear Sir The Christian name of the wife of the first Earl of Belvedere was Mary.[2] She was the daughter of Lord Molesworth. She never lived in Belvedere College, however. After the divorce court proceedings she

---

[1] For the taking over of *Dubliners* and *Exiles* by the Egoist Press. A new edition of the former appeared in 1922 and of the latter in 1921. *Chamber Music* was taken over later from Elkin Mathews and a new edition published in August 1923. In 1924, when the Egoist Press suspended publication, these books, together with *A Portrait of the Artist*, were taken over by Jonathan Cape.

[2] See II, p. 193, n. 7.

was confined in Gaulstown, Co. Westmeath, the old seat of the family, near Belvedere House by the shore of Lough Ennel, a new residence just completed by the Earl. The Countess Mary died about 1780. Belvedere House (now Belvedere College) was not completed and occupied by the second Earl (the builder of it), until 1786. Yours faithfully,   Charles Doyle S.J.

From Bernard Shaw to Sylvia Beach[1]

10 October 1921   *10 Adelphi Terrace, London, W.C.2*

Dear Madam, I have read several fragments of *Ulysses* in its serial form. It is a revolting record of a disgusting phase of civilisation; but it is a truthful one; and I should like to put a cordon round Dublin; round up every male person in it between the ages of 15 and 30; force them to read it; and ask them whether on reflection they could see anything amusing in all that foul mouthed, foul minded derision and obscenity. To you, possibly, it may appeal as art: you are probably (you see I don't know you) a young barbarian beglamoured by the excitements and enthusiasms that art stirs up in passionate material; but to me it is all hideously real: I have walked those streets and known those shops and have heard and taken part in those conversations. I escaped from them to England at the age of twenty; and forty years later have learnt from the books of Mr. Joyce that Dublin is still what it was, and young men are still drivelling in slackjawed blackguardism just as they were in 1870. It is, however, some consolation to find that at last somebody has felt deeply enough about it to face the horror of writing it all down and using his literary genius to force people to face it. In Ireland they try to make a cat cleanly by rubbing its nose in its own filth. Mr. Joyce has tried the same treatment on the human subject. I hope it may prove successful.

I am aware that there are other qualities and other passages in *Ulysses*: but they do not call for any special comment from me.

I must add, as the prospectus implies an invitation to purchase, that I am an elderly Irish gentleman, and that if you imagine that any Irishman, much less an elderly one, would pay 150 francs for a book, you little know my countrymen. Faithfully,   G. Bernard Shaw

---

[1] The text of this letter is taken from Sylvia Beach, *Shakespeare and Company* (New York, 1959), p. 52, except that the word 'several' in the first sentence has been restored from a typed copy among Joyce's papers.

To VALERY LARBAUD   MS. Bib. Municipale, Vichy

11 October 1921   [*Paris*]

Dear Larbaud: I am still waiting for *Penelope*. Perhaps it will come
tomorrow.[1] Meanwhile I send you enclosed. Can you read between the
lines?[2] Io, si. Sincerely yours   JAMES JOYCE

To HARRIET SHAW WEAVER   MS. British Museum

13 October 1921   *rue de l'Université 9, Paris VII*

Dear Miss Weaver: Enclosed is a copy of a letter which I saw only
yesterday. Copies of the prospectus were sent to Mr W. B. Yeats, Mr
George Moore and of course they did not reply. This will not prevent
them however from subscribing for the book anonymously through a
bookseller in common with the elderly Irish gentleman. Sincerely yours
                                                       JAMES JOYCE

P.S. Perhaps I 'ought to add' that I win a bet (made six months ago)
thanks to Mr Shaw's letter.[3]

To VALERY LARBAUD   MS. Bib. Municipale, Vichy

20 October 1921   [*Paris*]

Dear Larbaud: Herewith the *Penelope* episode, uncorrected and incomplete but perhaps enough to allow you to get a general idea of it.
I hope you will like it. Kind regards   JAMES JOYCE

To VALERY LARBAUD   MS. Bib. Municipale, Vichy

30 October 1921   *rue de l'Université 9*

Dear Larbaud: My typist has sent you extracts (of course uncorrected)
from the beginning and middle of *Ithaca*. In a few days she will send you
extracts from the end. I shall send you the proof of the Messianic
[scene] from *Circe* when I get it back.

I finished *Ithaca* last night so that now the writing of *Ulysses* is
ended, though I have still some weeks of work in revising the proofs.
Sincerely yours   JAMES JOYCE

    [1] From the typist.
    [2] Joyce sent Larbaud a copy of Shaw's letter. He felt sure that Shaw had subscribed
to the book anonymously. (*Letters*, ed. Gilbert, p. 173.)
    [3] Joyce had bet Sylvia Beach a silk handkerchief against a box of Voltigeurs (a brand
of small cigars) that Shaw would not subscribe.

To Harriet Shaw Weaver   MS. British Museum

1 November 1921   *rue de l'Université 9, Paris VII*

Dear Miss Weaver: A fortnight ago I sent you by registered post a set of proofs (receipt enclosed). Did you receive them safely? If so will you please send them back, preferably in two or three registered letters as printed matter often takes weeks to reach here. I have two new sets to send but should like to know that the first reached you.

I have now finished the *Ithaca* episode and with that the writing of *Ulysses*. What remains to be done is the revision of proofs of the last four episodes. The printer says he can set it all by 15 November and bring it out, he hopes, by the end of the month. I intend to do nothing in the way of revision of proofs for two days as I feel very tired and listless. I shall begin again on Thursday and the fault will be the printer's not mine if the book is not out in a few weeks.

Those few weeks, however, are a trouble to me materially. About 400 subscriptions are made, I believe, but no part of the money will be available till the notices go out towards the end of the month to the effect that the book is ready. I should be glad to have these three weeks free in order to complete the revision of the last proofs. The landlord is already somewhat dubious I am afraid. I have scarcely energy enough to write more precisely but if there is any small amount forthcoming in the way of royalties I should be greatly relieved to have it by return. If I can get over these few weeks in peace I am quite willing to do any active work which society may assign me.

A coincidence is that of birthdays in connection with my books. *A Portrait of the Artist* which first appeared serially in your paper on 2 February finished on 1 September. *Ulysses* began on 1 March (birthday of a friend of mine, a Cornish painter)[1] and was finished on Mr Pound's birthday,[2] he tells me. I wonder on whose it will be published.[3]

I am sending this by airmail and, if not too much trouble for you, would be glad to have a line from you in reply.

With kind regards and apologies for the somewhat fatigued and certainly boring contents of the present sincerely yours James Joyce

[1] Frank Budgen, who was half Cornish; Joyce preferred to regard him as totally a fellow Celt.

[2] 30 October.

[3] Joyce had already made up his mind that it should appear on 2 February 1922, his own birthday.

To VALERY LARBAUD   MS. Bib. Municipale, Vichy
6 November 1921   *rue de l'Université 9, Paris*

Dear Larbaud: Many thanks for those kind words of dedication which
I saw yesterday with pleasure.[1] I recognised in the story many points we
discussed during *notti bianche*.[2] Expected to see you last night at *The
Kid*[3] and hope you are not ill. Possibly I may see you tonight. If not I
shall post you my scheme of *Ulysses*[4] and proposed programme for the
readings[5] Sincerely yours   JAMES JOYCE

To VALERY LARBAUD   MS. Bib. Municipale, Vichy
11 November 1921   [*Paris*]

Dear Larbaud: Here is my copy of the book so far for you to look
through to refresh your memory. I should like to have it back as soon as
possible—even piecemeal—as I need it to refer to. One copy of each
page proof coming in will also be sent you. I add the unrevised pages
(galley) of the Messianic scene from *Circe*. Can you fix Wednesday
23 Nov. as date of conference?[6] The translations of passages chosen by
you have been made. I went over them with Benoit-Mechin.[7] Kind
regards   JAMES JOYCE

To VALERY LARBAUD   MS. Bib. Municipale, Vichy
[*About 15 November 1921*]   [*Paris*]

Dear Larbaud: Hope you are better. Can you let me have that little
plan I gave you of *Ulysses*. I shall amplify it and send it back next day.
Please let me have it tomorrow Sincerely yours   JAMES JOYCE

[1] Larbaud dedicated his *nouvelle*, '*Amants, heureux amants*,' *Nouvelle revue française*
XVII.98 (1 November 1921) 522–56, 'To James Joyce, my friend, and the only begetter
of the form I have adopted in this piece of writing. V.L. Paris, novembre 1921.'
[2] 'Sleepless nights.'   [3] A film of Charlie Chaplin.
[4] The elaborate plan of *Ulysses* was circulated among only a few of Joyce's friends and
reviewers until Stuart Gilbert included most of it in *James Joyce's* Ulysses (London, 1930).
A typed copy of it is reproduced complete in *A James Joyce Miscellany*, ed. Marvin
Magalaner (Carbondale, Illinois, 1959), opposite p. 48.
[5] Larbaud asked Joyce to select passages from *Ulysses* to be read at a *conférence*.
[6] This was not held until 7 December 1921.
[7] Jacques Benoist-Méchin (b. 1901), French historian and man of letters, and later an
important official in the Laval government. He was at this time a young man of twenty,
full of enthusiasm for Joyce's work, and he translated the passages from *Ulysses* which
Larbaud wished to read in his *conférence*.

To FRANK BUDGEN (Postcard)   MS. Yale

[*23 November 1921*][1]   [*Paris*]

Dear Budgen: Let me know what day you arrive. Can you bring me a
little book on palmistry? I enclose 10 francs. Hope you come soon. I
have a lesson for you here perhaps. Eye attack threatening but hope to
Christ not. Please reply by return. Can you find what is the price of a
book published about a year ago *My Three Husbands*, author unknown.[2]
Sincerely yours   JAMES JOYCE

Glad you liked Ithaca.

To VALERY LARBAUD   MS. Bib. Municipale, Vichy

26 November 1921   [*Paris*]

Dear Larbaud: Can you dine with me tonight? I hope so as I want to
show you and comment on the new plan and discuss this matter which is
rather delicate, I think, and important. As we shall dine at our end and
I shall be at work all day would it be too much to ask you to call for me,
say, at 7.30?

I have seen the notice of your séance and am glad and honoured to
see our names associated for my first (or possibly last?) appearance
before a French public Bien des choses   JAMES JOYCE

To ARTHUR POWER[3]   MS. S. Illinois (Croessmann)

[*? November 1921*]   [*Paris*][4]

Dear Power Here are the episodes with cuts and blunders. I have two
later ones in typescript and will give them next week.   J.J.

From SHERWOOD ANDERSON[5]   TS. Private

3 December 1921   *Chicago, Illinois*

Dear Mr. Joyce:— I am writing this note to make you acquainted with
my friend Ernest Hemingway, who with Mrs. Hemingway is going to

[1] This date is written on the postcard in another hand.
[2] *My Three Husbands*, a fairly amusing book by an anonymous woman author, was
published by Methuen in London in May 1921.
[3] Arthur Power (b. 1891), a young Irish writer who had met Joyce in the Bal Bullier
at the celebration that took place about 10 April 1921, the day Joyce and Sylvia Beach
signed a contract for the publication of *Ulysses*.
[4] The letter is on stationery of Shakespeare and Company at 8 rue Dupuytren.
[5] Sherwood Anderson (1876–1941), the American writer, had met Joyce during the
late spring or summer of this year.

Paris to live, and will ask him to drop it in the mails when he arrives there.

Mr. Hemingway is an American writer instinctively in touch with everything worth while going on here and I know you will find both Mr. and Mrs. Hemingway delightful people to know.[1]

They will be at 74 Rue du Cardinal Lemoine. Sincerely,

SHERWOOD ANDERSON

To VALERY LARBAUD   MS. Bib. Municipale, Vichy

[*About 14 December 1921*]   [*Paris*]

Dear Larbaud: The following passages in the *Cyclops* episode are new or so amplified as to be new. Will you read them?

Inisfail (parable of S. Michan's)	p. 282 et seq.
Cyclops	p. 284 et seq.
Execution	p. 293 et seq.
Lecture attendance	p. 304
Forester's Marriage	p. 312 et 313
Cyclop's [sic] Handkerchief	p. 317 et 318

Hope you are well and that Fargue[2] was not too bored the other night by my 'conférence' Sincerely yours   JAMES JOYCE

To ALESSANDRO FRANCINI BRUNI   MS. S. Illinois (Croessmann)

30 December 1921   *rue de l'Université 9, Paris VII*

Caro Francini: Grazie delle tue lettere.[3] La fotografia ti sàra mandata direttamente—forse domani. Io non ho un momento libero. Sono nato in 1882 a Dublino. Il mio primo libro era *Chamber Music* (*Musica da Camera*). Quell'articolo apparve nel *Fortnightly Review* Aprile 1900 sull'ultimo dramma di Ibsen *Quando noi morti ci destiamo*. Quel motivo

---

[1] On 9 March 1922 Hemingway wrote Anderson (MS. Newberry Library), 'Joyce has a most goddamn wonderful book. It'll probably reach you in time. Meantime the report is that he and all his family are starving but you can find the whole celtic crew of them every night in Michaud's where Binney and I can only afford to go about once a week.

'Gertrude Stein says Joyce reminds her of an old woman out in San Francisco. The woman's son struck it rich as hell in the Klondyke and the old woman went around wringing her hands and saying, "Oh my poor Joey! My poor Joey! He's got so much money!" The damned Irish, they have to moan about something or other, but you never heard of an Irishman starving.'

[2] Léon-Paul Fargue (1878–1947), the French poet, had helped Benoist-Méchin with the translation of passages for Larbaud's *conférence*.

[3] Francini wrote asking for some information he needed for a lecture on Joyce which he was to give in Trieste on 22 February 1922.

liturgico è l'introito[1] per tempo pasquale '*Vidi aquam egredientem de templo a latere dextro*'.[2] Il monastero al quale alludi è forse Einsiedeln? Scrivimi ancora se hai tempo. Per un esemplare d'*Ulisse* non so. Vedrò. Prima si era deciso a non dare esemplari alla stampa. Si criticherà e si venderà lo stesso eppoi è troppo caro. L'esemplare a buon prezzo costa 300 lire e pesa 2 chili. Poi si decise a fare 18 esemplari su carta inferiore per certi critici che sono molto in vista ma di questi 18 solo 2 sono destinati all'Italia. In somma vedrò. Spero avrai successo colla tua conferenza—ma quando incontri un triestino (oltre il bar. Ralli che ha sottoscritto) che pagherà 300 lire per un libro di Zois[3] accendi una candela a Sant'Antonio Taumaturgo.

Ogni bene e felicità a te ed ai tuoi nell'anno nuovo   JAMES JOYCE[4]

To VALERY LARBAUD   MS. Bib. Municipale, Vichy

5 January 1922   [*Paris*]

Dear Larbaud: Many thanks for New Year's wishes and those succulent chocolates. We shall meet on Saturday, I hope. Pound wants to do an article on Ramon Gomez de la . . . de la. . . .[5] In a shop[6] at the corner of rue Jacob, rue Furstenberg you will see a picture of Molly *avec le vieux lion.*[7]

Σάς ευχαριστώ πολύ δία τήν ευγενίαν σάς ό φίλος τόυ[8]

JAMES JOYCE

[1] Not the Introit but the Asperges. Joyce persisted in this error in his book.

[2] Quoted by Stephen Dedalus in *Ulysses* at the beginning of the *Circe* episode, pp. 563–64 (431).

[3] The Triestine way of pronouncing Joyce.

[4] (Translation)

'Dear Francini: Thanks for your letters. The photograph will be sent to you directly —perhaps tomorrow. I don't have a moment free. I was born in 1882 in Dublin. My first book was *Chamber Music* (*Musica da Camera*). That article appeared in the *Fortnightly Review* for April 1900 on the last play of Ibsen, *When We Dead Awaken*. That liturgical theme is the Introit for Paschal time, '*Vidi aquam egredientem de templo a latere dextro*'. The monastery to which you refer is perhaps Einsiedeln? Write me again if you have time. As for a copy of *Ulysses* I don't know. I'll see. It was first decided not to give copies to the press. They will review and buy it anyway. Besides it is too expensive. The cheap copy costs 300 lire and weighs two kilos. Now it's been decided to print 18 copies on cheaper paper for certain well-known critics but of these 18 only 2 are intended for Italy. So I will see. I wish you success with your lecture—but when you find a Triestine (other than Baron Ralli who has subscribed) who will pay 300 lire for a book of Zois light a candle to Saint Anthony the Worker of Miracles.

All good wishes to you and your family for the new year   James Joyce'

[5] Ramon Gomez de la Serna (b. 1891), Spanish novelist, dramatist, critic, and aphorist, in whom Larbaud was much interested.

[6] Joyce and Larbaud used to play a game of spotting Bloom and Mrs Bloom in Paris cafés.

[7] 'With the old lion,' that is, with *Leo*pold Bloom.

[8] In modern Greek: 'I am extremely grateful to you for your generosity. Your friend.'

To MYRON C. NUTTING (Postcard)   MS. Northwestern

9 January 1922   [*Paris*

Dear Nutting: Miss Beach would like to have that colour tomorrow if possible. The blue is all right but possibly a little faded as the flag was exposed for some time in the sunlight.[1]

Many thanks and kind regards to Mrs Nutting and yourself

JAMES JOYCE

To ROBERT MCALMON   MS. Pearson

23 January 1922[2]   [*Paris*]

Dear McAlmon: Here pp. 683 to end is *Penelope* in uncorrected semi-final form. Please excuse me to Miss Hamnet.[3] I shall not be quite free till Wednesday and am in a state of energetic prostration. Can you tell Giorgio where we can meet tonight say at 7.30 or tomorrow at 12 noon? If he doesn't find you please send me a *pneu*.

Ulysses is supposed to appear on Saturday or Monday. Sincerely yours   JAMES JOYCE

To FRANK BUDGEN   MS. Yale

31 January 1922   *rue de l'Université 9, Paris VII*

Dear Budgen: *Ulysses* will probably be published the day after to-morrow. You will get your copy as soon as the post-batch arrives. I have been working on the last proofs till this morning and am exhausted.

Thanks for your good wishes for my birthday and please give our regards to the Suters. My wife is better but the excitement has made her very nervous.

Was it you who sent me *My Three Husbands*.[4] If so how much do I owe you?   JAMES JOYCE

From MAURICE DARANTIÈRE[5]   TS. Buffalo

1 February 1922   *Maurice Darantiere, Maistre imprimeur, A Dijon*

Trois exemplaires de Ulysses sont remis au courrier de ce soir comme Lettres Express à l'adresse de Miss Beach.[6]

[1] Joyce wished to have *Ulysses* bound in the colours of the Greek flag, white on blue. The binders had great trouble in finding the right blue; to help them Joyce sent a Greek flag to his friend, the artist Myron C. Nutting (b. 1890, an American who lived in Paris from 1919 to 1929), and asked him to mix the exact shade for them to copy.

[2] Joyce misdates 1921.

[3] Nina Hamnett (1890–1956), English painter and author of two books of reminiscences.

[4] See p. 54.   [5] Maurice Darantière was Joyce's much tried printer in Dijon.

[6] This letter did not satisfy Joyce, who attached much talismanic importance to

L'officine toute entière est heureuse d'avoir lu votre lettre du 30 janvier. Elle est heureuse de vous offrir le premier exemplaire à la date du 2 Février.   MAURICE DARANTIERE.[1]

From STANISLAUS JOYCE   MS. Buffalo

26 February 1922   *via Sanità 2, Trieste*

Dear Jim, I received 'Ulysses' in good order. Many months before I was sent an imperfect typescript of 'Circe'. When I got your letter enclosing copy of Shaw's almighty opinion I brought it to Benco, whom I succeeded in seeing after having called at the 'Nazione' several times. He read the letter carefully and mumbled that it was 'very interesting, very interesting indeed' but he didn't think it would interest his readers. When I received 'Ulysses' I likewise hastened to him and offered to lend it to him even before I had read it myself. He was very polite but he was very busy. He said he would ask me for it when he had time to read it. My impression is that he does not like the later developments of the book. Who is Silvio,[2] anyhow?

I suppose 'Circe' will stand as the most horrible thing in literature, unless you have something on your chest still worse than this 'Agony in the Kips'. Isn't your art in danger of becoming a sanitary science. I wish you would write verse again. The last few things you have written are of so much finer a quality than your early verse that no one can doubt what you might do if you tried again. I should think you would need something to restore your self respect after this last inspection of the stinkpots. Everything dirty seems to have the same irresistable attraction for you that cow-dung has for flies. I recognize, of course the almost unlimited adaptability of your style: the flabby Dublin journalese, with its weak effort to be witty, or suitable to the morning after the night before, and only too well, the obscene ignorant scrawl of 'Penelope', but in the return of 'Ulysses' I don't understand the intention of the catechism.[3]

Francini has read a conferenza-caricature on you in the hall of

receiving the first copy of his book on his fortieth birthday, 2 February. At his behest Sylvia Beach telephoned Darantière to say that the post was too uncertain. The printer then offered to dispatch more copies by the conductor of the Dijon–Paris express, due to arrive in Paris at 7 o'clock in the morning of the crucial day. Miss Beach met the train and received a bundle containing two copies, one of which she brought to Joyce, the other exhibited in her shop.

    [1] (Translation)

      'Three copies of *Ulysses* have been sent tonight by express post to Miss Beach.

      The entire shop is happy to have read your letter of 30 January. It is happy to present you with the first copy on 2 February.   Maurice Darantière.'

    [2] That is, Silvio Benco.

    [3] The *Ithaca* episode.

Filarmonica.[1] You may easily guess that he has been out of a job for some time and was trying to turn an honest penny. He goes to Florence to-morrow to take up a job on the 'Nuovo Giornale'. The hall was about half-full. Anybody to whom I have spoken about it was dissatisfied, but I am sending you the booklet so that you can judge it for yourself. He swore to me before the lecture that it was a caricature in good taste and 'worthy of the subject'. Instead, it was vulgar and silly and worthy of the 'Coda del Diavolo'.[2] It did neither him nor you nor my own apparently negligible self any good. Dagli amici mi guardi Iddio.[3] These people know each other.

In December last you promised to send me back the money I gave you as soon as the book was off your hands. So far I have got nothing. I bought those ten pounds two years ago at over ninety lire to the pound, so that I will lose in any case. If you want the money, keep it; but I don't think it possible that you want it. You got money on your arrival in Paris. Your last letter announced a further gift of two thousand pounds. You cannot be in need of ten pounds for two years. I am. In fact this seems to me only part and parcel of the careless indifference with which you have always acted in affairs that concerned me. I am no longer a boy.

I hope Nora has quite recovered from her accident—of which I have heard different accounts. Remember me to her and to Georgie and Lucia.   STANNIE

To FERDINAND REYHER[4]   MS. S. Illinois (Feinberg)

14 March 1922   *rue de l'Université 9, Paris VII*

Dear Reyher: Many thanks for your continued interest in my books. The few press copies (18) of *Ulysses* have all been disposed of. The edition at 150 francs is sold out and Miss Beach would not like to part with any *édition de luxe* at 350 or 250 on these terms. Moreover, the translation would take nearer 10 years than 1 year. Let the translator begin on *The Portrait* (English rights belong to The Egoist Press)

---

[1] Alessandro Francini Bruni, *Joyce intimo spogliato in piazza* (Trieste, 1922). The title means, 'Joyce Stripped in the Marketplace.' Francini delivered the lecture in the Sala della Società Filarmonico-Drammatica.

[2] *La Coda del Diavolo* ('The Devil's Tail'), a newspaper published in Trieste from 1909 to 1915 under the editorship of Vittorio Cuttin. Its contents were generally scurrilous or disgusting.

[3] 'God protect me from my friends.' The Italian proverb goes on: 'from my enemies I protect myself.'

[4] Ferdinand Reyher, American writer, author of *The Man, the Tiger, and the Snake* (New York and London, 1921), and of *David Farragut, Sailor* (New York, 1953).

which is already translated into French, Swedish and Spanish. If you
would pass this information on to him and to his firm they can both get
to work when they have acquired the rights.

I am going away shortly for a holiday but you can always write c/o
Miss Beach here. I hope you are enjoying yourself. I rarely see anybody
as I am still busy (a chore) helping in sending out copies. With many
thanks and regards Sincerely yours   JAMES JOYCE

To ROBERT MCALMON   MS. Pearson

17 March 1922   *rue de l'université 9, Paris*

Dear McAlmon: I send back your article[1]—many thanks. I corrected
the title of Flaubert's book in it and added a footnote—Miss Beach's
address. She doesn't know what paper it could go to and as it's all about
ME I can't send it anywhere myself. What about *Broom*?[2] The editor
Loeb is in Paris, I hear. I suppose the *Gargoyle*[3] is useless. As regards
Dial Pound, Eliot and Colum are all doing or have done articles in it so
I fancy they are full up. A new number of *The Tyro*[4] is out but a review
to be of service to me should appear shortly. I suppose your father-in-
law[5] could not place it anywhere? The 150 franc edition is out of print,
there remain only 250 and 350 francs copies. Matters are in a dreadful
tangle with Darantière however. We can't get press copies out of him
and Miss Beach leaves for Dijon tonight. I have not had a day's peace
since the book came out. If the press copies came and if the rest of the
edition were quickly disposed of accounts would be settled up quickly
and I could at last lie back. As it is Miss B. the Greek girl[6] and I make
frantic endeavours to hasten that consummation.

I will send any other notice I get. Let me know what you do with the
notice. Thanks for sending it. It's all right. Are there any 250 or 350 fr
candidates[7] down there? Sincerely yours   JAMES JOYCE

[1] Joyce had importuned McAlmon to write a review of *Ulysses*. It does not seem to have been published.

[2] *Broom*, 'an international magazine of the arts,' was founded in Paris in November 1921 by Harold A. Loeb (b. 1891). It continued until January 1924.

[3] *Gargoyle*, a little magazine published in Paris from August 1921 to about October 1922. The editor was Arthur Moss.

[4] *The Tyro*, 'a review of the arts of painting, sculpture and design,' edited by Wyndham Lewis, was published in London in 1921–22. There were only two issues.

[5] Sir John Ellerman.

[6] Myrsine Moschos, assistant to Miss Beach in Shakespeare and Company.

[7] That is, candidates for copies of *Ulysses*. Of the 1,000 copies of the first printing of *Ulysses*, the first hundred, signed by the author, were priced at 350 francs; the next 150, on *vergé d'arches*, at 250 francs; and the rest, on less costly linen paper, at 150 francs.

To Stanislaus Joyce[1]   TS. S. Illinois (Croessmann)

20 March 1922   *rue de l'Université 9, Paris VII*

Dear Stannie, My solicitor will send you a cheque for 10£ on the 25 instant. I am sorry to hear you are pressed for money. How do you manage it? Living in a furnished apartment without a family, of exemplary habits and giving all the lessons to all the pupils. My case is different. Except for the four months I lived in Larbaud's flat and the first six weeks I pay between 2500 and 3000 lire a month rent. The last six months' work on Ulysses I did in this bedroom where three of us sleep without a desk, without books, etc.

I did not receive the copy you promised of Joyce Spogliato in Casa. I am sure it was very funny and quite suited to the distinguished audience.

Miss Weaver has made me another gift of £1500 in addition to the £2000 and the previous £5000 making £8500 in all, as well as the reversion of a country house somewhere. Nobody of my admirers in Trieste subscribed for Ulysses, except Baron Ralli. The first English notice appeared last week, and the day after 148 copies were ordered. The edition, 750 copies, at 150 francs, is out of print since Wednesday last. There remain only 50 copies of the de luxe and about 80 of the 250 franc, so the bowsies had better hurry up.

I have now to arrange for the private English and American editions, out of which I expect to make as much again. The Paris edition brings me 82,000 net. It is a pity the fisarmonici[2] did not know these funny details, or perhaps it is just as well. They might have laughed themselves to death.

I was entertained to lunch last Friday by the British and Irish press of Paris, Admiral Sir Heaten Ellis[3] in the chair. The Dail Eirann Minister of Publicity[4] called on me and asked me if I intended to return to Ireland at present. I told him not for the present. One redeemed city (and inhabitants thereof) will last me for a few years more. He has proposed a resolution to his Irish cabinet to send my name to Stockholm as candidate for the Nobel prize. He will probably lose his portfolio without obtaining the prize for me.

I have to remain here sometime yet to sign the last of the de luxe

---

[1] From an incomplete copy. The whereabouts of the original is not known.

[2] A play on 'fisarmonica' (accordion) and the 'philharmonic' hall where Francini gave his lecture.

[3] Vice-Admiral Sir Edward Heaton-Ellis (1868–1943).

[4] Desmond Fitzgerald (1889–1947), Irish politician, was Minister for Publicity from 1918 to 1922, for External Affairs from 1922 to 1927, and for Defence from 1927 to 1932.

copies and to arrange with the publishers of the English and American editions and to have some of the chief errors and omissions rectified on the plates. After that I must get a holiday somewhere for a few months. As soon as money and time allow me to settle down I shall visit your hospitable city to collect a few odds and ends: pardon, to make a bundle of several things I could not put into my trunk on the occasion of my departure from Trieste.

Nora has quite recovered from the shock—it was hardly an accident [typescript breaks off]

To HARRIET SHAW WEAVER   MS. British Museum

20 March 1922   *rue de l'Université 9, Paris VII*

Dear Miss Weaver: Many thanks for the plan.[1] Besides misprints I see with surprise that it is in part mislined making nonsense of the middle of the scheme. I shall have the omitted lines inserted, the whole retyped and send it back to you.

I suppose you saw the article in the *Daily Herald*[2] of last Friday. I could get only 2 copies here so that if you have a few I should like to have two or three. The artist's impression of me struck me so forcibly that I thought the only thing to be done was to send you a recent photograph which I hope you received.

Is it possible to find out diplomatically whether there is a copy of *Ulysses* in the British Museum Library? An order came from the Greek manuscripts department but it may have been private. Another order, it seems, from the library was transmitted by a bookseller. If they have no copy I shall present one, of course. But if they have one already it is useless to waste a copy.

I suppose a notice or notices will appear this week. Mr S. P. B. Mais of *Daily Express* who got a copy says he will write an 'appreciative article'.[3] The question of press and library copies which has been worrying me has been solved at last but not until Miss Beach went down to Dijon. She came back yesterday and everything seems to be in order now. With kindest regards sincerely yours   JAMES JOYCE

[1] The scheme of *Ulysses*.
[2] George Slocombe, 'The Week in Paris,' *Daily Herald* (London), 17 March 1922, p. 4.
[3] S. P. B. Mais, 'An Irish Rebel: and Some Flappers,' *Daily Express* (London), 25 March 1922.

To [NORA BARNACLE JOYCE][1]   MS. Private

[April 1922] 8.30 a.m. Thursday   *[Paris]*

My darling, my love, my queen: I jump out of bed to send you this.
Your wire is postmarked 18 hours later than your letter which I have
just received. A cheque for your fur will follow in a few hours, and also
money for yourself. If you wish to live there (as you ask me to send two
pounds a week) I will send that amount (£8 and £4 rent) on the first of
every month. But you also ask me if I would go to London with you. I
would go anywhere in the world if I could be sure that I could be alone
with your dear self without family and without friends. Either this must
occur or we must part forever, though it will break my heart. Evidently
it is impossible to describe to you the despair I have been in since you
left. Yesterday I got a fainting fit in Miss Beach's shop and she had to
run and get me some kind of a drug. Your image is always in my heart.
How glad I am to hear you are looking younger! O my dearest, if you
would only turn to me even now and read that terrible book which has
now broken the heart in my breast and take me to yourself alone to do
with me what you will! I have only 10 minutes to write this so forgive me.
Will write again before noon and also wire. These few words for the
moment and my undying unhappy love.   JIM

To JACQUES BENOIST-MÉCHIN   MS. Benoist-Méchin

8 April 1922   *rue de l'Université 9, Paris VII*

Dear Mr Mechin: I am glad to know that you have received your copy
of *Ulysses* safely and that your manuscript of the music on pp. 643–644[2]
has been decently reproduced. It was very kind of you to take all that
trouble and to have endured so patiently the hearing of Molly Bloom's
characteristic songs *qui ne sont plus dans le mouvement.*[3] I hope the
reading may relieve in some measure the monotony of your life down
there. With renewed thanks Sincerely yours   JAMES JOYCE

---

[1] Nora Joyce insisted, against her husband's wishes, on taking the children with her
and going to Ireland on 1 April 1922. She seems to have threatened not to come back.
Once in Galway, she telegraphed to him for funds. But the Civil War fighting made her
return about the end of April to Paris.
[2] The music for the ballad of 'The Jew's Daughter', *Ulysses*, pp. 809–10 (690–1).
[3] 'Which are no longer in fashion.'

To MYRON C. NUTTING   MS. Northwestern

24 April 1922   [*Paris*]

Dear Nutting: I am sorry I was not free the other evening but to tell
the truth I am anything but a pleasant messmate at present. Thanks
for thinking of me. The only news of any weight is enclosed.[1] Will you
please return it when read Sincerely yours   JAMES JOYCE

To MRS MYRON C. NUTTING   MS. Northwestern

26 April 1922   *rue de l'Université 9, Paris*

Dear Mrs Nutting: The address[2] is c/o Miss Casey, 5 Nun's Island,
Galway. Sincerely yours   JAMES JOYCE

To HARRIET SHAW WEAVER   MS. British Museum

30 April 1922   *rue de l'Université 9, Paris*

Dear Miss Weaver: Thanks for copies of the *Nation*. Mr Murry's
article[3] is very useful for I think it will break the boycott.[4] I met him
casually a few days ago at lunch and he wrote me the enclosed[5] afterwards. He tells me he has written a second article and wants to do a
third.

I am glad to hear you are having a long holiday in the country. Mine
has not come yet. I send you a copy of the *New York Herald* with a
second article.

I enclose the letter but when you write perhaps you would be good
enough to send it back.

I am glad to hear that Miss Marsden has finished her book[6] and beg
you to tender her my respectful congratulations. With kindest regards
sincerely yours   JAMES JOYCE

[1] Probably a newspaper clipping reporting an outbreak of fighting in Galway, where
Joyce's wife and children were staying.

[2] Of Nora Joyce in Galway.

[3] J. Middleton Murry, 'Mr. Joyce's "Ulysses",' *Nation and Athenaeum* (London),
XXXI.4 (22 April 1922) 124–25.

[4] Joyce attributed the paucity of reviews of *Ulysses* in England to a covert boycott.

[5] A letter to Joyce from Murry, undated, says in part, 'I feel that I did not make a
sufficient apology for the inadequacy of my article upon "Ulysses". Long before writing
it I had made up my mind that it was quite hopeless for me to try to say anything really
worth saying about it within the limits of space imposed upon me, and that I must con-
fine my attention to the business of helping it to get a hearing. My article has no other
merit whatever.' He concluded by inviting Joyce to tea.

[6] Dora Marsden was embarked on a series of books purporting to solve the mystery of
life in terms of a philosophy in which space was mother and time father.

To ERIC PINKER   MS. S. Illinois (Feinberg)

17 May 1922   *rue de l'Odéon 12, Paris VI*

Dear Mr Pinker: Allow me in the first place to offer you my condolence
on the sudden death of your father.[1] I would have done so before but I
did not know that the agency was still in existence until I heard
casually shortly before receipt of your letter that it was being carried on
by his son.

   As regards the question in your letter I cannot consent to any
alteration of the text of *Ulysses*.

   I shall feel obliged if you can give me any information concerning the
theatrical manager whose name is mentioned on the enclosed slip.

   I expect to be in London in a week or ten days and shall call on you
if I stay there, as is probable, for a few days. Sincerely yours

                                                     JAMES JOYCE

To RICHARD WALLACE   MS. Wallace

15 August 1922   [*Paris*]

Dear Wallace Thanks for your kind note. Am writing this beside the
window with half an eye. Have got leave to start for London on Thursday
but am not yet cured. The nebula in the pupil will take some time yet to
disappear. There have been other reviews of *Ulysses* but I can't send
them as they are packed up in cases and stored. I am glad to hear you
are living so well and so cheaply there.[2] The German motto ought to be
—'tis better to have fought and lost than never to have won at all. I
have to stay in London for a week or perhaps two in order to do some
business with various people and then I shall go somewhere if put into a
train. 1000 drops of stuff in my eye, profuse nightly perspirations and
pain have made me for the moment very fatigued and irritable so that
if there is any undue noise or confusion travelling I shall get out of the
train and sit or lie on the rails. I would enjoy indeed a bottle of
Rüdesheimer with you. May it greatly increase your tranquil serenity
but in case of bad dreams resulting therefrom you can turn Hindenburg's

---

   [1] James B. Pinker died on 8 February 1922, his sons Eric, James, and Ralph succeeding
to his business. In the year before his death his relations with Joyce had deteriorated. At
Joyce's request, Miss Weaver had more and more taken over responsibility for his
books, and Pinker had felt that he was being put aside. Joyce justified his neglect of
Pinker on the ground that Miss Weaver and Pound had been his *de facto* agents from the
start, and that Pinker, when he submitted Joyce's manuscripts, never succeeded in
placing them.
   [2] In Germany.

face to the wall. Please excuse this ill written letter. I hope you will continue to enjoy yourselves. My kindest remembrances to you both

JAMES JOYCE

[Enclosure]   *Turf*[1] *Rue de l' Université*

Dearest Lilian: I hope you are having a good time. Are you getting fat? We are off on Thursday am fed up with Paris rotten weather everything dull since you left. I am sorry we could not have gone on to Germany. However I hope we shall soon meet again. I will write to you from London with best love to you both from us Irish   NORA

To THEODORE SPICER-SIMSON (Dictated letter)   TS. Princeton

25 August 1922   *Euston Hotel, London N.W.*

Dear Simson, Your letter was forwarded to me and we are both very sorry to have missed you. Unfortunately the condition of my eyes has been aggravated during the journey and at the moment I do not know whether I must remain in London to be operated (which I dread) or go on to the South of England or return to Paris.[2] I am in fact waiting for a reply from my Paris doctor as the men I saw here were very pessimistic. In these circumstances I don't know what can be done about your suggestion of including me in your forthcoming Book of Portraits of Writers.[3] The only thing I can suggest for the moment is that you call on my publishers in Paris 12, Rue de l'Odeon and ask for a bundle of all the sketches and photographs which were made about the time of the publication of Ulysses. Even if I go back to Paris, to put myself again in my Doctor's care, I don't think that I could possibly pose for you. In any case will you please drop me a line and if you call on my publishers, might I ask you to tell Miss Moschos of the state of things, but add that no allusion should be made to the urgency of an operation in any letter addressed to me as I have not informed my wife of the gravity of the case.

It would be a pleasure for me to meet you again after 20 years, and perhaps if all goes well I may be back in Paris cured. In the meantime, many thanks for your kind expression concerning my books. Sincerely yours,

JAMES JOYCE

[1] A private joke about Nora Joyce's pronunciation of the French word 'Neuf'. To prevent her saying 'Nef', Wallace suggested she pronounce it to rhyme with 'Turf'.

[2] Joyce and Nora crossed to London on 13 August 1922. The journey made his eyes worse. He consulted two London ophthalmologists, Doctors Henry and James. They warned him that the fluid in the left eye had begun to organize and become immovable, and recommended an immediate operation. Joyce wrote to his Paris ophthalmologist, Dr Louis Borsch, and decided to return to Paris. He left England in mid-September.

[3] Theodore Spicer-Simson, *Men of Letters of the British Isles* (New York, 1924). A medallion portrait and brief characterization of Joyce appear on pp. 94–96.

To ROBERT MCALMON   TS. Pearson

2 September 1922   *Euston Hotel, London N.W.*

Dear McAlmon, I am sorry I could not see you this morning when you
called but it takes me nearly an hour to do all the different dressings for
my eye. Will you please thank Lady Ellerman for her kind invitation
and give my excuses explaining why it is impossible for me at present to
go out anywhere.

I am not by any means a social attraction. My wife tells me you are
leaving for Paris on Monday. I should very much like to see you before
then as I have a few messages to intrust to you It is possible that I may
get a telegraphic call to a Doctor this evening at the hour you proposed
coming 6 p.m. so that if I am not there I should like to see you to-morrow
morning at quarter past eleven for a few minutes.

As you see my journey here has turned out disastrous and I should
like to explain a couple of matters preferably in conversation. Kind
regards,   JAMES JOYCE

To HARRIET SHAW WEAVER   MS. British Museum

4 October 1922   *9 rue de l'Université, Paris VII*

Dear Miss Weaver: I saw Dr Borsch yesterday after having waited two
and a half hours. He says that probably both iritis and persistence of
that nebula are due to root abscesses of teeth which should be drained
or removed. He does not think in any case that I will have such an
attack again as the eye reached a crisis which he says I got over. He
wants to correct the right lens of my glasses and will then let me go to
Nice on Monday or Tuesday. He says that if the stay there and the
dental operation (which in his opinion will not provoke an eye attack)
do not dissipate the nebula sufficiently a slight operation—not iridectomy or iridotomy but sphincterotomy will probably restore a great
part of former vision.

I am sending back a copy of press notices. I met Mr Jaloux[1] who said
he sent you a few phrases. I have indicated the places where he and
John Eglinton enter the chorus. The lines cancelled can be used by them.
I think this change ought to be made at once as both reviews are
important. . . .

I hope Dr Borsch is right. The prospect is not cheerful but I will let
them (dentist and oculist) have their way in the hope that I may get

---

[1] Edmond Jaloux (1878–1949), the French critic.

back my sight. His opinion coincides with that of Dr James in the main
for whom as for Dr Henry see *Ulysses* p. 243, l. 8.[1] With kindest regards
sincerely yours   JAMES JOYCE

To HARRIET SHAW WEAVER   MS. British Museum
(Dictated to Lucia Joyce)

27 October 1922   *Hotel Suisse, Nice.*

Dear Miss Weaver Thanks for the advance (£120).[2] I took a flat on
Wednesday and payed luckily only a small sum (£2) as I had not the
money in my pocket. An hour afterwards I felt the first sign of trouble
in my eye and the following day I was again in the doctor's hands, one
recommended to me by Dr Borsch in case of need.[3] He attributes the
relapse chiefly to the rain and wind-storms of the past week. It had not
rained for nine months before my arrival. I am to have the visit of five
leeches in an hour from now and he hopes that by relieving the congestion the attack will not develop. There is no tension. He thinks that as
soon as practicable I ought to be operated as the risk is too great. My
sight has improved very much even during the inflammation. By raising
my head to a certain angle I can see as well through the bad eye as
through the good. This means that there is a clear space in the lower
part of the nebula on the lens. It seems the operation is not likely to
have as damaging an effect as if it had been made when the sight was
almost totally effaced.

    Will you please confirm your instructions which I sent to Mr
Darantiere.

    I now close this letter as my daughter who is writing it is not such a
distinguished english writer as her troublesome father, thank God. With
kindest regards sincerely yours   JAMES JOB JOYCE

To HARRIET SHAW WEAVER   MS. British Museum

25 November 1922   *26 Avenue Charles Floquet, Paris VII*

Dear Miss Weaver: My eyes have not been and are not well. I hope to
keep down whatever is threatening. I am very tired. Dr Borsch says he

[1] '. . . Henry and James's wax smartsuited freshcheeked models, the gentleman Henry,
dernier cri James.' *Ulysses* p. 326 (253). Henry & James was a clothing shop at 1, 2, and
3 Parliament Street in Dublin.
    [2] The advance was on royalties of the new English edition of *Ulysses*.
    [3] Joyce had intended to winter on the Côte d'Azur; on 13 October they were at
Marseilles and by 17 October they had reached Nice. But bad weather had an injurious
effect upon his eye, in which blood accumulated and a nebula formed. Dr Louis Colin,
whom Joyce consulted in this emergency, applied leeches to drain the blood and dosed
the nebula, to dissolve it, with a strong and painful dionine solution (salicylate of soda).
Part of the nebula disappeared and the condition was temporarily alleviated.

would prefer to operate in 6 weeks or so if the eye can be kept calm. If!

I enclose letter from Dijon which disposes of the trial threat. I have not seen Miss Beach since but suppose things are better.[1] I too had a friendly letter from her inviting me to meet Larbaud and Fargue but I did not go. I shall write to the former as soon as I am over this.

The leaflet is all right except that the *Quarterly* should come I think after Mr Huddleston[2] and is that phrase I asked about in it. I can't read the print with this light. Please send me some copies. I approve of your sending press copies to Mr Wells, also to Mr Bennett (who is entitled to one). I suggest in each case you put a slip marked 'Nation' (date) or 'Outlook'—with the publisher's compliments. Mr Hemingway writes for the *Toronto Star*. Mr Lewis ought to get a press copy (not for review). I promised him one and tried during my illness (when was I last well?) to have one sent to him. He did not answer. I heard he was in Venice.

I think you ought to inquire about those Quarterlies. Everything else sent me to Nice was forwarded. Strange to say the writer whom I mentioned in my letter asking for them—Mr Marcel Proust—died this day week. His name has often been coupled with mine. People here seem to have expected his death but when I saw him last May he did not look bad.[3] He looked in fact ten years younger than his age.

I don't think Mr Aldington ought to be asked to write a second article. I met Mr Hueffer.[4] He apologised in a way for his article[5] which, he says, was written at your dictation.[6] I am glad you have taken to writing the favourable criticisms. It seems to me I wrote most of them so far—I mean I see my own phrases rolling back to me. I think the English Review comes out about the 26 or 27 of the month. Will you send me 2 copies please?

[1] Sylvia Beach told Joyce that, as someone had warned her, the second edition of *Ulysses* imitated the first so closely that it might subject her to court action for publishing a bogus first edition. He wrote to Maurice Darantière at Dijon, the printer, and was confirmed in his own view that '*Ulysses* (1st edition) is not a unique edition i.e. luxe, except perhaps for the signed 350 franc copies which, as you may remember, I declined to repeat. . . . The second edition is differentiated in size and weight and is plainly marked a second edition in two places for any buyer who can read.' (*Letters*, ed. Gilbert, p. 196) The argument over this point was part of a larger quarrel between Joyce and Miss Beach (*ibid.*, pp. 195–97).

[2] Sisley Huddleston (1883–1952), English journalist, and the author of several books on life in Paris. His review of *Ulysses* in the *Observer*, 5 March 1922, was the first important one in England.

[3] Several varying reports of this meeting are given in Ellmann, *James Joyce*, pp. 523–524.

[4] Ford Madox Hueffer (later Ford Madox Ford).

[5] Ford Madox Hueffer, ' "Ulysses" and the Handling of Indecencies,' *English Review* (London) XXXV (December 1922) 538–48.

[6] Miss Weaver notes, 'I cannot recall that event.'

I am sure you are anxious to be away in Cheshire. King Beaver will never find you there. He will start in the shires of Northumberland, Cumberland, Westmoreland, Durham etc.

My eye now warns me to stop. I send a correspondence from a Dublin paper between Mr Buck Mulligan and Mr Leslie. The only intelligent person in it is the labourer on Mr Leslie's estate who is evidently a compatriot of the narrator of the Cyclops. With kindest regards sincerely yours   James Joyce

To Ford Madox Ford   MS. Roland Loewe

10 January 1923   *Avenue Charles Floquet 26, Paris VII*

Dear Hueffer: The name and address of the Nice doctor are:

> Dr A Colin
> rue Gioffreddo 30
> Nice

hours 2–4 p.m. If you see him you may tell him I have postponed the 'dionine' experiment till after the holidays—16 inst—then the other abscesses are to be lanced and then closed (that is, the iridectomy operation in February). You can have confidence in him, I think.

I am glad you are having a pleasant stay down there. I suppose you never go to Mentone but if you do I have a favour to ask. On the bridge that is between France and Italy there are some old Italian women who sell shell cameos (camées de coquilles) for about 10 francs. I should like to have one at your choice for the one I bought there and had mounted on a gold circlet the *femme de menage* has stolen together with a nice brooch and God knows what else. Don't give yourself the least trouble about this, only if you happen to be there perhaps you will buy one. The Italian woman will probably begin by asking a few thousand for it just to make talk.

Many thanks in advance and kind regards Sincerely yours
                                                              James Joyce

To Valery Larbaud   MS. Bib. Municipale, Vichy

17 January 1923   *26 Avenue Charles Floquet, Paris*

Dear Larbaud: We are sorry to hear you don't go out but could you make an exception and dine with us on Saturday next at 8? If you are on a special diet let us know. Miss Beach and Miss Monnier will come also Fargue. I have a series of operations in front of me—three no less—so I should like very much to see and meet you before the damned things begin.[1] Will you let me have a word in reply? *Spero di si*[2]

Sincerely yours   JAMES JOYCE

To VALERY LARBAUD   MS. Bib. Municipale, Vichy

5 February 1923   *26 Avenue Charles Floquet, Paris VII*

Dear Larbaud: Thanks for the copy of *Echantillons* which I shall now try to read with my back to the light—and also for the kind dedication. I am sorry you were not with us the other night and hope your health is better. I am well enough except for my sight. No fewer than three operations to be faced and of course I have been putting it off. But I shall begin next week.

An Italian version of *Ulysses* modelled on yours is to be brought out in Rome as soon as possible so when your work and health allow could you let me have a copy of your plan,[3] e.g.—

Telemachia
I (entire)
II (recension)[4]
III (fragments)
etc

In this way the two versions would be similar though not identical since recensions would differ and the fragments chosen could hardly be the same.

I hope you approve? Sincerely yours   JAMES JOYCE

To HARRIET SHAW WEAVER   MS. British Museum

26 February 1923   *26 Avenue Charles Floquet, Paris VII*

Dear Miss Weaver: At last I have some kind of good news though not much. I did not write before because I was not sure whether the

---

[1] In July 1922 Dr Louis Berman (1893–1946), a well-known New York endocrinologist then visiting Paris, examined Joyce at Ezra Pound's instigation. He proposed endocrine treatment for Joyce's arthritic back, and after one look at the patient's teeth insisted upon their being X-rayed at once. They proved to be in such bad condition that he advised complete extraction. Two dental operations were thereupon scheduled, to be followed by an eye operation, a sphincterectomy (the sphincter being the oval muscle surrounding the eyelid). The ophthalmologist was Dr Louis Borsch.

[2] 'I hope so.'

[3] Joyce had hoped that Larbaud would undertake the translation of *Ulysses* into French, but Larbaud felt it would require too much time. He agreed, however, to translate portions of it, and to fill in the interstices with summaries.

[4] I.e., summary.

condition would persist. The dionine treatment prescribed by Dr Colin of Nice[1] has dissipated a fair part of the film. Dr Borsch however will not apply it in the strong solution which the Nice doctor prescribed partly I suppose because he is older and more prudent but also because he knows better the pusillanimous nature of his patient. He prefers to continue the treatment gradually and to wait and see if the film will thin more. He does not believe the dionine will dissipate the film wholly nor was Dr Colin positive of that either. He was however as you see a very clever man and all the London doctors who said the film was 'organised' (that is not fluid but irremovable) were wrong. Unfortunately this does not mean any improvement in my power to read or write and for this reason. I had before 1/10 of normal vision in that eye. Now I have 1/7 or 1/6 but this is only good for longrange vision. It enabled me a few nights ago to see the lights of the Place de la Concorde which before had been only a blur. Dr Borsch believes that after the operations I will have 1/2 of normal vision. Personally I am sceptical about the effect of the dental one but since Dr Borsch will not do his operation till the dentist has done his let it be so. The latter will get to work as soon as Dr Borsch is convinced that the dionine can do no more. The threatened attack in the right eye has been kept under partly by Dr Borsch's local treatment, partly by Dr Colin's cure.

Can a copy of *Ulysses* (2nd edition) be sent to my brother Charles Joyce? If so it ought to be numbered. The copy Mr Rodker sent me to work on is unnumbered. Does he know the numbers of the copies sequestrated?[2] I think this point is important in such an edition.

No press notices of the second edition have reached me. I know nothing about the French and Italian versions but then I rarely see anybody except a few people whom I asked here for diplomatic reasons and in acknowledgment of services rendered to my book among them Mr Huddleston of *The Observer* who is now Paris representative of *The Times*.

The weather here has been atrocious, bleak, damp, cold etc. I hope it is better in your part of the world. I wonder if you ever weigh in one hand the smaller Oxford blue volume against the Greco-Bavarian

[1] See p. 68, n. 3.

[2] The first English edition of *Ulysses*, published by John Rodker for the Egoist Press, consisted of 2000 copies and appeared on 12 October 1922. About five hundred of these were seized and confiscated by the customs in New York. In late January 1923 Rodker published a second English edition, identical with the first except for a note reading, 'This edition of 500 copies is specially reprinted to replace those destroyed in transit to the U.S.A. No .' These are the copies which are said to have been seized at Folkestone by British authorities. John Rodker told this editor that only 400 copies had actually been seized; this number is more likely since several copies have survived. See also Slocum and Cahoon, p. 27.

telephone directory[1] in the other. If you wish any elucidation I shall be glad to give it—before I forget it myself! Though I shall feel like Eneas when invited by Dido to tell his tale '*Infandum, regina, iubes renovare dolorem*'.[2] Nevertheless he told it.

With kindest regards and best wishes and some hopes for a good result of all this treatment sincerely yours   JAMES JOYCE

P.S. An Irish 'Who's Who' has just been issued. It contains 2500 names but not mine.[3]   J.J.

To HARRIET SHAW WEAVER   MS. British Museum

28 March 1923   *26 Avenue Charles Floquet, Paris VII*

Dear Miss Weaver: These few lines will let you know that the conjunctivitis ended yesterday. No bad effects have followed. Dr Borsch thinks it is useless to prolong the dionine treatment (which, however, still does good) and so on Tuesday next I go into hospital.[4] . . .

I am rather sceptical as to the elimination of arthritis by removal of teeth or abscesses. However if it should turn out well I shall be the first to admit it. Everything depends on the success of Dr Borsch's operation, it seems to me and as he thinks this other indispensable I consent to it.

In spite of my eye attack I got on with another passage by using a charcoal pencil (*fusain*) which broke every three minutes and a large sheet of paper.[5] I have now covered various large sheets in a handwriting resembling that of the late Napoleon Bonaparte when irritated by reverses. If my muddy mind is clear enough and if I can find a stenographer I shall try to send you the 'exegesis' of the Scylla and Charybdis episode before I go into hospital.[6]

---

[1] A joking reference to *Ulysses*.

[2] Virgil, *Aeneid*, II, 3: 'Unutterable woe, O queen, you urge me to renew.'

[3] *Thom's Irish Who's Who*, a biographical book of reference of prominent men and women in Irish life at home and abroad (Dublin, 1923).

[4] For the dental operations. The first took place on 4 April 1923, the second a few days later.

[5] Joyce announced to Miss Weaver, in a letter of 11 March 1923, that he had begun work on a new book (*Finnegans Wake*): 'Yesterday I wrote two pages—the first I have written since the final *Yes* of *Ulysses*. Having found a pen, with some difficulty I copied them out in a large handwriting on a double sheet of foolscap so that I could read them. *Il lupo perde il pelo ma non il vizio*, the Italians say. The wolf may lose his skin but not his vice or the leopard cannot change his spots.' (*Letters*, ed. Gilbert, 202.) The first passage was the King Roderick O'Conor fragment, pp. 380–82 in the published book.

[6] The explanation is perhaps among Harriet Shaw Weaver's papers but has not yet come to light.

I hope you got the *Sporting Times*.[1] I enclosed it in a copy of a Paris theatrical paper lest its latent heat might evaporate.

I think I got over this last attack (I hope it is the last attack) very well though I was frightened at the beginning. With kindest regards sincerely yours   JAMES JOYCE

To HARRIET SHAW WEAVER   MS. British Museum

30 March 1923   *26 Avenue Charles Floquet, Paris VII*

Dear Miss Weaver: Many thanks for your letter and the article in the *Manchester Guardian*. I shall send a few lines of formal thanks to Mr Gwynn[2] who after sixteen years of literary criticism has discovered my existence. One half of his article is taken almost verbally from the text of *Ulysses*, the other half consists of phrases which I myself set in circulation. They now come back to me. You ask me to whom I wish copies to be sent. The copies of *Ulysses* which I presented to certain of my fellowcountrymen and fellowcountrywomen were either unacknowledged or locked up or given away or lent or stolen or sold and, it seems, in all cases unread. Nevertheless it remains part of my policy to inflict notices of myself upon the recipients. Therefore if the stamping is not too tiresome I would ask you to be kind enough to send copies to. . . .[3]

I hope Mr Jaloux's[4] article will appear on 1 April—a pleasant anniversary. During my illness I think I managed to arrange for an article in *La Revue des Deux Mondes*.[5] When I have got one into *La Revue de France* I shall cease—to the relief of my Paris admirers. In my opinion however my name would be absent from the *Manchester Guardian* (as from the Irish *Who's Who* and the official history of the Irish Literary Movement and the playbills of the Abbey Theatre) but

---

[1] A writer with the pen-name of Aramis wrote on 1 April 1922 in the *Sporting Times* (London), a newspaper subtitled affectionately *The Pink 'Un*, that Joyce, while a writer of talent, had in *Ulysses* 'ruled out all the elementary decencies of life' and indulged in the 'stupid glorification of mere filth. . . . The main contents of the book are enough to make a Hottentot sick'.

[2] Stephen Gwynn, 'Modern Irish Literature,' *Manchester Guardian*, 15 March 1923, 36–40.

[3] Miss Weaver's transcription does not give the names.

[4] Jaloux's article, which appeared in the *Revue de Paris* on 1 April 1923, related Joyce to Rabelais, and found beneath the encyclopedic air and formal oddities a 'vast and genuine beauty'.

[5] Louis Gillet (1876–1943), 'Littératures Etrangères: Du Coté de chez Joyce,' *Revue des Deux Mondes* 28 (1 August 1925) 686–97. It was uncomplimentary but Joyce wrote Miss Weaver that he was pleased that his three years of planning had borne fruit. 'The tone of the article does not matter much,' he said. (*Letters*, ed. Gilbert, p. 232.)

for certain articles in English reviews and these would not have been published but for previous articles in French reviews.

Please present my compliments to Miss Marsden. I hope you will have a pleasant Easter. With kindest regards sincerely yours

JAMES JOYCE

To EMILIO CECCHI[1]   MS. Cecchi

2 April 1923   *26 Avenue Charles Floquet, Paris VII*

Egregio collega, La ringrazio sentitamente dello trafiletto. Spero abbia già ricevuto l'esemplare 'stampa' che pregai la casa editrice a Londra di spedirle. Leggerò con molto interesse il suo articolo sul *Convegno*; però siccome entrerò domani all'ospedale per una operazione all'occhio (iridectomia), e non so dove andrò a finire dopo, La prego di volere inviare l'esemplare (oltre quello destinato a Londra) alla casa editrice qui: Shakespeare & Co, 12 rue de l'Odéon, a mio nome. Da un pezzo non ho notizie di Linati. Se lo vede però me lo saluti. Spero che il tordo—o se mi permette di rettificare la sua allusione ornitologica—lo struzzo non gli abbia fatto male.[2]

Con distinti ossequi e ringraziamenti mi creda dev/mo JAMES JOYCE[3]

To MRS WILLIAM MURRAY   MS. National Library

3 April 1923   *c/o Shakespeare and Co, 12 rue de l'Odéon, Paris VI*

Dear Aunt Josephine: Here at last is the list.[4] I shall be very glad if you will please fill it up in your free moments and return it registered to

[1] Emilio Cecchi (b. 1887), the distinguished Italian critic and short-story writer, had written a brief article on *Ulysses* in the Rome newspaper, *La Tribuna*, 2 March 1923. He intended to write a longer one in *Convegno* but did not do so.

[2] In his article Cecchi objected that Italian interest in Joyce was confined to his minor works. He reminded his readers of the gluttonous host who, at a table heaped with thrushes and potatoes, urged the potatoes on the guests so as to keep the thrushes for himself.

[3] (Translation)

'Dear colleague, I thank you warmly for the clipping. I hope you have already received the review copy which I asked my London publisher to send to you. I shall read with great interest your article in *Convegno*; but since I go into hospital tomorrow for an eye operation (iridectomy), and do not know where I shall end up afterwards, I beg you to be so good as to send the copy (aside from the one intended for London) to my publisher here: Shakespeare and Company, 12 rue de l'Odéon, in my name. I have had no news of Linati for some time. If you see him remember me to him. I hope that the thrush—or, if you will allow me to correct your ornithological allusion—the ostrich has done you no harm. With respectful regards and thanks believe me faithfully yours   James Joyce'

[4] Joyce had written Mrs Murray on 21 December 1922, 'I have been trying to collect my notes as well as my poor sight will allow and I find several names of people connected with the family who were of the older generation when I was a boy. I wonder if I sent you

above address. I hope all with you are well and that you got over the Easter all right. I am in no hurry for the book but would like to have it back in a few months.

Kindest regards from all and many thanks in advance   JIM

To HARRIET SHAW WEAVER   MS. British Museum

28 May 1923   *26 Avenue Charles Floquet, Paris VII*

Dear Miss Weaver: I hardly know what to write. Dr Borsch tells me the eye[1] is clearing slowly and that it takes a certain time but that it is sure, if slow. I suppose he is right but the improvement which he perceives I cannot see or see very slightly as it is still a long way from reading vision. . . . As for the dentist he is equally optimistic and has even begun to test me for the permanent plate. I know that both these doctors are the best in their branches in Paris and are very conscientious and so all I can do is to assent. But I wish it were all over. . . .

The weather here ever since my operations has been dreadful. Nevertheless I have gone through some of my notes with what sight I have.

I will end this now and send it off. It is thundering and my daughter is playing the piano. She has made good progress. With kindest regards sincerely yours   JAMES JOYCE

P.S. I think this is the anniversary of my eye attack.

To HARRIET SHAW WEAVER   MS. British Museum

10 June 1923   *26 Avenue Charles Floquet, Paris VII*

Dear Miss Weaver: I enclose a cutting which is not true.[2] My small flat is all upside down with ten cases of books and manuscripts, three sacks of newspapers, four trunks, four valises, three hatboxes etc. I expect to leave Paris on Saturday.[3] The dentist has now supplied me with the

an exercise book with the names of these persons at the tops of the pages would you be kind enough (whenever you have a spare moment and anything occurs to your mind) to scribble down in pencil or pen anything noteworthy, details of dress, defects, hobbies, appearance, manner of death, voice, where they lived, etc just as you did for the questions I sent you about Major Powell—in my book Major Tweedy, Mrs Bloom's father? They all belong to a vanished world and most of them seem to have been very curious types. I am in no hurry. You could send me back the book in six months if you like but I would feel greatly obliged if you could fill in any details for me as you are the only one who is likely to know anything about them.' *Letters*, ed. Gilbert, p. 198.

[1] Dr Borsch performed the sphincterectomy on 28 April 1923.

[2] A newspaper reported he was blind.

[3] Joyce and his wife and daughter went to London in mid-June 1923 for a holiday. They had decided to spend the summer at Bognor in Sussex.

permanent set. . . . Till today I found it difficult to eat and talk. As
regards the sight it seems to be getting very slowly better. I can now do
some reading and have raced through many accumulated books and
notes. It will take many months to heal completely, Dr Borsch says. . . .
There is something fantastic in the huge disorder that now surrounds
me. I shall be glad to escape from it anywhere for the moment. I feel in
much better health however. With kindest regards sincerely yours

JAMES JOYCE

To CLAUD W. SYKES   MS. Yale

11 June 1923   *26 Avenue Charles Floquet, Champ de Mars*
Tél: Ségur 16–81

Dear Mr Sykes: Many thanks for your letter. As you may have heard
I have been in hospital and have just come through three operations.
The report of my blindness is not accurate. It is believed that the last
operation will give me good sight and I can write and read a fair amount
even now. We are leaving Paris for the summer. If you are passing here
before 15 instant[1] will you please write or ring me up?

With kind regards from us all to Mrs Sykes and yourself sincerely
yours   JAMES JOYCE

From W. B. YEATS   MS. Buffalo

26 June [1923]   *82, Merrion Square, S., Dublin*

Dear Joyce: Have you any wish to revisit Dublin? If so will you spend
a few days with us? If you will come soon as we may be flitting to
Galway in a couple of weeks. My wife and I have a great admiration for
your work and there are many people here who share our admiration.
Perhaps you would like to meet some of them—a new literary generation.[2] Yrs s   W B YEATS

To SYLVIA BEACH[3]   MS. Buffalo

12 July 1923   *Alexandra House, Clarence Road, Bognor*
(Sussex) England

Dear Miss Beach: Will you please order the following books (American)
for me:

[1] Joyce went with his family to London on this date.
[2] Joyce was pleased by the invitation but declined it. The previous August, in reply to
a letter from Lady Gregory, he had vehemently declined to be considered a part of the
Irish literary movement.
[3] From a typescript made by Miss Beach.

1) English Speech and Literature by E. Vizetelly[1]

2) Ireland's Part in the Making of Britain by O. J. Fitzpatrick ?[2]

Perhaps Brentano's has them. Also can you get me any information about

1) New Book of Kings by   Davidson[3]

2) The Complete Peerage (8 vols) edited by Lord Howard de Walden.

A dreadful thunderstorm passed by here on Monday. Luckily we got only the fringe of it—quite enough—but London was terrified. It is very hot. My complexion is now cinnabar and rosbif à l'anglaise and sienna and extra ochre and deep walnut etc. I have also catalogued about 40 pp. of notes in spite of the heat wave.[4]

Giorgio's telegram and subsequent letter about the flat were decisive against our taking it. I made an alternative proposal that we take it and barter it, if unsuitable—that is, dispose of the bail without profit in exchange for a more suitable flat of similar size but of a much dearer rent. He has not written about that so I suppose it is off. In any case, will you please thank Mme Tisserand for keeping it open for me and give her from my account 100 francs which I shall settle at our next meeting. As Giorgio has nothing to do I hope he will find what we want. He knows what will suit, I presume.

I had to visit the oculist twice in London with these — glasses. The improvement of sight is so slow that I have given up thinking about it. Lucia will go to Deauville about the end of the month I think. I expect to go to Cornwall then. In any case it would be useless for either of us to return to Paris now—worse than useless for me as I know nothing about flats except that they are presumably flat not hilly.

You will be glad to hear that Miss Weaver made me a couple of days ago the very great gift of another £12,000 (twelve thousand pounds) equivalent at today's exchange rate of 936,000 frs. This throws some light on the situation. In view of benefactions of various provenences it ought to be pointed out that the sum for which the MS of *Ulysses* was acquired is equivalent to the interest for *6 weeks* on the total sum (£21,000) made over to me by her.

Mme du Pasquier[5] wrote hopefully about Exiles being played in the

[1] E. Vizetelly, *Essentials of English Speech and Literature* (New York and London, 1915).

[2] Benedict Fitzpatrick, *Ireland and the Making of Britain* (New York and London, 1922).

[3] John Morrison Davidson, *The New Book of Kings* (Boston, 1884).

[4] These were notes left over from *Ulysses*, which Joyce expected to be useful in his new work.

[5] Mme Hélène du Pasquier was one of three translators of *Dubliners* into French. Their work was published under the title *Gens de Dublin*, with a preface by Valery

Elysian Fields.[1] Is not this adding a new horror to eternal punishment?

Yeats wrote me a pressing invitation to stay with him in Dublin where, he says, there are many who share his admiration of me and a new literary generation anxious to meet me. I thanked him amicably and declined.

Please thank Miss Monnier also for the trouble she took. I am sending Fargue a funny advertisement which please translate for him while he fans himself with his hat.

Many thanks to yourself for your telegram and letter but as I am not on the spot (and should be only in the way if I were) it is better to work through Georgio who is reputed to be the best living authority on the manners, customs, institutions, privileges, perquisites, hereditary and acquired domestic characteristics of the Joyce family abroad. With kind regards yours sincerely   JAMES JOYCE

To HARRIET SHAW WEAVER   MS. British Museum

20 July 1923   [*Bognor*]

Dear Miss Weaver: May I trouble you to make three copies of this[2] at your leisure? Please keep one yourself for in moving today I have lost one of your typed sheets and I should like to have a complete set of these scattered passages[3] when needed. I am now on the third floor. Over me, thank goodness, is the roof.

With kindest regards and many thanks   sincerely yours
                                                            JAMES JOYCE

To HARRIET SHAW WEAVER   MS. British Museum

2 August 1923   *Bognor*

Dear Miss Weaver: I send you this as promised—a piece describing the conversion of S. Patrick by Ireland. You may keep the other rough drafts. With kindest regards sincerely yours   JAMES JOYCE

Larbaud (Paris, 1926). She also translated *Exiles* in collaboration with a man named Baernaert, according to Sylvia Beach, but this translation was not published.

[1] Her hope was that Hébertôt (pseudonym of André Daviel) (b. 1886), director of the Théâtre des Champs-Elysées, would produce it there. But he did not.

[2] The passage on King Roderick O'Conor (later *Finnegans Wake*, pp. 380–82).

[3] The other passages were on St Kevin, Berkeley, and Tristran and Iseult (later pp. 604–6, 611–12, 384–86).

To Harriet Shaw Weaver   MS. British Museum

19 August 1923   Victoria Palace Hotel, 6 rue Blaise Desgoffe, Paris

Dear Miss Weaver: We are staying here. Hotels are full up and we have
had two days of a wild house chase.[1] Dr Borsch will not be back till 6
September. My dentist is also out of town. So is Mr Davidson[2] whom I
cannot see till Tuesday. He turns out to be a friend of mine (or acquaintance). I had not connected him with the affair. I telephoned to Mrs
Davidson who told me that her husband got a wireless message from
Miss Lewisohn who is the proprietress of a New York theatre asking
him to telegraph to me and then to her as they want to put the play into
rehearsal. This message came from mid ocean as they had bought the
play to read on the boat. Many thanks indeed for so kindly typing those
clauses. They will be very useful. I shall suggest they be forwarded,
filled in, sent back and then forwarded to Mr Pinker for ratification if
he thinks the terms adequate. Mr Pound has a good opinion of these
people. I shall write to you on Tuesday or Wednesday. With kindest
regards and many thanks sincerely yours   James Joyce

To Harriet Shaw Weaver   MS. British Museum

23 August 1923   Victoria Palace Hotel, 6 rue Blaise Desgoffe, Paris

Dear Miss Weaver: I have now seen Mr and Mrs Davidson (the latter
wants to do my head—he is not a barber but a sculptor) and have
heard a long enthusiastic story. In the middle of it a letter arrived from
Miss Lewisohn. I sent her your contract and asked her to fill in or strike
out as she pleases. I tried to look interested but my thoughts were
elsewhere. This is a great mistake, I know, and I should not do it if I
knew better where I was. Of course I have broken my promise and have
begun drafting other parts in spite of the heat, noise, confusion and
suffocation. My son arrived this morning. When he is rested I think we
shall leave him here to hunt around and go away to some quiet place for
a week or so. Tours, I think. Perhaps it will be better for you to write
12 rue de l'Odéon. I sent you a copy of the *Freeman* with a review of Dr
Collins's pretentious book.[3]
     It is better to say nothing about one's impressions on arriving here in

     [1] A letter on this theme to T. S. Eliot is in Appendix, vol. III.
     [2] Jo Davidson (1883–1952), the American sculptor. He had urged Alice and Irene
Lewisohn, founders of the Neighborhood Playhouse in New York, to produce *Exiles*.
They did so, in 1925, when it ran from 19 February to 22 March.
     [3] See p. 33, n. 4.

present circumstances. Mr Davidson swears he will get us a flat with the aid of an Indian friend. Thaumaturgy of [some] kind is needed. With kindest regards sincerely yours   JAMES JOYCE

From J. F. BYRNE   MS. Private

8 October 1923

Dear Joyce: If you care to write me I shall be glad to hear from you. You may take up the thread as with the Byrne you last met in Dublin in 1909.[1]   J. F. BYRNE

To LILY BOLLACH   MS. Stanford

10 October 1923   [*Paris*]

Dear Miss Bollach: After our interview the other evening it seems to me very unfair of me to have inflicted on you such difficult work. It is very kind of you to undertake but I think you are doing so at too great a sacrifice. The text must be impossible for a foreigner and I ought to have known it. However as you are doing this piece may I ask to make this one addition?

On the last page of the *prose* part (before the verse begins) after the words 'oremus prayer' and before the words 'for navigants etc' please insert these words: 'to Peregrine and Michael and Farfassa and Peregrine'[2]

With many apologies and kind regards sincerely yours

JAMES JOYCE

To MRS RICHARD SHEEHY[3]   MS. Texas

21 October 1923   *12 rue de l'Odéon, Paris*

Dear Mrs Sheehy: I am grieved to read in a recent Irish paper of the death of my old schoolfellow Dick Sheehy. I hope you will allow me to send you this message of sympathy in remembrance of our friendly companionship in boyhood and youth. Sincerely yours   JAMES JOYCE

---

[1] An allusion to Byrne's having reassured Joyce when Cosgrave impugned Nora Joyce's fidelity. See II, p. 235.

[2] *Finnegans Wake*, p. 398. The names are those of the Four Masters.

[3] See II, p. 191, and *Letters*, ed. Gilbert, p. 205.

To HARRIET SHAW WEAVER   MS. British Museum

2 November 1923   Victoria Palace Hotel, 6 rue Blaise Desgoffe, Paris

Dear Miss Weaver: You will be disappointed when you open this. It is
not new MS but the fair copy of Mamalujo[1] which I forgot to send. I
have since worked over the typed copy again and have now definitely
abandoned it. I could not do much these last weeks as my wife has been
attending the dentist for some unpleasant work—now finished. I have
prepared a nice intricate Mah Jongg puzzle for myself and shall start on
it on Monday. Mr Quinn was here and wants another 150 pages of
printed matter = about 500 pages of MS which he says I did not supply,
as he is proposing, I believe, to sell *Ulysses*. He already has the entire
MS and, as you will see by the enclosed, does not know (though I
supplied him with the list of names of episodes) that *Ithaca* and
Penelope are the two last episodes.

I send you a prospectus of Mr Ford's (he does not wish his other name
to be used) new review.[2] I have declined again to let any of the pieces be
printed but have allowed my name to go on the contributors' list.

Mr Bird[3] of *Three Mountains Press* came to me with a proposal about
bringing out at once a third (or fourth) edition of *Ulysses* to be sold
directly here. I sent him to Miss Beach who then said she wanted to do
it and said she was waiting for me to suggest it. I did not do so because
I was not sure of her attitude and also because I did not know what my
proposal might entail for her.

Does the British Moslem Society publish any propaganda paper? If
so I should like to see a copy.

My son will sing next Sunday in a chapel of one of the four masters
(S. Luke's) at the request of the choirmaster who was struck by his
voice, it seems, at the *Schola Cantorum*. I don't know what he is going to
sing. I suppose it will not be the third strophe of the Leinster evangelist.[4]
With kindest regards sincerely yours   JAMES JOYCE

P.S. I have written in the additions.   J.J.

[1] Joyce's nickname for the Four Evangelists, Matthew, Mark, Luke, and John. This
section is now pp. 383–99 of *Finnegans Wake*.

[2] Ford Madox Ford (Hueffer) edited the *transatlantic review*, a new monthly magazine
in Paris, with the text in English and French, from January 1924 to January 1925.
Joyce eventually allowed him to include (in the April 1924 issue) the first fragment of
Finnegans Wake to be published, the Mamalujo episode.

[3] William Bird (1889–1963), born in Buffalo, New York, went to Paris in May 1921 as
European manager of the Consolidated Press. He founded the Three Mountains Press
and published Hemingway, Pound, and other writers during the 1920s. After the second
World War he edited a newspaper in Tangier.

[4] *Finnegans Wake*, p. 399.

To Harriet Shaw Weaver   MS. British Museum

19 November 1923   *Hotel Victoria Palace, 6 rue Blaise Desgoffe,*
Paris (Montparnasse)

Dear Miss Weaver: Thanks for your letter and press cuttings. I suppose you have seen Mr Eliot's article in the Dial.[1] I like it and it comes opportunely. I shall suggest to him when I write to thank him that in alluding to it elsewhere he use or coin some short phrase, two or three words, such as one he used in speaking to me 'two plane'. Mr Larbaud gave the reading public about six months ago the phrase 'interior monologue' (that is, in *Ulysses*). Now they want a new phrase. They cannot manage more than about one such phrase every six months —not for lack of intelligence but because they are in a hurry.

Thanks also for *Arabia Deserta*[2] and the *Querschnitt*.[3] I wish I could go away somewhere and read the former for my own pleasure but alas in spite of all I said I am working overtime again. My eye is still bandaged but gives me no trouble. I hope to be all right by the middle of the week.

I do not know how long we shall be here. I hope not for Christmas. A certain princess Murat[4] to whom I was introduced (I had hardly shaken hands when I began to recite *Je cherche un appartement de cinq ou six pieces, trois chambres, salon, salle à manger*) promised she would find me one when she comes back from London. However I caught the cold in my eye on a wildgoose chase to Versailles on a similar errand. Nevertheless I cannot stop now for I must try to block out (roughly, at least) certain parts of the book before my next holiday. The passages typed represent twice or three times as much, the rest being already written in the sense that additions will be made all over the present text from notes to which I have now no access. . . . With kindest regards sincerely yours   James Joyce

[1] T. S. Eliot, 'Ulysses, Order, and Myth,' *Dial* LXXV.5 (November 1923) 480–83.

[2] Charles Montagu Doughty's *Travels in Arabia Deserta* (1888) was republished in 1920–1921.

[3] Several early poems of Joyce (*Chamber Music*, xii, xv, xxvi, xxix, xxxvi) had been published in *Der Querschnitt(* Frankfurt a.M.) III.3/4 (Fall 1923) 157–59.

[4] Princess (Marguérite) Murat (1886–1956).

To FORD MADOX FORD (Postcard)   MS. Roland Loewe

13 December 1923   *Victoria Palace Hotel, 6 rue Blaise Desgoffe,*
                                                    Paris (VIᵉ)

Dear Ford: When sending me the T. R. could you let me have also the
October *Criterion*[?] Miss Beach will send you a copy of 4th edition of
Ulysses Sincerely yours   JAMES JOYCE

To FORD MADOX FORD (Postcard)   MS. Roland Loewe

17 December 1923   *Victoria Palace Hotel, 6 rue Blaise Desgoffe,*
                                                    Paris (VIᵉ)

Dear Ford: Thanks for T.R. Can you let me have the *Criterion* for a
few days? Sincerely yours   JAMES JOYCE

To VALERY LARBAUD   MS. Bib. Municipale, Vichy

17 December 1923   *Victoria Palace Hotel, 6 rue Blaise Desgoffe,*
                                                    rue de Rennes

Dear Larbaud: Thanks for your new book[1] with the very kind words
about me in it. I want to show you what I have done in the hope that it
may continue to interest you. I shall have a fair lot ready in a week or so
and perhaps you would like to see the typescript. How I write in
present circumstances I don't know—influence of *ad maiorem dei
gloriam*,[2] perhaps.

   I was sorry to hear your health was not good but the last reports are
more favourable. As soon as I have once more presented my credentials
(MSS) to you can we not have a quaresimal[3] dinner somewhere together?
I hope so.

   With very kind regards and my sincere thanks sincerely yours

                                                   JAMES JOYCE

To LILY BOLLACH   MS. Yale

18 December 1923   *[Paris]*

Dear Miss Bollach: I am dreadfully sorry about last night and to hear
that you waited so long too. You must have a nice opinion of my manners
but really I was prevented at the very last moment when I could not

---

   [1] Valery Larbaud, *Amants, heureux amants* (Paris, 1923). This included the earlier
dedication. See p. 53, n. 1.
   [2] That is, his Jesuit education. He quotes the Jesuit motto.   [3] 'Lenten.

even telephone to you not knowing your number. All I can do is to apologise and hope you are not too annoyed.

I called and got the typesheets—all done to my astonishment! They are excellently done too. Many thanks.

Can you meet me on Monday at 6.15 at the same place (I went there today at 1.45 as your concierge told me to do)? I shall go in any case but it would serve me right if you made me wait an hour before you came yourself.

With renewed apologies and many thanks sincerely yours

JAMES JOYCE

To ROBERT MCALMON   MS. Pearson

[*19 December 1923*]   *Victoria Palace Hotel, 6 rue Blaise Desgoffe,*
                                        Paris (Montparnasse)

Dear McAlmon: My solicitors write that they will send a cheque for £60 to you at your London address next week. As Christmas is now only six days off can you let me know whether you were able to make the arrangement you suggested.

I hope you are having a good time. Will there be Swedish as well as American punch in your next work. A fourth edition of *Ulysses* comes out next week.[1]

Jed haabe det De vil have et godt Jultid derop i det gamle Norge. Paa gensyn![2] Sincerely yours   JAMES JOYCE

P.S. Norge is the Danish name for Sweden (copyright in the United States by J.J.).

To ROBERT MCALMON   MS. Pearson

5 January 1924   *Victoria Palace Hotel, 6 rue Blaise Desgoffe, Paris*

Dear McAlmon: I confirm my telegram 'Cheque received etc'. Has that cheque come through? There is a lot of mail for you lying at Miss Beach's. She is away. Miss Moschos does not know what to do with it. Perhaps the cheque is here. My solicitors usually send it registered. Would it have been delivered, if so? In France, I think not. Send me a line in reply if you can as soon as this reaches you if it does. Pound was in hospital for threatened appendicitis but comes out tomorrow. He leaves for Italy on Tuesday. The 4th edition of *Ulysses* is out. We are

---

[1] Actually this was the second printing for Shakespeare and Company, the second and third 'editions' having been made for the Egoist Press.

[2] 'I hope that you will have a good Christmas there in that old Sweden. To our next meeting!'

threatened with a flood here but the rise is less today. 1924 begins well.
In haste sincerely yours   JAMES JOYCE

To NORA BARNACLE JOYCE[1]   MS. Private

[? 5 January 1924][2]   *[Paris]*

Dear Nora: The edition you have is full of printers' errors. Please read
it in this. I cut the pages. There is a list of mistakes at the end   JIM

To ETTORE SCHMITZ   MS. Fonda Savio

30 January 1924   *Victoria Palace Hotel, 6 rue Blaise Desgoffe,*
                                          Paris, rue de Rennes

Caro amico, Sono andato alla stazione ma nessun treno era in arrivo
(nemmeno ritardato) nell'ora indicatami. Ne ero molto dispiacente.
Quando ripasserà per Parigi? Non potrebbe pernottare qui?
   Grazie del romanzo con la dedica.[3] Ne ho due esemplari anzi, avendo
già ordinato uno a Trieste. Sto leggendolo con molto piacere. Perchè si
dispera?[4] Deve sapere ch'è di gran lunga il suo migliore libro. Quanto
alla critica italiana non so. Ma faccia mandare degli esemplari di
stampa a

   1) M. Valery Larbaud   chez Nouvelle Revue Française
                          3 rue de Grenelle
                          Paris
   2) M. Benjamin Crémieux   chez Revue de France
                             (troverà l'indirizzo su un esemplare)
   3) Mr T. S. Eliot, Editor 'Criterion'
                          9 Clarence Gate Mansions
   4) Mr F. M. Ford 'The Transatlantic Review'
                          27 Quai d'Anjou
                          Paris

[1] Although Nora Joyce had been given the first copy of *Ulysses*, she had never
consented to read it. Joyce evidently had reason to feel she was more amenable now.
   [2] The date must be that of the fourth printing, January 1924, because this was the first
to have corrections bound in at the end.
   [3] Schmitz had sent a copy of *La Coscienza di Zeno* (Bologna, 1923) with the inscription:
'27.12.23. Many thanks for your kindness. My best wishes to you and your family. Do
not get angry—please—about the papers on which I write my wishes. E.S.' The volume
is now at Buffalo.
   [4] Schmitz wrote Joyce in January 1924 that he was discouraged by the reception of his
book and felt that he had again done a foolish thing, and at an age—sixty—when one
hates to cut a foolish figure.

Parlerò o scrivero in proposito con questi letterati.[1] Potrò scrivere di più quando avrò finito. Per ora due cose mi interessano: Il tema: non avrei mai pensato che il fumare potesse dominare una persona in quel modo. Secondo: il trattamento del tempo nel romanzo. L'arguzia non vi manca e vedo che l'ultimo capoverso di *Senilità* 'Si, Angiolina pensa e piange ecc . . .'[2] ha sbocciato grandemente alla chetichella.

Tanti saluti alla Signora se si trova costì. Spero avremo il piacere di veder loro fra breve.

Una stretta di mano   JAMES JOYCE

PS. Anchè, Mr Gilbert Seldes[3] 'The Dial' (indirizzo?) *New York*'[4]

To VALERY LARBAUD   MS. Bib. Municipale, Vichy

[*? February 1924*]   *S. James's Palace, Dungeon 76, Luteatia*[5]

Dear Larbaud: Thanks for the transmitted invitation. I regret I am not free. May I ask you, by the way, to be rather reticent about my new

---

[1] Joyce was as good as his word; he succeeded in stirring up Larbaud and Crémieux in particular, and the result of their advocacy was that Schmitz, until then snubbed by Italian critics, began to receive serious consideration.

[2] The last sentence in *As a Man Grows Older* says, 'Yes, Angiolina thinks and sometimes cries, thinks as though the secret of the universe had been explained to her or the secret of her own existence, and is sad as though in all the whole world she could not find one solitary *deo gratias*.'

[3] Gilbert Seldes (b. 1890), American writer and editor.

[4] (Translation)

'Dear friend: I went to the station, but no train was due (nor any overdue), for the hour which had been indicated. I was very sorry. When will you be coming through Paris again? Could you not spend the night here?

Thank you for the novel with the inscription. I now have two copies, having already ordered one in Trieste. I am in the process of reading it with great pleasure. Why are you discouraged? You must know that it is by far your best book. As far as the Italian critics are concerned, I do not know. But have review copies sent to 1) M. Valery Larbaud, c/o *Nouvelle Revue Française*, 3 rue de Grenelle, Paris; 2) M. Benjamin Crémieux, c/o *Revue de France* (you will find the address on a copy); 3) Mr T. S. Eliot, Editor *Criterion*, 9 Clarence Gate Mansions; 4) Mr F. M. Ford, *The Trans-atlantic Review*, 27 Quai d'Anjou, Paris. I shall speak or write to these men about the matter. I shall be able to write more when I have finished it. At the moment two things interest me. The theme: I would never have thought that smoking could dominate a person in that way. Secondly: the treatment of time in the novel. There is no absence of wit in it and I notice that the last line of *As a Man Grows Older*: "Yes, Angiolina thinks and weeps, etc . . ." has impressively developed in privacy.

Greetings to Signora Schmitz if she is there. I hope we shall have the pleasure of seeing you before long.

A handshake   James Joyce

P.S. Send a copy also to Gilbert Seldes, "The Dial" (address?) New York.'

[5] Mocking for Victoria Palace Hotel. Luteatia is a corruption of Lutetia, Latin for Paris. If not inadvertent, it may mean (by a scramble of languages) 'the place where one eats well'.

book? Lucia has done an 'articolessa' on Charlie Chaplain[1] [sic] which she will send you tomorrow. It is about the same length as himself.

Did you get the 'Coscienza di Zeno'? Kind regards Sincerely yours
                                                       JAMES JOYCE

What is the date?

To A. J. LEVENTHAL ['LAWRENCE EMERY'][2]   MS. S. Illinois
                                                    (Croessmann)

8 February 1924   *Victoria Palace Hotel, 6 rue Blaise Desgoffe,*
                                              Paris, Montparnasse

Dear Sir: Allow me to thank you for the friendly notice of my book *Ulysses* which appears in the first number of your review. Sincerely yours   JAMES JOYCE

To ROBERT MCALMON   MS. Pearson

[?18 February 1924]   *Hotel Victoria Palace, 6 rue Blaise Desgoffe,*
                                              Paris (Montpartnasse)

Dear McAlmon: There is no chance of my getting away and the legacy bore[3] is still hanging on. Is it possible for you to make an arrangement as before which I would then settle on next quarter day (25 March). We are still 5 weeks off that and I am again pressed. I cannot write to Miss Weaver first because the matter is out of her hands and also because she is staying with Miss Marsden now and I don't think she likes the tone of my last effusions though Larbaud to whom I read it thinks they are the strongest pages I have written. The task I have set myself is dreadfully difficult but I believe it can be done. O dear me! What sins did I commit in my last incarnation to be in this hole?

I hope you are enjoying yourself down there. You ought to visit the walled town of Vence (Station Cagnes). If you do call on A. Kerr Bruce,[4] Le Petit Mas. He will give you a good Scotch and soda. If you see them give them our regards. I like Cannes too especially to drive (horse not auto) round the bay.

----

[1] Lucia Joyce's article, touched up by Larbaud, appeared in the Belgian review, *Le Disque vert*, which devoted a double number to Chaplin in 1924.

[2] A. J. Leventhal (b. 1896), Irish writer and lecturer in French at Trinity College, Dublin, signed a review of *Ulysses* in the *Klaxon* (Dublin) (Winter, 1923–24) 14–20, with the penname of 'Lawrence K. Emery'. Joyce was gratified to be favourably noticed in Ireland.

[3] Miss Weaver had promised to assist Joyce with a legacy she was about to receive from the estate of an aunt.

[4] A Scotsman, at one time manager of the Havas Agency in Paris.

My sight is not very good today as the weather is changing. So I shall end this.

Of course I never heard or saw anything of Princess Murat since.[1] I am not able to do these jobs and write in the half dark at the same time.

Please remember us to Dr and Mrs Williams.[2]

Kind regards to yourself and many thanks   sincerely yours

JAMES JOYCE

P.S. *Ulysses* is selling very well but I don't care to bother Miss Beach.

To FORD MADOX FORD (Postcard)   MS. Roland Loewe

25 February 1924   [*Paris*]

Dear Ford: As it is already the 25th can you please let me have my typescript back and the first proofs?[3] I should like to check them Sincerely yours   JAMES JOYCE

To FORD MADOX FORD   MS. Stanford

6 March 1924   [*Paris*]

Dear Ford: It is now 5.30 and there is no sign of the proof promised me for Tuesday evening. As arranged I must revise this proof again and be sure that my revisions are made even if the piece has to be held over for another number. Will you please see that I get it at once. Sincerely yours   JAMES JOYCE

To FORD MADOX FORD   MS. Roland Loewe

14 March 1924   [*Paris*]

Dear Ford: Thanks for your note and for the trouble Mrs Ford and yourself took to check my proof. However, as it seemed to me almost impossible that you could revise such a tricky proof I went to Clarke's. The foreman had gone and the clerk could not find my proof. He said he thought it might be on the machine. I asked him to telephone to me tomorrow morning and then drove to Quai d'Anjou but, not finding you, left my name. My checking of the proof would mean a delay of about an hour and much relief to myself. I hope it is still possible. I

[1] See p. 83.
[2] William Carlos Williams (1883–1963), American poet.
[3] See p. 82, n. 2.

explained in a letter to Mrs Ashworth that I could not go to the printer's on Thursday but would go on Friday. Sincerely yours

JAMES JOYCE

To HARRIET SHAW WEAVER   MS. British Museum

15 March 1924   *Victoria Palace Hotel, 6 rue Blaise Desgoffe,*
                                              Paris (Montparnasse)

Dear Miss Weaver: I hope none of the MS[1] was lost. It is eleven pages. The first words are 'O tell me' the last 'waters of. Night!' I shall send you two pages which have been written round again to replace. But they do not change the piece. It should be read in successive runs. On Monday I shall try to start Shaun the Post.[2] This would make the second part of the book fairly complete with the letter. The first part[3] is not written yet.

You did not say if you liked the piece?[4] I read it to Mr Larbaud who was enthusiastic about it. I think I shall fall all of a heap after the Shaun piece. It has been such a struggle. With kindest regards and many thanks sincerely yours   JAMES JOYCE

To FORD MADOX FORD   MS. Roland Loewe

[? *16 March 1924*]   [*Paris*]

Dear Ford: The proof (sent me without the former one to check it by!) is quite impossible. I glanced over it. Not only has it not been read but many of the most glaring blunders are still in it. I gave the typescript to you, as you remember, under pressure and on the distinct understanding that I could write in notes to which I had not then access. I think it is due to me to hold over the piece for your next issue as the printer seems to be still learning his trade. If you can call today before 5 I shall explain to you why in my opinion it is necessary to make these apparently trifling additions.

Your maid does not know where I can find you. I thought it better to drive up here in the hope of finding you rather than send a pneu. Sincerely yours   JAMES JOYCE

[1] An early draft of *Anna Livia Plurabelle* (*Finnegans Wake*, pp. 196–210).
[2] That is, Book III (four chapters long), pp. 403–590.
[3] That is, Chapters I–IV of Part I.
[4] Miss Weaver's attitude towards *Finnegans Wake* was a little reserved from the start, but Joyce was eager for her approval.

To Robert McAlmon   MS. Pearson

24 March 1924   *Victoria Palace Hotel, 6 rue Blaise Desgoffe, Paris*

Dear McAlmon: I must ask you to overlook my discourtesy in not
acknowledging and replying to your letter, with cheque (frs 2120). I
have been working myself silly and revising proof of the four masters or
evangelists for the T.R. What a job, too! What is your address? Is this
right? I want to return you the money. Miss Beach says you are coming
on here. Will you please drop me a line? I hope you have had a good
sunny time. Sincerely yours   James Joyce

To Valery Larbaud   MS. Bib. Municipale, Vichy

24 March 1924   [*Paris*]

Dear Larbaud: Will Mrs Nebbia[1] and yourself dine with us on
Thursday, calling here at 8.15? We hope so. Enclosed is revised typed
copy of Anna Livia. Have you heard the four masters bit? It will be in
the Transatlantic Review next number.[2] I read you a mere sketch a
year ago. But perhaps you read it in the folder. But I don't think you
had time.

   I am nearly stunned by this way of life. O, mon dieu! Did Miss Beach
send you the N.Y. Times?[3] I think it ought to be answered. Sincerely
yours   James Joyce

To Lily Bollach   MS. Stanford

24 March 1924   [*Paris*]

Dear Miss Bollach: I am dreadfully late in acknowledging receipt of
the second typescript which you rushed off for me so promptly. It was
very kind of you indeed as it was a mere whim of mine to have it for that
day.[4] I apologise also for the delay in remitting you enclosed (frs 70.–)

---

   [1] Signora Maria Nebbia, Larbaud's longtime friend.
   [2] As Joyce wrote Robert McAlmon early in 1924 (*Letters*, ed. Gilbert, p. 209), 'Ford
has come so often to the well and talked about support given me in the past that I have
consented to give him the four masters bit (which is only a sidepiece) for his next number.
The review is very shabby in my opinion.'
   [3] Ernest Boyd, 'Order Established in the Literary Chaos of James Joyce, A Guide to
"Ulysses" and Its Author,' *New York Times Book Review* (2 March 1924) 7. Boyd
was reviewing Herbert Gorman, *James Joyce: The First Forty Years* (New York,
Huebsch, 17 March 1924). He attacked some of Larbaud's views of Joyce. See p. 109,
n. 2.
   [4] Presumably his birthday, 2 February.

for your excellent work. The spelling 'eygs' is all right—a mixture of Danish and English which is intentional.[1] My excuse for all my discourtesy is that I have been revising proof after proof of a passage which will appear next week in the transatlantic review—the piece about the four old men typed by you some months [ago].[2] So I hope you will forgive me. I shall of course send you a copy of the review immediately it comes out. I hope I may be able to see you this week as there is another small matter I want to bother you about. With renewed apologies and many thanks sincerely yours   JAMES JOYCE

To ETTORE SCHMITZ   MS. Fonda Savio

1 April 1924   *Restaurant des Trianons, Paris*

Caro amico: Buone notizie. M. Valery Larbaud ha letto il Suo romanzo. Gli piace molto. Ne scriverà una recensione nella *Nouvelle Revue* Française. Ne ha scritto anche ad una sua amica la Sig. Sibilla Aleramo della *Tribuna*.

Tanti saluti alla Sua Signora ed a Lei una stretta di mano.

JAMES JOYCE[3]

To HARRIET SHAW WEAVER   MS. British Museum

6 April 1924   *Victoria Palace Hotel, 6 rue Blaise Desgoffe,*
Paris (Montparnasse)

Dear Miss Weaver: For some days past I have not been allowed to read a line on account of a secretion in the conjunctiva—scarcely any inflammation, no pain and it seems no danger. Dr Borsch says I must limit my work in present conditions to a half or a third. I have been working ten hours a day in semi-dark for the past seven months. I am to be operated on when the fine weather comes I suppose in May. He says it will be much simpler and have a good result.

I hope to resume with Shaun tomorrow. I had done about a third. But he (already a dawdler) will be longer on the road.

I asked Miss Beach to send you the *Transatlantic Review*. You will notice revisions in it. I also send you an article by Mr Ford.

---

[1] 'Eygs' appears twice in the *Anna Livia Plurabelle* section, *Finnegans Wake*, p. 199.
[2] *Finnegans Wake*, pp. 383–99.
[3] (Translation)
   'Dear friend: Good news: Mr Valery Larbaud has read your novel. He likes it very much. He will write a review of it in the *Nouvelle Revue Française*. He has also written a friend of his concerning it, Signora Sibilla Aleramo of the *Tribuna*.
   Greetings to your wife and to you a handshake.   James Joyce'

Mr Gorman's book on me[1] arrived. It is well and carefully written but it reminds me of so much labour and strife that I am afraid it was in part responsible for a nervous collapse I had a few days ago. I went out today and feel better.

I am glad you are going to rid yourself of the worry of the publishing business but, of course, mistrustful of your successor.[2]

Can you get Mr Gorman's book in Brentano's, London. I suppose so.

This has been a dreadful winter and the prospect of ending it in a clinique is the only proper finale. But I hope there is something better beyond.

Miss Beach will send your copy of *Ulysses* to London by some trustworthy messenger, if she has not done so.[3] I have not seen her for a while as my general expression is not a pleasant one to offer to anybody's gaze, though, strangely enough, the Shaun the Post piece is very amusing—to me, at least. It is extremely hard to write.

I hope you are well after your stay in the country and that you will not be bored by this letter. With kindest regards sincerely yours

JAMES JOB

To FORD MADOX FORD   MS. Roland Loewe

8 April 1924   *Victoria Palace Hotel, 6 rue Blaise Desgoffe,*
Paris, Montparnasse

Dear Ford: Many thanks for the kind mention of me in Sunday's *Chicago Tribune*. I hope the issue is selling well.

The *Egoist Press* is going out of business and Mr Jonathan Cape wants to acquire copyright of all my books at once. He has forwarded a contract to me and suggests that I submit it to you. May I trouble you to let me know what you think of it. The royalty 15% seems to me rather low. The *Egoist Press* paid me 25% and *Shakespeare* and Company 66% of net profit. Sincerely yours   JAMES JOYCE

P.S. Miss Weaver writes that it is not easy to get your review in London?

---

[1] See p. 91, n. 3. Herbert Gorman (1893–1954) began as a reporter for newspapers in Springfield, Massachusetts, and continued his journalistic career from 1918 to 1928 in New York City. He wrote biographies of Longfellow, Hawthorne, Dumas, and Mary Queen of Scots, and a long series of historical novels. His connection with Joyce began in 1917 when he wrote a perceptive review of *A Portrait of the Artist* for the *Springfield Union*. The two men did not meet until about 1926. Joyce authorized Gorman to write a biography of him, and this appeared, after many delays, in 1939 in New York.

[2] It was just at this time that Harriet Shaw Weaver turned over the publishing rights to Joyce's first four books (not including *Ulysses*) to Jonathan Cape.

[3] This was a copy of the fourth printing of January 1924

To Lily Bollach   MS. Stanford

24 April 1924   [*Paris*]

Dear Miss Bollach: I wanted to write to you several days ago but I have
had a rather bad nervous collapse from overwork. I have again a request to
make which, I am sure, will bore you greatly. Mr Valery Larbaud asked
me to let him have a copy of the Anna Livia piece (enclosed) and I have
also promised one to a relative[1] in Ireland who has done a good deal of
research for me. So could you make three fresh copies of it without the
blanks in the paging? If so, I shall be extremely obliged though I can
imagine how tiresome it is to type the same thing three or four times
over. Mr Larbaud leaves for Italy in a few days but if you are pressed
for time please let me know. I shall call on your concierge in any case.

With this is a copy of the French translation of my first novel which
I beg you to accept with many thanks for your promptness and
courtesy.

Apologising for the short notice I am giving you Sincerely yours
                                                        James Joyce

To Valery Larbaud   Bib. Municipale, Vichy

2 May 1924[2]   *Restaurant des Trianons, Paris*

Dear Larbaud: Here is one of the pieces of verse[3] I spoke to you of.
Tomorrow I will send you Anna Livia corrected. It is already typed but
I revise the typescript always Sincerely yours   James Joyce

To Lily Bollach   MS. Stanford

21 May 1924   [*Paris*]

Dear Miss Bollach: Do you think you could manage to type these
verses (the first I have written for six years) and leave six copies with
your concierge by tomorrow (Thursday) evening? I should be much
obliged to you if you could. Also I should like to know how much I owe
you and must apologise for not having settled with you before now. I
should be very glad if we could meet some evening as, unfortunately, I am
going to make another trip (into a hospital) and I wanted to arrange

[1] Michael Healy.
[2] The date is written in another hand, probably Larbaud's.
[3] Probably the two poems written in Zurich in 1917 and 1918, 'A Memory of the
Players at Midnight' and 'Bahnhofstrasse'.

another matter with you before I do so. Are you free on Friday evening at 6.30 p.m. at the usual place? I shall feel glad if you will let me know. With many thanks sincerely yours   JAMES JOYCE

To VALERY LARBAUD   MS. Bib. Municipale, Vichy

22 May 1924   *Victoria Palace Hotel, 6 rue Blaise Desgoffe*
                                                              (rue de Rennes)

Dear Larbaud: All my books and MSS are packed up[1] (Anna Livia with them) so I cannot find what I promised. It is impossible to work any longer in this hotel. However, I send you a short poem—the first I have written for six years.[2] I hope it reaches you before you leave for Genoa. Sincerely yours   JAMES JOYCE

To LEON FLEISCHMAN[3]   MS. Joseph Mitchell

27 May 1924   *Victoria Palace Hotel, 6 rue Blaise Desgoffe,*
                                                          Paris (Montparnasse)

Dear Fleischman: I am sorry you could not dine with us before you sailed. I hope you will find Mrs Fleischman[4] quite recovered from her illness. Will you please give her our kind regards. As we spoke about my American publisher I enclose a letter which I will ask you to return. You will see that in one year not a single copy of *A Portrait of the Artist* has been sold in the United States. My annual income apparently from sales in America is about 30$. Sincerely yours   JAMES JOYCE

To ROBERT McALMON   MS. Pearson

30 May 1924   *[Paris]*

Dear McAlmon: May I introduce a friend of mine, Mr Patrick Tuohy,[5] an Irish painter who did a portrait of my father and is finishing one of

---

[1] Joyce packed up his manuscripts so as to rest his left eye, at Dr Borsch's order.

[2] 'A Prayer' in *Pomes Penyeach*.

[3] Leon Fleischman (1890–1946) was the Paris representative of the American publisher Boni and Liveright. He wrote a book, *Refractions* (New York, 1929). (Joyce regularly misspelt his name as Fleischmann, and this slip has been corrected.)

[4] Mrs Fleischman (née Helen Kastor) (1895–1963) was later divorced from her husband and married Joyce's son George on 10 December 1930.

[5] Patrick Joseph Tuohy (1894–1930), Irish artist, was the son of a well-known Dublin ophthalmologist. Chiefly because he recognized the name, Joyce commissioned Tuohy in 1923 to paint a portrait of John Stanislaus Joyce in Dublin. This proved very successful. In May 1924 Tuohy asked Joyce to pose, and when he consented, demanded innumerable sittings. Joyce put up with Irishmen gladly, but he found Tuohy's conversation boring, and did not greatly like the portrait. Tuohy committed suicide in New York in 1930.

me. You may find him interesting. His accent, which is very Dublin, may be perhaps a little difficult to understand. sincerely yours,

JAMES JOYCE

To MYRON C. NUTTING   MS. Northwestern

[? *30 May 1924*]   *Restaurant des Trianons, 5 Place de Rennes (VIᵉ),*
Gare Montparnasse, Paris

Dear Nutting: This is to introduce Mr Patrick Tuohy who has painted my father. He will show the photograph.[1] I like it and would like to have your opinion of it. He would like to see your portrait of my wife and also the sketch of me.[2] Sincerely yours   JAMES JOYCE

To HARRIET SHAW WEAVER   MS. British Museum

2 June 1924   *Victoria Palace Hotel, 6 rue Blaise Desgoffe,*
Paris (Montparnasse)

Dear Miss Weaver: Many thanks indeed for your kind letter. I enclose one of a different tenor. Its weatherbeaten appearance shows the energy with which I put it into my pocket. We have been here for nine months and I am only one week in arrears. . . . This Norwegian must have been reading my MS surruptiously [sic], I fear.[3]

Mr Tuohy has added still another complication by insisting on remaining another week. I have now given him 26 sittings. He was to have left today but last night he begged for two more and as he is forfeiting his salary as professor at the Dublin school of art I consented. He will telegraph to you when he arrives in London and bring you the portrait.[4] He has to get a special cage made as the paint will not be dry.

I am to see Dr Borsch at 6 p.m. and will add a postscript to this to tell you what is decided about the operation.[5] The posing has tired me but I think it would be well to go into the clinic and have it over. There are so many problems[6] to be solved that I can face only one at a time. Perhaps in there staring up at darkness I may solve the second.

[1] The original is now at the University of Buffalo.
[2] These two pictures are now at Northwestern University.
[3] The enclosed letter must have been from Joyce's landlord, who evidently had a Norwegian name. In *Finnegans Wake* the hero, Earwicker, comes from Scandinavia to invade Ireland, so Joyce was elaborately comparing this advent with his landlord's fiscal encroachment.
[4] The portrait of James Joyce, which Tuohy was taking on to Dublin to exhibit.
[5] To forestall glaucoma, Joyce submitted to his second iridectomy on the left eye on 10 June. The first was in Zurich in 1917. He had now had five eye operations in all.
[6] In *Finnegans Wake*.

John Stanislaus Joyce, father of James Joyce, painted by the Dublin
artist Patrick Tuohy in the early 1920s (p. 95).

Joyce's passport photograph in Paris.

Right: Jenny Serruys, later Mme Bradley. *Below, left:* A recent photograph of Mme William Aspenwall Bradley. *Below, right:* William Aspenwall Bradley.

Sylvia Beach.

John Rodker, James Joyce, Sylvia Beach, and Cyprian Beach, in Shakespeare and Company, about 1921.

Valery Larbaud.

Announcement of Valery Larbaud's lecture on Joyce in Adrienne
Monnier's bookshop, 7 December
1921 (pp. 53-54).

LA MAISON DES AMIS DES LIVRES
7, rue de l'Odéon, Paris - VIe — Tél.: Fleurus 25-05

Mercredi 7 Décembre
à 9 h. précises du soir

SÉANCE CONSACRÉE A
L'ÉCRIVAIN IRLANDAIS

JAMES JOYCE

CONFÉRENCE PAR

M. VALERY LARBAUD

Lecture de fragments de ULYSSES
traduits pour la 1re fois en français

— *Nous tenons à prévenir le public que certaines des pages qu'on lira son*
d'une hardiesse d'expression peu commune qui peut très légitimement choquer.—

Cette séance étant donnée au bénéfice de JAMES JOYCE,
le droit d'admission sera, exceptionnellement, de 20 francs par
personne. Nous serions particulièrement reconnaissants envers
les personnes qui voudraient bien dépasser la somme fixée.

Les places doivent être retenues à l'avance. Nous rappelons qu'elles sont limitée
à cent.

Robert McAlmon and James Joyce, in a pencil portrait by Paul-Emile Bécat, Paris, 1921.

Ezra Pound, John Quinn, Ford Madox Ford, and James Joyce in Pound's rooms in Paris, 1923.

Lucia Joyce, drawn by Myron C.
Nutting, 1923.

Myron C. Nutting.

A drawing of Richard Wallace,
1923, by Myron C. Nutting.

Lucia (left) and Nora Joyce (right), with two unidentified persons, in Galway, April 1922.

Joyce, Mrs Joyce, and George at a restaurant, early 1920s.

Harriet Shaw Weaver, about 1923. (*Photograph by Man Ray.*)

Does Mr Huebsch's account mean that no copy of my novel was sold in the United States in one year and that my total royalties come to 30 $. I have written to a friend of mine, a Mr Fleischman, formerly a partner in the firm Boni and Liveright, to try to take the books off Mr Huebsch's hands. They are not even in his catalogue, Miss Beach says, and yet copies of the *Transatlantic Review* with Mamalujo in it fetch 18 $.50, visitors report.

The weather is dreadful today and 'my sight is growing thicker on me with the shadows in this place'.[1] My memory too is dulled. I cannot remember accurately the first page of Shaun and he is not here to aid me. I revised the new press cuttings for Miss Beach. I hope you received the Nouvelles Littéraires.[2] Mr Larbaud has great courage. On the same page you will see a notice about *Commerce* in which a translation of the first 12 pages of *Ithaca* as far as 'Old Ollebo M.P.' will appear.[3]

I expect a letter from the solicitors in the morning and I shall then write to them and to you. In the meantime it is useless for me to say anything but that if I had been in your place and in my present mood I would have thrown the fire irons (including the fender) at the spectral bore seated in that armchair. With kindest regards sincerely yours

JAMES JOYCE

P. S. The operation, Dr Borsch says, ought to be done. He cannot do it on Wednesday as Mr Tuohy wants that day. It will be made on Saturday.

J.J.

To VALERY LARBAUD   MS. Bib. Municipale, Vichy

6 June 1924   *Victoria Palace Hotel, 6 rue Blaise Desgoffe,*
Paris VII

Dear Larbaud: I must thank you for the allusion to me in that interview. But how am I ever to live up to it?

I had a letter from 'Italo Svevo' this morning. He is in despair about his book. If you manage a short note on it somewhere or, as you suggested, give some pages of it in the second number of *Commerce* you would do

[1] In the version of *Anna Livia Plurabelle* which Joyce sent Miss Weaver on 8 March 1924, one of the washerwomen says, 'My sight is getting thicker on me with the shadows in this place.' See Fred H. Higginson, *Anna Livia Plurabelle: The Making of a Chapter* (Minneapolis, 1960), p. 46. In *Finnegans Wake*, p. 215, the sentence became, 'My sights are swimming thicker on me by the shadows to this place.'
[2] Frédéric Lefèvre, 'Une Heure avec M. Valery Larbaud,' *Nouvelles Littéraires* III.85 (31 May 1924) 1–2.
[3] *Commerce* (Paris) I (Summer 1924) 123–58, contained part of the *Telemachus*, *Ithaca*, and *Penelope* episodes of *Ulysses*, in the translation of Valery Larbaud and Auguste Morel. A smaller selection from *Ithaca* was used.

much more for him than my mention of *Les Lauriers sont coupés* did for Dujardin.

I am very glad you liked the prayer. Pleasant holidays! sincerely yours   JAMES JOYCE

From ETTORE SCHMITZ[1]

10 June 1924   *Trieste*

Caro amico, grazie per la Sua del 6. Mi dispiace tanto di sentire che Lei ha di nuovo bisogno di farsi torturare. Spero di sentire presto che sta bene.

Parto domani per Londra. Ringrazi Larbaud da parte mia e gli dica che può fare del mio romanzo tutto, persino tradurlo per intero. (Buona l'idea?).[2] Non scrivo a Larbaud solo per l'esperienza fatta che i letterati hanno in genere una cattiva 'nursery', (almeno gl'italiani) e non usano rispondere. Di quei tre romanzi che mandai ultimamente in Italia pare nessuno sia giunto a destinazione. Io ho il grande torto di occuparmi ancora del mio romanzo. Tanto più che lo faccio solo col Suo intervento e che Lei, a questo mondo fra soddisfazioni e seccature grandi (quella dell'operazione) ha già abbastanza da fare. Fatto questo passo presso il signor Larbaud, lasciamolo correre ambedue (il romanzo).

Mi sono procurato l'Ulisse. Al mio ritorno lo leggerò capitolo per capitolo tentando di viverlo. Ho la promessa di Suo fratello che dopo ogni capitolo lavorato a fondo mi concederà la sua assistenza. Credo che dopo di Lei non potevo trovare un assistente migliore.

Io spero che a Londra non dovrò rimanere che quattro settimane.

Saluti cordiali anche alla Sua Signora ed anche da parte di mia moglie.

Suo devotissimo   ETTORE SCHMITZ

A proposito di Suo fratello: Mi disse che fra poco Le scriverà. Sta benissimo e mi consegnò due giornali che di Lei parlano.[3]

---

[1] The text of this letter is taken from 'Carteggio . . . Svevo–Joyce', ed. Harry Levin, *Inventario* II.1 (Spring 1949) 123–24.

[2] Larbaud wrote Schmitz a little later, in an undated letter, that he was arranging to publish some of *La Coscienza di Zeno* in French translation in the new review, *Commerce*, and was also planning a critical article on Schmitz's work for some other review. Italo Svevo, *Corrispondenza con Valery Larbaud, Benjamin Crémieux e Marie Anne Comnène* (Milan, 1953).

[3] (Translation)

'Dear friend: Thank you for your letter of the 6th. I am very sorry to hear that you must again undergo your tortures. I hope to hear soon that you are better.

I leave tomorrow for London. Give my thanks to Larbaud and tell him he can do anything with my novel that he wants, even translate it in its entirety. (Good idea?) I refrain from writing to Larbaud only because it has been my personal experience that

To HARRIET SHAW WEAVER   MS. British Museum

11 July 1924   *Hotel de France et Chateaubriand, Saint-Malo*

Dear Miss Weaver: Many thanks for your letter of some days ago. I left Paris after a final interview with Dr Borsch. I am to go back there in a couple of months to see the result of the operation and to get other glasses. Meanwhile I am to continue the treatment here or wherever we stop. No further operation, he says, is necessary or would do any good. The sight will come back, he says. I will say nothing more on this subject till then.

I left Paris in the usual whirl of confusion. The first fragments of *Ulysses* translated are to appear in *Commerce*, a *revue de luxe* this month. Mr Larbaud being away the fragments chosen were insufficient. I asked to have others added. When this was done the princess di Bassiano[1] objected to some of the passages. This I overruled. (This correspondence must now cease. AUTHOR.) Then the French printer who set *Penelope* (or part of her) struck out punctuation but put in accents. I insisted on their deletion. This caused fright. In the end, at the suggestion of Miss Monnier or the other two editors Mr Larbaud was telegraphed to. He replied bilingually to make sure there would be no mistake: Joyce a raison Joyce ha ragione.[2] This gem now blazes brightly in my crown.

Then Mr Cape and his printers gave me trouble. They set the book[3] with perverted commas[4] and I insisted on their removal by the sergeant-

men of letters have generally had a poor upbringing (at least the Italians), and they do not usually answer. Of those three novels which I sent recently to Italy, it would seem that none has reached its destination. I confess it as a great fault that I am still concerned about my novel. All the more so since you are the only one to help me and you, between great satisfactions and annoyances (the operations), already have enough to keep you busy in this world. After taking this step with M. Larbaud, let's both let it go (the novel).

I have secured a copy of *Ulysses*. After my return I shall read it chapter by chapter, attempting to live it through. I have your brother's promise that after I have worked over each chapter thoroughly he will give me his assistance. I think that next to you I could not have a better guide.

I hope that I will not have to stay in London for more than four weeks.

Cordial greetings to you and to Mrs Joyce from myself and from my wife. Your faithful   Ettore Schmitz

About your brother: he said that he will write you soon. He is in good health and he gave me two newspapers which speak of you.'

[1] Marguerite (Chapin) Caetani, Princess of Bassiano (1881–1963), was born in New London, Connecticut. She came to Europe to study singing and married Roffredo Caetani, Prince of Bassiano and later Duke of Sermoneta. She published the reviews *Commerce* (1924–32) in Paris and *Botteghe Oscure* (1948–60) in Rome.

[2] 'Joyce is right' (in French and Italian).

[3] Jonathan Cape issued in 1924 a new edition, with type reset, of *A Portrait of the Artist*.

[4] Joyce preferred dashes to quotation marks.

at-arms. Then they underlined passages which they thought undesirable. But as you will see by the enclosed: They were and, behold, they are not.

The Neighbourhood Playhouse of New York sent me a contract agreeing to all my terms of last year: advance of $ 250, limit of 1 year or retainer of $500 for another, accounts weekly and stipulation as to production.[1] I have signed and am returning it.

I shall have other news of an unusual kind to send you on Monday when I get back a letter which I sent for typing. I prefer to send it than to tell you and I had copies made at once for obvious reasons. All I will say is that it gave me great satisfaction to receive it.[2]

I shall defer till then more homely news about this part of the ancient empire of the Celts.

I hope you are well in London with this heat. There is a Breton fair on under my windows. I was very glad to get my heels out of Paris in spite of the unsatisfactory result of the operation. It had become almost unbearable especially after the arrival of the teams a week or so ago. I am staying here as it is the best place to look around from and find out where to go. My wife and both my children are with me. They also need a very good rest. The fair is rather noisy (I hope I shall not steal a set of bagpipes from one of the Lower Breton delegates) but perhaps a fall from pandemonium to silence would have stunned me. With kindest regards sincerely yours   JAMES JOYCE

To W. B. YEATS   MS. Yeats

12 July 1924   *Hotel de France et Chateaubriand, Saint-Malo*

Dear Yeats: Many thanks indeed for your very kind letter of 5 instant. I am sorry that I am again obliged to decline your invitation but unfortunately I have just undergone another eye operation (the third) and the result will not be known for a few months. I must then return to Paris to have my sight tested and I am not yet sure where I shall be in September and October.

Let me thank you for your intervention in my favour with the committee you mention[3] but, more than for that, for the expression of friendly admiration with which you have honoured me. Sincerely yours

JAMES JOYCE

[1] The Neighborhood Playhouse produced *Exiles* on 19 February 1925. It continued for 41 performances, ending 22 March.

[2] A second invitation from W. B. Yeats to stay with him and his wife in Ireland.

[3] Yeats had evidently interceded in Joyce's behalf with the Tailteann Prize committee in Dublin, but Joyce was ineligible because not resident in Ireland. In awarding the prizes, Yeats nevertheless singled out *Ulysses* as 'more indubitably a work of genius than any prose written by an Irishman since the death of Synge'.

To ALESSANDRO FRANCINI BRUNI (Postcard)   MS. S. Illinois
                                                (Croessmann)

23 July 1924   *Hotel Chateaubriand, S. Malo*

Caro Francini: Mi trovo qui dopo un'altra operazione all'occhio del
quale non si sa ancora il risultato. Spero che questa ti trova in buona
salute ed anche la signora e Daniele.[1] Mia moglie Giorgio e Lucia sono
con me. Non so dove andremo da qui. Siamo sempre senza casa!
   Saluti cordiali alla famiglia ed a te una stretta di mano

                                                JAMES JOYCE[2]

From STANISLAUS JOYCE   MS. Buffalo

7 August 1924   *Trieste   Via Sanita 2, I*

Dear Jim, I hope you will have so far recovered from your recent
operation as to be able to read this without difficulty. I received Lucia's
card telling me that you were getting on well. Do your many doctors
hold out any hope of having done with the job one of these days? At
this distance I cannot understand the necessity for so many operations.
The same paper that speaks of your eye trouble amongst the social
events, says that Tuohy has done your portrait. Very quickly, it seems.
I am glad you have let him. His portrait of Pappie is a wonderful study
of that little old Milesian. I am especially glad that Tuohy is not that
irritating kind of clever painter that sees in his sitter only a type. The
likeness is striking. The face, the pose, the hands especially I recognize
and looking at them I feel that I know how they have come to be so.
Compared with this portrait, Augustus John's of Hardy (which I used
to like) now seems to me wooden.
   I have to thank you for a list of things: the Transatlantic Review, the
French translation of your novel, Gorman's study of you and many
papers.
   Gorman's study is also a very satisfactory performance. He seems to
be impressed by your importance in modern literature, whereas Boyd
wishes to impress people with his own importance as a critic and to deny
as far as he can that you were 'discovered' abroad. And yet in dealing

---

[1] Francini's son.
[2] (Translation)
   'Dear Francini: I am here after another eye operation the result of which is not yet
known. I hope this finds you in good health and your wife and Daniele too. My wife,
Giorgio, and Lucia are with me. I don't know where we will go from here. We are
always homeless!
   Kind greetings to your family and to you a handshake   James Joyce'

out justice he is by no means uninfluenced by the current of hostile opinion still against you in Dublin. Gorman speaks of his work as 'not definitive'. As I like the tone of book I should be glad to supply him with information on certain points, if he intends to amplify what he has written. He does not mention 'The Holy Office' (your break with the mummers) or 'Gas from a Burner' for instance. A pupil of mine who saw the book lying on my table said 'A very different work from Sig. Francini's,[1] I imagine!'—that awfully funny lecture on you, tutta da ridere. You have read it so I need not enlarge on its imbecility as criticism. If he had blurted out his meaningless vulgarities with a certain riff-raffish humour, he might have carried it off, but he is not the man to do so. He kept mumbling over them and skipping paragraphs while people were quietly getting up and walking out as if after some kind of unholy communion. He has committed that 'bêtise' of his before quitting Trieste but he has left me to pay for it. I had had a misgiving before he delivered it and had asked him to let me see it. He swore earnestly and volubly that there would be nothing to object to in his caricature. I don't acquit him of a certain amount of malice in the affair and you by your silly horseplay with him and with[2] Silvestri here after your return helped to bring it on yourself. To hell with him, anyhow. As far as I am concerned I'll live it down; you it doesn't hurt. He wrote to me from Florence saying that he had to deliver a lecture before I don't know what society. At first I was not inclined to answer, then thinking it better he should speak about your work than you, I sent him registered and express an eight-page analysis of ULYSSES (much like Gorman's) so that the audience might not go away with the idea that you belong to the [word missing] category. He never acknowledged receipt of it. A pupil of mine who was in Florence called at the Nuovo Giornale and wrote to him. No answer. After a long time he scribbled a few lines to say that there had been a large gathering of the English colony but that during the lecture these 'straitlaced English' (inglesi puritani) kept filing out of the hall. I am now thoroughly sick of this bloody fool.

I have received one instalment of your yet unnamed novel in the Transatlantic Review. I don't know whether the drivelling rigmarole about half a tall hat[3] and ladies' modern toilet chambers[4] (practically the only things I understand in this nightmare production) is written with the deliberate intention of pulling the reader's leg or not. You began

---

[1] See pp. 58–59.
[2] The manuscript of the letter ends here and is continued on a typed copy with lacunae.
[3] *Finnegans Wake*, p. 387.   [4] *Ibid.*, p. 395.

this fooling in the Holles Street episode[1] in ULYSSES and I see that Wyndham Lewis (the designer of that other piece of impudent fooling 'the Portrait of an Englishwoman') imitates it with heavy-hoofed capering in the columns of the 'Daily Mail'. Or perhaps—a sadder supposition—it is the beginning of softening of the brain. The first instalment faintly suggests the Book of the Four Masters and a kind of Biddy in Blunderland and a satire on the supposed matriarchal system. It has certain characteristics of a beginning of something, is nebulous, chaotic but contains certain elements. That is absolutely all I can make of it. But! It is unspeakably wearisome. Gorman's book on you practically proclaims your work as the last word in modern literature. It may be the last in another sense, the witless wandering of literature before its final extinction. Not that I imagine that literature will ever die as long as men speak and write. But they may cease to read or at least to read such things. I for one would not read more than a paragraph of it, if I did not know you.

What I say does not matter. I have no doubt that you have your plan, probably a big one again as in 'Ulysses'. No doubt, too, many more competent people around you speak to you in quite a different tone. My only excuse for saying what I think is that it is what I think, and it is so little pleasure to me to say that this is perhaps the chief reason why I cannot bring myself to write to you. Why are you still intelligible and sincere in verse? If literature is to develop along the lines of your latest work it will certainly become, as Shakespeare hinted centuries ago, much ado about nothing. Ford in an article you sent me suggests that the whole thing is to be taken as a nonsense rhythm and that the reader should abandon himself to the sway of it. I am sure, though the article seems to have your approval, that he is talking through his half a tall hat. In any case I refuse to allow myself to be whirled round in the mad dance by a literary dervish.

I wrote to you in much the same strain when you sent me 'Ulysses', and yet a good part, the greater part of it I like. I have no humour for the episodes which are deliberately farcical: the Sirens, the Oxen of the Sun; and as the episodes grow longer and longer and you try to tell every damn thing you know about anybody that appears or anything that crops up my patience oozes out. The talent however is so obvious that I almost take it for granted. Dublin lies stretched out before the reader, the minute living incidents start out of the pages. Anybody who reads can hear the people talk and feel himself among them. At every turn of this, the longest day on record, there are things to give him

---

[1] The *Oxen of the Sun* episode.

pause. There is many a laugh but hardly one happy impression. Everything is undeniably as it is represented, yet the 'cumulative effect' as Grant Richards would say, makes him doubt truth to be a liar. You try to shift the burden of your melancholy to the reader's shoulders without being yourself relieved. To me you seem to have escaped from the toils of the priest and the king only to fall under the oppression of a monstrous vision of life itself. Where so much has been recorded, I object to what has been omitted. There is no serenity or happiness anywhere in the whole book. I suppose you will tell me ironically that this is my chance and my work;[1] to set to and write up all the eucharistic moments of Dublin life. It is not my business. Yet in these same surroundings that you describe I have not rarely been penetrated by a keen sense of happiness. I cannot exploit these moments either in prose or verse, but the fact remains that they have been.

In the Tyrone Street episode,[2] for instance, the relation or at least the analogy between the imagination in the intellect and the sexual instinct in the body (my fixed idea, by the bye, old chap, explained to you first in Dublin apropos of Yeats' phrase 'world troubling seaman',[3] which I corrected to 'world-troubling semen', and later in Trieste to you and Francini when I pointed out the resemblance between the 'Bacchanals' of Euripides and Ibsen's 'Ghosts')[4] is worked out with a fantastic horror of which I know no equal in literature painting or music, but not more fantastically horrible than some of the manifestations of the instinct with which it deals. It is undoubtedly Catholic in temperament. This brooding on the lower order of natural facts, this re-evocation and exaggeration of detail by detail and the spiritual dejection which accompanies them are purely in the spirit of the confessional. Your temperament, like Catholic morality, is predominantly sexual. Baptism has left in you a strong inclination to believe evil. For of all the manifestations of Circe, the most benign, that which has inspired poets of all kinds for thousands of years (including the poet of 'Chamber Music') is

[1] See II, p. 280, n. 4. This was evidently a catch-phrase used by both brothers.
[2] The *Circe* episode.   [3] Yeats, 'The Madness of King Goll.'
[4] In a talk for the British Broadcasting Corporation, Stanislaus Joyce explained that he had told his brother that the interest of Euripides' play lay in the implication 'that the imagination is to the mind what the sexual instinct is to the body, something joyous and uncontrollable, apparently foolish and effeminate, but in fact, in both cases indispensable and terrible when thwarted, something which it is death to hide. Without one, the mind is pedantic and sterile, joyless and void of human sympathy; without the other, the body is but a labouring machine'. Joyce replied, in a letter which has not survived, that the episode did not deal with the sexual instinct but with the locomotor apparatus. Stanislaus Joyce comments: 'Perhaps it is pride of authorship, but I was and am unconvinced. All through the episode there is a parallelism between what happens in fact, which is mainly sexual, the scene being laid in a brothel, and what happens in the imagination.'

represented by a couple of lines by Yeats, murmured by a student in drunken slumber.[1] This is bias. The close however, with dream figure of Bloom's young son and the suggestion that children are the real lambs who take away just these sins of the world is so unexpected and so unexpectedly tender, that one reader at least could not read it unmoved.

The clerk said that it would be necessary for you to prove your British citizenship with your birth certificate and passport first and then Georgie would have the right to apply either for British or Italian Citizenship. This has been confirmed by the Consul here. It seems even those who have resided in Italy for more than ten years may have to apply even for the Citizenship they already possess. If they try to force Italian citizenship on me, they will find that I have [word missing] it pretty smartly. In the end the clerk who got nice when I got nasty, suggested a declaration in a form which I enclose. I enclose also a card from a German gentleman who thinks you are giving 'Ulysses' away with a pound of tea.

Regarding my visit to Paris, it would be very difficult for me to go in Spring. I had intended to go this September but if you are away, of course I won't. Besides Schaurek has again borrowed over three thousand lire from me for his trip to Bohemia and then to Venice. I expect to be repaid this month. Much will depend on that. How are you enjoying yourself in Saint Malo? The famous Carnac[2] must be somewhere near there, I suppose? You could take a leaf out of Renan's book[3] and meditate on old ancient Celtic civilization there and in Ireland before Logue's predecessors came over in their come-to-bed half a tall hats to swap the kingdom of Heaven for the Kingdom of Ireland. Where (except in operetta) could you find a more burlesque title than [words missing]? Is he anything to the Mayor of Cork[4] who committed suicide on the King's Threshold?[5]

Another point regarding your cinematographic psychological analysis. It is often obscure and it should not be so. Thought may be inconsequent, desultory, heterogeneous—anything you like—but never obscure to the thinker. How could it be so? Yet in 'Ulysses', Bloom's wool-gatherings as often as not leave the reader guessing. This is a mistake, in my opinion and vitiates the whole book. I have the right, I think, to make this observation as, of the two, I first attempted to

---

[1] At the end of the *Circe* episode, Stephen Dedalus, who has been knocked down, mutters some fragments of Yeats's 'Who Goes with Fergus?', originally a song from *The Countess Cathleen*.

[2] Carnac, a village in Brittany, famous for its megalithic monuments.

[3] He refers to Renan's *Souvenirs d'enfance et de jeunesse*.

[4] See p. 16, n. 4.   [5] A play by Yeats (1904).

write out the rambling thoughts—and of a person lying awake in bed, too—until he fell asleep. This in my diary, under the date of Monday, the 18th July 1904, I still have.[1] You chucked it aside with a contemptuous phrase: 'the youthful Maupassant'. At that time you were writing, to my entire satisfaction, about 'the faith that in the Middle Ages sent the spires singing up to Heaven'. You were wrong. No writer so artificial as Maupassant suggested it to me. It was the description of the death of a Russian lieutenant in Tolstoy's story 'Sebastopol' that gave me the idea. I have forgotten the lieutenant's name[2] because I have not seen the book since then. You need not grudge me these small claims. After all, the hint, to which I myself attached no importance at the time, is nothing. The work is all.

You see I write rarely but with a vengeance. Remember me to Nora, Lucia, and Georgie.   STANNIE

To SYLVIA BEACH   MS. Buffalo

17 August 1924   *Hotel de France et Chateaubriand,*
                                         Grand Café Continental, Saint Malo

Dear Miss Beach: Here are two enclosures. The card may be answered by a copy of press notices and a prospectus. As for the draft from New York (for which I already signed a receipt) I know nothing of it. I gave your address. We leave here tomorrow morning for Quimper, Hotel de l'Epée. I should be glad if you could send me 1000 francs there as I shall arrive there with only a few hundred. If the New York draft arrives could you forge my name payable to yourself and remit me the rest? Or if not send it to me and I will return it. Am I right in thinking that I am now 2000 francs in your debt? From Quimper I shall write to London for more money, I have £200 there loose in cash, luckily, as I shall need it to continue our journey. I expect to be able to return to Paris at the end of next week but only for a week as I have to go to London.

Up to today Camille Jullian's book[3] has not come. I sent you two loads of books last night. Did you receive the *Irish Times*? What is wrong about *Commerce*? Has that dog,[4] who is so fond of raw posteriors,

---

[1] See *The Dublin Diary of Stanislaus Joyce*, ed. George Harris Healey (London and Ithaca, New York, 1962), pp. 108–110.

[2] Praskukhin.

[3] Camille Jullian, *De la Gaule à la France, Nos origines historiques* (Paris, 1922).

[4] At a luncheon celebrating the founding of *Commerce* and the publication in the first issue of selections from *Ulysses* translated by Morel and Larbaud, Joyce had hardly sat down when the Princess di Bassiano's dog entered and put his big paws on Joyce's shoulders. The princess, when she understood that her guest had an inordinate fear of

eaten the first batch? *Limbes*[1] is a good word but the French equivalent is not *ventre* but *entrailles*—at least that is what the priest here said while reciting a *Hail Mary* before a shrine in the Assumption procession.[2]

I suppose you have Mr Murry's new book,[3] reviewed in *Criterion*? It seems to be a parody of the interior monologue of *Ulysses*. Is it good? The extract I read is rather feeble I think

My brother from Trieste will shortly be coming to Paris. He writes that the interior monologue was used by Tolstoy in *Sebastopol*, by one of the characters in that story, a soldier. I have no doubt it was. And also by holy Job when seated on the acropolis of Israel.

Did I tell you that in giving his award at Dublin Sir John Lavery[4] passed over the portrait of my father[5] (second prize) and gave the first prize to a painting by Mr Keating. The press says the award was 'keenly criticised'

I should like to have that book of Jullian's as soon as possible. With kindest regards and thanks   sincerely yours   JAMES JOYCE

To HARRIET SHAW WEAVER   MS. British Museum

7 October 1924   Victoria Palace Hotel, 6 rue Blaise Desgoffe, Paris

Dear Miss Weaver: We returned here a couple of days ago. Another mountain came to Muhammad—my brother from Dublin[6] whom I had not seen for twelve years. He went away last night. Strange to say like Shaun[7] his work is postal night duty. I had an interesting conversation with Mr Morel[8] in Carnac and Vannes. I suppose you received *Commerce*. I arrived here to find a first class battle in progress between one of the editors Mr Fargue and princess Somebody[9] on the one hand

dogs, removed it. She said it was harmless, although she allowed that once it had chased a plumber out the window. 'I had to buy the man a new pair of trousers,' she laughed. Sylvia Beach, who recounts this incident in *Shakespeare and Company*, p. 143, says that Joyce shuddered and whispered to her, 'She's going to have to do the same thing for me.'
    [1] 'Limbo.'
    [2] *Le fruit de vos entrailles est béni.*
    [3] J. Middleton Murry, *The Voyage* (London, 1924). It was reviewed by 'F.M.' in the *Criterion* II (April 1924) 483–86.
    [4] The *Irish Times* of 5 August 1924 reported that Seán Keating's 'Homage to Hugh Lane' had received the Tailteann Gold Trophy, the judge being Sir John Lavery (1856–1941), the Irish artist.
    [5] By Patrick Tuohy.   [6] Charles Joyce, then living in London.
    [7] In *Finnegans Wake*.
    [8] Auguste Morel, French poet and translator. He afterwards undertook to translate the whole of *Ulysses*, a task in which he was aided by Stuart Gilbert and supervised by Valery Larbaud and Joyce himself.
    [9] Marguerite Caetani, Princess di Bassiano.

and Miss Beach and Miss Monnier on the other. Thank goodness I am
out of it. Mr Larbaud is here but I have not seen him yet. I know his
first words will be: have you something to read to me? No. O!

My sister-in-law is a devotee of S. Patrick and keeps his statue on her
mantelpiece. She gave me a pocket breast-plate in the new Irish colours
with part of his famous prayer on it cut in the form of a shield.[1] At the
top is a cross and at the end are the words: all rights reserved. This
must be the first case of copyright in the history of humanity.

I hope that in a day or two I shall have fixed up something about a
flat so that we can leave for London. During these last two days the
sight of my eye has been wretched. I see less than before. It is very
irritating. I cannot understand why part of this deposit cannot be
removed when they can remove everything else in the eye. I shall try to
see the doctor tomorrow or Tuesday.

The fourth edition of *Ulysses* is sold out. The fifth will appear at the
end of the month.[2] With kindest regards sincerely yours

                                                                JAMES JOYCE

To MRS WILLIAM MURRAY (Telegram)   MS. National Library

1 November 1924   *Paris*

Deeply grieved to hear of your illness but we all hope you will come
through it safely all our wishes for speedy recovery[3] and my kindest
remembrances   JIM

To VALERY LARBAUD   MS. Bib. Municipale, Vichy

4 November 1924   *8 Avenue Charles Floquet, Paris VII*

Dear Larbaud: Are you going out yet? If so, and if Mrs Nebbia is with
you can you both dine with us on Saturday next at 8 p.m. here? We hope
so. Don't make a mistake about the number. It is the same street but
number *eight* and we are on the fifth floor left. There is a lift. Will you
let me know in any case. Sincerely yours   JAMES JOYCE

From VALERY LARBAUD   MS. British Museum

6 November 1924   *71 rue du Cardinal Lemoine, Vᵉ*

Dear Joyce, Many thanks for your kind letter. I am much better, and
we accept with great pleasure your invitation for Saturday night at

[1] *Finnegans Wake*, pp. 231, 486.
[2] According to Slocum and Cahoon, the fifth printing of *Ulysses* was dated September
1924.
[3] Mrs Murray did not in fact recover.

8 o'c. I hope I shall have the great treat of hearing some new chapters of your book.

An embarrassing question arises from the fact that I am no longer on speaking terms with Miss Beach (a complicated *imbroglio* of frustrated interests): What about Morel's translation? And the part I was to play in that affair?[1] But we shall discuss that question and reach a conclusion.

Maria sends her regards to you and Mrs Joyce. Yours faithfully

V. LARBAUD

To VALERY LARBAUD (Postcard)   MS. Bib. Municipale, Vichy

9 November 1924   *8 Avenue Charles Floquet, Paris VII*

Dear Larbaud: I sent a card to Morel. Will you please let me see the reply you are printing in the N. R. F.[2] as soon as possible. I forgot to say last night that the Deutsche Verlag (Stuttgart) wants to do a translation of *Ulysses* under direction of Curtius.[3]

I hope Mrs Nebbia and yourself found a car easily.   J.J.

To HARRIET SHAW WEAVER   MS. British Museum

9 November 1924   *8 Avenue Charles Floquet, Paris VII*

Dear Miss Weaver: It was very good of you to send all those notices in the midst of your rush. How politely Brother Jonathan tries to place the blame for his blunder on your shoulders and what a nice sweet neat amiable little letter Mr Bennett sent. I wish the novel had been published without these critical remarks on its jacket.[4] The other cuttings are of a piece.

I am sorry Mr Lewis was in a bad mood. Did you mention the portrait to him? I wonder why Mr Eliot had to fly over here to see what Shaun

[1] The question of ultimate authority in making the French translation of *Ulysses* became increasingly complicated. Morel did the initial labour and Larbaud reviewed it, during the early stages. Then Stuart Gilbert was brought in. By what Joyce called the Trianons treaty (an understanding arrived at in the Paris restaurant, Les Trianons, in 1928), Larbaud was designated final arbiter.

[2] Valery Larbaud, 'A Propos de James Joyce et de "Ulysses": Réponse à M. Ernest Boyd,' *Nouvelle Revue Française*, XII.136 (1 January 1925) 5–17. In *Ireland's Literary Renaissance* Ernest Boyd attacked Larbaud's statement, in his lecture on Joyce of 7 December 1921, that with *Ulysses* 'Ireland makes a sensational re-entry into European literature'. Boyd asserted that Larbaud knew nothing of Irish literature and disregarded Joyce's relationship to his nation's culture. Larbaud in his reply, which Joyce urged him to make, protested that he was being quoted out of context.

[3] Ernst Robert Curtius (1886–1956), eminent German critic and scholar. He wrote frequently on Joyce, his principal work being *James Joyce und sein Ulysses* (Zurich, 1929). In his *Französischer Geist im neuen Europa* (Berlin and Leipzig, 1925), p. 216, he writes of Joyce's influence on Larbaud.

[4] Miss Weaver arranged with Jonathan Cape that he should take over the copyrights of Joyce's books and republish them. When the new edition of *A Portrait of the Artist* appeared, the jacket included an encomium from Arnold Bennett. Bennett wrote in

calls the proprietoress.[1] Mr Larbaud tells me he is invited to a dinner there for that occasion consisting of steak and a pound and a half of bacon with some chops followed by beefsteak with a splendid onion and fried bacon and grilled steak.[2]

I enclose a letter which explains everything. As I expected the temperature is on the rise. I am now deep in the confidence of both camps. Larbaud has now definitely broken with Fargue who is closely connected with Ippolita (M—d—e la Pr—nc—ss d— B—st—n—.[3] I give her this name because that is the name of a lady who throws somebody or herself under an Italian goods train[4] set in motion by signor Gabriel of the Annunciation[5] who is sentimentally championed by Larbaud who has been denounced by Miss Monnier who is helped by Miss Beach. Larbaud has been warned not to walk, run or creep through the rue de l'Odéon. Ippolita told several people that A.M. was a bookseller and A.M. told me about Ippolita and several people and V.L. told me about A.M. and Fargue and Ippolita and then we had some steak followed by fried bacon with rashers and two pounds of Ippolita which was quite tender after the goods engine followed by a splendid muddle.

My wife went to see Dr Borsch. The result: tomorrow he is not free, Tuesday is a holiday. I shall see him on Wednesday. He says he will have to make a larger operation—similar to that in Zurich—that I am highly nervous and in consequence of repeated attacks there is a great deal of secretion. He said I will get back my sight! It is very weak today so I shall not write much more.

I think that at last I have solved one—the first—of the problems presented by my book. In other words one of the partitions between two of the tunneling parties seems to have given way.

I shall be glad to have *Penguin Island*.[6]

With many thanks and kindest regards sincerely yours

                                                    JAMES JOYCE

great irritation to the *Times Literary Supplement* to say that the quotation was from his review of *Ulysses*, and that he did not admire *A Portrait of the Artist* at all.

[1] Princess di Bassiano was financing Eliot's review, the *Criterion. Finnegans Wake*, p. 406.

[2] Compare Shaun's 'stockpot dinner of a half a pound of round steak very rare' and an avalanche of other dainties in *Finnegans Wake*, p. 406.

[3] Princess di Bassiano.

[4] Probably the works of Joyce are meant by this metaphor of Italian goods, though he may also be glancing at Schmitz's.

[5] Gabriele D'Annunzio, here as elsewhere acknowledged by Joyce as a formative influence.

[6] Joyce had asked Miss Weaver to procure a copy of Anatole France's *Penguin Island* (1908) for him. She informed him on 7 November 1924 that she was reading it herself before sending it on.

To Valery Larbaud   MS. Bib. Municipale, Vichy

20 November 1924   *8 Avenue Charles Floquet, Paris VII*

Dear Larbaud: Thanks for the typescript. It almost finishes the question but there are just two points I would like to discuss. Can Mrs Nebbia and yourself come here and have tea on Friday 29 at 4.30. We could discuss it then. Morel has done, it seems, 100 pages of *Ulysse*. I shall look up this matter of the German rights before you come. I am not free till the 28 as on the 27 I have to read part of the *Sirens* for a gramophone record.[1]

There is bad news too. I have cataract. The doctor did not tell me till a few days ago. I am to be operated on the 31.[2] *Et j'en ai marre!*[3]

Kind regards from us to Mrs Nebbia and yourself Sincerely yours

James Joyce

To Ettore Schmitz and Family (Postcard)   MS. Fonda Savio

22 December 1924   *8 Avenue Charles Floquet, Paris VII*

Buon Natale ed ogni bene auguro a Lei ed a tutta la famiglia dal quartetto triestino[4]   James Joyce[5]

To Harriet Shaw Weaver   MS. British Museum

23 December 1924   *8 Avenue Charles Floquet, Paris VII*

Dear Miss Weaver: I have leave to read a little but not to write. This is not to tell you a long tale about my eyes but to wish you a happy Christmas. I send you a little book. I hoped it would be *Gens de Dublin* but it is not out yet.

In a few words. The cataract was removed—difficult in an eye which has withstood attacks for eighteen years. I saw splendid sights for a minute or so. Dr Borsch says the sight cannot come back quickly but it will come. 'The readiness is all.'[6] There is to be an electric cure when the broken window of my soul can stand more shocks. He is positive as to the result.

[1] Sylvia Beach had arranged that Joyce make a gramophone recording of the speech of John F. Taylor, which is quoted in the *Aeolus* episode of *Ulysses*, pp. 179–81 (141–43). It did not turn out well and only a few copies were made. Rhein-Verlag has recently (1961) issued this recording under the title, *James Joyce Spricht*.

[2] Actually, 29 November (Joyce's sixth eye operation, for removal of cataract).

[3] 'And I'm fed up!'   [4] An allusion to a well-known Triestine chamber music ensemble.

[5] (Translation)

'Merry Christmas and every good wish to you and all the family from the Triestine quartet.   James Joyce'

[6] *Hamlet* V. ii, 234.

I am still bandaged up—had prolonged cinema nights[1] and am *extrêmement fatigué*.

When I am better and can see, yes, I should like to go to the south for a little.

I will send you all the news in my next letter.

Many good wishes from all here. I hope you will enjoy your Christmas in the country and send you my kindest regards. Sincerely yours

JAMES JOYCE

To HARRIET SHAW WEAVER   MS. British Museum

30 December 1924   *8 Avenue Charles Floquet, Paris VII*

Dear Miss Weaver: I hope this reaches you in time to wish you a happy New Year. We got over Christmas well enough in spite of my occluded eye. Since Saturday there is (I am almost afraid to say it) a small, but definite return of some kind of vision in my eye. Dr Borsch says it has been a great battle but apparently he thinks it is over. I can make out objects dimly even without a lens. Of course I must have one to replace that extracted and another to correct my sight. Well, I hope.

There is some mixed news. The princess sent me a cheque [for] 825 francs when I was in the clinique for the piece in *Commerce*. I endorsed it to Mr Morel who wants it. There was a meeting of editors. V.L. offered his hand to L.P.F. In presence of all John Henry[2] Fargue turned his back and walked away over the asphodel fields. The princess wept on L.P.F.'s new overcoat who then wrote to V.L. three times, *comme ça*: Odysseus, you have treated me badly. V.L. replied: My dear Achilles etc etc. So now they meet.

The *Anglo-American* review seems important. There is a strong attack on me in *Les Marges* but temperate towards me personally. A book of parodies from Dublin of AE, WBY etc even inserts a note before the parody of me, apologising for 'this poor attempt' etc.

I am sorry to see that Mr William Archer is dead. He was very kind to me at one time. I am afraid he forgot it and me.[3]

I suppose you are having the usual deluge. The weather is against me.

For some reason or other I am dreadfully tired. Fatigue, fatigue, fatigue. I suppose it will pass soon. Perhaps it is *Ulysses* or 2 years and 8 months of eye worry or four operations so soon after one another or

---

[1] Joyce wrote Miss Weaver on 27 June 1924 (*Letters*, ed. Gilbert, p. 216) that 'whenever I am obliged to lie with my eyes closed I see a cinematograph going on and on and it brings back to my memory things I had almost forgotten'.

[2] Really Léon-Paul.

[3] Joyce's efforts to interest Archer in his books had proved unavailing.

600 drops of iodine and as many more of scopolamine in about a month.

I hope the new year brings us all health and a glimpse of the sun.

With kindest regards and renewed good wishes from myself and all this household sincerely yours   JAMES JOYCE

To LILY BOLLACH   MS. Stanford

18 January 1925   [*Paris*]

Dear Miss Bollach: I intended to have written to you before now but to my surprise on my return to Paris I had to undergo another operation on 29 November, this time for cataract! If you are not too busy I should be much obliged if you could type some more of my incomprehensible MS. If convenient to you we can meet at the corner of Avenue Gabriel tomorrow (Monday) at 6.30 or so. If not will you please leave word for me what hour and place will suit you. With kind regards Sincerely yours
JAMES JOYCE

To VALERY LARBAUD   MS. Bib. Municipale, Vichy

2 February 1925   *8 Avenue Charles Floquet, Paris VII*

Dear Larbaud: I enclose typescript which you may like to see. When you have read it I would be glad to have it back and hear what you think of it.

I was to have gone to the clinic today. It seems I have to undergo some kind of a supplementary operation still (big or small, I don't know).[1] Is it not a frightful bore?

I hope you are well. If all goes well I hope Mrs Nebbia and yourself will come to dinner here soon before they throw us out next month— but you not like [sic] a meal presided over by a cyclops?

Thanks for the N.R.F.[2] It removes all the breadcrumbs very neatly, I think. Sincerely yours   JAMES JOYCE

To HARRIET SHAW WEAVER (Dictated)[3]   MS. British Museum

23 February 1925   *Clinique des yeux, 39 rue du Cherche Midi*

Cher Mademoiselle Weaver je me trouve ici depuis 8 jours le trouble dans mon œuil persiste mais l'on m'assure que ce n'est pas l'Iris et quil n'y aura pas de consequence je n'en sais rien la douleur est parfois

---

[1] Joyce's seventh eye operation was postponed by Dr Borsch because of conjunctivitis and then episcleritis in the good (right) eye. These were serious enough to put Joyce in the eye clinic from about 15–25 February 1925.

[2] See p. 115, n. 8.   [3] Raymond's spelling and punctuation have been preserved.

intolerable et principalement Vendredi la nuit. Le docteur m'a assurer maintenant que le crise est passée. je lespère bien.

On a donne la 1ᵉʳ de ma piece a New-York jai recu un télegrame d'un ami qui me disait quel a ete bien acceuillie je conte que se sera un succès destame. Il fait un temps atrosse ce qui retarde baucoup ma guerison. J'ai toujours le cinéma pour m'amuser il ne sesse jamais.

Je vous dicts ma lettre par Raymond le fils de mon infirmiere il a dix ans il est bien gentil de mecrire cette lettre je lui donnerait un petit cadeau quand il la portera a la poste. Bien Cordialement a vous

JAMES JOYCE[1]

To HARRIET SHAW WEAVER   MS. British Museum
(Dictated to Lucia Joyce)

26 February 1925   *8 av. Charles Floquet, VIIᵉ*

Dear Miss Weaver I came back here yesterday fairly well to have a rest before the operation and to try to revise the piece for Mr Eliot.[2] The operation was to be Monday but a violent rainstorm came on during the night which has set me back a little and this morning they think it must be put off for a couple of days. With this attack in the good eye I am practically helpless but I managed to do some revision even in the dark as I want to send off the piece before I go back.

The conjunctivitis turned into what is called episcleritis. This, Dr Borsch says, can be terribly painful but unlike iritis is not dangerous in itself and leaves no traces. I was sent to the clinic. Six leaches were applied but nevertheless the pain especially during the nights was bad. On Friday night I really thought I was as near unreason as my worst critics think me but they gave me some morphine which gave me relief.

[1] (Translation)
   'Dear Miss Weaver: I have been here for eight days. The pain in my eye persists but I am told that it is not the iris and that there will be no bad effects. I don't know about that. The pain has been sometimes unbearable, especially Friday night. The doctor assures me the crisis is over. I certainly hope so.
   The première of my play has been presented in New York. I had a cable from a friend who said that it was well received. I suppose it will be a *succès d'estime.* The weather is atrocious and is slowing my recovery. I have always the cinema for amusement; it never stops.
   I am dictating this letter to Raymond, my nurse's son. He is ten. He is very nice to write this letter for me. I will give him a little present after he posts it. Cordially yours
                                                                James Joyce'
[2] The fifth chapter of *Finnegans Wake* (pp. 104–25) was published in an early form by T. S. Eliot under the title, 'Fragment of an Unpublished Work,' in *Criterion* III.12 (July 1925) 498–510.

This crisis is now past but I wish the whole thing was over. I don't think *Exiles* was a great success.[1] There is neither a motor car nor a telephone in it. I will try to send you the MS[2] by Mr McAlmon if I see him. I should be glad to hear Mr Muir's article[3] read to me before I send off the piece which is an indirect reply to criticisms.

I will end this now as my eye is a little troublesome. I shall see Dr Borsch tonight and hope fervently I will soon have definite good news to send. With kindest regards sincerely yours   JAMES JOYCE

To HARRIET SHAW WEAVER   MS. British Museum
(Written with black pencil in large letters)

7 March 1925   [*Paris*]

Dear Miss Weaver This is the most I can do so please forgive the style of paper and pen. My lease of this flat[4] was up on the 15 instant but as there seemed no prospect of getting away I asked to have it renewed for two months. An X ray examination is to be made first to see whether any of the old abscesses have reformed[5] and if so it is to be removed before the other operation (capsulotomy) is done. He[6] is positive that I will have good sight. I cannot see a word of print yet. It is very boring. Mr Eliot wrote to say that April no[7] had gone to press. Mr Auguste Morel helps me and with him, some red ink and a magnifying glass I shall have the piece ready before the tooth and eye act starts.

I enclose programme of *Exiles* and a few notices. Mr Boyd has a reply to Mr Larbaud in the N.R.F.[8] Miss Beach would like to have the programme afterwards. The weather keeps bad here, it is against me. The only touch of the south is a young cat, biscuit-coloured, I have from Marseille. He is deeply bored by the Paris murk but eats a lot of bread and butter and the *Daily Mail*. Not knowing what to do I make *vocalizzi* at the piano and octogenarian's exercises with an elastic stretcher I found in my son's room.

---

[1] See p. 100, n. 1.

[2] See next page, n. 2.

[3] Edwin Muir, 'James Joyce: The Meaning of *Ulysses*,' *Calendar of Modern Letters* (London) I.5 (July 1925) 347–55.

[4] At 8 Avenue Charles Floquet.

[5] The X-ray indicated that there was an imbedded fragment of tooth.

[6] Dr Louis Borsch.

[7] Of the *Criterion*.

[8] Ernest Boyd, 'A Propos de James Joyce et de "Ulysses", Réponse à l'article de M. Valery Larbaud,' *Nouvelle Revue Française* XXIV.13 (March 1925) 309–13.

I wanted to send you a new book[1] by Mr Pound, a large paper edition of the kind you do not like much but will wait till I can write better.

I wish I could do more but it is useless to think until these new troubles are over, but I will send you the Criterion piece (new version) as soon as I can.

I hope the snow and gales do not roam around you as they do through the Eiffel tower here. With kindest regards sincerely yours

JAMES JOYCE

To ERNEST WALSH (Dictated letter)   TS. Yale

13 March 1925   *8 Avenue Charles Floquet, Paris, France*

Dear Mr Walsh, I am glad to hear that you are now in better health and hope the climate down there will do you good. Evidently you did not get a letter which my daughter, Lucia, sent you while I was in hospital to the Grand Hotel, Bayonne. In that letter she explained to you that I was in the hospital and that I could not publish anything in any review until a piece which I am sending to the Criterion, London, had first appeared, as I had promised Mr T. S. Eliot to give him the preference. When it appears (July next) I shall send you something[2] and if you wish you may use my name as that of a future contributor.

I am enclosing a typescript which a friend of mine[3] sent to me in the hope that you may like it or at least get into communication with him. He was at one time art critic for the New York Herald here and he delivered a series of lectures in Dublin on modern French painters and also a lecture on Ulysses at Oxford. He is an Irishman and I think he may be of some use to you. I am answering the other part of your letter on a separate sheet as you may wish to print it.

Many thanks for the kind expression contained in your letter. Please give our regards to Miss Moorhead and accept the same for yourself. Sincerely yours   JAMES JOYCE

P. S. Unfortunately I have to return to the clinic in a week in order to undergo another but less serious operation, after which I hope I shall be able to work with more ease. At present I am unable to read or write.

---

[1] *A Draft of XVI. Cantos of Ezra Pound* (Paris, January 1925). This expensive edition of 180 copies was published by the Three Mountains Press.

[2] Joyce eventually contributed the Shem section (*Finnegans Wake*, pp. 169–95) to *This Quarter*, I.2 (Autumn–Winter 1925–26) 108–23.

[3] Arthur Power.

To Ernest Walsh[1]

13 March 1925   *8 Avenue Charles Floquet, Paris, France*

Dear Mr. Walsh: I am glad to hear that the first number of your review[2] will shortly appear. It was a very good thought of yours dedicating this number to Mr. Ezra Pound and I am very happy indeed that you allow me to add my acknowledgement of thanks to him to the others you are publishing. I owe a great deal to his friendly help, encouragement and generous interest in everything that I have written, as you know there are many others who are under a similar debt of gratitude to him. He helped me in every possible way in the face of very great difficulties for seven years before I met him, and since then he has always been ready to give me advice and appreciation which I esteem very highly as coming from a mind of such brilliance and discernment.

I hope that your review, setting out under so good a name will have the success which it deserves Sincerely yours,   James Joyce

To Harriet Shaw Weaver   MS. British Museum
(Dictated to Lucia Joyce)

25 March 1925   *8 Av. Charles Floquet (7e)*

Dear Miss Weaver Thanks for remembering me and in connection with St Patrick. I was able just to finish the revision of the piece for Mr Eliot but fear it would have to be copied out again as I doubt whether any typist would make it out. There was little or no improvement in the sight of the right eye until the last few days when fresh trouble broke out in it and the dental operation fixed for yesterday had to be put off again. The X-ray photograph showed what is called a sequester and this has to be removed but I do not know when nor does anybody else.

I have now been put on a starvation diet by way of adding to my present pleasures. The weather here renders my cure almost impossible once an attack has set in. I am also advised to walk eight or ten kilometers a day. If I can do this with one eye sightless and the other inflamed in today's thick damp fog through the traffic of Paris on an unfed stomach I shall apply for the legion of honor. I should like to hear Vico[3] read to

[1] This typewritten letter was reproduced photographically in *This Quarter* (Paris) I.1 (Spring 1925) 219.

[2] Ernest Walsh lived to edit only two issues of *This Quarter*. The third (Spring 1927), edited by Ethel Moorhead after his death, retracted the dedication of the first issue to Pound, and contained an attack instead by the new editor.

[3] Giambattista Vico (1668–1744), Neapolitan philosopher and historian. His book, *La Scienza nuova* (1744), offered a cyclical theory of history and a new conception of the

me again in the hope that some day I may be able to write again. I put
an advertisement in the Mail for a reader but got not even one reply
though I have often seen advertisements from Italians in it. I sent the
disc[1] to London by Mr McAlmon. If you have a gramophone you ought
to get some discs of John MacCormack. I have some which are very
good. I suppose you will soon be back in London.

Give my best greetings to Miss Marsden. With kindest regards
sincerely yours   LUCIA JOYCE, JAMES JOYCE

To LILY BOLLACH   MS. Texas
(Written with black pencil in large letters)

1 April 1925   *[Paris]*

Dear Miss Bollach Will you please excuse my silence and impoliteness.
I have been very ill three times, with my eyes. Have still to undergo
another operation. I want to give you some MS next week if I am better
but I am not well enough yet—the MS I told you of.

I enclose 100 frs as part of my debt with very many apologies. Please
let me know if you are still free for next week, I hope.

Please write with a heavy black pencil. I cannot distinguish one word
of print or pen but can pencil with a magnifying glass

Apologising for this dreadful letter Sincerely yours   JAMES JOYCE

To ROBERT MCALMON   MS. Pearson

8 April 1925   *8 Avenue Charles Floquet, Paris*

Dear McAlmon May I ask you to buy and send me by a trusty messenger
these 2 discs and also to order for me the 2 pieces of music. They are for
Giorgio. I add the name of publisher. This is my best writing—already a
progress. One operation today at 5.30 and the last (I hope) on Tuesday
next. Enclosed is 150 francs. I would like to have these as soon as you
can. Perhaps you could 'phone the people if place out of your way.

What about the proofs[2] and my silly idea ?[3]

relationship between history and imagination. Joyce read it in Trieste and used it cen-
trally in *Finnegans Wake.*

[1] Of his reading from *Ulysses.* See p. 111, n. 1.

[2] See next page, n. 4.

[3] In a letter of 4 April 1925 to McAlmon (*Letters*, ed. Gilbert, p. 226), Joyce wrote, 'A
rather silly idea came to me about your book which I send on for what it is worth. Is
there to be any preface or introduction? It seems to me there is a certain resemblance
between the group of writers who collected around Pound, I mean W.L. [Wyndham
Lewis], T.S.E. [Eliot], H.D. [Hilda Doolittle] etc., and the writers of the Yellow Book
Row of half a century ago who collected around Arthur Symons; if he is still writing do
you think it will be amusing to have a few pages of preface by him?'

Best Easter greetings from us all. Sincerely yours and with thanks

JAMES JOYCE

Gustav Holst
  'At the Boar's Head' (Opera in 1 act: just published piano and voice score)

Liza Lehmann
  'In a Persian Garden (Verses of Omar Khayam voice and piano)

Frederick Delius
  The Mass of Life (*price only*)

from Walsh, Homes & Co
    148 Charing + Rd.

To HARRIET SHAW WEAVER   MS. British Museum
(Written with black pencil in large letters)

11 April 1925   [*Paris*]

Dear Miss Weaver: These lines to wish you a happy Easter. The dentist's operation is over—so let us say no more about it. Dr Borsch's operation was fixed for Tuesday. Now it seems he is going away for some days but it is not sure. I shall know at 3.30. In any case I hope he will do it by Thursday.[1]

The piece for the *Criterion*[2] nearly drove me crazy. It came back from the typist (to whom I was too blind to explain its labyrinths) in a dreadful muddle. Yesterday with 3 magnifying glasses and the help of my son we chopped it up and today Mr Morel will come and sew it up on his sewing machine. I want to send it off before I go into the clinic. I shall send you a copy, I hope, by Monday. If impatience is a sign of imminent health I am very sound. With kindest regards sincerely yours

JAMES JOYCE

To ROBERT McALMON   MS. Pearson

[*?25 April 1925*][3]   [*Paris*]

Dear McAlmon Please give me a day or so more to check that proof?[4] The dreadful weather these last days made my eyes impossible. Sincerely yours   JAMES JOYCE

---

[1] Joyce's seventh operation, a capsulotomy, was performed by Dr Louis Borsch about 15 April 1925. It was to remove the front wall of the left eye's capsule and lens. The capsule is the posterior sheath of the eyeball.

[2] See p. 114, n. 2.

[3] The date is probably the same as Joyce's letter to Harriet Shaw Weaver (*Letters*, ed. Gilbert, p. 227), where he says, 'I have some proofs to correct for Mr McAlmon. . . .'

[4] 'From Work in Progress,' *Contact Collection of Contemporary Writers* (Paris, 1925), pp. 133–36. Afterwards *Finnegans Wake*, pp. 30–34.

To HARRIET SHAW WEAVER   MS. British Museum
(In rather large handwriting)

1 May 1925   [*Paris*]

Dear Miss Weaver: I am glad to hear you are coming over but as I dream all day of the Euston Escorial[1] and the heavenly landscape of smoky engines I cannot understand anybody coming here.

I am no worse, possibly a little better but it is almost impossible for me to recover in this climate. The odds are too heavy and yet I am reluctant to go away an 'unfinished job'. I can write this and even see a few of the letters! It is the first of December today (winter time) and the light is dazzling.

Have you time to ask these people (Vocalion) to send me the records marked. I want the *Martha* one for Mr Morel,[2] the bass for my son and the English tenor one for myself. The day is awfully long and boring and all I can do is to listen to a few records and scribble an odd note. My reason for troubling you is that shops here ask a month or two to import new discs yet a London shop sent me a disc lately (the de Reszke[3] quartet in an English fourpart song—cf. Mr Earwicker's speech p.1. 'our fourposter singing Etc'[4]—which gave my ear and brain great pleasure) in three days!

I 'wrasted the page redhanded'[5] from the Sunday Times but I hope you will be able to join the fragments.

You will find a good article on me in the new London review *The Calendar* for April.[6] I 'rush for the post'[7] and end this abruptly as I see I have quoted myself several times. I hope you are feeling well after your stay in the country. With kindest regards sincerely yours

                                             JAMES JOYCE

P.S. It is better to have the discs sent through Miss Beach. She manages the customs better than I could.   J.J.

---

[1] A mocking reference to the Euston Hotel (near Euston Station), where Joyce usually stayed when he went to London.

[2] Presumably to help Morel with the translation of the *Sirens* episode, where Friedrich von Flotow's opera, *Martha* (1847), is prominent.

[3] Jean de Reszke (1850–1925), Polish-born tenor. John Stanislaus Joyce had been complimented on occasion as having a voice like Jean de Reszke's.

[4] *Finnegans Wake*, p. 533, in the section called *Haveth Childers Everywhere*.

[5] '... wrasted redhandedly. . . .' *Finnegans Wake*, p. 122.

[6] Bertram Higgins, 'The Natural Pander: Leopold Bloom and Others,' *Calendar of Modern Letters*, I.2 (April 1925) 139–46.

[7] *Finnegans Wake*, p. 430.

To Valery Larbaud   MS. Bib. Municipale, Vichy

[?1 June 1925][1]   *2 Square Robiac (192 rue de Grenelle)*[2]

Dear Larbaud: Arthur Symons would like to meet you. Can you put off your journey for a day and dine with us on Monday? I hope so. If you can please call at the Hotel Castile, 37 rue de Cambon at 8 on Monday. Au revoir cordialment votre   James Joyce

To Léon-Paul Fargue   MS. S. Illinois (Feinberg)

13 June 1925   [*2 Square Robiac, 192 rue de Grenelle, Paris VII*]

Cher Fargue: Nous voilà finalement installés ici. Voulez-vous me faire savoir avec un mot ou bien téléphoner (Ségur: 95.20) quand nous pourrons visiter votre fabrique[3] pour choisir les coupes—préférablement après mardi? Merci d'avance   Cordialement votre

James Joyce[4]

To Harriet Shaw Weaver   MS. British Museum

8 July 1925   *2 Square Robiac, 192 rue de Grenelle, Paris VII*

Dear Miss Weaver: I could not write till now (not even now) as I have been getting into ever deeper Liffey water. I want to leave the piece with Miss Beach for the September *Calendar.*[5] I have taken immense pains with these three pieces, I hope they justify it. The richer they are the less hard will be the other parts of the book if . . . and when . . .[6] I have still several days more to work on Anna Livia and then I need to go away for a rest. . . .[7]

I saw Dr Borsch. He is surprised I cannot see better, is positive I will see. I asked if another operation might be necessary. He said: I think not.

The article by Mr Muir[8] is not a reprint.

---

[1] The year 1925 is written on the letter in another hand, probably Larbaud's. See p. 118, n. 3. This letter was probably written before Larbaud left (early in June?) for his summer holidays.

[2] Joyce had taken a flat at this address in March and moved into it at the end of May.

[3] Fargue had inherited a glass factory established by his father.

[4] (Translation)

'Dear Fargue: Here we are moved in at last. Would you let me know by note or else telephone (Ségur 95.20) when we can visit your factory to choose the cups—preferably after Tuesday? Thank you in advance. Cordially yours   James Joyce'

[5] Joyce had agreed to let the *Calendar of Modern Letters* (London), a review founded in March 1925, publish *Anna Livia Plurabelle*. But the English printers boggled at it, and Joyce withdrew it in September. He then arranged to publish it in the *Navire d'argent* (Paris) I.5 (October 1925) 59–74.

[6] Joyce's ellipses.   [7] Omission by Miss Weaver   [8] See p. 115.

I walk an hour in the morning and the same in the evening with determination. I wish I had finished this piece and was sitting in a railway carriage. I hope you are having a pleasant stay up there. . . .

Do you want me to send on the typescript. I should prefer not for a reason which I shall explain later. With kindest regards sincerely yours

JAMES JOYCE

To HARRIET SHAW WEAVER   MS. British Museum

21 July 1925   *2 Square Robiac, 192 rue de Grenelle, VIIe*

Dear Miss Weaver: The *Criterion* is out. The piece for *This Quarter* has now gone to press and I have sent off the piece for the *Calendar*. We are leaving for Fécamp (Normandy) address: Hôtel des Bains. I saw Dr Borsch. I have to undergo another operation when I come back in September. He says it is boring but the only course and in the end I will see, he says.

I am going to ask the seabreezes at the coast what they think about it all. With kindest regards sincerely yours   JAMES JOYCE

To RICHARD WALLACE (Postcard)   MS. Wallace

Postmarked 27 July 1925   [*Fécamp*]

Dear Wallace: Auguste Morel is making a copy of that plan of *Ulysses* for you and I gave him your address. I hope you enjoyed your trip. We are leaving soon for Rouen. Weather bad but not as bad as in Paris J.J.

To SYLVIA BEACH   MS. Buffalo

[*31 July*] *1925 S. Ignaceous'* [*sic*] *Day   Grand Hotel de la Poste, Rouen*

Dear Miss Beach: I hope you will have a pleasant time. Here it rains and rains! The Anna Livia sign is a simple equilateral triangle or delta Δ. Before you go can you make the few more changes enclosed and also order that interesting book. Will you leave Δ with Miss Moschos in case I think of anything else? I hope you won't have storms. What a summer! I sent the photo to L. M.[1] Did you send Criterion[2] to Pound and Larbaud? I think I promised it but 2 Square Robiac drove a lot out of my head. Also has V. L. *Contact* selection.[3] I have a rather large change

[1] Unidentified.
[2] See p. 114, n. 2.
[3] Joyce apparently wished to know if Sylvia Beach had sent Valery Larbaud a proof of the fragment from *Finnegans Wake* (pp. 30–34), which was to be included in McAlmon's *Contact Collection of Contemporary Writers*.

to make on the fourth last page of ⌐[1] so I hope Walsh sends me the proof quickly as I want to banish the whole Earwicker family from my mind.

I am sorry to give you trouble again at the last moment but it is a disturbed time.

Give my best wishes also to Miss Monnier for a pleasant holiday With kindest regards sincerely yours   JAMES JOYCE

Δ

p 13 l 5	before Lily	insert Snakeshead	
"	" Laura	" Fountainoy	
"	after Lappin	" and Flora Ferns and Fauna Fox-Goodman[2]	
p 7 l 19	cancel God insert Goggle		
p 8 ls 1, 2	cancel Go easy and insert Lisp it slaney and crisp it[3]		
p 4 l 3	cancel rhyme! insert cushingloo!		
p 3 l 11	cancel God insert Chalk[4]		
p 8 l 20	cancel Spit on the iron insert Spitz on the iern[5]		
p 10 l 16	cancel what insert more		
	" and " but[6]		
p 1a l 4	" Paleillyou! insert Pwllhyllyou![7]		
p 4 l 21	cancel God insert Close[8]		
p 5 l 2	" So " Shoal[9]		
p 7 l 8	" run " aston[10]		

Queer Fish
by
L. Boulenger
(Partridge 3ˢ/6ᵈ)[11]

To HERBERT GORMAN   MS. S. Illinois (Croessmann)

31 July 1925   *Grand Hotel de la Poste, Rouen*

Dear Mr Gorman: Your letter has just reached me. Will you please telegraph or write to me immediately on your arrival as I want to go to the south of France, Bordeaux, as soon as possible. I intended to go on

---

[1] Joyce's symbol for the *Shem* chapter (*Finnegans Wake*, pp. 169–95).
[2] *Finnegans Wake*, p. 212.   [3] *Ibid.*, p. 206.   [4] *Ibid.*, p. 200.   [5] *Ibid.*, p. 207.
[6] *Ibid.*, p. 208. The 'But' was subsequently dropped.
[7] Not in the book.   [8] *Ibid.*, p. 201.   [9] *Ibid.*, p. 202.   [10] *Ibid.*, p. 205.
[11] Joyce's description of above corrections.

Tuesday next as the weather here is very bad and I need a rest between one operation and [another] operation. I am here with my family.

I hope you will forgive me for not having written to you before. I shall explain to you the reason when I have the pleasure of meeting you. Allow me in the meantime to express my very grateful thanks.[1] Sincerely yours   JAMES JOYCE

To W. S. KENNEDY, Chairman,   MS. Texas
Incorporated Stage Society, London

8 August 1925   *Grand Hotel de la Poste, Rouen*

Dear Sir: I am much honoured by the proposal of your committee to produce my play *Exiles* during the next season of your society and willingly give you my permission. Particulars of the performances in Munich and in New York will be sent you in a week or so by my French publisher. The play, as far as I know, has never been given in Dublin Sincerely yours   JAMES JOYCE

Address: 12, rue de l'Odéon, Paris VI

To ERNEST WALSH   MS. Yale

10 August 1925   *Grand Hotel du Raisin de Bourgogne, Niort*

Dear Mr Walsh: The enclosed will explain my telegram. Many thanks for your kind reply and message. My sight is worse and I have to go to Paris at the end of September to undergo another (the 7th) operation on my eyes. I want to correct the proofs of these two pieces while I can as after the operation I shall not be able to do anything for a long while, I suppose. The editor of *The Calendar* wishes to publish his piece on 1 October. Can you let me have a proof of your piece early in September and fix the date of appearance of your review before the 1 October? In that case he will set his piece now and I can check both and be finished with them as I should like to have a few weeks of rest before I reenter the clinic. We are leaving for Arcachon. My address had better remain: 12 rue de l'Odéon, Paris.

I hope your own health keeps good. Please accept for Miss Moorhead and yourself our kind wishes sincerely yours   JAMES JOYCE

To HERBERT GORMAN (Telegram)   TS. S. Illinois (Croessmann)
13 August 1925   *Arcachon*
Staying here please telegraph or write your plans   JAMES JOYCE
                                              Hotel Regina Palace

---

[1] For Gorman's book, *James Joyce: His First Forty Years.*

To ERNEST WALSH   MS. Yale

15 August 1925   *Regina Palace Hotel et d'Angleterre, Arcachon*

Dear Mr Walsh: You have not replied to my letter from Niort so I am
sending this express. The piece for the October *Calendar* will be
announced in the September *Calendar* and appear on 1 October with a
footnote (v. *The Criterion* (July), *This Quarter* (September)). My sight
is getting worse, I think, so I shall be very glad if you will have the piece
set at once and sent to me. I will correct it and the other piece at the
same time. I must have a few weeks complete rest before I return to
Paris for the operation. I can write but cannot see well what I write or
read. Will you please telegraph me the word 'arranged' if you can do
this? It does not matter if your review is delayed a few days after 30
September so long as it is dated September and referred to as above.

Please do not send your cheque to me here but make it payable to
Myrsine Moschos and send it to 12, rue de l'Odéon as Miss Beach is on
leave till 20 inst. I have told Miss Moschos about it. Send the proofs,
please, registered to Miss Beach at the same address.

Many thanks for your kind message. I am glad you found the piece
suitable.

I regret having to trouble you but hope you will understand my case
Sincerely yours   JAMES JOYCE

To SYLVIA BEACH   MS. Buffalo

[*?22 August 1925*][1]   *Regina Palace Hotel et d'Angleterre, Arcachon*

Dear Miss Beach: I hope you are back safe in Paris and enjoyed your
holiday. I had to rob 3000 francs from you but I wrote to Walsh to send
my cheque in name of Miss Moschos and to Eliot to send the other
payable to you. Between these delays and no proofs and the unexpected
long journey down here with four breaks I feel more fatigued than when
I left Paris. I hope they send you those cheques to cover my advance.
I draw 11.000 francs in ten days but do not know how to arrange till
then. My sight is getting so bad in the good eye even that I am beginning
to think I have an incipient cataract in it too. I want to correct both
proofs as soon as possible. Hold Δ till my next letter arrives—probably
Saturday morning—with last corrections and then send it off registered
please. You will see by Walsh's letter that *This Quarter* may not appear
for months yet and I cannot hold up the *Calendar* indefinitely. Walsh's
review *may* come out on time. In any case please suggest that the

[1] The postmark indicates the date was the 22nd, and Joyce was at Arcachon in August 1925.

Editor of *Calendar* add a footnote at the beginning of the piece to the effect (v. *The Criterion*, (July 1925), *This Quarter*, September, 1925) That is all I can do. What do you think of Gorman's letter[?]

As you see, *Exiles* is to be given by the Stage Society.[1] I said you would supply particulars of the performances. You know the story

New York: ? ?!
Paris: ? ? ? ? ? ? ?
Italy: translated by Carlo Linati ? ? ?
Germany: given at Schauspielhaus Munich. Producer: Elizabeth Koerner. Complete fiasco. Row in theatre. Play withdrawn. Author invited but not present. German Foreign Office did not allow his entrance. Thank God.

Arcachon is a very nice place. It is near Dax. I ought to go there and get into the *fontaine chaude* and stay in it and never trouble everybody no more.

It is a pity Darantière is so slow about U. *VI*,[2] isn't it With kindest regards sincerely yours   JAMES JOYCE

To VALERY LARBAUD (Postcard)   MS. Bib. Municipale, Vichy

23 August 1925   *Regina Palace Hotel, Arcachon*

Dear Larbaud: Thanks for your card. Am here looking for sunlight which is shy of us. Will go to Dax after for a week or so before returning to Paris to fight my seventh operation. Good wishes from us all to Mrs Nebbia and yourself   JAMES JOYCE

The Stage Society (London) gives Exiles in January or February.

To HERBERT GORMAN   MS. S. Illinois (Croessmann)

[About 4 September 1925]   *2 Square Robiac, 192 rue de Grenelle,*
                                                        Paris VII
                                          Telephone: Ségur 95:20

Dear Mr Gorman: I hope you received the photograph I sent you. As regards the 'broadsheets' you mention I cannot reply until I see the exact text or a reproduction of it with details of type etc.[3] I never give

---

[1] On 14 and 15 February 1926, with W. G. Fay directing.

[2] The sixth printing of *Ulysses* took place in August 1925, probably at the end of the month.

[3] Probably 'The Holy Office' or 'Gas from a Burner'. Gorman wished permission to reprint one or the other in an enlarged edition of his book.

interviews and therefore your proposal in that direction leads me to suggest that it would be well if we could meet on other terms before you go back. I shall be very happy to give you any information I can on matters of fact or to let you see any documents or criticisms etc. We shall be in Paris on Sunday or Monday. I understand you should sail on the following Saturday. From where? If it is from a French port perhaps something could be arranged. Your letters are in my trunk on the way to Paris. Sincerely yours   JAMES JOYCE

To HARRIET SHAW WEAVER (Postcard)   MS. British Museum

Postmark 6 September 1925   *[Paris]*

Dear Miss Weaver: Just a line to say we got back last night to this semi-arctic clime. On arriving I find that the *Calendar* printers flatly refuse to compose Madame Anna Livia. Miss Beach thinks I ought to see Mr Gorman before he returns to U.S.A. so I am proposing to meet him halfway at Boulogne—where the Patricks come from. A Milan publisher wants to present *U.* to the Italian public and three Greeks called on Miss Beach with a mysterious book for me which they are sending. With kindest regards sincerely yours   JAMES JOYCE

To HERBERT GORMAN (Telegram)   TS. S. Illinois (Croessmann)

8 September 1925   *Paris*

Boulogne risky can you arrive here Wednesday my guest leave Thursday morning wiring fare   JOYCE

To STANISLAUS JOYCE   MS. Cornell

28 September 1925   *2 Square Robiac, 192 rue de Grenelle, VIIᵉ*

Dear Stannie: I was very glad to hear the good news of your engagement for we have had only bad news lately, Aunt Josephine's death, Nora's uncle's (Tom) and her sister (Annie). When are you to be married? At least I have a house now and it ought to be easier for you to pay us a visit. Can you come this autumn, for example? I will send you the fare and you could pass a pleasant time here. I have to undergo another eye operation this month, but I will time it according to your answer. Let me have a line by return, if you can.

Tuohy's portrait of Pappie is touring U.S.A. I asked him to try to do a sketch of mother from photographs. He managed to get two faded ones. Has Eileen any? If so it would be advisable to send copies of any or all at once to him (Prof. P. J. Tuohy, Metropolitan School of Art, Kildare Street, Dublin), as he is thinking of going to Spain.

Thanks for Linati's article. I never hear from him but a Milanese firm wrote asking for Italian rights of *Ulysses*. I never give them till *A Portrait* is first translated. The Spanish and German translations of it appear in November. The English printer of *The Calendar* refuses to set up a piece of my new book. It comes out therefore complete (the piece) on Wednesday in a Paris review.[1]

Do you intend to settle down in Trieste? And are you going to take an empty flat? This above costs me 20,000 francs a year empty with *charges* up to 25,000. I spent about 120,000 francs on it up to now so may the devil beautify it.

The day after I got back here from Arcachon I got a slight attack in my eyes which are still dimmed with scopolamine so I cannot write very much yet. But I am writing so that you could make plans before the Berlitz-Biarritz season begins. Surely to God it is not necessary for you to give barking lessons to fioi-de-cani[2] from dawn till gutterdammerung! I saw Schmitz once or twice here and introduced him to a lot of people. Did George Antheil call on you? He has set *Cyclops* episode.

Give my regards to anyone who cares for them and first drop me a line in reply. Give our greetings also to our future sister-in-law and aunt[3] (respectively) who is younger than her nephew.   Jim

To Dámaso Alonso[4]   TS. Alonso

31 October 1925   *2 Square Robiac, Paris, France*

Dear Mr Alonso: Many thanks for your kind letter. As regards the Spanish title of my novel, from what you say it seems better to use the word Adolescente.[5] As you say the Spanish Joven is impossible. Nevertheless, I believe that the classical meaning of adolescence is a person between the ages of seventeen and thirty-one and this would cover only

---

[1] See p. 121, n. 5.

[2] 'Sons of dogs,' a Triestine epithet more affectionate than vituperative.

[3] Stanislaus was engaged to Nelly Lichtensteiger. The marriage took place on 13 August 1928.

[4] Dámaso Alonso (b. 1898), the eminent Spanish writer of both poetry and criticism. He was lecturing on Spanish language and literature at Cambridge in 1924 and 1925, and on his return to Spain in the latter year wrote to Joyce asking for interpretations of certain passages. Joyce's reply is taken from a photostat kindly supplied by Alan Cohn, who has also furnished the information in the notes.

[5] The translation, signed by Dámaso Alonso with the pseudonym Alfonso Donado, was published in Madrid in 1926 under the title, *El Artista adolescente (retrato)*. In a letter to Alan Cohn the translator wrote: 'You will see we had a sort of discussion about the Spanish title of the book. The one I chose never satisfied me. I must say I never could find anything better.'

the fifth chapter of the book and represents about one fifth of the entire period of adolescence, whereas in English at least, while the word adolescent is quite inapplicable to the person represented in chapters 1, 2 and even 3, the term young man can be applied even to the infant on page one, of course in joke. What is the usual description of self-portraits made in youth used in the catalogue of your Spanish picture galleries? The word autoritrato seems to me an insufficient description of a picture. The title of the French translation which I sent you, in order that you may consult it on doubtful points is taken from the catalogue of the Louvre.

As regards your question, please refer in all cases to the French translation.[1] I did not revise it but I helped the translator a good deal.

> Page 31:[2] This is a kind of foot-stool with two ears, stuffed without a wooden frame. The term is childish and popular. Compare the word 'hassock'
>
> Page 92:[3] An abbreviation of the word, made by schoolboys, 'translation'
>
> Page 105:[4] This is a kind of sweet meat made of a soft marshmellow jelly which is coated first with pink sugar and then powdered, so far as I remember with cocoanut chips. It is called 'Slim Jim' because it is sold in strips about a foot or a foot and a half in length and an inch in breadth. It is very elastic and can be eaten by two people at the same time.
>
> Page 119:[5] Schoolboy's abbreviation for problems set by a master to his class on the model of some theorum or problem in whatever book of Euclid's Geometry they are reading.
>
> Page 222:[6] A euphemism used by Cranley [sic] in as much as it begins with the same letter for a product of the body the mono-syllabic term for which in English is sometimes used as an exclamation and sometimes as descriptive of a person whom one does not like. In the French language it is associated with Marshal Cambronne[7] and the French (the females at least) sometimes use a

[1] 'In his letter,' writes Dr Alonso, 'Joyce referred me to the French translation. This I avoided as much as I could. I think my Spanish translation was closer to the original character of the novel than the French one. There is in some respects a likeness between Spanish and Irish people's idiosyncrasy.'
[2] 'Toasted boss.' Joyce is referring to page numbers in the Jonathan Cape edition of *A Portrait of the Artist* (London, 1924).
[3] 'Trans.'   [4] 'Slim jim.'
[5] 'Sums and cuts.'   [6] 'Sugar.'
[7] Pierre Cambronne (1770–1842), a French general at Waterloo who is said to have responded to an English order for surrender, 'Merde!' ('Shit!'). Joyce made a point of almost never using vulgar words in his letters (except to his wife); hence this roundabout explanation.

similar euphemism employing the [word] miel instead of the word used by the military commander.

Page 224:[1] He means nothing except that he affects to consider the name of the Middlesex philosopher as the name of a race horse.

Page 232:[2] Cranly misuses words. Thus he says 'let us eke go' when he means to say 'let us e'en go' that is 'let us even go'. Eke meaning also and having no sense in the phrase, whereas even or e'en is a slight adverbial embellishment. By quoting Cranly's misquotation Lynch gives the first proof of his culture. The word yellow (the second word) is his personal substitution for the more sanguine hued adjective, bloody.

Page 242:[3] A reference to Plato's theory of ideas, or more strictly speaking to Neo-Platonism, two philosophical tendencies with which the speaker at that moment is not in sympathy.

Unnumbered Page:[4] Translate this word for word. It means and is intended to mean, nothing.

Page 285:[5] An allusion to the New Testament phrase 'The light under a bushel'.

Page 285:[6] In rowing. Compare Rower's heart. The phrase of course suggests at once a disappointment in love, but men use it without explanation somewhat coquettishly, I think.

Page 232:[7] A form of procope for 'Damn your soul'.

I hope you will let me have a copy of this Spanish version when it comes out. If you send me your copy of the English when you have finished with it I shall be very happy to sign it for you, if you would like to do so. Sincerely yours,   James Joyce

P.S. Will you please address your reply to me here in Paris and not in Arcachon.   J.J.

[1] '—We'll have five bob each way on John Anthony Collins.' Collins (1676–1729) was an English deist.

[2] '—Let us eke go, as Cranly has it . . . Damn your yellow insolence.'

[3] In explaining *claritas* to Lynch, Stephen says that the connotation is rather vague. 'Aquinas uses a term which seems to be inexact. It baffled me for a long time. It would lead you to believe that he had in mind symbolism or idealism, the supreme quality of beauty being a light from some other world, the idea of which the matter was but the shadow, the reality of which it was but the symbol.'

[4] Probably, as Alan Cohn suggests, a reference to p. 277, where the squat student asks Cranly, 'Do you intend that now, . . . as *ipso facto* or, let us say, as so to speak?' Alonso had presumably not given the page of this quotation.

[5] 'Shining quietly behind a bushel of Wicklow bran.'

[6] 'When we came away father . . . asked me why I did not join a rowing club. I pretended to think it over. Told me then how he broke Pennyfeather's heart.' A rower's heart is said to be enlarged by rowing and so prone to attacks when the exercise is given up.

[7] '—Your soul!'

To Harriet Shaw Weaver[1]   MS. British Museum

5 November 1925   *2 Square Robiac, 192 rue de Grenelle, VII*

Dear Miss Weaver: I have been working very laboriously these last few weeks and have almost made a first draft of ∧d.[2] My cold has gone. Mr Walsh has been moving from Como, via Milan, via Genoa and Rapallo, via Mentone and now Grasse with my proofs and typescript and letters and Miss Beach's following him while he sends explosive letters full of what she calls 'guesswords' etc. Goodness knows what sort of text of mine he will offer to his readers if ever the second number comes out.[3]

Nobody here, not even Mr Ford, can solve the problem of *Two Worlds*.[4] Huge advertisements have appeared in several big American and English reviews, the former costing, I am told, $1000 each! I never wrote a letter or sent any MS to Mr Roth. He wrote (or roth) to me in 1921. I did not answer, I think. He also wrote to me on 25 September asking me to give him something and said he would buy the forests of Hudson Bay for paper etc. I did not answer. And yet number 1 apparently came out on 15 with a piece of mine in it. I have sent two cables to New York but have got no information yet. An American journalist told me that to cover the expense of such 'billing' there ought to be a circulation of hundreds of thousands of copies and the actual number is 450!

I am having queer experiences with editors. New press opinions of ∆[5] are: 'all Greek to us' 'unfortunately I can't read it' 'is it a puzzle?' 'has anybody had the courage to ask J. how many misprints are in it' 'those French printers!' 'how is your eyesight?' 'charming!'—This last from Mrs Nutting, who, however, heard me read it and indeed suggested my voice should be dished (misprint for 'disced').

Mr Antheil has received a copy of musical supplement to *This Quarter* with some pages of his Cyclops setting.[6] He has not shown it to me as yet. I believe Mr Pound got it published for him.

---

[1] Published in Gilbert, *Letters*, p. 236, but with first paragraph omitted.

[2] The incomplete triangle meant the book of Shaun (the third part of *Finnegans Wake*) while 'd' meant the fourth chapter of that part (pp. 555–90). For a complete list of Joyce's signs, see *Letters*, ed. Gilbert, p. 213.

[3] See p. 116, n. 2.

[4] Samuel Roth began to publish the available fragments of *Finnegans Wake* in *Two Worlds* (New York), a magazine which he edited from September 1925. This periodical concluded after eight issues, the first five of which contained Joyce's work, in September 1926. Meanwhile, in July 1926, Roth started *Two Worlds Monthly*, where more than half of *Ulysses* was serialized before the review ceased publication in October 1927.

[5] *Anna Livia Plurabelle.*

[6] 'Extract: Mr Bloom and the Cyclops,' from an opera based upon the *Cyclops* episode in *Ulysses*, by George Antheil, was published as a 26-page musical supplement to *This*

I shall go to see Dr Borsch (of whom I dreamed last night) tomorrow for the first time since I was ill and ask him to let me finish Ad before the next match. With kindest regards sincerely yours   James Joyce

To Herbert Gorman   TS. S. Illinois (Croessmann)

5 November 1925   *2 Square Robiac, 192 rue de Grenelle*

Dear Mr. Gorman: As we did not meet in Bologne [sic], much to my regret, I am sending you some rectifications for your book about me, which I hope will reach you in time for the English edition. You may incorporate them in the text or in footnotes, or in an appendix, but I should prefer you to do so as though the information, which deals with facts only, had been acquired by you in a personal conversation, and not as contributed by me.

I send you a copy of the Navire d'Argent, which I hope reached you safely and shall forward you in the next week or so, a copy of This Quarter containing another piece. As since the death of Mr. John Quinn, I have no agents in America, I should be very glad if you could give me any information concerning a quarterly review entitled 'Two Worlds' edited by Mr. Samuel Roth.

I look forward to the pleasure of seeing Mrs. Groman [sic] and yourself in Paris at an early date. Sincerely yours,   James Joyce

To Ettore Schmitz (Dictated letter)   MS. Fonda Savio

21 November 1925   *2 Square Robiac, 192 rue de Grenelle. VIIe*
                                                                    Parigi

Caro Schmitz, Scusi se la mia risposta ha tardato ma questi ultimi giorni avevo scopolamine negli occhi e anch'oggi preferisco dettar a Lucia. Essa vi ringrazia molto, tanto Lei che la signora Trevisani[1] ed io pure la ringrazio per il gentilissimo invito ma purtroppo non può accettarlo per il momento ed ecco perchè. Mercoledì o giovedì prossimo entro alla clinica dove devo subire un'operazione, la settima in tre anni (cateratta secondaria) ma conto di esser di ritorno per Natale, poi passate le feste vogliamo andare a Londra per la première ed unica

---

Quarter (Milan) 2 (Autumn–Winter 1925–26). Antheil (1900–1959) never finished the opera. The young and iconoclastic American composer was friendly with Joyce during the nineteen-twenties.

[1] A sister of Signora Schmitz, who had met the Joyce family in Zurich.

della mia commedia. In queste circostanze sarebbe difficile per Lucia di assentarsi. Ci rincrescie perchè sarebbe stato un soggiorno molto piacevole per lei, però l'anno prossimo spera di poter andar a passare qualche tempo a Trieste.

Ho parlato colla direttrice[1] del 'Navire d'argent' la quale m'assicurò che un brano del Suo libro sarà pubblicato nel numero di gennaio e febbraio presentato da Crémieux.[2] Continuo a lavorare malgrado l'ostacolo della vista.

Rassicuri la Sua Signora in quanto riguarda la figura d'Anna Livia.[3] Di lei non tolsi che la capigliatura e quella soltanto a prestito per addobbare il rigagnolino della mia città l'Anna Liffey che sarebbe il piu lungo fiume del mondo se non ci fosse il canal che viene da lontano[4] per sposare il gran divo, Antonio Taumaturgo[5] e poi cambiato parere se ne torna com'è venuto.

Tanti saluti cordialissimi a voi tutti quanti una stretta di mano

JAMES JOYCE[6]

---

[1] Adrienne Monnier. The *Navire d'argent* began publication in 1925.

[2] Benjamin Crémieux (1888–1944), French novelist and critic, was particularly interested in Italian literature.

[3] The reference is to Joyce's letter to Schmitz of 20 February 1924 (*Letters*, ed. Gilbert, p. 212), in which he wrote: 'A propos of names: I have given the name of Signora Schmitz [i.e., Livia] to the protagonist [Anna Livia Plurabelle] of the book I am writing. Ask her, however, not to take up arms, either of steel or fire, since the person involved is the Pyrrha of Ireland (or rather of Dublin) whose hair is the river beside which (her name is Anna Liffey) the seventh city of Christendom springs up....' Signora Schmitz protested this use of her name when she was told that the *Anna Livia Plurabelle* episode was a dialogue of two washerwomen; she probably feared Joyce might portray her as a kind of Molly Bloom.

[4] The Canal Grande in Trieste.

[5] The church of S. Antonio Taumaturgo facing the canal before it was partly filled.

[6] (Translation)

'Dear Schmitz: Forgive me if my answer has been long in coming, but the last few days I have had scopolamine in my eyes and even now I prefer to dictate to Lucia. She sends her hearty thanks to you and Signora Trevisani and I also thank you for your kind invitation, but unfortunately she cannot accept it at the moment and this is why. Next Wednesday and Thursday I shall be at the clinic where I must undergo an operation, the seventh in three years (secondary cataract), but I expect to be out for Christmas: after the holidays we hope to go to London for the "première" and the only performance of my play. Under the circumstances it would be difficult for Lucia to be away. We are very sorry because it would have been a delightful visit for her. Next year, however, she hopes to be able to spend some time in Trieste.

I have spoken with the editor of the *Navire d'argent* who assures me that a selection from your book will be published in the January and February numbers with a presentation by Crémieux. I continue writing in spite of the obstruction in my sight.

Reassure your wife with regard to the character Anna Livia. I have taken only her hair, and that merely as a loan, to adorn the little river of my city, the Anna Liffey, which would be the longest river in the world if it were not for the canal that comes from afar to join the celebrated divo, Anthony the Worker of Miracles, and then, having changed its mind, returns whence it came.

My cordial and best greetings to you all [and] a handshake   James Joyce'

To HARRIET SHAW WEAVER   MS. British Museum

23 November 1925   *2 Square Robiac, 192 rue de Grenelle, VIIe*

Dear Miss Weaver: I am not going into the clinic this morning. For the last week Dr Borsch has been treating the other eye with scopolamine for what he calls a suffusion and he will not operate till both are normal. The 'scopo' obstructs my sight in reading and I cannot finish Λd before Wednesday. I must do this before I go in if I am to have any peace. . . . My wife does not seem to like the idea of this operation but the nurse says that when Dr Borsch has made an operation which he considers final he tells the patient 'La nature fera le reste' and does not encourage the patient to try again. It is a dreadful bore especially now that my slow brain has got to work well after two months' labour. But I will rest for a couple of days and probably jump through hoop no 7 on Friday or Saturday.

Here is a cutting of Mr Mulligan[1] and there is Lalou's article in *Vient de Paraître*[2] and an article about Δ in the New Republic by Edmund Wilson.[3]

You must be having a bad time with all those troubles. I hope they are past and that your health is good.

Your MS[4] this time will be partly written by Lucia (who calls it 'cinese' (Chinese). I mean the penscript not the pencil draft. It will be finished tomorrow surely—of course only as a first draft but I perceive that I have written more of the book than I had thought. I am sending you the papers. Can you return them to Miss Beach for her files? I hope this house is worth all the outlay or even that my writing of late is? With kindest regards sincerely yours   JAMES JOYCE

To LILY BOLLACH   MS. Stanford

5 December 1925   *2 Square Robiac, 192 rue de Grenelle, Paris VII*

Dear Miss Bollach: Many thanks for your letter. I could not reply as my eyes were dilated with scopolamine and at twelve o'clock today I

---

[1] That is, of Oliver St John Gogarty. The clipping probably referred to his pilgrimage to Rome in October 1925 as one of a group headed by President W. T. Cosgrave.

[2] R.L. [René Lalou] (b. 1889), 'Ce qu'on lit. "From *Work in Progress*," ' a review of *Anna Livia Plurabelle* as published in *Navire d'argent*. Lalou's article appeared in *Vient de paraître*, 23 November 1925.

[3] Edmund Wilson, 'James Joyce as a Poet,' *New Republic* 44 (4 November 1925) 279–80. Wilson discusses the poetry in Joyce's prose, mainly in *Ulysses*, and ends with a long quotation from *Anna Livia Plurabelle*.

[4] Joyce determined to give Harriet Weaver the manuscript of *Finnegans Wake* as a partial return for her kindness to him.

enter the clinique for a 7th eye operation! Please excuse me. I have a long piece that I wanted you to be kind enough to type for me but it must wait till I come out when I hope you will not be so overworked. With many thanks Sincerely yours   JAMES JOYCE

From LUCIA JOYCE to   MS. British Museum
HARRIET SHAW WEAVER

17 December 1925   *2 Square Robiac, 192 rue de Grenelle, VIIe*

Dear Miss Weaver, My father has been home since Tuesday but we hardly know what news to send you. He has had no sight in the eye since the operation on account of the blood and he has pain and dizziness.[1] The dreadful weather also makes him very nervous. He is going to see Dr Borsch tonight and hopes he will soon have a better report of himself. He is glad to be at home and we do not know what would have become of him if he had come out of the clinic into a hotel. The doctor says he must have complete rest.

With kindest regards from my mother and myself sincerely yours
                                                        LUCIA JOYCE

To HARRIET SHAW WEAVER   MS. British Museum

31 December 1925   *2 Square Robiac, 192 rue de Grenelle, VIIe*

Dear Miss Weaver I have not leave to write but am sending this to wish you a very happy New Year. I have been having a poor time, more or less constant pain in the wound, allayed by aspirin and pilocarpin (antidote of scopo), no sight whatsoever and 'blues'. Dr Collinson[2] says he has not great hopes of it. Dr Borsch says I ought to see when the blood absorbs. It is doing so at about 1/20 of the normal rate. With kindest regards sincerely yours   JAMES JOYCE

P. S. Did you get H.C.E. ?[3]

[1] Joyce submitted to his ninth and tenth operations on 8 December and 12 December 1925, at the hands of Dr Borsch. He sometimes varied the count.
[2] Dr Arthur William Collinson (b. 1896), at that time assistant to Dr Borsch, now an ophthalmologist in Boston, Massachusetts.
[3] *Haveth Childers Everywhere.*

From ETTORE SCHMITZ[1]

15 February 1926   *London*

Caro Joyce, Scrissi all'indirizzo indicatomi mandando il biglietto. Mi si rispose che avevo dimenticato di rimettere la lettera Sua e mi si invitava di presentarmi al bigoncio con la stessa la sera della rappresentazione. Così feci e tutto finì bene: Ebbi due magnifici posti e, contrariamente agli usi del paese, a 'maca'. Lo debbo a Lei e grazie! Non del tutto a 'maca' perchè mi portarono via la sua lettera.

Tutta la sera fui accompagnato dal delizioso sentimento di assistere allo svolgimento di una Sua opera importante, tanto differente da tutte le altre Sue.[2] Molti anni or sono io lessi Exiles in manoscritto, quella cara calligrafia che tutti ora conoscono, che io amo ma che non so leggere correntemente se non è dedicata a segni italiani. Neppure la rappresentazione mi diede tutta la commedia il cui testo spero di avere questa sera. Specialmente l'ultimo discorso di Rowan che, suppongo, tanto importante per la rivelazione delle molle più misteriose che lo fanno agire, a me e a Livia sfuggì interamente forse anche perchè eravamo un po lontani dalla scena. Di solito a Londra sediamo tanto vicini agli attori che, quando diciamo: 'I beg your pardon', gli attori, se sono buoni, ripetono la frase. Ho fretta di avere il libro perchè giovedì tento di passare gratis al 'Debate on Exiles'[3] e vorrei aver capito l'opera interamente.

La Black Roberts[4] per me fu un'attrice indimenticabile. Non dev'essere mica facile di rappresentare una donna cui non deve mancare certa pratica della vita e farvi risonare l'ingenuità con la chiarezza di un suono di campana e con la misura che l'ingenuità deve serbare per essere sentita autentica. Invece di un applauso le mandai un bacio e, spero, lo avrà sentito almeno come quelli di Robert Hand.

Rupert Harvey[5] mi diede una grande sorpresa. Non so se sia voluto, ma si muove, siede, s'alza e guarda come Lei. Amerei ora di rivederlo in altra parte per intendere meglio questa. È certo un attore valoroso. Mi parve come un uomo che amerebbe di agire senza dover dar conto delle proprie azioni. Non c'è esitazione in lui, ma la spiegazione che concede è fatta sempre con voce moderatissima quasi desiderasse che qualche sua

[1] The text of this letter is taken from 'Carteggio ... Svevo–Joyce', ed. Harry Levin, *Inventario* II.1 (Spring 1949) 126–28.

[2] Schmitz attended *Exiles* at Joyce's request. The play was given by the Stage Society on 14 and 15 February 1926.

[3] Because of adverse comments, a public debate on the play was held by the Stage Society on 17 February.

[4] Gwaldys Black-Roberts is meant. She played the role of Bertha.

[5] Rupert Harvey (1887–1954), a prominent English actor, producer, and director.

parola non fosse intesa dai suoi interlocutori. Spesso ciò gli riuscì con me visto che parlò sempre in inglese.

Bene William Sta[c]k che all'ultimo momento assume la parte di Robert Hand. Però la sua parte è la più facile[1] delle tre.

Pubblico magnifico, ma qualche bestione doveva esserci. Accanto a me un signore disse: They want to force on us Italian ways. Degl'Italiani si sa, anzi, che sono gelosi anche quando non amano.

Molti applausi. Più fragorosi dopo il primo e secondo atto.[2]

Spero di vederla a Parigi, per qualche momento almeno, il 25 corrente. Suo affezionatissimo,   Ettore Schmitz

Ha visto l'articolo del 'Corriere della Sera' di G. Caprin dell'undici corrente?[3] Guai se continua così. Meno il furto mi rimprovera tutti gli altri delitti. Dio sa quello che penseranno Crémieux e Larbaud. E anche Lei vi figura, con rispetto, ma vi figura, povero Joyce![4]

[1] The text in *Inventario* reads 'difficile', but the translation there is 'easiest', and probably 'difficile' is an error in transcription.

[2] The review in the *Times* (London) on 16 February 1926 (p. 12, col. 3) concludes, after a mocking summary of the plot, that the characters are inhuman and fail to stir the audience's sympathy.

[3] G. Caprin, 'Una Proposta di celebrità,' *Corriere della Sera* (Milan), 11 February 1926.

[4] (Translation)

'Dear Joyce, I wrote to the indicated address and sent the card. I received an answer saying that I had forgotten to send your letter and was asked to present myself with it at the box office on the night of the performance. I did this and all ended well: I had two fine seats and, contrary to the custom of the country, "free of charge". I owe this to you. Many thanks! Not entirely "free of charge" however, since they took your letter away from me.

During the whole evening I had the delightful feeling of being present at the unfolding of one of your important works, so different from all your others. Many years ago I read *Exiles* in manuscript, in that beloved handwriting which everyone knows today, which I cherish, but which I cannot read fluently unless it is consecrated in Italian words. Not even the performance gave me all of the play, the text of which I hope to have this evening. Especially the last speech of Rowan which is, I suppose, very important for an understanding of the inner springs of his character and actions, eluded Livia and me entirely, perhaps because we were a little far from the stage. In London we usually sit so close to the stage that when we say "I beg your pardon", the actors, if they are good, repeat the words. I am anxious to have the book because on Thursday I shall try to get in gratis to the "Debate on Exiles" and I should like to have understood the work completely.

Black Roberts was for me an unforgettable actress. It must not be very easy to portray a woman who is not lacking in a certain experience of life and to depict at the same time her naiveté with the clarity of a bell and with that restraint which naiveté must possess in order to be felt as authentic. Instead of applauding I blew her a kiss and I hope she took as much notice of it as she did of those of Robert Hand.

Rupert Harvey greatly surprised me. I don't know whether it is intentional or not, but he moves, sits down, gets up and looks like you. I should now like to see him under other circumstances so as to be able to understand this better. He is certainly an able actor. He struck me as a man who wants to behave in such a way as not to be obliged to account for his actions. There is no hesitation in him but such explanation as he grants is made in a very low voice, as if he wished that some of his words would not be understood by his interlocutors. In my case he often succeeded, since he always spoke in English.

To HARRIET SHAW WEAVER   MS. British Museum

5 March 1926   *2 Square Robiac, 192 rue de Grenelle, VIIe*

Dear Miss Weaver . . . since you ask me I think there is a very very slight improvement of vision. He[1] is now using some kind of a new chemical stimulant (not chemical but acting by purely physical means, recently discovered here, I understand, synthol for massaging the temples and brow).

And as for *Exiles* the enclosed letter from my former partner in the English Players[2] throws a good deal of light on the production, especially the production in the auditorium. I am sorry I did not engage a stenographer to record the debate. . . .

Many thanks for Dowland's songs.[3] They at least are beyond question. I could never sing them but I could listen to them all day. I mean I have the voice but not the style. I hope something I have written may bear comparison with *Come silent night* for instance. I used the rhythm of William Bird's *Woods so Wild*[4] in describing Isolde in the last piece.[5]

A fine job on the part of William Sta[c]k who took over Robert Hand's role at the last moment. His role, however, is the easiest of the three.

The audience was magnificent, but there must have been some louts present. A gentleman next to me said, They want to force on us Italian ways. Italians, of course, are known for being jealous even when they are not in love.

Great applause. Loudest after the first and second acts.

I hope to see you in Paris, at least for a few moments, on the 25th of this month.
Your very devoted   Ettore Schmitz

Have you seen the article by G. Caprin in the *Corriere della Sera* of the 11th inst? It will be just too bad if he goes on in this way. Excepting theft, he reproaches me for all the other crimes. Heaven knows what Crémieux and Larbaud will think about it. And even you are in it, respectfully, but in it just the same, my poor Joyce!'
[1] Dr Louis Borsch.
[2] Claud W. Sykes had sent Joyce a full report on the production of *Exiles*. This is now among the Harriet Shaw Weaver papers in the British Museum.
[3] John Dowland.
[4] William Byrd (1540–1623), English composer. His song, 'Woods So Wild,' is as follows:

> Shall I go walk the woods so wild,
> Wand'ring, wand'ring here and there,
> As I was once full sore beguiled,
> Alas! for love! I die with woe.
> Wand'ring, wand'ring here and there,
> Alas for love—I die—with woe.

[5] In the fourth chapter of the book of Shaun, *Finnegans Wake*, p. 556, Isabel (Isolde) is described: 'night by silentsailing night while infantina Isobel (who will be blushing all day to be, when she growed up one Sunday, Saint Holy and Saint Ivory, when she took the veil, the beautiful presentation nun, so barely twenty, in her pure coif, sister Isobel, and next Sunday, Mistlemas, when she looked a peach, the beautiful Samaritan, still as beautiful and still in her teens, nurse Saintette Isabelle, with stiffstarched cuffs but on Holiday, Christmas, Easter mornings when she wore a wreath, the wonderful widow of eighteen springs, Madame Isa Veuve La Belle, so sad but lucksome in her boyblue's long

This, completed and revised, I read a week ago to a small audience. . . .
It produced stupefaction, I think. That evening I was exhausted to the
point of idiocy and since then, though I wanted to revise Λabc for Mr
Roth,[1] could not do so. Instead I read a few books and plays, the Life of
Sims Reeves,[2] Juno and the Paycock,[3] Figgis's Book on Blake.[4]

Please let me hear from you how your sister progresses. I hope she
will speedily recover and that you yourself will keep in good health.
With kindest regards sincerely yours   JAMES JOYCE

To IVAN OPFFER[5]   MS. Donald Gallup

9 March 1926   *2 Square Robiac, 192 rue de Grenelle VIIe*

Dear Opfer: Can you please ring me up (Ségur 95–20) as I should like
to know whether you are free or would like to do my son soon. He is free
at present as he has suspended his singing lessons owing to false
diagnosis of his voice and so could sit for you when you like.

I hope you have some good news from America Sincerely yours
                                                        JAMES JOYCE

To STANISLAUS JOYCE   MS. Cornell

26 March 1926   *2 Square Robiac, 192 rue de Grenelle, VIIe*

Dear Stannie: We are glad to hear you are coming and will all be very
glad to see you again.[6] On receipt of this will you either wire me or send
a card to say on what of next week you will probably arrive so that I may
make better arrangements than I was able to do in Eileen's case. The

black with orange blossoming weeper's veil) for she was the only girl they loved, as she is
the queenly pearl you prize, because of the way the night that first we met she is bound to
be, methinks, and not in vain, the darling of my heart, sleeping in her april cot, within
her singachamer, with her greengageflavoured candywhistle duetted to the crazyquilt,
Isobel, she is so pretty, truth to tell, wildwood's eyes and primarose hair, quietly, all the
woods so wild, in mauves of moss and daphnedews, how all so still she lay, neath of the
whitethorn, child of tree, like some losthappy leaf, like blowing flower stilled, as fain
would she anon, for soon again 'twill be, win me, woo me, wed me, ah weary me! deeply,
now evencalm lay sleeping.'

[1] A letter from Pound suggests that Joyce had made an arrangement of some sort with
Samuel Roth about the publication of *Work in Progress* (*Finnegans Wake*) in Roth's
Two Worlds (New York). It was Roth's unauthorized serial publication of *Ulysses*
beginning in July 1926, in *Two Worlds Monthly*, that led to legal proceedings.
[2] John Sims Reeves (1818–1900) was the leading English tenor of his time. Joyce read
Charles E. Pearce, *Sims Reeves* (London, 1924).
[3] Sean O'Casey, *Juno and the Paycock* (London, 1924).
[4] Darrell Figgis, *Paintings of William Blake* (New York, 1925).
[5] Ivan Opffer, American artist.
[6] Stanislaus Joyce visited his brother in April 1926.

weather is getting better here and Easter is generally very lively here so I think you will enjoy your stay. It is useless to open up any subject touched on in your letter as you are coming personally. Arrivederci

JIM

To HARRIET SHAW WEAVER   MS. British Museum

17 April 1926   *2 Square Robiac, 192 rue de Grenelle, Paris*

Dear Miss Weaver: . . . I have received a copy of the Spanish translation of A.P.O.T.A.A.A.Y.M.[1] and also of the German version. Would you care to have these, the German at least? Mr Rascher admits to having sold 9 copies of *Verbannte* and wants a million. . . .

I finished the revision of Λabcd yesterday. Today I copied out the sheets of Λa which were unreadable to have them retyped. Tomorrow and Monday I shall do, I hope, the same for Λb. Then Λc will take three or four days. Then the typing of these and the 'man of four watches' is complete. I am not sure for the moment how much I have done. I shall know when I read it. I am to read it Λab, interval, and Λc to a small group, this time including Antheil and a young American Galantière[2] who is preparing a course of lectures on *U.* I think I have done a good deal. My brother says that having done the longest day in literature I am now conjuring up the darkest night. I will send you Λd complete in typescript and the necessary new pages to insert into Λabc. Have you read *Le Culte des Héros*[3] yet? What do you think of it? Every time I read a piece I go round with the hat after begging those present to remember it and help me by finding things for me. They all seem to forget about it as quickly as possible except Miss Beach who knows how to whistle books out of the air.

How long do you stay in London? I hope your sister goes on well. With kindest regards sincerely yours   JAMES JOYCE

To LILY BOLLACH   MS. Stanford

2 May 1926   *2 Square Robiac, 192 rue de Grenelle, Paris*

Dear Miss Bollach: First of all, thanks for your Christmas card. I have undergone two more eye operations—the latter very severe—and could not write. Please excuse me. Can you meet me for a few moments at

[1] *A Portrait of the Artist as a Young Man.*

[2] Lewis Galantière (b. 1895), American writer and playwright, who was with the International Chamber of Commerce in Paris, 1920–27.

[3] S. Czarnowski, *Le Culte des héros et ses conditions sociales: St. Patrick, héro national de l'Irlande* (Paris, 1919).

7 p.m. next Tuesday, at the corner of Avenue Gabriel? I hope so as I have some work which I would ask you to type if you have any free time. I have written it out very clearly and large. I hope you are in good health and not overworked in your new office. With kind regards sincerely yours   JAMES JOYCE

To LILY BOLLACH   MS. S. Illinois (Croessmann)

16 May 1926   *2 Square Robiac, 192 rue de Grenelle*

Dear Miss Bollach: The phrase in my MS reads 'by that noblest of magistrates at his Saxon tannery with motto O'Neill etc'.[1] You are right about 'my face'[2] and 'too' One more change. In the speech that *precedes* the verse (Λc near end)

Day socker from vanfloats etc

for 'Magrath or MacManagh' read 'O'Bejorumsen or Mockmacmahonson'[3] Do you think you could leave part of it say Λab on Monday with your concierge so that I could be revising it in the meantime? You are having a terrible time with my MS, I am afraid. I am sorry to be the guilty cause and hope for your own sake it will soon be over.

Many thanks in any case. A copy of *Ulysses*, 1st edition, ordinary paper autographed was lot 203 at a book auction in the Salle Drouot yesterday. It was sold for 2750 francs. My American price would be higher. I hope you have yours. With kindest regards sincerely yours

JAMES JOYCE

To LILY BOLLACH   MS. Stanford

7 June 1926   *2 Square Robiac, 192 rue de Grenelle VIIᵉ*

Dear Miss Bollach: I have at last revised and sent off Λabcd. The work was excellently done and very promptly. Many thanks. Will you please let me know how many hours of dreadful labour it cost you and excuse please my delay in writing Sincerely yours   JAMES JOYCE

To HARRIET SHAW WEAVER   MS. British Museum

29 August 1926   *Hotel de l'Océan, Digue de Mer, Ostende*

Dear Miss Weaver: These rapid lines are to wish you many happy returns of your birthday. I hope they reach you in time as I have found the post here rather slow—2 days from Paris, a 5 hours run. I am sorry

---

[1] *Finnegans Wake*, p. 495.   [2] *Ibid.*, p. 459.   [3] *Ibid.*, p. 529.

to hear your sister had such a time in the storm[1]—a dreadful experience for an immobilised person! The only good thing is that sometimes a shock like that does good and in any case a visitation of that kind rarely recurs.

I am of a sudden overladen with work. Last week the entire typescript of *Ulysses* in German arrived and on top of it the German translator[2] to revise it with me. We work together all day practically, word for word. They want to bring it out in October!!!

I am sorry to hear of Miss Marsden's trouble and of course do not bother about the disk[3] in such circumstances. All the same I was glad to have your notes on my voice and would like more about my non-rhetorical accents when you feel so inclined.

I hope the German publisher won't rush the translation—and me.

With renewed good wishes and kindest regards sincerely yours

JAMES JOYCE

To HARRIET SHAW WEAVER   MS. British Museum

26 September 1926   *Hotel Astoria & Claridge, Bruxelles*

Dear Miss Weaver: Here is $\Delta 2$ MS and typescript.[4] Please let me know what you think of it, when read? The *Dial* proposed to delete one third of Λabcd![5] Lewis, it seems, has been to Paris and asked for the MS[6] and is coming here as he wants to see me. 'And I have done with you too, Mrs Delta'[7]—for the moment. She will babble anon. With kindest regards sincerely yours   JAMES JOYCE

[1] A chimneystack of her sister's house was struck by lightning.

[2] Georg Goyert (b. 1884) translated *Ulysses* into German. The first edition appeared in October 1927, the second in 1930. The publisher was Rhein-Verlag, then in Basel, later in Zurich.

[3] In a letter of 18 August 1926 (*Letters*, ed. Gilbert, p. 244), Joyce asked Miss Weaver to note the points of the Irish accent in his recording of Taylor's speech in *Ulysses*. He particularly wished her to notice the consonants.

[4] A revision of *Anna Livia Plurabelle*.

[5] Joyce declined and withdrew it.

[6] Wyndham Lewis planned to print some of *Finnegans Wake* in his new review, *The Enemy*, which began publication in January 1927 and ceased in 1929. But he changed his mind.

[7] A reference to a dream Joyce had, which he wrote out for Herbert Gorman: 'I saw Molly Bloom on a hillock under a sky full of moonlit clouds rushing overhead. She had just picked up from the grass a child's black coffin and flung it after the figure of a man passing down a side road by the field she was in. It struck his shoulders, and she said, "I've done with you." The man was Bloom seen from behind. There was a shout of laughter from some American journalists in the road opposite, led by Ezra Pound. I was very indignant and strode up to her and delivered the one speech of my life. It was very long, eloquent and full of passion, explaining all the last episode of *Ulysses* to her. She wore a black opera cloak, or *sortie de bal*, had become slightly grey and looked like *la Duse*. She smiled when I ended on an astronomical climax, and then, bending, picked up a tiny snuffbox, in the form of a little black coffin, and tossed it towards me, saying,

From Ettore Schmitz[1]

30 September 1926   *Trieste*

Caro amico, Le invio la 'Fiera letteraria' del 19 corrente con l'articolo di Montale[2] su Dubliners. Forse Lei non l'ha avuto ancora. Mi pare interessante. Montale non ricevette il ritratto che per lui Le avevo domandato. Deve essere andato smarrito.

Appartiene alla Sua famiglia un J. Joyce che nel 1850 pubblicò a Trieste 'Recollections of the Salz Kammergut, Ischl, Salzburg, Bad Gastein, with a sketch of Trieste?' Il libro fu scovato da mio genero per la sua collezione di storia patria.

Io vidi per un istante Suo fratello al bagno di mare e mi disse che si sposa in ottobre.[3] V'è la speranza di vedervi tutti qui?

Salutandola caramente, Suo devotissimo   Ettore Schmitz[4]

To Harriet Shaw Weaver   MS. British Museum

16 October 1926   *2 Square Robiac, 192 rue de Grenelle*

Dear Miss Weaver: On calling at Miss Beach's the other morning I got your letter of the 9 instant with its bad news. You say you are going to Guildford today so I hope you may receive this on arrival there. I am much distressed to hear of your brother's death in such a way. Surely, though a doctor, he must have neglected or misunderstood his case.[5] It

"And I have done with you too, Mr Joyce." I had a snuffbox like the one she tossed to me when I was at Clongowes Wood College. It was given to me by my godfather, Philip McCann, together with a larger one to fill it from.' Ellmann, *James Joyce*, p. 561.

'Mrs Delta' is Anna Livia Plurabelle, who, besides her fluvial association with deltas, had the Greek letter delta for symbol.

[1] The text of this letter is taken from 'Carteggio . . . Svevo–Joyce', ed. Harry Levin, *Inventario* II.1 (Spring 1949) 129.

[2] Eugenio Montale (b. 1896), the celebrated Italian poet and critic. His article was 'Cronache delle Letterature Straniere: "Dubliners" di James Joyce,' *Fiera Letteraria* II.38 (19 September 1926) 5.

[3] See p. 128, n. 3.

[4] (Translation)

'Dear friend: I send you the "Fiera Letteraria" for the 19th of this month with an article by Montale on *Dubliners*. Perhaps you have not already seen it. It strikes me as interesting. Montale did not receive the picture which I asked you for on his behalf. It must have gone astray.

Does a certain J. Joyce who in 1850 published at Trieste *Recollections of the Salz Kammergut, Ischl, Salzburg, Bad Gastein, with a Sketch of Trieste* belong to your family? The book was discovered by my son-in-law for his collection of history of the fatherland.

I saw your brother for a moment at the bathing beach and he told me that he is to be married in October. Can we hope to see you all here?

With friendly greetings, Your devoted   Ettore Schmitz'

[5] Miss Weaver's brother had died, as Joyce himself was to die, of peritonitis.

seems to me to have been similar to Wallace's whose life, I am sure, was saved by a timely operation last spring. It is very shocking to think of. You do not say whether the niece you speak of is his daughter or not. You will have a very gloomy return to your sister. I hope her case will not be aggravated by the death of her brother and that your family will be spared any of these dreadful troubles for a long time to come.

In these circumstances I shall not weary you with news and articles and gossip. I set to work at once on what you told me[1] and shall go on. I know it is no more than a game but it is a game that I have learned to play in my own way. Children may just as well play as not. The ogre will come in any case.

With my sympathy to you and your family and my kindest regards sincerely yours   James Joyce

To Ezra Pound   MS. Pound

[Early November 1926]   *2 Square Robiac, 192 rue de Grenelle*

Dear Pound: Miss Beach has sent you the typescript I had made for you. As you know the *Dial* accepted it for $650 and then cabled a refusal. It has now been accepted for publication in an annual which a number of American writers bring out in February for $200.[2] It is the whole of part 3 of the book. There are 4 parts, divided each into 4 sections.[3] Some of part 1 appeared in *Contact*, *Criterion*, *This Quarter* and *Le Navire d'Argent* (the end of that part). A piece of part 2 was in the *Transatlantic Review*. None of part 4 has been printed.

Please let me know what you think of it. The sign on the cover means nothing. It is to distinguish it from other similar books. I use the signs

[1] Joyce wrote Miss Weaver on 24 September 1926, from Brussels, 'A rather funny idea struck me that you might "order" a piece and I would do it. The gentlemen of the brush and hammer seem to have worked that way. Dear Sir. I should like to have an oil painting of Mr Tristan carving raw pork for Cornish countrymen or anicebust of Herr Ham contemplating his cold shoulder.' (*Letters*, ed. Gilbert, p. 245). On October 1 she replied: 'You have made a curious request indeed! Here then followeth my "order": To Messrs Jacques le Joyeux, Giacomo Jakob, Skeumas Sheehy and whole Company: Sirs: Kindly supply the undersigned with one full length grave account of his esteemed Highness Rhaggrick O'Hoggnor's Hogg Tomb as per photos enclosed and oblige Yours faithfully   Henriette Véavère'
The photographs were of the giant's grave at St Andrew's, Penrith. She enclosed a pamphlet by the Reverend James Cropper which urged that it was probably not a giant's grave at all. Her letter ended with an expression of some misgivings about *Finnegans Wake*, though this was put with great diffidence.
[2] This publication did not come about.
[3] Joyce modified this plan by treating the first eight chapters as Part I, the next four as Part II, the next four as Part III, and the last chapter as Part IV. See also *Letters*, ed. Gilbert, pp. 241–42, 246.

∧ ⊏ ∆ ⊓[1] etc through my notes instead of letters as they are quicker to make and read as references.

I hope Mrs Pound and yourself are well and that you especially are getting stronger down there Kind regards Sincerely yours

JAMES JOYCE

To STANISLAUS JOYCE   MS. Cornell

5 November 1926   *2 Square Robiac, 192 rue de Grenelle, Paris*

Dear Stannie: I enclose Lire 6000.—in draft on Trieste and Milan. I hope it reaches you in time with our best wishes to Nelly and yourself. Let me know if you get it. I am utterly overworking myself. Roth is pirating *Ulysses* (bowdlerized) in a new monthly magazine[2] of which he sells 50,000 copies a month. I have tried to enjoin the publication but there seems to be no remedy. The Germans, having given me four days at Ostende, to revise the translation with the translator (we did 88 pages) are now rushing the translation into print.[3] It is of course full of the absurdest errors and with large gaps. Such is financial literature. If they do not give me a délai, I shall ask Miss Beach to circularize the German press with a disclaimer.

I hope your arrangements are all made and that your marriage will soon come off and that it will be a very happy one.

Buona fortuna!   JIM

From EZRA POUND[4]   MS. Private

15 November 1926   *Rapallo*

Dear Jim: Ms.[5] arrived this A.M. All I can do is to wish you every possible success.

I will have another go at it, but up to present I make nothing of it whatever. Nothing so far as I make out, nothing short of divine vision or a new cure for the clapp can possibly be worth all the circumambient peripherization.

---

[1] The signs designate Shaun, Shem, Anna Livia Plurabelle, and Humphrey Chimpden Earwicker. See *Letters*, ed. Gilbert, p. 213.

[2] Samuel Roth reprinted 14 episodes of *Ulysses* in *Two Worlds Monthly*, from July 1926 to October 1927. Joyce succeeded in obtaining an injunction—only after the publication of the book had ceased—on 27 December 1928.

[3] See p. 142.

[4] The text of this letter is taken from *Letters of Ezra Pound*, ed. Paige, p. 202.

[5] Of the book of Shaun, *Finnegans Wake*, pp. 403–590.

Doubtless there are patient souls, who will wade through anything for the sake of the possible joke . . . but . . . having no inkling whether the purpose of the author is to amuse or to instruct . . . in somma. . . .

Up to the present I have found diversion in the Tristan and Iseult paragraphs that you read years ago . . . mais apart ça. . . . And in any case I don't see what which has to do with where. . . . Undsoweiter.

[Yrs ever   E P]

To HARRIET SHAW WEAVER   MS. British Museum

24 November 1926   *2 Square Robiac, 192 rue de Grenelle*

Dear Miss Weaver: The phrase about the Waterworld's face is mine own.[1] Please correct 'Sir Tristran, violer d'amores, fr'over the short sea, had passencore rearrived fra North Armorica on the scraggy isthmus of Europe Minor' etc.[2] I sent Λabcd to E.P. at his request and he has written turning it down altogether, can make nothing of it, wading through it for a possible joke etc. I sent you papers about the Roth affair. I have been greatly overworked and overworried these last few weeks and yesterday took to the sofa again. Today I restarted. One great part of every human existence is passed in a state which cannot be rendered sensible by the use of wideawake language, cutanddry grammar and goahead plot. I think you will like the piece better than sample. With kindest regards sincerely yours   JAMES JOYCE

To BERNARD SHAW[3]   British Museum

26 November 1926   *Paris*

Dear Sir: Allow me to offer my felicitations to you on the honour you have received and to express my satisfaction that the award of the Nobel prize for literature has gone once more to a distinguished fellow townsman Sincerely yours   JAMES JOYCE

---

[1] On 15 November 1926 Joyce sent Miss Weaver what became the opening lines of *Finnegans Wake* and explained their meaning in detail. The phrase, 'rory end to the regginbrow was to be seen ringsome on the waterface,' he glossed in part by saying, 'When all vegetation is covered by the flood there are no eyebrows on the face of the Waterworld.' (*Letters*, ed. Gilbert, p. 248.) She asked, in a letter to him written five days later, where this phrase had come from.

[2] In his letter of 15 November Joyce had a slightly different version: 'Sir Tristram, violer d'amores, had passencore rearrived on the scraggy isthmus from North Armorica. . . .'

[3] From a typescript made by Dan H. Laurence. He notes that this is the only congratulatory letter about the Nobel Prize that Shaw appears to have preserved.

To Lily Bollach   MS. Stanford

29 November 1926   *2 Square Robiac, 192 rue de Grenelle*

Dear Miss Bollach: A very tragic event in my family (the Italian branch of it)[1] and the worry and trouble of the piracy and lawsuit (see papers sent herewith) are my excuse for the delay in answering you. I shall be happy if I am able to do anything for your friend and shall bear his case in mind though I don't understand if you mean literary or commercial work. With kind regards sincerely yours   James Joyce

To Harriet Shaw Weaver   MS. British Museum

29 November 1926   *2 Square Robiac, 192 rue de Grenelle*

Madam i ave today finished the draft No 2 in nice MS of peece of prose y[r] rispected O/ to me which i will now give 1 coat of french polish to same which will turn out A 1 as desired

it is a very nice peece and i ope same will be found most sootable to your bespoke in question i am, Madam trly y[r]s   ⊏ (his mark)[2]

From Harriet Shaw Weaver   MS. Private

3 December 1926   *[London]*

To Mr. ⊏ Sir, Pleased to hear job completed barring coat 3 polish. Congratulate you on smartness in execution of order solicited, given and received a bare two months ago, days on sofa not excluded.

Further order: please to insert, incorporate or otherwise include in text of work now in hand or of any work hereafter to be in hand numpa one firstclass beauful phrase anent the face of waterworld[3] which it would be very many pities if same was to succomb or be drownded in note for private consumption on premises only. Yours ffly

REVAEW TEIRRAH

pp H.W.

[1] The sudden death in Trieste of Frantisek Schaurek, Joyce's brother-in-law.
[2] The symbol of Shem, i.e., James.   [3] See p. 146, n. 1.

To HARRIET SHAW WEAVER   MS. Private

5 December 1926   *[Paris]*

To t.r.[1] Mem: 5.12.926: Insertion desired duly made[2]
⌐ joiners hand
checked by   J.J.   overseer

Re ⊓[3] pp v to xxvi

To STANISLAUS JOYCE[4]   TS. S. Illinois (Croessmann)

15 December 1926   *2 Square Robiac, 192 rue de Grenelle*

Dear Stannie, The notary says it is useless to make a sworn statement
before him. I am to make a simple declaration, send it to you, who, as
curator, are to recognise it in a sworn statement as true.[5]

I am busy and worried. American lawyers refused to take up this case
but at last I have got one who says he will try to stop the publisher by
backstairs influence. The American press, to which my publisher cabled
and wrote does not publish cable or letter and continues to print Roth's
full-page advertisements, knowing them to be a swindle. He is pocketing
at least 1,000,000 francs a month.

I am also very hard at work.

Do not tell me for the moment any more details, but propose to me
some temporary plan and say what you suggest I do, say, till March. I
go then to Lugano for a week or so and we could meet. Many happier
returns of the 17th.[6] Regards to Eileen and children.   JIM

To MRS MYRON C. NUTTING   MS. Northwestern

17 December 1926   *2 Square Robiac, 192 rue de Grenelle*

Dear Mrs Nutting: Many thanks for your courteous thought. I
am glad you liked the piece I read.[7] I was not at all well and had a

[1] The last letters of 'Harriet' and 'Weaver'.
[2] '... and there's nare a hairbrow nor an eyebush on this glaubrous phace of Herr-
schuft Whatarwelter....' *Finnegans Wake*, p. 12. The word 'waterworld' appears on
p. 367.
[3] Symbol designating Earwicker and the first chapter of the book.
[4] From a typewritten copy.
[5] James and Stanislaus Joyce were trying to settle Frantisek Schaurek's affairs and to
help their sister Eileen determine her future course.
[6] Stanislaus was forty-two.
[7] About 14 December Joyce invited Eugene Jolas and Mrs Jolas, Elliot Paul, Myron C.
Nutting and his wife, Sylvia Beach, and Adrienne Monnier to hear the opening pages of
Finnegans Wake.

collapse myself after it like the old gentleman in it[1] but am better today.
I thank Nutting and yourself for coming Sincerely yours

JAMES JOYCE

To HARRIET SHAW WEAVER   MS. British Museum

21 December 1926   *2 Square Robiac, 192 rue de Grenelle*

Dear Miss Weaver: I enclose your piece. I read it a few days ago to a
small audience. Though I was partly smothered by a cold and in a state
of exhaustion it seems to have made an impression for the next day also
I received letters and bouquets! I performed a firstclass collapse for a
day and a half which I repeated on Saturday but today am feeling quite
well again.

I hope you will like it. I think it will make a good opening. With
kindest regards sincerely yours   JAMES JOYCE

To STANISLAUS JOYCE[2]   TS. S. Illinois (Croessmannn)

8 January 1927   *192 rue de Grenelle, Paris*

Dear Stannie, Yes, allright. I will arrange for £10 a quarter to be sent
to Eileen in Dublin from the time she arrives. As regards the rest of
6000 lire, you will have to use it, I am afraid. I have no money at present.
In fact, I got a loan off my April cheque to send that. My income is £18
a week, not quite £1000 a year. My books between New York and
London bring me in about £60 extra. *Ulysses* sold well there last five
years, but Roth has killed the sales here, too, and has (or will) pocket
the proceeds of 25 normal editions. Not a single daily or weekly in U.S.
published our cabled denial. I am engaged in a very costly law suit, but
will go on even if I lose it. I have organised an international protest to
make this a test case for the reform of U.S. law.[3] Please ask Benco to
sign enclosed (incomplete) lists and return to 12 rue de l'Odéon as soon
as possible. I wish he could get a few other good signatures: Praga,
Bracco, Panzini.[4] We cannot lose time. If Roth carries this through, the
pirates in America will make it the beginning of even worse.

Will you please send me Lecky[5] and Kettle's[6] two books?
I hope things are better now.   JIM

---

[1] That is, Finnegan.   [2] From a typewritten copy.
[3] For the text of this protest against the piracy of *Ulysses*, see pp. 151–53.
[4] Marco Praga (1862–1929), Milanese dramatist; Robert Bracco (1862–1943), Neapolitan dramatist; Alfredo Panzini (1863–1939), Italian essayist and novelist.
[5] William Edward Hartpole Lecky (1838–1903), the historian, was born near Dublin. The
book by Lecky which Joyce had left in Trieste was probably his *History of Rationalism*
(1865).
[6] Probably *The Day's Burden* (London, 1910) and *Home Rule Finance* (Dublin, 1911).

To HARRIET SHAW WEAVER   MS. British Museum

16 January 1927   *192 rue de Grenelle, Paris*

Dear Miss Weaver: These few lines are to show you how the protest is
going. Shaw, Yeats, Moore, Pound and James Stephens refuse to sign.[1]
Tant pis! It is impossible to get a reply from Lewis (who was so anxious
to have something of mine in his new review) so I have sent the piece to
New York to try to get American copyright. I am plunged again in
work. I want to try to finish Part I before 2 February or very soon after
and, if possible, get away for some weeks. I cannot work at Part 3 in
this way. It is too much. I must take it easier. Nobody else does it or a
tithe of it.

I feel greatly honoured by Einstein's signature, given so quickly and
simply. The lawcase in my name is proceeding in New York.

My eyes are about the same perhaps a wee bit better. Dr Borsch was
made *officier de la légion d'honneur* yesterday. With kindest regards
sincerely yours   JAMES JOYCE

To STANISLAUS JOYCE   MS. Cornell

[Late January 1927]   *[Paris]*

Dear Stannie: The protest will be mailed to the press 1 February. If
you have seen any signature added please wire name   JIM

[1] Yeats, Sturge Moore, and James Stephens signed the protest later. Bernard Shaw
wrote Sylvia Beach on 18 December 1926, in a letter now at Harvard, 'I do not quite
understand the protest you ask me to sign about Ulysses. Is it copyright in the United
States or not? I seem to remember its publication there in The Little Review. This was a
compliance with the printing clauses which ought to have secured copyright.
'It may be, however, that what the protest means is that a pirate publisher has fallen
back on the old law under which the copyright in Byron's Cain was voided: namely, that
there is no copyright in a blasphemous, seditious, or immoral publication. In that case
there is no effective remedy. . . . If, however, the work is in the public domain in America
by simple neglect to secure copyright, I am afraid there is nothing to be done. . . . I am
afraid Mr Joyce can do nothing but suggest to one of the American newspaper syndicates
an article by him on the subject. They could afford to pay him at least 1250 dollars for it.
'The protest is all poppycock: nobody that the pirate cares about will blame him for
taking advantage of the law. But Mr Joyce can point out that the law has produced an
absurd situation. Instead of suppressing the book, which is its object, it is inviting every
bookseller to rush out an edition of it, and thereby increase the author's reputation enor-
mously.'
Ezra Pound wrote to Joyce on 25 December 1926 to explain, 'My only reason for not
signing your protest is that I consider it misdirected. To my mind the fault lies not with
Mr. Roth, who is after all giving his public a number of interesting items that they would
not otherwise get; but with the infamous state of the American law which not only
tolerates robbery but encourages unscrupulous adventurers to rob authors living outside
the American borders, and with the whole American people which sanction the state of
the laws. The minor peccadillo of Mr. Roth is dwarfed by the major infamy of the law.'
(*Letters of Ezra Pound*, ed. Paige, p. 206.)

To VALERY LARBAUD   MS. Bib. Municipale, Vichy

26 January 1927   *2 Square Robiac, 192 rue de Grenelle*

Dear Larbaud: Will Mrs Nebbia and yourself dine with us and a small
party at Langer's, Champs Elysées, at 8 pm on Wednesday 2 February
next? It is my birthday and the anniversary (5th) of publication of
Ulysses and the international protest will be given to the press that day.
Miss Beach, Mlle Monnier, the MacLeishes,[1] Sisley Huddleston and
two Irish friends of mine make the party. Please let me know by return
as I have to reserve a table Kindest regards   JAMES JOYCE

Statement regarding the piracy of *Ulysses*[2]

2 February 1927   *Paris*

It is a matter of common knowledge that the ULYSSES of Mr. James
Joyce is being republished in the United States, in a magazine edited by
Samuel Roth, and that this republication is being made without
authorization by Mr. Joyce; without payment to Mr. Joyce and with
alterations which seriously corrupt the text. This appropriation and
mutilation of Mr. Joyce's property is made under colour of legal
protection in that the ULYSSES which is published in France and
which has been excluded from the mails in the United States is not
protected by copyright in the United States. The question of justifica-
tion of that exclusion is not now in issue; similar decisions have been

---

[1] Archibald MacLeish (b. 1892), the American poet, and his wife, Ada MacLeish, a
concert singer.
[2] The first draft of this statement was made by Ludwig Lewisohn at Joyce's prompting
and is said by Sylvia Beach to have been corrected by Archibald MacLeish. The statement as issued to the press bears some marks of Joyce's style. Lewisohn's draft is now at
Harvard, dated 23 November 1926, and reads as follows:
'The unauthorized serialization of the *Ulysses* of Mr. James Joyce by Mr. Samuel Roth
in his *Two Worlds* magazine is a matter of the gravest import not only to all writers but to
all honest men. A work is produced which has one mark, at least, in common with the
masterpieces of the past: it seems strange, revolutionary and dreadful to the conventional
mind. Hence the law, which expresses the conventional mind, fails for the moment to
protect that work under its aspect of property. The work cannot be printed and protected
in America. And now arises the peculiar situation that a man who appreciates this work
is unscrupulous enough to take advantage of the author's momentary helplessness in
order to rob that author of the legitimate fruit of his labors with the shamelessness of a
highwayman but quite without the highwayman's courage, since the law grants him a
temporary immunity. The issue is both morally and practically important. It involves
the good name of American publishing and of American literature. One's personal attitude toward *Ulysses* does not touch it. The undersigned colleagues and admirers and
friends of Mr. Joyce protest to American publishers and to American readers not pri-
marily in the name of an esoteric masterpiece but in the name of common honor and
honesty and of that security of the works of the intellect and the imagination without
which art cannot live.'

made by government officials with reference to works of art before this. The question in issue is whether the public (including the editors and publishers to whom his advertisements are offered) will encourage Mr Samuel Roth to take advantage of the resultant legal difficulty of the author to deprive him of his property and to mutilate the creation of his art. The undersigned protest against Mr. Roth's conduct in republishing ULYSSES and appeal to the American public in the name of that security of works of the intellect and the imagination without which art cannot live, to oppose to Mr. Roth's enterprise the full power of honorable and fair opinion.

(signed)

Lascelles Abercrombie
Richard Aldington
Sherwood Anderson
René Arcos
M. Arcybacheff
Ebba Atterbom
Azorin, *Président de l'Académie Espagnole*
C. du Baissauray
Léon Bazalgette
Jacinto Benavente
Silvio Benco
Julien Benda
Arnold Bennett
Jacques Benoist-Méchin
Konrad Bercovici
J. D. Beresford
Rudolf Binding
Massimo Bontempelli
Jean de Bosschère
Ivan Bounine, *de l'Académie Russe*
Robert Bridges
Eugène Brieux, *de l'Académie Française*

Bryher
Olaf Bull
Mary Butts
Louis Cazamian
Jacques Chenevière
Abel Chevalley
Maurice Constantin-Wéyer
Albert Crémieux
Benjamin Crémieux
Benedetto Croce
Ernst Robert Curtius
Francis Dickie
H.D.
Norman Douglas
Charles Du Bos
Georges Duhamel
Edouard Dujardin
Luc Durtain
Albert Einstein
T. S. Eliot
Havelock Ellis
Edouard Estaunié, *de l'Académie Française*
Léon-Paul Fargue
E. M. Forster
François Fosca
Gaston Gallimard

Edward Garnett
Giovanni Gentile
André Gide
Bernard Gilbert
Ivan Goll
Ramon Gomez de la Serna
Cora Gordon
Jan Gordon
Georg Goyert
Alice S. Green
Julian Green
Augusta Gregory
Daniel Halévy
Knut Hamsun
Jane Harrison
H. Livingston Hartley
Ernest Hemingway
Yrjo Hirn
Hugo von Hofmannsthal
Sisley Huddleston
Stephen Hudson
George F. Hummel
Bampton Hunt
Bravig Imbs
Holbrook Jackson
Edmond Jaloux
Storm Jameson

Juan Ramon Jimenez
Eugene Jolas
Henry Festing Jones
George Kaiser
Herman Keyserling
Manual Komroff
A. Kouprine
René Lalou
Pierre de Lanux
Valery Larbaud
D. H. Lawrence
Emile Legouis
Wyndham Lewis
Ludwig Lewisohn
Victor Llona
Mina Loy
Archibald MacLeish
Brinsley Macnamara
Maurice Maeterlinck
Thomas Mann
Antonio Marichalar
Maurice Martin du
    Gard
Dora Marsden
John Masefield
W. Somerset
    Maugham
André Maurois
D. Merejkowsky
Régis Michaud
Gabriel Miró
Hope Mirrlees

T. Sturge Moore
Paul Morand
Auguste Morel
Arthur Moss
J. Middleton Murry
Sean O'Casey
Liam O'Flaherty
Jose Ortega y Gasset
Seumas O'Sullivan
Elliot H. Paul
Jean Paulhan
Arthur Pinero
Luigi Pirandello
Jean Prévost, *de*
    l'Académie
    Française
C. F. Ramuz
Alfonso Reyes
Ernest Rhys
Elmer E. Rice
Dorothy Richardson
Jacques Robertfrance
Lennox Robinson
John Rodker
Romain Rolland
Jules Romains
Bertrand Russell
George W. Russell
    'A.E.'
Ludmila Savitsky
Jean Schlumberger
May Sinclair

W. L. Smyser
E. Œ. Somerville
Philippe Soupault
André Spire
Th. Stephanides
James Stephens
André Suarès
Italo Svevo
Frank Swinnerton
Arthur Symons
Marcel Thiébaut
Virgil Thomson
Robert de Traz
R. C. Trevelyan
Miguel de Unamuno
Paul Valéry, *de*
    l'Académie
    Française
Fernand Vandérem
Fritz Vanderpyl
Francis Viélé-Griffin
Hugh Walpole
Jacob Wassermann
H. G. Wells
Rebecca West
Anna Wickham
Thornton Wilder
Robert Wolf
Virginia Woolf
W. B. Yeats

To CLAUD W. SYKES   MS. Yale

10 February 1927   *2 Square Robiac, 192 rue de Grenelle,*
                                                            Paris

Dear Mr Sykes: Do you think you could spare any time to look
through the German proofs (page) of *Ulysses*. I told you about it. The
firm has rather rushed the translation and it would be a pity if it

contained bad errors as the French translation is almost a masterpiece, they say.

I am sending a letter of protest which will interest you

Kind regards to Mrs Sykes and yourself from us both Sincerely yours

JAMES JOYCE

To VALERY LARBAUD   MS. Bib. Municipale, Vichy

10 February 1927   *2 Square Robiac, 192 rue de Grenelle*

Dear Larbaud: Is Mrs Nebbia quite recovered now as my wife would like her to have tea some afternoon, and we ought to dine together one of these nights. By the way, ought not a footnote to appear to *Protée*[1] to say that this title is not in the original text? Sincerely yours

JAMES JOYCE

To HARRIET SHAW WEAVER   MS. British Museum

18 February 1927   *2 Square Robiac, 192 rue de Grenelle*

Dear Miss Marsden:[2] Before I write trying to explain what I am doing and why I want the case of Pound's soundness of judgment at the present

---

[1] The *Proteus* (*Protée*) episode of *Ulysses* appeared in the *Nouvelle Revue Française* XV.179 (1 August 1928) 204–26, in a translation by Auguste Morel and Stuart Gilbert reviewed by Valery Larbaud. Joyce had given names to the episodes in the book originally, but, perhaps because these insisted distractingly on the Homeric parallel, withdrew them before *Ulysses* was published.

[2] A slip for Weaver. It suggests Joyce's agitation of mind over several recent letters of Miss Weaver in which she objected to *Finnegans Wake*. On 29 January 1927 she wrote the protest, 'I wish Mr. Pound had signed it, considering that the book in question is *Ulysses* and not the present one. And perhaps when the present book is finished you will see fit to lend ear to several of your older friends (E.P. to be included in the number): but the time to talk of that matter is not yet.' Joyce replied on 1 February (*Letters*, ed. Gilbert, p. 249), 'Your letter gave me a nice little attack of brainache. I conclude you do not like the piece I did? It is all right, I think—the best I could do. I will gladly do another but it must be for the second part or fourth and not till after the first week in March or so, as the editors of *transition* liked the piece so well that they asked me to follow it up. . . . Do you not like anything I am writing. Either the end of Part I Δ is something or I am an imbecile in my judgment of language. I am rather discouraged about this as in such a vast and difficult enterprise I need encouragement.

'It is possible Pound is right but I cannot go back. I never listened to his objections to *Ulysses* as it was being sent him once I had made up my mind but dodged them as tactfully as I could. . . . He makes brilliant discoveries and howling blunders.'

Miss Weaver was distressed but held her ground. 'It seems to me you are wasting your genius,' she wrote on 4 February. 'But I daresay I am wrong and in any case you will go on with what you are doing, so why thus stupidly say anything to discourage you? I hope I shall not do so again.' He asked her to read some poems by Ralph Cheever Dunning, whom Pound was extravagantly praising, and on 11 February 1927 she agreed that the poems were disappointing.

moment more gone into. I am glad you agree about Dunning.¹ Some
time ago Mrs Symons asked me (from her husband)² if I had not written
any verse since *Chamber Music* and if it would collect. I said it would
make a book half as big but I did not trust my opinion of it as I rarely
thought of verse. There are about fifteen pieces in all, I think, and I
suppose someone someday will collect them. I mentioned this to Pound
and asked could I show him, say, two. I left them at his hotel. A few
days after I met him and he handed me back the envelope but said
nothing. I asked him what he thought of them and he said: They belong
in the bible or the family album with the portraits. I asked: You don't
think they are worth reprinting at any time? He said: No, I don't.
Accordingly I did not write to Mrs Symons. It was only after having
read Mr Dunning's drivel which Pound defends as if it were Verlaine
that I thought the affair over from another angle. They are old things
but are they so bad that *Rococo*³ is better than their poorness? ...
Remember me to Miss Marsden. With kindest regards sincerely yours

JAMES JOYCE

To EZRA POUND   MS. Pound

23 February 1927   *2 Square Robiac, 192 rue de Grenelle, Paris*

Dear Pound: My lawyer here Conner⁴ has had a cable from his partner
in N.Y.⁵ 'Have J. search his records to determine whether he sold
American copyright to Jane Heap as she claims'.⁶ Can you send me a
short typewritten note which I can show my lawyer here as to what I
gave you from Zurich for the review, how much you paid (£50?), etc?⁷
I should like it by return. Roth now offers me $1000 if I will sign a
statement to the effect that he offered me that sum before the publication. I do not intend to reply to him. Sincerely yours   JAMES JOYCE

¹ Ralph Cheever Dunning, English poet, had published *Hyllus, A Drama* (London,
1910), and *An Italian Tale* (Paris, 1913). The work which impressed Pound was *The Four
Winds*, published only in *Poetry* and the *transatlantic review*. Of this Pound wrote to
H. L. Mencken in February 1925, 'Dunning is 47, first case I have met where a chap has
done mediocre and submediocre stuff up to such an age, and then pulled the real thing.
(Mr Eliot don't like it, but then he don't see either Yeats or Hardy); possibly Dunning
is of our generation and concealed from the young.' *Letters of Ezra Pound*, ed. Paige,
p. 270.
² Arthur Symons.
³ A poem in *The Four Winds*.
⁴ Benjamin Howe Conner (b. 1878), an American lawyer in Paris.
⁵ Chadbourne, Stanchfield, and Levy, a law firm in New York.
⁶ The only parts of *Ulysses* which had been copyrighted in the United States were
those published by Margaret Anderson and Jane Heap in the *Little Review*.
⁷ Pound denied that the *Little Review* had paid Joyce anything, but said he himself
had turned over to Joyce as payment some money furnished by an admirer (possibly
Lady Cunard or John Quinn).

To Ezra Pound   MS. Pound

2 March 1927   *2 Square Robiac, 192 rue de Grenelle*

Dear Pound: Thanks. That declaration[1] ought to be enough. I cannot understand what she is doing (J.H.[2]). We have cabled several times and can get no answer. I assume she is trying to help me but she is really impeding my case. The whole affair is a most dreadful bore. They say Conner is a very competent lawyer. The lawyer who sent me the offer from Roth wrote again this morning. R. apparently circulated the rumour that he had compromised the case with me so I had a cable sent denying that also.

I enclose Collins's reply to Wallace which has just come. I hope it is of some use. By the way will you please send me back Λabcd, registered. I want to try to have it copyrighted in America.[3] I am publishing the first pages of the book (Λabcd is Part 3) in a Paris review.[4] When is the first number of *Exile*[5] to appear?

I hope Mrs Pound and yourself are well. Sincerely yours

                                                  James Joyce

To Georg Goyert   MS. S. Illinois (Croessmann)

6 March 1927   *2, Square Robiac, 192, rue de Grenelle*

Dear Mr Goyert: Two other persons are reading your translation and I shall collect and transmit their suggestions with mine, which are pencilled. Please send me a list of your doubtful points and can you write your letters *typed* on account of my sight. What is the fare and the time of the train journey to Paris from Witten. Surely they will allow us to meet before the translation comes out! Have you done the end of the *Oxen of the Sun*? Sincerely yours   James Joyce

[1] A formal declaration by Pound, made at the American consulate in Genoa, attesting that he had never authorized Samuel Roth to publish Joyce's *Ulysses* in *Two Worlds*. Roth had alleged in his own defence that he had received permission from Pound, who was acting as Joyce's literary agent.

[2] Jane Heap.

[3] Five books were published in the United States in editions of a few copies solely to protect American copyright. The first (*Finnegans Wake*, pp. 3–216) was copyrighted by Donald Friede, and published on 9 January 1928. The others were published by order of Joyce's law firm in New York. The second (pp. 282–304, 403–28), appeared on 24 July 1928; the third (pp. 429–73) on 4 October 1928, the fourth (pp. 474–554) on 15 February 1929, and the fifth (pp. 555–90) on 7 January 1930. The last four made up the Shaun section, Part 3.

[4] In *transition*.

[5] Pound founded the semiannual review, the *Exile*, in Spring 1927; it continued for four issues, the last being Autumn 1928.

To H ARRIET S HAW W EAVER   MS. British Museum

16 March 1927   *2 Square Robiac, 192 rue de Grenelle*

Dear Miss Weaver: In view of the enclosed[1] I have decided to publish my 13 pieces of verse (1904–1927) in a tiny volume like the Donne you gave me at 1/- one shelenk a copy and the title: *Pomes Pennyeach* [sic].[2] So they will be out of the way.

Darantière 'gave' my proofs years ago to a few in his works. There is to be an arbitrage and so on and more lawyers and so forth.

The P.E.N. club of London invited James the Punman to be guest of honour at a dinner in London on 5 April. As many English writers signed the protest I accepted. We leave here on 29 instant as it takes a week to cross the Woebegone.

The miners at Willingdone[3] also offered to pay my fare up there and give me a 'royal welcome' if I would speak to them. I won't speak but if I went to London I have been thinking of taking a trip Euston–Willingdone–Penrith[4]–Barrow[5]–Holyhead–Dublin–Galway etc. If circumstances allowed it, that is. My father has been writing to me for years. I don't like so much going to Ireland but I don't like to refuse him always.

Transition[6] is held up a week by legal formalities but I suppose, as you don't like ⊔[7] any better in his nice print frock[8] that he will not appeal to you even in his 39 articles of clothing.[9] As for me I am working away at the suite (I will sell my chances of going to London to end it all every word.[10] O go on, go on, go on![11]). The typescript is like a caviare sandwich. Besides trying to revise the German muddle[12] and patching up my wardrobe in order to look like a respectable litteratoor when I sit down at the dinnertable.

---

[1] Two letters from Archibald MacLeish, warmly praising Joyce's later poems.

[2] *Pomes Penyeach* was published by Shakespeare and Company on 7 July 1927. Thirteen large paper copies were also printed, according to Sylvia Beach (*Shakespeare and Company*, p. 175), and were distributed as follows: 1, Sylvia Beach; 2, Harriet Shaw Weaver; 3, Arthur Symons; 4, Valery Larbaud; 5, George Joyce; 6, Lucia Joyce; 7 Adrienne Monnier; 8, Claud W. Sykes; 9, Archibald MacLeish; 10, Eugene Jolas; 11' Elliot Paul; 12, Mrs Myron Nutting; 13, Joyce himself.

[3] A man named Wilson, apparently a mine owner in Willington, Northumberland, wrote Joyce an enthusiastic letter urging a visit.

[4] See p. 144, n. 1.

[5] Barrow-in-Furness, Lancashire.

[6] See p. 5. The first portion to be serialized was the first chapter of *Finnegans Wake*.

[7] Earwicker.   [8] A revised typescript.

[9] That is, its formal publication in *transition*. Earwicker's thirty-nine articles of clothing are mentioned in *Finnegans Wake*, pp. 534, 283, and elsewhere.

[10] *Finnegans Wake*, p. 206.   [11] *Ibid.*, p. 207.

[12] The translation of *Ulysses* into German

Please let me know if you approve of the publication.
<u>Rushing</u> for the Posht[1] With kindest regards sincerely yours

JAMES JOYCE

16. (Ho! Ho! Tomorrow is Potreek's Day, the sham rogue!) iii.927

To GEORG GOYERT   MS. S. Illinois (Croessmann)

Postmark 31 March 1927   *2 Square Robiac, 192 rue de Grenelle*

Dear Mr Goyert: I shall be absent from Paris (in London where the
P.E.N. Club is giving me a dinner)[2] from 3 to 9 April. I corrected the
sheet you sent me but cannot find it! Could you send me another. I am
very sorry for my carelessness. Sincerely yours   JAMES JOYCE

To RICHARD ALDINGTON   MS. Texas

[? *Late April 1927*]   *2 Square Robiac, 192 rue de Grenelle, Paris*

Dear Mr Aldington: During my absence from Paris your letter was
mislaid. I am writing to thank you for your suggestion[3] but suit was
entered against Roth on 23 March and I shall wait the result. I understand his magazines have been stopped.[4] I have to thank you also for
your signature to the letter of protest. I think it will have some effect.

Have you still the dossier of the *English Players* which I sent you
from Locarno?[5] If so I shall be very glad if you will send it to Miss
Sylvia Beach, 12 rue de l'Odéon, Paris. Sincerely yours   JAMES JOYCE

From STUART GILBERT[6]   MS. Private

9 May 1927   *42 Avenue Pasteur, Becon-les-Briyeres, Seine*

Dear Sir Some weeks ago, at the Shakespeare Library, I happened to
point out to Miss Beach a curious mistake in the translation of

[1] See p. 120, n. 7.   [2] On 5 April 1927. John Drinkwater presided.
[3] Aldington's suggestion, in a letter of 10 March 1927, was that Joyce either join with
the *Little Review* in sueing Roth for infringement of copyright, or else publish a bowdler-
ised version of *Ulysses* for the American market with a note explaining why he was
driven to this action.
[4] Roth suspended publication after the October 1927 issue of *Two Worlds Monthly*; by
that time he had printed more than half of *Ulysses*. Court proceedings went slowly, but
on 27 December 1928 Roth was enjoined from using Joyce's name in any way by Justice
Richard H. Mitchell of the Supreme Court of the State of New York.
[5] In 1919. Aldington lost the dossier and did not find it again.
[6] Stuart Gilbert had retired from the British Civil Service in Burma and was now making his home in Paris, where he still resides. Besides helping signally with the translation
of *Ulysses*, he wrote *James Joyce's* Ulysses (1930), edited the first volume of Joyce's
Letters (1957), and translated many other books.

'Ulysses' which appeared in the first number of '900'[1] and mentioned
that I had compared the translation with my 'Ulysses' and noted in the
otherwise excellent French version several discrepancies from your text.
She was kind enough to give me a hearing and asked me to submit a
note on these discrepancies. I enclose a note on some of these. There are
others, less apparent, which, nevertheless, might interest you, and I am
at your disposal, should you care to hear my observations.

If you would care, I am prepared to go through the French version
and, tentatively, to make suggestions. I fully appreciate your translator's
colossal task and his skill in execution and would assist without
officiousness and, I hope, with tact.

My reason for this demarche is that I hope the translation of
'Ulysses' may do for French literature what the original has done for
English and that nothing may be lost in transit. I am not out for any
remuneration or acknowledgement of any assistance I might give.

I enclose my card and, as further evidence of 'educational qualifications', add that I have an Oxford Honours Degree and converse
bilingually, my wife being French. yours faithfully   A. S. GILBERT

To SYLVIA BEACH   MS. Buffalo

27 May 1927   *Grand Hotel Restaurant Victoria, La Haye*

Dear Miss Beach: I return you herewith posthaste the pomes in their
proper order with correct dates and text and an addition to face p. 2
and if you fill in the titlepage it is all right but I should like to check a
final proof in bound proof. Has my brother not sent on the rest of the
MSS yet?[2] I am sorry I could not hear you.[3] There is a station (on 1950)
at Scheveningen but it runs in the season only for transmitting. There
is scarcely a soul there on account of the cold spell so we stay in the
town and tram it out: it is only about 10 minutes. Here it is very quiet
and dear but the people are very civil and obliging and not rapacious
really. It is the exchange and the small things do not hit them at all
though to us they seem terribly dear. The strand is wild and endless.
Unfortunately I had a dreadful time with a savage dog on Wednesday
25 inst. My wife and Lucia had gone for tea and I walked on a mile or so
and lay down on my overcoat reading the baedeker and trying to make
out the coastline when the brute rushed from Lord knows where at me.

[1] A translation of the *Calypso* episode by Auguste Morel appeared in *900: Cahiers
d'Italie et d'Europe* (Rome-Florence) I (Autumn 1926) 107–31.
[2] Joyce sent to Stanislaus Joyce for a number of his manuscripts; he wished to present
the manuscript of *Dubliners* and that of *Stephen Hero* to Miss Beach.
[3] Miss Beach spoke on the French radio about the publication of *Ulysses* in Paris.

I beat him off a few times. His owner ran up and his mistress and they got him down but he slunk round when their back was turned and attacked me again in the same way fully four times. It lasted I am sure a quarter of an hour. In my alarm my glasses got knocked and one of the lenses flew away in the sand. When Madame or whatever she was finally tugged the animal away howling the owner and I went down on our knees and after groping for a long time found the lenses. I feel so helpless with those detestable animals. Revolver? I suppose he would have me before I made up my mind to fire. Or carry stones in my pocket? If I could do the trick of gentleman into fox[1] I could save my breath better.

Thank Mrs Antheil for the words.[2] I shall use some of them. As regards the rest I will explain to her in Paris. I hope Ulysses IX[3] will soon ascend the papal throne. His motto is to be: *Triste canis vulpibus* = This 'ere dog will worry them there foxyboys. With kindest regards sincerely yours   JAMES JOYCE

To STANISLAUS JOYCE (Postcard)   MS. Cornell

10 June 1927   *Zaandam*

Best greetings from here. Berlitz was right after all[4]

JIM, LUCIA, NORA

To CLAUD W. SYKES (Postcard)   MS. Yale

10 June 1927   *Hotel Krasnapolsky, Amsterdam*

Dear Mr Sykes: What is your present address? A little book of my verse is coming out in a day or two and I think you may like to have a copy. How do you get on with my pieces in *transition*??? I get threats denunciations, jokes etc by every sending of press clippings.

Kind regards to Mrs Sykes and yourself Sincerely yours

JAMES JOYCE

P.S. I hope your work on *Ulysses* is over.[5] Amen!

---

[1] An allusion to *Lady into Fox* (London, 1922), a novel of David Garnett (b. 1892), the English writer.

[2] Presumably Russian words (since Mrs Antheil was from Russia), to be worked into *Finnegans Wake*.

[3] The ninth printing of *Ulysses* was issued this month.

[4] In emphasizing the spoken language; Joyce was learning Dutch.

[5] Sykes knew German well and had helped to revise Goyert's translation.

To HARRIET SHAW WEAVER   MS. British Museum

10 July 1927   *2 Square Robiac, 192 rue de Grenelle, Paris*

Dear Miss Weaver: Many thanks. The cheque has arrived and I had written to MacLeish[1] already on Saturday to have the proceeds of sale sent to Monro, Saw and Co.[2] News here goes from bad to worse. Wallace died on Tuesday and was buried on Thursday. . . . As for Roth he now issues an appeal to the American public to subscribe to a Samuel Roth defence fund in the name of the liberty of beauty, and to fight his case. I am described as a renegade jew with an 'organisation and vast funds' behind him.

I initialled your copy of the verses[3] as I thought a full signature in such [a] poor effort would look too ridiculous. The form is pleasing.

I am dejected enough by all these troubles. . . . That clergyman's name is Rev. James Cropper.[4] Ireland's Eye[5] (ey = island in Danish) is an islet off Howth Head. Phoenix Park[5] is rather close but it is a place not built by hands—at least not all—whereas □ is.[6]

I have been checking proof after proof and am tired. The dinner I had arranged for at Miss Beach's between J.J. and S.[7] is of course off for the present. The footnote about him in the book I send confirms my statement. Lalou's remark about my new work is in a very small minority indeed.[8] Do you remember was it you or I who sent to Mr

---

[1] Joyce asked Archibald MacLeish, who was returning to the United States, to offer the proof copy of *Dubliners* (the abortive Maunsel printing) to A. S. W. Rosenbach, the book dealer and collector. The sale was not effected.

[2] He was beginning to make inroads on the principal (in stocks) of the money Miss Weaver had given him, as well as using the income. The money to be obtained from the sale of the proofs was to be used to repurchase two blocks of stock that had been sold by Monro, Saw & Co. at his insistence. Miss Weaver was distressed, and Joyce tried to behave more providently.

[3] That is, of *Pomes Penyeach*, published five days before. See p. 6.

[4] The author of the pamphlet about the Giant's Grave at St Andrew's, Penrith. See p. 144, n. 1.

[5] While in London in April 1927 for the P.E.N. Club dinner, Joyce suggested that Miss Weaver try to guess the title of his book, which until publication was known only as *Work in Progress*. Over several months she tried different possibilities. In a letter of 28 June 1927 she proposed among others 'Ireland's Eye' and 'Phoenix Park'.

[6] Joyce's symbol for the title was a square. (*Letters*, ed. Gilbert, p. 213.) Since the action of the book was also circular, he probably had in mind squaring the circle, a scientific goal which also attracted Leopold Bloom.

[7] The initials of John Jameson and Son, a Dublin whisky; Joyce had formed the fantastic notion of having James Stephens finish *Finnegans Wake* for him. He wrote Miss Weaver on 20 May 1927 (*Letters*, ed. Gilbert, pp. 253–54) that JJ and S would in that case make 'a nice lettering under the title'.

[8] Renè Lalou wrote favourably about *Finnegans Wake* in a book entitled *Panorama de la littérature anglaise contemporaine* (Paris, 1929). Presumably he had earlier said something complimentary to Joyce in conversation.

Aldington the dossier of the English Players. I should like to have it back but he has not answered me. With kindest regards and thanks sincerely yours   JAMES JOYCE

To GEORG GOYERT   MS. S. Illinois (Croessmann)

Postmark 25 July 1927   *2 Square Robiac, 192 rue de Grenelle*

Dear Mr Goyert: Many thanks for E.S[1] and the rest. Prof Fey's article is good but Bloom wears a chapeau melon not a silk hat (he is not yet canonised!) and Mrs Purefoy is not a Putzfrau. 'Crab' is a slang word for a pubic parasite (Fr. morpion) 'Toby Tostoff' is bogus Russian from the verb 'to toss off' an expression for 'to masturbate'

We have just got back here. We had vile weather in Holland and here it is as bad.

Kind regards to Mrs Goyert and yourself   JAMES JOYCE

P.S. I will send N.R.F. when the piece appears.[2]

To HARRIET SHAW WEAVER   MS. British Museum

26 July 1927   *2 Square Robiac, 192 rue de Grenelle*

Dear Miss Weaver: I am glad you got the booklet[3] and did not dislike it. None of the others (Symons, Yeats, Pound, my father, brother etc) to whom I sent copies even acknowledged receipt of it. I expect Slocombe's[4] notice in the *Herald*[5] will be the last as it was the first. Miss Beach and Miss Monnier have gone to Savoy. I did not change lawyer because a) it was nearly impossible to find one to act, b) he is the most influential American in Paris except the ambassador, c) all the dossier is in his office in New York, d) his first act when Miss Beach retired was to send her his bill for services in her mother's case, e) I am not sure that I know all the facts of the case or that Miss Beach does, f) his letter was so callous in any case that I thought it better not to antagonise him. Her father and sister will be here in August. What the result will be I do not know.

It is now proposed that Miss Monnier is not to do successive editions of

---

[1] *English Studies* (Groningen, Netherlands).
[2] See p. 154.   [3] *Pomes Penyeach.*
[4] George Slocombe (1894–1963), English journalist, literary critic, and writer on history and art. Joyce told Slocombe he had the 'melancholy distinction' of being the only reviewer of *Pomes Penyeach*. George Slocombe, *The Tumult and the Shouting* (New York, 1936), p. 221.
[5] Slocombe, 'On the Left Bank,' *Daily Herald* (London), 14 July 1927.

Ulysse. I understand that the N.R.F. will do them, if needed. She will do a limited semi-private edition, I think.[1]

More kilos of abuse about ⊔⊔. Mr Shane Bullock[2] calls me a monster and Mr Ben Hecht[3] a Jack the Ripper. The review[4] has received letters from former friendly critics, Edwin Muir, [sic] deploring my collapse.

I am working night and day at a piece[5] I have to insert between the last and ⊏. It must be ready by Friday evening. I never worked against time before. It is very racking.

This house is shuttered up, ten out of twelve flats being left by absent families. I wish I saw some prospect of air and rest and relief from the storms and stifling heaviness but I see none. I enclose an explanation of one of the added phrases on p. 1 of last instalment. Two of your guesses were fairly near.[6] The last is off the track.[7] The piece I am hammering at ought to reveal it.[8] Please excuse this but I have Friday on the brain. With kindest regards sincerely yours   JAMES JOYCE

To HARRIET SHAW WEAVER (Postcard)   MS. British Museum

8 October 1927   *192 rue de Grenelle, Paris*

Dear Miss Weaver: I was quite ill last week, a collapse, but am all right. I am working very hard on the final revise of Δ on which I am prepared to stake everything.[9] When I send it off I will write. I wonder if I can get away even then. I am glad you like the new ⊏.[10] But I am utterly 'moidered' (Irish for confused in the head) by Anna Livia. I have spent at least another 150 at her toilet. With kindest regards sincerely yours   JAMES JOYCE

P.S. The eyes are all right.   J.J.

---

[1] The first printing of *Ulysse*, 1200 copies, was published in February 1929 by Adrienne Monnier, the second in January 1930 by J.-O. Fourcade. The third printing, also in 1930, was by her and Gallimard, and subsequent printings have been by Gallimard.

[2] Shane F. Bullock (1865–1935), Irish novelist.

[3] Ben Hecht (1894–1964), American playwright and novelist.   [4] *transition.*

[5] Chapter VI (*Finnegans Wake*, pp. 126–68). The chapter that follows is about Shem.

[6] 'Ireland's Eye' and 'Phoenix Park'.   [7] 'Dublin Bay.'

[8] Chapter VI is a series of twelve questions and answers. The answer to the first is 'Finn MacCool'. In a letter of 14 August 1927 (*Letters*, ed. Gilbert, p. 258) Joyce gave her a further clue: 'As to "Phoenix". A viceroy who knew no Irish thought this was the word the Dublin people used and put up the mount of a phoenix in the park. The Irish was *fiunishgue* = clear water from a well of bright water there.' With this help Miss Weaver did in fact guess 'Finn's Town' and 'Finn's City' in a letter of 17 September 1927. The subject is not mentioned further in the letters that have come to light; probably Joyce did not wish her to come any closer.

[9] He was revising *Anna Livia Plurabelle* for the November 1927 issue (No. 8) of *transition.*

[10] The Shem chapter (VII), *Finnegans Wake*, pp. 169–95.

To VALERY LARBAUD   MS. Bib. Municipale, Vichy

[*? 18 October 1927*]   *2 Square Robiac, 192 rue de Grenelle*

Dear Larbaud: Of course you are to have the casting vote in all
discussions.[1] I agree with every word of your letter to Miss Monnier.
The German translation[2] came out on Tuesday last. I could not write a
line on Svevo—or anything else.[3] I have just finished revision of Anna
Livia for transition no 8. What a job! 1200 hours of work on 17 pages.
She has grown—riverwise—since the night you heard her under the sign
of Ursa Minor. Her fluvial maids of honour from all ends of the earth
now number about 350 I think.[4]

I hope to see you soon here. Sincerely yours   JAMES JOYCE

P.S. And now for your address ? ? ?

To GEORG GOYERT   MS. S. Illinois (Croessmann)

19 October 1927   *2 Square Robiac, 192 rue de Grenelle*

Dear Mr Goyert: I have not yet seen the German *Ulysses*.[5] I do not like
at all the title *So Sind Sie in Dublin*.[6] It is not my point of view which
would be, if at all, *So Sind Wir in Dublin*.[7] But I like neither. If
'Dubliners' is impossible what about 'In Dublin Stadt' or 'Dublin an
der Liffey' ?[8]

Please let me know by return Sincerely yours   JAMES JOYCE

To ROBERT MCALMON   MS. Pearson

29 October 1927   *2 Square Robiac, 192 rue de Grenelle*

Dear McAlmon: Referring to our last conversation I am to read the
Anna Liffey piece here next Wednesday at 3.30 sharp on account of the

---

[1] Of the French translation of *Ulysses*.

[2] Of *Ulysses*, by the Rhein-Verlag in Basel.

[3] Larbaud had urged that Joyce, who had been so active in urging others to write
about Schmitz, do something of the kind himself. But Joyce had a long standing principle
not to write critical essays or prefaces, and he declined now as he would again after
Schmitz's death the following year.

[4] Joyce prided himself on the number of river names he could incorporate in the *Anna
Livia Plurabelle* chapter.

[5] Published 15 October 1927.   [6] 'What They're Like in Dublin.'

[7] 'What We're Like in Dublin.'

[8] 'In Dublin City' or 'Dublin on the Liffey.' The title Goyert eventually chose for his
translation of *Dubliners*, which was published by Rhein-Verlag in Basel in 1928, was
Dublin: Novellen.

light.[1] If you would care to hear it please come. We shall be glad to see
you Sincerely yours   JAMES JOYCE

To DANIEL BRODY[2]   MS. Brody

7 November 1927   *2 Square Robiac, 192 rue de Grenelle, Paris*

Sehr geehrter Herr Doktor: Die vier Bände der deutschen Ausgabe
meines 'Ulysses' sind mir einige Tagen vor angekommen. Gestatten Sie
dass ich Ihnen meinen besten Dank ausdrücke für Ihre höfliche
Gedacht. Die Ausgabe ist wirklich sehr schön und geschmackvoll und
hoffentlich wird sie auch in materiellem sowohl als in literarischem Sinn
ein Lohn für alle Ihre Bemühungen. Ich mochte Ihr Exemplär unter-
schreiben. Vielleicht können Sie es bei Gelegenheit nach Paris schicken.
In der Zwischenzeit sende ich Ihnen ein ganz kleines Bändchen[3] als
Gegengewicht zum 'homerischen Ungeheuer' Ihr ergebener

                                                              JAMES JOYCE[4]

To EZRA POUND   MS. Pound

[? 8 November 1927]   *2 Square Robiac, 192 rue de Grenelle, Paris*

Dear Pound: I have been a long time in replying to both your letters[5]
but I had not a moment for I was working all day on Anna Livia
(transition 8) which I had to read after in its final amended form,
putting in an extra 200 hours on the 1000 I told you of. And after that
I did not feel at all well, nervous collapse etc.

As regards Covici[6] it is kind of you to think of me. Roth has been
pirating the thing in transition also so it is being set up in 3 copies in
the U.S.A., 2 being sent to Washington and the 3rd to me so that I may
have legal copyright of it. Part 1 has just finished in transition and next

---

[1] Joyce finished this version of *Anna Livia Plurabelle* on 27 October. Early in November 1927 he read it to a group of about twenty-five friends, who were greatly impressed by
it.
[2] Daniel Brody (b. 1883 in Budapest) took over the Rhein-Verlag, Zurich, in 1926. He
published the German translation of *Ulysses*.
[3] *Pomes Penyeach.*
[4] (Translation)
'My dear Doctor: The four volumes of the German edition of my *Ulysses* arrived
here a few days ago. Allow me to express my thanks to you for your courteous thought.
The edition is really very handsome and tastefully done, and I hope your efforts on its
behalf will be rewarded in a material as well as a literary sense. I would like to sign
your copy. Perhaps you could send it to Paris when an opportunity offers. In the meantime I am sending you a very small book to counterbalance the "Homeric monster"
Yours sincerely   James Joyce'
[5] These letters have not come to light.
[6] Pascal Covici (1888–1964), American publisher. Pound suggested him as a publisher
for *Finnegans Wake*.

month I should begin to publish there serially also Part 3. But I do not intend to publish serially Part 2 or the shorter Part 4 when the 8 or 9 instalments of Part 3 are finished. Miss Beach, of course, has first claim on the right to publish but if my American copyright is secured I shall bear in mind your suggestion.

I cannot find the phrase you ask about either in Father Rickeby's[1] enormous edition of Aquinas or in the French one I have. The scholastic machinery of the process of thought is very intricate, *verbum mentale* and all the rest of it but I can find no such phrase as you quote. Perhaps it is used in logic or metaphysics. To my mind it does not convey as yet any very precise sense. These philosophical terms are such tricky bombs that I am shy of handling them, being afraid they may go off in my hands.

How is your health which is much more important. I heard from Bird that you had to undergo another operation. I hope it is not true or at least that it is well over and done with by now. I have nicely exhausted myself a goodly share of kicks (some of them aimed at me from that well of English undefiled, Tasmania!) and a few halfpennies of encouragement for which I am deeply grateful.

I hope Mrs Pound and your boy are well. Friendly regards from us all. With kind regards Sincerely yours   JAMES JOYCE

P.S. I forgot to send a little epigram I made after our last conversation, I think, about my new book. So here it is. I am writing it legibly.

> E.P. exults in the extra inch
> Wherever the ell it's found
> But wasn't J.J. a son of a binch
> To send him an extra pound?

The title I gave it (the epigram) was:

> Troppa Grossa, San Giacomone![2]

To MRS J. F. BYRNE   MS. Private

10 November 1927   *2 Square Robiac, 192 rue de Grenelle, Paris*

Dear Mrs Byrne, I am very glad to meet my old friend Byrne[3] after so many years and it is most kind of you to allow him to stay a few days.

---

[1] Joseph John Rickaby (1875–1932).

[2] 'Too heavy, great Saint James!' A parody of the Italian expression, 'Troppa grazia, San Antonio' ('Too much grace, St Anthony'), denoting too much of a good thing. St Anthony of Padua is known as a worker of miracles.

[3] J. F. Byrne visited Joyce for a few days in November. The two much enjoyed each other's company.

I hope you will not be annoyed if we press him to stay over the weekend
as the weather is very fine and he ought to see a number of things here
before he leaves. The change too will do him good. He will go back on
Monday or Tuesday unless you should wish him to return earlier. With
kind regards sincerely yours   JAMES JOYCE

To CLAUD W. SYKES (Postcard)   MS. Yale

19 November 1927   [*Paris*]

Dear Mr Sykes: I did not receive the letter you mention and thought
you might be still in Denmark. I have written to Rhein verlag to send
you one of my author's copies.[1] The edition was sold out in 3 weeks. Let
me know when it reaches you. Many thanks for your kind references to
my new work. I spent 1200 hours writing the piece in transition 8!
     Friendly regards to you both Sincerely yours   JAMES JOYCE

To G. MOLYNEUX PALMER   MS. National Library

29 November 1927   *2 Square Robiac, 192 rue de Grenelle VII, Paris*

Dear Mr Palmer: Will you please send six of your settings of *Chamber
Music* for middle voice, say, up to A flat or G natural to M. Slivinsky,
Au Sacre du Printemps, 3 rue Cherche-Midi, Paris, VII. I think I can
arrange with him to bring them out for you in a satisfactory way and
they would have a good sale here, I am sure. Have you set any of *Pomes
Penyeach*? Sincerely yours   JAMES JOYCE

To FRANK BUDGEN   MS. Yale

14 December 1927   *2 Square Robiac, 192 rue de Grenelle*

Dear Budgen: I see by a card sent to 12 rue de l'Odéon[2] that you are in
Paris. If you have not left will you please ring me up (Ségur 95–20)
before 11 a.m. on Thursday or Friday morning as I shall be glad to hear
from you.[3] I hope Suter[4] got the presentation copy of the German
Ulysses which I asked the publishers in Stuttgart to send him. Sincerely
yours   JAMES JOYCE

---

[1] Of the German translation of *Ulysses*.   [2] Sylvia Beach's bookstore.
[3] Joyce and Budgen had been out of touch for several years, and this was Joyce's
overture to renew their friendship.
[4] The Swiss sculptor August Suter (1887–1965), with whom Budgen often stayed in
Paris.

To FRANK BUDGEN (Postcard)   MS. Yale

13 January 1928   [*Paris*]

Thanks for letter and New Year's wishes which I return. I am sorry Mrs
Budgen and you had such a bad time. As for me the worst Xmas and
New Year I can remember. I have been and am painfully ill—inflammation of intestines—caused by overwork and worry. Ring me up
(Segur 95.20) any morning as I would like to talk with you. Did S¹ get
his Ulysses? I shall really have to go away and rest or I shall have a
worse nervous breakdown.   J.J.

To ELLIOT PAUL²   MS. British Museum

[*About January 1928*]   *2 Square Robiac, 192 rue de Grenelle*

Dear Mr Paul: If compatible with existing text and still possible make
the following changes please.
page 1. A Tullagrove etc has a septain inclinaison³
page 6   raucking his flavourite turvku in the smukking precincts of
         lydias⁴
"   7 wedgemidden of the stream⁵
         lying low on his rawside⁶
         And (something follows here which I forget but if compatible
         add) diesmal he was laying him long on his laughside⁶ Many
         thanks sincerely yours   JAMES JOYCE

P.S. Please have 3 copies of transition⁷ when out sent me by express. JJ

To VALERY LARBAUD   MS. Bib. Municipale, Vichy

19 January 1928   *2 Square Robiac, 192 rue de Grenelle*

Dear Larbaud: I got your pneu and shall follow your instructions. But
in that case I shall not call on the person in question⁸ till tomorrow
(Saturday) so that there may seem to be no connection between our two
visits. I shall call about another matter and introduce the principal

---

¹ August Suter.
² Elliot Paul (1891–1958), American novelist and journalist, a long-time resident of
Paris, and for a period Jolas's assistant editor on *transition*.
³ *Finnegans Wake*, p. 284.   ⁴ *Ibid.*, p. 294.
⁵ *Ibid.*, p. 297.   ⁶ *Ibid.*, p. 301.
⁷ *transition* 11 (February 1928) 7–18; these pages eventually became *Finnegans Wake*,
pp. 282–304.
⁸ Adrienne Monnier.

theme casually[1] but firmly. After which I shall write you to fix an appointment. It will be all right, I am sure. So don't worry. Sincerely yours   J.J.

To STANISLAUS JOYCE   MS. Cornell

Postmark 29 January 1928   *2 Square Robiac, 192 rue de Grenelle*

Dear Stannie: I am recovering from a painful illness—inflammation of the intestines aggravated by work and worry. I have no money. On the 14th inst. I had to sell out £300 more of stock but have not yet got my cheque from the lawyers. As soon as it comes I will send on the 600 francs. I was forbidden all work. Some months ago I suspended the free-mailing list of *transition* which was costing me about 400 francs a month. The person referred to is Miss Weaver who has come to Paris on account of it and my illness,[2] and this note was caused by my offer to James Stephens to take over the book.[3] To my surprise he expressed the most unbounded admiration for it. His words are too extravagant to repeat but he spoke very generously.   JIM

To the EDITOR of the *Revue Nouvelle*[4]

10 February 1928   *Paris*

Cher Monsieur, La demande que vous venez de me faire au sujet d'une contribution éventuelle de ma part à votre numéro spécial dédié à la mémoire de Thomas Hardy me touche profondément. Je crains malheureusement de manquer des titres nécessaires pour donner une opinion qui ait une valeur quelconque sur l'œuvre de Hardy, dont j'ai lu les romans il y a tant d'années que je préfère ne pas en faire le compte;

---

[1] The question of Larbaud's overall responsibility for the translation of *Ulysses* into French.

[2] Miss Weaver went to Paris in January and stayed into February. She had come to feel that her intervention in Joyce's literary life was ill advised, and wished to set matters right as much as she could, and to assure him that he could depend upon her support no matter what he wrote. Joyce spent long hours explaining the book to her, and she came to sympathize more fully with his aims and methods.

[3] Joyce, always fond of coincidences, was pleased to think that James Stephens's name was a combination of his own first name and that of Stephen Dedalus; he also learned that Stephens's birthyear, birthday, and birthplace (Dublin) were the same as his own. (In reality, Stephens was illegitimate and his surname, birthyear, and birthday were invented.) Joyce was discouraged enough to toy at least with the notion of having Stephens finish his book for him. (See p. 161, n. 7.) When he broached the matter more seriously, in July 1929, Stephens said he would do anything to help him, but insisted that Joyce himself would write it and that *Anna Livia Plurabelle* was 'the greatest prose ever written by a man' (*Letters*, ed. Gilbert, p. 282).

[4] This letter was published in a special Thomas Hardy number of the *Revue Nouvelle* (Paris) IV.38–9 (January–February 1928) 61. The text is taken from there.

et en ce qui concerne son œuvre poétique, je dois vous avouer que je l'ignore complètement. Il y aurait donc de ma part une singulière audace à émettre le moindre jugement sur la figure vénérable qui vient de disparaître: il vaut mieux que je laisse ce soin aux critiques de son pays.

Mais quelque diversité de jugement qui pourrait exister sur cette œuvre (s'il en existe), il paraît par contre évident à tous que Hardy offrait dans son attitude du poète vis-à-vis du public, un honorable exemple de probité et d'amour-propre dont nous autres clercs avons toujours un peu besoin, spécialement à une époque où le lecteur semble se contenter de moins en moins de la pauvre parole écrite et où, par conséquent, l'écrivain tend à s'occuper de plus en plus des grandes questions qui, du reste, se règlent très bien sans son aide.

JAMES JOYCE[1]

To HARRIET SHAW WEAVER　　　　　　　　　MS. British Museum

15 February 1928　　　　　　　*2 Square Robiac, 192 rue de Grenelle*

Dear Miss Weaver: You must have had a bad time on the Manche but O think of what you are away from here. Friede[2] has not replied. He told Antheil that I had concluded a pact with him and disposed of the book.[3] Miss Beach, as I suspected, seems to have believed this and still half believes it. Conner over the telephone today told me that it seems to him a second Roth affair and that for the moment I was completely in

[1] (Translation)
'Dear Sir, The request you have just made me for a possible contribution by me to your special issue dedicated to the memory of Thomas Hardy touches me deeply. I fear unfortunately that I lack the necessary qualifications to give an opinion about Hardy's work which would have any value, for I read his novels so many years ago that I prefer not to remember how many; and as for his poetical work, I must confess to you that I am totally ignorant of it. So it would be singularly audacious for me to render the least judgment upon the venerable figure who has just disappeared: it is better for me to leave this responsibility to critics of his own country.

But whatever diversity of judgment may exist about his work (if any does exist), it is none the less evident to all that Hardy demonstrated in his attitude of the poet in relation to his public, an honourable example of integrity and self-esteem of which we other clerks are always a little in need, especially in a period when the reader seems to content himself with less and less of the poor written word and when, in consequence, the writer tends to concern himself more and more with the great questions which, for all that, adjust themselves very well without his aid.　　　　　James Joyce'

[2] At the suggestion of Elliot Paul, Donald Friede (1901–1965) published a fragment of *Finnegans Wake* in January 1928 to forestall piracy. He took out the copyright in his own name rather than in Joyce's, a mistake to which Joyce responded with alarm. Friede sent a transfer of copyright in February.

[3] George Antheil reported nothing accurately, and no doubt converted Friede's desire to publish the whole of *Finnegans Wake* into the extravagant claim that a contract had been signed.

Friede's power and to proceed very carefully. This is what I tried to do. Hill, *transition*'s lawyer, wrote saying: You will see by the enclosed copy of Mr F.'s letter to me that he has ceded the copyright to Mr Joyce. There was no enclosed copy. He was cabled to but has not replied. I wanted the current issue of *t*. and the first $\frac{1}{2}$ of Λabcd which I had set up to reach my lawyers[1] before any other person could copyright them and have them set up there at my expense but Mr Jolas has been ringing up to say the printer had a special holiday etc and so *t*. 11 has gone to America. Miss Beach and Mr Jolas had a fine old set-to on the heels of which I arrived. There was an awful lot of snappy thunder in the air but I managed to keep to my point. Jolas has just written a very good article and while I want an explanation I don't want a quarrel which may be unnecessary. Miss Monnier is still grippée (so is Miss Moschos now) but when she gets better there will be a general brisking up of the artillery. Moreover my trunk's by no means the trunk he used to was and as for my poor brainbox why it's falling down all the time and being picked up by different people who just peep inside as they replace it and murmur 'So we thought'!

Lucia dances through it all.[2] She was very good, I think.

I am very glad you came to Paris for at least I know where I stand. Of which more anon.

I met the greatest editor in the world[3] in the office of the consulate of the greatest empire on earth.[4] He signed[5] the power of attorney, saved me 25 francs, took me home in a taxi and offered me an aperitif—unaccepted. The greatest surprise in history. With kindest regards sincerely yours   JAMES JOYCE

To STANISLAUS JOYCE   MS. Cornell

[*16 March 1928*]   *2 Square Robiac, 192 rue de Grenelle*

Dear Stannie: Eileen and the children stayed here 4 days. I paid for that and also 2nd class and cabin fares to Dublin about 3000 francs in all. They left for Dublin just a fortnight ago today but I never heard from them that they had arrived nor do I know where they are.

I hope things are going well with you. Schmitz was given a dinner here last night by the Pen Club.   JIM

[1] This stratagem of Joyce, to secure American copyright by registering an issue of *transition* with the Copyright Office before it was officially published, would probably not have satisfied legal requirements.

[2] Lucia Joyce was taking a course in the dance from Lois Hutton. On 19 February 1928 she played the part of a wild vine in a 'Ballet Faunesque' at the Comédie des Champs-Elysées. Joyce had probably seen a rehearsal a few days earlier.

[3] Possibly Lord Beaverbrook.   [4] The British Consulate.   [5] As witness, evidently.

To DONALD FRIEDE (Cablegram)   TS. John H. Thompson

20 March 1928   *Paris*

THANKS FOR DEED OF RELEASE COPYRIGHT RECEIVED
HAVE ALREADY MADE ARRANGEMENTS THROUGH
CHADBOURNE STANCHFIELD AND LEVY NEW YORK FOR
PRINTING PRESENT AND SUBSEQUENT INSTALMENTS
THERE TO PROTECT COPYRIGHT FOR ME[1]   JOYCE

To STANISLAUS JOYCE (Postcard)   MS. Cornell

Postmark 22 March 1928   *Hotel du Rhin, Dieppe*

Nora had a letter today from her mother to say that Eileen and the
children had been down in Galway and had gone back to Dublin; I
suppose. I have not yet heard from them but at least they reached
Ireland[2]

Best wishes to both of you   JIM

From ETTORE SCHMITZ[3]

27 March 1928   *Trieste*

Caro amico, qui ho trovato le due lettere per gli editori.[4] Non si può
essere più generosi di così.

Io vivo dei suoni che m'accompagnano da Parigi.[5] Uno sovrasta agli
altri: Anna Livia e il ritratto del Veruda.[6] Vorrebbe Lei averlo? Dica
in una cartolina postale la sola parola 'sì' ed io glielo invio. Senza il Suo
consenso non oso inviarLe il ritratto di mia moglie. Di lavori di Veruda

---

[1] Joyce's New York lawyers arranged for the publication of four fragments. Unfortunately none of these bore a notice of copyright, though one was inserted later in the
fourth. Joyce objected that his wishes had not been carried out and paid only a portion
of the legal fees.

[2] Mrs Eileen Joyce Schaurek decided it would be easier for her, as a widow, to live in
Ireland, and she took her two children back there at this time.

[3] The text of this letter is taken from 'Carteggio . . . Svevo–Joyce', ed. Harry Levin,
Inventario II.1 (Spring 1949) 130.

[4] One of the letters was to Jonathan Cape, the other to B. W. Huebsch, urging them to
publish Schmitz in English translation.

[5] Schmitz was honoured at a testimonial dinner of the P.E.N. Club in Paris in March
1928. Among those attending were Isaak Babel, Jules Romains, Ivan Goll, Jean Paulhan,
Benjamin Crémieux, and Joyce.

[6] Umberto Veruda (1868–1904), a well-known Triestine painter. A note in *Inventario*
suggests that Schmitz had Veruda in mind in depicting the sculptor Balli in *Senilità*.

io ne ho molti, e in quanto al soggetto io mi tengo caro l'originale.

Alla Sua signora i nostri ringraziamenti. Quando viene Lucia? Le stringo affettuosamente la mano, Suo devotissimo   ETTORE SCHMITZ[1]

To VALERY LARBAUD   MS. Bib. Municipale, Vichy

28 March 1928   *Grand Hôtel de la Poste, Rouen*

Dear Larbaud: I was sorry to have bad news of you but am glad to hear you are now better. We are snatching a few days' holiday in Dieppe and here but as soon as I return to Paris I shall put matters right with Miss Monnier—or I hope so. Gilbert wrote to me before I left Paris but I avoided the issue—though I personally found him quite obliging and well-intentioned—and shall abide by our 'Trianon treaty'[2] as the best way to avoid friction.

Svevo was entertained by the Paris Pen Club last week (Gesumaria, *che* vino e *che* cena!)[3] and our names were mentioned often by Romains[4] who presided as his godfather. If we had a literary 'grandson' what age would he be? Sincerely yours   JAMES JOYCE

To HARRIET SHAW WEAVER   MS. British Museum

28 March 1928   *Grand Hôtel de la Poste, Rouen*

Dear Miss Weaver: It is very dark in this salon to write. We left Dieppe last evening as neither my wife nor I has been over well. I fatigued myself to exhaustion point over Λa. I am glad you like the fable.[5] Chatto and Windus put out a prospectus which Miss Beach has announcing a colossal new work in the press by Lewis.[6] The text says 'the only work that can at all hold a card to it is ———'. You can supply the blank.

---

[1] (Translation)

'Dear friend, I found the two letters for the publishers here. It is not possible to be more generous than this.

I am living among the sounds which have accompanied me from Paris. One thing stands out above the rest: Anna Livia and the portrait by Veruda. Would you like to have it? Write on a postcard merely the word "yes" and I will send it to you. Without your permission I would not dare send you a portrait of my wife. I have many of Veruda's works and as far as the subject of this one is concerned, I fondly retain the original for myself.

Our thanks to your wife. When is Lucia coming? I shake your hand affectionately. Your devoted   Ettore Schmitz'

[2] See p. 109, n. 1.   [3] 'Jesus and Mary, *what* wine and *what* a dinner!'

[4] Jules Romains (b. 1885), French novelist and man of letters.

[5] The fable of 'The Ondt and the Gracehoper' (*Finnegans Wake*, pp. 414–19), was published in *transition* 12 (March 1928) 7–27.

[6] Wyndham Lewis, *The Childermass* (London, 1928).

I think I have managed to get Pound to testify in the Roth case. Roth's counsel raised his name frequently and a refusal on E P's part would be taken as a tacit admission that Roth was right. I enclose a letter from V.L.[1] (which please send back to my Paris address) and I shall have to patch up that too when I get back. I think I have also nipped in the bud a nascent unpleasantness between Antheil and Miss Monnier: The latter[2] had a kind of offer from the Cologne opera to put on the Cyclops in October if I would go there and be present at a reception. I hate these things but I agreed to go there as he is in a bad way and in poor health. Between ourselves as V L puts it I don't think he has written 20 bars of the piece in the last four or five years but I pretend to think it is getting on splendidly. The rest is now up to him. The Abbey Theatre has engaged him to do a ballet on Cuchulain fighting the waves.[3]

I have been reading about the author of 'Alice'.[4] A few things about him are rather curious. He was born a few miles from Warrington (Daresbury),[5] and he had a strong stutter[6] and when he wrote he inverted his name like Tristan and Swift. His name was Charles Lutwidge of which he made Lewis (i.e. Ludwig) Carroll (i.e. Carolus).

Yes I should like to see a few copies of that paper.[7] Dr Ellwood is the original of Temple in the Portrait. He is quite as accurate as ever, I see.

We return to Paris in a day or two. I hope the sea air did us some sort of good. It is madness to work till the very last instant for 15 months at a stretch as I do in Paris. I have lost 6 kilos in weight. But I hope to have determination enough to stop it and get off for a good spell of holiday. There are moments when I feel 20 but also half-hours when I feel 965. With kindest regards sincerely yours   JAMES JOYCE

To VALERY LARBAUD   MS. Bib. Municipale, Vichy

5 April 1928   *2 Square Robiac, 192 rue de Grenelle*

Dear Larbaud: I got back here Saturday and saw the matter through I think. At least by now you ought to have a letter from her[8] acquiescing in your conditions, which after all are nothing but the original arrangements, as I pointed out to her. Best wishes for Easter Sincerely yours

JAMES JOYCE

---

[1] Valery Larbaud.   [2] A slip for 'the former'.   [3] For Yeats's play, *Fighting the Waves.*
[4] Lewis Carroll and *Alice in Wonderland* appear frequently in *Finnegans Wake*, he as a lustful old man and she as a variant of Earwicker's daughter Isabel. See Adaline Glasheen, *A Census of Finnegans Wake* (Evanston and London, 1956), pp. 4, 23–24.
[5] Harriet Shaw Weaver, as Joyce knew, was also born near Warrington.
[6] In *Finnegans Wake* Earwicker is a great stutterer.
[7] Unidentified.   [8] Adrienne Monnier.

To ETTORE SCHMITZ   MS. Fonda Savio

6 April 1928   *2 Square Robiac, 192 rue de Grenelle, Paris*

Caro Schmitz: Di ritorno qui trovo la Sua gentile lettera. Ben volentieri accetto il Suo regalo e che l'immagine di Anna Livia mi porti e ricordi ed auguri. Spero che avrà buon successo con Cape o coi Viking, il primo pero, non comprendente inglese, è piu temibile.

Buona Pasqua alla signora ed a Lei da noi tutti   JAMES JOYCE[1]

To HARRIET SHAW WEAVER   MS. British Museum

8 April 1928   *2 Square Robiac, 192 rue de Grenelle*

Dear Miss Weaver: I don't think I am violating any confidence in enclosing V.L.[2]'s new letter since you do not know what it is about though a good dozen of people, if he is right, do here. (What English!) But as you were, luckily for me, present at one heated scene I want you to know that it's quite as warm as ever in Paris. I have, I think, smoothed over matters between V.L. and Her[3] but there remain to be rubbed down S.G.[4] (!) and A.M.,[5] the two translators who dislike each other and V.L. and are heartily disliked by him in return. Fortunately (??) they all like ME.

Ahem!

Pound has agreed to give evidence against Roth. Ford[6] has invited me to be godfather to his daughter (see Shaun's sermon) who is to be baptised a R.C. on Friday next. Svevo has sent me Veruda's portrait of his redheaded wife, Mrs S. (v. Anna Livia: her name is Livia S.). Mrs Jolas is going to U.S.A. Elliot Paul is married. Mr and Mrs Sage[7] are divorced etc. The transition people are beginning to bother me again for the June instalment but I have not energy enough to say yes, aye or no.

I have lost pounds and pounds of flesh. Weigh 8 st. odd which is nothing for one who would be a sixfooter if mangled out so I have to eat oyster, Turkish Delight, Butter Scotch, coal, strychnine, hypophosphates etc etc. Rodker came over. He wanted to publish Pt I and

---

[1] (Translation)

'Dear Schmitz: Upon my return here I found your kind letter. I will gladly accept your gift and may the portrait of Anna Livia bring me both memories and luck. I hope you are successful with Cape and Viking. The first, however, not understanding English, is more to be feared.

Happy Easter to your wife and to you from all of us.   James Joyce'

[2] Valery Larbaud.   [3] Adrienne Monnier.   [4] Stuart Gilbert.   [5] Auguste Morel.
[6] Ford Madox Ford. The godmother was Jenny Serruys Bradley.
[7] Robert Sage (1899–1962), an assistant editor of *transition* and a member of the staff of the Paris edition of the *Chicago Tribune* and then of the *New York Herald Tribune*.

then do a version of A.L.P. which I could not sanction. Now he wants to do a similar bit from Pt III with a preface, as I suggested, by a 100% Englishman. I have not agreed to anything yet as I shall have to talk it over with Miss Beach first. Antheil is gone—to work in the Cyclops' forge, I suppose.

I am not very well. Dieppe was too damp and I have sharp recurrences of pains. The doctor examined me, says I have no inflammation worth talking about but am nervously exhausted. I shall try to get away to 'Tristan da Cunha'[1] as soon as I can. But there is a great difference in the state of my mind since your visit so the spasms are only physical.

As it is Oyster Monday[2] I shall now close up my shell for the evening. With kindest regards sincerely yours   JAMES JOYCE

P.S. Please send back V.L.'s letter.

To HARRIET SHAW WEAVER   MS. British Museum

16 April 1928   *2 Square Robiac, 192 rue de Grenelle*

Dear Miss Weaver: I shall try to get away this week but I can scarcely go leaving the VL-AM mix-up as it is. Here is letter 4 from VL. I cannot find 3. He proposed André Maurois as reviser. I am utterly opposed to any such change. My relations of course are, as always, amicable. We were to have motored down with them and Fargue to Chartres Saturday but it rained too much. The French general elections are coming on which make me nervous like the stalwart hero I am. Ford's child has to be instructed in Xian doctrine, it seems. He offered me a little house he has in Toulon and asked us to dinner. I don't see much use for a sponsor at all if the child (who is a nice little girl anyhow) can remove the devil etc on her own account but I accepted his invitation as an act of friendliness. With kindest regards sincerely yours   JAMES JOYCE

To HARRIET SHAW WEAVER (Postcard)   MS. British Museum

26 April 1928   *Grand Hotel, Toulon (Var)*[3]

Dear Miss Weaver: A line to say I am here by Fr. Ford's[4] advice and am very pleased with it, him and myself. Am sending this off while awaiting mail forwarded from Paris. Kindest regards sincerely yours
                                                          JAMES JOYCE

[1] *Finnegans Wake*, p. 159.   [2] *Ibid.*, p. 407.
[3] The Joyces stayed in Toulon, part of the time in Ford Madox Ford's house, until about 8 May.
[4] Joyce liked to equate Ford with 'Father O'Flynn' in the Irish song, and even wrote two stanzas about him as 'Father O'Ford'.

To HARRIET SHAW WEAVER   MS. British Museum

28 April 1928   *Grand Hotel, Toulon (Var)*

Dear Miss Weaver: I think I have patched up the affair for a while and so am trying to rest a bit here. But transition has sent me a heap of proofs to revise for June and September[1] and Conner a new questionnaire and letter about the copyrighting of the new opus.

The explanation about the Austrian paper is. That Fiera invited me to go to Florence paying expense and my lecture fee to represent Ireland. I wrote declining on grounds of health (in Italian of the most courtly description) and suggested to Paolo Orano[2] that my place be taken by James Stephens concerning whom I wrote a fine panegyric, with the result that the honour was offered to him. Mr Stephens came to Paris and saw me and he accepted it of which I am very glad. As regards Ford and his daughter who, by the way, is named like her mother 'Stella' I shall write as soon as I have waded through a half dozen of my notebooks of revision. With kindest regards sincerely yours

JAMES JOYCE

To HARRIET SHAW WEAVER (Postcard)   MS. British Museum

20 May 1928   *[Paris]*

Dear Miss Weaver: I have returned here to a mountain of proofs, Δ and Λb and c. I am feeling rather lazy about it and will have to give myself some sort of a kick or prod up.[3] Count Shaun MacCormack sings here on Tuesday. I hope you have better weather than ours. Kindest regards sincerely yours   JAMES JOYCE

To FRANK BUDGEN   MS. Yale

27 May 1928   *2 Square Robiac, 192 rue de Grenelle, Paris*

Dear Budgen: On my return from a holiday in Toulon and Avignon I found your article here.[4] I took it to *transition* and it went to press today. I asked them to send you a cheque. I hope you get it soon.

Many thanks. I like it very much. I am sure it will make a good effect. It is all to the point.

[1] In the Summer 1928 issue of *transition* (No. 13) Joyce published *Finnegans Wake*, pp. 429–73. The next instalment came in the February 1929 issue.

[2] Paolo Orano (1875–1945), Italian writer and journalist, and an ardent fascist.

[3] Compare *Finnegans Wake*, p. 470.

[4] Frank Budgen, 'The Work in Progress of James Joyce and Old Norse Poetry,' *transition* 13 (Summer 1928) 209–13. It was included later in *Our Exagmination*, pp. 35–46. See p. 194, n. 1.

I have a lot to do for the next few days or so but will write to you again after no 13 comes out

I found that the oldest vignoble[1] in all Provence is the Clos S. Patrice which it seems was the original name of the wine now known as Chateauneuf du Pape. It is very good. When you next come this side we will drink health in it and other wines. Sincerely yours   JAMES JOYCE

To HARRIET SHAW WEAVER   MS. British Museum

3 June 1928   *2 Square Robiac, 192 rue de Grenelle*

Dear Miss Weaver: Will you please add in whatever you have on your copy of t.12 on the copy sent you on Thursday and tear out the pages and send them back. I am working desperately hard for t.13 as the final revision of Δ took a dreadful lot of time.

I have received two more offers from U.S.A. each of $11,000 in advance of 20% royalties. Not bad for a book which a year ago they called gibberish. t.13 contains an article by Budgen (very good) and one by Gilbert.[2]

Terrible storms here. I think you will like Λb when you see him in full dress. With kindest regards sincerely yours   JAMES JOYCE

To STANISLAUS JOYCE (Postcard)   MS. Cornell

26 June 1928   *[Paris]*

Dear Stannie: We may leave for Copenhagen in a few days.[3] Can you remember if you sent me my Danish Berlitz book? If you did I shall look for it. If not can you send it. It is a grey blue book.

I hope you are both well. Giorgio is down in the Pyrenees at Canterets Saluti cordiali   JIM

To VALERY LARBAUD   MS. Bib. Municipale (Vichy)

26 June 1928   *2 Square Robiac, 192 rue de Grenelle, Paris*

Dear Larbaud: Herewith the explanation. Both your versions of 'rognons etc' are much better.[4] I have asked Miss M. to get you

---

[1] 'Vineyard.'

[2] Stuart Gilbert, 'Prolegomena to *Work in Progress*,' afterwards included in *Our Exagmination*, pp. 47–75.

[3] Joyce did not realize his hope of going to Copenhagen until August 1936. In July 1928 he and his wife went to Salzburg with Stuart and Moune Gilbert.

[4] On 14 June 1928 Larbaud wrote Joyce:

'Two samples of what I am doing for the translation. These are extreme cases, though. Not to be shown, would give useless pain.   V.L.

Text: . . . *he liked grilled mutton kidneys | which gave to his palate a fine tang of scented urine.*

Ruggieri's catalogue. She says you can keep Circe till the rest of the book is sent which will be as soon as possible. She is going to have it printed in Chartres near which her people live so as to be in closer touch with the printer. I think we shall go to Denmark next week but you can always write here if you are in doubt as I shall leave my address. We went to Chartres the other day in Miss B's car i.e. my wife Miss B Miss M and I. I think I came with flying colours through some keen cross-examination by looking more like an idiot than usual. I saw S.G. once or twice and he has written an article on my 'Work in Progress' but A.M. I have not seen for 6 or 7 months, I think, 5 certainly.

I hope your health is good now. My wife says about three times a week, I must reply to that letter in the morning. What will she think of me! etc. She writes about four letters a year preceded each by 3 months of good resolutions. So there you are!

I hope we will soon have dinner all together under the patronage of S. Muscadet de Nantes. Una stretta di mano   JAMES JOYCE

To HARRIET SHAW WEAVER (Postcard)   MS. British Museum

30 June 1928   [*Paris*]

Dear Miss Weaver: Of course you didn't believe I was really finished with Λb for all. This week I have been cabling, phoning, writing express letters etc but at last he comes out Monday, only 31 days behind

---

A. Morel: . . . *il aimait . . . | qui gratifiaient ses papilles gustatives d'un fumet de chaix mâtiné d'un rien d'urine.*'

This is pure journalese, something for 'Moeurs des Diurnales', of the "comme dit l'autre" style.

"Fumet de chaix" is a *cliché*, while "a fine tang" is not. "Mâtiné de," another *cliché*. "d'un rien de" is both *recherché* and facile. The feeble strain of humour in the French sentence is vulgar; of the commercial-traveller sort; the way they talk when they try to talk "well".

I leave "gratifiaient" because it is etymologically right; I accept "papilles gusta-tives", though the expression is a little *prétentieuse*, more "learned" (cheap science) than the simple "palate" of the text, because it gives equilibrium to the French sentence and arrests the reader's attention on that aspect of Mr Bloom's physical life.

The rest I reject, and translate more literally: "d'une belle saveur" (= "fine tang") "un léger parfum d'urine" (= "of faintly scented urine".)

Thus in my interpretation the phrase stands as follows: . . . *il aimait . . . | qui gratifiaient ses papilles gustatives d'une belle saveur au léger parfum d'urine.*

Text: *Kidneys were in his mind as he . . .*

A. Morel: *Il songeait à des rognons tant en . . .*

Of course, this is the meaning, but it is not a literary translation of a literary sentence. The humourous side of the phrase in the text is lost. I translate:

Il avait des rognons en tête tandis qu'il . . .'

scheduled time.[1] I will send you a few shafts of moonlight on some of the duskier bits as soon as the text is released. With kindest regards sincerely yours   JAMES JOYCE

To F. SCOTT FITZGERALD[2]   MS. Princeton

11 July 1928   *2 Square Robiac*

Dear Mr Fitzgerald, Herewith is the book you gave me signed and I am adding a portrait of the artist as a once young man with the thanks of your much obliged but most pusillanimous guest. Sincerely yours

JAMES JOYCE

To STANISLAUS JOYCE (Postcard)   MS. Cornell

31 July 1928   *Hotel Mirabell, Salzburg*

Which S. Johann?[3] There are two near here. S.J. in Tirol and S.J. in Pangon (broken off[4]). Lucia is with the Duncan School[5] in Schloss Klessheim near here—a castle which belonged to Archduke Louis Victor or rather he belonged to it, domicilio coatto.[6] The people here say he was perfectly sane and a Guter Mann and that is family intrigue. Why so late as the 10th.[7] We may stay over a week or so more (8 days already yesterday). It must be easily the finest town of its size (35000) in Europe. We hope to meet you both. Giorgio is in the Pyrenees (Canterets).   JIM

To STANISLAUS JOYCE (Postcard)   MS. Cornell

Postmark 5 August 1928   *Salzburg*

We stay here a week or so more as Lucia is satisfied in the Duncan school. Then go probably to Vienna for a week. What is your address in S. J.? A friend of mine, one of the translators of *U*, Stuart Gilbert is a

---

[1] See p. 177, n. 1.

[2] F. Scott Fitzgerald (1896–1940), the American novelist. At a dinner party in Paris, to exhibit the awe he felt for Joyce, Fitzgerald offered to jump out a window. Joyce was more frightened than flattered, and seems to refer to the incident in this letter.

[3] Stanislaus Joyce, who was to marry Nelly Lichtensteiger on 13 August 1928, suggested to his brother a meeting at S. Johann in Austria, where he planned to take a wedding trip.

[4] Sankt Johann im Pongau. Joyce was not sure of the spelling, and wrote 'broken off' to indicate that the word was incomplete.

[5] Raymond Duncan's school of the dance.

[6] 'Forced residence.' Archduke Louis Victor (1842–1919) was a brother of Emperor Francis Joseph; because of his homosexuality and unreliability, his family obliged him to stay in his castle, Schloss Klesheim, and not leave it.

[7] The marriage was originally planned for a few days earlier.

few miles from there. Gasthof Einsiedeln Kitzbühel. He and his wife are coming on here about the 16th. He is writing a commentary on U.[1] Antheil also. His *Hero and the Cyclops*[2] is to be given at the Cologne Opera in the autumn and we are invited to go. I hope you will visit here.[3] It is worth it.   JIM

To BENJAMIN CONNER (Dictated letter)   TS. Léon

1 September 1928   *Munich*

Dear Mr Conner I have been ill with my eyes the last three weeks and could not write, so I am dictating the present letter.[4]

I was much relieved to receive the copies of parts 10 and 11 of Work in Progress and to know that the copyright of this portion of the book also has been properly taken out in my name in the United States. I hope you have received for this purpose also copies of Transition No 13 (the quarterly); if not, will you kindly ring up Miss Beach.

As regards the suit against Mr Roth, it would be foolish of me to oppose my opinion to that of your partners in New York, but if there is, in their opinion now, no case against him under copyright or property laws and no prospect of recovering any of the money he has probably safely disposed of, gained by misuse of my name and mutilation of my work, I suggest at least that they press for some judgment—nominal damages of one dollar, with an injunction against any further use of my name—which, when recorded, may establish a precedent in case law in favour of unprotected European writers, whose cause in this instance is mine also.

Believe me, dear Mr Conner, sincerely yours   JAMES JOYCE

To STANISLAUS JOYCE (Dictated postcard)   MS. Cornell

Postmark 9 September 1928   *Hôtel Continental, Le Havre*

Can you let me know in what book President Masyrac alludes to Ulysses?[5]

By return, please.

Kind greetings go to Nellie and yourself: not quite recovered yet, so dictating this.   JIM

---

[1] *James Joyce's* Ulysses (London, 1930).

[2] This, like Antheil's commentary on *Ulysses*, was never completed.

[3] James and Stanislaus Joyce and their wives met in Salzburg for several days during August.

[4] Another dictated letter, to Adrienne Monnier and Sylvia Beach, of 3 September 1928, is in Appendix.

[5] Thomas G. Masaryk, *Die Weltrevolution: Erinnerungen und Betrachtungen 1914–1918* (Berlin, 1925), p. 110.

To VALERY LARBAUD   TS. Bib. Municipale, Vichy
(Dictated letter)

[? 7 October 1928]   2 Square Robiac, 192 rue de Grenelle

Dear Larbaud: I suppose Miss Beach told you about my collapse.[1] I cannot see a single word of print and of course am dreadfully nervous on account of it. They are giving me injections of arsenic and phosphorous but even after three weeks of it I have about as much strength as a kitten and my vision remains stationary that is in the dusk with the light behind it.[2] They examined 'all the internal organs of the beast' and his blood pressure and found everything normal except his nerves. Apparently I have completely overworked myself and if I don't get back sight to read it is all U-P up.[3]

I passed on all your corrections with my suggestions to Miss Monnier. Morel I have not seen this long time but I shall write to him if and when I feel a little stronger. He has misunderstood here and there but it would be unfair to lay too much stress upon that in a work of such length and difficulty.[4] I am glad you liked my name for the little priest. I hope you will soon be in Paris so that we can have a chat. Did you get my telegram from Salzburg in time for your birthday—a very beautiful town and the most courteous people imaginable but the climate helped to play havoc with me.

I sent you through Miss Beach a copy of Tidbits with Miss or Mrs Ursula Bloom's advice on when to say yes, which must have amused you. Of course you have read all about Svevo's tragic death.[5] But I don't think he would have lived very long even in the normal course of things as his heart was seriously affected. I am glad we were able to do something for him, a great deal in fact for the German edition must be out by now and an American publisher has cabled for the American rights.

[1] While at Salzburg Joyce suffered a renewal of his eye trouble, but he was able to travel on to Frankfurt, Munich, and Le Havre. Back in Paris in September, he had a serious attack.

[2]   'She may very well pass for 42,
                      In the dusk with the light behind her.'
          The Judge's Song in Gilbert and Sullivan's Trial by Jury (1875).

[3] An allusion to the postcard received by Denis Breen in Ulysses, on which is written 'U. P.: up.'

[4] Joyce felt that Morel's translation was too coarse and violent. 'A little too much Madagascar here.' But he recognized his care and devotion. See his letter to Miss Weaver of 20 September 1928 (Ellmann, James Joyce, p. 616. The text in Letters, ed. Gilbert, p. 266, is abridged.).

[5] Schmitz died 13 September 1928 as a result of injuries sustained when the automobile in which he was being driven struck a tree near Treviso. His wife was also injured but recovered.

Nino Frank,[1] a friend of Bontempelli's[2] of 900, has been commissioned by the Florentine review Solaria to collect opinions for a special number to which you, Crémieux, Goll, Goyert and I are asked to contribute. In view, however, of the ill-timed polemic in the Italian literary press after S's death I think it impolitic that we should do so now at any rate, so I suggested to Crémieux and Frank to have this deferred for three or more months at least until the acrimony has spent itself and they have arrived at the firm conviction that la scoperta Francese[3] is a pure myth after which we shall all be much more amiable and it would not greatly matter who writes or what he writes. Please let me know what you think of this.

Anna Livia Plurabelle, which we read to each other under the sign of the great bear, rue Danau with our field marshall's cocked hats of coloured paper resplendant on our intelligent heads has come out in a limited edition for subscribers but though I have no control over these I have cabled the only begetter[4] to keep one of the reserve copies unnumbered for you if you would like to have it.

My wife joins me in sending all good wishes to Mrs. Nebbia and yourself and let us hope that we shall both be rid of dieting etc. in the near future. With kindest regards,   J.J.

To VALERY LARBAUD   MS. Bib. Municipale, Vichy
(Written in heavy black pencil)

16 November 1928   *Maison de Santé, 5 rue Édouard-Dumont,*
                                                            Neuilly-s/Seine

Dear Larbaud: These few lines to tell you my wife was operated on the 8 and has had now a 7 days radium treatment.[5] All has gone well up to the present. We go home in a day or so and then, after 15 days auto-vaccine treatment return here for 4 days more radium. This ought to

[1] Nino Frank (b. 1904), Italian writer and anti-fascist whose books were proscribed by Mussolini's regime. He has worked for UNESCO in Paris.

[2] Massimo Bontempelli (b. 1878), Italian poet and journalist, with whom Joyce had become acquainted in connection with the review *900*.

[3] Italian critics were slow to accept Italo Svevo's works, and they felt no gratitude for the French enthusiasm for a writer whom most of them had wished to disregard. 'La scoperta francese' ('the French discovery') was still not accepted.

[4] *Anna Livia Plurabelle* was published as a small book by Crosby Gaige in New York on 20 October 1928, at a price of $15. It had a preface by Padraic Colum. Though Joyce's letter speaks of the book as already published, he probably received an advance copy, and the reference to three weeks of eye trouble would make the probable date of this letter 7 October 1928.

[5] Nora Joyce had an exploratory operation for cancer; this was followed by radium treatments which proved ineffective. She returned to the hospital in February 1929 for a hysterectomy.

effect a definite cure. It has been a dreadful fortnight for all of us, however. As regards myself I can see my own handwriting in this black graphite but cannot see one word of any print but capitals!

I think you have not heard the 'prehistoire' to E. M.'s[1] article. He is not 'against us' naturally but feeling is too raw in Italian literary circles to make our intervention at present advisable. *Du reste, qui s'excuse, s'accuse.*

Thanks for your kind inquiries also from my wife.

Pardon this MS. Sincerely yours   JAMES JOYCE

To STANISLAUS JOYCE   MS. Cornell

15 December 1928   *Maison de Santé, 5 rue Édouard-Dumont,*
                                          Neuilly-s/Seine

Dear Stannie: Many happy returns of the 17. Nora was operated here on 8 November and has been undergoing a radium treatment since. She is making some progress. I can write this and almost see it but cannot read a word of print except capitals. Nonetheless am trying to work in this poor atmosphere (I am in the next room to her to keep her company). More anon Kind regards to Nelly and yourself from all   JIM

To FRANK BUDGEN   MS. Yale

[*15 December 1928*]   *Maison de Santé, 5 rue Édouard-Dumont,*
                                          Neuilly-s/Seine

Dear Budgen: Many thanks for your article[2] which Giorgio has just read to me. It is nice and hard like the nuts of Knowledge. I have been having a very anxious time with my wife who was operated here on 8 November last. I am in here to keep her company as the operation and still more the treatment make her highly nervous. She is getting on well these last weeks. As for myself I can write at last as you see but cannot see any print yet, not even my own, alas!

Jeg onsker Dem en glaedelig Jul og et godt Nytår. På gensyn![3]
Sincerely yours   JAMES JOYCE

---

[1] Eugenio Montale, 'La Morte di Italo Svevo: l'ultimo addio,' *Fiera Letteraria* (Milan), 23 September 1928.

[2] See p. 177, n. 4.

[3] (Translation from Danish)
'I wish you a merry Christmas and a happy New Year. Let us meet soon.'

Court Injunction[1]

27 December 1928

INJUNCTION

At a Special Term, Part II, of the Supreme Court, held in and for the County of New York, at the Court House thereof in the Borough of Manhattan, New York City, on the 27th day of December 1928.

PRESENT:

HON. RICHARD H. MITCHELL
JUSTICE.

JAMES JOYCE
             Plaintiff,

—against—

SAMUEL ROTH AND TWO WORLDS
PUBLISHING COMPANY INC.,
             Defendants.

Upon the summons, amended complaint and the answers thereto, the deposition of Samuel Roth, subscribed January 10, 1928, the deposition of James Joyce, taken March 8, 1928, the stipulation between the attorneys for the respective parties and consent of defendants thereto, both dated December 19, 1928, and all other proceedings heretofore had herein:

Now, on motion of Chadbourne, Stanchfield & Levy, plaintiff's attorneys, it is

ADJUDGED AND DECREED that the above-named defendants Samuel Roth and Two Worlds Publishing Company Inc., and each of them, their officers, assistants, agents and servants are hereby enjoined, under the penalty by Law prescribed, from using the name of the plaintiff for advertising purposes or for purposes of trade by

(a) Publishing, printing, stating or advertising the name of the plaintiff in connection with any magazine, periodical or other publication published by defendants or either of them;

[1] From an official photostat.

(b) Publishing, printing, stating or advertising the name of the plaintiff in connection with any book, writing, manuscript or other work of the plaintiff;

(c) Publishing, printing, stating or advertising, or otherwise disseminating the name of the plaintiff in connection with any book, writing, manuscript or other work of the plaintiff, including the book 'ULYSSES', in any issue of Two Worlds Monthly, Two Worlds Quarterly, or any other magazine, periodical or other publication, heretofore or hereafter published by defendants. Enter,

RICHARD H. MITCHELL
Justice of the Supreme Court
THOMAS F. FARLEY.
Clerk.

To HARRIET SHAW WEAVER   MS. British Museum

10 January 1929   *192 rue de Grenelle, Paris*

Dear Miss Weaver: My wife has just been examined by the three doctors and her case pronounced a complete success—one of the quickest and most satisfactory on record. . . .[1]

I am hopelessly overworked and my sight has got rapidly worse. Borsch told me last night that if it did not improve in a week or so that both eyes should be operated. I have not told my wife yet. I am to be seen by some other doctors first. I am very hesitent[2] about these operations and no wonder.

Enclosed are notices for Δ.

I can scarcely see this scrawl but I hope you can read it. I need another week's sight to finish Λc. With kindest regards sincerely yours

JAMES JOYCE

To STANISLAUS JOYCE[3]   TS. Cornell

26 January 1929   *192 rue de Grenelle*

Dear Stannie, Will you please send to Stuart Gilbert, 43 or 45 Avenue Pasteur, Becon-les-Bruyere, Paris, that German book if it is in Trieste,

---

[1] This conclusion was premature. See next page.

[2] The spelling of hesitancy with an *e* instead of an *a* was an echo of an incident often referred to in *Finnegans Wake*, the unmasking of Richard Pigott as a forger of Parnell's writing in 1889 by his misspelling of that word.

[3] This letter was probably typed by Joyce, who was learning to use a typewriter. A few missing letters have been supplied.

about Odysseus he wrote for.[1] Also the partial score of Samuel Butler's
Ulysses,[2] as he needs them both for his book.

I return to the clinic with Nora on the fourth where she has to
undergo another and larger operation which it is hoped and believed
will effect a radical cure, especially after the former results of the former
operation and radium treatment. My reading sight seems to have come
to an end but I was informed that both eyes should be again operated.
This will be operation nine and ten. Nevertheless with the help of about
ten assistants I was able to check the next installment for Transition
which comes out this week. Don't allude to this news about Nora in any
letter reaching me before the fifth proximo as she does not know it yet.

Best wishes to Nellie and kind regards from us all.   JIM

From VLADIMIR DIXON[3]   MS. Buffalo

9 February 1929   *27 Avenue de l'Opera, Paris*

Dear Mister Germ's Choice, in gutter dispear I am taking my pen
toilet you know that, being Leyde up in bad with the prewailent
distemper (I opened the window and in flew Enza), I have been reeding
one half ter one other the numboars of 'transition' in witch are printed
the severeall instorments of your 'Work in Progress'.

You must not stink I am attempting to ridicul (de sac!) you or to be
smart, but I am so disturd by my inhumility to onthorstand most of the
impslocations constrained in your work that (although I am by
nominals dump and in fact I consider myself not brilliantly ejewcatered
but still of above Avveroëge men's tality and having maid the most of
the oporto unities I kismet) I am writing you, dear mysterre Shame's
Voice, to let you no how bed I feeloxerab out it all.

I am überzeugt that the labour involved in the compostition of your
work must be almost supper humane and that so much travail from a
man of your intellacked must ryeseult in somethink very signicophant.
I would only like to know have I been so strichnine by my illnest white

---

[1] Albert Hartmann, *Untersuchungen über die Sagen vom Tod des Ulysses* (Munich,
1917). This book develops the theme of the son in search of the father. It is mentioned in
Stuart Gilbert, *James Joyce's* Ulysses (New York, 1952), p. 352. Another book by
Hartmann, *Magic*, was probably also familiar to Joyce. *Ibid.*, pp. 66, 359.
[2] Samuel Butler set to music a secular oratorio, *Ulysses*, with words by Henry Festing
Jones, shortly before his death in 1902.
[3] This letter, obviously composed if not written by Joyce himself but never acknowledged by him, was delivered by an unknown hand to Sylvia Beach's bookshop. The
address was that of Brentano's bookshop. Joyce urged her to include it in *Our Exagmination* (see p. 194, n. 1) where it duly appeared as the last word, pp. 193–94.

wresting under my warm Coverlyette that I am as they say in my
neightive land 'out of the mind gone out' abd unable to combprehen
that which is clear or is there really in your work some ass pecked which
is Uncle Lear?

Please froggive my t'Emeritus and any inconvince that may have
been caused by this litter. Yours veri tass   VLADIMIR DIXON

To HARRIET SHAW WEAVER (Postcard)   MS. British Museum

Postmark 12 April 1929   [*Paris*]

Dear Miss Weaver: I am very busy revising the fragment and don't feel
at all well, tiredness and intermittent pains. Have you a copy of Blast
II[1] and is it possible to have that Welsh-English dictionary? I hope you
are now back in London. I hope to finish my revision in a week or so.
With kindest regards sincerely yours   J.J.

To HARRIET SHAW WEAVER (Postcard)   MS. British Museum

Postmark 18 April 1929   [*Paris*]

Dear Miss Weaver: Thanks for Blast II but what I want is the English-
Welsh part! The queer allusion to me is in the illustration of that hotel
catalogue of marvels.[2] Have you seen the new number of W.L.'s
Enemy?[3] A lot of it was read to me but I should prefer the book
advertised in *Pearson's W*.[4] 'Want to join the police?' That, at least is
about something. Kindest regards   J.J.

P.S. How small I can write.

    [1] *Blast*, a review edited by Wyndham Lewis, began publication in June 1914 and ceased
with the second issue in July 1915. It was an angry statement of the Vorticist position.
Joyce's interest in *Blast* is probably explained by Lewis's book, *Time and Western Man*
(London, September 1927), which contained a full scale attack upon Joyce. Since the
two men had been friendly, Joyce was surprised as well as offended. Presumably he
wanted to see *Blast* in order to discover with what presuppositions Lewis had started his
advertising career.
    [2] Joyce had heard that his name was mentioned in a pamphlet advertising the Gros-
venor House Hotel, Park Lane.
    [3] *The Enemy* 3 (January 1929) 9–84 contained a long essay by Lewis on 'The Diabolical
Principle', in which he remarked, among other things, on Joyce's 'polygluttonous
volume (always "in progress"—Continuous Present)'. He advised both Joyce and Gertrude
Stein to get out of English and concoct a new tongue to amuse themselves.
    [4] *Pearson's Weekly*.

To Harriet Shaw Weaver (Postcard)   MS. British Museum

26 April 1929   [*Paris*]

Dear Miss Weaver: Giorgio made his debut last night (v. programme).[1]
He had no stage fright and even scowled round on the pianist when the
latter (wilfully, he says) made a mistake. He sang quite well. I am
working night, noon and morning. C. K. Ogden is doing the preface.[2]
G.S.[3] [sic] has sent an article of his *Ulysses* work to the *Fortnightly*
which wished to see it when he, at my suggestion, wrote to W. L.
Courtney (died Nov. '28). E. P. dines with us tonight. More anon. You
will scarcely recognise my fables now. Picasso was too busy to do me so
Brancusi did it.[4] I was awake nearly all last night trying to solve a
problem in elementary mathematics—all this for a word or two. With
kindest regards sincerely yours   James Joyce

To the Editor of *Solaria*[5]

31 May 1929   *Parigi*

Caro collega, la ringrazio anzitutto d'avere avuto il gentile pensiero
d'associarmi al tributo d'omaggio offerto dalla rivista *Solaria* alla
memoria del mio vecchio amico Italo Svevo. E aderisco molto voltentieri
quantunque io creda che ormai la sua sorte letteraria debba rimanere
affidata unicamente ai suoi libri, e che l'emettere guidizi in proposito
riguardi soprattutto i critici del suo paese.

   Mi sarà sempre grato il pensare che il caso m'ha concesso l'occasione

---

   [1] George Joyce made his debut on 25 April 1929 by singing two songs of Handel at a
Concert of the Studio Scientifique de la Voix of Professor George Cunelli.
   [2] Harry Crosby (1898–1929) and Caresse Crosby (b. 1892), the founders of the Black
Sun Press, persuaded Joyce to let them publish a fragment of *Finnegans Wake*. He
arranged for them to do *Tales Told of Shem and Shaun*, to include 'The Mookse and the
Gripes' (*Finnegans Wake*, pp. 152–59); 'The Muddest Thick That Was Ever Heard
Dump' (pp. 282–304); and 'The Ondt and the Gracehoper' (pp. 414–19). When they
thought the book should have an introduction, Joyce proposed Julian Huxley and
J. W. N. Sullivan. Neither of these was available, so he proposed C. K. Ogden (1889–
1957), the inventor of Basic English and co-author with I. A. Richards of *The Meaning
of Meaning*. Ogden accepted the invitation. The book was published in Paris on 9
August 1929.
   [3] A slip for S.G., Stuart Gilbert. The *Fortnightly Review* accepted his essay.
   [4] Pablo Picasso declined the Crosbys' invitation to do a portrait of Joyce for a frontispiece, saying he never did portraits by order. They then approached Constantin Brancusi
(1876–1960), who did a sketch of Joyce which they considered too conventional. When
they asked for another, Brancusi produced a curleycue drawing which he said was a
'Symbol of Joyce' and expressed the '*sens du pousser*' ('the feeling of thrusting') which
he thought a principal characteristic.
   [5] The text is taken from *Solaria* (Florence) IV.3–4 (March–April 1929) 47, where the
letter appears in a section entitled 'Omaggio a Svevo'.

d'aver avuto parte, per quanto minima, alla accoglienza che un pubblico suo e internazionale ha fatto a Svevo negli ultimi anni della sua vita. A me rimane la memoria d'una persona cara e un'ammirazione di lunga data che con gli anni, anziche affievolirsi, matura.

JAMES JOYCE[1]

To SIGNORA LIVIA SCHMITZ   MS. Texas

14 July 1929   *Imperial Hotel, Torquay*[2]

Gentile Signora: La copia che Schmitz mi mandò non era la bella e non sono sicuro di averla perchè mi parlò nella sua lettera della sua intenzione di pubblicare la conferenza[3] in una rivista. Però, non appena tornato a Parigi in settembre, cercherò fra le mie carte. È possibile anche ch'io abbia passato le copie a Miss Beach per il suo archivio in attesa dell'articolo stampato. Ma essa pure è in vacanze, ma gliene parlerò al mio ritorno. Dove si trova la copia dalla quale Schmitz lesse? Non avrebbe potuto leggere quella che mi mandò. Forse la diede al Linati o al Ferrieri? Non mi sembrerebbe inverosimile.

Grazie per i due libri. Non li avevo visti prima.

Saluti cordiali anche da parte di mia moglie dev^mo   JAMES JOYCE

PS. Questa volta ho scritto l'indirizzo *tout court*![4]

[1] (Translation)
'Dear Colleague: I thank you very much for your kindness in associating me with the review *Solaria*'s tribute to the memory of my old friend Italo Svevo. And I willingly consent, although I believe that now his literary fate should be entrusted entirely to his books, and that passing judgement on them should be the concern mainly of critics of his own country.
It will always be pleasant to me to remember that chance gave me an opportunity to have a part, however small, in the recognition that his own country and an international public accorded Svevo during the last years of his life. I retain the memory of a lovable person, and an admiration of long standing that matures, rather than weakens, with the years.   James Joyce'
[2] A letter written from Torquay to T. S. Eliot, of 2 July 1929, is in Appendix.
[3] Svevo lectured in the rooms of the review *Convegno* in Milan on 26 March 1927. A translation by Stanislaus Joyce of the lecture was published by James Laughlin in a private edition (Christmas, 1950).
[4] (Translation)
'Dear Signora: The copy Schmitz sent me was not the final one and I am not sure that I have it, since he mentioned in his letter his intention to publish the lecture in a review. However, as soon as I am back in Paris in September, I shall search among my papers. It is also possible that I passed on the copy to Miss Beach for her archives while awaiting the printed article. She too is on holiday, but I shall speak to her on my return. Where is the copy from which Schmitz read? He could not have read from the one he sent me. Perhaps he gave it to Linati or Ferrieri? This would not seem to me to be unlikely.
Thank you for the two books. I had not seen them before.
Cordial greetings from my wife and myself devotedly   James Joyce
P.S. This time I have written just the address.'

To CARESSE CROSBY (Postcard)   MS. S. Illinois (Croessmann)

Postmark 17 July 1929   *Imperial Hotel, Torquay,*
                                                    England

Dear Mrs Crosby: Before you leave Paris for that well earned rest can
you see that the full number (25 and 25) press and author's copies have
been left with Miss Beach. She was 10 or 13 short when I left
   With kind regards to Mr Crosby and yourself Sincerely yours
                                                      JAMES JOYCE

To GEORG GOYERT (Postcard)   MS. S. Illinois (Croessmann)

Postmark 20 July 1929   [*Torquay*]

Sehr geehrter Herr Goyert: Können Sie mir ein Paar Seiten Ihrer
Ubersetzung ALP. schicken? Hier habe ich, Gott sei Dank, Zeit genug
und möchte sehen ob uberhaupt eine Ubersetzung davon möglich ist.[1]
   Freundliche Grüsse auch an Ihre Frau Gemahlin von uns beiden
                                                      JAMES JOYCE[2]

From EDOUARD DUJARDIN   MS. Buffalo

22 July 1929   *3 rue Notre Dame des Champs, Paris VI*

   Cher et illustre Monsieur Joyce, Je vous remercie de penser à la
traduction des 'Lauriers sont coupés', et je fais immédiatement envoyer
le livre a M. Eric Pinker.[3]
   Ma femme et moi, nous sommes en train d'achever la lecture
d'Ulysse' . . . Que vous dirais-je? si ce n'est ce que je vous disais déja
le jour du déjeuner?[4] le sentiment de nager dans un océan de spiritualité,

---

[1] Goyert's translation of *Anna Livia Plurabelle* did not appear until after Joyce's
death, when it was published in *Die Fähre* (Munich) I.6 (1946) 337–40.
   [2] (Translation)
      'Dear Mr Goyert: Could you send me a few pages of your translation of ALP? I
have some free time here, thank God, and I want to see whether a translation of it is
really possible.
      Friendly greetings, to your wife as well, from us both   James Joyce'
   [3] Joyce's letter to Eric Pinker, his literary agent, about an English translation of
Dujardin's *Les Lauriers sont coupés*, is on p. 192. He informed Dujardin of the plan with
his accustomed deference to the originator of the *monologue intérieur*. Dujardin, who
was grateful for the fame Joyce had brought him in his old age, responded in the same
style.
   [4] Adrienne Monnier's 'Déjeuner Ulysse', a luncheon held to commemorate the publication of *Ulysses* in French in February and also the twenty-fifth anniversary of Bloomsday
on 16 June, took place on 27 June 1929 at the Hotel Léopold in Les Vaux-de-Cernay, a
village beyond Versailles. The guests included Dujardin, Paul Valéry, Philippe Soupault,
Jules Romains, Léon-Paul Fargue, Sylvia Beach, Samuel Beckett, Thomas McGreevy,
George Joyce, and Helen Fleischman.

le même que j'ai éprouvé à vingt ans la première fois que j'ai entendu (sans savoir l'allemand) les quatre journées du 'Ring des Nibelung', c'est-à-dire quelque chose qui fait comprendre ce que les mystiques dénomment la vision en Dieu.

En ma plus fervente admiration,   Dujardin[1]

To Eric Pinker   MS. S. Illinois (Feinberg)

[*About 25 July 1929*]   *Imperial Hotel, Torquay*

Dear Mr Pinker: Mr Edouard Dujardin is sending you from Paris a copy of his book *Les Lauriers Sont Coupés* which, he thinks, might be translated into English. He was a friend of Huysmans, Zola, Manet and of Mr George Moore. First published nearly 40 years ago it went into a second edition in 1924. It has a curious history—told in a preface by Mr Valery Larbaud—with which my name is associated. I hope you may find a London publisher for it. But for the reason above mentioned Mr Dujardin does not wish that it be issued by any publisher who publishes books of mine, either here or in America.

This will be my address (or Euston Hotel, London, after 1 September) for the next two months, I expect, as I am taking a holiday and a rest. Sincerely yours   James Joyce

P.S. Dujardin's address is 3 rue Notre Dame des Champs, Paris VII

To Frank Budgen (Postcard)   TS. Yale

[*? Early August 1929*]   *Imperial Hotel, Torquay*

Let me know when you can if you got the books[2] alright. What you think of Ogden and Brancusi and if you have picked a passage in Alp.[3] You ought to glance at Tomlinsons London River[4] too. Splendid weather down here and hope you have a good holiday.   J.J.

---

[1] (Translation)

'Dear and illustrious Mr Joyce, Thank you for thinking of the translation of *Les Lauriers sont coupés*, and I am having the book sent to Mr Eric Pinker at once.

My wife and I are just finishing *Ulysse*. What can I say, beyond what I said to you the day of the luncheon? The sensation of swimming in an ocean of spirituality, the very one I experienced at twenty when I first heard (without knowing German) the four days of *The Ring of the Niebelungs*, something, in fact, which makes understandable what the mystics call the vision in God. With my most fervent admiration

Dujardin'

[2] Probably *Anna Livia Plurabelle* (New York, 1928) and *Tales Told of Shem and Shaun* (Paris, 1929).

[3] Joyce wanted Budgen to do a painting based on *Anna Livia Plurabelle*, for presentation to Miss Weaver. He chose a passage which, in a later version, became pp. 206–207 of *Finnegans Wake*.

[4] H. M. Tomlinson, *London River* (London, 1921).

James Joyce photographed by Sylvia Beach on Bloomsday, 1925.

Joyce on the 'wild and endless' strand at Scheveningen, Holland, 1927 (p. 159).

Nora Joyce in the 1920s.

cia Joyce (at left) with two other dancers, 1928 or 1929.

Samuel Beckett in Paris, about 1928.

Drawing of Joyce by Wyndham Lewis, 1921.

Joyce painted by Patrick Tuohy in 1924.

Joyce in a drawing by Brancusi, 1929.

drawing of Joyce by his daughter Lucia, about 1930.

Scott Fitzgerald's sketch of a dinner party at Adrienne Monnier's flat. The mermaids at left and right are Mlle Monnier and Sylvia Beach. In between are Lucie and André Chamson, Zelda Fitzgerald, and her husband, who kneels before 'St James' (p. 180, n.2).

Joyce with Stuart and Moune Gilbert.

The Joyces and Lucia (left) with the Gilberts in Strasbourg, 1928.

The 'Déjeuner Ulysse', held at the Hotel Léopold in Les Vaux-de-Cernay on 27 June 1929, with Adrienne Monnier as hostess (p. 191, n.4).

From FRANK CROWNINSHIELD[1] to CARESSE CROSBY   TS. S. Illinois
                                                  (Croessmann)

12 August 1929   *'VANITY FAIR', Graybar Building, New York*

Dear Mrs Crosby, You were truly angelic to send me that interesting
Joyce book,[2] which has just reached me.

Would it be a good idea, perhaps, to use little quotations from it in
Vanity Fair? If so, we should have to explain a few things: first, how
long has Joyce been at this new book,[3] and how soon after Ulysses
(1922) did he conceive it.[4] How long will it be, in words?[5] When will it
be published?[6] Who will publish it?[7] Are the sketches in it to be
consecutive and interrelated?[8] How is Joyce's health?[9] Where is
he?[10]... Yours   FRANK CROWNINSHIELD

To FRANK BUDGEN (Postcard)   MS. Yale

Postmark 15 August 1929   *Royal Hotel, Bristol*

Dear Budgen: Choose any part of 'Proteus' that you prefer[11] but I
doubt that a few well chosen words from A.L.P. *on* the picture itself
not the frame? Here with a glimpse of Sykes' Avenue Kind regards
                                                        JAMES JOYCE

From GEORGE MOORE[12]   MS. Buffalo

11 September 1929   *121 Ebury Street, London, S.W.1.*

Dear Mr. Joyce, When we look back upon our lives, our lives seem
fateful. I never understood why I avoided reading 'Ulysses,' for I was

---

[1] Frank Crowninshield (1872–1947) was editor of *Vanity Fair* (1914–1935). Text from
a typed copy.
[2] *Tales Told of Shem and Shaun* (Paris, Black Sun Press, August 1929).
[3] On a copy of this letter, Joyce answers: '7 years. Since October 1922. Begun at Nice.'
[4] Joyce answers, 'Eight months after publication of *Ulysses*.'
[5] Joyce answers, 'about 2/3 of it has appeared.'   [6] Joyce answers, 'I cannot say.'
[7] Joyce leaves this question unanswered.
[8] Joyce answers, 'It is all consecutive and interrelated.'
[9] Joyce answers, 'Health good enough. Eyes again very weak.'
[10] Joyce answers, 'On holidays in Torquay (Devon) and London.'
[11] For the painting Joyce had commissioned.
[12] George Moore had gone to Sylvia Beach's bookshop one day when Joyce was there,
and afterwards wrote her saying he would have liked to meet him. Joyce arranged a
meeting in London. The two men treated each other with studied politeness, though
Moore's had a slight edge to it. So, when Joyce offered him a copy of the French translation of *Ulysses*, Moore replied, 'I shall be delighted to accept any book you choose to
send me, but I hope you don't mind my reminding you that I can read English.'

curious to read it, and when I was in the Nursing Home somebody whose name I cannot recall at the moment sent me a present of a reading desk, and I wondered what could have put it into his head to send me such a useless piece of furniture. Now I know! I am reading 'Ulysses,' and if you were here for a longer time and could dine with me, we would talk about the French, which I think wilfully exaggerated in places.

Thank you for sending the book; I look forward to reading it all the winter. And I have to thank you, too, for the volume of essays explaining your new work in progress.[1] The best of these seems to me to be by Stuart Gilbert.[2]

Padraic Colum has written a very pretty introduction[3] to the still unpublished work, and I remember him as you remember him at the outset of his career, when everything seemed against him. Very sincerely yours,   GEORGE MOORE

PS I still hope to see you before you return.

To VALERY LARBAUD (Postcard)   MS. Bib. Municipale, Vichy

[? *Late September 1929*]   [*Paris*]

I cannot make out A.B's[4] attitude. Do you ever correspond with him. If *W.inP.*[5] is all wrong why does he for ever return to it? Are you coming to Paris soon?   J.J.

PS. Morel is married.

To VALERY LARBAUD   MS. Bib. Municipale, Vichy

[*20 September 1929*]   *2 Square Robiac, 192 rue de Grenelle*

Dear Larbaud: Have just got back here and hope we meet soon. Is this a good Spanish publisher?[6] Please return it (the letter) and let me know

---

[1] The collection of essays on *Finnegans Wake* by Samuel Beckett, Marcel Brion, Frank Budgen, Stuart Gilbert, Eugene Jolas, Victor Llona, Robert McAlmon, Thomas McGreevy, Elliot Paul, John Rodker, Robert Sage, and William Carlos Williams, published under the title, *Our Exagmination round His Factification for Incamination of Work in Progress*, by Shakespeare and Company (Paris, 1929).

[2] Stuart Gilbert, 'Prolegomena to Work in Progress,' pp. 47–75.

[3] Colum wrote the 'Preface' to *Anna Livia Plurabelle* (New York, 1928).

[4] Arnold Bennett criticized the language of *Anna Livia Plurabelle* in 'Books and Persons', *Evening Standard*, 19 September 1929.

[5] *Work in Progress* (*Finnegans Wake*).

[6] Larbaud, in a letter of 22 September 1929, thought not.

if you approve. What about Gilbert's chapter of his *Ulysses* book for
the *Revue de France*. I suppose you got the *Fortnightly*.[1] Have arranged
for the English translation of *Les Lauriers sont Coupés* with a preface
by George Moore.[2] Kindest regards to both   J.J.

From GEORGE MOORE   MS. Buffalo

11 October 1929   *121 Ebury Street, London, S.W.1.*

Dear Mr. Joyce, I have delayed writing to thank you for sending me the
Italian translation of Yeats's poem from 'The Countess Cathleen'[3] for I
wished to write you a long letter about 'Ulysses.' But there is so much to
be said about the book that I shall have to wait till I meet you in Paris
in the spring. If I began to tell you my doubts about the inner monologue
I should fill three or four pages.

Looking forward to renewing under the skies of our election the
acquaintance begun in London, I am, Very sincerely yours,

GEORGE MOORE

---

[1] With Stuart Gilbert's article, 'An Irish Ulysses: *The Hades Episode*,' *Fortnightly
Review* CXXVI. N.S. 751 (1 July 1929), 46–58.

[2] But see p. 197.

[3] Joyce translated, in collaboration with his Triestine friend Nicolò Vidacovich, both
Yeats's *The Countess Cathleen* and Synge's *Riders to the Sea*. See II, pp. 298, 321–22.
He mentioned the translations to Nino Frank, who wrote Vidacovich to ask if copies
survived. Subsequently the Synge translation was published in *Solaria* IV.9–10
(September–October 1929), 3–16. Vidacovich's letter to Frank, now at Northwestern
University, suggests more precisely the terms of the collaboration, and is here translated:

23 June 1924   *Via Mazzini 13, II.p, Trieste (11)*

'Dear Sir, Your very kind letter of this month afforded me great pleasure, recalling
to me that happy time when James Joyce, not famous as yet, gave me lessons in English and initiated me in the Irish revival, making me acquainted with Yeats, Synge,
and others.

By coincidence, just a few days before I received your letter, I came upon the copy of
Synge's *Cavalcata al mare* (*Riders to the Sea*) which was offered to Sainati. I thought I
remembered accurately that Joyce and I had made the translation together. So please
ask him if that is so, and if it is, my name ought properly to be included too.

As for Yeats, I translated the whole first act of *The Countess Cathleen* into verse with
the assistance of Joyce, who explained the most difficult passages to me. This first act
was sent, as a draft, to the author, who showed it to Antonio Cippico. Cippico, as far as
I can remember, did not dislike the translation, but remarked that he would prefer the
verses to be less literary, as it were, and better suited to be spoken in the theatre.
Meanwhile Linati published his prose translation, and my work stopped there. If it is
of any interest to you, I enclose a draft of my translation.

Please remember me cordially to James Joyce and believe me Yours sincerely,

Nicolò Vidacovich'

To STANISLAUS JOYCE (Postcard)   MS. Cornell

Postmark 13 October 1929   *[Paris]*

Dear Stannie: I think it must be a copy you, I or Eileen gave to someone in Trieste which is in the revue. Meanwhile please send me three
copies in a letter and the new photo and Prezioso's address. The other
copies as you suggest. John Sullivan[1] sends you his regards. He is to
dine with us on Tuesday. Please reply by return.   JIM

To ERIC PINKER   MS. S. Illinois (Feinberg)

7 November 1929   *[Paris]*

Dear Mr Pinker: Many thanks for cheque (£7.9.)
    I saw Mr George Moore before I left London and he told me he would
write a preface for Dujardin's book if you got a publisher for it. Mr
Stuart Gilbert, one of the translators of the French *Ulysse*, has offered
to translate it. Will you please tell me if you have offered it to the
Mandrake Press, 41 Nursery Street, and, if so, whether they will do it?
Sincerely yours   JAMES JOYCE

To CARESSE CROSBY (Telegram)   TS. S. Illinois (Croessmann)

12 December 1929   *Paris*

Deeply shocked by dreadful news[2] please accept my sincere sympathy
                                                   JAMES JOYCE

To JO DAVIDSON (Cablegram)   TS. Library of Congress

3 May 1930   *Paris*

SULLIVAN[3] TRIUMPH DUBLIN ENGAGED COVENT
GARDEN RECORDING COLUMBIA   JOYCE

[1] John Sullivan (d. c. 1958), was a Corkman, of a Kerry family, who at the age of
twelve went to Rouen. He received a musical education and became a leading tenor of the
Paris Opera. Stanislaus Joyce met him in Trieste and was pleased to find him reading *A
Portrait of the Artist*. He wrote his brother and Joyce arranged to meet Sullivan in
Paris. When he heard Sullivan sing in *Tannhäuser*, he became a violent partisan and
spent much time during the next three years in trying to win for his friend the fame he
deserved.
    [2] The suicide of Harry Crosby in New York on 10 December 1929.
    [3] John Sullivan was engaged to sing at Covent Garden on 20 June 1932, but the
arrangement was mysteriously cancelled. The gramophone recording he made for Columbia did not turn out well and was not put on sale, though a few copies of it survive.

From George Moore   MS. Buffalo

10 May 1930   *121 Ebury Street, London, S.W.1.*

Dear Mr. Joyce, My anxiety will be great till I hear from you that the
Swiss oculist[1] promises you the sight of one eye. One eye is quite
sufficient; a man is as well off with one as with two. Now about
Dujardin.[2] I enclose a copy of a letter I have written to him, and hope he
will understand that the human mind is not like a weathercock and
cannot be diverted from one subject to another. I may live for a few
more years, and if I do I shall naturally devote them to my own work.
Moreover, I know nothing of the question which apparently agitates
France, the discovery of the monologue interieure. In England we don't
believe that any discovery has been made. We think, rightly or wrongly,
that the monologue interieure existed from time immemorial.

    With many wishes for your recovery, I am, Very sincerely yours,

GEORGE MOORE

Report of Dr Alfred Vogt on Joyce's eyes[3]

June 1930

REPORT.

Left eye. A ninth operation was performed on this eye for tertiary
cataract by Professor Alfred Vogt at Zurich on the 15th of May 1930.
The growth was cut through horizontally, but the proposed operation
could not be completed as the vitreous body, most of which seems to
have been lost during the last two operations, threatened to collapse
completely by emergence or during the acute attack of Scopolamine
poisoning which immediately followed the eighth operation. The
dangers attendant on the ninth operation were successfully avoided as
was an excessive hemorrhage. Ten days after the operation an attack of
mechanical iritis due to the presence of blood occurred but lasted only
ten hours and did not leave any exudate. A week later leeches were

[1] Professor Alfred Vogt (1879–1943) in Zurich. Several friends urged Joyce, whose
sight was now fading badly, to put himself in Vogt's care, since this ophthalmologist was
known to achieve results which were frequently spectacular. Joyce went to Zurich in
April to consult him, and Vogt promised that the sight of at least one eye would be saved.
Joyce relayed this prognosis to George Moore. (See also letter from Lucia Joyce to Sylvia
Beach, 16 April 1930, in Appendix.)

[2] Moore and Dujardin having been friends in youth, Joyce asked Moore during their
meeting early in September 1929 if he would write a preface to an English version of *Les
Lauriers sont coupés*. Moore consented but now thought better of his decision.

[3] This report, unsigned, is typewritten on the stationery of Georges Borach, a friend of
Joyce in Zurich. A few slips in spelling have been corrected.

applied which successfully removed all the blood from anterior chamber of the eye. On the 3rd of June it became possible to make a microscopic examination. This revealed that the incision made, contrary to what happened in other operations, had remained open and unclogged by exudate but that blood had entered into the vitreous body, which a much operated eye would take some months to eliminate. It also revealed however that at the last operation the back wall of the capsule of the lens had not been removed, possibly because its removal was too difficult and that in the time intervening between the eight and the ninth operation, $1\frac{1}{2}$ years, it had been gradually overclouded so that it is now in a condition of almost *secondary cataract*, thereby occluding practical sight. At some future date which Professor Vogt cannot yet fix a tenth operation (capsulotomy) should be performed.

Right eye. This has not suffered appreciably in consequence of the operation on left eye, it still presents a complicated cataract on which an eleventh operation must ultimately be performed.

General observations.

It has been decided to defer the 10th operation till middle of September 1930. The operation just performed will probably produce a slight amelioration of vision in the left eye, which before had a seeing power of 1/800 to 1/1000. On the other hand the seeing power of the right eye, estimated some month ago at 1/30, diminished constantly but slowly as the cataract developed. The most favorable factor in the case is, that, according to all medical opinions, in both eyes, optic nerve and periphery of the retina functioned perfectly normally. It is also, Professor Vogt believes, that the macula also is *normal* and that is, if the two operations still necessary are made with special instruments and when the eyes are in a non-glaucomatous condition, that there is every hope of obtaining ultimately a fair measure of clear and practical vision.

From NORA BARNACLE JOYCE   MS. British Museum
to HARRIET SHAW WEAVER

Postmark 15 June 1930   *St Gotthard Hotel, Zurich*

Dear Miss Weaver: I could not write till now as the doctor put off testing my husband's sight till this morning. He examined it for nearly an hour and found a great progress in the sight so that, though he would prefer us to remain for a fortnight more so as to observe it he does not want us to have any more hotel expenses and has prescribed temporary glasses and will allow my husband to travel to Paris as soon as these are made. My husband asks you not to speak of his eyes to anyone till I write again.[1] Of course he is greatly disappointed we cannot be with you at Covent Garden for the 20th but he hopes we may be there for the second or last performance of Romeo. He begs you to send him to Paris address Morning Post and Daily Telegraph of Thursday last. Kindest regards from us both   Nora Joyce

From John Sullivan to Jo Davidson   TS. Library of Congress

23 June 1930   *Theatre National de l'Opera, 1 rue Glück, 1, Paris*

Mr. John Sullivan presents his compliments and encloses herewith a copy of a challenge[2] which he is sending to the press.

[Enclosure]
To the Editor 'New York Herald'   *Theatre National de l'Opera,*
1 rue Gluck, 1, Paris

De la Musique avant toute chose . . .

Your musical critic Mr. Louis Schneider, in his notice of the recent performance at the Paris Opera of *Guillaume Tell*, with Mr. Lauri-Volpi in the tenor role, informs the numerous readers of your journal that this was an exceptional performance, such as only a really great artist could have given. As I have, for many years, sustained this part, notably the most difficult ever written for the tenor voice, at the National Academy of Music here, where I am to-day *titulaire du rôle*, I claim the right, under your favor, to state publicly in these columns that Mr. Lauri-Volpi, quite departing from the tradition upheld at this theatre for the last hundred years by all who have preceded him, cut out more than half of the singing part assigned to him by the composer. To be precise, all the arduous recitatives, without one exception, were suppressed. The duet with Tell in the first set was reduced to one third of its length and vocal difficulty, as was the duet with the soprano in the second act and

---

[1] Joyce wanted to keep his recovery secret because he was concocting a publicity stunt to aid his friend, the tenor John Sullivan. On 30 June 1930 he attended a performance of *Guillaume Tell*, with Sullivan singing the role of Arnold, at the Paris Opera; in the middle of it, according to newspaper accounts, 'A sudden hush fell . . . when a man in one of the boxes, whom many recognized as James Joyce, . . . dramatically leaned forward, raised a pair of heavy dark glasses from his eyes, and exclaimed: "*Merci, mon Dieu, pour ce miracle. Après vingt ans, je revois la lumière.*" ' He reported that his doctors had given him permission to take off his dark glasses only during the opera. Sullivan was duly mentioned in the press notices of this extraordinary event.

[2] The challenge, which follows, was apparently written by Joyce, who probably also thought up the scheme of a vocal duel.

the celebrated and trying trio which immediately follows. As if this were not enough, Mr. Lauri-Volpi most prudently avoided the perilous duel with the chorus which was written to form the climax of the whole Opera.

These being the facts, I courteously invite Mr. Lauri-Volpi to sing this part in its entirety and as it was composed by his fellow countryman Rossini and as I myself have sung it over two hundred times throughout France, Belgium, Spain and North and South America, but especially in all the principal cities of Italy. I had, indeed, the honor of being chosen by Mr. Tullio Serafin when this Opera was revived by him at the San Carlo Theatre of Naples in 1923, after a lapse of thirty four years, during which time no tenor had been found in all Italy to sustain the part after the death of the celebrated Tamagno. If Mr. Lauri-Volpi will sing this role, without transpositions or omissions at any Paris theatre or concert hall, where I may be allowed to sing it also, I am willing to accept Mr. Louis Schneider as judge. Nay more, to facilitate him in coming to his verdict, I shall be most happy to present to him an elegantly bound edition of the operatic score, feeling sure that such an eminent musician will welcome this opportunity of becoming re-acquainted with a masterpiece which he would appear to have very successfully forgotten.

Et tout le reste est . . . publicité.[1] Sincerely yours

(Signed) JOHN SULLIVAN[2]

[1] 'And all the rest is . . . publicity.'

[2] The version sent to the French press was a little different, but also reads as if Joyce had written it:

39 rue de Clichy, Paris

DÉFI

De la justice avant toute chose!

Le critique musical du New York Herald à Paris, M. Louis Schneider ayant rendu compte à ses nombreux lecteurs de la représentation à l'opera du Guillaume Tell de Rossini avec M. Lauri Volpi tenant le rôle d'Arnold comme d'une représentation digne d'un grand artiste, je me permets en ma qualité de titulaire depuis des années de ce rôle à l'Académie Nationale de Musique d'affirmer que M. Volpi s'est permis de couper un peu plus de la moitié de son rôle, en supprimant les recitatifs, diminuant le trio et évitant totalement le duel perilleux contre le choeur final. En outre je défie M. Lauri Volpi de chanter ce rôle tel que son compatriote Rossini l'a écrit et comme moi-même je l'ai chanté des centaines de fois dans toutes les villes principales de la France, de la Belgique et de l'Italie même, où cet opéra enseveli à cause du manque du tenor capable de le chanter après la mort du celèbre Tamagno qui le chanta pour la dernière fois en 1889, a été ressuscité pour moi en 1922 au théâtre San Carlo à Naples, sous la direction de M. Tullio Seraphin. Je propose donc à M. Volpi de chanter ce rôle integralement sans transpositions ni coupures dans n'importe quelle salle de Paris où je pourrais le chanter aussi. Je laisse comme arbitre des deux executions M. L. Schneider lui-même auquel j'offrirai pour cette occasion un exemplaire de la parution originale de cet opéra élegamment reliée, convaincu du reste qu'un amateur de musique comme il semble l'être ne pourra trouver que fort agréable de refaire connaissance directe avec un chef d'oeuvre qu'il semble avoir en grande partie oublié.   (Signé) John Sullivan

To Valery Larbaud (Postcard)   MS. Bib. Municipale, Vichy

28 July 1930   [*England*]

Dear Larbaud This is one of the first p.c's I have been able to write for about 2 years.[1] I hope you have better news to send me Cordialement votre   James Joyce

To Stanislaus Joyce (Postcard)   MS. Cornell

3 August 1930   *Randolph Hotel, Oxford*

Herewith W. Pater's photograph.[2] I can write this but scarcely see it.
                                                                      Jim

To Herbert Gorman (Postcard)   MS. S. Illinois (Croessmann)

2 September 1930   *Hotel de la Plage, Étretat*

H.C.E.[3] was sent to you c/o your banker, Haymarket. Has Colum answered yet?[4] Please ring up my hotel after 10 p.m. and get address of Charles Stevens, night porter.[5]   J.J.

To Harriet Shaw Weaver   MS. British Museum

6 September 1930   *Étretat, Les Golf Hotels*

Dear Miss Weaver: Herewith the cheque with many thanks. My money was wired to Dover while we were crossing to Calais. Miss B. left Paris and it took a long time to get it back. Paris was a furnace so we left after 4 days but I had time to arrange about the 2nd Czech edition of *U.* and the first of A.L.P. I hope you got the former and also S's record through Schwarz.[6] I suppose you saw H.H.'s note in the *Daily Telegraph* the Monday after we left.[7] I should like 2 copies of it. I managed to get Antheil's setting of *Nightpiece* and sent it on to him.[8] All will go well if

[1] A postcard to Sylvia Beach of 18 July 1930 is in Appendix.
[2] Really the knocker on the main gate of Brasenose College, Oxford, in the shape of a distorted face with a swollen (brazen) nose.
[3] *Haveth Childers Everywhere.*
[4] Gorman had asked Colum to help him with information for his life of Joyce.
[5] Joyce wished to send the night porter a copy of *Ulysses*. See p. 206.
[6] See p. 209, n. 3.
[7] This had to do with *The Joyce Book*, a book of Joyce's poems with the musical settings by different composers, which Herbert Hughes was editing. It was not published until March 1933, by the Sylvan Press and Oxford University Press in London.
[8] George Antheil's setting of 'Nightpiece' in *The Joyce Book*.

John does not hold up the plan.[1] Tuohy, who painted my father and me, has just committed suicide in New York. We shall remain here only a few days more. It is a charming spot and we have had 9 days of unbroken sunlight so that my lumbago has almost gone but I hear they had ghastly weather all July and August.

Yes, we escaped that Paris thunder storm, thank goodness. I hope you are able to read this. My pen keeps running along on the offchance that you will be able. When in Paris I started a subscription for Sage[2] but as his father has come along with aid that is over which saves me a lot of work. The poor fellow has now pleurisy as well.

With apologies for this scrawl and kindest regards sincerely yours

JAMES JOYCE

P.S. The manager and cashier of the *Lord Warden* hotel at Dover are great admirers of mine and accompanied us down to the boat. Here it is the same, the manager being one Ramon Joyce, a member of a Portugese-French branch of the family.   J.J.

To JAMES B. PINKER   MS. S. Illinois (Feinberg)

9 September 1930   *Étretat (S.I.), Les Golf Hotels,*
                                      'La Plage' & 'La Rotisserie'

Dear Mr Pinker: I agree on condition that A.L.P. is published before the 31 December next.[3] But please ring up T. S. Eliot at Faber and Faber's on the proposal as also about his plan of publishing H.C.E. in the same miscellany.[4] This should appear before the end of February 1931 as the fourth and final fragment[5] is to be published in an *edition de luxe* as usual first in Paris in April next. These fragments from what reviewers call *Work in Progress* really have no title but for convenience' sake a few words taken from the text have been put on the title page.

I wrote all this letter with my own hand and can even make out the words but I hope it is legible to others Sincerely yours   JAMES JOYCE

[1] Augustus John was to do a drawing to serve as a frontispiece to the book.

[2] Robert Sage.

[3] *Anna Livia Plurabelle* was published by Faber & Faber as Criterion Miscellany No. 15 on 12 June 1930. Joyce is perhaps referring to the third reprint of this booklet, which took place in October 1930.

[4] *Haveth Childers Everywhere*, Criterion Miscellany No. 26, was published by Faber & Faber on 8 May 1931.

[5] Joyce may have had in mind *The Mime of Mick Nick and the Maggies*, which, however, was not published until 1934. But it is more likely that at this time he planned to publish a *Chapelle D'Izzied* fragment; see p. 209.

To Mrs Herbert Gorman   MS. S. Illinois (Croessmann)

5 October 1930   *192 rue de Grenelle, Paris*

Dear Mrs Gorman I return with this A.S.'s[1] letter and enclose one from my Scotch cousin[2] who may be yours also. My wife wants to know if you could see the place she writes of so that we might form an idea about price etc. Her idea now is to have a summer residence in London so as to avoid the hundreds of pounds I spend yearly in hotel bills there. I cannot get any satisfaction about that A.L.P. disc and I wish Mr Gorman could bring the matter up in conversation if and when he meets T.S.E.[3] The idea was Ogden's but he is now quite off it and a sale of 5 discs a year is absurd.[4] I hope you are over your indisposition by now. Sullivan will sing *Guillaume Tell* for the last time at the opera on 8 and 17 instant. Is it likely you can come. I have put off my Zurich operation till after that. At last I got Beecham and Lady Cunard into the theater last week to hear him.[5] B told me after the opera it was the most amazing tenor voice he had ever heard and that he would do all he could for him in London. Thank Mr Gorman for his letter. I can write this but not see it well and I hope you can read it. My eyes were not injured in the taxi crash,[6] thank goodness. Kindest regards to you both from 4½d[7]   J.J.

To James Stephens (Postcard)   MS. Donald Gallup

6 October 1930   *192 rue de Grenelle, Paris*

Dear Stephens: I hope you got the A.L.P. disc I sent you *safely*. Perhaps you could see Ogden (address Royal Societies' Club). He and T. S. Eliot have some scheme about making records of writers. The H.M.V. factory is not progressive enough. You ought to read or speak some of your work or perhaps we can still manage our 2-sided disc. Sullivan had a delirious reception in Marseille Sincerely yours

JAMES JOYCE

[1] Arthur Symons. He agreed to write an 'Epilogue' to *The Joyce Book*.
[2] Unidentified.   [3] T. S. Eliot.
[4] Joyce recorded the last pages of *Anna Livia Plurabelle* for C. K. Ogden at the Orthological Institute in London during August 1929. Sales were disappointing.
[5] Joyce's intricate manoeuvres to persuade Sir Thomas Beecham to attend *Guillaume Tell* when Sullivan was singing the role of Arnold are described in Ellmann, *James Joyce*, pp. 638–40.
[6] Joyce was in a taxi crossing the Esplanade des Invalides in September 1930 when a private car ran into it. 'I was flung violently forward and then as violently back but escaped any glass in the eye. I had a big bump on my forehead and a bad pain in my back, but the doctor who examined me said there was no internal injury.' *Letters*, ed. Gilbert, p. 294.
[7] See p. 205.

To Herbert Gorman   MS. S. Illinois (Croessmann)

11 October 1930   *192 rue de Grenelle, Paris*

Dear Mr Gorman: Please thank Mrs Gorman for kindly visiting that house but from the description of the entrance it would not suit. I return P.C.'s[1] letter but nothing of the kind I suggested seems to have been done. I enclose 4 letters, one to Sullivan, three to me which will show what I have been doing. I was with Kahn[2] at the opera this week, with Beecham last week and as you see Richard Guinness[3] is coming over for the last performance. If you are coming wire me beforehand. The Scala of Milan yesterday invited Sullivan to sing *Guillaume Tell* there in the full version which Lauri-Volpi cut by half and also *Tannhauser*. He goes to Lyon, Marseilles and Barcelona for a few months and then the Paris opera is reviving *La Juive* for him in February.

Please send me back these letters by return though you may copy them if you wish—they are themselves copies. Have you got your copy of H.C.E. Babou[4] has the receipt from the P.O. It was sent registered two months ago c/o your banker. We hope to see you both over here.

Our kindest regards to you both in the meantime. Sincerely yours

JAMES JOYCE

To Herbert Gorman (Cablegram)   TS. S. Illinois (Croessmann)

13 October 1930   *Paris*

GUINNESS PREVENTED FROM COMING THEN SEATS FREE
WIRE IF YOU WISH ME RETAIN   JAMES JOYCE

To Mrs Herbert Gorman   MS. S. Illinois (Croessmann)

22 October 1930   *192 rue de Grenelle, Paris*

Dear Mrs Gorman: Do you know a Scotch shop in London which sells plaid ties? If so I should like you to buy me one and send it. The plaid I prefer (I think it is the Murray) has a lot of red in it as a ground and of

[1] Padraic Colum. He agreed to write a brief essay, 'James Joyce as Poet,' for *The Joyce Book*. Gorman acted as intermediary in making the request.

[2] Otto Kahn (1867–1934), American financier and patron of the arts, especially of music, whom Joyce was endeavouring to interest in Sullivan.

[3] Richard Guinness (b. 1888), Irish industrialist and patron of the arts.

[4] *Haveth Childers Everywhere* (eventually pp. 532–54 of *Finnegans Wake*) was published by Henry Babou and Jack Kahane in Paris and New York in June 1930.

course blue and white and yellow all over it. They made me buy a suit to go to Zurich in and I can't find here a tie such as I want.

Augustus John came here I think on Friday and I am to sit for a week so it seems we shall have left for Zurich when you come. You missed something on Friday night which you cannot ever have heard in your life and will never hear again.[1] We were so sorry you were not with us.

With many thanks and kindest regards to you both. Sincerely yours

$4\frac{1}{2}$d[2]

To HARRIET SHAW WEAVER   MS. British Museum

22 October 1930   *192 rue de Grenelle, Paris*

Dear Miss Weaver: . . . The 3rd French *Ulysse* comes out on the 15.xi. Sullivan has gone away for 4 or 5 months and I began to write the 2nd part[3] on Sunday last—but with what labour! It is always like that when I start a fresh bout. I have exchanged my old machine for a Remington portable and hope to learn how to use it myself.[4] I sent the letters off to the Abbey Theatre. We had another letter from Dr Tibbles.[5] If his *Vi-Cocoa* still exists I would like to have a packet of it. There is one last copy of *Music and Letters*[6] I would like sent to my brother Stanislaus, whose address is 6 via Cesare Battisti, Trieste.

I hope you are well. How long are you staying in London? My lumbago is quite gone but I can't sleep at night. With kindest regards sincerely yours   JAMES JOYCE

P.S. I should like you to *enquire only* if copies of *Apes of God*[7] are to be had and at what price.

---

[1] That is, John Sullivan singing in *Guillaume Tell*.

[2] See p. 203.

[3] Joyce was now writing the first chapter of Part II (*Finnegans Wake*, pp. 219–59).

[4] He did make some progress with it.

[5] Dr Sydney Granville Tibbles (1884–1960), an ophthalmologist in London. Joyce humorously confused him with the Dr Tibbles who recommended Vi-Cocoa and is mentioned in *Ulysses* and *Finnegans Wake*.

[6] A friend of Joyce in Paris, Edgardo Carducci, published an article, 'The Tenor Voice in Europe,' in *Music and Letters* XI. 4 (October 1930) 318–23. In the course of it he praised John Sullivan, saying among other things, 'I owe it to Mr. James Joyce if I have been able to understand a voice like that of Mr. Sullivan, the most remarkable tenor of our generation and perhaps the only one which can be called a genuine survivor of those golden ages. . . .' He attributes to Joyce also the idea that Sullivan's voice is a kind of synthesis of the principal developments in the tenor tradition.

[7] *The Apes of God*, by Wyndham Lewis, was first published in a limited edition by the Arthur Press in London, June 1930.

To HERBERT GORMAN   MS. S. Illinois (Croessmann)

28 October 1930   *192 rue de Grenelle, Paris*

Dear Mr Gorman: Please thank Mrs Gorman very much for the Scotch
plaid ties, one of which I will wear for the portrait if Augustus John
allows me. A copy of *Ulysses* was sent in the French F.O.[1] bag in care of
Mr Poliakoff (whom you can ring up after Wednesday) 49 Queen's Gate
Gardens. Before you leave London may I trouble you to fetch it and
give it to the night porter of the Euston from me, explaining the delay
as the diplomatic courier is not always available. He is on duty only
from 10.30 p. m. and his name is Charles Stevens.

The enclosed has just come from Ogden. Will you read it quickly and
pass it on to T.S.E, asking him to return it to me at once. I wish to know
whether F & F's scheme has dropped (as seems to be the case) before
replying to C.K.O.

In great matutinal haste and with my thanks Sincerely yours
                                              JAMES JOYCE

To HERBERT GORMAN (Postcard)   MS. S. Illinois (Croessmann)

30 October 1930   *Paris*

Dear Mr Gorman: If there are two copies of *U* at Mr Poliakoff's the
unsigned one is for the porter. To see whether it is signed or not he
should slip off the tirage[2] band without breaking it and the chemise[3] and
replace afterwards. A. J.[4] started my portrait a few days ago with that
highly treasonable Stuart royal tie.[5] Kind regards   JAMES JOYCE

To SIGNORA LIVIA SCHMITZ   MS. Texas

25 November 1930   *Carlton Elite Hotel, Zurich*

Dear Mrs Schmitz: I am here again seeing prof. Vogt about my eyes
but he cannot operate them at present owing to their state and that of
the weather here so that I must come back in the spring for a very
difficult operation on the right eye.

I am writing to your friends in Paris to telephone me there after

---

[1] Foreign Office. *Ulysses* could not be sent by ordinary mail.
[2] A paper band indicating which printing of *Ulysses* this copy was.
[3] Wrapper.   [4] Augustus John.
[5] One of the ties sent him by Mrs Gorman.

Saturday and shall explain to them what my idea is about the preface
to Schmitz's book.[1]

I hope you are quite well and all the other members of the family.

With friendly remembrances also from my wife. Sincerely yours

JAMES JOYCE

To GEORGE ANTHEIL (Postcard)   MS. David Diamond

Postmark 25 November 1930   [*Carlton*] *Elite Hotel, Zurich*

Have been visiting my oculist here, prof. Vogt but operation is put off
till spring. Herbert Gorman and I are at work pruning Act I of *Cain*[2]
for you[.] Go ahead in the meantime. Will write you more on my return
to Paris on Saturday   JAMES JOYCE

To STANISLAUS JOYCE (Postcard)   MS. Cornell

Postmark 26 November 1930   *Elite Hotel, Zurich*

Are here for a few days to see Vogt who has put off operation till spring.
My sight has slightly improved. Kind greetings from all   JIM

To MICHAEL LENNON[3]   MS. S. Illinois (Croessmann)

27 November 1930   *Carlton Elite Hotel, Zürich*

Dear Mr Lennon, I suppose you have seen about the treasury grant for
opera. I sent a great deal of material to Mr Snowden[4] and I think this is
now the moment for you to try the persons you suggested. If attention
be made to our friend in the press his stage name 'Sullivan' by which he
is known abroad should be used in preference to his real name which
often confuses readers as they think of Denis O'Sullivan. I also think
his Christian name may be dropped. Nobody ever uses Enrico or
Giacomo when alluding to Caruso or Lauri-Volpi and Sullivan is a 'divo'.

I have been here consulting my doctor who finds I have made progress
but postpones operation till the spring owing to the bad weather so I am
returning to Paris today. Sincerely yours   JAMES JOYCE

[1] After Schmitz's death in 1928, Joyce wrote his widow offering to do what he could to
further Schmitz's literary reputation. She asked him to write a preface for an English
translation of *Senilità*. See pp. 213, 241.
[2] Joyce urged George Antheil to compose an opera based on Byron's *Cain* with
John Sullivan in the title role.
[3] Michael Lennon (b. 1891), now a retired Irish District Justice.
[4] Philip Snowden (1864–1937), who became Viscount Snowden, a government
minister with an interest in music.

From DR ALFRED VOGT   TS. Private

1 December 1930   *Zürich*

Hochverehrter Herr Joyce! Besten Dank für Ihren freundlichen Brief.
Ich freue mich sehr, konstatieren zu können, dass das Ergebnis meiner
Operation schon jetzt ein erfreuliches ist, und dass die neue Pupille, die
ich setzte, sich noch weiter vergrössern wird. Die Hauptsache ist jetzt,
dass Sie sich keiner Erkältung aussetzen, damit nicht ein Rückfall der
Iritis eintritt.

Ich kann dann später zunächst die Entfernung des Stars des *rechten*
Auges in Angriff nehmen, und schliesslich—unter allen Vorsichtsmass-
nahmen—das Nachstarhäutchen des linken Auges spalten, sofern dies
noch nötig erscheinen wird.

Mit herzlichen Grüssen und Wünschen Ihr   VOGT[1]

To HARRIET SHAW WEAVER   TS. British Museum
(Typed by Joyce)[2]

22 December 1930   *192 rue de Grenelle, Paris*

Dear Miss Weaver First of all I wish you a happy Xmas. You know
part of the news. My wife and daughter-in-law are[3] at present on the
most affectionate terms. We were at the marriage which was private but
her stupyd lawyer forgot to insert at the mairie the clauses of the
contract of separation des biens which by my son's request had been
made a few days before so that my son becomes by French law the
monarch of all he surveys. I enclose another letter from Hughes who is
going farther every time. He means well but I am in a very awkward
position with Milhaud[4] and Jarnach[5] whom I have to meet tonight at a
concert not to speak of Antheil who, it seems, at Pound's suggestion is

---

[1] (Translation)
   'My dear Mr Joyce, Many thanks for your friendly letter. I am very happy to be
able to state that the result of my operation is already favourable and that the new pupil
which I put in will enlarge itself further. The main thing now is that you should not
expose yourself to any colds, so that iritis will not recur.
   Then later I will be able to begin first the removal of the cataract from the *right*
eye, and finally, with all due precaution, the splitting of the post-cataract membrane of
the left eye, insofar as this may still be necessary.
   With cordial greetings and good wishes Yours   Vogt'
[2] Joyce's typing errors have been preserved.
[3] George Joyce married Helen Kastor Fleischman on 10 December 1930. Nora Joyce
at first disapproved of the marriage because of a disparity in age, but soon grew fond of
her daughter-in-law.
[4] The composer Darius Milhaud (b. 1892).
[5] Philipp Jarnach (b. 1892), French-born conductor and composer, whom Joyce had
met in Zurich during the first World War.

backing out of Byron[1] and wants me to write a new peppy libretto for him. I wired refusing and sending him a polite ultimatum either to go ahead with my adaptation or let me hand it over to Stravinsky to which he has not yet replied. Mrs Colm has started a scheme with an American publisher for the issue of a Joyce anthology under which I am to get 10,000 dollars she swears but in the meantime the man who at Colm's suggestion has just brought out an edition de luxe of my essay on Mangan with a preface by C.[2] having got wind of Schwarz's[3] unauthorised first edition of the same is coyly declining to cable the stipulated (9000 francs. I had no end of trouble between Faber and Faber and Babou and Kahane. By an oversight of Miss Beach's I signed over to the latter the exclusive rights for H.C.E. so that I had to hold F and F's book[4] due this week but got permission to bring it out in April by giving B and K an option on the next fragment. I am still suffering from insomnia which is a dreadful bore and I will not be able to complete the first draft before the end of the year if even then. Gorman is engaged on a biography of me for which I have to supply him copiously with information and I am also trying to explain to Miss Monnier's sister[5] who knows no English the text of Chapelle D'Izzied (the next fragment)[6] for which she is to do a hieroglyph preface. Also I have to help Colm with his preface for Hughes's[7] book besides assisting at the seances of the French translation of A L P.[8] Things are in a bad mess here on account the the banco-political scandal and my royalty reserve dropped with a bang just when wedding, Xmas and New Year announced themselves so that I have to realise another £100 immediately and would be greatly convenienced if M and S[9] could advance me half of it the moment they enetter [sic]

[1] The opera Joyce had urged George Antheil to write, with Byron's *Cain* as libretto. But he refused to edit the text in any way except to suggest small excisions, and would not allow his own name to appear on the programme. Pound advised Antheil that the subject was impossible.

[2] This edition has not been traced.

[3] Jacob Schwartz, proprietor of the Ulysses Bookshop (London), published *James Clarence Mangan* on 7 March 1930, in an edition of 40 copies not intended, as he informed Joyce, for sale.

[4] Faber & Faber published *Haveth Childers Everywhere* on 8 May 1931, Babou and Kahane having published their edition in Paris, at the Fountain Press, in June 1930.

[5] Mme Paul Bécat (Marie Monnier), an artist and weaver.

[6] This did not appear.

[7] *The Joyce Book*, ed. Herbert Hughes (London, 1933). Padraic Colum's essay, 'Joyce as Poet,' is on pp. 13–15.

[8] Samuel Beckett (b. 1906) and Alfred Péron (d. 1945) began to translate *Anna Livia Plurabelle* into French late in 1930. When Beckett had to go back to Ireland, Paul Léon, Eugene Jolas, and Ivan Goll revised their work under Joyce's supervision. Philippe Soupault was also enlisted later, and Adrienne Monnier as well. The final version was published in the *Nouvelle Revue Française* XIX.212 (1 May 1931) 633–46.

[9] Monro, Saw & Co.

their office after the Yuletine alltoobrief respite from me. Sullivan has caused delirium in Marseille and has left to sing at the San Carlo of Naples, probably the greatest lyrical theatre in the world but the dunderheads of Covent Garden are still dozomg over him. I hope you got safely his new disc I sent you. One side is poora and the other only fair as . . . is a wretched firm but of course S. wanted the money and took this offer. Will you please return H8s letter to Miss Beach?

This machine is my new toy and that's my weakness now[1] but the big one I gave Miss Monnier in exchange for it is the bane of her life. My eyes being tired I shall now stop. thanks for so promptly returning letter for Colm who wanted it.

With renewed good wishes of a crispnessnice and kindest regards. sincerely yours,   James Joyce

From Louis Gillet   MS. Buffalo

7 January 1931   *17 rue Bonaparte*

Cher Monsieur J'ai été bien touché de voir que vous aviez gardé le souvenir de mon vieil article[2] sur votre *Ulysse* et que vous aviez la bonté de ne me pas m'en témoigner de rancune.[3] Je reconnais avec regret que cet essai n'était pas entièrement sympathique. J'ai beaucoup réfléchi depuis, ou plutôt votre ouvrage s'est installé dans mon esprit et y a fait son domicile : j'en mesure mieux l'importance et l'interêt extraordinaires. Je suis loin de le 'classer' encore, mais je sais bien qu'il occupe une place dominante dans la littérature anglo-américaine, et peut-être dans la littérature universelle, depuis dix ans. Je ne puis m'empêcher de reconnaître la valeur d'un phénomène.

J'ai eu l'occasion de revenir incidemment plusieurs fois sur le sujet, peut-être avec plus de justice que je n'avais fait tout d'abord. Mais je me propose depuis longtemps de faire mieux si je puis et de profiter pour cela des divers ouvrages qui ont été édité sur vous (en particulier ceux de R. E. [sic] Curtius et de Gilbert Stuart [sic]). Je voudrais commencer par le problème que pose votre nouveau poème, le terrible problème du langage, ou plutôt de l'individualisme de l'expression : la refonte totale de tous les éléments de l'esprit, la manière dont vous avez pour faire

---

[1] An allusion to the popular song, 'Yes, Sir, That's My Baby.'

[2] Louis Gillet, '*Littératures Ètrangères. Du Côté de chez Joyce,*' *Revue des Deux Mondes* (Paris) Seventh Period, 95th year, 28 (1 August 1925) 686–97.

[3] Joyce had considered the article useful even though hostile, because any attention from this august review was of value. See p. 74. He met Gillet early in January 1931 at a reading of Edith Sitwell's, and received Gillet's apologies for his earlier article with good grace.

apparaître dans la forme des mots des milliers d'associations, pour créer une musique nouvelle, une sorte de *fieri* à la mesure du *cosmos*. Cette tentative m'étonne autant qu'elle me séduit. J'y ai beaucoup réfléchi déjà mais avant de rien entreprendre je voudrais m'assurer d'être d'accord avec vous; j'aimerais de lire avec vous quelques pages du *Work in Progress*.

Je pars ce soir pour quelques jours, je vous demanderai un rendezvous à mon retour. Je bénis Miss Sittwell [sic], quoique je goûte peu son *rubbish*, et je bénis surtout la bonne Sylvia Beach, puisque j'ai eu grâce à elle la fortune de vous rencontrer, et de vous rencontrer indulgent et magnanime.

Veuillez agréer cher Monsieur l'assurance de mes sentiments de dévouement et de vraie admiration.   Louis Gillet.[1]

To Valery Larbaud   TS. Bib. Municipale, Vichy
(Typed by Joyce)

10 January 1931   *192 rue de Grenelle, Paris*

Dear Larbaud I rang up the hotel at S.Malo and they told me you had left for Paris.If you are really here can we dine any night this coming week at the Trianons with Arnold Bennett?[2] He is at the Marignan and very desirous of meeting you again after so long as am I too.

---

[1] (Translation)
'Dear Mr Joyce, I was deeply touched to see that you had remembered my old article on your *Ulysses* and that you were kind enough to bear me no ill will on account of it. I recognize with regret that this essay was not entirely favourable. I have thought about it a good deal since then, or rather your work has settled itself in my mind and made its home there: I am better able to measure its extraordinary importance and interest. I am far from "classifying" it yet, but I am well aware that for ten years it has held a dominant place in Anglo-American literature and perhaps in world literature. I am unable to avoid recognizing the value of a phenomenon.

I have had occasion to take up the subject several times in passing, perhaps doing it more justice than I did at first. But I have intended for some time to do better if I could and certainly to profit from the various works which have been published on you (especially those of R. E. Curtius and Gilbert Stuart). I should like to begin with the problem posed by your new poem, the terrible problem of language, or rather of individuality of expression; the total recasting of all the elements of the mind, the way you have of bringing into the form of words thousands of associations, of creating a new music, a sort of *becoming* on a cosmic scale. This endeavour astonishes me as much as it beguiles me. I have thought about it considerably already but before undertaking anything, I should like to be sure of being in agreement with you; I should like to read with you a few pages of *Work in Progress*.

I am leaving tonight for a few days, I shall ask you for an appointment on my return. I bless Miss Sitwell although I derive little pleasure from her "rubbish," and I bless especially good Sylvia Beach, since, thanks to her, I had the chance to meet you and, when I did, to find you indulgent and magnanimous. With devotion and sincere admiration,   Louis Gillet'

[2] Joyce had not despaired of winning over Bennett to his cause. See p. 194.

Herewith are a few pages of the French A.L,P. which may amuse you. Please bring them along.

Ihope you are well. I have not slept decently for a long time and my sight seems to have become temporarily much worse.

With kind regards sincerely yours   JAMES JOYCE

From VALERY LARBAUD   MS. Buffalo

20 January 1931   *71 rue du Cardinal-Lemoine Vᵉ*

Dear Joyce, Thanks to you and to Mrs Joyce, in the name of both of us, for those beautiful flowers. We received them on the first day my wife was able to leave her bed. She is much better now, but I cannot say the same of myself; and my last interview with my doctor left me under the impression that he was growing pessimistic about me.[1]

I hope you are better, and able to work. I wish I could see you. Toutes nos amitiés,   V. LARBAUD.

From JOHN STANISLAUS JOYCE   MS. Cornell

31 January 1931   *25 Claude Road, Glasnevin, Dublin*

My dear Jim I wish you a very happy birthday and also a bright and happy New Year. I wonder do you recollect the old days in Brighton Square, when you were Babie Tuckoo, and I used to take you out in the Square and tell you all about the moo-cow that used to come down from the mountain and take little boys across?[2]

I will write to Georgio in a few days, when he returns from his honeymoon.[3] I see by the photo that he too wears glasses? I suppose he needs [them] but if possible he should not use them. I hope Lucia's sight is all right, give her my fond love and also to Nora. I often hear from Mr Healy, who's generous gifts I should be glad if *you* would also acknowledge. Again, my dear boy, may God bless you is the prayer of Your fond and loving   FATHER

---

[1] During the nineteen-thirties Larbaud became progressively paralysed and never recovered his health.

[2] 'Once upon a time and a very good time it was there was a moocow coming down along the road and this moocow that was down along the road met a nicens little boy named baby tuckoo.' These are the first words in *A Portrait of the Artist*.

[3] See p. 208, n. 3.

To Jo Davidson   TS. Library of Congress

8 February 1931   *192 rue de Grenelle, Paris*

Dear Davidson, I enclose the original with translation of the Genoese and Neapolitan notices of Sullivan which you kindly promised to forward to general Dawes[1] with a covering note of your own. I understand from Sullivan that the Chicago Opera of which General Dawes is a patron is in search of renors [tenors] for the coming season. I hope these notices may bring about as they should Sullivan's engagement. Many thanks to you in any case for what you have tried to do. Sincerely yours.   James Joyce

To Signora Livia Schmitz   TS. Fonda Savio

11 March 1931   *192 rue de Grenelle, Paris*

Dear Mrs. Schmitz: I enclose a letter from my friend Mr. Ford[2] which please return to me when read. Will you see that the publishers communicate with him as soon as possible. He is very well known in America and his introduction ought to be of great help.

If Mr. Herbert Gorman who is writing my life has written to you, you may reply to him if you feel inclined to do so, as he has my authorisation. If my brother who lives at number 6 via Cesare Battisti has a telephone, can you please ring him up? He has also been written to by Mr. Gorman but has not replied and my son sent him about ten days ago a very extraordinary letter which had been forwarded to me from some person who calls himself Gianni Corte, living in Via del Teatro Vecchio, Capodistria who seems to be either a madman or a blackmailer or a practical joker or all three combined.[3] My brother was asked to have this matter investigated but he has not replied to that either. The letter was addressed to me in a wrong name somewhat like my own and

---

[1] Charles Gates Dawes (1865–1951), Vice-President of the United States 1925–29, Ambassador to the Court of St James 1929–32. He was a Brigadier-General. Dawes, who played the piano and composed a little, was an active patron of the Chicago Grand Opera Company.

[2] When Signora Schmitz asked Joyce to write a preface to *Senilità* in an English translation by Beryl de Zoëte, Joyce dictated a reply to his daughter (*Letters*, ed. Gilbert, pp. 298–99), explaining that he never wrote prefaces or gave lectures or interviews. Moreover, a preface by him would damn the book because his present style of writing was considered by readers in England and America to be '*una vera senilità*' (a true senility). He proposed instead that Ford Madox Ford would be qualified to write a preface both by his reputation and by his being 'of a certain age'. Joyce promised to do his best to have the book prominently reviewed and to arrange for its translation into other European languages. Ford was agreeable but Signora Schmitz declined. Eventually Stanislaus Joyce wrote a preface describing his brother's enthusiasm for Schmitz's novels.

[3] Gianni Corti proved to be insane.

to my publishers also wrongly spellt at an incorrect address, but the french post managed to deliver it. Will you therefore please ask my brother or if he is too busy my sister-in-law to let us have a letter as soon as possible.

With kind remembrances from us all, and best wishes for the success of 'As a Man Grows Older' sincerely yours   James Joyce

To Herbert Gorman   TS. S. Illinois (Croessmann)

[*? 19 March 1931*]   [*Paris*]

Dear Gorman, I enclose two letters just received. The letters from the two Italian solicitors I have sent on to Paul Bourget. Will you please ring me up when convenient? I hope you were not too fatigued by the last supper.[1] I hope at least that it was an unbloody sacrifice, however unnecessary, on your part. Sincerely yours   James Joyce

To Michael Lennon   TS. S. Illinois (Croessmann)
(Typed by Joyce)

29 March 1931   *192 rue de Grenelle, Paris*

Dear Mr Lennon, I am moving from this address on the 10-th prox. qnd hqve been so busy that I have not hqd time to reply to your kind letter.In the intervql between the first qnd second communication from Mr Fitz Gerald[2] I sent on to General Dawes copies of Sullivan's recent Genoese and Neapolitan notices with typed english translation.It so happens that the Russian American sculptor Davidson is doing his head and mine at the same time for s show in London in June. I cannot find General Dawes's letter, either I sent it om to Sullivan and he has not returned it or he has returned it and I have packed it up in one of my numerous cases of books. anyhow his attitude was much more help-ful than that of the British ambassador here or the Irish minister.He said he had written personnally to Insul[3] forwarding him the papers and asking him to investigate qnd if possible take up Sullivan's case. Of course if more pressure can be broughtt to bear through Mr Vincent[4] so much the better. My warm thanks for all the trouble you have taken, Sincerely yours   James Joyce

[1] A letter of late March 1931 from Herbert Gorman to Joyce (a copy of which is in a private collection) helps to date this letter. He says in part: 'The supper on Saint Patrick's Day tired me but not too much. I was all right the next day. It was the first time I was up and out and the mere idea of freedom exhausted me as much as anything else.'

[2] Desmond Fitzgerald.

[3] Samuel Insull (1859–1938), utility magnate, whose principal cultural interest was the Chicago Civic Opera.

[4] Unidentified.

To HARRIET SHAW WEAVER   MS. British Museum

11 April 1931   *Hotel Powers, 52 rue François 1ᵉʳ, Paris*

Dear Miss Weaver: This holy Saturday ceremony began at 8 a.m. and ended at 2 p.m.[1] These few lines are just to let you know our address. I had a bad night but think I am beginning to feel somewhat rested. I hope your crossing was a smooth one. It is useless to discuss my present condition with Miss Beach. As she does not know what my motive is [a blot here]

(That was the hotel pen that interrupted) she naturally regards my acts in a wrong light and has no idea of what I have to face in the way of expenses over there. I shall think the matter over more carefully as regards dates as soon as we or rather my wife is rested and I am better. With kindest regards sincerely yours   JAMES JOYCE

To VALERY LARBAUD   MS. Bib. Municipale, Vichy

13 April 1931   *Paris*

Dear Larbaud: My son is now married as perhaps you know and my flat has become too noisy of late years so I have given it up, stored my things and am leaving Paris till late in the autumn when I shall come back and rent a much smaller one. I hope you are better by now and that it may be possible for us to meet (if not to dine though *purtroppo*[2] I too am on a regime after [a] miniature collapse) before [I] leave in the next few days.

Kindest remembrances to Mrs Larbaud and yourself from us both
                                                JAMES JOYCE

P.S. I have quite a different opinion about the Svevo preface.[3]

To STANISLAUS JOYCE   MS. Cornell

14 April 1931   *Hotel Powers, 52 rue François 1ᵉʳ, Paris*

Dear Stannie: The telegraphic address is on top. Please wire me the word 'yes' or 'no' if you have received a *second* letter from Gorman and again the same word rispettivamente whether you agree to his proposal to have the letters or passages you deem most important copied at his

---

[1] Joyce refers to the move from their flat at 2 Square Robiac, 192 rue de Grenelle, to the Hotel Powers. He intended to spend six months in England and to establish permanent domicile there. Miss Beach evidently felt that the move was a mistake.

[2] 'Unfortunately.'

[3] Larbaud wrote Joyce on 15 March 1931 that Signora Schmitz had written him two long letters asking him to persuade Joyce to write a preface for *Senilità*. He hoped Joyce 'could give her this satisfaction'.

expense at once and forwarded to him here: address: Hotel Place de l'Odéon, Place de l'Odéon, Paris.[1] I never promised Schmitz or his wife any such thing.[2] I do not write prefaces. I hope the ceremony of the 26 will be a crowning affair for whenever I mentioned S's name to any of my semi-literate pupils they laughed in my face. Will you please get the information Giorgio asked for *re* Corti and his brother as soon as possible and send it to him so that the *prefecture de police* here may send orders to the frontier?[3] I am sorry you share his opinion of my recent writings.[4]

Am leaving for England in a day or two when I recover from a nervous breakdown I had. Permanent address: 12 rue de l'Odéon, Paris. I shall explain my plans later. I am not coming back to Paris probably till late autumn.

Kindest regards to Nellie and yourself.   JIM

To STANISLAUS JOYCE   MS. Cornell

15 April 1931   [*Paris*]

Dear Stannie: Another Triestine lunatic turned up last night in the person of Bruno Veneziani.[5] His sisters and Eileen also told me he was in a madhouse. He says he has just come to Paris to stay and study something and has just given a concert in Milan. He wants advice etc, letters of presentation to Gide, Milhaud etc. I feel inclined to give them. He seems normal enough socially at least, and it would make up for the *prefazione mancata*.[6] Please add a word yes or no to your wire as I leave here in a day or so. In haste   JIM

---

[1] Stanislaus Joyce sent copies of most of his letters from his brother to Herbert Gorman. They are now in the Croessmann collection at the Southern Illinois University Library.

[2] Literally true, but Joyce had written Signora Schmitz on 24 September 1928 (*Letters*, ed. Gilbert, p. 270), 'Please remember me if at any time my help can serve to keep alive the memory of my old friend for whom I had always affection and esteem.'

[3] Corti had said in his letter he would kill Joyce, so the frontier police were to be instructed not to let him enter France.

[4] Stanislaus Joyce had written his brother, 'With the best will in the world I cannot read your work in progress. The vague support you get from certain French and American critics, I set down to pure snobbery. What is the meaning of that rout of drunken words? It seems to me pose, the characteristic you have in common with Wilde, Shaw, Yeats, and Moore. You want to show that you are a superclever superman with a superstyle. It riles my blood to see you competing with Miss Stein for the position of Master Boomster. But whereas she never had anything to lose, you have—knowledge of what you write, breadth, sanity, and a real style, which was a registering instrument of rare delicacy and strength.' (MS. Buffalo)

[5] A talented but erratic brother of Signora Schmitz.

[6] 'The missing preface,' which Joyce had declined to write to *Senilità*, published under the title *As a Man Grows Older* (London and New York, 1932).

To HARRIET SHAW WEAVER   MS. British Museum

17 April 1931   [*Hotel Powers, Paris*]

Dear Miss Weaver: I shall begin my fifth hegira[1] on Sunday[2] and hope
to arrive in London Whittington-like that evg. (w.p.).[3] Will you please
retain rooms for us at Garland's (Lucia comes too). If detained at
Calais I shall countermand by wire. I am a good deal better and only
wish I could stay at this inn for another week. With kindest regards
sincerely yours   JAMES JOYCE

P.S. I suppose I may have mail sent to your address for a day or so?

To ROBERT MCALMON   MS. Pearson

27 April 1931   *Hotel Belgravia, Grosvenor Gardens,*
                                          Victoria, London S.W.1

Dear McAlmon: It will be all the better if you can arrange with a good
American house like the Putnam you mention or Lippincott because
then Curtis Brown could arrange simultaneously at this side. He thinks
the subscription a very good idea to cover large advertising and also
because the book[4] is so long (E.P. says it is 1½ *Ulysses*) and times so bad.
I thought from our telephone talk that you agreed as for yourself if need
be. I have also got one of the best agents in London whom I have just
seen, Curtis Brown, 6 Henrietta Street, Covent Garden, to take the
matter in hand. He is sending me a letter to him which I am to sign and
he will send copies of this letter to those who are invited to join in the
list. Can you send him the address of MacLeish and Brancusi, with the
Christian name of the latter. He is writing at once to E.P. for the MS.
I hope this is all right. The person I saw at Curtis Brown's is a Mr
Pollinger[5] who knows E.P. well and is, I think, quite trustworthy. He
proposes the firm of Martin Secker. Sincerely yours   JAMES JOYCE

P.S. If you go away from your present address let him have some
permanent one to write to.   J.J.

---

[1] His other trips to London since 1920 were in 1922, 1923, 1927, and 1930.
[2] 19 April 1931.
[3] 'Weather permitting.'
[4] Ezra Pound's *Cantos*, which had not yet found a commercial publisher. McAlmon was
doing his best to help.
[5] Laurence Edward Pollinger (b. 1898), then with Curtis Brown and now head of a
literary agency of his own, Laurence Pollinger Ltd.

From ANDRÉ GIDE   MS. Buffalo

30 April 1931   *Cuverville au Caux*

Cher Monsieur Quelle émotion de recevoir une lettre du grand Joyce! J'ai écrit aussitôt à Mr Bruno Veneziani mes regrets de n'être pas à Paris présentement et de devoir remettre à un peu plus tard le plaisir de le rencontrer. Ah! que je serais heureux de pouvoir vous y revoir également! Vous me laissez fort incertain de votre adresse, mais, après avoir balancé plusieurs jours, je me décide à confier ce mot à notre amie Sylvia Beach—ne voulant pas vous laisser ignorer combien se réjouit d'apprendre que vos yeux vont sensiblement mieux votre admirateur attentif et affectueux   ANDRÉ GIDE.[1]

To EZRA POUND (Typed by Joyce)   TS. Pound

7 May 1931   *Hotel Belgravia, Grosvenor Gardens, London*

Dear Pound I had another talk with Mr Pollinger of Messrs Curtis Brown's yesterday.He seems to me to be a sincere wellwisher of yours and I hope you will send him the Ms and leave it in his hands for a few months, allowing him to shape the scheme I suggested to him as he thinks best.He believes it will be a help in view of the length of your book and the state of the market and would ensure extensive advertising by a trustworthy firm.

I wrote a long express letter to Mrs Dyer[2] asking her to send invitations to Miss Rudge[3] and you for her evening and telling her about your Villon opera[4] but my daughter-in-law does not say that you were there.MRS Dyer8s telephone number is ;Trocadero 12,o4.

---

[1] (Translation)
'Dear Sir What a pleasure to receive a letter from the great Joyce! I wrote at once to Mr Bruno Veneziani of my regret at not being in Paris and at having to defer for a little while the pleasure of making his acquaintance. It would be delightful indeed if I might see you then as well. You leave me very uncertain of your address, but after hesitating for several days I have decided to entrust this note to our friend Sylvia Beach—not wishing to let you be unaware of how much the news that your eyes are definitely better delights your attentive and affectionate admirer   André Gide'

[2] Mrs Louise B. M. Dyer, Australian patron of music. She founded the Lyre Bird Press in Paris 'for the purpose of publishing rare or little-known musical works in fine editions', including the works of Couperin and Purcell.

[3] Olga Rudge, American musician and a long-time friend of Pound.

[4] Joyce urged Mrs Dyer to stage Pound's opera, *Villon*. This work has never been published in its entirety, but parts of it appeared in *Townsman* (London) I:2 (April 1938) 12–18, and *New Directions in Prose and Poetry* III (1938) (Norfolk, Connecticut).

YOU Mentioned Manon.There is a very good tenor Gerard singing this at the Trianon Lyrique. He sings the Ah fuyez, douce image with great effect.PERHAPS YOU COULD GO WITH Gorman. heterodaktylographically yours   JAMES JOYCE

To Mrs May Joyce Monaghan   MS. Yale

11 May 1931   *28B Campden Grove, Kensington, London*[1]

Dear May: I hope you and yours are well. I have rented this flat till 25 Sept. when we go back to Paris. Will you please let me know by return of post whether you received a letter from Mr Herbert Gorman asking you questions in connection with the biography of me he is writing.[2] It is important for me to know this at once. My sight is a little better. I can write, as you see, and walk with prudence but alas! cannot read.

Kind greetings from Nora Lucia and myself   JIM

To Stanislaus Joyce   MS. Cornell

12 May 1931   *28B Campden Grove, Kensington, London*

Dear Stannie: The above address will find me even if we go away till 25.ix when we return to Paris. I want to know have you sent the connotatoi[3] of Mr Corti and his redentissimo[4] brother to Giorgio and have you sent me the press report of Cav. Pasini's speech[5] and is it safe for me or Giorgio to recommend Rosso Veneziani[6] to people in Paris. His two sisters, Mrs Schmitz and Mrs Bliznakoff, told us with deep sighs that he was hopelessly off his head. If Mrs S. told you I promised to write a preface for any book of I.S. she lies.[7] When I see Cav. P's

---

[1] The Joyces settled at this address about 10 May, intending to return to it each year.

[2] Herbert Gorman began work on his authorized biography of Joyce in December 1930. (See letter to Gorman, 27 January 1931, in Appendix.)

[3] 'Official description.'

[4] The extreme opposite of irredentist; hence, in this context, reactionary.

[5] At a ceremony in honour of Schmitz which took place on 27 April 1931. Ferdinando Pasini (b. 1876) was an Italian critic.

[6] Bruno Veneziani had red hair.

[7] See p. 207, n. 1, and p. 213, n. 2.

discourse I shall see his publisher here who has written me several times. Did you get H.C.E. and the N.R.F. ?[1] Salve!   JIM

To Jo DAVIDSON   MS. Library of Congress

13 May 1931   *28B Campden Grove, Kensington, London*

Dear Davidson: We have this place here for the summer months but will probably go to Bournemouth either in June or July before returning to Paris in the autumn.

My agent, Mr Ralph Pinker, who says he knows you heard you did my head and asked me to ask you if he could have a photograph of it. I am simply passing on this request without comment.

Is there any news from General Dawes or from Otto Kahn? Sincerely yours   JAMES JOYCE

To STANISLAUS JOYCE   MS. Cornell

22 May 1931   *28B Campden Grove, Kensington, W.8, London*

Dear Stannie: Have you sent the description of Corti to Giorgio and the whereabouts, if known, of C's brother? Have you sent me the *Piccolo* for the 27 April[2] and is it possible to have a few Triestine papers about the 'vision' affair?[3]

I am making this short so that you may read it while running from one son of an italo to another. Best greetings   JIM

To DESMOND HARMSWORTH[4]   MS. Harmsworth

17 June 1931   *28B Campden Grove, Kensington, W.8*
                                                   Tel. Western 1966

Dear Mr Harmsworth: From the enclosed letter it would seem that you are looking for me in connection with the publication of Pound's book which I have been trying to arrange. If this is so perhaps you can ring me up here some morning? Sincerely yours   JAMES JOYCE

---

[1] *Haveth Childers Everywhere* and the French translation of *Anna Livia Plurabelle*. The latter appeared in the *Nouvelle Revue Française* XIX.212 (1 May 1931) 633–46.

[2] On 26 April 1931 a bust of Ettore Schmitz, executed by the Triestine sculptor Giovanni Meyer, was officially presented to the city of Trieste and placed in a public garden.

[3] Probably a news report about Joyce's recovery of his sight.

[4] Desmond Harmsworth (b. 1903), painter and publisher.

To DANIEL BRODY   MS. Brody

26 June 1931   *28B Campden Grove, Kensington, W.8*

Dear Mr Bródy: Many thanks for your friendly joint card of good
wishes for Bloomsday. I am answering it through you because I want to
thank you also for your flowers last year on the same date. And also I
wish to ask a favour of you. Will you please destroy the record I sent you
of Sullivan in *Guillaume Tell.* I sent out about twenty of these without
having heard them and now that I have heard them I find them atrocious.
Such a record can do him only harm and I am trying to avoid that by
asking my friends to destroy them.

  Please give my kind regards to Mrs Bródy Sincerely yours
               JAMES JOYCE

To PADRAIC and MARY COLUM   MS. N.Y. Public Library
                    (Manuscript)

18 July 1931   *28B Campden Grove, Kensington, W.8*

Dear Colm and Mrs Colm: ... As regards your kind Dublin offer I
cannot make up my mind to cross the second channel. My sight is too
weak. I have not enough funds even if I draw these advances. I have not
a friend in Dublin on whom I could rely. Please thank your sister.
Perhaps if you were here we might talk it over. And too much publicity
was given that Kensington ceremony.[1] It was very thrilling when the
registrar refused to function saying we should go and get divorced but
after production of lawbooks by my solicitor he did the deed. While I
was signing the roll the King was signing the new law the English call
the Marry-Your-Aunt Bill.[2] He should now sign a Marry-Your-Wife
Bill Sincerely yours   JAMES JOYCE

To STANISLAUS JOYCE   MS. Cornell

18 July 1931   [*London*]

Dear Stannie: The *Piccolo* does not contain either in report or Pasini's
speech any allusion to the telegram I sent that morning or to your

---

[1] Joyce and Nora Barnacle were married on 4 July 1931 at the Registry Office in
Kensington. To avoid talk he concocted a story of a previous marriage, but the journalists
and photographers gave embarrassing publicity to the ceremony.
 [2] The Marriage (Prohibited Degrees of Relationship) Bill made legal the marriage of a
man with his deceased wife's niece by marriage and of a woman with her deceased
husband's nephew by marriage. It was passed by the House of Commons in May and by
the House of Lords in July, and received Royal Assent on 31 July 1931.

presence among the professors or to Larbaud and Miss Monnier or to myself.[1] Whoever eventually writes the preface to *Senilità* should mention that fact.[2]

Thanks for your wire. The other branches of the family (Paris excepted) expressed consternation. I had offered my nephew George[3] who is workless £1 a week if he would help me with my notes from 2 to 5 pm every day but his stepmother (he is 21) took from him the *Exagmination* I had lent him and we were given to understand that our influence etc etc. The Press Association by the way but particularly the *Sunday Express* made a most spirited attempt at blackmail but funked it at the end, the rumour having gone around that I had come in for a big sum which would enable me to fight them for libel. The affair as you know is as clear as mock turtle.[4] Having eloped with my present wife in 1904 she with my full connivance gave the name of Miss Gretta Greene which was quite good enough for il Cav. Fabbri who married us and the last gentleman in Europe il conte Dandino who issued the legitimate certificates for the offspring, but this full connivance voided the marriage in the eyes of English law see Hargreave's[5] Laws of England page 471–2 and the second ceremony was thought advisable to secure the inheritance under will. I have a slight cough this morning so please forgive me if I now desist.

With best Xmas wishes to Mr and Mrs Joyce from Mr and Mrs Ditto MacAnaspey[6] and here's jumping that bucket as Tinker said to his gipsy[7] I remain, dear professor, matrimonially yours

MONICO[8] COLESSER[9]

From HARRIET SHAW WEAVER to JOHN SULLIVAN   MS. Sullivan

19 July 1931   *74 Gloucester Place, London, W.1*

Dear Mr. Sullivan, Mr. Joyce has asked me to write to you once again for him, to give you his address—28b Campden Grove, Kensington, London, W.8—and to say that he has had so much worry and business the last two months that he prefers not to write to you himself just now or his family would imagine he was launching another crusade on your

---

[1] At the ceremony in honour of Ettore Schmitz on 26 April 1931. See p. 220, n. 2.
[2] Stanislaus Joyce did so in the Introduction, p. xii.
[3] Son of Charles Joyce.
[4] See p. 221, n. 1.
[5] Really Halsbury's.
[6] A catch phrase of Joyce's father, meaning simply 'ditto'.
[7] Traditional gipsy marriage ceremony.   [8] See p. 439, n. 8.
[9] An absurd teacher of German at the Berlitz School in Trieste.

behalf which would wear him to a shred several degrees more threadlike than even his present appearance makes.

He has spoken to many people here about you and has come to the conclusion that there is nothing further to be done with regard to Covent Garden or the Carl Rosa company. One possibility, however, of a different nature has occurred to him, but he would like your opinion of it before making any move in the matter. It is this. He has made the acquaintance of the high commissioner of Ireland—Mr. Dulanty[1]—a great admirer of his—and has talked to him a great deal about you and, with your permission, would like to make the following suggestion to him. It is the last string he can think of to pull in your interests. Would you, if it were possible to organize here a small Franco-Irish contingent of influential people to subscribe between them a sum of, say, £700 as a guarantee to Mr. Lionel Powell against possible eventual loss if he were to engage—under the patronage of the high commissioner and the French ambassador—the Queen's Hall, London, for two nights in October or November for two performances of *Guillaume Tell* in concert form if Sir Thomas Beecham could be got to redeem a part of his word and conduct the orchestra—if that could be done would you, Mr Journet[2] and Mr Gromen[3] be available to come over for these performances which might be looked upon as a belated centenary?

The minor parts could be filled from here and as regards the soprano Mr. Joyce has met a Mrs. Malcolm (Australian) who sang for several years in Italy under a stage name and whose husband is a cousin of Mr. Hugh O'Niel[4] of the Ulster parliament who might also be got to patronize the affair. Mr. Joyce himself would have nothing to do with it beyond setting it going. He has spoken to several critics, including Mr Hughes[5] and Mr Newman[6] and they have promised to write the performance up.

As Mr Dulanty is leaving on holiday within a week Mr Joyce begs you to answer by return—to himself at the address given above. Yours sincerely   HARRIET WEAVER

---

[1] John Whelan Dulanty (1881–1955), High Commissioner of Ireland in London, 1930–50.

[2] Marcel Journet (1867–1933), French bass.

[3] A French baritone.

[4] Sir Hugh O'Neill, Baron Rathcavan (b. 1883), Speaker of the House of Commons of Northern Ireland, 1921–29, and M.P. for Ulster, 1922–50.

[5] Herbert Hughes was music critic of the *Daily Telegraph*.

[6] Ernest Newman (1868–1959), the biographer and music critic, wrote for the *Sunday Times*.

To IVAN GOLL[1]   MS. Goll

30 July 1931   28B Campden Grove, Kensington, W.8 (Angleterre)

Cher Monsieur Goll: Nous avons ici le reçu de la poste pour le disque
envoyé recommandé. On croît que la censure l'a suivi et que c'est inutile
d'envoyer un autre.

Maintenant aussi à Francfort la *Frankfurter Zeitung* du 19 juillet
publie une page entière de texte de J. J., auteur d'Ulysse, traduite du
manuscrit anglais par Irene Kafka. Qui est-elle? Où a-t-elle trouvé ce
manuscrit que le journal m'attribue? Je l'ignore. Je ne la connais point.
Je n'ai jamais écrit cette sotte nouvelle qui s'appelle *Vielleicht ein
Traum*.[2]

Je n'ai jamais été en correspondance avec la Frankfurter Zeitung.

Vielleicht ein Traum aber bestimmt eine Schweinerei. Cordialement
votre   JAMES JOYCE[3]

To JONATHAN CAPE   MS. S. Illinois (Feinberg)

30 July 1931   28B Campden Grove, Kensington, W.8

Dear Mr Cape: It was very unfortunate that I intruded on you as I did
today. I had not heard of your sad news. We both have a pleasant
memory of our meeting with your amiable and kind wife in Paris. Please
accept our sincere sympathy.[4] Sincerely yours   JAMES JOYCE

To GEORG GOYERT   MS. S. Illinois (Croessmann)

31 July 1931   28B Campden Grove, Kensington, W.8

Dear Mr Goyert: As you are my official translator in Germany voilà
une histoire pour vous.[5]

[1] From a typewritten copy.

[2] The *Frankfurter Zeitung* published on 19 July 1931 a translation by Irene Kafka of a
story, 'Perchance a Dream,' by Michael Joyce, originally published in the *London
Mercury*. The newspaper attributed it to James instead of Michael Joyce, and to James
Joyce the 'error' appeared disingenuous.

[3] (Translation)

'Dear Mr Goll: We have kept the postal receipt for the disc sent by registered
mail. It has probably been stopped by the censorship and it is useless to send another.

Now in Frankfurt, too, the *Frankfurter Zeitung* of 19 July has published a whole
page of text by J. J., author of *Ulysses*, translated from the English manuscript by Irene
Kafka. Who can she be? Where has she found this manuscript which the newspaper
attributes to me? I know nothing of it. I do not know her at all. I never wrote that silly
story which is called *Vielleicht ein Traum*.

I have never communicated with the *Frankfurter Zeitung*.

Perchance a Dream but definitely an outrage. Cordially yours   James Joyce'

[4] Jonathan Cape's second wife, Oliva Viola James Cape, had just died.

[5] 'Here is a story for you.'

Joyce with the tenor John Sullivan.

David Fleischman,
Helen Joyce's
son by her first marriage.

Helen Kastor Fleischman, who
married George Joyce on 10
December 1930.

Helen Fleischman, George, Nora, and James Joyce, Paul Ruggiero,
and Frau Borach, in Zurich after Joyce's eye operation, May 1930.

Joyce, Paul Léon, and C. P. Curran in Paris.

Lucie Léon, about 1930.

Paul Léon.

A recent photograph of Mrs Maria Jolas.

Maria and Eugene Jolas with their daughters Betsy and Tina and a Russian governess, in 1932.

B. W. Huebsch, Joyce's American
publisher, in a late photograph.

Joyce with Philippe Soupault, one of his French translators.

Joyce with Augustus John, 1930 (pp. 205-206).

The Joyces with their solicitor, on the day of their marriage in London, 4 July 1931.

Joyce and his wife in the 1930s.

The Frankfurter Zeitung (19 July 1931) published *Vielleicht ein Traum*, a fragment by J.J. author of *Ulysses*, with an editorial note to say it is translated from the English MS by Irene Kafka.

I do not know either the editor or Irene Kafka. I never had any such MS. and I never wrote the text or anything like it.

??? Sincerely yours   JAMES JOYCE

PS. I have nobody to read your handwriting here so please reply by typed letter.   J.J.

From STANISLAUS JOYCE   MS. S. Illinois (Croessmann)
to HERBERT GORMAN

8 August 1931   *Via Cesare Battiste 6, Trieste*

Dear Mr. Gorman, I enclose a small sheaf of letters representing, so far as I can judge, about one tenth of the letters to be copied. The work goes on very slowly. I don't type and have no typewriter myself, but a friend of mine, who has a fair knowledge of English, has kindly helped so far. As he finds my brother's handwriting difficult to read, I dictate and he types. In this way a rather long letter of 6–700 words takes an hour and a half, ten long postcards take three hours. I have given practically all my spare time to this job and to the far less pleasant one of sorting the letters out of a heap in a mouldy old packing-case.

I have received an offer to do the work from an Englishman. He offers one shilling per thousand words, so that the present enclosure would cost about 8/-. If this suits you—plus postage and expenses—the whole thing could be done in a couple of weeks. I shall be glad if you will let me know as soon as possible. I have not the faintest notion what the usual typing expenses are, but I am sure my friend's charges would not be excessive.

As for the matter of the letters, there are three cycles: matter of Rome, matter of Pola, matter of Trieste—like the old romances. *Matter of Trieste:* While Jim and his family were in Dublin I moved 'carefully and horizontally' into a smaller, newer cleaner flat, instead of bothering about legal actions and so on. My brother has still illusions about the law. When he returned to Trieste after the collapse of his hopes of getting anything he might write published in Dublin, he lived in the new flat—via Donato Bramante 4—until the outbreak of the war, working sanely and soberly and living more comfortably than ever before. He finished 'The Portrait of the Artist', wrote 'Exiles' and planned and began 'Ulysses.' At the beginning of the war he was able

through the influence of two Greek gentlemen, Count Sordina and
Baron Ambrogio Ralli, to get to Switzerland on parole, these two
gentlemen standing guarantee for him. In Zurich a German doctor
advised him to drink wine because he was anaemic. Knowing what I do
of German doctors during the war, I think it not impossible that the
advice may have been given in bad faith. At any rate the advice was
accepted with enthusiasm, and his health, which was good in Trieste,
has suffered ever since.

When my brother came to the Berlitz School in Trieste there was
already a teacher here with whom the manager quarrelled. The manager
offered the position to me through my brother, who wanted me to come
for a holiday, as he wished to have someone to talk to. I left Dublin on
the 24th Oct. 1905 and arrived here a few days later. At that time I was
not yet twenty-one, my brother was twenty-three, so that we were both
very young. I have lived here since then, never returning to Ireland and
never leaving Trieste except when during the war I was interned in
Austria as a civil prisoner. In 1909 it had been arranged that I was to
take a trip to Dublin and bring Georgie with me. At the last moment my
brother wanted to go, as I had always inwardly suspected he would. He
was met at the station of Westland Row in Dublin by a family group
who asked him 'Where's Stannie?' It's a question I have often asked
myself. Yours very truly   STANISLAUS JOYCE

From the EDITORS of the *Frankfurter Zeitung*
to ERNST HITSCHMANN[1]   TS. Private

13 August 1931   [*Frankfurt*]

Sehr geehrter Herr, wir haben Ihnen für Ihren Brief zu danken.
Inzwischen haben wir einen kleinen Artikel 'Michael und James'
veröffentlicht, der das Versehen richtig stellt. Wir sollten meinen, dass
Herr Joyce mit dieser Erklärung zufrieden sein könnte. Wir sind ja in
der Tat an der Namensverwechslung unschuldig. Sie ist uns fatal genug.
Was Irene Kafka betrifft, so hat sie schon mancherlei für uns über-
setzt und dies ist die erste üble Erfahrung, die wir mit ihr machen. Sie
würden uns zu Dank, verbinden, wenn Sie uns mitteilen wollten, welche
Gründe Sie veranlassen, uns vor der Dame zu warnen. In vorzuglicher
Hochachtung.   FEUILLETON-REDAKTION
                                                  der *Frankfurter Zeitung*[2]

[1] A German lawyer interceding on Joyce's behalf.
[2] (Translation)
 'Dear Sir, Thank you for your letter. In the meantime we have published a little
article, "Michael and James," which puts the blunder right. We should suppose that

To STANISLAUS JOYCE   MS. Cornell

22 August 1931   *28B Campden Grove, Kensington, W.8*

Dear Stannie: Am almost sure I heard the Schmitzes say a Kafka had translated some of his things. The F.Z. refuses to apologise and prints what I sent you from Dover.[1] All the chief literary agencies in London have been rung up. None has ever heard of Michael Joyce.[2] The British Museum catalogue has been searched for past 80 years. No record of any book of his. There is, however, a magazine run by the Cunard, P & O, Ellerman lines etc to encourage ocean cruises on their vessels. It is called *The Blue Peter* and a Michael Joyce is a contributor to it. In addition to writing begging letters I have refused thousands of pounds for years past because I would not write for the press on commission and now one of the leading European newspapers goes and puts my name under a fraudulent shoddy piece of journalese and will not even apologise for it. They had the thing in their hands for months, made no effort to get into touch with me or my publisher, never sent me a copy of the paper it appeared in or tried to pay me the big fee they knew I would be entitled to, infringed my German publisher's contractual rights, refused to apologise when written to and published under a displeasing title an article which is mean, silly, impertinent and untrue. I'm going to sue them anyhow so that's that. I hope you will be able to get the facts into the press. If so, send me 4 copies of any paper it appears in.

I am sorry you have to toil amid that damn dreary correspondence and hope you are soon 'through' with it. Three hoots for Furtofranco[3] Greetings to you both.   JIM

P.S. You know, you advised me to proceed against Roth and not 'play the gentle Jesus always'. I did, though I presaw the result. Aha! Huff![4]

Mr Joyce would be satisfied with this explanation. In any case we are not responsible for the change of names. It is certainly unpleasant for us. As for Irene Kafka, though she has translated a lot of things for us this is the first bad experience we have had with her. We should be grateful to you if you would advise us what grounds there might be to warn us against the lady. Faithfully yours, The Editors of the *Frankfurter Zeitung*'
[1] 'Michael und James.'
[2] Michael Joyce (b. 1903), now well known as a writer, was then a young man who had published several stories in the *London Mercury* and was beginning to achieve recognition. Among his later works are *My Friend Hobhouse* (London, 1948), *Edward Gibbon* (London, 1953), and *Samuel Johnson* (London, 1955).
[3] 'Frankfurter' inverted. The meaning in Italian would be 'open theft'.
[4] Exclamations Stanislaus Joyce might be presumed to make on reading this letter.

To T. S. Eliot   MS. Faber

27 August 1931   *London*

Dear Eliot: Isn't this a nice letter.[1] I have used your name in a letter my solicitors are sending. A copy of this will be sent you before it is dispatched. If you disapprove I will have the phrase deleted. I used yours and O'Casey's, coupling them with my own, rather than G.B.S. or H.G.W.[2] etc because we are more or less of an age and represent three clearly different branches of writing. I suppose I am letting myself in for another big bill for costs but here goes!

Excuse me for not having rung up. I have been strangely unfit these last few days.

What about the proofs and what has your sales manager done with my versicles?[3] Sincerely yours   James Joyce

P.S. What do you think I should ask for Japanese rights?[4]

To Michael Joyce   MS. Michael Joyce

6 September 1931   *28B Campden Grove, Kensington, W.8*

Dear Mr Joyce: I thank you for your kind and considerate letter[5] which is a refreshing change after my recent experience. The Frankfurter

[1] Joyce enclosed a copy of a letter from Irene Kafka to Monro, Saw & Company, of 17 August 1931, which read as follows:

'Hotel de France Wien 1. Schottenring 3.

   Dear Sir, I am in receipt of your letter of the 15th inst. And I am a little astonished that now after four weeks and after having given so much explanations to everybody concerned you should not have been informed how all this happened. It was much more harmless as what you may fancy. The said text *was* from Joyce. But not from James Joyce, the author of Ulysses. It has been translated from me out of the English typescript of *Michael* Joyce, whose short stories I translate and publish for some years already. Now my new secretary had been mistaken and she thought that there could only exist one sole Joyce, the author of Ulysses. So she wrote James instead of Michael, as I had dictated to her. And I did not remark that as I controled her writing. And I got a terrible shock when the paper came. Of course I wrote an explanation to the Frankfurter Zeitung at once and I sent to them the original English type-script out of which I did translate for consideration. And then I got a letter from Rhein-Verlag in Munich and explained to them the matter as it happened. And I gave the same explanation to Mr James Joyce's friend Mr Georges Borach who wrote to me from Zurich. I asked him to put the expression of my deepest regret before James Joyce that it [is] all I can do in this painful affair. My Secretary has been quite broken as she heard the trouble she caused quite unconsciously. But I know that a similar thing never more shall occur. I beg you to state this and to take you also all my apologies for yourself and for Mr James Joyce. Yours sincerely,   Irene Kafka'

[2] Bernard Shaw or H. G. Wells.
[3] See p. 247, n. 1.   [4] For the Japanese translation of *Ulysses.*
[5] Michael Joyce sent James Joyce a letter sympathizing with him over the misuse of his name.

Zeitung and the translator seem to have treated you with almost as scant courtesy as they have used towards myself.

I am still, however, nearly as much in the dark as the person in your story. Am I to understand from your letter that the translator obtained a copy of the December issue of the *London Mercury* and translated your story without authorization from you? Or did you send her the issue and has she merely omitted to inform you of its publication in Germany? I, myself, learnt of the publication as you did, by chance Sincerely yours   JAMES JOYCE

To MICHAEL JOYCE   MS. Michael Joyce
8 September 1931   *28B Campden Grove, Kensington, W.8*

Dear Mr Joyce: I do not wish to trouble you with correspondence in this matter unnecessarily but it would be of great help to me if you could inform [me] on what date (approximately) you sent your story to Miss Kafka and whether it was the December issue of the *London Mercury* you sent her for translation.

I thank you in advance and shall ask my agent to notify you of any developments in the case. Sincerely yours   JAMES JOYCE

To ERNST ROBERT CURTIUS   MS. Yale
[About 17 September 1931][1]   *Lord Warden Hotel, Dover*

Dear Professor Curtius: I thank you for your letter. Three weeks have now passed and though you and my English solicitors and my literary agent in Vienna have all written to the paper and the translator neither one nor the other has offered me privately or publicly one word of excuse or explanation. I am determined however that the matter shall not stop here Sincerely yours   JAMES JOYCE

To HARRIET SHAW WEAVER   MS. British Museum
1 October 1931   *'La Résidence', 41 Avenue Pierre 1er de Serbie, Paris*

Dear Miss Weaver: I saw Miss Beach. . . . She had had confirmation that Roth had brought out and sold off to someone else an edition of 10,000[2] and suggested to me that Hemingway's lawyer would take up the case over there. I declined to have anything more to do with lawyers.

---

[1] A letter from Joyce to Sylvia Beach written in mid-September 1931, before leaving London, is in Appendix.

[2] Of *Ulysses*. Roth's pirated edition of *Ulysses*, published in 1929, was printed from new plates which followed with slight deviations the ninth printing (May 1927) by Shakespeare and Company. Joyce accepted a rumour that another pirated edition had been made by photographic reproduction, but Slocum and Cahoon, pp. 28–29, declare that this 'almost certainly never existed.'

I said Pinker's opinion was that the only way to stop Roth was to get a U.S. publisher to take the book. She asked did I want that. I said if Roth went on for 3 years more the American market, already crippled, would be killed outright. She said a U.S. edition meant shutting her shop and rearing chickens but that she would do it if it was my wish. . . .

[Mrs Colum's] idea is that the U.S. publication ought to be made at once as it would mean the Nobel Prize for me and an English publication the year after.

The sheepish premier[1] did not bleat yesterday and the numbskull[2] who smokes the pipe neither. Why doesn't W.L.[3] do something since the pound's gone ezra.

Strange to say I am trying to write.

I hope someone takes your flat and that we take someone's. Kindest regards sincerely yours   JAMES JOYCE

From MONRO, SAW & COMPANY   TS. Private

6 October 1931   *44 Queen Victoria Street, London*

Dear Mr. Joyce, With regard to the letter you sent me for me to send on to Dr. Rothschild[4] in order that he might send it to the Frankfurter Zeitung, it appears to me that the letter was drafted by you to be written by us and if a letter at all on these lines was written by Dr. Rothschild it would have to be revised in its various references to ourselves and to our legal advisers in Frankfurt. I take it you have a copy of it and I have the following comments to make:—

Paragraph

With regard to/(1), the quotation 'by James Joyce the author of the great English novel ULYSSES and translated from the original manuscript by Irene Kafka.' This would, of course, have to be in German and not in English.

Paragraph (2), the words beginning 'The text you published was, according to your statement to Dr. Daniel Brody Director of the Rhein Verlag, in your possession for two months before you published it.'

We do not appear to have in our possession any information showing

---

[1] Ramsay MacDonald. Joyce called him Ramshead MacDullard. See p. 234.

[2] Stanley Baldwin (1867–1947), at this time serving under Ramsay MacDonald in the coalition National Government.

[3] Wyndham Lewis.

[4] Dr Willi Rothschild, a German lawyer in Frankfurt, was asked by Monro, Saw & Co. to look into the matter of Irene Kafka's allegedly deliberate misuse of Joyce's name. On 19 September 1931 he wrote advising that a suit for damages would be futile; the maximum amount to be expected if the case were won would be £25. He explained that in Frankfurt the slip would be regarded as trifling, and that a lawsuit on account of it would seem vindictive and exacting, unworthy of a writer of repute.

that this statement was made and accordingly that the manuscript was in the possession of the newspaper for two months.

With regard to the statement that the signature is a forgery, there is no signature to the document.

With regard to the paragraph reading as follows:—'Firstly you send us a letter of explanation stating that Irene Kafka had made an error in the Christian name of the writer and that you had come to an agreement with the Rhein Verlag as to what *reparation* you were going to make.' We have not seen any letter of explanation to the effect mentioned and the Frankfurter Zeitung did not write that they had come to an agreement with the Rhein Verlag. What they said was that they would take the necessary steps in conjunction with the Rhein Verlag to put the matter in order which is somewhat different.

Throughout it would be necessary to make quotations from the newspaper in German.

With regard to the paragraph at the top of page 3, there is no concluding statement such as is suggested and the whole of this paragraph is paraphrasing of the article which, though substantially correct, is not exactly what was stated.

With regard to the next paragraph, it is suggested that the matter had not yet been but would be placed in the hands of your legal friends in Frankfurt, which is not now a correct statement.

With regard to the various questions you ask, I cannot see any use in asking these questions. Some of them might be useful questions to ask in a Court in cross examination.

The proposed letter is so full of statements which are open to question that the Frankfurter Zeitung, if they wished to reply to it, could reply in such a way that you would get no satisfaction at all and in my opinion it might only lead to a long correspondence without any satisfactory result to you. My own view is that if Dr. Rothschild, knowing the conditions in Germany, does not think it advisable to take proceedings it is very little use writing to the newspaper for an apology.

The newspaper has already inserted an article which, in their view, explained the matter and it does not appear to me to be likely they will insert another article unless forced to do so by proceedings.

Under the circumstances mentioned I am altogether opposed either to my firm writing the letter in the terms of the draft you sent us or to my firm asking Dr. Rothschild to do so. Although I regret very much the trouble and inconvenience you have been caused over this matter, I feel that, having regard to Dr. Rothschild's advice, it is no use pursuing it further. Yours sincerely,   F. R. D'O. Monro

To T. S. Eliot   MS. Faber

[*About 15 October 1931*]   *2 rue Saint Philibert, Passy, Paris*
                                                    Tel. Auteuil 17.28

Dear Eliot: I have mislaid in moving here the proof you sent me.[1] The opinion here is that it is good but that the slightly larger and heavier one you spoke of sending would be better. Can I have a page?

I saw Miss Beach. She says Roth has brought out a new American edition of *Ulysses* (10,000 copies!?) and she stands by her terms,[2] however, I suppose you saw that the U.S. government has taken the ban off several books from Boccaccio backwards and forwards. Miss Beach is surprised not to have heard from you about the book of essays.[3]

I have started work again as well as one can in rather uncertain circumstances. The people to whom I ceded my flat in London let me down very badly. They cried off the contract they had agreed to thereby worsting me out of £100. There is no redress, according to my solicitors. Also according to the same and this Frankfurt colleague there is none in that Michael & James case except that I have to pay fees and expenses in London Vienna and Frankfurt amounting to £48. So that's that.

I hope Mrs Eliot and yourself are well. We are still somewhat knocked about like Cromwell's ruins.[4] Sincerely yours,   JAMES JOYCE

To Harriet Shaw Weaver   MS. British Museum

27 October 1931   *2 Avenue Saint Philibert, Passy, Paris*

Dear Miss Weaver: The report[5] is all right, thank goodness, so that's that.

I finished pulling together the first 8 episodes last night and as I am quite fatigued and it is a splendid day Giorgio is taking us out for a long country drive. . . . To my great relief I find that much more of the book is done than I had hoped for. Soupault[6] who has been on a lecture tour in the U.S.A. told me yesterday that the government would have no

[1] Of a sample page of *Finnegans Wake*, which Faber & Faber had contracted to publish.
[2] Sylvia Beach asked that any American publisher of *Ulysses* pay her $25,000 for ceding her rights.
[3] *Our Exagmination*.
[4] An allusion to a line in a popular song, 'I'm one of the ruins Cromwell knocked abaht a bit.'
[5] On his health.
[6] Philippe Soupault (b. 1897), French writer, a good friend of Joyce in the 1920s and '30s, who collaborated in the French translation of *Anna Livia Plurabelle*. His *Souvenirs de James Joyce* was published in Algiers in 1943.

chance of winning a suit against *Ulysses*. He said it is on the extension lecture program for many universities and actually prescribed for the M.A. degree for next year in the New York university. So let them take off the ban and I suppose England will follow suit as usual a few years later. And Ireland 1000 years hence.

May I ask you to put through two telephone calls before you leave London. . . .

Please return *Four* to Léon. The writer should not have used O.G.'s[1] letter in an article. The latter is a swimmer, boxer, cyclist, aviator, motorist and of course I cut a poor figure, eyeless etc. Still the world begins from an egg. Enough of them and all alien annoyances. I have a job on hand. Kindest regards sincerely yrs   JAMES JOYCE

To STANISLAUS JOYCE   MS. Cornell

19 November 1931   *Paris*

Dear Stannie: Please return these samples of my daily mail *by return*. What am I to do about that cursed madman in C.[2]? Any use my writing to his chief constable there? Why the hell don't they put him in an asylum?

As for Annie[3] her brother keeps a string of racers and hunters and they won't let their children mix with mine. If I had the Lsd free I'd send it but I think the scheme harebrained (10 rooms! I cannot let my flat of 3!) I said I would pay his railway fare to Riviera if she could get any money to keep them there. Greetings.   JIM

To HARRIET SHAW WEAVER   MS. British Museum

21 November 1931   *2 Avenue S. Philibert, Passy, Paris*

Dear Miss Weaver: Gorman leaves for U.S.A. on 26 returning February. He has to deliver a series of lectures on me. It is true that he and Mrs G. are being divorced. He, in fact, is engaged to be married to another divorced woman but this must not be known yet. I hear he has some stepchildren. Apart from this he wants to know when you expect to have access to your letters and I the same with regard to the MS of *W.i.P.*

L.P.F.[4] is now in favour again and on visiting terms.[5] I met him outside a cafe. He was very friendly to me, took down address and telephone number etc. I won a large box of cigars from Miss Beach who

---

[1] Oliver St John Gogarty.   [2] Capodistria. Gianni Corti is meant.
[3] Annie Hearne Joyce, Charles Joyce's second wife.
[4] Léon-Paul Fargue.   [5] With Adrienne Monnier and Sylvia Beach.

bet that Sullivan ('the most immoral man she had ever heard of') had run off to South America with his mistress. He is, in fact, in Nice engaged for a big season there in *Mastersingers*. Mrs S. was here to tea chattering away gaily as usual about her two curious children. I gave the boy a lot of my ties as, like Giorgio, he is inclined to dandyism.

Jarnach[1] continues to hold up the O.U.P. book. I got Lucia (by a ruse) to make me elaborate capitals for the poems and sent them over.[2] H.H.[3] said it was too late. The book was set up. Now I have shown them to Mrs Crosby who admires them and proposes to make a very expensive edition of only 25 copies, facsimile of my handwriting.[4] I would let Lucia draw the whole amount. I have to speak to Miss Beach about this as she has the world rights and also the original MS which I gave her along with that of *Dubliners*.

Pinker writes asking what is *Pomes Penyeach* (is it by me?) and Faber and Faber who were to have sent me a larger type proof sent me on Nov. 20 (excuse this loose leaf)[5] on Nov 20 a proof pulled on Oct 16 which is identical with the proof pulled on 21 Sept.[6] Why doesn't Ramshead Mac Dullard do something about it all, find a formula or something of that sort of thing.

Another prospective tenant for 'Chicken from Barkers'[7] wanted me to buy a shopful of china including a dozen eggcups etc. I wonder what kind of early Victorian breakfast parties she wanted to give. Several letters were exchanged and then she altered her intentions.

The madman in Trieste[8] has started writing to me again violent letters. At 8.30 on Tuesday Harold Nicholson[9] will lecture on me over the London radio.[10] He has written a broadcast pamphlet in which he calls me 'the Einstein of English fiction'.

I am stitching away like a cobbler.

[1] Philipp Jarnach. See p. 208.

[2] Joyce was encouraging Lucia Joyce to design *lettrines* or elaborate capital letters like those on illuminated manuscripts. He hoped to use these in *The Joyce Book* (London, 1933).

[3] Herbert Hughes, editor of *The Joyce Book*.

[4] This edition of *Pomes Penyeach*, with initial letters designed by Lucia Joyce, and the poems in facsimile of Joyce's handwriting, was published not by Mrs Crosby but by Jack Kahane (Paris, Obelisk Press) and by Desmond Harmsworth (London) in October 1932. Mrs Crosby published the *Collected Poems* in New York in 1936, but without the initial letters and the facsimile handwriting.

[5] 'A small sheet of paper, the other sheet being full.' (Miss Weaver's note on the typed copy.)

[6] Of *Finnegans Wake*.

[7] An allusion to his Kensington flat and a family joke.

[8] Gianni Corti.

[9] Sir Harold Nicolson (b. 1886), English man of letters and diplomat.

[10] This talk was called off by the British Broadcasting Company at the last moment; Nicolson protested strongly and at last was allowed to give it on 6 December 1931.

People are alarmed about S.G.[1] I took him to the opera and have induced him to see Dr Fontaine[2] of whom he is shy. *Il y a des hommes comme ça.*[3] Kindest regards sincerely yours   JAMES JOYCE

To T. S. ELIOT   MS. Faber

22 November 1931   *2 Avenue S. Philibert, Passy, Paris*

Dear Eliot: I was waiting for the proof[4] promised me when we decided that the one pulled on 21 September was not clear enough. It has now (21 November) reached me and apparently was pulled on 16 October and is identical with that of 21 September, see enclosed. I suppose that ends the matter.

Do you want to set up part 1. ?[5] If so, I could send it.

Has anything been arranged about the volume of essays ?[6]

I cannot make up my mind about Zurich yet.

With kind regards to Mrs Eliot and yourself sincerely yours
                                                            JAMES JOYCE

To HARRIET SHAW WEAVER   MS. British Museum

27 November 1931   *Passy*

Dear Miss Weaver. . . . Miss Monnier gave a big dinner in my honour to hear the radio. London was put on at 8.30 sharp. Nicholson announced at once that pressure had been brought to bear on him etc etc and that the expected talk on J.J. could not take place. The company expressed itself volubly in French about the B.B.C. directors etc after which we all went in to table and had a merry meal. . . .

I am working very hard. Everything seems now to be well disposed.

It is strange that my presence has this effect and my absence produces a violent reaction. For instance, there has appeared in the *Catholic World* (N.Y.) an article—leader—on me which Colum and his wife say is so vulgar and scurrilous that they will not show it to me.[7] They are both indignant over it. Guess who the writer is. Michael Lennon who helped me so much in the Sullivan affair, who asked me for a signed copy of *Ulysses*, whom I invited to Llandudno,[8] whom I entertained

---

[1] Stuart Gilbert.

[2] Dr Thérèse Bertrand-Fontaine, who was Joyce's physician until he left Paris for the last time in 1939.

[3] 'Some men are like that.'   [4] Specimen pages of *Finnegans Wake.*

[5] *Finnegans Wake*, pp. 3–216.   [6] *Our Exagmination.*

[7] Michael J. Lennon, 'James Joyce,' *Catholic World* CXXII (March 1931) 641–52.

[8] In July or August 1930.

with Hughes to dinner and talked with till 1 a.m., who afterwards wrote
asking me if I would allow his wife to call on me on her way through
Paris etc.

   Pourquoi?

   With kindest regards sincerely yours   JAMES JOYCE

To CARESSE CROSBY   MS. Library of Congress

28 November 1931   *The Lancaster, 7 rue de Berri, Paris*

Dear Mrs Crosbie [sic]: James Stephens is in Paris for a few days. If
you want to see him his address is:

                11 rue Campagne Première
                         Montparnasse.

   I hope you received the initials from Herbert Hughes and also the
3 poems my son took the printer's yesterday.

   I enclose a galley page of the Oxford University Press edition of
Pomes Penyeach which you may be interested to see—Colum's preface.[1]
Will you be so good as to return it to me? Sincerely yours

                                                           JAMES JOYCE

Tel. Auteuil 17.28

To HARRIET SHAW WEAVER   MS. British Museum

18 December 1931   *2 Avenue S. Philibert, Passy, Paris*

Dear Miss Weaver: I enclose a letter received from Conner which
please return when read. What a fine muddle I have got myself into and
how pleasant it is to be called a swindler by an American lawyer! There
is a crisis in the B.B.C. precipitated by H.N.[2] and Mr Alfred Noyes[3] has
started a polemic about me in the *Times*, T.S.E.[4] says. He considered
Huebsch's terms 'ludicrous'. I am sending a copy of my letter to Conner
also to the Viking Press. Pinker has been bungling things in firstrate
fashion and I see by the morning paper that there is a strong movement
afoot in England to introduce prohibition as in the U.S.A. If this bill is
passed I hope it will be applicable to the solid food cooked in the
country.

   In the middle of all this Messrs Monro Saw write me that they want
6d (sixpence) to give to the Insurance people who say they simply must
have a look at my furniture every Saturday with a dark lantern.

---

[1] *The Joyce Book* is meant.   [2] Harold Nicolson.
[3] Alfred Noyes (1880–1958), English poet and man of letters.   [4] T. S. Eliot.

There are three persons in the Blessed Trinity but it is only on occasions such as this that the Third Person should be invoked. Kindest regards sincerely yours   JAMES JOYCE

From EZRA POUND   TS. Private

21 December 1931   *Rapallo, Via Marsala, 12 int. 5*

EZRA POUND

21 Dec. 1931   Anno X[1]

Dear Jhayzus Aloysius Chrysostum Greetin's of the season to you and to yr wives and descendents legitimate and illigitimate (se*lon*).

Blarney Castle, it come into me mind. Do you know anything, apart from the touchin' ballad; about it. I mean when did fat ladies from Schenekdety or Donegal first begin to be held by their tootsies with their hoopskirts falling over their priavtes to in public osculate: he [the] said stone

and for what reason? fecundity? or the obverse?
Whose stone, in short, was it?

I regret not havin had the opporchunity to sing you my last ditty when in Paris, or rather the last before I went thither, composed for yr/ special postprandial dilectation and then, domme, I forgot it. At least I think I forgot it, I can't remember having performed it.

When you get an address send it on; or come down and watch the icicles forming on the edge of the mare Thyrenno. benedictions   E.P.

SONG FOR INFORMAL GATHERINGS
(to the familiar lyric measure)

O Paddy dear an' did you hear
The news that's going round,
The Censorship is on the land
And sailors can be found
ExPurgating the stories
That they used to tell wid easé
And yeh can not find a prostichoot
Will speak above her knees.

[1] Of the Fascist regime.

I met Esmond Fitzguggles[1]
And the ole souse says to me:
'I fought and bled and died, by Xroist!
'That Oireland should be free,
'But you mustn't now say "buggar" nor
    "bitch" nor yet "bastard"
'Or the black maria will take you
'To our howly prison = yard.'

'They've had up the damn boible
'To examine its parts an' hole,
'And now we know that Adam
'Used to practice birt = controll,
'In accardance wid St. Thomas
'And dhe faders of the church,
'And when pore Eve would waant to fuck
'He'd lambaste her wid a birch.'

'We must prothect our virchoos',
Lowsy Esmong says to me,
'And be chaste, begob, and holy
'As our Lord was wont to be.
'And we must select our language
'So that it shall not offend
'The fat ould buggerin' bishops
'Or their woives, worrld widout end!'

Sure I t'ought of Mr Griffeth
And of Nelson and Parnell
And of all the howly rebels
Now roastin' down in hell
For havin't said 'Oh, deary me!'
Or 'blow' or even 'blawst'
An' I says to lowsy Esmond:
'Shure owld Oireland's free at last.'

                    O'Donal Hugh Red O' Donnel.

[1] Desmond Fitzgerald. See p. 61, n. 4.

To EZRA POUND   MS. Pound[1]

1 January 1932   [*Paris*]

Extracr (sic) from The Groves of blarney (Air: The Bells of Shandon) by
Richard Milliken[2]

> And there's a stone there that whoever kisses
> HE never misses
> To grow eloquent.
> 'Tis he may clamber to a lady's chamber
> Or become a member
> Of sweet parliament.
> A clever spouter
> He'll soon turn out or
> An out-and outer to be left alone.
> Don't seek to hinder him
> Or to bewilder him
> Sure, he's a pilgrim from the Blarney stone.

Extract from Work in Progress, Part I, section6
(it is the second of the four masters ,who here represents Munster,
answering. He has been asked a riddle .What Irish capital city of six
letters ,beginning with D and endung with N etc etc' but he answers)
Dorhqk. and, sure, where can you have such good old chimes anywhere ,
and leave you, as on the Mash and how 'tis I would be engaging you
with my plovery soft accents and descanting upover the scene beunder
me of your loose vines in theirafall with them two loving loofs brace-
letting the slims of your ankles and your mouth's flower rose and
sinking ofter the soapstone of silvry speech'[3]
Dear Pound: There is nothing phallic about the Blarney stone, so far as
I know. The founder of the castle was a cunctator (or perhaps it was the
defender of it). He kept on inventing excuses, parleys etc during its
siege, I think in the time of Essex. The stone is flat and so far as I can
remember let into the wall a few feet below a window. I never understood
why it could not have been kissed from a ladder. I heard there were
double bands of elastic to fasten the women's dresses. I did not kiss
the stone myself.

I hope you had a pleasant *ceppo*.[4] Ours was saddened by the death of

---

[1] The quotations are typed by Joyce, the letter proper is in his handwriting.
[2] The stanza is actually by Frances Sylvester Mahony ('Father Prout') (1804–66), and
was written as an addendum to Richard Alfred Millikin's poem.
[3] *Finnegans Wake*, p. 140.   [4] Ceppo di Natale, 'Yule log.'

my father in Dublin[1] He loved me deeply, more and more as he grew
older, but in spite of my own deep feeling for him I never dared to trust
myself into the power of my enemies

It has been a great blow to me.

We send you and Mrs Pound our best wishes for the New Year
sincerely yours   JAMES JOYCE

To HERBERT GORMAN (Postcard)   MS. S. Illinois (Croessmann)

14 January 1932   *Paris*

Dear Gorman: I have sent you the sad news of my father's death which
is a great blow to me. I hope you are well. Please send Lennon's article
as you promised.[2] Bonne Année   JAMES JOYCE

To GEORG GOYERT   MS. S. Illinois (Croessmann)

12 February 1932   *2 Avenue Saint Philibert, Passy, Paris*

Dear Mr Goyert: Many thanks for your kind message of congratulation
on my fiftieth birthday and for the flowers. I did not see these until the
lady who brought them had gone and could not then thank as she left
no address.

I hope things are going not too badly with you. As for me I expect to
be a grandfather at any moment. With friendly regards sincerely yours
                                                              JAMES JOYCE

To EZRA POUND   MS. Pound

13 February 1932   *2 Avenue Saint Philibert, Passy, Paris*

Dear Pound: As you live là-bas can you tell me what I ought to do.
Italian papers, *Il Mattino* (Naples),[3] *La Fiera Letteraria*[4] etc have
several times published translations of things of mine. They never
consult me, inform me or pay me. I see that *Il Convegno* last October
or so published Rossi's translation of Episode 1 of *Ulysses*.[5] Didn't I
write you something about that when you were here? Of course, they
pay me nothing. What do you say? Is it all right? Sincerely yours
                                                              JAMES JOYCE

[1] John Stanislaus Joyce died on 29 December 1931.

[2] See pp. 235–36. Joyce evidently wanted several copies of Lennon's article, to illustrate
his predicament *vis à vis* Ireland.

[3] This translation has not been found. Slocum and Cahoon, p. 121, D76.

[4] 'Un Caso penoso,' a translation by Giacomo Prampolini of 'A Painful Case', was
published in *Fiera Letteraria* (Milan) IV.23 (3 June 1928) 5.

[5] 'Ulisse 1° Episodio,' a translation by Alberto Rossi, was published in *Convegno*
(Milan) XII.9–10 (October 1931) 476–502.

To STANISLAUS JOYCE (Telegram)   TS. Cornell

15 February 1932   *Paris*

GRANDSON BORU [sic] TO DAY NAME STEPHEN JAMES =
                                                      JIM

To STANISLAUS JOYCE   MS. Cornell

29 March 1932   *Paris*

Dear Stannie: I return preface[1] typed and amended. If it is all right
send it on but do not mention me as I do not want to be made use of.

You have not made this point of dialect or lingua clear to an English
reader. And I wish it were a little clearer than it is that Schmitz was
very careful of his money. Imagine yourself in Manchester reading this
preface and you will understand what [I mean.] What have you done
with Miss Weaver's photographs and that of Baroness S. Leger?[2]

Sorry to hear you have been ill and hope you are better.

Kind regards to Nelly and yourself   JIM

P.S. Also my relations with S were quite formal. I never crossed the
soglia[3] except as a paid teacher and his wife became longsighted when
she met Nora in the street.

To BENNETT CERF[4]   TS. Cerf

2 April 1932   *2 Avenue Saint Philibert, Passy, Paris*

Dear Mr Cerf, I thank you very much for your message conveyed to me
by Mr Robert Kastor.[5] You ask me for details of the story of the
publication of *Ulysses* and since you are determined to fight for its
legalisation in the United States and to publish what will be the only
authentic edition there, I think it just as well to tell you the history of

[1] The preface by Stanislaus Joyce to Svevo's *As a Man Grows Older.*
[2] A woman who lived and made dolls on the Isola da Brissago in the Lago Maggiore.
Joyce heard that she was known as 'Circe' and so made her acquaintance in 1919. She
was of central European extraction; her claim to a title has not proved verifiable.
[3] 'Threshold.'
[4] The text of this letter is taken from the prefatory matter of James Joyce, *Ulysses*
(Random House, Modern Library, New York, 1961), pp. xiii–xv. Bennett Cerf (b. 1898),
publisher and writer, founded Random House in 1927. At Cerf's request Joyce wrote this
letter to serve in lieu of an author's preface to the edition first published in 1934.
[5] Robert Kastor (b. 1892), a New York investment broker, brother of Mrs Helen
Joyce. Kastor helped to arrange for the publication of *Ulysses* by Random House.

its publication in Europe and the complications which followed it in America, although I was under the impression that they were already well known. As it is, however, they have given my book in print a life of its own. Habent sua fata libelli![1]

You are surely well aware of the difficulties I found in publishing anything I wrote from the very first volume of prose I attempted to publish: *Dubliners*. Publishers and printers alike seemed to agree among themselves, no matter how divergent their points of view were in other matters, not to publish anything of mine as I wrote it. No less than twenty-two publishers and printers read the manuscript of *Dubliners* and when at last it was printed some very kind person bought out the entire edition and had it burnt in Dublin—a new and private *auto-da-fé*.[2] Without the collaboration of the Egoist Press Ltd. London, conducted by Miss Harriet Weaver *The Portrait of the Artist as a Young Man* might still be in manuscript.

You can well imagine that when I came to Paris in the summer 1920 with the voluminous manuscript of *Ulysses* I stood even slenderer chances of finding a publisher on account of its suppression after the publication of the eleventh episode in the *Little Review* conducted by Miss Margaret Anderson and Miss Jane Heap. These two editors were, as you probably remember, prosecuted at the instance of some society and as a result further publication in serial form was prohibited, the existing copies were confiscated and, I believe, the fingerprints of the two ladies were taken. The completed manuscript, however, was offered to one of your colleagues on the American market but I greatly doubt that he even took the trouble to glance at it.

My friend Mr Ezra Pound and good luck brought me into contact with a very clever and energetic person Miss Sylvia Beach who had been running for some years previously a small English bookshop and lending library in Paris under the name of Shakespeare and Co. This brave woman risked what professional publishers did not wish to, she took the manuscript and handed it to the printers. These were very scrupulous and understanding French printers in Dijon, the capital of the French printing press. In fact I attached no small importance to the work being done well and quickly. My eyesight still permitted me at that time to read the proofs myself and thus it came about that thanks to extra work and the kindness of Mr Darantière the well-known Dijon printer *Ulysses* came out a very short time after the manuscript had been

---

[1] 'Books have fates of their own.' Terentianus Maurus, *De litteris syllabis et metris Horatii*, l. 1286.
[2] See II, p. 319, n. 3.

delivered and the first printed copy was sent to me for my fortieth birthday on the second of February 1922.

You are however in error when you think that Shakespeare and Co. never published anything before or after *Ulysses*. As a matter of fact Miss Sylvia Beach brought out a little volume of thirteen poems of mine entitled *Pomes Penyeach* in 1927 and also a volume of essays and two letters of protest concerning the book I am engaged in writing since 1922. This volume was brought out in 1929 and it bears the title of *Our Exagmination round his factification for incamination of Work in Progress*.

The continental publication of *Ulysses* proved however to be merely the beginning of complications in the United Kingdom and the United States. Shipments of copies of *Ulysses* were made to America and to Great Britain with the result that all copies were seized and burnt by the Custom authorities of New York and Folkestone. This created a very peculiar situation. On the one hand I was unable to acquire the copyright in the United States since I could not comply with the requirements of the American copyright law which demands the republication in the United States of any English book published elsewhere within a period of six months after the date of such publication, and on the other hand the demand for *Ulysses* which increased every year in proportion as the book penetrated into larger circles gave the opportunity for any unscrupulous person to have it printed and sold clandestinely. This practice provoked a protest signed by one hundred and sixty-seven writers of all nationalities and I even obtained an injunction against one[1] of these unscrupulous persons in a New York court. I am enclosing copies of both these documents which may interest you. This injunction, however, proved of no avail as the enjoined defendant resumed his practice very soon again under another name and with a different mode of procedure, namely a photographic forgery of the Paris edition which contained the falsification of the Dijon printer's imprint.[2]

It is therefore with the greatest sincerity that I wish you all possible success in your courageous venture both as regards the legalisation of *Ulysses* as well as its publication and I willingly certify hereby that not only will your edition be the only authentic one in the United States but also the only one there on which I will be receiving royalties.

Personally I will be very gratified if your enterprise is successful as it will permit American readers who have always proved very kind to me to obtain the authenticated text of my book without running the risk of

[1] Samuel Roth.   [2] See p. 229, n. 2.

helping some unscrupulous person in his purpose of making profit for himself alone out of the work of another to which he can advance no claim of moral ownership.

There may be some other points in which you are interested and I hope that should you be over in Europe again this year you will oblige me by communicating with me either direct or through my son so as to enable me to elucidate any point you may still be in doubt about. Yours sincerely JAMES JOYCE

To the MAYOR OF FLORENCE   TS. Private

9 April 1932   *2 Avenue Saint Philibert, Passy, Paris*

Magnifico Podestà Anzitutto Le chiedo venia se non rispondo che oggi e se la mia risposta si presenta sotto questa forma agghindata e stinta ma la pregiatissima Sua lettera inoltrata da Londra mi è pervenuta con qualche ritardo ed in fatto di calligrafia sono un vero imbrattacarte. La ringrazio del cortese invito nonchè delle generose parcelle di viaggio offertemi ed apprezzo altamente l'onore che un tale invito proveniente dal primo cittadino di tanta città mi conferisce.

Mi duole assai di non essere in grado di accettare e di dovere rinunciare al privilegio di parlare dinanzi ad un auditorio amichevole nella capitale toscana. Purtroppo le fate che s'inchinarono sopra la mia culla mi tolsero il dono della facondia, vanto di molti miei connazionali e mi lasciarono in sua vece una 'lingua di lana in bocca baggiana'.[1] La prego dunque di tenermi per iscusato.

Se mi è lecito proporre un altro nome credo che il mio amico, il poeta americano Ezra Pound, il quale ha tradotto in inglese le opere di un grande scrittore fiorentino, Guido Cavalcanti, potrebbe benissimo rimpiazzarmi. Il suo indirizzo è: 12 via Marsala, Rapallo dove abita da dieci anni.

Nel mentre porgo a Lei, al chiarissimo rettore della regia Università di costì ed al comitato da Loro presieduto i miei sinceri ringraziamenti. La prego, Magnifico Podestà, di gradire i sensi dei miei piu doverosi ossequi. JAMES JOYCE[2]

[1] A play on the expression, 'lingua toscana in bocca romana'—'the Tuscan tongue in a Roman mouth'—which Italians consider the perfection of their language.

[2] (Translation)
'Your Honour the Mayor: First of all I ask your pardon for not replying until today and then in this bedizened and faded form, but your most esteemed letter forwarded from London reached me after some delay and as for handwriting I am a mere scribbler. I thank you for your courteous invitation as well as the generous travelling expenses offered me and I value highly the honour that such an invitation, coming from the first citizen of such a city, confers upon me.

To VALERY LARBAUD   MS. Bib. Municipale, Vichy

13 May 1932   *Hotel Belmont et de Bassano, Champs-Elysées, Paris*

Dear Larbaud: Lucia had a bad *crise de nerfs* at the Gare du Nord so I
had to take the trunks off the train, abandon our journey to London
and definitely give up my Kensington flat.[1] So here we are in a hotel
again, after 12 years in Paris!

I talked about you a few days ago at lunch with de Lanux[2] who is
having a show here of his soldiers. The enclosed *bêtise*, written only for
the sake of the rhymes, is the result.[3]

Thanks for the print. I had it framed in silver. I am sending this to
your country address though you seem to be cruising in the mezzogiorno.[4] Sincerely yours   JAMES JOYCE

To CONSTANT HUNTINGTON[5]

22 May 1932   *2 Avenue Saint Philibert, Passy, Paris*

Dear Mr Huntington I do not think I can usefully add anything to
what my learned friend, the professor of English at the University of

> I regret very much being unable to accept, and having to forego the privilege of
> speaking before a friendly audience in the Tuscan capital. Unfortunately the fates
> who bent over my cradle deprived me of the gift of eloquence—the ornament of many
> of my compatriots—and left me in its stead 'a woollen tongue in a foolish mouth.' I beg
> you therefore to excuse me.
>   If it be permissible for me to propose another name I think that my friend, the
> American poet Ezra Pound, who translated into English the works of a great
> Florentine writer, Guido Cavalcanti, might replace me excellently. His address is:
> 12 via Marsala, Rapallo, where he has lived for ten years.
>   On this occasion I offer my sincere thanks to you, to the very distinguished rector
> of the royal university there, and to the committee over which you preside. I beg you,
> Your Honour the Mayor, to accept this expression of my deepest respect.
>   James Joyce'

[1] Joyce let his flat at 28B Campden Grove, Kensington, for the fall and winter of 1931–
1932, and intended to return there in the spring. With his wife and Lucia he went to the
Gare du Nord on 17 April 1932, but Lucia screamed that she hated England and refused
to go. After forty-five minutes Joyce had their baggage removed from the train.
  Lucia was now clearly schizophrenic, but Joyce refused to consider her more than
temporarily insane, and from now to the end of his life exhausted every possible cure in a
futile effort to make her well.
[2] Pierre de Lanux (b. 1887), French historian, collected toy soldiers, as did his friend
Valery Larbaud.
[3] It is reproduced in Peter Spielberg, *James Joyce's Manuscripts and Letters at the
University of Buffalo* (New York, 1962), pp. 26–27.
[4] 'South.'
[5] Constant Huntington (d. 1962) was Chairman of G. P. Putnam's Sons Ltd., London.
He had asked Joyce to offer some direct comment on Schmitz's book. The text of this
letter is from a typewritten copy in a private collection. Another copy, bearing the date
30 May 1932, is at Cornell.

Trieste (see titlepage) has written in his preface to Senilita, (As) A man grows older.[1]

With regard to the other book[2] by the author of Senilità the only things I can suggest as likely to attract the British reading public are a preface by sir J. M. Barrie, author of My Lady Nicotine, opinions of the book (to be printed on the back of its jacket) from two deservedly popular personalities of the present day, such as, the rector of Stiffkey[3] and the Princess of Wales and (on the front of the jacket) a coloured picture by a Royal Academician representing two young ladies, one fair and the other dark but both distinctly nicelooking, seated in a graceful though of course not unbecoming posture at a table on which a book stands upright, with title visible and underneath the picture three lines of simple dialogue, for example:

Ethel: Does Cyril spend too much on cigarettes!

Doris: Far too much.

Ethel: So did Percy (points)—till I gave him Z E N O. Sincerely yours

JAMES JOYCE

To JOHN SULLIVAN   MS. Texas

26 May 1932   [*Paris*]

Please sign and send off this[4] if all right.   J.J.
Paris

P.S. Sign 'J. Sullivan'[5] for the love of music—

To HARRIET SHAW WEAVER   MS. British Museum

8 June 1932   *Paris*

Dear Miss Weaver: . . . a letter from Tokio this morning to say that 2 Japanese editions of *U* appeared there on 5 February 1932.[6] Up to date 13,000 copies have been pirated, the gross receipts being 170,000 frs to

[1] Joyce had proposed *A Man Grows Older* as the English title for Schmitz's book. See *Letters*, ed. Gilbert, p. 298.

[2] *La Coscienza di Zeno* (1924).

[3] Rev. Harold Francis Davidson (1875–1936), Rector of Stiffkey, was tried and convicted on various charges of immoral behavior in March and July 1932.

[4] Probably a letter, though Sullivan thought it was a copy of 'From a Banned Writer to a Banned Singer', which was published in the *New Statesman and Nation* N.S. III.53 (27 February 1932) 260–61, and in *Hound & Horn* (New York) IV (July–September 1932) 542–46.

[5] Sullivan had usually called himself O'Sullivan until Joyce took him in hand and made him drop the O' as pretentious.

[6] The editions were published by two Tokyo publishers, Dai Ichi Shobo and Iwanami Shoten. The first, in two volumes, appeared in 1931 and 1934 respectively; the second, in five volumes, was published from 1932 to 1935.

date. One of the publishers asked my terms last June. It seems there is a
10-year law limit to protect European copyright after which period any
book is free. I asked T.S.E. to get the opinion of his sales manager (the
same who made no use of my advt rhyme[1]). He gave his profound opinion
that I should demand a very high advance of very high royalties (how
much I forget) and said nothing of the 10-year law. The Japanese
considered the terms exorbitant, waited till the 2 February jubileed by,
and went ahead. No news from U.S.A. With kindest regards sincerely
yours   JAMES JOYCE

To EDOUARD DUJARDIN   MS. Texas

26 June 1932   *2 Avenue Saint Philibert, Passy, Paris*

Cher Monsieur Dujardin: Les choses ne vont pas bien. On a même
proposé l'isolement total pour ma fille, proposition contre laquelle tout
mon instinct se révolte.[2] Il y aura justement demain une consultation
entre les médicins et je propose d'emmener ma fille de cette maison et de
l'envoyer à l'étranger accompagnée par son infirmière et une famille de
notre connaissance afin qu'elle puisse se distraire.[3]

Je ne veux pas que l'on parle trop de cette affaire mais dans les
circonstances je ne pourrai absolument rencontrer et causer avec des
personnes réunies à une fonction comme le diner de demain soir.[4] L'idée
d'y présider ne m'était jamais agréable. J'y serais allé comme invité avec

[1] Joyce wrote rhymes for the use of Faber & Faber in advertising *Anna Livia Plurabelle* and *Haveth Childers Everywhere*. For the former:

> Buy a book in brown paper
> From Faber & Faber
> To see Annie Liffey trip, tumble and caper.
> Sevensinns in her singthings,
> Plurabelle on her prose,
> Seashell ebb music wayriver she flows.

For the latter:

> Humptydump Dublin squeaks through his norse,
> Humptydump Dublin hath a horrible vorse
> And with all his kinks english
> Plus his irismanx brogues
> Humptydump Dublin's grandada of all rogues.

The sales manager, W. J. Crawley, was hesitant. In the end the verses were used only on
a mimeographed publicity release, to which was prefixed a note: 'The sales department,
puzzled as such departments are wont to be, have sought some light on the two James
Joyce contributions to Criterion Miscellany. Below the explanations offered are passed
on that you may be able to derive similar enlightenment.' Joyce was annoyed.

[2] Lucia Joyce was now a patient at Dr G. Maillard's clinic at l'Hay-les-Roses.

[3] Joyce had to go to Zurich to see Dr Vogt, and on 3 July 1932 he took Lucia, along
with her nurse, from the clinic to Feldkirch. They were to stay there under the supervision of Eugene and Maria Jolas, while he went on to Vogt.

[4] Dujardin asked Joyce to preside at a meeting of the P.E.N. Club.

grand plaisir si la présidence avait été confié à un de vos collègues français. Je suis trop sensible du bon accueil qu'on a fait à mes écrits ici en France pour oublier que je suis un invité et pas un hôte.

Je vous souhaite une soirée très agréable. J'y serai présent en esprit: mais nous viderons encore des coupes ensembles *in terra viventium* [sic].

Veuillez accepter mes excuses et me croire cordialement votre

JAMES JOYCE[1]

To PAUL LÉON[2]   TS. Faber

12 July 1932   [*Zurich*]

Prof. Vogt saw my eyes on Monday 10 July. He says I should have come to him before and is afraid it is now too late. The right eye was still operatable 20 months ago. Now the cataract is total and unfortunately complicated with glaucome (secondary) and a partial atrophy of the retina. I was wrongly advised, he says, to put an atropine in it which was pure poison. He says I must not even rub it. Retina and optic nerve were normal when he saw it in November 1930 but are not so now. He intends to observe it for some days and then decide whether he will allow it to go blind (erblinden) or attempt two very difficult operations in succession, the first early in September. In the latter course I may have to face a 5–6 months residence in Switzerland. This means a total cessation of work, a great deal of nervous tension and a considerable expenditure of money. I am writing to Vogt a letter explaining the events from April 1931 which prevented me from coming here to be visited and operated. He added that seeing the complicated condition

[1] (Translation)
'Dear Mr Dujardin: Things are not going well. They have even proposed that my daughter be kept in total isolation, an idea my whole nature revolts against. In fact there will be a consultation of doctors tomorrow and I am proposing to take my daughter out of that establishment and to send her across the border in the company of her nurse and a family we know so as to give her a change.

I should not like the affair to be much spoken of but in the circumstances I absolutely cannot mingle and talk with people gathered for an occasion like the dinner tomorrow night. The notion of my presiding at it has never pleased me. I would gladly have come as a guest if the chairmanship had been entrusted to one of your French colleagues. I am too cognizant of the fine reception my books have been accorded in France to forget that I am a guest and not a host.

I hope you will have a very pleasant evening. I shall be there in spirit: but we will have other occasions to drain our glasses together in the land of the living.

Please accept my excuses and believe me cordially yours   James Joyce'
[2] Paul Léon sent this copied excerpt of a letter he had received from Joyce to T. S. Eliot. The whereabouts of the original is unknown. Some words have evidently been slightly miscopied.

of the neglected eye, he was reluctant to touch the other but that he would have done so had glaucoma and retinary atrophy not intervened in the other, resultant from interocular pressure unchecked [illegible word][1] by operation.

To STANISLAUS JOYCE   MS. Cornell

14 July 1932   *Carlton Elite Hotel, Zurich*

Dear Stannie: If that review wishes to reproduce a black and white of one of the 'lettrines' you yourself should write to:

> Monsieur J. Kahane[2]
> Chez Herbert Clark et Cie
> 335 rue S. Honoré
> Paris

asking first his permission, and then asking him to have the lettrine 'O' (of the poem 'Simples') photographed at $\frac{1}{2}$ size, the expenses to my charge. I do not wish the request to come through me.

Lucia is summering at Feldkirch with some friends,[3] Hotel zum Loewen.

I am here about my eyes. Their state is aggravated owing to my delay in coming, due to one damn worry after another. In fact Vogt fears the eye he could have perhaps saved 20 months ago must go blind. However, I am under observation.

Best regards to Nelly and yourself   JIM

P.S.

Giorgio is at

> La Ferme du May
> S. Jean-Cap Ferrat
> Alpes Maritimes
>   France.

To MR and MRS ROBERT KASTOR (Postcard)   MS. Kastor

16 July 1932   *Elite Hotel, Zurich*

With best wishes to yourself and family for a sunny holiday.[4] If you want any rain please say so and I shall send any amount of it. Sincerely yours   JAMES JOYCE

[1] Léon's note.
[2] Jack Kahane, of the Obelisk Press. See p. 234.
[3] Eugene and Maria Jolas.
[4] The Kastors were at Cap Ferrat with George Joyce and his family.

To HARRIET SHAW WEAVER   MS. British Museum

22 July 1932   *Carlton Elite Hotel, Zurich*

Dear Miss Weaver: To continue and conclude. . . . My father sent me a message by a friend in the curious roundabout delicate and allusive way he had in spite of all his loud elaborate curses (he is quoted on the jacket of an amusing book *Lars Porsena* or *The Future of Swearing*)[1] that if I thought fit he would like a tombstone to be placed on his grave bearing the names of himself and my mother. He left the wording to me and did not mention his two sons, daughter and mother also buried there. Poor foolish man! It seems to me his voice has somehow got into my body or throat. Lately, more than ever—especially when I sigh.

Jolas sends good news from Feldkirch but I never know whether these letters are rigged or not. Lucia writes announcing her arrival with the nurse on Friday next. I hope she does not decide to stay. I wish she would not come. She runs the risk of two more station scenes.

I thought if she sent three letters GBS to Shaw on the 26th (they have the same birthday) he might like her talent. But I am afraid Shaw has lived too long on the boreal side of La Manche to appreciate silly things like that. Perhaps he is right too.

I have had no reply from F and F. No doubt they will have several bored meetings of all the bored members.

The reason Goll's[2] article is so rubbishy is not because Goll is not a poet of sorts. Tuohy's portrait[3] is a failure. Colum's article is also.[4] So is Lewis's personal one[5] (though his hostile criticism is by far the best that has appeared).[6] And as for Pound's pen pictures—heaven preserve us! *Es tut mir leid aber es ist nichts zu malen.*[7]

I cannot get a reply out of Collinson.[8] . . . With kindest regards sincerely yours   JAMES JOYCE

[1] Robert Graves, *Lars Porsena, or The Future of Swearing and Improper Language* (London, 1927). Graves refers to John Stanislaus Joyce on p. 92.

[2] Ivan Goll, 'James Joyce,' in *Die Weltbühne*, 1932.

[3] Of James Joyce.

[4] Padraic Colum, 'Portrait of James Joyce,' *Dublin Magazine*, n.s. VII.2 (April–June 1932) 40–48.

[5] In the *Enemy*. See p. 188, n. 3.

[6] In *Time and Western Man*.

[7] 'I'm sorry but there is nothing to paint.' A comic distortion of '*Nichts zu machen*' ('Nothing doing').

[8] Regarding his own eyes or possibly regarding an operation on Lucia to correct a strabismus.

To Frank Budgen   MS. Yale

1 August 1932 Bundesfeier[1]   *Carlton Elite Hotel, Zurich*

Dear Budgen: Up to now my idea has not worked badly. Lucia, apart from initial melancholy, has stayed down there a month and will stay on till she goes back to Paris in September.

For myself the news is not good. Vogt is naturally annoyed with me. He does not believe he can save the right eye from going blind. I should have left everything else aside and come back before while it was still operatable. He will return for a few hours to Z'ch in a fortnight and may let me know definitely then. Of course, he says, it might need 2 or 3 operations (which would make the baker's dozen)—a major and some secondary ones. He is, of course, the only man in Europe who can do it but what about me in my present Wirbel[2] of worries.

What a climate! Platzregen[3] all the time.

Do not let yourself be discouraged by anything I may have said about your book.[4] I hope you will go on with it. But if you had 28 years' experience of English publishers you would proceed very warily with them as I do. Besides, public houses solemn promises are not quite as lasting as the Rütlischwur.[5] A pity you could not have talked more with S.[6] He would have gone on for hours about painting probably.

Did you know of a little habit the Helvetians have on their national day. They cut off all the draught wine, will serve only full bottles (whole) of wine in bottle and this à l'écarté[7]—like Horseshow whisky in Dublin? Or is this new? Half the streets of Z'ch are ripped up. I seem to be always coming back here.

What trouble my eyes have given me! We had Ruggiero to dinner the other night. Still loquacious on the subjects of frog cooking, Abdul Hamid,[8] Armenians, etc.

If I knew Sargent's address in Lugano I would send him a card
Sincerely yours   JAMES JOYCE

[1] The Swiss national day.   [2] 'Vortex.'   [3] 'Downpours.'

[4] Budgen was now writing *James Joyce and the Making of 'Ulysses'*, about the years they had spent in Zurich. It was published by Grayson & Grayson (London, 1934), and republished with some additional material as a paperback by Indiana University Press (Bloomington, Indiana, 1961). At first Joyce thought Budgen's book must necessarily duplicate material in Gorman's biography or Gilbert's critical study, but he changed his mind as Budgen proceeded with it.

[5] The oath taken on 1 August 1291 at Rütli which laid the basis for the Swiss constitution.

[6] John Sullivan.

[7] Usually 'à l'écart,' 'off to the side,' 'privately.'

[8] Abdul Hamid II (1842–1918), Sultan of Turkey from 1876 until his deposition in 1909.

To ROBERT MCALMON   MS. Pearson

[August 1932?]   *[Zurich?]*

Dear McAlmon: I have 7 names good each for a subscription[1] of £10, payable about October next, (i.e. myself, you, T.S.E., H.W. etc) and have given in 7 others of whom I am morally sure. (Lady Cunard, her daughter, WL, Antheil and Mrs Herbert Gorman). I am sure I can find easily another 6. That will make £200 and we can probably run it up to £300 but if when called on you happen to be short I can easily cover the two names and we can settle it some time or other. As a matter of fact, I am your debtor.

As regards Gorman (or rather Mrs Gorman whose name I give) I think you must be misinformed. Colm who knows them well for years told me they had fairly ample means. I always found her very free-handed but there is of course no earthly reason why she is obliged to subscribe. I wish you could help him with his book. People are unnecessarily hostile to him. I hope he is well and yourself the same sincerely yours   J.J.

To ALFRED BERGAN[2]   MS. N.Y. Public Library (Manuscript)

5 August 1932   *Carlton Elite Hotel, Zurich*

Dear Mr Bergan: I hope this finds you in good health and that you excuse me for not having written to you before but my daughter has been rather ill and I myself am here on account of my wretched eyes. I may have to submit to two more operations, making the full dozen, or the right eye may be left to go blind—the devil or the deep sea.

It was very kind of you to act as you did about poor Pappie's will and if you will let me know the cost of the tombstone I shall send a cheque for it. The names of my parents are John Stanislaus and Mary Jane.

I wonder what became of all the signed editions of my books I sent to Pappie. Apart from any material value (the first Paris edition of *Ulysses* signed is worth about £35) I do not want them to be in the hands of strangers.

You are in this book by name[3] with so many others of Pappie's

---

[1] The subscription was to the facsimile edition of *Pomes Penyeach* with initial letters by Lucia Joyce.

[2] Alfred Bergan was a lifetime friend of John Stanislaus Joyce. In *Ulysses* he appears as assistant to the sub-sheriff of Dublin, Long John Clancy, a position he actually held. Later he became a solicitor's clerk in the office of David Charles.

[3] In the *Cyclops* episode.

friends. I remember very well your singing *One of the Family* and *Sister Susie's Playing*. You always made the same mistake in one line of the latter, a mistake prompted by politeness and encouraged by conviviality, for you sang 'would make both you and I sick' instead of 'would make both me and you sick'.

My grandson Stephen was born a month after Pappie died. I wrote a little verse about it[1] and if I ever publish it I will send you a copy. No man could be worthy of such intense love as my father had for me

With many remembrances and all good wishes sincerely yours

JAMES JOYCE

From C. G. JUNG[2]   TS. Private[3]

[? *August 1932*]   *Küsnacht-Zürich, Seestrasse 228*

Dear Sir,   Your Ulysses has presented the world such an upsetting psychological problem, that repeatedly I have been called in as a supposed authority on psychological matters.

Ulysses proved to be an exceedingly hard nut and it has forced my mind not only to most unusual efforts, but also to rather extravagant peregrinations (speaking from the standpoint of a scientist). Your book as a whole has given me no end of trouble and I was brooding over it for about three years until I succeeded to put myself into it. But I must tell you that I'm profoundly grateful to yourself as well as to your gigantic opus, because I learned a great deal from it. I shall probably never be quite sure whether I did enjoy it, because it meant too much grinding of nerves and of grey matter. I also don't know whether you will enjoy what I have written about Ulysses because I couldn't help telling the world how much I was bored, how I grumbled, how I cursed and how I admired. The 40 pages of non stop run in the end is a string of veritable psychological peaches. I suppose the devil's grandmother knows so much about the real psychology of a woman. I didn't.

[1] 'Ecce Puer.'
[2] Carl Gustav Jung (1875–1961), the eminent Swiss psychologist, wrote an article about *Ulysses* in 1930. Dr Daniel Brody, director of Rhein-Verlag, considered the possibility of publishing it in the first issue of a new magazine he planned to found, and submitted it to Joyce for his approval in late September 1930. Joyce sent a curt wire '*Niedrigerhängen*' ('Make a show of it,' literally, 'Hang it lower'). But his friends Ivan Goll and Valery Larbaud wrote Brody privately that the use of it would be inadvisable, and in any event Brody decided not to start the magazine. Jung amended the unused article and published it as 'Ulysses: Ein Monolog', in the *Europäische Revue* (Berlin) VIII.9 (September 1932) 547–68, and then included it in his *Wirklichkeit der Seele* ... (1933). For Joyce's principal objection to Jung's article, see p. 262.
[3] From a typewritten copy.

Well I just try to recommend my little essay to you, as an amusing attempt of a perfect stranger that went astray in the labyrinth of your Ulysses and happened to get out of it again by sheer good luck. At all events you may gather from my article what Ulysses has done to a supposedly balanced psychologist.

With the expression of my deepest appreciation, I remain, dear Sir, Yours faithfully   C. G. Jung

To Harriet Shaw Weaver   MS. British Museum

6 August 1932   *Carlton Elite Hotel, Zurich*

Dear Miss Weaver ... Here is a letter from Dr Codet[1] and you will receive from Borach a letter the nurse sent by hand through Jolas written to her by Lucia, though unsigned and unfinished. It is a disquieting document. Will you please return it to me c/o Borach. My wife has not seen it.

She insisted on going to F[2] though Lucia wrote up a perfectly normal letter to me this morning saying she wanted to see me too and that I should not be left alone and that she and the nurse would come to Z'ch.

She has worked on at her alphabet and has now reached 'O'. Jolas says that 3 or 4 of the letters are astounding. What I find disquieting in the letter is not so much its exaltation. Each phrase could bear a rational meaning and some of the phrases are very fine. It is the lack of even casual connections. She has however gained 3 kilos, about ½ stone in 3 weeks. Also when she heard vaguely of what Vogt said she had a violent fit of crying and said she should come to Z'ch to stay with her mother. Anything, even weeps, which takes them out of absorption in themselves is a good sign. She could not gain in weight unless her mind were fairly free.

My wife has gone to see if any plans can be made ahead. She does not think Lucia wants to leave us definitely yet and thinks we should prepare a Paris home. I will tell you more when she comes back.

What kind of wandering willies are going flat-hunting these days? I mean your tenant too. My cook[3] stays on by the month as his 'chef', the ambassador, is expecting to be moved.

Do you mind sending Codet's letter to Giorgio, La Ferme de May, Saint Jean-Cap Ferrat, Alpes Maritimes, France? He telephoned

---

[1] One of the doctors at l'Hay-les-Roses. He wrote Joyce agreeing that Lucia might improve in less clinical surroundings.
[2] Feldkirch.   [3] The tenant of his Kensington flat.

today from Geneva, near where his stepson[1] is at camp. They are all well.

I hope you have no more storms like the Monday one. A cloud burst here yesterday and gave me a great fright and a drenching. With kindest regards sincerely yours   JAMES JOYCE

To LUCIA JOYCE   MS. Private

8 August 1932   *Carlton Elite Hotel, Zurich*

Cara Lucia: Forse che andrò a Feldkirch dopo tutto. Dipende da Londra. Devo tornare al consolato brittanico domani. Il sig. Monro è assente da Londra ed il suo socio doveva mandarmi un anticipo su certi fondi che vendo. Come sto non ho abbastanza per andare costì e pagare la nota già dovuta. Avrò soldi fra qualche giorno. Ma *se* l'anticipo mi arriva domani o mercoledì mattina forse farò un salto là fino a sabato per vederti. Credevo fosse uno di quei maledetti luoghi in montagna popolato di temporali.

Qui si scoppia dal caldo. Che il diavolo pigli l'estate e le vacanze! Borach e sua madre sono partiti. Beran[2] cenerà con me stasera. È una persona che ha molto *charme*. Ti manda ed a mamma i suoi saluti.

Potrei forse lavorare con Jolas laggiù. Ecco un idea. Però, come sempre, la bocca spalancata per la pioggia di quattrini. Hai un bell'imbecille di padre. Eccoti un piccolo epigramma un poco—ma non molto—satirico che ho mandato a Giorgio per la sua festa. Quest'altro anno devo farmi un altro che principerà: *Ventisei il ventisei*. Brauchbar e Ruggiero sono anche via. Domani sera, se non parto, dovrò cenare col vecchio ambulante che vende il *Zirri-zittig*,[3] *Morgenblutt*.[4] Ti mando questo espresso perchè ti giungera presto e che mi piace buttar via soldi.

Dovrei vedere il prof. Vogt sabato. Lui è (naturalmente) arrabbiato con me perchè non son andato prima da lui.

Sono contento che sei ingrassata. Eri troppo magra.

Arrivederci presto ad ogni modo

Tanti saluti a mamma vi abbraccio tutt'e due   BABBO[5]

---

[1] David Fleischman (b. 1919), the son of Helen Fleischman (Joyce) and Leon Fleischman.

[2] The Swiss poet Felix Beran (1868–1937).

[3] The *Neue Zürcher Zeitung* in Zurich-German spelled phonetically.

[4] Mispronunciation of *Morgenblatt*, a Zurich newspaper. Morgenblutt would mean 'Morning Blood'.

[5] (Translation)

'Dear Lucia: Perhaps I will go to Feldkirch after all. It depends on London. I must go back to the British consulate tomorrow. Mr Monro is away from London and his partner was to send me an advance on certain stocks I am selling. As of now I don't have enough to go there and pay the current bill. I will have money in a few days. But

To Stanislaus Joyce (Postcard)   MS. Cornell

Postmark 17 August 1932   [*Feldkirch*]

Got yr. Verona card. Hoped you might be near here in Tyrol. When you
get back to T.[1] can you get Lucia La Storia della Scrittura or dell'Alfa-
beto (Biblioteca del Popolo, Sonzogno) 15c She is doing an alphabet
for another book.[2] Best wishes to both   Jim

To Alfred Bergan (Dictated letter)   TS. N.Y. Public Library
                                                          (Manuscript)

[*? Late August 1932*]   *Hotel zum Löwen,*
                                        Feldkirch (Vorarlberg), (Austria)

Dear Mr Bergan, Thanks very much for your letter. I return you, as
you wish, the catalogues. I prefer Design No. 120 which is the simplest,
and enclose the inscription. Will Messrs. Harrison please let me know
the total cost, and also when the headstone can be erected, and the
manner and time of payment which they desire?

I am staying here with my wife and daughter who, I am glad to say, is
much better, but must return to Zurich in a week or so and then to
Paris. But any letter sent me here will be forwarded.

I remember quite well Mr. Harding,[3] and heard from our common

---

if the advance comes tomorrow or Wednesday morning perhaps I will take a jaunt up
there till Saturday to see you. I thought it was one of those wretched mountain places
populated by thunderstorms.

Here we are bursting with heat. Devil take summer and holidays! Borach and his
mother have left. Beran dines with me this evening. He is a very charming person. He
sends his greetings to you and mama.

I could perhaps work with Jolas down there. That's an idea. But, as always, with
my mouth wide open for the rain of coins. You have a fine imbecile of a father. Here is
a little epigram, a bit—but not very—satirical which I've sent to Giorgio for his birthday. Next year I will have to write another which will begin, 'Twenty-six on the twenty-
sixth.' Brauchbar and Ruggiero are also away. Tomorrow evening, if I don't leave, I
will have to dine with that old peddlar who sells the *Zirri-zittig, Morgenblutt.* I send
this to you by special delivery because it will reach you quickly and because I like to
throw money away.

I am to see Prof. Vogt on Saturday. He is (of course) angry with me because I didn't
go to him sooner.

I am glad you are getting fatter. You were too thin.

I will see you soon in any case.

Greetings to mama I embrace you both   Babbo'

[1] Trieste.

[2] *A Chaucer A.B.C.*, with Lucia Joyce's *lettrines* and a preface by Louis Gillet, was not
published until July 1936.

[3] Patrick Harding. See II, p. 244.

friend Patrick Hoey[1] in Ostend a few years ago a very amusing description of the attendance at his funeral.

I am very grateful for all the trouble you are taking on my behalf. Sincerely yours,   JAMES JOYCE

P.S. Would it be possible to have the whole done in white marble, gravestone and headstone, or is this for some technical reason, or on account of some regulation in the cemetery, not advisable?

To JOHN SULLIVAN   MS. Texas

25 August 1932   *Hotel Löwen, Feldkirch*

Dear Mr Sullivan: What bad luck! Still, try Hariot for *La Juive*. They must do the centenary revival[2] at the Opéra and who is to sing Eliezar if not you? By the way, is *Le Prophète* in your repertory or does the part suit you and how long is it since you sang it? They are giving it at Zurich in September and October and Borach suggested writing the chef d'orchestre to have you invited as *Gast* for 1 night at 10,000 or 12,000 frs (French). Of course nothing may come of it as usual.[3] However I said I would write to you. Though how the little Stadttheater is going to stage Acts 4 and 5 (unless you supply the explosion) I don't know. But ce sont leurs oignons.[4]

Lucia, I think, is out of the danger zone but will need many months of surveillance. She and her friend are going in a week or so to Vence on condition that we go to Nice for a few months so as to be near them. So we said yes. Will you be singing thereabouts in the autumn?

The news in the English press that I have been operated is not correct. I have to go up to Zurich in a week or so to see Vogt who will then say definitely whether he can safely touch the eye or not. What a misfortune that all my worries did not leave me free to go to him 12 months ago. He could have saved the eye then in all probability. But I have had one damned thing after another.

You may reply here as your letter will be sent on to my Zurich hotel when I leave. Good luck as always Sincerely yours   JAMES JOYCE

[1] Patrick Hoey, a chemist's assistant who worked in Graham's Pharmacy in Westmoreland Street. He was a well-known man about town, good at after-dinner speaking and singing.

[2] Jacques Fromental Halévy, *La Juive*, an opera in five acts (1835).

[3] Sullivan received the invitation and sang in Zurich as arranged.

[4] 'Those are their onions,' i.e., that is their business.

To Alfred Bergan   TS. N.Y. Public Library (Manuscript)
(Dictated letter)

1 September 1932   *Hotel zum Löwen, Feldkirch, Austria*

Dear Mr Bergan: A few hours after I wrote you I had misgivings about
the date (May was my Mother's birth and marriage month) so I wrote
to my sister, Mrs. Shaurek, 16 Mountjoy Square, to call at Harrison's
and alter it. I hope this has now been done. I should like model 2, which
I have marked and am returning illustration of.[1] I should also prefer to
make one remittance instead of two, that is, £48–10–0 to cover
Harrison's bill and the maximum of cemetery fees. Will Messrs.
Harrison agree to pay these fees for me, out of the check so made up?
And also, will they put the work in hand now, and when do they undertake to finish it and have it erected?

　　This letter is purely a business one, which I am dictating. I shall
reply to the other parts of your letter in a few days. Sincerely yours,

                                              James Joyce

From W. B. Yeats   TS. Buffalo

2 September 1932   *Riversdale, Willbrook, Rathfarnham, Dublin*

My dear Joyce Bernard Shaw and I are busy founding an Academy of
Irish Letters, we are nominating the first members, twenty-five, who
have done creative work with Ireland as the subject matter, and ten who
have given adequate grounds for their election but do not fall within
this definition. The creators Academicians, the others Associates. When
we began talking over members we found we had to make this division
or we should have been overrun with people from England or Scotland
with a little Irish blood and a great desire to acquire a national character.

　　Of course the first name that seemed essential both to Shaw and
myself was your own, indeed you might say of yourself as Dante said 'If
I stay who goes, if I go who stays?'[2] Which means that if you go out of
our list it is an empty sack indeed. By the end of next week I shall have
the signed form of nomination and I will send it to you with a copy of
the rules. I would however think it a great thing if you would trust us so
far as to give your assent when this letter reaches you. It will have to be
sent on from your London Solicitor's and I am alarmed lest your name

---

[1] Joyce was selecting his father's gravestone.
[2] Dante, says Boccaccio, was asked to undertake an embassy to Pope Boniface VIII,
and responded, 'If I go, who remains? If I remain, who goes?' Paget Toynbee, *Dante
Alighieri* (London, 1900), p. 155.

does not reach me in time. There will be no subscription, the little money wanted apart from fifty pounds Shaw has given us will be raised by lectures. The Academy will be a vigorous body capable of defending our interests, negociating with Government, and I hope preventing the worst forms of censorship. All the writers here who are likely to form our Council are students of your work.[1] Yrs Sy   W B YEATS

To HARRIET SHAW WEAVER   MS. British Museum

22 September 1932   *Hotel Métropole, Nice*

Dear Miss Weaver: We are all here. Lucia and the nurse came over from Vence today. There is a lot of news but I am busy trying to get on alone with W i P for Transition.[2] I will continue in pencil for there is something wrong with this ink.

I saw Vogt again on Saturday. He injected I don't know what and I had to go back in 3 hours. It was a test for tension. The result was favourable and he then said he could wait (bad eye). There was no room in the anterior chamber as it was, he would have to cut through the lens to work. This might produce a traumatic iritis which would probably pass over to good eye and perhaps undo all. He says the capsule will shrink in about $1-1\frac{1}{2}$ years and so leave him some space. . . . He changed my glasses and insists I am to come back to see him every 3 months during that $1-1\frac{1}{2}$ yr.

Yeats and Shaw have written me a very complimentary letter asking me to accept nomination as member of the New Irish Academy of Letters. I am declining. Live abroad, bad sight etc.

The Albatross Press (rival of Tauchnitz) has been bombarding me with phone calls, telegrams etc from Germany to Z'ch, Geneva and here. They want to take over Miss Beach's continental rights whether Cerf wins the U.S. case or not.[3] They would sell at $\frac{1}{4}$ her price but pay

[1] When Joyce did not reply at once, a second (printed) letter, signed by Bernard Shaw and Yeats, followed. Joyce's answer, dated 5 October 1932, thanked Yeats: 'It is now thirty years since you first held out to me your helping hand.' He wished success to the Academy, but said, 'My case, however, being as it was and probably will be, I see no reason why my name should have arisen at all in connection with such an academy: and I feel quite clearly that I have no right whatsoever to nominate myself as a member of it.' (*Letters*, ed. Gilbert, p. 325)

[2] Joyce was now working on the first chapter of Book II (*Finnegans Wake*, pp. 219–259), which was published in *transition* 22 (February 1933) 49–76.

[3] The Albatross Press, with headquarters in Hamburg, offered to publish *Ulysses* in Europe. Joyce signed a contract with this publisher which assigned a share of the book's royalties to Sylvia Beach. The new edition was issued under the imprint of the Odyssey Press in December 1932, and had the advantage of being corrected by Stuart Gilbert. In its fourth printing it became, as James F. Spoerri has shown, the most accurate text of *Ulysses*.

only half as much royalties. Of course the sales would be infinitely more numerous. I have not yet replied. With kindest regards sincerely yours

JAMES JOYCE

To STANISLAUS JOYCE (Postcard)   MS. Cornell

28 September 1932   *Hotel Métropole, Nice*

Congratulations on your *début*.[1] Lucia's book[2] is out and is exquisite. Did that initial appear?[3] I suppose nobody in T.[4] bought a copy. *Tant pis pour eux.*[5] Kind greetings.   JIM

To ALFRED BERGAN   MS. N.Y. Public Library (Manuscript)

1 October 1932   *Hotel Métropole, Nice, France*

Dear Mr Bergan: Can you please let me know whether you received from my Solicitors the cheque (£48.9.9.) for Messrs. Harrison? Also if the inscription has not yet been made I should like to check the wording.

It is very good of you to have offered to see this matter through. I do not think you are the last of Pappie's friends for I know that Mr Devan is still alive. It is strange that after such a long absence I continue to think of all those people, though I have met so many others in different lands.

I hear that the little poem I spoke of is published in a New York weekly.[6] I shall ask my agent to send you a copy. Sincerely yours,

JAMES JOYCE

To FRANK BUDGEN   MS. Yale

9 October 1932   *Hotel Métropole, Nice*

Dear Budgen: I thank Mrs Budgen and yourself and the Suters for your message but never believe anything an Englishman tells you in the press or an Irishman in a bar about me. I was not operated: after 5 weeks study of the case Vogt decided it was too difficult and dangerous even for him. But I have to go back to Z'ch every 10 or 12 weeks for a year or a year and a half as he is observing some process and will not trust any

---

[1] Stanislaus Joyce's preface to Svevo's *As a Man Grows Older* (London, 1932).
[2] *Pomes Penyeach*, with Lucia Joyce's *lettrines* (Paris and London, October 1932).
[3] See p. 249.   [4] Trieste.   [5] 'So much the worse for them.'
[6] See p. 253. 'Ecce Puer' was published in the *New Republic* (New York) LXXIII.939 30 November 1932) 70.

other doctor. Damn well right too. I wish I had met him ten years ago. And talking of press reports I got a pile of clippings a few days ago about a reading of A.L.P. by Miss Allgood[1] to be given in a London theatre. I heard nothing about it. A few vague words with her some 15 months ago. And of an Irish academy of letters including myself. As for that I had a letter from Yeats and Shaw but declined to send in my name.

I wish you and Sargent could see Lucia's book of lettrines at Harmsworth's shop. Please go with him and if you like them as I know you will a line would please her greatly. The enclosed is a little silly but rather graceful—I mean the picture of myself and daughter and of Wilhelm Meister. There is something Mignonesque about her and, if it comes to that, I do not mind being called a 'harmonieux vieillard' when there are so many inharmonious young striplings about.

Here (if I can find it) is a letter I had from Jung.[2] But please send it and the cutting back *bei Gelegenheit*.[3] The letter of course is privileged. Have not replied yet.

How about your book? Is it 'marching'? If I can throw any obscurity on the subject let me know. Sincerely yours   JAMES JOYCE

To JOHN SULLIVAN (Postcard)   MS. Texas

9 October 1932   *Hotel Métropole, Nice*

Are you engaged anywhere in this sector as we may stay on here and did you get any offer from Zurich.[4] I spoke to the chef d'orchestre Kalisco, a Viennese.   J.J.

To FRANK BUDGEN (Postcard)   MS. Yale

[*About 18 October*] *1932*   [*Nice*]

Useless to drag Sargent down to Harmsworth's. Have just heard the Dover Customs have seized and impounded all the English copies (10) as 'silk luxury goods' (on account of the green silk casings) and are demanding Chinese ransom prices!

Oh oh Pound Sterling!   J.J.

---

[1] Sara Allgood (1883–1950), Irish actress.
[2] Pp. 253–54.
[3] 'At your convenience.'
[4] See p. 257, n. 3.

To ALFRED BERGAN   MS. N.Y. Public Library (Manuscript)

18 October 1932   *Hotel Métropole, Nice, France*

Dear Mr Bergan: I am very sorry but I cannot read the corrected date on enclosed. Will you tell me what it is so that I may reply? We will be leaving here in a few days for Orange so I should like a line by return. Sincerely yours,   JAMES JOYCE

To GEORG GOYERT   MS. S. Illinois (Croessmann)

22 October 1932   *Hotel Lord Byron, Champs-Elysées, Paris VIIIᵉ*

Dear Mr Goyert: I hope *you* can read *my* writing. I can write my own writing but cannot read anybody else's!

Have just arrived here from Nice. After 12 years in Paris we are without a flat and all my books are packed up so I cannot lend you my copy of *T.T. of S. and S.*[1] Perhaps Borach or Bródy could.

But surely you cannot have finished A.L.P. yet?

I am sending you a notice about Lucia (my daughter) which may amuse you. She has great talent.

Is there any chance of your coming to Paris. We spent part of the summer in Feldkirch, a nice old town. I liked the people very much—old-fashioned and polite.

I am trying to work. I must go back to Zurich every 3 months to be examined by Vogt.

Did you see Jung's article and his letter to me. He seems to have read *Ulysses* from first to last without one smile. The only thing to do in such a case is to change one's drink![2]

Our regards to all your family sincerely yours   JAMES JOYCE

From PAUL LÉON to RALPH PINKER   TS. S. Illinois (Feinberg)

26 October 1932   *27 rue Casimir-Périer (VIIᵉ) Littre 88–89*

Dear Mr Pinker, Some time ago Mr. Joyce has been approached by Warner Bros. in view of obtaining his consent to the filming of Ulysses. I went to see the gentleman who is the manager of their Paris Office. This gentleman seemed very eager to have the film done as quickly as possible. Mr Joyce was at the time away from Paris and on my referring

[1] *Tales Told of Shem and Shaun* (Paris, 1929).
[2] After these words Joyce marks, 'v. *Ulysses*—episode Eolus.' On p. 157 (123) in the *Aeolus* episode, Ned Lambert talks to Simon Dedalus about a particularly florid passage in Dan Dawson's latest speech, 'What about that, Simon? he asked over the fringe of his newspaper. How's that for high?
—Changing his drink, Mr Dedalus said.'

the matter to him he asked me to give a dilatory answer. I did so and never heard again from Warner Bros. Now we learn that there have been several press news published in the States about the forthcoming filming of Ulysses.

I have taken the matter up with Mr Joyce who in fact tells me that he is in principle opposed to the filming of Ulysses and would like the news in the paper to be denied. I must also add that I had warned Mr Cerf of the proposal in case there was some idea of pirating Ulysses. Mr Cerf replied to me that he considered the firm so first class that there could not be any piracy in it and that on the contrary he considered the filming of Ulysses as very beneficial for the circulation of the book. He naturally takes the material point of view, Mr Joyce on the contrary takes the literary point of view and is therefore opposed to the filming as irrealisable. Before however giving this answer which is an absolute and flat refusal I have advised him first to find out what our position is as regards the filming rights. Should the filming rights in the States also not belong to him then naturally there is no use refusing and it would be better to come to some arrangement. Should however the film rights belong to Mr Joyce then he would absolutely refuse.

Could you perhaps find out what the exact situation is?

Mr Joyce has at last heard from Gorman who has probably been wakened up by your letter to your brother many thanks. Sincerely yours

PAUL LÉON

To ALFRED BERGAN   MS. N.Y. Public Library (Manuscript)

27 October 1932   *Hotel Lord Byron, Champs-Elysées, Paris*

Dear Mr Bergan: Your letter has followed me up from Nice. I could not read the pencilled date in the inscription but now that everything is right can you let me know when the stone can be erected?[1]

[1] In accordance with John Joyce's wish that his wife's name as well as his own be engraved on his headstone, James Joyce wrote the simple inscription:

IN
LOVING MEMORY
OF
JOHN STANISLAUS JOYCE
OF CORK
BORN 4TH JULY 1849
DIED 29TH DEC. 1931
AND OF HIS WIFE
MARY JANE
OF DUBLIN
BORN 15TH MAY 1859
DIED 13TH AUGUST 1903

Yesterday I sent you an article about my daughter which may amuse you. I never receive journalists, French or English. The one who wrote this article seems to think I am 80 years old. I am, however, a grandfather and here is a bad snapshot of myself and my first grandson, Stephen James, taken a month ago at Nice.

There is a point on which I should like to have your advice. An American writer[1] is doing a biography of me and he wants information about my ancestors. You may remember the family portraits (now in the possession of my son Giorgio). These represent besides Tuohy's splendid portrait of my father (born at Cork, 4 July 1849) my grandfather, James, born, I think in Fermoy,[2] who married Ellen O'Connell, second cousin to Dan, and my great grandfather James[3] who married Anne McCann of Ulster. The American writer wants to go back a few more generations on the Joyce side. Is my father's birth registered also at Charlemont Hse and could I find in that entry the date and place of the birth of my grandfather James (approximately 1828 at Fermoy, Rose Cottage) and if I found that would it have the date and place of birth of my great grandfather from which I could obtain the information required? Or should enquiries be made at Cork and Fermoy? The publishers would pay a small fee for research, I suppose. Sincerely yours

JAMES JOYCE

To FRANK BUDGEN   MS. Yale

29 October 1932   *Hotel Lord Byron, Champs-Elysées, Paris*

Dear Budgen: The British Customs have now decided to send back the whole English edition[4] to Paris after 3 weeks muddle-headed correspondence. There is however one solitary copy at Bumpus's in Oxford Street so you and Sargent could see it there. Tell me how you like it. She has done a whole alphabet since and I think the letters would stand well before the 23 stanzas of Chaucer's alphabet-poem which begins 'Almighty and almerciable queen' (i.e. the Madonna)   J.J.

[1] Herbert Gorman.

[2] James Augustine Joyce (1827–1866), a salt and lime manufacturer near Cork. He married Ellen O'Connell, possibly a distant relation of Daniel O'Connell. He died at the age of only thirty-nine, and left one child, John Stanislaus Joyce (father of James).

[3] James Joyce, great-grandfather of the writer, was also a salt and lime manufacturer.

[4] See p. 260, n. 2.

To DANIEL BRODY   MS. Brody

3 November 1932   *Hotel Lord Byron, Champs-Elysées, Paris VIIIe*

Dear Mr Brody: My son has just read me your letter over the telephone.
I have not given permission to any firm in the U.S. or elsewhere to film
Ulysses. I received from Messrs W B Yeats and Bernard Shaw an
invitation to become a member of the new Irish Academy of Letters but
declined it. I was not operated by Vogt in August. I have to return to
Zurich every 3 months to be under observation by him for the next 12 or
18 months and then he will see whether he can operate or not. You may
keep the designs until the Christmas season if you think there is a
reasonable prospect of doing something with them. I received a letter
from Goyert and referred him to you. It may interest you to know that
the British Customs seized the whole 10 copies (9 sold in advance) of the
English part of my daughter's book of *lettrines* on account of the 'carton'
classing it as 'silk luxury goods' and demanding a Chinese ransom of £4
per copy on a book which already costs £12 a copy. No wonder the £ is
at 82 in the shade. Sincerely yours   JAMES JOYCE

To F. V. MORLEY[1]   MS. Faber

3 November 1932   *Hotel Lord Byron, Champs-Elysées, Paris VIIIe*

Dear Mr Morley: You probably saw my correspondence with Eliot
about my daughter's *lettrines* some months ago. I am giving you a Paris
notice and a prospectus—this latter, simply as information. Only one
copy of the book is to be seen in London as the British Customs at
Newhaven seized all the copies sold to English buyers—10—and
demanded Chinese ransom at the rate of £4 per book, the book costing
already about £12. If you call at Bumpus's shop in Oxford Street (?)
you can get the *lettrines* and if they interest you I have a proposal to
make with regard to my daughter's work. Please let me hear from you as
soon as you can.

    I shall write to you about myself shortly. I have been through a most
trying time for the past year and especially the past half year. Sincerely
yours   JAMES JOYCE

[1] Frank Vigor Morley (b. 1899), writer, and a director of Faber & Faber.

To F. V. MORLEY   MS. Faber

10 November 1932   *Hotel Lord Byron, Champs-Elysées, Paris*

Dear Mr Morley: It was very kind of you to act so promptly. You are
right in saying that such work is not for the English market. In fact this
pochoir[1] reproduction can be done only in Paris and even here only by
two or three firms. Some of the *lettrines* had to be done over sixteen
times. As regards my daughter's alphabet which is now complete it is in
the same style but more mature. The *lettrines* were designed to stand as
initials for Chaucer's poem in ottava rima, *A.B.C*, translated from the
French of Guillaume de Deguilleville, a poem in praise of the Madonna,
beginning 'Almighty and almerciable queen'. Mr Holroyd Reece[2] of the
Albatross Press admires those *lettrines* very much and he wrote to
Messrs Burns and Oates about them. I hope that this firm or perhaps
the O.U.P. will decide to print the poem with the initials which however
would have to be done over here.

Apart from this very elaborate and costly work I think that she is
capable of doing things simpler and more utilisable. This was why I
presumed on so short an acquaintance and asked you to inspect the
book. Neither writer or publisher (Miss Beach) of P.P. is taking any
royalty or payment in connection with this edition and 33% of the net
profits will go to my daughter. I asked her if she had anything else to
show and she gave me the enclosed.

I am painfully aware that I am already a burden to your firm on
account of my tardiness but if I could secure for her any kind of work
(she had a bad nervous breakdown some months ago but has come
through it well and is full of desire to express herself in this form of art
which she has chosen) it would be an immense relief to me. It would
probably enable me to go ahead with my own work and so fulfil my
engagements towards your firm. If you yourself are unable to commission
her perhaps you can direct me to the proper quarter.

I do not know where the British and American papers get their scare
headlines about me. I have never given an interview in my life and do
not receive journalists. Nor do I understand why they should consider
an unread writer as good copy.

As you see I can write. Unfortunately I cannot read except with a
very strong magnifying glass. I went to Zurich in July and Professor
Vogt (probably the greatest eye-doctor in the world) found that my

---

[1] Stencil-plate.
[2] John Holroyd-Reece (b. 1897), publisher, author, and translator, headed the holding
company that controlled Albatross and Tauchnitz editions.

sight had somewhat improved. I have to return to him every three months for a year or a year and a half to be under constant observation. He is afraid to touch the bad eye until the process of amelioration in the other has reached its highest point. As these wretched eyes of mine have already been operated on ten times (unfortunately not by him, except the last time) after about 25 years of recurrent inflamations it is a very delicate case to handle.

I am glad to hear you are bringing out another fragment of W. i P.[1] But the first part of this letter is the most important at the moment. I shall be extremely grateful for any help or suggestions which you offer me.

Please give my regards to Eliot[2] when you write to him. Sincerely yours   JAMES JOYCE

From PAUL LÉON to HARRIET SHAW WEAVER[3]   MS. British Museum

4 January 1933   *27 rue Casimir Périer, Paris 7ᵉ*

Dear Miss Weaver, I am again writing to you on a subject which Mr Joyce feels incapable of doing himself and which is perhaps better judged by an outsider in the present conditions and under the strain he is living in.

The point is that he cannot meet the current monthly budget with his monthly income. It is not the flat alone which costs with the additional expenses some 2.000 alone, but he has to keep a companion for his daughter which salary, board and lodging put together amounts to some 2.000 again. If you add to this extra expenses necessitated by doctors' visits, some work undertaken by his daughter etc. he can barely meet the first of the necessities commanded by the situation. He is extremely reluctant to have again to avail himself of money obtained from the selling of his stock but he is afraid it has become a necessity. His flat in London has been vacated by the 15th of last

---

[1] *Two Tales of Shem and Shaun*, including 'The Mookse and the Gripes' (*Finnegans Wake*, pp. 152–59) and 'The Ondt and the Gracehoper' (pp. 414–19), but excluding 'The Muddest Thick That Was Ever Heard Dump' (pp. 282–304) which was printed in the Paris edition of 1929. Faber & Faber published the book on 1 December 1932 and priced it at 2s. 6d.

[2] T. S. Eliot was Charles Eliot Norton Professor at Harvard University at this time.

[3] Paul Léon's letters to Harriet Shaw Weaver were written under two aspects: he was first and foremost a sympathetic friend, and he was also a spokesman for Joyce in matters which Joyce did not wish to take up himself. He would not have written such a letter as this one without at least implied authorization; it represents, though with some filtering and perhaps even change of emphasis, Joyce's attitude.

month and the new application by a new tenant had to be refused for want of references and guarantees. So that this month the quarter's rent had to go out Mr Joyce's own pocket which reduced by half his monthly allowance. In these circumstances he begs you again to instruct Messrs. Monro Saw & Co. to sell another £100 of his stock in order to enable him to pass through this month.

I hope that by the end of February, as I wrote you, the first royalties due on Ulysses will begin coming in and this will certainly ease the situation at least materially which otherwise is just as indefinite as it was. From what I hear from Mr Joyce—as I have personally no direct means of judging—the situation has to a great extent exhausted him both physically and morally. He tries to react by working very hard, at least as much as he has the chance, but I have seen him suffering so deeply and with such disastrous effects on his strength that my impression is that he is sometimes at the end of his forces. As every exceptional personality his pains cut deeper into his system than with us—but his recovery—as he often does recover—is the more admirable. In spite of this rather sombre picture I am drawing I think his attitude is the correct one and some slight results are beginning to tell. There is no reason to give up hope and that is the reason why I am writing that the situation is uncertain though not by all means irretrievable.

The Odyssey edition of Ulysses seems to have reached a wide circle of persons. Mr Pinker has just written to him about an offer for an Italian translation of Ulysses and Mr Joyce has received another one for a Spanish translation—which is then due to reach the South-American Market.

Mr Joyce's relations with the Odéon quarter are very good. I think I am going to see Miss Beach to-day about the publication of some documents on Mr Joyce for a new French Review 'Le Minotaure' which I will not fail to have sent to you.

I think I have kept you au courant of all the situation and beg you to accept my best wishes for a happy New Year with kindest regards Sincerely yours   PAUL LÉON

May I raise the following points. From Messrs. Monro Saw & Co's letter I see that Mr Joyce is selling South African stock—is it advisable to do so since now S.A. has gone of[f] the gold standard? I am merely putting a question since I do not know what effect it has had on S.A. stock.

Mr Joyce would like to have the money if possible by the end of the week.

From Paul Léon to Harriet Shaw Weaver   TS. British Museum

17 March 1933   *27 rue Casimir-Perier (VII), Littre 88–89, Paris*

Dear Miss Weaver, I did not write to you before as I was expecting some development in the situation which however did not take place.

First of all I want to thank you for the sending of the copies of the Hull Daily Mail and may I ask you to have one copy of it sent to Mr Pinker (Talbot House Arundel Street Strand) and another to Mr Holroy[d] Reece (Casa Beata, Via Monte Allegro, Rapallo, Italy). May I also trouble you in the future whenever there are news of that importance to send two copies to me for Mr Joyce and the other three to Mr. Reece, Mr. Pinker and to Mr Cerf (20 East 57th Street, New York c/o Random House—I have sent to Mr Cerf one of the copies you forwarded to me).

Secondly I hope you have kindly undertaken the settlement of the London flat problem which Mr Joyce reminded me again to-day he would like to see terminate as rapidly as possible and definitely.[1]

Thirdly and the most important part of this letter is Mr Joyce's state of health which permit me to treat in full sincerity as I consider his recent second breakdown as a second warning which should not be lightly over looked.

There is no doubt that Mr Joyce has had an almost unbearable time to stand lately the result of which is now telling. What he needs principally is I firmly believe some absolute rest and this he is not only not getting now but seems to despair of getting ever. I know for a fact that he had placed great hopes in your sojourn in Paris, however when he saw that you were taking a different attitude both within the circle of his immediate surroundings as well as outside his house he gave up what seemed the only hope to make a clean breast of it with you which led to his reticence in his conversations with you.[2] I do not think that he will be capable to pull through all these troubles unless he finds somebody he can absolutely trust and rely upon and this is what he had hoped to find in you. As an instance let me come back upon the question of his rest and visit to Zurich. The visit to Zurich is necessary everybody agrees as well as a good rest for several weeks I should say but he has neither the hope nor the assurance that it will ever be possible to realise either of them. Mr.

[1] Joyce had given up hope of maintaining a London residence.
[2] Harriet Shaw Weaver went to Paris shortly before this letter was written. Her visit did not go well, in part because she was dismayed by Joyce's drinking.

Borach has written a letter in a different tone suggesting a kind of kidnapping and taking Mr Joyce away, but I feel sure that unless somebody intervenes, I mean somebody with authority nothing will come out of it. The principal difficulty is, in my opinion that Mr Joyce is too considerate and will never press the point to its logical conclusion. Another example is the way he is constantly pestered by people asking for his help and aid which having not the strength to refuse he is trying to do in the best possible manner and which is not at all warranted either by his occupations or by his present state of health and nerves.[1] I could name you several of them, there are: Budgen, Goll, Sullivan, Dujardin and Pelorson. One is doing a German translation of A.L.P.,[2] the other going to Rome to lecture on the Interior Monologue,[3] the third writing a book on Mr Joyce[4] etc. etc. and Mr Joyce has to speak to all, give directions, indications which in his case amounts to practically dictating every word that is written. As a result he finishes these meetings exhausted loses appetite and sleep and is incapable to react in his home life so as to make his own life and his own interests the predominant problem of the household. I do not wish that you should have the impression I am complaining about anybody or anything, on the contrary I am absolutely certain that the situation is attempted to be handled in the way everybody understands it but the fact remains that nobody understands it as Mr Joyce does and unless somebody intervenes in his favour and intervenes strongly he will never obtain the necessary rest and quiet which are so essential for his work. On the contrary since he is a little better these last few days he is irritable which is usually a sign of better health but weaker nerves. He is seeing Dr Debray to-morrow afternoon, I hope I will be able to write to you a more detailed account of his physical condition after he sees Mr Joyce— however I am sure that whatever his physical condition, his nerves should be handled with extreme care. I again beg you not to take all the above in a bad part on the contrary I understand that Mr Joyce for one thing appreciates greatly that as a result of your kind intervention the material problem is at least for the next few months assured and that is one source of constant worry that is less.

I will keep you au courant of anything that happens and please believe me very sincerely yours,

PAUL LÉON.

[1] Actually Joyce was often cheered up by such work. See p. 286.
[2] Ivan Goll was translating *Anna Livia Plurabelle*.
[3] Edouard Dujardin.
[4] Frank Budgen.

About Mr Budgen—for completion of his book he must go to Dublin in order to paint Chapel Izod (I am not sure of my spelling) the source of the Liffey to illustrate his book.[1] As however he has already received £50 in advance from his publishers I believe Mr Joyce will have to finance the trip.

To JAMES STEPHENS   MS. Stanford

21 March 1933   *42 rue Galilée, Paris, XVI*

Dear Stephens: Herewith a photo of your quasi namesake and his grandfather.

To return for a moment to G.M.'s funeral I read that the British Prime Minister was there. This is more than can be said for the I.F.S.[2] or I.R.A.[3] or whatever their initials are. You told me you knew him[4] and sometimes met him socially. I know nothing about him except this one fact and that some English doctor operated on his eye. I think you ought to tell him about Vogt.[5] All the oculists I tried in London, eight or nine, were quite incompetent. Sincerely yours   JAMES JOYCE

From PAUL LÉON to HARRIET SHAW WEAVER   MS. British Museum

21 March 1933   *27, rue Casimir-Périer, Paris VII*ᵉ

Dear Miss Weaver I have received your letter this morning and let me thank you most sincerely for it. I will write to you in answer to it more fully—I mean giving you the doctors opinion and the general state

---

[1] Joyce wanted Frank Budgen not only to paint Chapelizod, but also to see what this suburb of Dublin now looked like. Its name is often derived from Chapelle d'Yseut, and Joyce associated it with Earwicker's daughter Isabel as well as with Iseult of Ireland. Earwicker, the central character of *Finnegans Wake*, is an innkeeper in Chapelizod. Frank Budgen describes his trip to Chapelizod in *James Joyce and the Making of 'Ulysses'*, pp. 310–11.

[2] Irish Free State.

[3] Irish Republican Army.

[4] That is, Eamon de Valera (b. 1882), then President of the Executive Council of the Irish Free State.

[5] De Valera was in fact told about Vogt and eventually submitted to an operation by him. Joyce was very conscious of De Valera's career and eye trouble, and of the fact that they were born in the same year. As John Garvin has pointed out, De Valera is frequently mentioned in *Finnegans Wake*.

of affairs now as soon as I will have a chance to speak with Mr Joyce. In the meantime he begs me to tell you of his gratitude for the interest you have and are showing.

This is merely to bother you with another request. As there has appeared a notice in the Paris Intransigeant (our Evening Standard[)] about Prof Vogt and Mr Joyce would you kindly send me the papers you mentioned over the phone about Vogt. I hope I am not giving you too much trouble Thanking you again Believe me Sincerely yours

PAUL LÉON

Can you also if you possess send me *the date* of the issue of the Semaine à Paris referring to the dancing competition in the Bal Bullier in which his daughter took part.[1]

From PAUL LÉON to HARRIET SHAW WEAVER   TS. British Museum

23 March 1933   *27 rue Casimir-Perier (VIIᵉ), Littre 88–89*

Dear Miss Weaver, I had a more lengthy conversation with Mr Joyce to day and I am therefore hurrying this letter to you as I would like it to reach you before you leave for the week-end.

Mr Joyce wishes me first of all to give you an account of his last interview with doctor Vignes about his daughter. The doctor is distinctly pleased and hopeful—an objective proof of the good achieved by the treatment is the fact that whilst up to now Miss Joyce was losing some 500 gramms weekly during the month of her treatment she has not lost anything at all. The doctor prescribes that she should continue the same treatment for another month and is adding to the treatment absorption of sea-water for the time being by the mouth but later by injection. Added to this hopeful news Mr Reece telephoned me the other day saying that Messrs Burns and Oates were willing to do Miss Joyce's alphabet for the poem of Chaucer on a commission basis and I am going to have a more detailed conversation with him in a few days.

I am glad to be able to give you this account as it leads me to Mr Joyce himself, and to his state and the effect his daughter's health has on his nerves. Somewhere about a week before the doctor's opinion was taken she had something of a kind of relapse but fought it through

---

[1] Miss Weaver has written on the letter, '17–24 May 1929.'

herself without any aid from outside which is a good sign. But of course
these days of tension were chosen for conversations of the kind that she
would not recover, that her treatment had only superficial results and
that Mr Joyce was wrong on insisting on it etc. etc. this could not but
have a bad effect on his nerves and may have added to the strain which
eventually led to the collapse the other day. I was present Saturday last
at the visit of Dr Debray whom I had warned that he would find Mr
Joyce in a bad shape. The reason for it was that some kind soul had
informed Mr Joyce that it would be useless for him to go to Zürich for
he had ruined his eyes definitely and that Vogt would never agree to
operate him again. This remark was not even, I consider, heartless but
chiefly tactless and led to a complete breakdown. The doctor had
examined him very minutely found his bloodtension absolutely normal
(14 high and 8 low) for his age. He attributed his weakness to the delay
necessary for the recovery. He promised him a full recovery of his forces
in five or six days which in fact is coming true as Mr Joyce in the last
two days is really feeling stronger. But to show you how nervous Mr
Joyce is I can tell you that having slept badly in the previous days he
felt strong pains in the back of his head due probably to insufficiently
reconstituted blood circulation naturally Mr Joyce got a fright and
thought immediately of meningitis. All these bad thoughts are due in a
small degree to the fact that he is yet unable to concentrate his mind on
his work but that is only one part of it the other brings me to the
allusion you make in your letter. I mean drinking. I have seen Mr Joyce
several times having had too much to drink and as the above opinion
about his going to Zürich was partly based on the same ground I made
it a special point to bring in the conversation with the doctor to this
matter. Dr Debray is resolutely and absolutely of the opinion that drink
has nothing to do with his collapse. It may have perhaps weakened Mr
Joyce's resistance but it is in no way the cause of anything in his health.
He examined his liver and digestive tube and he emphatically says that
they are in a perfect order and absolutely not of the types he knows to
be necessarily the consequences of an abuse of drinking. I was very glad
that he was so emphatic about it as I had noticed that Mr Joyce of late
had fallen under the influence of so many reproaches of too much drink
that he was himself beginning to believe in the fact that he was under
the influence of alcoholic poisoning. After the opinion of the doctor I
can absolutely reassure you in this respect. And I can add that the
doctor even advised him to take some wine at meals (as a matter of fact
Dr Vignes has prescribed wine during meals to Miss Joyce too) some
quarter of a litre but Mr Joyce up to now has not taken any at all.

Among the many things that have perhaps added to the impairment of
his sight people seem to forget that a great deal has been done by his
work and this is certainly no cause of complaint. To achieve any sort of
success in this respect is to try and give back to Mr Joyce as much of his
sight as is possible. As a matter of fact from what I know Vogt was
hopeful and advised Mr Joyce to come and see him every three months
and now there are already six months since he was seen. I consider it an
absolute necessity for Mr Joyce *to go to Zürich* as it happens to
coincide not only with the problem of his sight but also with a much
needed change of atmosphere and air which cannot but have a good
effect on his nerves and general health. Dr. Debray advised him to quit
Paris for a week or two going even as near as Fontainebleau but since
Zürich is necessary for the eyes I think we have no choice. Now how to
arrange it? Although I could have accompanied Mr Joyce during the
Easter vacations I do think that both materially and morally he needs
Mrs Joyce to accompany him and the problem then is limited to the
fact what to do with Miss Joyce during the week or fortnight that her
parents will be away. Could anyone take care of her during that time in
Paris (as she must not I think leave her doctor for the moment) remains
to be seen. But physically I think Mr Joyce is decidedly better and were
it not for a still subsisting pallor which annoys and frightens him I think
he would admit that he feels better.

I would like merely to add a few words about his general state of mind
during the last year and first of all in connection with the rue de l'Odéon.[1]
You know all the developments and using what I think an utmost
forbearance Mr Joyce has succeeded during all this time to escape an
open break. This does not alter the fact however that at the root of the
things he has been maltreated and this cannot but have a decisive
influence on the relations. You know Mr Joyce better than I do and for
a longer time and you know too that since the 12 or 13 years he has been
living in Paris in a very artistic and literary surrounding he has managed
not to quarrel with anybody nor to have any quarrels forced on him. He
assumed the same attitude with the rue de l'Odéon but there were facts
which could not help proving the contrary. You say in your letter that
you found Mr Joyce very elusive—personally I think his attitude was
even harsh towards you and I can explain it only by the fact that he
felt and knew that people were trying to misconstrue themselves and

[1] Joyce's relations with Sylvia Beach and Adrienne Monnier had been strained by a
letter Mlle Monnier wrote him on 19 May 1931. She protested against the way that she and
Miss Beach had, as they felt, been put upon. Joyce treated the attack with deliberate
casualness, and forbore to state grievances of his own.

the facts making the best of your very kind disposition and patient character. He decided that it was better to let others speak and he himself assumed an attitude of perfect mutism.

But even this problem of the relations with the rue de l'Odéon is but of secondary character compared to the real worries which have beset him during the last year. Seeing him as often as I do I think I am right that the principal worry by far overshadowing all other problems has been the state of health of his daughter. You cannot imagine how this has affected him especially as in the position he is he had often to act singlehanded even against the opinion of the doctors and of his immediate family. It is always easier to give up a case as hopeless or to attribute something to an exterior reason as for instance the wine than to go to the root of the thing. And here Mr Joyce has rebelled and acted as he personnally thinks best. At present even when Miss Joyce is I think, decidedly better he comes across great difficulties and this improvement is entirely due to Mr Joyce. And as regards himself though I repeat I find him much stronger he still perhaps as a reaction varies from states of great irritation and impotent fury to sudden lachrimose fits. These happily are very rare now, I prefer him furious to the state of dejection he was in last week.

Finally and to wind up I think the voyage to Zürich of prime necessity and if you could do something in this respect your interference would be a blessing. For I do think Mr Joyce belongs to his work and unless he is able to do it he will not get well. All other considerations apart if he is given a chance of calm and continuous work he will be able to force the other problems and people to adapt themselves to his life.

I do not wish to wind up this letter without thanking you again for your very kind letter and to tell you that you should not be mistaken in interpreting my perhaps harsh words. I am writing to you in this manner because I have the impression that you can do a lot by words and acts and it is this consideration which gives me the courage to write to you in this way and I have absolutely nothing but the most respectful thoughts. With kindest regards very sincerely yours,   PAUL LÉON

I have received the New Statesman and the Sunday Times with the cuttings—the latter being a wrong reference. Maybe it was the Observer.

To ARNOLD BAX[1]   MS. Texas

29 March 1933   *42 rue Galilée, Paris V*ᵉ

Dear Mr Bax: Forgive me for my delay in writing to thank you for your
setting of my verses[2] in the O.U.P. book.[3] I find it very evocative and
the slightly Norwegian strain that runs through it very suitable. It has
also the merit, rare nowadays, of being singable.

I have received a letter to which I have not yet replied from a Mr
Anthony Bax and am wondering if he is a relative of yours as I suppose
the name is rather uncommon.

Thanking you again for the pleasure your music has given me, believe
me to be Sincerely yours   JAMES JOYCE

From PAUL LÉON to   TS. British Museum
HARRIET SHAW WEAVER

25 April 1933   *27 rue Casimir-Perier (VIIᵉ), Littre 88–89*

Dear Miss Weaver, Again it has been some time since I have written
and beg to be excused but every day I keep putting it off hoping always
to have some better news to report. Here are the latest developments.
On Friday night Mr Joyce suffered from a very acute attack of colitis
and could not sleep at all with the result that in the morning he could
not move from tiredness and from the continuing soreness of all his
inside and muscles. I saw him in the morning (I mean Saturday) and he
was in a rather desperate condition. After I had gone in the afternoon
the attack came back this time it was so extremely acute that Mrs Joyce
and Miss Joyce got alarmed. You cannot imagine how strong these
pains can be and how utterly helpless and strengthless they leave Mr
Joyce. His son was called up and eventually in the absence of Dr
Debray Dr Fontaine was asked to come. She came only by six o'clock
when the spasmodic attack had passed. She thoroughly examined Mr
Joyce and to our general relief found that there was nothing the matter
with him at all. She does not think that he suffers from colitis but on the
other attributes the dreadful spasms to a disequilibrium of the system
of the sympathetic nerve with the focus of the dislocation in the
epigastric part of his stomach provoking the terrible pains. She did not
think it necessary to prescribe any particular diet and on the contrary

[1] Sir Arnold Trevor Bax (1883–1953), English composer. He was particularly fond of
Irish subjects.
[2] 'Watching the Needleboats at San Sabba.'   [3] *The Joyce Book*, pp. 21–23.

declared that the state of his intestines was infinitely better than they were when she last saw them i.e. 3 or 4 years ago. In this part of her diagnostic she in fact confirmed what Dr Debray told me. But she insisted perhaps even more emphatically than he did that absolute and complete calm was necessary in fact a restcure was not only advisable but thoroughly needed. Since this visit Mr Joyce seems to be physically better but morally the problem gets more and more entangled everyday and this is what in fact I have to write to you about.

Naturally his downheartedness is probably due to a certain degree of the attack of his physical and nervous state as every one of this attacks leaves him the worse and the weaker for it. But what is worst is the moral effect. If I were to describe his state today I would call it that of a listless disgust and apathy in connection with the most vital problems of his life and work. The latter is even not considered today and whenever I mention the subject Mr Joyce merely waves his hand in despair and resignation. Secondly there is the voyage to Zürich which is in my opinion so absolutely necessary for his eyes, for his nerves for his health in fact for everything and which tallies so well with the needed rest cure. In this respect I meet difficulties of a twofold character. First of all in his immediate surroundings the opinion seems to prevail that he has as much sight as he wants and that therefore a voyage to Zürich is an unnecessary expense. Today Mr Joyce himself is in such a state that he merely submits to the inevitable. For independently that he may be influenced or not influenced by these opinions he raises the problem of money. He has none left and has asked me today to write to you asking you to direct his solicitors to sell the last £100.–.– available on the last power of attorney immediately and send him the proceeds as quickly as possible. I beg you kindly to do so as in the present circumstances when money is altogether scarce I doubt if I will be able to obtain for him an advance from the bank where I usually get it as we are nearing the end of the month settlements and he has practically no money left. But this as you know does not settle the question of principle. With the reduced income he has to look forward and he can hardly be allowed to go on selling the stock he has. I think it is greatly due to this state that his mind is so unsettled and that his health is so shattered. He has arranged to stay in the flat until the 15 of May—after these £100.–.– he may drag in the same flat until the 15 of June possibly but afterwards he absolutely does not know what to do and his usual remark is 'let everything go to pieces'. And this is not merely a pose but a constant idea and almost an obsession. He hopes to have gained by that time sufficient strength to face the worst but how on earth he is going to collect energy and strength I am absolutely at a loss to say. But he is so weak now and so listless that I have not the courage to take away any of his illusions.

There is one point also that permit me to touch upon and which concerns directly myself. I am rather loth to play the role that events have forced upon me. I may be mistaken but I have a feeling that I am not particularly welcome in Mr Joyce's home. Though personally I have nothing but a good feeling towards them it seems and I think it could be justified that there seems to have remained a small grudge against me in connection with last year's events in which owing to my family connection I have had to play a part.[1] As a result I am received only when Mr Joyce insists personally on it or when he actually needs me for his health or otherwise. This places me in a false position and in connection with the communications I have to give you this falsity is intensified. I have today suggested to Mr Joyce that may be it would be better if you were to correspond with him direct but was unable to obtain a decisive answer from him. Please forgive me for writing you this, I hope you will understand, but I certainly will continue to keep you au courant of Mr. Joyce's health, but perhaps in a less personal way.

In order to wind this up. The expected relapse in Miss Joyce's health has not come though she seems to have given up entirely her work in bookbinding and in attending the Marie Laurencin class.[2] So Mr Joyce hopes for the best without being very reassured.

May I terminate with a prayer. I do emphatically consider that the voyage to Zürich is of prime necessity and I go even so far as to say that unless it is undertaken in whatever circumstances it will be possible Mr Joyce will not get well or capable to resume his work unless he goes there.

Please excuse me if any words or expressions I have used may seem harsh to you they are certainly not meant to hurt you in any way and believe me with kindest regards Very sincerely yours.

PAUL LÉON

[1] Paul Léon, out of sympathy for Lucia Joyce, had encouraged his young brother-in-law, Alexander Ponisovsky (1901–1944), to take an interest in her during the early months of 1932. Ponisovsky proposed marriage to her early in March 1932 and was accepted. The engagement party ended, however, in Lucia's collapse. She stayed for some days with the Léons before returning to her parents' flat. The engagement was of course broken off, but Nora Joyce bore a grudge, irrationally if maternally, against the Léons on this account.

[2] Since the doctors insisted that the worst danger in Lucia's condition was apathy, her parents encouraged her to take up bookbinding and also a class in painting with Marie Laurencin (1895–1956), the French artist.

To VALERY LARBAUD   MS. Bib. Municipale, Vichy

4 May 1933   *42 rue Galilée, Paris (Etoile)*

Dear Larbaud: They tell me you are at present in town and I am
writing to know, first of all, if you are both well, as I hope you are, and
secondly whether you purpose staying here through the summer or not.
I suspect you will not stay here and as I myself purpose setting up
residence permanently in Paris again after a break of two years I
wondered whether your flat would be rentible during June–August. I
should like to have a small quiet flat to work in all the summer while my
wife is house-hunting and then to move into fixed quarters about
September. All my furniture is stored here. I am in a *meublé* as I gave up
my Kensington flat as unsatisfactory. We are only three and even Lucia
may be away part of the summer. But even if you do stay on or do not
wish to let your place I should be glad to see you or even hear from you.

The leaflet enclosed may interest you.

Do you know L. Gillet. He often asks me about you but I have no
news to give him.

I suppose you know that Miss B. is no longer my publisher. The
Albatross Press took over *U* and it is having a big international sale in
its 13th edition. *Honi soit qui mal y compte!* Sincerely yours

JAMES JOYCE

From PAUL LÉON to FRANK BUDGEN[1]   TS. Budgen

7 May 1933   *27 rue Casimir-Perier (VIIe), Paris*

Dear Mr Budgen, Miss Weaver, who is here at present, Hotel Galilee,
Rue Galilee, Paris XVIe, would prefer the picture from the sketch No. 1,[2]
her birthday is the 1st of September.

I have been asked to acknowledge receipt of your letters and am glad
you liked your stay over the water. I sent you by request a volume
about dreams which I should like to have back however as I would like
to read it myself.[3] In a day or two I shall send you, or perhaps Miss
Weaver will, the text of a play by André Obey,[4] author of *Noë* which is
having a great success here called LOIRE, the chief character is Anna
de la Loire and her five daughters—tributaries. You will find the
resemblance very striking in many parts.

---

[1] This letter was partly dictated by Joyce, as the phrasing makes clear.

[2] A sketch by Budgen of the Thames between Kew and Richmond. Joyce bought it to
give to Harriet Shaw Weaver.

[3] Frank Budgen does not recall what this book was.

[4] André Obey (b. 1896), French playwright.

Your runner up Mr Louis Golding[1] has an article which you should read on the subject you are treating in the April-XIXth century, probably a chapter from his book.

Details of the portrait gallery are: Giorgio (TUOHY pastel) Lucia (Laurencin—unfinished) James (oil—TUOHY) ditto (monotype Silvestri) Helen (oil Marchand) Nora (oil—Budgen) ditto (oil Silvestri) John (oil—TUOHY) James (sanguine Aug. John) James (grandfather of my client) Ellen, born O'Connell, grandmother, James ditto as a boy i.e. the grandfather, James Great-grandfather, Anne, born McCann—great grandmother. These last five are all in oil representing various generations of the family and are by Comerford[2] of Cork.

If you will send me registered your chapter on W.i.P. it will be read and commented on.

As regards the Nausicaa chapter you will receive a ponderous volume of some six hundred large pages on the origin and history of what he chooses to call 'Le Manteau de Tanit'.[3] He believes that this subject should be treated by you with IMMENSE seriousness, respect, circumspection, historical sense, critical acumen, documentary accuracy, citational erudition and sweet reasonableness. He had great difficulty in obtaining it again through his brother from part of his library left behind in Italy and he requests that you will not lend it to anybody as he advertised for it here but could not get a copy. Sincerely yours,

PAUL LÉON

To FRANK BUDGEN (Postcard)   MS. Yale

29 May 1933   *Hotel Habis [Zurich]*

Sending you a parcel of books. Please acknowledge receipt. Sorry about the photo. Did you get the big book from Léon? Had 2 consultations with Vogt.[4] Another on Wednesday. *Scheussliche Wetter Ein Platzregen Grüsse*[5]   J J.

[1] Louis Golding (1895–1958), English man of letters. His article, 'A Sidelight on James Joyce,' appeared in *Nineteenth Century* CXIII.674 (April 1933) 491–97. He also published a critical study entitled *James Joyce* (London, 1933).

[2] John Comerford (c. 1792–1832).

[3] 'The Mantle of Tanit.' Tanit (Tanith) was virgin goddess of the moon to the Carthaginians. The book, which has not been traced, was about women's drawers. For Budgen's treatment of the subject see *James Joyce and the Making of 'Ulysses'*, pp. 212–14 and the reproduction of his painting of the *Nausicaa* episode, opposite p. 218.

[4] Joyce was persuaded by Sigfried Giedion (b. 1893), the Swiss architectural authority, and his wife, Carola Giedion-Welcker, the art critic, to go to Zurich with them on 22 May 1933, so as to consult Professor Alfred Vogt about his eyes.

[5] 'Dreadful weather A downpour Greetings.'

To STANISLAUS JOYCE   TS. Private

30 May 1933   *Zurich*

1st consultation

Left eye, the good one, slightly improved since Sept. 1932. No exudate
or precipitation in gap. Artificial gradually opening upwards. Rate of
progress slow. This is an advantage as rapid rate of progress might
bring complications. It wd continue 3 or 4 yrs until pupil reached 4 mm.
Could be hastened by operation but far too dangerous. After 3 yrs a
tiny operation (removal of outer film) may be possible and advisable.
Prognosis good.

2nd consultation

Right eye disimproved. Cataract almost completely verkalkt (calcified),
no vision. Little sensibility to light. Retina (invisible, certainly in part
atrophied. Test of injection made at 1st consultation however gives not
unfavorable result as regards probability of glaucoma. Therefore
operation still possible—if not made, eye will be blind. If it is made—
very difficult; also dangerous for operated eye which may go blind
during op. because of loss of vitreous. If it succeeds still no means of
knowing what vision eye may obtain, this depending on retinal condition. For such an operation greatest tranquillity needed.

Asked advantage of such an operation, Vogt said 2 eyes better than 1.
Asked about retour d'age and my physical state, Vogt said he found me
looking younger and better (!!!) But that I shd have complete calm.
Asked if op. might imperil left eye, V. replied (reversing what he said in
Sept. consultation) that if there was a traumatic iritis in right eye after
op. wd probably extend to left and undo all the good he believed.

Refused to advise, but sd if in my place and cd be sure of operator like
himself wd run risk.

I am to reflect and let him know in few days. He wd operate now or in
Sept.,[1] when in any case I must return to Zurich to have my eye
examined.

To STANISLAUS JOYCE (Postcard)   MS. Cornell

6 July 1933   *Evian-les-Bains*

We stay here a few weeks and then go to Zurich for August. Any chance
of our meeting during the summer?   JIM

---

[1] The operation was postponed for various reasons and in fact never took place.

To CAROLA GIEDION-WELCKER   MS. Giedion-Welcker

8 July 1933   *Le Grand Hotel, Évian-les-Bains (Haute-Savoie)*

Dear Mrs Giedion[1]: Can you let me know whether your kind offer of
the villa for August is still open and, if so, the exact dates of your leaving
and return. I delayed writing till now as I never know what is going to
occur.

   If words are not complete in this epistle blame the ink not the drink.
I am writing in a blaze of sunshine tempered by a pitch black room.

   And à propos of handwriting can you put me in touch with Mr Pulver[2]
and what does he charge for an opinion? I have something I feel
inclined to submit to him.

   Friendly regards to Mr Giedion and yourself sincerely yours

                                                   JAMES JOYCE

To DANIEL BRODY   MS. Brody

8 July 1933   *Le Grand Hotel, Évian-les-Bains*

Dear Mr Bródy: My best thanks, however belated, to Mrs Bródy and
yourself for your kind remembrance of Bloomsbury Fair. I heard part of
Mr Birrell's lecture before leaving 'Paname' and I liked it. If I knew his
address I should write to him to thank him for so kindly making me a
gift of the typescript.

   I am sorry about the delay Frau A. L. P. finds in making her bow to
the German public but agree with you that, as things and people are
just now, the least said the soonest mended.

   With best wishes for the summer vacation Sincerely yours

                                                   JAMES JOYCE

To STANISLAUS JOYCE   MS. Cornell

13 August 1933   *Hôtel Richemond, Genève*

Dear Stannie: I got your wire of 2 August but no letter since then. Did
you write? I ask because the crétin of a concierge in Z'ch has misdirected half my mail. I wish you would drop me a line for I might still
be able to fix up something. This is the finest city for its size that I have
ever seen and beautifully situated on the banks of the Rhone and the
shores of Lake Leman.

   If you wrote I am sorry but you will have to write again.   JIM

   [1] Joyce's regular misspelling of Giedion as Gideon has been corrected in these letters.
   [2] Max Pulver (b. 1889), a well-known graphologist. Joyce wished to show Pulver some
of Lucia's handwriting.

To FRANK BUDGEN   MS. Yale

21 August 1933   *Hôtel Richemond, Genève*

Dear Budgen: I am sorry but the state of health, to say nothing of
other worries, in which I find myself will not permit me to read the
proofs of your book to which I wish every possible good success. Kindly
notify your publishers of this fact as they might use my name in this
connection in their advertisements in which case I should have to ask
my agent in England to contradict their statement in the press.

I shall write you about the picture tomorrow. Sincerely yours

JAMES JOYCE

To FRANK BUDGEN   MS. Yale

28 August 1933   *Hôtel Richemond, Genève*

Dear Budgen: I will write to you about your book in a day or so.

Friday 1 September is Miss Weaver's birthday. Will you please *now*
ring her up and fix an hour for Thursday when you can deliver the
picture.[1] *This as from yourself*

I will pay for the frame extra. Let me know the amount. If it is framed
tant mieux. If not what about a bog oak one[2] but beware of those
swindlers in 'Paddy and his pig' shops. Either they will sell you black
painted deal or promise you faithfully to have it ready for Thursday etc
and then leave you in the lurch. It is a lustreless black fossil wood. One
of my countless walking sticks is of bog oak, possibly you remember it.

I hope Sargent saw that doctor and that all is right with him.
Sincerely yours   JAMES JOYCE

From LUCIA JOYCE to FRANK BUDGEN   TS. Budgen

3 September 1933   *42 rue Galilée, Paris*

Dear Mr. Budgen, We are just back from Geneva and my father sends
you the following suggestions. Keep a close hold on your american
wrights. The Continental wrights he believes he can arrange for you
with the Albatross Press who have published him. For this purpose get
your publishers to send a copy to his agent Pinker to be forwarded at
my father's request to Mr. Reece. Have nothing to do with Tauchnitz
but have a copy sent to Mr. Daniel Brody Rheiverlag 35 a Koniginstrasse

---

[1] See p. 279. The painting showed the Liffey, with the bridge at Chapelizod in the fore-
ground, and a broken wall in the distance.

[2] Joyce, as Frank O'Connor noted, had in his Paris flat a picture of the city of Cork
framed in cork. But Budgen was not able to find any bog oak.

Munich his german publishers. He says if all the germans have gone daffed by then a Swiss firm might do the translation. In any case copys should go to Dr. Edward Corrody literary editor of the N Z Z[1] and Prof. Bernard Fehr[2] of the University of Zurich 24 Eleonora Strasse both of whom are personal friends of his. He suggests as motto for your book these lines of Godfried Kellers Ich will spiegeln mich in jenen Tagen, die wie Lindenwipfelwehen entflohen, wo die Silbersaiten angeschlagen, zart doch bebend gab den ersten ton.[3]

With regard to the Zunfthaus the Safran one was the Guild of dyers. The Zimmerleuten one is now quiet chic with the french chef named Michel who can serve you Kangaroo-schwanzsuppe[4] which is a change from the Zurich cuisine at wartime.[5]

The frase of the latin mass which you could not read is on Ulysses page I. The old catholics Augustiner Kirche are a good example of a Mooks gone Gripes.[6] They separated from Rome in 71 when the infallibility of the pope was proclaimed a Dogma but they have since gone much more apart. They have abolished auricular confession they have the eucarist under two species but the faithful received the cup only at Whitsun. I see no prayers to the B V M or the saints in their prayer book and no images of her or them around the church. But most important of all they have abolished the Filioque clause in the creed concerning which there has been a schism between western and eastern christendom for over a thousand years, Rome saying that the Holy Ghost proceeds from the father and the son. Greece and Russia and the East Orthodox churches that the procession is from the father alone, ex patre without Filioque. Of course the dogmas subsequently proclaimed by Rome after the split are not recognized by the east such as the

---

[1] Dr Eduard Korrodi (b. 1885), Swiss author, literary critic for the *Neue Zürcher Zeitung*.

[2] Bernhard Fehr (1876–1938) was professor of English at the University of Zurich from 1927 until his death.

[3] A slightly inaccurate quotation from Gottfried Keller's poem, 'Jugendgedanken':

> Ich will spiegeln mich in jenen Tagen,
> Die wie Lindenwipfelwehn entflohn,
> Wo die Silbersaite, angeschlagen,
> Klar, doch bebend, gab den ersten Ton,
> Der mein Leben lang,
> Erst heut noch, widerklang,
> Ob die Saite längst zerrissen schon. . . .

('I want to see my mirrored image in those days / Which fled like the flutterings of the tops of lindens, / When the silver cord, struck, / Clear, yet quivering, gave its first note, / Which resounded all my life, even today, though the cord snapped long ago.')

[4] 'Kangaroo-tail soup.'

[5] Budgen discusses the guilds briefly in his book (p. 25), but without using the extra details Joyce furnished him.

[6] For this fable see *Finnegans Wake*, pp. 152–59.

Immaculate conception. See the Mooks and the Gripes that is West and east, paragraph beginning when that Mooksius and ending Philioquus.[1] All the grotesque words in this are russian or greek for the three principal dogmas which separate Shem from Shaun. When he gets A and B on to his lap C slips off and when he has C and A he looses hold of B. My father hopes you will enjoy Ascona the most boring place in Switzerland and not fail to visit Geneva by far its most beautiful and elegant city. Sincerely yours,   LUCIA JOYCE

From PAUL LÉON to   TS. British Museum
HARRIET SHAW WEAVER

23 September 1933   *Paris*

Dear Miss Weaver, I feel very guilty indeed for not having written to you before but I find it very difficult also owing to Mr Joyce's distrustful attitude to give you a correct picture of the situation which varies almost from hour to hour and actually from day to day that I keep postponing my letter to you always hoping to be able to give you better news. I think, however, that now I must write to you as clearly as possible.

Mr Joyce returned as you know some three weeks ago and almost as soon as he arrived he collapsed with those terrible pains which have poisoned his existence during the last several years. He was confined to bed for a week. Dr Debray who was alone in Paris came to see him and relieved the pains which were sometimes continuous from seven to eight hours by laudanum compresses. Mr Joyce had lost seven kilos during the summer. His diagnosis was decidedly that the causes of the pains were due to nerves and as you know the hell which Mr Joyce has been going all through the summer and which was however he says but a culmination of continuous worry in the last four or five years there is little reason to be surprised that his nerves gave way at last. I left Paris for ten days in the beginning of September and during this time things seem to have been physically better though I did not hear from Mr Joyce who did not write to me. Dr. Debray whom I saw before I left was unusually outspoken for a doctor on the subject of members of Mr Joyce's family and overofficious friends who put 'une interpretation trop facile' on the case, an interpretation which he did not share and which no doctor would agree with after 48 hours examination. At present though the pains reappear now and again they do not last as rule for more than 45 minutes or an hour. A certain relief has been

[1] *Finnegans Wake*, p. 156.

brought I must say by the stay here of Mr Budgen who came with the proofs of his book[1] through which Mr Joyce went with him and Mr Gilbert. It is a long time since I have seen Mr Joyce so interested in anything as he has been in this work making suggestions, remembering points etc. Even after Mr Budgen's departure he kept dictating me various suggestions to be wrought in the text. I think he has finished now. And though he had one day of pains whilst Mr Budgen was here it did not seem to affect him as much as usual. Now instead of making progress with his own book he is trying to help Mr Gilbert in a translation of some French novel[2] which the latter is doing into English and this work seems to take much of his time in the afternoon.

All this concerning the physical state of Mr Joyce himself, as far as the other members of his family are concerned, I think that up to quite recently things had been better but just the day before yesterday there was a scene which affected Mr Joyce greatly and which again rendered him very nervous. It is probably this sense of incertitude which keeps his nerves on edge all the time.

Morally however his state is greatly influenced by the material incertitude in which he is living. He came home to find the £ down to almost 78 and the $ to 16, his son and daughter in law prepared to store their furniture and go and live in Vienna. The latter however he succeeded in dissuading them from doing. In spite of the general financial panic and the state of alarm caused in this country by the events on the other side of the Rhine Mr Joyce seems to be determined on getting an unfurnished flat as the only means of terminating his long neglected book which I believe can only be achieved in some conditions of comfort and ease surrounded by his books which at present are scattered in some three or four different places in two countries.

I thought I had arranged with Albatross[3] for Mr Joyce getting now a substantial advance. They sent in however something like one thousand francs alleging that they are entitled to settle quarterly and the large sales having taken place only in the last two months. So they are postponing their settlement to the end of the year. The sales are actually satisfactory—1,000 copies in July and 600 copies in August of the cheap edition and 200 each of these months of the bound edition. They are going to print a new issue of the cheap edition (4,000 copies) next month as with their various depots they have but 1,000 left on hand.

---

[1] *James Joyce and the Making of 'Ulysses'.*

[2] Edouard Dujardin, *Les Lauriers sont coupés*, was translated by Stuart Gilbert under the title *We'll to the Woods No More*, and published by New Directions (Norwalk. Connecticut, 1938).

[3] The Odyssey Press edition of *Ulysses*, published 1932.

The Werner Laurie[1] proposal is the fifth which seems to have fallen through and this naturally has affected Mr Joyce. Besides the Ulysses case in America which was to be tried in New York on the 22nd last has again been postponed and Mr Joyce wishes to wait until there is some decision in America before he presses anybody in Europe.

This is the greatest detail I can write to you now. I hope to be able to write to you more as soon as I get a good talk with Mr Joyce meaning as soon as he will be freer to give me more of his time but this is not easy to do for many reasons and in fact he does not seem to wish to write at all when it is a question of repeating endlessly the same inconclusive story. Believe me sincerely yours,   PAUL LEON.

P.S. I forgot also to write to you that he has still to fight against pressure brought to bear on him from all sides with regard to placing his daughter under a certain restraint in a sanatorium which he absolutely refuses to do and he has placed her in the care of a doctor here and has engaged a girl-companion for her. The opinion of this doctor is that she ruined her nervous system by five years dancing strain something which he always combated and tried to discourage as far as he could while recognising her great talent. He tells me that she is encouraged by certain people to go and pass the winter alone in Zürich—this he regards as lunacy but every time I meet him some new origin of her condition has been discovered the only thing which does not vary is the fact that he is the culprit. I am writing you this of my own initiative and almost against his express wish for he considers it is quite useless to make these continual long explanations. As a matter of fact it is he who should go to Zurich at the end of the month.

To STANISLAUS JOYCE   MS. Cornell

18 October 1933   *42 rue Galilée, Paris (Etoile)*

Dear Stannie: Thanks for the two books. I have looked here and there through one *G di D.*[2] I wanted them chiefly for the files. They have played me the same trick as Roth and the Japanese (20000 copies of *U* in Japanese sold in Japan in 6 months): but there is nothing to be done. So the Tokyo lawyer says. The best thing in the O.U.P. book is Bliss.[3] J.S.'s poem is good too.[4]

[1] T. Werner Laurie considered briefly the possibility of publishing *Ulysses* in England but gave it up.
[2] *Gente di Dublino*, the Italian translation of *Dubliners* by Annie and Adriano Lami, was published in March 1933 by Edizioni Corbaccio, Milan.
[3] The setting of 'Simples' by Arthur Bliss in *The Joyce Book* (London 1933).
[4] James Stephens, 'Prologue,' *ibid.*, p. 11.

I should have gone to Zurich today but have to put it off, being slightly *grippé*. Hope to go next week. I have to see Vogt 3 times a year *circa*. My case is on in the U.S.A. and am expecting a cable every day. Meanwhile H.H.[1] has given me a cross. This blessing is valid.[2] 'Quaecumque benedixerunt, benedicantur.'[3]—but only, I think, for that copy and that reader. *Buon pro gli faccia!*[4]

France has become very dear with the paralysed £ at 78 but I suppose one has to pay a premium for this district. The grandson is hale and hearty. A man named Michelesse (?) called here. I had no book to give his firm, of course. He seems all right but what a funny lingo he speaks! Why not write direct to Putnam's? The manager, Huntington, is very agreeable. It is only the usual woolliness of English publishers. I had a letter from Poppie. She was operated, the usual thing, I expect, but is now better. Did you get your teeth seen to? You should. You will feel much better afterwards. Budgen has done a book on me, with drawings. You will get a copy. As for Gorman, *spurlos verschwunden*.[5]

Best wishes to you both from all the six J's   JIM

To JOHN SULLIVAN   MS. Texas

18 October 1933   *42 rue Galilée, Paris*

Dear Mr Sullivan: Have just got your wire thanks, but wait your letter to know whether if you finish in Bordeaux on 24 and sing in Avignon on the 26 you will still be able to fit in this Zurich trip as you kindly offered, afterwards, I mean, though in the present theatrical season and with the trouble you have at home I think it unlikely. Mrs Sullivan rang up and I hope the news she is expecting from Prof Lancet (?) on Friday will be better. Anyhow I am glad to hear of your *cachets*. The enclosed should cause you to laugh in at least $3\frac{1}{2}$ octaves. La bénédiction des poignards n'est rien à côté de vous.[6] The *Minotaure*[7] which had my open letter to you[8] in the MS for publication found it too difficult to translate. Good luck sincerely yours   JAMES JOYCE

[1] Herbert Hughes.

[2] Joyce enclosed a letter to Sylvia Beach from DeWitt Eldredge, 18 September 1933 (now at Cornell), telling her how he held a copy of *Ulysses* under his coat while the Pope was blessing him.

[3] 'Whatsoever things they have blessed are blessèd.'   [4] 'Much good may it do him!'

[5] 'Vanished without a trace.'

[6] 'The blessing of the swords is nothing beside you.' Joyce was referring to a particularly loud scene in Act IV of Giacomo Meyerbeer's *Les Huguenots*.

[7] A French little magazine. See p. 268.

[8] 'From a Banned Writer to a Banned Singer,' first published in *New Statesman and Nation*, n.s. III. 53 (27 February 1932), 260–1. It is printed with explanatory notes in *Critical Writings*.

From PAUL LÉON to F. V. MORLEY   TS. Faber

19 November 1933   *27 rue Casimir-Perier (VIIᵉ), Paris*

Dear Mr Morley, Please find enclosed the several points concerning the
circulation of ULYSSES in Great Britain which seem to me to have
some bearing on a possible publication of this work in England. There
are of course several others to be added, that of cases of Ulysses being
sold under the mantel in fact at all booksellers in England. But the
principals are mentioned in the appended notes. Naturally I am
constantly following the matter up and as soon as anything new turns
up I will let you know.

I cannot refrain from thinking that it would be time to do something
about bringing out ULYSSES in England. I am sure (and I am not
talking without reasons) that should the H.O.[1] be approached you will
find the authorities (though naturally unwilling to commit themselves
or promise anything) less difficult to be talked to on the matter than
they ever have been. In fact I think that unofficially they would hint
that personally they will not start a case and ban the book. Of course
the Director of Public Prosecution is at the mercy of letters from
private persons who will complain but I am sure that he will think twice
before starting a case himself.

Obviously the winning of the case in America will constitute a strong
card in our game but I do think that even independently of this something should be done in England. From the cuttings concerning L.
Golding's book[2] you will see how public opinion is being prepared
independently from us. Unless something is actually started right away
it will mean a terrible amount of time wasted, for you must not forget
that there is a constant stream of copies going to England which take
away the readers of the eventual British publication.

I hope you will find your way in devising some scheme; it will not
mean great investment of capital since a case can be provoked following
the American precedent of having a copy of the current edition seized
by the Customs authorities.

Please remember me to Mrs Morley and believe me sincerely yours,

PAUL LÉON

Mr Joyce, whom I have just seen, wishes me to tell you that in view of
the lack of courage which he has met with up to now, he is strongly
advised to undertake the publication of Ulysses in G. B.[3] himself—

---

[1] Home Office.   [2] See p. 280, n. 1.   [3] Great Britain.

Notes on the circulation of the English edition of ULYSSES
in England.

1). In the last week of April or in the first week of May 1932 there
appeared in the Evening Standard an interview with one of the keepers
of the British Museum. This gentleman is quoted as saying (the
question he was interviewed on was 'banned books') and emphasizing
that ULYSSES was not a banned book that they took it off their
catalogue at their own discretion and that they never made any difficulty in giving it to the reading public in fact to any person who had a
valid reason to alledge for reading it. In fact Ulysses had been read so
much that they had to acquire several copies and had them bound.
Their proceedings would naturally had been different if ULYSSES had
been under a ban of a decision taken by a Court.

2) I do not know the details of the seizure of the 499 copies of the second
edition of Ulysses by the Custom Authorities at Folkestone (The entire
edition was of 500 copies). You may obtain the entire correspondence
exchanged between the customs and the then editor of ULYSSES Mr
John Rodker from this gentleman (whose address can be found in the
P.O. Directory). The Customs at the time refused to send the copies
back to France and the Chief of the Folkestone Customs Office is supposed to have destroyed them all. As a matter of fact, there are strong
reasons (among which words said by the Custom Officers themselves)
showing that this was not done and a copy of this edition can, I am sure
be found on sale in London. It is an open secret that Ulysses is sold in
London. Mr Stuart Gilbert at the time in India had a copy sent to him
from Oxford from Messrs Blackwell to Burma—This copies [sic] bears
the imprint: Printed for the Egoist Press by John Rodker, Paris.

3) Finally last year ULYSSES was placed as a text book in Cambridge
on the list of a young professor's lectures on Modern English Litterature.
The course took actually place and it is an open secret that a copy of
Ulysses is easily obtainable (though expensively) at any bookseller of
the University cities. In fact the course would have passed unnoticed
had not this young lecturer applied to the Home Office to obtain a copy
officially. As a result his course and his private life were investigated by
the H.O. authorities and the Director of Public Prosecution went so far
as to warn the Vice-Chancellor of the unheard of thing that was going
on in the Cambridge University. The Vice-Chancellor showed this
letter to several persons including the incriminated professor. It

contained amidst vehement protests about the indecency of Ulysses the humourous offer to forward a copy of ULYSSES for the Vice-Chancellor's private and personal edification.

4) The B.B.C. censor refused to allow Mr Harold Nicholson's lecture discussing ULYSSES over the Radio. Only after three weeks of continual tergiversation and under the threat of Mr Nicholson's resignation did he finally give way with the condition that the title of Ulysses would not be mentioned.

From PAUL LÉON to HERBERT GORMAN   TS. S. Illinois (Croessmann)

22 November 1933   *27 rue Casimir-Périer (VIIᵉ), Paris*

Dear Mr Gorman, Mr Joyce wishes me to write to you on the following matter: He is being pestered by his American publishers about the inclusion in the American edition of ULYSSES of a chart which he had drawn up eleven years ago establishing the parallel episodes between ULYSSES and the ODYSSEY. This chart which had been written for Mr Valery Larbaud at the time, had an absolutely private character and was not meant for publication, least of all as an addition or interpretation of the text. It had been communicated to you confidentially and nobody in America knew of its existence at least as far as the publishing circles are concerned.[1]

The present publishers of ULYSSES have obtained it, as they tell us, from you and despite the repeated and absolute refusal of Mr Joyce to allow them to print it in their edition they keep on insisting on its inclusion.

This chart was communicated to you for the purposes of the biography of Mr Joyce which you intended to write at the time. I do not know if you intend to use it still or to write the biography at all but as you have thus been instrumental to this new plan would you please be good enough to write to Random House, to your editor and to Mr Joyce himself stating that the chart was communicated to you and that you showed it and as it seems parted with it without any authority and much to Mr Joyce's annoyance as it seems the only way to put an end to their perpetual insistence. Sincerely yours,   PAUL LÉON

[1] Herbert Gorman had not, in fact, given the chart to Bennett Cerf. The culprit may have been Edmund Wilson.

From T. S. ELIOT to MONRO, SAW & COMPANY   TS. Faber

28 November 1933   *Faber & Faber, 24 Russell Square, W.C.1*

Dear Sirs, I understand from Mr. James Joyce that you are his solicitors in this country, and we are now his English publishers. We shall be publishing his WORK IN PROGRESS when it is completed, and are meanwhile exploring the possibility of bringing out a new edition of ULYSSES. I am therefore writing to you to ask you to be so kind as to provide us with such facts in the history of the case as may be in your possession, and as would be relevant to this venture.

First of all, I am told categorically by Mr. Joyce that ULYSSES is copyright in this country, and in his own name. I should be obliged if you could confirm this statement from your own knowledge. If this is so, the situation is materially different from that in America.

Together with my colleague Mr. Morley, I went to Paris last week and discussed matters with Mr. Joyce and with his Paris solicitor, M. Paul Leon. Subsequently M. Leon sent us a memorandum of the relevant facts in his possession, but these leave gaps which must be filled before we can proceed further.

We are anxious to find out all the facts about the publication of the first edition of ULYSSES. It seems that after vain attempts by Miss Harriet Weaver to persuade a British printer to produce the book for her, she had it printed in Paris as published by the Egoist Press Limited, of London, of which she was proprietor. I have the impression that it was this edition of 499 copies which was seized by the Customs authorities at Folkestone. According to M. Leon's memorandum, however, the consignment seized at Folkestone was a second edition, and he tells me nothing about the first edition. I presume that it was shortly after this seizure that Miss Weaver abandoned her attempt, and the book passed into the hands of Miss Sylvia Beach in Paris. In my own acquaintance with the case there is a complete gap between Miss Weaver's first attempts to get the book printed in this country, and Miss Beach's production of the book in Paris. Miss Beach sent me by post a copy of her first edition, which some years later I unfortunately lost: that is to say, it was borrowed or stolen.

We are most anxious to know through whose intervention this book was first brought to the attention of the Customs or any other civil authorities in Britain, and to what legal process of condemnation it was submitted. I should like to be quite clear as to the legal differences between this case and that of books which have been condemned, or, according to newspaper slang, 'banned', after being printed and published in this country. Not until we are thoroughly acquainted with the case shall we be in a position to conjecture in what way, if in any, proceedings against a new publication of the work in this country after more than ten years' lapse of time, might be instituted.

There are possibly some gaps in the history of the case which could be completed by Miss Weaver, or possibly Mr. John Rodker, but I am sure that you will agree that it is best that we should first obtain all the information possible from yourselves, as Mr. Joyce's legal representatives here, before enquiring elsewhere.

I think that my name will be known to Mr. Monro, as I had some communication with him a year and a half ago, on quite a different matter. Yours faithfully,   T. S. ELIOT
                                                                          Director.

To T. S. ELIOT   MS. Faber
5 December 1933   *42 rue Galilée, Paris XVIième*

Dear Eliot: No, I had heard nothing at all though one of your replies at lunch struck me. As you wrote me through your office I prefer to wait till I see you over here again to allude to the matter. Thanks for writing to me.[1] One needs a huge lot of patience in these cases.

It is I who should excuse myself. I forgot you were not there for all night. Anyhow Léon and I stayed on a long time after with the *patronne*, L. explaining to her all about *Ulysses* (which he has not yet read!).

Sullivan is still in the *midi* so I have not gone to Zurich.

Let me know when you come over next—but in advance. And also excuse my delay in replying. Sincerely yours   JAMES JOYCE

To STANISLAUS JOYCE   MS. Cornell
[About 8 December 1933]   *42 rue Galilée, Paris (Etoile)*

Dear Stannie: Thanks for your wire of felicitations.[2] Broken-backed Britain next.

Who are the enclosed? If you know them say I got the letter after a 2 months' circular tour of all my former addresses in Europe.

Now touching Xmas, as poor Pappie used to begin. Can you come here for the week. What does for four, girl included, can do for six. You ought to get a *ribasso* on the rlwy. Besides you can see Stevie. Also Sullivan if he's back from Marseilles. We all hope you can come. Lucia is much better (touching wood) in excellent health but as *stramba*[3] as a

---

[1] Eliot had informed Joyce that he and his wife had separated.

[2] Stanislaus Joyce congratulated his brother by telegram on the decision of Justice John M. Woolsey, of the United States District Court in New York, that *Ulysses* was not obscene. Woolsey's decision was announced on 6 December 1933.

[3] 'Extravagant.'

March hare and as proud as ever she can be. But devil a hapworth else that I can see after her ten doctors.

Anyhow send me a word by wire. Nora has made 4 plum puddings so there's enough to go round. I would like you to hear Giorgio's voice. He ought to come out next year. I got Lucia to study singing after 8 years' of talking. Don't talk to her either about dancing or diseases. She is beginning to forget about both, thank the Lord.

Ulysses will come out in N.Y. on 15 January next.

Send me the wire anyway and I hope you can arrange it.   JIM

Santa Lucia[1] '33 Her candle is burning quietly in the drawing room. She has had rather a job looking after my occhi.[2]

From T. S. ELIOT[3]   TS. Faber

11 December 1933   [*London*]

My dear Joyce, Many thanks for your letter. It does not now look as though I should be able to get over to Paris again this year, but I hope to come during January or February. I will not fail to let you know in advance, so that we may have an evening together. Meanwhile, if you should leave Paris for Zurich, I hope you would be able to get word to me.

I am delighted to hear that the censorship of ULYSSES in America appears to have lifted. I do not suppose that this will have any direct influence on the situation here, nevertheless it is a useful parallel to be able to draw. A few days after I got back from Paris, I wrote to Monro, Saw & Co. to ask them to be so kind as to let me have an account of the history of ULYSSES so far as they have knowledge of it. I have had an acknowledgement of my letter, but no reply: after I hear from them, I shall also try to get in touch immediately with Miss Weaver and with Rodker, to find out if they have any material facts to add to the dossier.

Yours very sincerely,   T. S. ELIOT

To T. S. ELIOT   MS. Faber

18 December 1933   *42 rue Galilée, Paris (Etoile)*

Dear Eliot: Thanks for your letter but the U.S. ban does not 'seem' to be lifted. It is lifted. I have here counsel's brief (100 printed pp) and the judge's ruling, about 12 pages. He states that his ruling is as legally valid as a decision by judge and jury, both parties having agreed to have the case tried before him alone. He orders that his ruling be filed.

---

[1] Santa Lucia, to whom Joyce had lit a candle on this, her day, is the patron saint of eyesight.   [2] 'Eyes.'   [3] From a carbon copy.

Three-fourths of the text was published in the N. Y. Herald Tribune of 7 December. The U.S. attorney-general, immediately after the decision, stood up and said he accepted the judge's ruling with great satisfaction and that the state would not appeal from it to a higher court. The defendant, Cerf, then said he would publish the book with an account of the proceedings (I suppose like the *édition définitive* of *Madame Bovary*) on 19 January next.

My solicitors don't understand very clearly why they were written to. No more do I. I told you I am the absolute owner of the copyright and property rights in England.

En somme, one half of the English-speaking world has given in. The other half, after a few terrifying bleats from Leo Britannicus, will follow—as it always does.

I am sorry you are not coming over. Anyhow I wish you a happy Xmas and good luck in the coming year. Sincerely yours JAMES JOYCE

To ALFRED BERGAN   MS. N.Y. Public Library (Manuscript)
20 December 1933   *42 rue Galilée, Paris XVI*

Dear Mr Bergan, I hope you will accept the enclosed and drink two toasts, one to Judge Woolsey and the other to me. I sent you also the N.Y. edition, just in here, which gives his ruling almost in full.

With this I also enclose a little Xmas card done by my daughter, Lucia. Sincerely yours,   JAMES JOYCE

From T. S. ELIOT[1]   TS. Faber
28 December 1933   [*London*]

My dear Joyce, Many thanks for your letter of the 18th. I am very glad to have further news about the early publication of ULYSSES in New York.

I am sorry that your solicitors do not seem to have understood the nature of my enquiry, as I wrote very fully. They could get a little more enlightenment, I hope, if they would write to me; so far, I have had nothing from them but an acknowledgement of my letter, but I suppose that they quite correctly applied to you first for your authorization to communicate with me. The major point was certainly not the matter of copyright, as I understood from you quite clearly in conversation that ULYSSES is copyright in this country, and that it is copyright in your name. The point is simply that in going ahead with the matter, we should wish to have a lawyer of our own at hand who was completely conversant with the whole history of the case, from Miss Weaver's first

[1] From a carbon copy.

attempts to get the book printed here, down to the Customs prohibition. The data which M. Leon provided are not adequate for the first part of this history. All I wanted from Monro Saw & Co. was that they should tell me all they knew of the history of the case, just as Leon wrote to Morley to give him all that he knew of it. I hope that they are willing to do so, and then, as I said, I propose to pick up what details I can from Miss Weaver and John Rodker.

Hoping to see you early next year, and with best wishes for the new year to you, to Mrs. Joyce, and to your family. Yours ever sincerely,

T. S. ELIOT

To FRANK BUDGEN   MS. Yale

30 December 1933   *42 rue Galilée, Paris*

Dear Budgen: Best wishes for '34. Fix up with U.S. as quickly as possible and let them go ahead,[1] irrespective of Boots Ltd. This will wake your own people up. Since things are going on between Soupault and you I prefer not to intervene.[2] We had dinner a week ago and I am well enough, shall meet at a New Year's Eve party. Grippe ever since 7 Dec and then had larynx tracheite. Better today. What a year! Fog, illness, disaster, madness. Do not rely too much on G.G.[3] as principal article. If he is on the loose he will have to write for his English masters. As for the piracy rumours you pass on my N.Y. publisher is quite prepared on that score. Sending your papers. Again happy '34 to Mrs Budgen yourself and Sargent   J.J.

From GEOFFREY FABER to DONALD SOMERVELL[4]   TS. Faber[5]

5 January 1934   *24 Russell Square, London W. C. 1*

My dear Donald, I want your advice—if possible your help—in an obscure matter, not without its importance for English letters. I don't really know if it falls within the Solicitor-General's province; if it doesn't I feel sure you will tell me what authority we ought to approach, and perhaps even give us a line of introduction.

The question I am raising is that of the publication of James Joyce's ULYSSES in England. As I expect you know, this book was originally published—and is still published—in Paris. Arrangements were made for a part of the original Paris edition to be published in London by a small firm called THE EGOIST PRESS (whose publications we took

---

[1] For an American edition of *James Joyce and the Making of 'Ulysses'*.
[2] Possibly an arrangement for the translation of Budgen's book into French.
[3] Probably Gerald Griffin, journalist and critic.
[4] Donald Bradley Somervell, Baron Somervell of Harrow (1889–1960), was Solicitor-General from 1933 to 1936.   [5] From a carbon copy.

over some time ago, but after the ULYSSES affair). Practically the whole of the consignment from Paris to the London publishers was seized by the Customs—I suppose by instructions from the Home Office—as 'obscene'. Copies imported from Paris are still liable to be seized, though they have always been obtainable quite easily from London booksellers. They can, in fact, now be bought at little more than one would have to pay in Paris.

Whatever the legal definition of obscenity may be, it has always been felt by most competent English critics that the term could not intelligently be applied to ULYSSES, which is certainly a work of genius and, in the opinion of many, much the most important literary work of art produced in English during the present century. The fact that it should have been classed by the police or the Home Office or the Customs authorities with pornographic literature has seemed, to those who hold the opinion I have suggested, to constitute a considerable slur on the intelligence of the authorities. Sooner or later the publication of ULYSSES in England is inevitable; and the question has now been raised in an acute form by its open publication in the U. S. A.

The position in the U. S. A. has been not dissimilar from that in this country. That is, the Customs seized all copies which came into their hands. Their action in doing so has recently been made the subject of a test case, heard by Judge Woolsey. The Judge gave a remarkable, and extremely intelligent judgement, to the effect that ULYSSES was not an obscene book and might be admitted into the United States. As the result of this judgement, the book will shortly be published in the U. S. A.

Naturally this decision has encouraged Mr. Joyce and his advisers to hope for English as well as American publication. My firm is particularly interested in this situation, because we are now Mr. Joyce's official publishers in England—we have issued parts of his unfinished book WORK IN PROGRESS and shall publish the book when it is finished. For some time Mr. Joyce has been pressing us to publish ULYSSES, and matters have now come to a head because (as we have just heard) another London firm has made him an offer to publish ULYSSES in the form of a six months' option.

I had intended to sound out official opinion in this country before long, but this communication obliges me to act more quickly than I had intended. We are, in fact, asked for an immediate reply in the form of a definite offer. That is, of course, of no interest to the English authorities, but it will explain to you why I am writing to you personally and informally in the matter. For any opinion or assistance you can give us I should be exceedingly grateful.

I have to go down to Wales this afternoon, and shall be away for ten days or so—whereas our answer to Joyce's agent cannot be delayed for more than two or three days. But in my absence the matter will be handled here by two of my directors—Mr. T. S. Eliot (of whom you know) and Mr. F. V. Morley. Is it asking too much of you to say that I should be very grateful if you could give Eliot and Morley an opportunity to see you for a quarter of an hour? They know the contents of this letter, and are—if anything—more familiar with the facts than I am myself. Either of them can be got on the telephone here on Monday morning. Yours ever,   Geoffrey Faber.

P. S. I enclose a copy of the American SATURDAY REVIEW OF LITERATURE containing Judge Woolsey's judgement.

From T. S. Eliot to Harriet Shaw Weaver[1]   TS. Faber

5 January 1934   [*London*]

Dear Miss Weaver, The question of the publication of ULYSSES in this country has again arisen, and I am anxious to supplement my meagre knowledge of the early facts in the case with a possible view to discussing the matter with a high official. My impression is that the reason why ULYSSES was not printed in this country was simply that you were unable to find a reputable printer to undertake it. I believe that after that you had an edition of 500 copies printed in France with the imprint of the EGOIST PRESS, London, and that 499 of these were the consignment which was seized at Folkestone. I should like to know if this is correct, and furthermore anything that you could tell me about the circumstances of the seizure: by what authorities, and if possible through what channel the book was drawn to the notice of the authorities. The question of the legal position is at present rather obscure.

If and when you are in town, it would be a pleasure to me to see you again, and no doubt it would be easier to discuss these matters in conversation than by letter. But if you are at present in the country, I should be very grateful for all the information that you care to give me in a letter.

With all best wishes for the new year, Yours sincerely,   T. S. Eliot

From Donald Somervell to T. S. Eliot   TS. Faber

6 January 1934   *11 Cornwall Terrace, Regent's Park N W 1*

Dear Eliot, I have had a letter from Geoffrey re Ulysses and he has asked me to write or see you. As I am just off for a week or so I am afraid that I can't see you so write. I have been on to the Home Office

[1] From a carbon copy.

and if you or Geoffrey would write or telephone to J. F. Henderson of the Home Office he would see you and give any assistance he can. He is in charge of that department. In case there is a muddle Mr Hacking's (The Under Sec) Private Sec told me that he would let Henderson know and that H would be glad to see you and give you any help he could.

I daresay they may not be able to be very helpful and I am not sure even if they were definitely prepared to say they would *not* move whether they could in fact stop a private person instituting a prosecution or whether they have any control outside the London area. These anyhow are points which he could tell you. I am very vague about the initiation of prosecutions, though I expect I ought to know about it; but I expect the Home Office could not as a matter of practical politics prevent or undertake to prevent the case going to the Court if there was a demand for having it so tested. However Henderson should be able to let you know the general position.   DONALD SOMERVELL

From HARRIET SHAW WEAVER to T. S. ELIOT   TS. Faber

7 January 1934   *74 Gloucester Place, W.I*

Dear Mr. Eliot, I will gladly give you any information I can as to the early facts of the attempt to publish *Ulysses* in this country.[1] And, as I agree with you that it would be easier to discuss the matter in conversation than by letter, I will ring up tomorrow afternoon to try to make an appointment with you.

Thank you for your good wishes for the new year. Please accept mine in return. Yours sincerely   HARRIET WEAVER

[1] Miss Weaver appended the following history:

'ULYSSES

1st Printing (Shakespeare and Company, Paris): February 1922 (1000 numbered copies)
2nd Printing (Egoist Press, London): October 1922 (2000 numbered copies, of which 500 burned by New York Post-office Authorities).
3rd Printing (Egoist Press, London): January 1923 (500 numbered copies, of which 499 seized by Folkestone Customs Authorities).
4th–11th Printing (Shakespeare and Company, Paris) January 1924–May 1930.
First issued by the Odyssey Press: December 1932.

A copy of the 2nd printing was sent to the British Museum in accordance with the English Copyright laws. It was not catalogued but can be seen by special request. (See note of Mr Leon's.)

The above particulars as to Printings are copied from the first Odyssey Press edition and the date (January 1923) given for the 3rd printing is incorrect. I cannot remember the exact date (Mr Rodker had the particulars) but it was certainly later in the year than January. Nearly 1500 copies had been sold (in Paris and London) before a ban was heard of.

The title page of the 2nd and 3rd editions bore the impress: Published for the Egoist Press, London by John Rodker, Paris.'

From T. S. ELIOT[1]   TS. Faber

9 January 1934   *[London]*

Dear Joyce, Morley will have written to-day to Léon, but here is the matter as things seem to be at the moment.

I think it was understood when we saw you in Paris that Faber & Faber were prepared to publish 'Ulysses' as soon as publication proved feasible. We had of course been pursuing enquiries when Leon's letter of the other day arrived, asking for a decision within five days.[2] My own enquiries might, in one direction, have proceeded quicker if I had thought to ask you to instruct Monro, Saw to let us have any information in their possession about the history of the case. Perhaps they have none, but they did take a long time to reply that they had no authority from you to communicate with us. I doubt whether this matters much, because I gather from Miss Weaver that nobody knows much about the confiscation at Folkestone, except for what little Rodker may know, and I have not yet been able to see him.

But the history of the case, although we want as full a chronicle as possible, is not the main line of investigation. It is impossible to get any positive statement from the Home Office, and nobody else will have any more success in that than we; but what can be done, and is a slow and delicate business, is to take the official temperature. We speeded things up as much as possible in order to be able to make some reply by the time that Léon wanted it; but our enquiries are not complete, and could not be completed within that time.

While I appreciate your desire that 'Ulysses' should be available before WIP appears, and of course agree as to the desirability, I do not feel that it is so vital as you may think. I learn that copies come through constantly from Paris, and so far I have not heard of a single instance of confiscation. The effect of publishing 'Ulysses' here of course will be to open up a new public; but I am convinced that there is a very large public indeed familiar with the book—though only in part in possession of it—which is quite ready for WIP the moment it appears.

My impressions are that the general atmosphere is steadily becoming more favourable. Now, if there were *no* symptoms of change, I should say: as well try the book now as any time. But I believe that there will be much better chances of success in six months or a year's time. What I have in mind is, that public opinion can change and is changing; but a

---

[1] From a carbon copy.

[2] Paul Léon, after John Lane The Bodley Head made a definite offer for *Ulysses*, wrote to Faber & Faber asking for a counter-offer within five days.

decision of a high court is a different matter; and I am afraid that premature attempts might actually delay the general availability of the book. I say a *high* court, because it would be bad for both publisher and book, if a publisher undertook to publish it without being ready to go on fighting for it. If it were published, and the publisher then lay down tamely under a mere magistrate's decision, the effect would be bad. But if on the other hand the magistrate's decision were sustained, there would be a legal precedent difficult to break for a long time.

I do not think that the other publisher will be able to gather any more assurance than we, or will be able to find out any more than we are finding. If he succeeds, I shall be as delighted as anybody. But if he abandons the attempt, we should like, when his option expires, to have an option for the following period, or periodically until the way is clear.

I should have written before, during this time, had I thought that I had enough information to bother you with. As soon as I have any further news, I will write to you at once. Yours ever sincerely,

T. S. ELIOT

To FRANK BUDGEN (Postcard)   MS. Yale

1 April 1934   [*Ventimiglia*]

Please excuse my long silence Going to Monte Carlo.[1] Will write you from there. I have had a good deal of illness in the household lately.[2] Hope your book is going well. Yes, thanks. I got the *House by the Churchyard*[3] Tutti saluti   JAMES JOYCE

To MME FRANCE RAPHAEL   MS. Raphael

24 April 1934   [*Paris*]

Dear Mrs Raphael I am very sorry to hear of the dreadful accident. Your niece says you are now out of danger. But what a frightful shock! It is well you are not disfigured, and I understand that it is not likely to leave any serious trace.

[1] René Bailly, a French industrialist married to an Irishwoman from Galway, invited the Joyces to accompany them on a motor trip to Zurich by way of Monte Carlo and Neuchâtel.
[2] See p. 304, n. 5.
[3] J. Sheridan Le Fanu, *The House by the Churchyard* (1863). Most of the incidents take place at Chapelizod, and there is also a scene in the Phoenix Park. Joyce frequently refers to it in *Finnegans Wake*. In 1937 he had Budgen read the book for him so as to refresh his memory of certain incidents. (*Letters*, ed. Gilbert, p. 396.)

I do hope you will get some compensation in spite of the lack of witnesses and that your suffering is not too great.

Let me thank you once again for your quick and excellent transcriptions. You have rendered me a very great service.[1]

With my very best wishes for your speedy and complete recovery sincerely yours   JAMES JOYCE

To CAROLA GIEDION-WELCKER   MS. Giedion-Welcker

25 April 1934   *42 rue Galilée, Paris*

Dear Mrs Giedeon: I enclose a letter of Lucia's (written at a bad time) and I think you ought to add the more recent card you received. Also two *lettrines* of hers which, of course, should be returned with the letter. Give no indication except that she is a young woman of 27[2]

I met my publisher[3] from the U.S. here and he informed me that the sales now stand at 35,000 but that my compatriot correligionists and the puritan prohibitionists are infuriated and have compelled the state attorney to file an appeal at the eleventh hour.

I hope Mr Giedeon and yourself and the children are well. We are back here, resting after our rest. I gave your messages to the Jolases and also to Miss Beach

By the way, will you please send me Pulver's opinion c/o Mr Paul Léon, 27 rue Casimir-Périer, Paris, VII? with the bill, of course.

Friendly greetings to you both from my wife and myself. Sincerely yours   JAMES JOYCE

To FRANK BUDGEN   MS. Yale

25 April 1934   *42 rue Galilée, Paris, XVI*

Dear Budgen: I've just come here to Paris from the rainy southern shore. I to Monte Carlo went but I never played a cent.[4] I saw Vogt in Z'ch. The right eye-lens almost calcified. He can't make up his mind. Two operations at least needed and he is not sure of the result. If good, I could see with a lens as well as most people. But any upset in the eye during the operation might pass to the other and close me up entirely.

---

[1] Mme Raphael used to transcribe Joyce's small and almost illegible notes into an over-sized handwriting so that he could refer to them easily in spite of his defective vision.

[2] Joyce was pursuing his plan to have the graphologist Max Pulver report on Lucia's handwriting.

[3] Bennett Cerf.

[4] In the music hall song, 'The Man Who Broke the Bank at Monte Carlo,' the words are: 'I to Monte Carlo went, / Just to pay my winter's rent.'

The other eye has slightly improved. He gave me a different glass to see better with. Have to go back in autumn.

Yes, the sales of *U* in *U.S.A.* are remarkable. 33,000 in 10 weeks. But you saw the latest development due to pressure from my infuriated correligionist compatriots and the puritan prohibitionists. Z'ch booksellers retail your book at 15 frs (almost £1) and find few buyers therefore. Could you buy in a copy for me at trade price if your contract allows it or if not at the full figure and have it sent to:

> Paul Ruggiero
> 48 Waffenplatz
> Z'ch

and let me know the amount. By the way, did you ever get a M.O. for 10/- or a banknote for 50 frs (French) about 2 months ago for some songs for Giorgio. He forgot to ask you.

I didn't remember about Fleiner[1] when I was in Z'ch. We were both upset by the tragic death of my friend Borach.[2] Next time I go I shall ring him up.

A young Frenchman Armand Petit Jean[3] has written a book, an amazing study of W.i.P. I never even saw him. It will be out in July. He is only 20 and began it 3 years ago!

I enclose something about Lucia but prefer not to discuss her case here. It is too long and complicated. She'll get all right they say. One needs all Job's patience with Solomon's wisdom and the Queen of Sheba's pinmoney thrown in. Please don't talk about it over there.

Not much news here except what you see in the press. I posed for J. E. Blanche[4] and he showed the portrait while I was away. I met Blaise Cendrars[5] who sent you his greetings. He says you were a fine singer in those days.

I spoke with the Sargents over the wires of course. He seems to have grown worse. It's a dreadful pity. Anyhow I hope Marseille does him good. Did he go there in search of quiet? If so, his life's work is all before him.

I'm a wretched correspondent but write whenever you feel disposed or want anything over here. I am sorry we did not meet this time. I was

[1] Professor Fritz Fleiner (1867–1937) was from 1915 to 1936 professor of administrative and constitutional law at the University of Zurich.

[2] Georges Borach was killed in an automobile accident in March 1934.

[3] Armand Petitjean, French critic. This book did not appear.

[4] Jacques Emile Blanche (1862–1942), French painter and writer. His portrait of Joyce is in the National Portrait Gallery in London.

[5] Blaise Cendrars (1887–1961), Swiss poet and man of letters. He and Budgen had met often in Paris in 1911–12.

swept off by a French friend of ours in a car to make my first motor trip, about 2500 Km. It was pleasant but I think I prefer Puffing Billy to Swaggering Bob.[1] *Schöne Grüsse*[2] Sincerely yours   JAMES JOYCE

To FRANK BUDGEN   MS. Yale

2 May 1934   *42 rue Galilée, Paris*

Dear Budgen: The other M.O. went astray. *Tant pis.* Here is one to settle your outlay with thanks and hopes for its safe arrival. I suppose Ruggiero will write to you. I met Cendrars in the studio of Fernand Léger.[3] Matisse, by the way, has been engaged by a N. Y. Book Club which is bringing out for subscribers an *edition de luxe* of *Ulysses* to do 20 illustrations.[4] What do you think of this? I hope your book sells off so that they may do a cheaper edition soon. People tell you your book is so interesting, they must read it etc. and then they don't buy it. It is useless. I have a grocer's assistant's mind. Friendly greetings sincerely yours   JAMES JOYCE

To LUCIA JOYCE   MS. S. Illinois

[Late May 1934]   *42 rue Galilée, Paris (Etoile)*

Cara Lucia: Non ti ho scritto prima perchè credevo forse meglio lasciarti in pace laggiù. Ma il dott. Humbert ci ha mandato notizie di te. Siamo molto contenti di apprendere che Nyon[5] ti piace. Spero che la 'bise'[6] non sia troppo attiva in questa stagione. In quanto alle lezioni di disegno puoi prenderne 2 o 3 volte alla settimana. Quel famoso libro[7] deve escire in Olanda alla fine di questo mese, *dice* l'editore.

    [1] That is, the train to the automobile. Joyce is playing on 'Staggering Bob', the name given to a newborn calf.
    [2] 'Friendly greetings.'
    [3] Fernand Léger (1881–1955), the French painter, had become friendly with Joyce.
    [4] The Limited Editions Club published *Ulysses* in an edition of 1500 copies on 22 October 1935. It contained six etchings with accompanying sketches by Matisse.
    [5] Lucia Joyce first went to Les Rives de Prangins, a sanatorium at Nyon under the direction of Dr Oscar Forel (b. 1891), on 30 July 1933. After a few days she appeared so panic-stricken that Joyce, against Forel's advice, withdrew her on 4 August. But her wild behaviour obliged him to send her there again in February 1934, and this time she remained until 15 September of that year.
    [6] French for 'north wind'.
    [7] *The Mime of Mick Nick and the Maggies* (*Finnegans Wake*, pp. 219–59) was published by the Servire Press in the Hague, Holland, in June 1934. The initial letter, the tailpiece, and the cover were designed by Lucia Joyce, and copies 5–29 were signed by both her and her father. The thousand copies which comprised the total edition were distributed under three other imprints besides that of the Servire Press: Messageries Dawson, Paris; Faber & Faber, London; and the Gotham Book Mart, New York.

Qui poche novità. Giorgio ha venduto il suo Rolls-Royce o Jolls-Joyce[.] Stevie sta benone; Helen pure. Mamma ed io anche. Niente di straordinario, salvo che giorni fa perdevo un biglietto da mille franchi. Lo credevo perduto per sempre ma dopo qualche ora fu ritornato ed indovina da chi. Dalla signora del quarto piano—quella che pestava i piedi ogni sera quando si suonava dopo le 10 ore. Le mandai qualche fiore ed essa ci invitò a prendere il tè!!! Era molto affabile. Sembra bellina. Peccato che ha una voce come un ranocchio.

Hai domandato uno *Stabat Mater*[1] di Lablache.[2] Ebbene da Durand non ne sanno niente. Lablache, del resto, era un cantante—il Chialiapin[3] del suo tempo—nato a Napoli di padre francese e madre irlandese. Non mi consta che abbia scritto della musica. Hai cambiato il nome, forse?

Speriamo che hai trovato qualche compagnia allegra. Facci sapere di quando in quando come stai. Ti farà del bene di restare là per ricuperare. L'ambiente qui non è ideale certo.

Salutami il dott. Forel, prego. Al dott. Humbert scriverò anche domani. Mama ti raccomanda d'ingrassare se puoi. Se hai bisogno di qualche cosa scrivici. Dunque, sta bene, divertiti e riposati. Ti abbracciamo   BABBO[4]

---

[1] This hymn was written by Jacobus de Benedictis, who died in 1306.
[2] Luigi Lablache (1794–1858), Franco-Italian (and Irish) bass.
[3] Fyodor Ivanovich Chaliapin (1873–1938), the Russian bass.
[4] (Translation)

'Dear Lucia: I have not written you before because I thought it would be better to leave you in peace down there. But Dr Humbert has sent us news of you. We are very glad that you like Nyon. I hope the "bise" is not too active this season. As for the drawing lessons you can take them two or three times a week. That famous book is going to be published in Holland at the end of this month, or so the editor says.

Nothing new here. Giorgio has sold his Rolls-Royce or Jolls-Joyce. Stevie is well; Helen too. Mama and I too. Nothing unusual except that a few days ago I lost a thousand-franc bill. I assumed it was gone for ever but a few hours later it was found and guess by whom. By the lady on the fourth floor—the one who used to stamp her feet every evening when we played the piano after 10 o'clock. I sent her some flowers and she invited us to tea!!! She was pleasant. She looks pretty. Pity that she has a voice like a frog's.

You asked for a *Stabat Mater* by Lablache. Well at Duran's they have never heard of it. Lablache, besides, was a singer—the Chaliapin of his time—born in Naples of a French father and an Irish mother. He is not known to have written any music. Did you misunderstand the name perhaps?

We hope you have found merry company. Let us know from time to time how you are. It will do you good to stay there and recuperate. The atmosphere here is certainly not ideal.

Please give my regards to Dr Forel. I will be writing Dr Humbert tomorrow. Mother urges you to fatten up if you can. Write if you need anything. So keep well, enjoy yourself and rest. We embrace you   Babbo'

To GEORGE and HELEN JOYCE[1]   MS. Kastor

1 June 1934   *42 rue Galilée, Paris*

Dear Giorgio and Helen: I will write you in English language. We
expect a letter from you by tomorrow (via S.S. *Bremen*) but I send this
off today. Also the fragment of W. i. P. I hope you send us good news,
that you are all three well and happy. We are both somewhat dazed by
the heavy heat here. I work every day alone at my big long wide high
deep dense prosework. We went to hear Gigli[2] (who sang in a gymnasium,
Palais des Sports, but has a beautiful voice. He imitates MacCormack
but has an ampler organ—not so true.) S.[3] in *La Favorite*[4] (this time he
surprised us all by his acting). *La Machine Infernale*,[5] very well given.
Mrs E.J.[6] and Mrs Nora J. went to the *Folies Bergères* while E.J. and I
went to see a Palestine company playing *Jacob and Rachel* in . . .
Hebrew, not Yiddish. It was very remarkable and barbaric.

I enclose this letter from S. to Pitt Sandborn.[7]

We have not yet made any summer plans. What a bore. Will let you
know as soon as we do.

They called in a German specialist at Nyon and he advised them to
treat Lucia as if she had something or other, though there is no trace of
it. And this apparently is doing her good. She sent me a silk tie she
knitted. She doesn't seem to know the kind of collars I wear. But it's
otherwise very nice and I'll get it altered. I hope the book cheers her up.
It is very well done.

We are looking for a flat. I am having my teeth fixed. But you are the
people to send the news. Gillet did not get into the Academy. There was
a spoiled vote. So he has to run again. Carducci[8] came around and let
me hear his *Norma*.[9] I am going to speak to Mrs Dyer about it. He
brought the Contessa with him.

Our best wishes to you both and regards to your host and trilingual
greetings to your lively charge. I shake all your amalgamated hands
several times over in rapid succession with that charming grace for which

---

[1] George and Helen Joyce sailed for the United States on 19 May 1934 and did not
return until September 1935.

[2] Beniamino Gigli (1890–1957), Italian tenor.

[3] John Sullivan.

[4] Gaetano Donizetti, *La Favorite* (1840).   [5] Jean Cocteau's play (1934).

[6] Mrs Eugene Jolas.

[7] John Pitts Sanborn (1879–1941), music critic for several New York newspapers in
turn, and therefore someone who might help George Joyce secure singing engagements.

[8] Edgardo Carducci, who set Joyce's poem, 'Alone,' to music in *The Joyce Book*, pp.
59–61.

[9] Vincenzo Bellini, *Norma* (1831). Carducci may have adapted the opera in some way.

I have always been noted and blow to you in valediction my parento-legal blessings from this little old log cabin down the Seine.   BABBO
PS Dears Helen and Giorgio

I hope you are having a fine time we are quite well, Paris misses you both lots of love to Stevie   NORA

From NORA BARNACLE JOYCE to   MS. Kastor
GEORGE and HELEN JOYCE

[*About 15 June 1934*]   *42 rue Galilée, Paris*

Dear Helen e Giorgio, Thanks for letters and postcard I got quite dizzy looking at that tall building. When I think it takes such a long time for a letter to reach you. I simply keep putting off writing, we are very glad to hear you are having such a good time.

We seem to have taken your place here as far as late hours is concerned we have been to see many things with the Jolases gene is missing Giorgio so much so the other evening he had a little too much to drink and forgetting himself turned round and gave the usual clap on the back to Jim Maria promptly reminded him it was his father who was there. We had a bit of a heat wave here luckily it did not last. I spend most of my time flat hunting. Carducci took me out to Neuilly to see some wonderful ones but they were all let Mrs Dyer invited us to an evening party I must say it was very smart she had the most wonderful buffet everything on the table was from the colonies I must tell you the funniest part of that was when I was getting into the new evening dress Jim thought the back was a bit too decolleté so he decided he would have to stich up the back of the dress can you imagine the result? of course he stiched it all crooked so I had to undo the stiches again I decided it was better [to] have a bare back I wish you could have seen him stiching my skin back bone altogether.

The news of Lucia is better Schwester rang up and I asked her in to have tea she wept copiously about Stevie she seems to be missing him very much I am not so sure she likes her present job but I did find her not looking so well as a matter of fact when she came in through the door she looked very dishevelled her hair was hanging around her she had a bunch of flowers in her hat and another at her waist and if I dont mistake she had a bunch in her bosom I hop[e] you have found a summer camp for David[1] is he feeling better

Does Stevie ever mention us give him a big kiss. We have just got back from the races and there was a little boy just like him running

---

[1] David Fleischman.

around. Giorgio we are very well I hope you will do something about your voice Best love to all saluti best regards to your family   NORA

Dear G & H: I have taken a flat near the park Monceau, 6 rooms 15000. Will write you both tomorrow. Just back from Prix des Draps. Good luck to you both   BABBO

To HARRIET SHAW WEAVER   MS. British Museum

10 July 1934   *42 rue Galilée, Paris*

Dear Miss Weaver: I delayed answering your letter as I wanted to have some definite news to send. I have it now. I have signed a lease for an empty flat—this after daily search for the past 4 months. It is in the first street to the right off Ave. Bosquet, turning your back to the river, 7 rue Edmond Valentin. We have work to do in it but I expect it will be habitable by September. Civil strife is reported to be in the air here and general Armageddon to be mobilising outside but I can't help it. My forty months of wandering in the wilderness must come to an end. It is risky for I don't know how the appeal court will rule in N.Y. and my rent-paying power depends on the judges. But my wife's nerves were giving out and, though I have been working about 5 to 7 hours a day for some time—as much as I can do in such heat—I need more elbow room.

... But now listen to this. Two years ago I arranged with Burns and Oates through Mr Holroyd Reece (of Albatross Press in Europe) to publish Lucia's alphabet for Chaucer's A.B.C. I agreed to pay them £225, to get Gillet to write a preface and have it done into English. This was done but they showed no sign of life so I got the Hague Press which did the last fragment to take on the job. Now for six months I have been writing a good dozen letters to have the *lettrines* sent back. All kinds of excuses. They are in London, in Grasse, locked up in Paris etc. Now it seems Reece does not know where they are. The blockheads have lost them. They keep on writing vapid letters in the style of Pinker and Cape, about 'getting into touch' and 'lose no time' 'how very much we feel' but the letters are not to be found. And the Xmas market the Dutch publisher had in view is now lost. Voila!

I have also been making vigorous efforts to get rid of Pinker, but Léon hangs on to one leg here and Mr Monro to the other in London so that I have had to give up the idea. . . .

We don't know what to do with ourselves this summer and I wish it were over. Thanks for the list of errors in the fragment. That is rather a pity.

This may interest you. Léon began to read to me from a scientific publication about Irish trees. The first sentence was to the effect that

the oldest tree in the island is the elm tree in the demesne of Howth
Castle and Environs.[1]

I hope you are keeping well and I am glad to have something positive
to report instead of my usual wail. With kindest regards sincerely yours

JAMES JOYCE

To GEORGE and HELEN JOYCE   MS. Kastor

13 July 1934   *42 rue Galilée, Paris*

Dear Giorgio and Helen: These few lines, I hope, find you well. They
are just to tell you we started moving our things into the new empty
flat I have taken yesterday. 5 rooms, lift, private telephone, chauffage,
4th floor, clear outlook as right opposite is a hotel particulier of 2
storeys. Little or no traffic in the street which has only 12 houses and is
not a suite of any other street. It is no 7 rue Edmond Valentin, between
avenues Rapp and Bosquet. If you stand at beginning of Av. Bosquet
with your back to the river and walk towards Ecole Militaire the 1st
street you pass on the right is a section of rue de l'Université. The
second is rue Edmond Valentin. That's it. rent 11,500. I am now the
tenant but workmen will be in till end of August, I think. The heating
system is being changed on all the floors and we are repapering and
cleaning generally. Only one flat on each landing and this cornerless and
quite bright.

So that's that.

I hope you will not cable Lucia on the 26th as she does not know yet
you are in U.S.

The heat here has been filthy (34 in the shade) but I suppose N.
Yorkers find that cool.

Our plan is to put all the workmen on the job and then leave for Spa
(Belgium) perhaps with the Gilberts.

The Jolases will be off for the south on the 19th but meanwhile Mrs
Jolas had to rush off to Saint Honoré as Tina there has swallowed a
hairpin.

We hope to have a letter from you in the morning as two big boats got in.

Meanwhile I send this off. How is Stevie standing the heat, also his
papa and mama. The Baillys are leaving for a Baltic cruise. Yes, thanks,
I will take some ice. Tante belle cose a tali belle persone[2]   BABBO

Ce soir on danse dans les rues!!![3]

---

[1] An interesting coincidence, since in *Finnegans Wake* the elm tree is associated with
Anna Livia Plurabelle, and Howth Castle and Environs with H. C. Earwicker.

[2] 'Best wishes to the best people.'

[3] 'They dance in the streets tonight [for Bastille Day]!!!'

To CAROLA GIEDION-WELCKER   MS. Giedion-Welcker

22 July 1934   *Grand Hotel Britannique, Spa, Belgique*

Dear Mrs Giedion: Your letter came just as we were leaving Paris for here. Thanks for settling that bill and many thanks for again offering us your villa for the summer. But we are taking only a short holiday. I have at last rented an empty flat and as soon as the workmen have finished in it we have to go back to start moving in. This would be a charming place here but for the rain which we brought with us, it seems. Anyhow, I hope you both enjoy your holiday. I am tired of the summer before it begins.

After a very long delay Mr Pulver sent back Lucia's letters, saying that pressure of work prevented him from giving an opinion on the handwriting of the person in question. Taking this with what you told me I think it not unlikely that he has a strong suspicion who it is. If then he does not want to give an opinion it may be because he resents having been approached in such a veiled way or because what he has to say is too unpleasant for him to write.

The news we have about her is slightly better but it is all very slow and confused. They really know as much about these cases as the layman.

Our address in Paris, as from the 15 September, will be:

> 7 rue Edmond Valentin
> Paris VII

but you can always get my telephone number if you ring up Miss Beach or Paul Léon. Be sure to do so when you are there next time.

Our kind regards to both Mr Giedion and yourself Sincerely yours

JAMES JOYCE

To GEORGE and HELEN JOYCE (Postcard)   MS. Kastor

22 July 1934   *Hotel Britannique, Spa (Belgium)*

Here's my hotel and my news is coming.   BABBO

To HARRIET SHAW WEAVER   MS. British Museum

28 July 1934   *Grand Hotel Britannique, Spa, Belgique*

Dear Miss Weaver: Will you please send back the enclosed when read. I don't know what to do about the *lettrines*. I have now lost the Xmas market for the book. They meant months of work, 3 at least, apart from their value. What a softheaded idiot! If any notice of my fragment appeared in the English press in which Lucia's name is mentioned will you please send it to me. The Dutch firm was willing to do the Chaucer poem without any money from my side.

We came here a day or two ago to allow a brigade of workmen time to set in order, clean, paint etc a flat which had been occupied for 20 years by the same people and to allow my wife time and space to repair her very exhausted nervous system. This place (my choice) is easily the most charming one of its kind we have ever seen but the weather is not good and, worst of all, the newsboys keep careering round the streets shouting out about 'l'Autriche'. I am afraid poor Mr Hitler-Missler[1] will soon have few admirers in Europe apart from your nieces and my nephews, Masters W. Lewis and E. Pound.[2] My wife is making a cure of baths which, I think, will do her good. Did Léon send you a bundle of MS ?[3] Indispensable for the Xmas fire.

I am still on the watch for news from the U.S. courts. I fancy they will rise on the 31 instant for the long vacation. I think the delay is a good sign.

I read of the usual terrible thunderstorms in England this summer. Thank Jupiter, we have escaped so far.

I have been working very hard and hope to get on quickly once I am in dock again.

I suppose you are as usual superior to weather conditions and in the goodest of health. With kind regards sincerely yours   JAMES JOYCE

To GEORGE and HELEN JOYCE   MS. Kastor

30 July 1934   *Grand Hotel Britannique, Spa (Belgique)*

Cari fanciulli: We have been here now 11 days. Before your wire came I had arranged for both telegrams to be sent to Lucia in both our absences.[4] I warned your concierge not to *rébuter* a wire if one came on the 27.[5] It did as you will see by Lucia's reply to my telegram today of inquiry whether she had sent a telegram on the 27. I hope the birthday passed off all right. We are taking the waters here and I wish I could

[1] A play on 'hit or miss'.
[2] The range of Pound's sympathies expanded from Mussolini to include some aspects of Hitlerism. Wyndham Lewis in 1931 published a series of articles in *Time and Tide* which were incorporated in his book, *Hitler* (London, 1931). He reversed these pro-Nazi views in 1939 with two books, *The Jews, Are They Human?* (London, March 1939) and *The Hitler Cult* (London, December 1939).
[3] Of *Finnegans Wake*.
[4] Joyce thought his daughter would be upset if she knew that either her father or her brother was away from Paris. He made sure that congratulatory telegrams from her brother and himself were sent to her from Paris on her twenty-seventh birthday, 26 July.
[5] George Joyce's birthday.

persuade my wife to take the carbo-gaseous baths which are said to be very soothing to the nerves. Perhaps I shall.

Helen, you are wrong if you think your cousin is in Germany. I mean Mr Hertz.[1] A few nights before we left Paris I was dining in Fouquet's when at 11.30 in he walked. He had been stopped at Amsterdam by bad news from wherever his place is and at once took the night *avion* for Paris and made straight for Fouquet's. Léon was there too so we had a chat. He seemed to have been deeply disappointed in America (much to our surprise) and as for Germany he became inarticulate. He left for Vichy or somewhere near next day. He said he would go to Denmark but did not care to cross Germany. Where he is now, I don't know.

I am glad to hear that Stevie sits on the beach with his face towards the old world, *quand même*. While I think Giorgio might have chosen *un andantino allegro*[2] rather than an *andante capo*[3] for his bass viol interlude in the last letter, considering the susceptible nature of one, at least, of the addressees, it is or should be patent that the conduct of public affairs in all the great countries of the world between Russia and America both included makes stupid, boring, irritating, backward England seem like a land still inhabited by non-bloodthirsty *homines sapientes*. I shall go there too when and if France gets unlivable-in but not till then. So I had to take a flat.

Enclosed are many things. I am running with this to the post for the boat. We are both well and hope you are. My regards to Mr Kastor.

Caro Giorgio, ti scriverò domani[4]

Dear Helen, I will write you the day after tomorrow

Caro nipotino, ti scriverò überübermorgen[5]

Shake and shake and shake   BABBO.

To STANISLAUS JOYCE   MS. Cornell

31 July 1934   *Grand Hotel Britannique, Spa (Belgique)*

Dear Stannie: Let me know how and where you are. I hope you got over that last bout of renal cattarh. We are here taking the waters as they did a long time ago. It is rather quiet and old-world, thank the lord. I have rented a new flat (empty) in Paris and the workmen are fixing it up. From, say, 1 September or 10 my address will be: 7 rue

[1] Wilhelm Herz (b. 1891), a Swiss relative of Helen Joyce. He has since Americanized his name to William Hartley.

[2] The sense is 'a slightly animated and cheerful . . .'.

[3] 'A slow (and cheerless) conclusion.'

[4] 'Dear Giorgio, I will write you tomorrow.'

[5] 'Dear little grandson, I will write you the day after the day after tomorrow.' (A combination of Italian and German.)

Edmond Valentin, Paris VIIe (tel: Invalides 50.38). It is between where I lived before, rue de Grenelle, and the Eiffel Tower.

People tell me not to settle down as there is going to be a brand new war but I am tired of paying 3 rents à la fois so I took it.

I send you the *Irish Times*, O G's poem on p. 7 may interest you though the picture of him as a baker's roundsman delivering 2 loaves, 2 turnovers and a crown in through the skylight seems odd.[1] Also Diarmuid and Grainne on p 15 are instructive.[2]

I am sending the money by the month to Eva. Am still without news from U.S. As you know after the judge's ruling in my favor on 6 December last the book came out but 3 months after the government, urged on by certain elements, lodged an appeal at the 11th hour. The case came up before the court of appeal 9 weeks ago. 3 judges without a jury decided to consider the case at their leisure. I think the U.S. courts rise today for their long vac. (the British are high too) so perhaps I shall hear nothing till October.[3] I have a contract also with John Lane, London, and he writes his lawyers have advised him to run the gauntlet next autumn and bring it out.

So I hope there's no fighting nor no nothing.

Did you get the fragment of my new book *The Mime of Mick Nick and the Maggies* with designs by Lucia. If not, I'll send you one.

She is still at Nyon. I believe she is getting better but it is slow. All the young girls or women or most of them seem to be off the key a little.

Giorgio and family are summering and simmering in New York (c/o Mr Adolf Kastor, 1239 Broadway). They aren't staying there, of course, but at Long Branch, a sort of N.Y. Brighton.

I hope to have some news of you. Best wishes to Nelly and yourself from us both   JIM

To T. W. PUGH[4]   MS. Pugh

6 August 1934   *Grand Hotel Britannique, Spa, Belgique*

Dear Mr Pugh: I am here on holiday away from books of reference so am trusting to memory as regards your address.

In the first place I hope you are well and that when you next visit

---

[1] Oliver Gogarty, 'The Mill at Naul,' *Irish Times* (21 July 1934), 7. In the poem Gogarty says that, prompted by thoughts of the ruined flour mill, he can 'let my love descend to spread / Through lowly roofs the gift of bread.'

[2] A picture of two prize swine appeared on p. 15.

[3] The United States Circuit Court of Appeals ruled on 8 August 1934 that *Ulysses* was not lewd or immoral. See next page.

[4] Thomas W. Pugh (b. 1883), of an old Dublin family of glassmakers that is mentioned in *Finnegans Wake*, was introduced to Joyce by Padraic and Mary Colum. He had read

Paris you will come to see me. My address there is now: 7 rue Edouard Valentin, Paris VIIe (Tel: Invalides 50.38).

My American publisher would like to have for a circular he publishes some photographs of scenes mentioned in *Ulysses* so I wonder if you would consent to have some of yours reproduced. I remember Kiernan's but he would also like to have the Martello Tower (Sandycove), Holles Street Hospital and the view of the Strand at Sandymount showing the Star of the Sea Church. Of course he would use your name and I take it these things are paid for.

There is still another matter in which you could aid me. Apart from the usual U.S. edition there is to be brought out before Christmas an *édition de luxe* with a preface by some writer and a series of 30 illustrations by the French painter Henri Matisse. He is at present in the south of France doing them. He knows the French translation very well but has never been in Ireland. I suppose he will do only the human figures but even for that he would perhaps need some guidance.[1]

Do you know any illustrated weekly published in Dublin about 1904 or before that time? If I could have some back numbers (the picture pages only) to show him when I go back to Paris he might be able to conjure up the past better. If you can find any back papers please let me know what they cost and I shall remit you the amount.

With many thanks in advance sincerely yours   JAMES JOYCE

PRESS RELEASE FROM THE NEW YORK HERALD   [*Paris*]

8 August 1934

U. S. Loses 'Ulysses' Appeal;
Court finds Ban hurting Art.

(By Wireless to the Herald).

New York. Tuesday.

The United States Circuit Court of Appeals, by a 2-to-1 decision, today ruled that James Joyce's 'Ulysses' is neither a lewd nor an immoral book and that its importation is proper. The decision upholds that of

Ulysses many times and knew the Dublin of 1904 in all its aspects exceedingly well. Mary M. Colum tells how Pugh, at Joyce's request, read some of the *Cyclops* episode in a low Dublin accent; Joyce remarked, 'I can read it in a more low-down Dublin accent than that.' Mary and Padraic Colum, *Our Friend James Joyce* (New York, 1958), pp. 168–69.

[1] Matisse's etchings for the Limited Editions Club *Ulysses* were based upon the Odyssey. Of Joyce's book he admitted privately, 'I haven't read it.'

Federal Judge John M. Woolsey, admitting the book for sale in this country, against which the Government, through United States Attorney Martin Conboy, appealed.

The dissenting opinion was handed down by Judge Martin T. Manton, who presided at the hearing of arguments. Judges Learned Hand and Augustus N. Hand in the majority opinion held that 'art certainly cannot advance under compulsion to traditional forms.'

Previously, the three Judges had heard Morris L. Ernst,[1] appearing for Random House, Inc., which has issued an American edition of the work, praise the book as 'a great work of fiction' and its author as a 'majestic genius'.

Conboy argued that the volume is undeniably obscene and immoral and that Judge Woolsey had erred in giving it a clean bill in the United States District Court a year ago.

'No reasonable man applying the proper rule of law would come to any conclusion other than that "Ulysses" is obscene,' Conboy told the Court. 'Taking the test of obscenity which has been established in the Federal Courts and applying it to the numerous passages of grossly obscene matter with which this book fairly reeks, there can be no doubt that the District Court erred in its determination that "Ulysses" is not obscene.'

Accompanying the brief was a list of references to certain portions of the volume selected as being particularly obscene in the opinion of the government. These passages were the same which the government had quoted in every similar brief since March, 1918, when Margaret Anderson first printed 'Ulysses' in her magazine, 'The Little Review'.

Judge Woolsey held that the book was not written to exploit obscenity and that nowhere did it tend to be an aphrodisiac. The court admitted 'Ulysses' was not an easy book to read or understand and that it had to be considered from a proper approach and not with Joyce's imitators in mind.

To HELEN JOYCE   MS. Kastor

9 August 1934   *Grand Hotel Britannique, Spa, Belgique*

Dear Helen: Thanks for your long letter. Why you give me grammatick lessons. He was me friend Le Hon[2] send you that wire. Le Hon very nice chap but he not know the Englisch grammatick like me and you, missus.

---

[1] Morris L. Ernst (b. 1889), well-known for his legal work in censorship cases.
[2] Paul Léon (in pidgin English). He had cabled to ask the decision of the Circuit Court of Appeals.

Also why for you make me big speechstuff about Frankee Doodles?[1] *'Pipe pas!'*[2] But, say, you's grown to be a swell orator, missus. I'll tell the woyld you is.

I got you both's wire about the appeal ruling.[3] Three cheers for me, says I to meself, says I.

Answers to questions, put or not put. The Vail[4] family has another daughter. The Gilberts are not here. They are lying in wait outside Paris for a cheap excursion train which would bring them here about the 16 to 20 inst. Jean Wright is her correct maiden name. Gillet's son-in-law died of cancer of the marrow on the first anniversary of his marriage. The Sullivans have rented an empty flat in the rue Juliette Lambert. I paid over to a solicitor (Mrs Jolas's) the money I was able to collect including Mrs Bailly's who paid like a goodhearted person, I think, so that ends that. I paid in yours too as it was no use bothering you.[5] Don't send me it. Time enough, when you come back to Paris.

Lucia seems to have fallen for some undesirable gent in the Nyon shop who either lives in Dublin or London. They are being kept apart and he is going away. This has for the moment upset her. But they say it will soon pass. I see nothing crazy in that, as women go.

Beckett has brought out his book *More Pricks than Kicks.*[6] One of the characters is named Lucia but it is quite different.[7] She is a cripple or something. Haven't time to read it. But looked at it here and there before quitting Paris. He has talent, I think.

Am glad to hear Stevie gets on well. The accounts of U.S.A. in the European press (heat and Dillinger[8] etc) are so lurid that we are glad to know you are enjoying yourselves.

You can write here even if we go on to Luxembourg. Cologne is only 14 hours away. Pity we dare not visit it. Moltissimi saluti   Babbo

[1] Helen Joyce had evidently extolled the American attitude to *Ulysses*, and so 'Yankee Doodle'.

[2] 'Sh' (like a parent telling a child to be quiet).

[3] See pp. 314–15.

[4] Laurence Vail, an American writer living in France, then married to Kay Boyle.

[5] A subscription by friends of John Sullivan.

[6] Samuel Beckett, *More Kicks than Pricks* (London, May 1934).

[7] Lucia Joyce had been in love with Beckett before her engagement to Ponisovsky.

[8] John Dillinger (1903–1934), the Chicago gangster.

To FRANK BUDGEN (Postcard)   MS. Clive Hart
[?9] *August 1934*   *Spa*

This looks as if I had sciatica. Just spoke with Matisse. He is now
doing an Eolus plate but I am to meet him in Paris in September. By
the way, my new address is 7 rue Edmond Valentin Paris VII (tel.
Inval: 50:38) am now going to continue my repose   J.J.

To FRANK BUDGEN   MS. Yale

13 August 1934   *Grand Hotel Britannique, Spa, Belgique*

Dear Budgen: I meant to write you a much longer letter than this but
am rushing it off for I have a fit of ague for the past 24 hours and my
eyelids are thick and smeared with protective salve. Must leave this
pretty but all-too-humid spa for drier Luxembourg. But write here. I'll
get it.

I thought Matisse's ideas would interest you. When sending back
Léon's letter tell me what you think. They are pretty much the same as
yours? He is to ring me up from Paris today with a string of queries.
O Lord, the one day I feel so shivery-shaky!

What I really want to show are the 2 enclosed letters. I thought, about
2 years ago, I had arranged through Holroyd Reece, manager of the
Albatross Press, and his friend a Mr Stanley Morrison of Burns &
Oates for the latter to bring out Chaucer's *A.B.C.* poems with a preface
by Louis Gillet and Lucia's lettrines. B & O were to do it on a commission I being prepared to agree to pay 225 £ and to pay for the preface
and its translation. I did this and waited about 4 years. No move. Then
the Dutch firm who have just brought out the 4th fragment of W i P (by
the way, have you it or do you want it?) offered to bring out the book
without any payment from me and pay royalties. I tried to get the
lettrines back so as to deliver them in July and thus catch the Xmas
market. Eight months' correspondence. Useless. Now it seems the idiots
have lost the *lettrines*. Do you know anything of Mr Morrison? Anyway
if these letters are lost I think I ought to sue them?

Urge on your publisher to bring out a cheap reprint of your book and
as soon as possible. I am sure there will be a much bigger demand for it
after the U.S. result. The government can still carry the case to the
U.S. equivalent of the House of Lords. But I doubt it. A pity that when
I win after 18 years struggle the $ drops 50%. Such is life.

Now I am going to cover myself up like the babes in the wood
sincerely yours   JAMES JOYCE

To GEORGE JOYCE   MS. Kastor

13 August 1934   *Grand Hotel Britannique, Spa, Belgique*

Caro figliolo: Lasciamo da parte le gravi questioni sollevate nella tua lettera. È uno spreco di tempo discuterle. Cosa fatta capo ha.[1]

Siamo qui da quasi un mese ma comincia a fare un tempo impossibile, umido, coperto, ecc. Andremo a Lussemburgo per qualche settimana. Mama ora sta un pò meglio. Era molto esaurita perchè ha fatto tanto a Parigi per via dell'appartamento.

Ci è stato una lieve ricaduta di Lucia ma passerà presto. Però, credo che un'intervista personale col *Forel*, coi dottori e colle infermiere oramai s'impone prima di combinare un programma per l'inverno. Dunque gli scrissi in questo tempo e se egli non va in vacanza passeremo per Basilea a Ginevra prima di entrare di nuovo a Parigi. Ad ogni modo Lucia resterà dove si trova fino al vostro ritorno come telo promisi.

Confermo il mio dispaccio d'ieri suggerito da Leone. Ma anche se questo trasferimento s'effettua in tutto o in parte la mia intenzione a proposito resta invariata. Per spiegare il panico di Leone bisognerebbe vedere i giornali europei al riguardo degli stati uniti. In questo mondo tutti questi si vogliono un bene di Dio.

Ho avuto una risposta dal Sig. Pugh a Dublino. E fra qualche settimana spero avere una serie di 6 fotografie genuine che si possono sostituire alle fotografie attuali. Matisse mi ha telefonato stamane da Parigi per avere certi dettagli. Gliene diedi e devo incontrarlo a Parigi fra 5 settimane.

Incoraggiati dal esito delle cose in America (ohibo! 18 anni di lotta, vittoria finale ed ... il dollaro perde 50% del suo valore all'estero) gli editori inglesi si sono decisi a far stampare e pubblicare quanto prima una prima edizione di 1000 e 100 firmati a 30/- e 3 ghinee risp., poi in '35 3000 a 15 scellini ed in '36 edizione illimitata a $8\frac{1}{2}$ scellini.

Quì termino la prima partita della mia lettera dove si tratta di sbarazzare il terreno delle faccende più materiali e continuerò domattina. Ti abbraccio   BABBO[2]

_____

[1] From Dante, *Inferno* 28, l. 107: 'Capo ha cosa fatta' ('A thing once done has an end').

[2] (Translation)

'Dear son: Let us put aside the serious questions raised in your letter. It is a waste of time to discuss them. What's done is done.

We have been here almost a month but the weather begins to be impossible, damp, overcast, etc. We will go to Luxemburg for a few weeks. Mama is a little better. She was totally exhausted because she had so much to do in Paris about the flat.

To GEORGE and HELEN JOYCE   MS. Kastor

[*Mid-August 1934*]   [*Vervins*]

This spring is called after the famous Dublin warrior (the iron duke)[1]
because it is so 'ferruginous'. Souppault was expelled from Germany for
his articles. Gillet left of his own accord. S[2] is now apparently in dear
old Vienna where the dear waltzes come from. I suppose the Vails are
there for a holiday too. I chose Spa. Everyone in Paris 'spat' when I
spoke of it. Talk of *La Juive*[3] and Fécamp and still this mother of many
gentler daughters can hold her own easily against them. (Says he!)

[Unsigned]

To STANISLAUS JOYCE (Postcard)   MS. Cornell

[*Mid-August 1934*]   [*Vervins*]

Sir Arthur W. was never here but the strongest of the ferruginous
springs is called after him the *Duc de Fer*. We may go on to Luxembourg
for a week. We are within an hour or so's train ride of Aix-la-Chapelle
where Charlemagne is buried and Cologne. But I dislike going over the
border even on a half-day motor coach trip. I wish everyone was as good
humoured and as good tempered as me and you. Don't go to Austria for
your holidays whatever you do.   JIM

Lucia suffered a slight relapse but that will soon be over. I think however that a
personal interview with *Forel*, the doctors and the nurses is essential before making any
plans for the winter. I therefore wrote to him lately and if he is not on holiday we shall
go through Basle to Geneva before we go back again to Paris. Anyway Lucia will stay
where she is until your return as I promised you.

I confirm my telegram of yesterday which Léon suggested. But even if this transfer
takes place entirely or in part my intention remains unchanged. To explain Léon's
panic you would have to see the European newspapers on the subject of the United
States. We all wish each other well in this world.

I had a reply from Mr Pugh in Dublin. For some weeks now I have been hoping to
have a series of six authentic photographs which could be substituted for photographs
of the present day. Matisse telephoned me this morning from Paris for some details. I
gave them to him and I am to meet him in Paris in five weeks' time.

Encouraged by the outcome of things in America (Ugh! 18 years of struggle, final
victory and . . . the dollar loses 50% of its value abroad), the English publishers have
decided to print and publish as soon as they can a first edition of 1000 and 100 signed
copies at 30 shillings and 3 guineas respectively, then in 1935 3000 copies at 15 shillings
and in 1936 an unlimited edition at 8 shillings and sixpence.

Here ends the first section of my letter in which I have tried to clear away the most
essential matters and I will continue tomorrow. I embrace you   Babbo

[1] Arthur Wellesley, Duke of Wellington (1769–1852).
[2] John Sullivan.
[3] Halévy's opera *La Juive* takes place in Constance, a Black Sea resort.

To GEORGE and HELEN JOYCE   MS. Kastor

21 August 1934   *Grand Hotel Brasseur, Luxembourg*

Dear Giorgio and Helen: This is only business. Here are 3 groups of
letters.

1) *Cerf*: In case the govt intends to take the case to the Supreme Court[1]
would it not be well to take the active side now. If Judge Manton[2] is
'notorious' why not direct public attention to the grave judicial error he
made (at least so I think) in calling out page, chapter and verse of the
book in an open court. If a publisher had used similar tactics in advertising his wares what would this judge have said of him? I think you
ought to see Colm anyhow.

Nyon: We are to go on there in a week. I shall not make any changes
till you return but it is about time I knew what is going on. I have
besides an 8-page letter from Lucia, received today. I will send this on if
I can read it or find anyone who can. My wife can read some parts. It is
scribbled in pencil. Lucia seems to sit by the window all day. This too is
the second 'titre d'essai'[3] in the way of injections 'à par hasard'.[4] How
many more.

Lettrines: It is the opinion of Gillet, Jolas and Budgen that there is
something sinister behind this 'loss'.[5] Reece was extremely put out by
Cerf's move in publishing *Ulysses* in the U.S. and then tried to do a
little 'gun-running'—which failed. I can have the written opinion of
Van der Pyl and Gillet (2 of the foremost French art critics) of Matisse
(who admires her work very much) of Fernand Leger and of J-E Blanche.
Unfortunately no press notice of her cover etc for my fragment appeared
in the English press because all the available copies were sold out before
its publication and Faber and Faber or Feebler and Fumbler did not
circulate the 35 press copies because they did not want to be bothered
by requests for copies they could not supply.

I fully expect to hear that I am wrong and perhaps I am too. Please
return all these letters carefully to Léon.

I am glad you are all so well and sunburned. I am at present attending
night school where they teach 'em how to make pothooks. After which I
take out a course of lectures in political science and European history
and military strategy. Then I am doing a correspondence to learn

---

[1] The government decided not to appeal the decision of the Circuit Court of Appeals.
[2] See p. 315.
[3] 'Experiment.'
[4] The meaning is, 'with a remote chance of being effective.'
[5] See p. 308.

how to send perfectly clear straightforward transatlantic cablegrams.

This is a lovely quiet rose-growing part of dirty old Europe so we shall probably leave it tonight or tomorrow.

I thank you for the cabled money. It is in Paris.

As a result of the U.S. court's decision the English publisher, egged on by his countless lawyers, crawled out with a project for immediate publication (the one I suggested a year ago) and is bucking up his shirtsleeves for a splendid stand. These are fine fellows when you get to know them after 30 years.

In addition to S's[1] daughter and Gillet's son-in-law Mrs Bailly's son is dead after 3 days of 'fièvre cérébrale'.[2] I hope after this 3rd victim the only allbones will take a nice long holiday on the Styx riviera.

O won't we have a merry time, drinking whisky, beer and wine, on Coronation, Coronation Day![3]

Good night, dear children. Nighty night, everybody   BABBO

To GEORGE JOYCE   MS. Kastor

28 August 1934   *Grand Hotel Monney, Montreux (Suisse)*

Caro figliolo, Le lettere qui accluse devono essere rimesse a volta di corriere a Léon. Come vedi l'edizione inglese sta per salpare.

Pregai Forel di preparare Lucia per la nostra visita. Egli disse di no, che avrebbe (lui) un'intervista con noi soli prima. Mi disse dunque di venire domenica alle $2\frac{1}{2}$ alla *sua* villa *Hautes Rives*, Lucia essendo alla sua *Les Eglantines* e che ad allontanarla ci penserebbe lui come voleva parlare con noi prima di acconsentire ad un incontro. Arriviamo alle $2\frac{1}{2}$ alla casa di *Forel*. Mama vede subito piantata sull'erba davanti la porta, Lucia. Mama mi dice: Entriamo presto prima che ne veda. E fila dentro. Io seguo come posso, l'atrio essendo pieno di gente. Mi credevo salvo ma sento la voce di Lucia gridare: Babbo! Babbo! Ed un momento dopo era addosso a me, abbracciandomi e singhiozzando. La calmai e poi essa inseguì mama. Io, allora, furibondo lanciavo una filza di moccoli contro un dottore che mi stava vicino. Sembra che avevano detto a Lucia che venivo alle $2\frac{1}{2}$. Che cosa pensate voi di questa storiella.

Il resto segue.

Mama trovò Lucia molto bene, il viso più tondo, i capelli non più grigi

---

[1] John Sullivan.   [2] 'Brain fever.'
[3] Sung also by Buck Mulligan in the first episode of *Ulysses*, pp. 11–12 (11).

ecc. Era molto affettuosa con mama, baciandola ecc. Povera e cara figliola!

Basta per oggi. Ti dirò le mie impressioni quando la rivedrò domani.

Ti abbraccio   BABBO[1]

Dear Helen and Stevie Many greetings to yiz!   BABBO

From ALLEN LANE to RALPH PINKER   MS. S. Illinois (Feinberg)

29 August 1934   *John Lane The Bodley Head Limited,*
                                        Vigo Street, London, W.1

Dear Pinker In reply to your letter of August 28th and, as promised on the telephone to-day, I am writing to put the exact position with regard to this proposed first publication of Joyce's ULYSSES here before you.

We have, as you know, taken several opinions from barristers and others in authority on the probable result of publication here. This has, in addition to the time involved, cost us a not inconsiderable sum of money. Having decided that there was no possibility of getting a definite opinion as to whether there would be a prosecution or not, we then attempted to find a printer who would undertake the work.

We were unsuccessful and, in order to get around this, we have had to form a separate company to undertake the printing. This, in order to make it strictly legal, has necessitated preparing Articles of Association and I should think that our fees on this alone will certainly not be less than thirty guineas.

Then we feel that for safety's sake the only way in which we can produce the book in the first instance will be in a strictly limited edition at not too low a price. As I explained to you on the 'phone to-day, the

---

[1] (Translation)

'Dear son: The enclosed letters should be sent off to Léon by the next post. As you see the English edition is now sailing along.

I asked Forel to prepare Lucia for our visit. He said no, he would have an interview with us first. He told me therefore to come on Sunday at 2:30 to his villa Hautes Rives, while Lucia was at Les Eglantines, and he would keep her away so he could speak with us before allowing us to see her. We arrived at 2:30 at Forel's home. Mama saw Lucia at once, standing on the grass near the door. Mama said to me: Quick, let's go in before she sees us. And she slipped in. I followed as best I could, the entrance being full of people. I thought I had made it when I heard Lucia cry, 'Babbo! Babbo!' And in a moment she was upon me, hugging me and sobbing. I calmed her and then she went on to mama. I stayed to swear violently at a doctor who happened to be near. It seems they had told Lucia I was coming at 2:30. What do you think of this little tale?

More to follow.

Mama found Lucia very well, her face fuller, no more grey hairs, etc. She was very affectionate with mama, kissing her etc. Poor, dear girl!

Enough for today. I will tell you my impressions when I have seen her again to-morrow. I embrace you   Babbo'

number we print will have to be large enough to be able to refer to it at a future date should an objection be raised to a subsequent larger edition and small enough to ensure that there would not be many copies lying around in booksellers' shops for any length of time after publication. We feel that the number to be aimed at is between 1000 and 1500 copies and the length of the work, together with the words of appreciation from prominent literary figures and the report of the two American cases, will not be far short of 1000 pages. This being the case, I cannot think that it is conceivably possible for us to show a profit on this first publication taking into consideration:

(a) our legal expenses.

(b) the expenses of formation of the new printing company

(c) the very large composition bill we shall have to face

(d) the author's advance of £200 which will have to be, for the purpose of our accounting, worked out over this first printing.

In addition to this, as we will not be able to bring out another edition for 12 months from the original date of publication, we shall have either to make stereos from the standing type or pay rent on it for that period. This, as you will realise on a book of this length, will mount up to a considerable sum.

In these circumstances I do think that we should let the present royalty, as stipulated in our contract, stand, the only alternative being that we should have to issue it in the first instance in an unlimited edition which, in my opinion, would be fatal to the prospects of the book in this country. Yours sincerely,   ALLEN LANE

To CAROLA GIEDION-WELCKER   MS. Giedion-Welcker

2 September 1934   *Hôtel Richemond, Genève*

Dear Mrs Giedion: We hope you have quite recovered from your accident. When are you likely to be back in Zurich or are you there already? I wish we could meet you in order to discuss our great difficulty with you. We found Lucia after 7 months of the clinic almost on the verge of collapse. Utter despair. The doctor says after all that time he can make no diagnostic. They are helpless in the case. The only hold she seems to have on life is her affection for us. She is under restraint, that is, her windows are barred, and she is always *surveillée*. But I feel if she stays there she will simply fade out. We are alone here, not knowing a soul. Our kind regards to you both. Sincerely yours

JAMES JOYCE

To FRANK BUDGEN   MS. S. Illinois (Feinberg)

2 September 1934   *Hotel Richemond, Genève*

Dear Budgen: I am here and am faced with a terribly difficult problem
about Lucia. After 7 months of the clinic she seems on the verge of
collapse. The doctors can make no diagnostic. Completely stumped.
You can perhaps help me. Some time ago you wrote me of some case
you heard of. It was a friend? and your letter spoke of a treatment for
reduction of white blood corpuscles.[1] Lucia has 4 times the normal
number of these. They say there must be a source of infection. They
have put her to tests for syphilis, tuberculosis, glands, etc., but the
result is always the same, negative. If this seat of infection could be
found and treated they think the battle might turn. If you have time
drop me a line and give me any details you know of. With friendly
greetings sincerely yours   JAMES JOYCE

P.S. I note that your royal reader[2] has been and gone and engaged his
royal self with a Greek Princess. Please arrange for the removal of the
six of the blood royal who stand between him and the throne to enable
you and me to become fashionable awfurs.

To FRANK BUDGEN   MS. Yale

5 September 1934   *Hotel de la Paix, Genève*

Dear Budgen: Thanks for prompt reply. Lucia's condition is called
leucocytosis. Is that the same as F's[3] friend. I hope he is not away on
leave. Very likely he is. Was a high altitude part of the treatment. If so
why have these doctors kept her down by the lake? At the end of 4
years they are as much in the dark as ever. No, there is no sign of her
lettrines.   [Unsigned]

To CAROLA GIEDION-WELCKER   MS. Giedion-Welcker

7 September 1934   *Hotel de la Paix, Genève*

Dear Mrs Giedion: In case there is a hitch in the negotiations between
Drs Forel and Loy, to whom I am trying with Forel's full approval to
transfer her, I must have some reserve. Here is a wire of advice from my

---

[1] Budgen had written Joyce of a treatment for leukaemia.
[2] The Duke of Kent took a copy of Budgen's book with him on a tour of South Africa.
[3] Professor Fritz Fleiner

friend Léon. Can you get me the correct name and address of this doctor who is evidently a psychiâtre

I received a long and very friendly letter from Mrs Fleiner giving me the name of the Z'ch doctor who is an authority on blood diseases. It is Prof Näggeli.[1] But this of course is the purely physical side.

I was advised at Nyon not to speak of the Davos suggestion for some time yet Thanks anyhow sincerely yours   JAMES JOYCE

To FRANK BUDGEN   MS. Yale

8 September 1934   *Hotel de la Paix, Genève*

Dear Budgen, I got a long and very friendly letter from Mrs Fleiner of which I will write you when I have made the inquiries it involves.

Can I ask you to do me a pressing favour?

I received Lucia's lettrines this morning from those bunglers. At once wired to my Dutch publisher who is to do them (he did my last fragment). He was leaving for London and wired me to send them there to 'Basil Street Hotel'. This address seems to me rather queer so I shall send them registered to you, writing him at the same time that you will hand them to him personally. Show him your book. I am telling him of it. His name is Carl ver Hulst. I want the lettrines out in time for the Xmas market, if possible. Tell me what you think of them. Sincerely yours

JAMES JOYCE

PS. Could you ring up Miss Weaver and let her see the lettrines as you are on your way to deliver them?

To FRANK BUDGEN   MS. Yale

22 September 1934   *Carlton Elite Hotel, Zurich*

Dear Budgen, Many thanks for your kind and prompt action. I have brought Lucia here. She is in Meyer's private clinic.[2] Prof Naeggeli (the blood specialist) saw her today and as soon as he has finished his examination I will write again. What will be your address in the *midi* and from when? Sincerely yours   JAMES JOYCE

---

[1] Professor Theodor Naegeli (b. 1886), a noted Swiss surgeon and blood specialist.

[2] Lucia Joyce was transferred from Forel's clinic at Nyon to Burghölzli, the mental asylum in Zurich, on 20 September 1934. Apparently Professor Maier, of Burghölzli, had a private clinic adjacent to the public asylum. On 28 September Joyce had her transferred to Dr Brunner's private sanatorium at Küsnacht, where Dr C. G. Jung was on the staff.

To T. W. PUGH   MS. Pugh

22 September 1934   *Carlton Elite Hotel, Zurich*

Dear Mr Pugh: Many thanks for sending me so promptly the photographs which are now in New York. Please let me know what I owe you
for them. I am glad you liked the little fragment[1] I asked my British
publisher to send you. Unkind people tell me it sounds just as well if
read backwards. But the designs,[2] I think, are very charming. Sincerely
yours   JAMES JOYCE

To GEORGE JOYCE   MS. Kastor

29 October 1934   *Carlton Elite Hotel, Zurich*

Caro Giorgio: Ebbi tre giorni o quattro il seguente dispaccio[3] 'George
presented your letter have just met him and sweet wife Lily and I send
you friendliest greetings we all drank to your good health will do everything possible'.

Dunque! La sua protezione dovrebbe esserti utile anche se la
situazione è troppo avanzata. Sarebbe per più tardi. Ad ogni modo non
dimenticare di ringraziarlo a nome mio. Sono contento anche che hai
visto Sandbourn. Pare che sia un uomo che veramente sa qualchecosa
del canto come George Pioche a Parigi.

Scribacchio questo per raggiungere l'Ile de France e cercherò di
scrivere a voi due domani in inglese.

Per il cinema sta bene, suppongo.[4] I nostri piani sono come i vostri
sempre nell'aria. Jung mi disse giorni fa mediante il suo assistente che
ha visto Lucia di nuovo dopo un mese ed è molto incerto sul da farsi.
Disse: il padre deve capire che interverrò se lui lo desidera ma che
un intervento psicoanalitico in questo caso particolare è molto difficile
e potrebbe anche cagionare un peggioramento definitivo. Desidera
vedermi mercoledì. Questo appunto è sempre stato il parere del padre
sopradetto. Jung personalmente fece una buona impressione su me.
Credo che abbia avuto molti successi con altri casi. Or ora il dott.
Brunner mi telefonò che Lucia era benissimo, è stata fuori oggi in
automobile e giocava al bigliardo. Speriamo continui così.

[1] *The Mime of Mick Nick and the Maggies.*
[2] By Lucia Joyce.
[3] From John McCormack. Joyce hoped the singer would further George Joyce's
musical career.
[4] George Joyce had urged his father to consider having *Ulysses* made into a film, and
particularly recommended a scenario by S. J. Reisman and Louis Zukofsky (b. 1904),
American poet.

Hai cantato per MacCormack e Pitt Sandbourn? Non intercalare
l'acca nelle vocali 'cuo-h-ore' ecc. Hai le vocali naturali di un italiano
ma appoggia bene sulle consonanti iniziali. Pensa alle parole, ti supplico.
Il canto non é che un linguaggio alato. Quella canzone 'Philadelphia'
dovrebbe essere cantata come un contadino, grosso e lordo, cammina.
Un tipo che va piano e va lontano.[1] Antheil ha perso l'occasione della
sua vita quando non scrisse l'opera Cain di Byron per Sullivan. Forse
non ne era capace. Ma salutalo da parte mia. Non più andrà farfallone
rumoroso[2] ma mi è stato sempre simpatico.

Corro correndo drio la nave. Ti abbraccio   BABBO

Salutami anche quella buona pasta americana che è Colm e sua moglie
che spero stia meglio.[3]

[1] Italian proverb, 'Who goes slowly goes far.'
[2] A play on Mozart, Le Nozze di Figaro, where the words are, 'Non più andrai farfallone amoroso.' ('Amorous butterfly, you will fly no more.') Joyce changes 'amorous' to
'noisy'.
[3] (Translation)
  'Dear Giorgio: I had two or three days ago the following cable: "George presented
your letter have just met him and sweet wife Lily and I send you friendliest greetings
we all drank to your good health will do everything possible."
  So! His protection should be useful to you even if the season is too far advanced. It
would be for later on. Anyway do not forget to thank him in my name. I am glad too
that you have seen Sandbourn. He seems to be someone who really knows singing like
George Pioche in Paris.
  I scribble this so as to catch the Ile de France and will try to write both of you
tomorrow in English.
  As for the film all right, I suppose. Our plans like yours are up in the air as usual.
Jung told me through his assistant some days ago that he saw Lucia again after a
month and is very uncertain about what to do. He said: the father must understand that
I will intervene if he wants me to but that a psychoanalytic intervention in this particular case is very difficult and might even cause a definitive deterioration. He wants to
see me on Wednesday. This in fact has always been the opinion of the above-mentioned
father. Jung personally made a good impression on me. I believe he has had many
successes with other cases. Just now Dr Brunner telephoned me that Lucia was very
well, was out in an automobile today and played billiards. Let us hope she will go on
this way.
  Have you sung for MacCormack and Pitt Sandbourn? Don't intercalate an 'h'
between vowels 'cuo-h-ore' etc. You have the natural vowels of an Italian but emphasize
the initial consonants. Think of the words, I entreat you. Singing is only language with
wings. That song 'Philadelphia' should be sung in the way that a big, heavy peasant
walks. A fellow who goes slowly and goes far. Antheil missed the chance of a lifetime
when he did not write the opera on Byron's Cain for Sullivan. Maybe he wasn't
capable of it. But greet him from me. He'll fly no more, the noisy butterfly, but he has
always been friendly to me.
  I run patter-clatter after the ship. I embrace you   Babbo.
Greetings also to that good sort of American Colm and to his wife who I hope is
feeling better.'

To GEORGE and HELEN JOYCE   MS. Kastor

20 November 1934   *Carlton Elite Hotel, Zurich*

Dear Giorgio and Helen: This in reply to your letter of 27 ult. We were
glad to hear all the exciting news and we want more. Giorgio should
take some valerian before he sings. Do not be downcast if a lull follows.
It is often like that and you cannot always rely on people's pushing.
But there was no doubt in my mind after 2 February last that Giorgio
has a firstclass voice. I don't want to criticize or advise you from here
but are you not neglecting Pitt Sandborn. The press is very important
and S. says he is the best critic of voices in America. When I hear of
some definite result I think I shall write to MacCormack thanking him.
I shall write to Giorgio separately.

We have no news. As reports from Kusnacht are favorable we contem-
plate going back to Paris though I don't like leaving Lucia alone for the
Xmas. We tried for a small furnished flat here to tide us over but could
not find one. My flat in Paris is of course only waiting to be occupied.
The expenses are very high. Kusnacht is like Prangins 7000 a month
and Jung's bill for October was 3600. So hurry up as I want the loan of
a million.

Ask Colm to write to me. How is Mrs Colm? Did you see Soupault?
Have you taken a flat as you spoke of doing? Mrs Jolas has not heard
from you. The photos of Stevie are not good. Take a few more. I should
like you to have a group taken. You don't say what those radio stations
pay. I am sorry to hear of MacSwiney's[1] death. He seemed to me a loyal
and straightforward henchman of MacCormack. I gave him my ALP
disc and he promised me McC's record of *Come into the Garden, Maud.*
Can you get this over there?

You are having a great honeymoon over there, it seems. Send me a
programme if you go to the opera. Is it opera? I hope you will have a
pleasant Thanksgiving dinner next Thursday, is it? We are arranging
to have the scar on Lucia's face taken away and covered by a plastic
surgeon here. This at her own insistent request. They say this is a good
sign. The 7 November was the last day for the U.S. govt to appeal
against the Circuit Court. Did they? Léon sent a cable to Cerf who did
not reply. I understand that the English edition is being printed. The
Gilberts have gone to London for some months to save money as
Gilbert is terribly afraid the British Overseas Empire is going to capsize.

---

[1] Denis McSweeney (d. 1934), John MacCormack's business manager for over
twenty-five years.

Otto Kahn told me the Irish element in U.S. counts for nothing culturally. Have you not tried some Jewish melomaniacs?

Please help me to draw up the invitation list for my approaching birthday. As everybody is everywhere I must arrange for a special aeroplane service. However, you can send the presents in the usual way. Please inform all your rich relatives about the date. Yes, that is a good idea. I am a little tired of wearing starched collars and I would like to try a diamond necklace.

Did Jacques-Emile Blanche ever exhibit my portrait over there? I think it's awful except for the splendid tie I had on. As you, Helen, write all the time about politics you ought to buy Slocombe's book *Crisis in Europe*. In it he foretold the murder of the King of Servia. We met Huddleston in Geneva. He is afraid to cross in a ferryboat over the lake.

Well, talk about scrambled eggs but what about this epistle.

Tante belle cose and my regards to Mr Kastor   BABBO

To GEORGE JOYCE   MS. Kastor

21 November 1934   *Carlton Elite Hotel, Zurich*

Caro Giorgio: Spero che qualche cosa di concreto sia avvenuta dopo la tua ultima lettera. Però, come scrissi ieri, non bisogna illudersi. È certo che l'appoggio di McCormack ti gioverà molto forse soltanto per il reclame. Quanto agli ufficiali della squadra irlandese (la quale, del resto, è stata ben battuta dai cileani tranne il cavallo dal fausto nome *Blarney Castle* montato dal capitano Ahearn) essi saranno buoni giudici delle parti deretane di un puledro ma in fatto dell'arte canora Dio ci liberi. Dovresti pensare anche alla piazza inglese che paga bene ed ha sempre bisogno di buone voci sopratutto per gli amatori che si parano alle feste musicali di Leeds, Sheffield, Norwich ecc. Ho una lettera di Beecham a Lionel Powell il più grande impresario di Londra. A proposito feci la conoscenza ieri del ex-regisseur[1] dell'opera di Berlino (espulso perchè ebreo) ed egli sarà molto interessato nel tuo caso. Il tuo timor panico passerà probabilmente nel momento del tuo battesimo di fuoco alla ribalta. L'idea di debuttare per mezzo del microfono non mi dice gran che ma meglio là che affatto. Ti prego però di stare attento a quel vizio dell'acca. Kieppura[2] era qui venerdì scorso. Pessima scuola, comportamento ignobile, gusto poco nulla, ma una bella voce intonata ed estesa,

---

[1] Dr Hans von Curjel (b. 1896), director of the Krolloper in Berlin, 1927–31, has been a producer and director in Zurich since 1933.

[2] Jan Kiepura (b. 1902), Polish tenor.

facile e naturale. Ma qualche ciucco [sic] gli ha insegnato il canto: 'forma-h-a diviná' 'misti-h-ico serto' ecc. E ciò durante tutta la serata. Figurati! Entusiasmo sprecato. Era accompagnato dalla Tonhalle alla stazione da uno stuolo di ammiratori o piuttosto ammiratrici che circondava il suo Rolls e cantò il suo congedo dai gradini. Si torna all'antico davvero.[1] Stasera andremo a sentire la nuova opera di Respighi *La Campana Sommersa* basata sul dramma di Hauptmann.

Sorriderai se ti dico che siamo stati, mama ed io, 'a scuola' come diceva il sig Tramontana. Vale a dire all'Università, ma si, è proprio nei banchi degli studenti nel bel mezzo della classe. Una volta per sentire un teologo ed un'altra per sentire il prof. Fleiner parlare dello stato tedesco. È il rettore. Eravamo da lui a pranzo ed a cena. È un vecchio erudito, dicono, ma gagliardo, un amico di Budgen della cui intelligenza pare avere una altissima opinione. E chi si vede accanto a noi sul banco ad ascoltare anche lui? Paul Suter che dopo aver fabbricato i dadi Krassi a Winterthur fino alle 5 del pomeriggio va all'università alle $6\frac{1}{2}$. Anche lui è in cuori coi Fleiner. E tutti questi professori attempatelli suonano il pianoforte o cantano tenore. E tutti sembrano apprezzare molto il vino di Fendant ed un buon piatto di Hasenpfeffer.

Non so se credi alla chiaroveggenza. Ad ogni modo ascolta ascolta [sic] questo dialogo e notane la data 25 9mbre.[2] Luogo: Kussnacht.

Lucia: Pensavo tutto il giorno a MacCormack. Perchè è stato fatto conte invece di te. Tu sei molto più grande. È ingiusto. Pensavo di scrivere al papa.

Io: Attenti alla grammatica.

Lucia: È un vecchio rimbambito. Ma sul serio fino a quando durerà l'ostilità fra te e l'Irlanda?

Io: A me lo domandi?

Lucia: Voglio riconciliarvi io. È ora che qualche grande personalità irlandese venga a stenderti la mano dopo tutto ciò che hai fatto.

La mattina seguente alle 7 il portiere dell'albergo mi portò il dispaccio, la prima e sola comunicazione ch'io abbia mai ricevuto da lui, ed il giorno dopo l'*Irish Times* di Dublino pubblicò un lungo articolo abbastanza favorevole sull'ultimo mio frammento,[3] il primo articolo su me apparso nella stampa irlandese da venti anni a questa parte. Te lo mando. Mostralo a Colm. Non dissi nulla di ciò a Lucia perchè non voglio incoraggiarla nei sui sogni. Ma, prescindendo dalla profezia, le parole stesse sono fulminanti. Ella ha delle volte la sapienza del serpente e l'innocenza del colombo.

---

[1] See p. 27, n. 2.   [2] Either this date is incorrect or the letter was written over several days.
[3] 'James Joyce's Experiment with Language,' *Irish Times*, 27 October 1934.

Non trovo qui Vanity Fair. Mi riconobbe il pizdrul quando vide la
fotografia? Suppongo che parla con accento americano. Se così è (in
malora lo stylo!) pieghiamo il capo. Ti saluto, o giovincello!

La signora Giedion lässt Sie grüssen. Mama è dal barbiere. Sta per
nevicare. Andró da Huguenin[1] e mangerò quello che i toscaneggianti
chiamano un panino gravido. Coraggio e buona fortuna! Ti abbraccio

BABBO[2]

[1] Huguenin Restaurant, at 39 Bahnhofstrasse, Zurich.
[2] (Translation)
'Dear Giorgio: I hope that something positive has happened since your last letter.
But as I wrote yesterday, there is no use deceiving oneself. The support of Mac-
Cormack will certainly be useful if only for the publicity. As for the officials of the
Irish team (which besides has been beaten by the Chileans except for the horse with the
lucky name *Blarney Castle* with Captain Ahearn in the saddle) they may be good
judges of the hind parts of a colt but when it comes to the art of singing God help us.
You should also think of the English market which pays well and is always in need of
good voices, above all for the virtuosi who appear at the music festivals of Leeds,
Sheffield, Norwich etc. I have a letter from Beecham to Lionel Powell, the greatest
impresario in London. By the way I also met the ex-director of the Berlin opera
company (expelled as a Jew) and he will be much interested in your case. Your stage
fright will probably vanish at the moment of your baptism of fire before the footlights.
The idea of making one's debut before a microphone doesn't seem right to me but
better there than not at all. Please watch those troublesome 'h's'. Kieppura was here last
Friday. Wretchedly trained, horrid behaviour, little or no taste, but a lovely voice,
extended, easy and natural. Some jackass taught him to sing 'forma-h-a divina'
'misti-h-ico serto' etc. And this throughout the evening. Think of that! Wasted enthusiasm. He was accompanied from the Tonhalle to the station by a crowd of admirers or rather admiresses who surrounded his Rolls and he sang his farewell from the
steps. It was really as in the old days. Tonight we will go to hear the new opera of
Respighi, *The Sunken Bell*, based on a play of Hauptmann.
You will smile if I say that mother and I went 'to school', as Mr Tramontana used to
say. That is, to the university, in fact, and on the students' benches in the middle of the
classroom. Once to listen to a theologian and again to hear Prof. Fleiner speak of the
German state. He is the rector. We had lunch and dinner with him. He is, they say, an
old scholar, but full of vigour, a friend of Budgen of whose intelligence he has a very
high opinion. And whom should we see sitting on the bench next to us listening too?
Paul Suter who after making Krassi screws at Winterthur until five in the afternoon
goes to the university at 6:30. He too is good friends with the Fleiners. And all these
oldish professors play the piano and sing tenor. And all seem to appreciate properly the
wine of Fendant and a good plate of Hasenpfeffer.
I don't know whether you believe in clairvoyance, but anyway listen listen to this
dialogue and note the date, 25 November. Place: Kussnacht.
Lucia: I was thinking all day about MacCormack. Why was he made a count
instead of you. You are much greater. It is unfair. I was thinking I might write to the
Pope.
I: Mind your grammar.
Lucia: He is an old dotard. But seriously, how long will the hostility between you and
Ireland last?
I: You ask *me* that?
Lucia: I want to reconcile you: it is time that some influential Irishmen should come
and shake hands with you after all you have done.
Next morning at 7 the bellhop brought me a cable, the first and only message I have
ever received from him, and the day after the *Irish Times* of Dublin published a long
and rather favourable article on my last fragment, the first article which has appeared
about me in the Irish press for twenty years. I am sending it to you. Show it to Colm.

To George and Helen Joyce   MS. Kastor

6 December 1934   *Carlton Elite Hotel, Zurich*

Dear Giorgio and Helen: This being San Nicolò I hope you have given
Stevie something in our name. You are too far away to send him anything. Here are some clippings for you. There is a good *cavatina* or
cantabile for bass in the first act of Haendel's *Saul* 'Wie beb' ich vor
Zorn'. Giorgio ought to learn this bass part. It is very dramatic and Saul
always is in a deuce of a temper about one thing or another. In fact he
never expresses any sentiment except sceptical mistrust and *bile*. The
bass named Tapolet was quite good and the baritone named Book
excellent. He sings Samuel.

It is stifling Föhn[1] weather and I have an unpleasant attack of
tracheitis. We have almost decided to have Lucia's scar removed here
next week. The removal of your things has begun. It is quite a work in
progress too. The very greatest, nay the most religious, care will of
course be taken of the vacuum cleaner and the icebox. I am in a hurry to
catch the boat as usual.

Herewith best wishes for your forthcoming marriage anniversary
which we shall confirm by cable. Tante belle cose   BABBO

To Frank Budgen   MS. Yale

18 December 1934   *Carlton Elite Hotel, Zurich*

Dear Budgen: I sent you today Matisse's drawings. Will you and
Sargent please look at them and tell me what you think of them? And
send them back for I have to return them.

I simply cannot write letters. We have been here in Z'ch 3 months.
Näggeli is stumped: can make nothing of the case physically. Psychically
she is supposed to be in the hands of Jung. If anything lies ahead of us
except ruin I wish someone would point it out. The few friends we have

I did not say anything to Lucia about it because I don't want to encourage her in her
dreams. But, apart from the prophecy, the very words are striking. She has sometimes
the wisdom of the serpent and the innocence of the dove.

I cannot find *Vanity Fair* here. Did the little man recognize me when he saw the
photograph? I suppose he speaks with an American accent. If so (curse this fountain
pen!) I will resign myself. I greet you, young man!

Mrs Giedion sends her regards to you all. Mama is at the hairdresser's. It is going to
snow. I will go to Huguenin's and eat what those who pretend to be Tuscans call a
pregnant roll.

Courage and good luck! I embrace you   Babbo'
[1] South wind.

leave Z'ch on the 22 so we shall pass our 30th Xmas together alone or
31st rather. The doctors say: go away. When we try to go she throws a
fit or something and so we hang on. Giorgio and Helen are still in N.Y.
I am trying to write something for the next number of transition. You
can imagine how easy it is.

We saw the Fleiners a few times—a very charming old couple. I told
him I got the idea of the technique of the newest fragment[1] from one of
his lectures I was at. I won the final appeal in the U. S. Schluss.[2]

I hope Sargent is better and the weather too. Give him and Mrs
Sargent our kindest remembrances.

And I hope you yourself are enjoying the very best of health and Mrs
Budgen.

As for us we are two poor Godforsaken gipsies on the roadside.

A happy Xmas nevertheless to all of you Sincerely yours

JAMES JOYCE

P.S. Perhaps you could send a line to Lucia. She never gets a letter.
Sanatorium Dr Brunner, Kusnacht, bei Z'ch.

We have a friend in Vence to whom you could give our news and
regards. His name is Bruce, Villa des Chardons. Scotch of course. I hope
he is well.

To ALFRED BERGAN   MS. N.Y. Public Library (Manuscript)

20 December 1934   *Carlton Elite Hotel, Zurich*

Dear Mr Bergan, This is the only way I can invite you to drink to both
our healths this Christmas so please let it pass.

We are still detained here and cannot return to Paris till after New
Year. I hope you are in good health and spirits. Giorgio (my son) gave
his first concert over the radio in New York a week ago[3] and he too will
not be back in Paris till the Spring. MacCormack says he has a
magnificent bass. How glad Pappie would have been of this. There have
been voices on both sides of our family for several generations, but
nobody ever really made a career out of it. McGuckin[4] used to say
Pappie had the best tenor voice in Ireland in his time. You never heard
him at his best. He had a voice very like that of Jean de Reszke. We
used to have merry evenings in our house, used we not?

---

[1] *The Mime of Mick, Nick and the Maggies* (The Hague, 1934).   [2] 'Finish.'
[3] For the National Broadcasting Company.
[4] Barton McGuckin (1852–1913) was the leading tenor of the Carl Rosa Opera Company. He heard John Stanislaus Joyce sing about 1875.

In answer to your question. No, I am not interested in Irish Sweepstake tickets. I suppose the staircases in all the hospitals in Dublin are now made of solid gold. The only decent people I ever saw at a racecourse were the horses. The late Shah of Persia when invited by King Edward to go to Goodwood replied: I know that one horse runs quicker than than [sic] another but which particular horse it is doesn't interest me.

With all good wishes to you for a merry Xmas and a happy New Year and with friendly remembrances sincerely yours   JAMES JOYCE

To GEORGE JOYCE   MS. Kastor

24 December 1934   [*Zurich*]

The Croppy Boy[1]

(Il ragazzo dai cappelli tagliati, il giovine tosato, nomignolo dato ai giovini ribelli irlandesi nel 1798 (Ninety Eight) dalla guarnigione inglesi [sic])[2]

> Good men and true in this house who dwell
> To a country bouchel (boy) I pray you tell
> Is the priest at home and can he be seen
> I would speak a word with Father Breen.
>
> The priest's at home and he may be seen
> Tis aisy talking with Father Breen
> So just step inside until I see
> If the holy father alone may be.
>
> The youth has entered a lonely hall
> What a solemn sound makes his low footfall
> And the gloomy chamber is chill and bare
> With a vested priest in an oaken chair.
>
> The youth has knelt and confessed his sins
> *In nomine Dei* the youth begins
> And at *mea culpa* he beats his breast
> And in broken murmurs confesses the rest.

---

[1] By William B. McBurney (d. about 1892), who wrote under the name 'Carroll Malone'. Joyce's version is inaccurate in places.

[2] '(The boy with cropped head, the tonsured young fellow, a nickname given to the young Irish rebels of 1798 by the English garrison.)'

I cursed three times since last Easter Day
And at masstime once I went to play
I passed the churchyard one day in haste
And forgot to pray for my mother's rest.

I bear no hate to a living thing
But I love my country beyond the King
So bless me, father, and let me go
To die, if God has ordered it so.

The priest said nought but a rustling noise
Made the youth look up in wild surprise
And before his eyes there sat in the chair
A yeoman captain with fiery glare.

With fiery glare and with fury hoarse
Instead of a blessing he breathed a curse
'Twas a good thought boy to come here and shrive
For one short hour is your time to live.

On yonder river two tenders float
The priest's in one if he isn't shot
I hold this house for my lord the King
And Amen, say I, may all traitors swing!

At Geneva barracks that young man died
And at Passage they have his body laid.
Good people, who hear this in peace and joy,
Breathe a prayer, drop a tear, for the Croppy Boy.

(Questa canzone era il il cavallo da battaglia del grande basso leggiero irlandese William Ludwig.[1] La generazione attuale l'ignora. È un nobile e semplice poema musicale, profondamente sincero e dramatico. Bisogna, quando lo canti, tenere il bilancio egualmente fra il capitano ed il giovine. L'ultima strofe si canta su un tono solenne ed impersonale. L'effetto di questra strofe, resa da una voce come la tua, è eletrizzante [sic]. Altro che *I Due Granatieri* e *La Canzone del Volga*! Non è una canzone patriottica come *Wearing of the Green*. Potresti cantarlo a Sheffield come a Cork. Studia ogni parola e ne farai un capolavoro)[2]

---

[1] William Ludwig (1847–1923), Irish baritone.

[2] '(This song was the battle charger of the great Irish light bass, William Ludwig. The present generation does not know it. It is a pure and noble musical poem, profoundly sincere and dramatic. When you sing it, be sure to hold the balance equal between the captain and the young man. The last stanza is sung on a solemn and impersonal note. The effect of this stanza, when rendered by a voice like yours, is electrifying. A far cry from

Shule Aroon

A buacaillin aluinn, eibin, óg
(a voocalin aulin eevin oge
o young lad, pretty, pleasant, young)
bao leatan oo cnoide, bao bear oo póg
(broad was thy heart, sweet thy kiss,
bodh lahan dho creeye, bodh dhyas dho pogue)

(These two lines are enough for Colm to tell you the rest.
Aggiungo le parole inglesi. Ci sono decine di varie versioni di questa
canzone)[1]

> I'll dye my petticoats I'll dye them red
> And round this wide world I'll search my bread
> Till friends and foes will think me dead
> Ir go béit tu mo muinnin nlean
>
> I wish I were on yonder hill
> 'Tis there I'd sit and cry my fill
> Till every tear would turn a mill
>
> I wish I wish I wish in vain
> I wish I had my heart again
> And vainly think I'd not complain.
>
> Refrain (after each verse)
> Phonetic
>   Shule shule shule aroon
>   Shule go siukar ogars shule go kewn
>   Mo lane gou misha ogus elya lyum
>   Is go dikey thoo mawoorneen slawn.

The Yellow Ale[2]

As I was going the road one fine day,
(O the brown and the yellow ale!)
I met with a man that was no right man
(O love of my heart!)

The Two Grenadiers and *The Volga Boat Song*! This is not a patriotic song like *Wearing
of the Green.* You could sing it just as well at Sheffield as at Cork. Study every word of
it and you will make it into a masterpiece.)'

[1] 'I am adding the English words. There are dozens of different versions of this song.'

[2] An Irish folksong. Joyce's version leaves out some of the connections. A fuller version in Irish has been found by Roger McHugh; its refrain line is '*Cuach mo lionndubh
bui*', 'O my flagon of yellow porter.' This version was translated by Lady Gregory in the
Celtic Christmas, the supplement to the *Irish Homestead* published at Christmas 1901.

He asked was the woman with me my daughter
(O the brown etc)
And I said that she was my married wife
(O, love etc)

He asked would I lend her for an hour and a day
And I said I would do anything that was fair.

So let you take the upper road and I'll take the lower
And we'll meet again at the ford of the river.

I was walking that way one hour and three quarters
When she came to me without shame.

When I heard her news I lay down and I died
And they sent two men to the wood for timber.

A board of holly and a board of alder
And two great yards of sack about me.

And but that my own little mother was a woman
I could tell you another pretty story about women

PS. Farò copiare la musica di queste tre canzone quanto prima. Ti
abbraccio   BABBO

Vigilia di Ceppo 1934 Z'ch
5 ore del pomeriggio e tutti i negozi chiusi!!!!¹

To LUCIA JOYCE²   MS. S. Illinois

[*About 27 December 1934*]   [*Zurich*]

Cara Lucia: Curioso! Stamane arriva una cartolina di Natale da
Hughes. E cos'era? La Ballynure Ballad che hai cantato ieri. Te la
mando.

Eccoti anche un paio di biglietti per *Il Flauto Magico* domenica
dopopranzo.

Non era tanto male dopo tutto il nostro piccolo natale assieme, non è
vero? E così si andrà da bene in meglio.

---

¹ 'PS. I will have the music of these three songs copied as soon as possible. I embrace
you   Babbo'
Christmas Eve 1934 Zurich
5 o'clock in the afternoon and all the shops closed!!!!'
² Lucia Joyce was at Dr Brunner's sanitorium at Küsnacht, but was allowed to join her
parents in Zurich on Christmas Day and the day after.

Devo scrivere una lunga lettera a Giorgio per non perdere il piroscafo che parte posdomani.

Quindi troncherò questa letterina qui. Tanto più che devo vestirmi per andare sentire *I Maestri Cantori*. Ti abbraccio   BABBO[1]

To GEORGE JOYCE   MS. Kastor

27 December 1934   *Carlton Elite Hotel, Zurich, Switzerland*

Caro Giorgio: Pazienza! Sono cose che succedono. Lascia che Stephens e MacCormack vadano verso il loro tramonto. Per te è ancora l'alba. Credo il contratempo [sic] sia dovuto in prima linea all'imbecille d'ufficiale della N.B.C. A proposito non hai fatto che cambiare l'ordine delle lettere. Banque Nationale de Crédit[2] ed ora National Broadcasting Corporation.

Ho un appuntamento stasera coll'ex-regisseur dell'opera di Berlino[3] ed egli metterà giù la musica delle tre canzoni già inviate. Devo scrivere a Hughes pregandolo di scrivere un accompagnamento per 'Molly, I can't say' o piuttosto diciamo 'The Quilt'. Non voglio fare questo senza una parola tua prima. Sembra che io abbia fatto un pappero telegrafando al conte papalino ma credevo che la lettera di Helen era un rimprovero.

Come canzoni per basso ti propongo Off to Philadelphia, Ruddier than the the Cherry, Angels Ever Bright and Fair (Hændel) Wie duftet doch der Flieder (la bell'aria del gelsomino di Sachs)[4] Revenge, Timothy Cries [?], The Cruiskeen Lawn, (credo vuol dire la piccola brocca bruna) e un'ottima canzone per basso.

Madame Gautier può cantare quello che vuole. The Joyce Book per me è un grandissimo mistero. 18 artisti hanno collaborato per fare omaggio a me: e si doveva darmi il ricavo netto. Il ricavo è stato nettissimo, cioè, un nettissimo niente. Ma credo che (il caso di Darius Milhaud mi fa pensare) che anche la musica appartiene a me.

30 o 40 musicisti almeno hanno messo in musica i miei poemetti. Il migliore è Molyneux Palmer. Dopo lui Moeran e Bliss. *Bright Cap* del primo ti andrebbe bene per un bis.

---

[1] (Translation)
'Dear Lucia: How strange! This morning a Christmas card came from Hughes. And what was it? The Ballynure Ballad that you sang yesterday. I send it to you.

Here also are a pair of tickets to *The Magic Flute* for Sunday afternoon.

Our little Christmas together was not so bad, was it? And so things will get better and better.

I must write a long letter to Giorgio so as not to miss the boat, which sails tomorrow.

I will break off this note to you now, then. Especially since I must dress to go hear *Die Meistersinger*. I embrace you   Babbo'

[2] George Joyce had been employed in this bank in Paris for a time.

[3] Dr Hans von Curjel.   [4] In the last act of *Die Meistersinger*.

Belle arie per voce grave nelle Melodie Irlandesi di Thomas Moore sono 'O Ye Dead' (cantata da Plunket Greene[1]), Silent, O Moyle' con accompagnamento di arpa. 'The Time I've Lost in Wooing' (per bis).

Curiosa coincidenza. Al mio primo concerto pubblico ero anche piantato in asso. Il pianista, cioè la pianista è andato via nel bel mezzo del concerto.[2] Anche io ho cantato 'Down by the Sally Gardens' ed ho ricevuto esattamente 10 dollari cioè 2 ghinee come te. A proposito è scozzese quello N.B.C.! Perchè 10 $ a Dublino nel 1914 dovrebbero essere altro che 10 $ per te a Nuova York nel 1934.

Si. Colm è una brava pasta di ragazzo. Leale e senza invidia. Bisogna abituarsi a questi scacchi: quanto ne ho avuti con Sullivan! Ma va avanti. MacCormack è certo volubile ma è od era molto occupato e non ti farà del male. Un po' di rabbia non nuoce. Quell'ufficiale della N.B.C. doveva chiudere la bocca all'ora giusta a Stephens ed a Colm i quali ti hanno fatto passare un cattivo quarto d'ora, il primo per troppa compiacenza in se stesso, l'altro per isbadataggine.

Ti manderò tutto il mio repertorio un poco alla volta. Oggi aggiungo due appunti per te.

Ballynure Ballad. Bally vuol dire città. Non so cosa significa il resto. Somiglia a un qualchecosa. Città del? È, credo, nella contea di Antrim. Ad ogni modo nella provincia di Ulster, oggi Northern Ireland o Le Sei Contee. Gente mescolata: irlandesi, inglesi e molti scozzesi d'origine. Duri e caparbi, forti bevitori e lavoratori, ostilissimi al papa e tutte le sue pompe ed opere. 'The 5th day of November' è Guy Fawkes' Day. La rima inglese suona:

> Please to remember
> The 5th of November
> Gunpowder Treason and Plot

Infatti si brucia ancora oggidì in pubblico l'effige di Fawkes che tentò nel regno di Giacomo 1° coll'aiuto di altri cattolici e gesuiti (?) di far saltare in aria il parlamento inglese. Il tipo che va a vedere l'orrendo fuoco di quella pira, parte in istato sincero, e torna verso sera alquanto brillo. È un bravo protestante. I due tipi dietro la siepe sono forse cattolici: od una ragazza cattolica con un protestante poco convinto. Ad ogni modo hanno una bella pazienza. Passare tutto un pomeriggio di novembre nebbioso in un fossato irlandese. *De gustibus non est disputandum.*

Silent, O Moyle: Moyle è quella parte del mare irlandese che ora si chiama il Canale di San Giorgio. Le tre figlie di Lir (Nettuno Celtico e

---

[1] Harry Plunket Greene (1865–1936), Irish bass-baritone.
[2] The incident formed the basis for the story in *Dubliners*, 'A Mother.'

l'origine del Re Lear di Shakespeare) furono cambiati in cigni e devono sorvolare quelle acque plumbee per secoli finchè il suono della prima campana cristiana in Irlanda non rompa l'incanto. Segue domani Ti abbraccio   BABBO[1]

[1] (Translation)

'Dear Giorgio: Be patient! These things happen. Let Stephens and MacCormack go towards their sunset. For you it is still dawn. I think the contretemps is due first of all to that imbecilic N.B.C. official. By the way, you have merely changed the order of the letters. Banque Nationale de Crédit and now National Broadcasting Corporation.

I have an appointment for this evening with the ex-director of the Berlin opera and he will set down the music for the three songs already sent. I must write to Hughes, asking him to write out an accompaniment for "Molly, I can't say" or rather for, shall we say, "The Quilt." I don't want to do this without a word from you first. Apparently I blundered by telegraphing the papal count but I had the notion that Helen's letter was a reproof.

As songs for a basso I propose 'Off to Philadelphia,' 'Ruddier than the Cherry,' 'Angels Ever Bright and Fair' (Handel), 'Wie duftet doch ein Flieder' (the fine aria of the jessamine by Sachs), 'Revenge,' 'Timothy Cries [?],' 'The Cruiskeen Lawn,' (I think it means the little brown jug) is an excellent song for basso.

Madame Gautier can sing what she likes. The Joyce Book is a very great mystery to me. 18 artists have collaborated to do me honour: and the net profit was to revert to me. The profit has been very net, that is, a very net nothing. But I believe (the case of Darius Milhaud makes me think so) that the music also belongs to me.

30 or 40 musicians at least have set my little poems to music. The best is Molyneux Palmer. After him are Moeran and Bliss. *Bright Cap* by the former would serve you well for an encore.

The lovely arias for deep voices among Thomas Moore's Irish Melodies are 'O Ye Dead' (sung by Plunket Greene), 'Silent, O Moyle' with harp accompaniment, 'The Time I've Lost in Wooing' (for an encore).

Strange coincidence. In my first public concert I too was left in the lurch. The pianist, that is the lady pianist, had gone away right in the middle of the concert. I too sang 'Down by the Sally Gardens' and I received exactly 10 dollars or 2 guineas, like you. By the way, that N.B.C. is Scotch! Because $10 in Dublin in 1904 should be more than $10 for you in New York in 1934.

Yes. Colm is a good sort. Loyal and without envy. One must get used to reverses. How many I experienced over Sullivan! But go right ahead. MacCormack is certainly talkative but he is or was very busy and won't do you any harm. Getting a bit angry doesn't hurt. That N.B.C. official should have told Stephens and Colm to shut their mouths at the right moment. They've given you a bad quarter of an hour, the first because of complacency and the other through mere carelessness.

I will send you all my repertoire a little at a time. Today I am just adding two notes for you.

Ballynure Ballad. Bally means city. I don't know what the rest means. It sounds like the city of ? I think it is in county Antrim. At any rate in the province of Ulster, today Northern Ireland or the Six Counties. A mixed breed: Irish, English, and many Scottish in origin. Tough and tenacious, hard drinkers and hard workers, very hostile to the Pope and all his pomps and works. "The 5th day of November" is Guy Fawkes' Day. The English rhyme goes:

> Please to remember
> The 5th of November
> Gunpowder Treason and Plot

In fact, to this day they burn publicly the effigy of Fawkes who tried, during the reign of James I, with the aid of other Catholics and Jesuits (?) to blow up the English Parliament. The fellow who goes to see the horrid flames of that pyre, leaves in a sober mind and comes home rather tight in the evening. He is a good Protestant. The two

To GEORGE and HELEN JOYCE   MS. Kastor

8 January 1935   [*Zurich*]

Dear G and H. Here's the Land of Saints and Sages.[1] H. Find
Ballynure in Antrim. G. Find Joyce Country in County Galway. I
thought it might be useful or instructive to locate any places mentioned
in any Irish songs G. sings. Is this a trick of memory. Now, only this
instant, I think I forgot a verse in *The Croppy Boy*? Did I? How strange
memory is! Anyway I write it out. It comes after 'my mother's rest'[2]
Tante belle cose   BABBO

To HELEN JOYCE   MS. Kastor

18 January 1935   *Carlton Elite Hotel, Zurich*

Dear Helen: Just got your letter. First, I hope your father is by now
well on the mend. Give him our best wishes. Also am glad to hear about
David.[3] As for Stevie he sounds all right at this distance. Does Mme
Gautier sing bass herself and how many hundred years training are
necessary before a singer can face an American public? Don't be down-
hearted, my dear little children. Everyone has an uphill time at first.
You said you were sending us a clipping: There is none in the envelope.
If Giorgio is irritated by the article think of this. This morning I
received a proposal from the London firm which is supposed to be
bringing out *Ulysses*. They want me to compose 735 headlines for the
735 pages e.g. p. 1, 'On the Top of the Tower', p. 2, 'A Morning Shave'
'Theological Talk' 'The Inner Man Satisfied' 'Arrival of the Milkmaid'.
As Mrs Colm would ask: Can you beat it?

Lucia is as I told you with a nurse in Villa Elite. But I am sending
away the nurse on Sunday or Monday as my sister Eileen is coming from

behind the hedge are Catholic perhaps or a Catholic girl with a not very ardent Protestant. Anyway they really have a good deal of patience. To spend a whole foggy
November afternoon in an Irish bog. *De gustibus non est disputandum.*

Silent, O Moyle: Moyle is that part of the Irish Sea which is now called St George's
Channel. The three daughters of Lir (the Celtic Neptune and the original of Shake-
sheare's King Lear) were changed into swans and must fly over those leaden waters
for centuries until the sound of the first Christian bell in Ireland breaks the spell.

More tomorrow. I embrace you   Babbo'
[1] A map of Ireland was enclosed.
[2] Joyce did leave out a stanza, actually the fifth rather than, as he thought, the sixth:

> At the siege of Ross did my father fall,
> And at Gorey my loving brothers all.
> I alone am left of my name and race;
> I will go to Wexford and take their place.

'The Croppy Boy' is one of the songs sung in the *Circe* episode of *Ulysses*.
[3] David Fleischman.

Dublin to try out a stay of a month or so with Lucia's [sic] at Lucia's constantly repeated request. Have just wired her her fare. Please ask all the jews in America to get up a subscription for me as I am planning to enter the poorhouse on S. Patrick's Day next.

So please cheer up, do. And send me a group photograph like the last lovely one we had taken. I think you were the nicest of all, Helen.

Goodbye. I have now to run in my slippers all the way to Cherbourg to catch that boat.

Caro Giorgio: Buona fortuna! Or su! Corajo! Avanti, Savoya! Salutami il piccolo.[1]

Remember! Remember!! Remember!!!

The 2nd of February[2]

is

C O M I N G

Mi spiego? Tante belle cose[3]   BABBO

To GEORGE and HELEN JOYCE   MS. Kastor

[*About 18 February 1935*]   *7 rue Edmond Valentin, Paris VII*

Dear G and H: This is only part of a letter. The enclosed explain themselves. Lucia and Eileen (who get on very well together) are spending some time with Miss Weaver as her guests.[4]

About Irish songs, I suggest

1) Buy Hughes's Irish County Songs[5] (2 vols) (they are nearly all Ulster songs) at Steinway Hall, 111 W. 57th Street.

2) Buy Moore's Irish Melodies and learn the following

    a) Fly not yet

    b) O, ye dead

3) Quick we have but a second (this needs a lot of breath)

4) The time I lost in wooing

5) Silent, O Moyle

(this is a lovely air but G. should study the legend of Lir's daughters)

---

[1] 'Dear Giorgio: Good luck! Cheer up! Courage! Forward, Savoy! Remember me to the little one.' Joyce uses the Triestine spelling, 'corajo,' instead of the usual Italian, 'coraggio.' 'Forward, Savoy!' was the Italian battle cry in the first World War; Joyce was amused by the Triestine modification of it to 'Avanti, cagoia' (snails).

[2] Joyce's fifty-third birthday.   [3] 'Do I make myself clear? Best wishes.'

[4] This visit went badly because of Lucia's deranged state of mind. She stayed in London from 15 February to 16 March 1935, when she left with her aunt Mrs Eileen Schaurek for Bray.

[5] Herbert Hughes, *Irish Country Songs*, 4 vols. (Dublin, 1909).

2) [sic] I shall try to get from London and send at once

    The little Red Fox by Arthur Somervell

    The Queen of Connemara by Alicia Needham

    Trottin' to the Fair ⎫ all by Villiers Stanford, the composer of

    Drake's Drum   ⎬ Molly Brannigan and Father O'Flynn.

    Eva Toole   ⎭

All these songs used to be sung by Plunket Greene, a well known Irish bass.

Next, I have an enormous collection of Irish folk music collected by Petrie[1] and another lot by Joyce (P.W.)[2] I shall send this out soon.

Suggestion

1935 is the centenary of the death of Bellini and of the birth of Allen Foley[3] our Irish bass, the Chialiapin of his time. He sang all Lablache's parts, (who was ½ Irish too his mother came from Cork and his [father] was born at Naples. I shall try to get the bass arias from Bellini's operas but they are usually with chorus. However this could be dodged. The centenary will certainly be celebrated in U.S.

La Forza del Destino—if G. likes the bass in this I will try to get him aria either Del mondo i di or Non imprecare I suppose he means.[4]

Have been all day hunting up music. We have been here a week.

All your portraits plus the big one of my wife by F.B.[5] which she ripped out of the frame are at the enclosed address. I am having them insured for 50,000 fr. as I believe T's[6] portrait of my father is very valuable.

Lucia's address is c/o H.W. 74 Gloucester Place, London W.1. Your very dusty dirty and tired   Babbo

Hope S.J.J. had a merry time on 15th.

P.S. There are no arias sold separately of *Kittege*[7]; the whole score costs 180 francs. Copy out the bass air in act III. But I sent the bass air[8] from Glinka's 'Vie pour le Tsar' which the Japanese bass sang well—his only good number. He wore a kimono and scarlet vest. I suppose the Nipponese evening dress but was a freak voice for me

[1] *The Complete Collection of Irish Music as Noted by George Petrie*, ed. C. V. Stanford (London, Irish Literary Society, 3 parts, 1902–5).

[2] Patrick Weston Joyce, *Irish Peasant Songs in the English Language* (London, Dublin, New York, 1906).

[3] Allan James Foley (1835–1897).

[4] Giuseppe Verdi, *La Forza del destino* (1862). The two arias are the duet, 'Del mondo i disinganni,' and the trio, 'Non imprecare, umiliati,' both in Act IV.

[5] Frank Budgen.   [6] Patrick Tuohy.

[7] Nikolay Andreyevich Rimsky-Korsakov (1878–1940), *Kitezh*, first performed in 1907.

[8] Susanin's aria, 'This Is No Time to Dream,' in Michael Glinka, *A Life for the Czar* (1836).

O Ye dead.[1] The 2nd verse of this should be sung almost in a whisper.

Am sending Goosens' settings of some of my verse.[2] I wish I could find Palmer's[3] which are much finer music or even Moeran's.[4]

I am afraid G. Antheil the famous composer who wrote those splendid operas *Ulysses* and *Cain* has made off with P. W. Joyce's collection of old Irish airs.   BABBO.

To GEORGE and HELEN JOYCE   MS. Kastor

19 February 1935   *7 rue Edmond Valentin, Paris 7ᵉ*

Dear G and H: I sent round your books and original editions in a box marked B.O. to the rue Claire and will leave the key with your solicitor. The portraits have been renovated my father's varnished and all insured. I will attend to this.

Lucia went to London as Paris was too full of unpleasant memories for her and also to see Beckett. She met him a few times and they had dinner together. More anon, as Willy Shakespeare saith. Eileen is with her having got indefinite leave from her job in the Dublin 'Sweepstake'. I pay her salary. They are living near Miss Weaver at the Ascot Hotel, York Street–Baker Street.

Souppault[5] just rang me up. I am to see him tomorrow at 5 p.m. He says you are having a festive time but it seems to me though you are both doing your best you are up against difficulties all the time and stupid people. Don't be discouraged. Also don't be annoyed at all the music I send. I know G. can't sing it all over then and there but it is well to have it. I sent also the *Cry of the Deer* (S. Patrick at Tara). This consists of 1) the invocation of the Trinity (the shamrock) 2) the so-called Breastplate (Corazza) of S.P. a prayer to Christ. The former is good oratorio style, the latter somewhat tedious and theatrical. The composer's real name is Harold White a Dublin man who wrote an opera called *Shaun the Post.*[6]

You don't seem to go much to the opera. I hope you liked *Siegfried*

---

[1] By Thomas Moore.

[2] *Chamber Music*, Six Songs for Medium Voice, Music by Eugene Goossens (London, 1930).

[3] H. Molyneux Palmer's settings were not published.

[4] *Seven Poems by James Joyce* set to music by E. J. Moeran (London, 1930).

[5] Philippe Soupault had been in the United States and was to return there during the summer of 1935. Joyce made clear to Soupault how unhappy and even ill he was because of his son's absence from Paris, and Soupault was a kind of ambassador from father to son, to encourage the latter to return.

[6] Harold Robert White (1872–1940?), Irish composer, organist, and singer. His opera, *Shaun the Post* (1924), was based on Dion Boucicault's play, *Arrah na pogue*.

with Melchior[1] but I suppose if they put on *Floradora* with George
Robey in the name part the horsehoers[2] would not notice. I went to
hear Rimsky's *Kittege* again at the Opéra Comique with Zaporoyetz as
Prince Yuri. Che splendore di voce. Ampia, estesa, facile e maestosa.
Se Sullivan era il rei dei fort *tenors*, Z– è l'imperatore dei *basses nobles*.[3]
But he gets only a few hundred francs a night. Of course his voice is
probably unsuited to many more flexible parts, Mephisto, for instance.
And his part lasts about 10 minutes. But it is majestically beautiful,
better than 6 years ago. I never met anybody in London who had even
heard of him. So there you are. MacCormack is touring California and
is to give a silver jubilee concert in N.Y., I think, on Easter Day. I also
see that Mr Pinza,[4] the bass, and Mrs are having some trouble probably
over a Mrs Presnitz. This joke is lost on you, H, but 'pinza' is a gateau
brioche and presnitz a kind of mince pie in Trieste.

It is awful weather and it gives me cramps.

A propos of the S.B.[5] sale of my MSS (of which I am still officially
ignorant) I am journalistically informed that the rumour is current over
there that she, by her generous sacrifice of all her rights in *U* to me,
resigned herself to abject poverty. Frailty, thy name is woman.

Why don't you send me a photograph of Stevie? I asked several
times. But there is something you asked me for too and I forgot it. I got
an offer from some impresario to make a lecture tour in the U.S. What on
earth do these people want to be lectured to all the time about? Every
old fool in Europe goes over to lecture to them about something or
other. And they lap it up like soup.

This is quite a different kind of flat from the Grenelle one: much
more *signorile*[6] but still simple. Big high rooms. My wife had to lengthen
all the curtains. Also very quiet. Except for the squad of children
upstairs. But that noise I don't dislike. Still I hope someone makes them
a present of a carpet or two.

Tara era il Mecca o Gerusalemme degli antichi irlandesi. L'isola era
una pentarchia = 5 re. Uno per ognuna delle 4 provincie, Ulster,
Munster, Leinster, Connaught ed il quinto il re supremo (áro.rí)[7]
era incoronato a Tara. S. Patrizio andò là a confrontare i preti druidici,[8]
come fece Moisè in Egitto. Fece ogni genere di miracoli anche. Ogni

[1] Lauritz Melchior (b. 1890).   [2] A deliberate distortion of 'showgoers'.
[3] 'What splendour of voice. Ample, outstretched, unstrained, and majestic. If Sullivan
was the king of strong tenors, Zaporoyetz is the emperor of noble basses.'
[4] Ezio Pinza (1892–1957), Italian bass.
[5] Sylvia Beach. Joyce had given her some manuscripts some time before.
[6] Upper class.   [7] The fifth province was originally Meath.
[8] *Finnegans Wake*, pp. 610–13.

fuoco doveva spegnersi in Irlanda salvo il fuoco reale a Slane, credo.
Patrizio suscitò l'ira dei druidi accendendo il fuoco pasquale. Era il
sabato santo.[1]

I see the little Lord Mayor of Dublin Alfie Byrne is going to N.Y. for
the 17th. Every day I open the *Irish Times* I see him and his golden
chain in some photograph or other. He has been Lord Mayor for 7 years
but before him Mr 'Larry' O'Neill was Lord Mayor for 15 years. In my
time the Lord Mayor was elected by members of the corporation to whom
he owed money so that they could get a garnishee order on his salary.

O yes I remember now. You said you had a film taken, isn't that it and
if I would like it. Yes, by all means.

No, I don't think Mme Jolas is angry with you nor the Gilberts. Sink
both these little worries in the bosom of the Atlantic.

Giorgio, so che canti stasera ma non so a che ora e come potrei udirti.
Buona fortuna ad ogni modo.[2]

My wife is out but I send greetings from us both to G, H and S.

Gradite, cari pargoli, i sensi dei miei più doverosi ossequi[3]   BABBO.

P.S.

Caro Giorgio: Ti mando le arie d'Oroveso e di Rodolfo.[4] Non posso
avere le altre oggi. Se questa serie di 'broadsheets' ti sembra interessante
sottoscrivi. Accluso un ritaglio concernente il mobile conto. A quanto
pare tutto va bene a Londra. Mandai Lucia da uno specialistica per le
glandole. Pare abbia una deficenza di secrezione adrenale. A parte ciò
questo medico sostiene che lo scontro nel taxi c'entra per molto nel suo
caso. Mandami buone novelle. Tanti saluti a Helen ed a Stevie. Ti
abbraccio   BABBO[5]

---

[1] 'Tara was the Mecca and Jerusalem of the ancient Irish. The island was a pentarchy
=5 kings. One for each of the four provinces, Ulster, Munster, Leinster, Connaught
and the fifth, the high king (ard ri), was crowned at Tara. St Patrick went there to
confront the druid priests, just like Moses in Egypt. He did every kind of miracle, too.
Every fire in Ireland was supposed to be extinguished except the royal fire at Slane, I
think. Patrick roused the druids' ire by lighting the Paschal fire. It was Holy Saturday.'
[2] 'Giorgio, I know you are singing this evening but I do not know at what time or how
I can manage to hear you. Good luck anyway.'
[3] 'Accept, dear little ones, the expression of my most dutiful homage,   Babbo.'
[4] From Vincenzo Bellini, *Norma* (1831), and Giacomo Puccini, *La Bohème* (1896),
respectively.
[5] (Translation)
'P.S. Dear Giorgio: I am sending you the arias of Oroveso and Rodolfo. I cannot obtain
the others today. If this series of "broadsheets" looks interesting to you subscribe to it.
I enclose a slip about the furniture bills. Apparently everything is all right in London.
I sent Lucia to a gland specialist. It seems that she has had a deficiency in adrenal
secretion. On this point the doctor thinks the taxi accident has made a lot of difference
in her case. Send me good news. Greetings to Helen and Stevie. Fondly   Babbo'

To LUCIA JOYCE   MS. National Library

26 February 1935 Tuesday   [*Paris*]

Cara figliola: Scusami di non averti scritto. Ed anche oggi non lo posso
perchè i miei occhi sono minacciati sia dal maltempo sia dalla polvere
dei vecchi libri che arrangiavo. È meglio dunque essere prudente.
Scusami anche presso la Sig.na Weaver. Eileen tornerà venerdì. Siamo
così contenti di sapere che tutto va bene costì. Brava, Lucia!

Adesso vuoi fare una piccola commissione per me? Ti mando 5
scellini. Va o telefona a

> Boosey and Co
> 295 Regents Street

e comanda per me di mandare per la posta due esemplari della canzone:
'Off to Philadelphia' di Battison Haynes (tono di do maggiore = C)

Costa 2 scellini ognuno dunque ti basterà.

Grazie

Ce [sic] noia avere occhi come i miei! Sempre allarmi! Ti abbraccio

BABBO[1]

To GEORGE and HELEN JOYCE   MS. Kastor

26 February 1935   [*Paris*]

Dear G and H: I can't write much as my eyes are troubling me—either
the awful damp or the window open or the dust of the books I was
unpacking. All your pictures are safe in the rue Claire, also a box of
all the 1st editions etc so carefully ticketed by Giorgio. Will send policy
of insurance on Saturday. Here's the receipt anyhow. And a letter from
L. You will see by the tone and writing that she is getting on well.

Am glad S[2] had a good party after all. Send us a photograph. Also to
hear your father, H,[3] is better.

Now for the songs.

[1] (Translation)
'Dear daughter: Excuse me for not writing. And today too I cannot because my
eyes are threatened either by the bad weather or the dust of the old books that I have
been arranging. So it is better to be careful. Please give my apologies to Miss Weaver.
Eileen will come back on Friday. We are so glad to know that everything is well with
you. Brava Lucia!
Now will you please do a little errand for me? I am sending you five shillings. Go
or telephone to Boosey and Co., 295 Regent's Street, and have them send me by mail
two copies of the song: 'Off to Philadelphia' by Battison Haynes (key of *do* major = C).
They cost two shillings each, so you will have enough.
Thank you
What a nuisance to have eyes like mine! Alarms all the time! Fondly   Babbo'
[2] Stephen Joyce.   [3] Helen Joyce.

I have found Philadelphia for you at least have just written L[1] in London where she can get it. I send today the songs promised. I had a new copy made of 3 settings of my verses by Palmer, made about 25 years ago but better than any of the subsequent ones, viz,

Gentle Lady

At That Hour

Donnycarney (this one has been set by at least 12 composers)

Will send them also on Saturday.

Blatherskite (vuol dire bubbole, fandonie, millanterie)[2] is not Irish at all but Scotch American. I suppose the song meant is Maggie Lauder. In Ireland the word is blatherumskite. Perbacco! Meritava proprio studiare 6 anni per cantare simile robaccia.[3]

Silent, O Moyle. Of course I know it, IT. You must have heard me sing it often. The best setting is by Sir Henry Bishop. It goes very well with a harp accompaniment. But *O Ye Dead* is the song for G.

Little Red Fox (An Modereen Ruadh) a charming little fanciful song. Moore (Thomas) used it in the melody *Let Erin Remember*. This melody is about Lough Neagh under which there is said to be buried a kind of Atlantis. Others say Finn MacCool in anger took a sod of turf out of Ireland and flung it in the sea, thus making 1) Lough Neagh 2) Isle of Man.

Non mi sento bene. Malora, questi vechi![4]

Queen of Connemara. Pity they sent this in the higher key by mistake. None of these songs is much, really. There is a very nice song by Hughes to words of Colum. 'O Men from the Fields'. Try for this. It sounds a bit Russian. I suppose the Blatherskite is that tawdry thing supposed to be 'to an ould ancient air of ould Ireland' after all, about women and kissing. O dear!

If he sings *Silent, O Moyle* though the man you mention, H, named Fisher has good ideas, such as the harp suggestion, he almost always smothers the melody and there is some flaw in his harmonic ear. Bishop keeps the line of the air free.

But I should like to hear Giorgio sing *O ye Dead.*[5] Some fool marked the 2nd verse (the reply of the ghosts) as F. This is nonsense.

Enough of yellow paper, Irish wails and my sticky eyes. If only I had a

---

[1] Lucia Joyce.

[2] 'Meaning blather, yarns, braggadocio.'

[3] 'My goodness! It was worth six years of study to sing this kind of rubbish.'

[4] (Translation)
    'I don't feel well. Devil take these old fellows!'

[5] According to Stanislaus Joyce, this song of Moore's gave his brother the theme of the story in *Dubliners*, 'The Dead.' In the second of the two stanzas, the dead speak in a whisper to express their pining for life.

fine *basso profondo* but not to sing B. Kyrie eleison, Gospodi pomilyou, Miserere Nobis O Lord, have mercy on U.S. Tante belle cose   BABBO

To MRS EILEEN JOYCE SCHAUREK   MS. National Library

13 March 1935   *7 rue Edmond Valentin, Paris*

Dear Eileen: One letter to save time so you may read this to Lucia. Your letter of Tuesday bears no address and if I had not asked Lucia where she was living when she telephoned I should not know where to send this. I hope the address is correct. In your letter you urge me to arrange for your departure for Ireland as soon as possible. In your wire of a few hours later you urge me to telegraph forbidding such a departure. The letters I receive from you and Miss Weaver are all contradictory. Lucia told me she wants a man to accompany her from Holyhead at least. I can think of nobody today. On Monday or Tuesday of next week there is a young Irishman here named Murphy who could pick her up in London. But it is a long wait for her. Curran, the only person I know in Dublin, could not leave his job. Anyhow I enclose the £2 Lucia asked for. How much do you pay in the boarding-house? . . .

Where does Lucia want to go to in Ireland—that earthly paradise? I enclose a letter from Galway from which you or she can draw what conclusions you like. But if she wants to go there or to Bray all right. In the last ten days I have sent with enclosed £15, £3 to you in Dublin £3 refund to Miss Weaver who sent them to you £1 and £5 to Lucia and now £2. When you want more as of course you will (and I forgot the £2.13. cheque) state plainly the amount. Nora thinks you ought to leave on receipt of this as there is a spell of good weather on. And alone as you did from here. She is not very keen on Lucia's going to Galway as she anticipates trouble when her people find out that she doesn't go to holy mass, holy confession, holy communion and holus bolus. However she thinks the air will do her good. Also Irish eggs are famous all over the world.

Miss Weaver wrote to me that Lucia had been rude to her. I shall be much obliged if you will let me know exactly what took place and by return.

While you stay with Lucia I will pay your salary £2 a week and of course pay for both your board unless some other person does so.

[Unsigned]

P.S. Have just had a ring up from Mr Murphy. He leaves Paris on 18 but stays in London a few days and will not leave for Dublin till the 21st

To MRS EILEEN JOYCE SCHAUREK[1]

[16 March 1935]   *7 rue Edmond Valentin, Paris 7ᵉ*

Dear Eileen: I am sorry you had such an alarm and your daughters too.
The affair seems mysterious. Is the bungalow on the top of Bray Head
and what could any burglar hope to get by entering the house of any
member of the Joyce family? I am short of cash this week end but on
Tuesday will wire £5 more, £2 for you and £3 for Lucia. She must get
used to handling money even if she spends some badly. Millions of
women do that. The scenes that scared you and Miss Weaver are
nothing to speak of. Her mother stood four years of very much worse
than that. Lucia says Charley's wife and Alice talked to her a lot about
Jesus Mary and Aunt Josephine. If these two females are so damn pious
how is it they bear no children? I shall write Lucia tomorrow as in any
case you won't get this before Monday. She also says Miss Weaver stole
a bottle of cognac. Possibly the strain is driving her to drink.

You have not answered any of my questions but this is excusable in
the circumstances. I want to know exactly (apart from the £2 a week I
will send you in lieu of your salary) what I have to pay as weekly board
for you and Lucia. Mr Murphy will stay in London from Tuesday to
Thursday or so but I will send you more details when I know them.

I hope you have by now got over your fright. Anyhow things like that
rarely happen twice in the same place. You are wrong in wanting to
conceal the fact of your wiring from Lucia. The only way to get on with
her is to be perfectly straightforward and honest as she is herself in
spite of her loony ways. Greetings   JIM

P.S. I did not know that Irish Paddies celebrate their *onomastico*.[2]
However, if it gives you and him pleasure, I will send him a line for
tomorrow. I mean Patrick.

To MRS EILEEN JOYCE SCHAUREK   MS. National Library

[? 17 March 1935]   *7 rue Edmond Valentin, Paris*

Dear Eileen: There is one other thing I can do about the crossing if
you really go. If you wire me in advance by what train you leave Euston
I shall try to get a travel agency to telephone the purser of the boat at
Holyhead to look out for Lucia and attend to her on the passage. But I
must know well in advance. Greetings   JIM

[1] From a photostatic copy.
[2] 'Saint's day.' Mrs Schaurek's third child was named Patrick.

To GEORGE and HELEN JOYCE   MS. Kastor

19 March 1935   *7 rue Edmond Valentin, Paris 7ᵉ*

Dear Giorgio and Helen: I left the keys with Mr Bodington. The policies[1] will follow when they arrive. The reason I took these steps is that a single signed 1st edition of *U* fetched 2700 frs in the Salle Drouot last year, that Schwarz told me 10,000$ was offered for my father's portrait when it was hung in N.Y. and that Marchand's[2] picture will also be worth more than you gave for it in all likelihood.

I hope all went off well on the 11th. Lucia tells me she had a letter from you about it. Her present address is c/o Miss Eva Joyce, 12 Mountjoy Square, Dublin. But she may go on to Galway for a short stay.

I sent the Dupan collection. There is none for *voix grave*. So I sent the best I could: *voix moyenne*: I shall not write any more today about the art of song.

I enclose a letter from Mr Kastor and another which present a curious contrast. Perhaps in a leisure moment you could look up number 2 and see if there is anything behind it.

Souppault[3] called here. He was very pessimistic about things in the U.S. But I think everyone is like that in all lands today. But he was very optimistic about Giorgio which is good to hear. Also he told us the child was flourishing. One other item of news I pass on to you with reserve. He said that Cerf was neglecting *Ulysses* in favour of Miss G. Stein and that in several of the towns where he lectured his hearers could not get copies of it ? ? ?

As regards the Beach sale of my MSS I am told the rumour is abroad on both sides of Brendan's herring pond[4] that she, by generously sacrificing all her rights in my favour, has reduced herself to starvation.

Mrs Bailly has gone to London and wanted us to go with her. After her return she goes to Dublin, she wants B. to close up shop, sell his business sell his flat and live in dear old Ireland in the morning.[5]

I think that's all the news I have this day of Our Lord (it is really S. Joseph's) but hope to have a good budget of news in your next.

About your chair, Helen. Every time I enter the refectory I bow to it. Also on leaving the refectory after refection. We are on the best of terms.

---

[1] Of insurance.   [2] Jean Hippolyte Marchand (1883–1940), French painter.
[3] See p. 344, n. 5.
[4] The Atlantic Ocean, which St Brendan, according to legend, was the first to cross, *Finnegans Wake*, p. 213.
[5] An echo of 'Off to Philadelphia'.

My cordial salutations to you both not forgetting the Society of Jewses (quip borrowed from W. i. P.)[1]   BABBO

P.S. Photos just arrived. They are very good. The little boy is very good-looking. Giorgio in the paper has exactly the same pose as I have in Silvestri's picture.

Di nuovo

BABBO

To LUCIA JOYCE   MS. S. Illinois

26 March 1935   *7 rue Edmond Valentin, Paris 7ᵉ*

Cara Lucia: In attesa della tua risposta alla mia lettera ti mando ancora 3 sterline, dunque 5 in tutto. Ho ricevuto ieri un dispaccio da Eileen che non spiega niente. Se le devi del denaro pagalo. È inutile sprecare il denaro telegrafando quando una lettera arriva in 24 ore. Insomma scrivimi chiaramente e dì a Eileen di fare lo stesso.

La Jolas mi ha mostrato la tua lettera che mi pare gaia, ed un poco satirica. Tanto meglio. Vuol dire che vai meglio?

Quanto al 'pony' vuoi imitare forse il famoso Yankee Doodle?[2]

Queste poche righe in fretta   Ti abbraccio   BABBO[3]

To LUCIA JOYCE   MS. S. Illinois

[About 7 April 1935]   *7 rue Edmond Valentin, Parigi 7*

Cara Lucia: Grazie della tua lettera. Ti ho spedito ieri in una busta 2 lire sterline. Non ti ho scritto ed oggi non posso scriverti a lungo perchè ho lavorato tutto il giorno. Vedo con piacere che sei sempre contenta costì e che il luogo ti va bene. Non ti ho mandato il giornale perchè credo che l'hai già visto.

---

[1] 'Then he caught the europicolas and went into the society of jewses.' *Finnegans Wake*, p. 423. The reference is to Helen Joyce's Jewish relatives.

[2] Lucia Joyce had asked for money to buy a pony. Her father treated the request as a joke.

[3] (Translation)

'Dear Lucia: While waiting for your reply to my letter I send you three more pounds, making five in all. I received a telegram from Eileen yesterday which explained nothing. If you owe her money pay it. It is useless to waste money telegraphing when a letter reaches here in 24 hours. So write me clearly and tell Eileen to do the same.

Mrs Jolas showed me your letter which seems to me gay and a bit satirical. So much the better. Does it mean you feel better?

As for the pony, do you perhaps want to imitate the famous Yankee Doodle?

These few lines in haste   I embrace you   Babbo'

Mi parli del defunto cavaliere Fernandez,[1] della di lui consorte e d'altre persone più o meno degne. Confesso però che la me[n]zione dei loro nomi suscita una fiammella alquanto fioca in questo cuore che va invecchiandosi. C'è dunque a Bray una gentildonna che si chiama Mazza: Ma perchè non si chiama Ombrellino?[2]

Mi consigli di andare al circo. Dove? Nell'anfiteatro o nella pista? Sono pronto a tutto.

Ti manderò tutti i libri che vuoi ma bisogna dirmi quali. Segui forse il mio cattivo esempio trascurando l'acqua della Moyle? Ma io mi lavo religiosamente ogni volta che la luna è in quintadecima.[3]

In risposta alle tue domande non sono in carteggio col Byrne ma credo che Carducci abbia letto Carducci[4] perchè io leggo Giacomo Giocondo.[5] Giorgio ora sta bene, Helen sta benone, ed il loro bambino benissimo.[6] [Manuscript breaks off]

To GEORGE JOYCE (Postscript to a missing letter)   MS. Kastor

[*About 10 April 1935*]   [*Paris*]

Pregai dunque Curran d'indagare.

Ieri sera ebbi una lettera da Lucia. Di Bray dice 'è un luogo magnifico pieno di fiori'. Insomma è contenta e spero sulla buona via.   B.

Giorni fa dovevo far rinnovare il mio passaporto. L'impiegato mi disse

[1] A young man in whom Lucia Joyce had been interested. He was the brother of Yva Fernandez, who collaborated in the translation of *Dubliners* into French.

[2] 'Mazza' in Italian means 'club'.

[3] In *Ulysses* Stephen Dedalus is notorious for not taking baths.

[4] That is, Edgardo Carducci, Joyce's musician friend in Paris, had read Giosuè Carducci, the poet.

[5] A mock-translation of Joyce's name, literally: James Joyful.

[6] (Translation)

'Dear Lucia: Thanks for your letter. I sent you yesterday two pounds in an envelope. I have not written and cannot write today at length because I have been working all day long. I am pleased that you continue to be happy there and that the place is good for you. I haven't sent you the newspaper because I think you have already seen it.

You speak of the defunct cavalier Fernandez, of his spouse and of other more or less worthy people. I confess however that the mention of their names arouses but a dim flame in this heart which is aging. So there is a lady in Bray named Mazza? But why isn't she named parasol?

You advise me to see the circus. Where? In the stands or in the ring? I am ready for anything.

I will send you all the books you want but you must tell me which. Are you perhaps following my bad example in neglecting the water of the Moyle? But I wash myself religiously every time the moon is in her fifteenth day.

In reply to your questions, I am not corresponding with Byrne but I think Carducci has read Carducci because I read Giacomo Giocondo. Giorgio is well now, Helen very well, and their child tremendously well.'

che aveva ordini di mandare gente come me alla legazione irlandese.[1]
Insistetti ed ottenni un altro. Ti avverto ma fa come credi.[2]

To FRANK BUDGEN   MS. Yale

15 April 1935   *7 rue Edmond Valentin, Paris 7ᵉ*

Dear Budgen: Please let us know by return are the names of the boxers
'Jack Sharkey and Jimmy Wilde' mentioned toward the end of the
fragment correct.[3] By the way please send back that proof and do not
show it.

Excuse my rather unsociable mood. It is a dreadful strain. A few days
ago for example we had 3 express letters and 1 telegram. Curran
apparently got scared.[4]

O la la!

My wife thanks for your letter. Sorry you had such a bad time going
over. Sincerely yours   JAMES JOYCE

To LUCIA JOYCE   MS. National Library

4 May 1935   *7 rue Edmond Valentin, Parigi 7*

Cara Lucia: Siccome le banche saranno chiuse domani e sarebbe forse
troppo aspettare fino a lunedì ti mando qui accluse 2 lire sterline.

Scusa la brevità di questa letterina. Spero che stai sempre bene.

Ti ho mandato un'altra novella[5] di Tolstoy: Incontro con un amico di
Mosca nel Caucaso: che spero ti piacerà. È un racconto singolare.
Credo che il suo cognome in russo significa 'grande'. Lo merita.

---

[1] Irishmen who carried British passports were encouraged to exchange them for Irish
ones. But Joyce preferred to remain a British subject.

[2] (Translation)
'So I asked Curran to enquire.
Last night I had a letter from Lucia. She says of Bray, "It is a splendid place, full of
flowers." She is happy then and I hope on the right road.
Some days ago I had to renew my passport. The clerk told me he had orders to send
people like me to the Irish Legation. I insisted and got another. I want to let you know
but do as you like.'

[3] A new fragment of *Work in Progress* was to appear in *transition* 23 (July 1935)
109–29. It comprised pp. 260–75 and 304–08 of *Finnegans Wake*. On p. 307 Joyce lists
among the subjects for themes, 'Compare the Fistic Styles of Jimmy Wilde and Jack
Sharkey.'

[4] C. P. Curran had been asked by Joyce to keep an eye on Lucia's situation in Ireland.

[5] On 27 April 1935 Joyce sent Lucia Tolstoy's story, 'How Much Land Does a Man
Need?' He said of it (*Letters*, ed. Gilbert, p. 364) that in his opinion it was 'the greatest
story that the literature of the world knows'.

Ho paura che i doganieri irlandesi ti faranno pagare un forte dazio sulla medicina mandatati. Ma non fa niente se ti fa bene. Ti abbraccio

BABBO[1]

To LUCIA JOYCE   MS. National Library

[9] *May 1935 Thursday*   *7 rue Edmond Valentin, Paris 7*

Cara Lucia: Non ho ricevuto nessuna notizia da parte tua riguardo alla spedizione di due libri nè dell'invio di due somme di denaro, quattro lire sterline in tutto. Spero che il tuo silenzio non sia dovuto a cattiva salute. Ad ogni modo ti mando accluse altre due sterline. Due righe in risposta ci farebbe piacere.

La ragione per la quale Curran non è andato da te è che sua madre morì giorni fa ed ebbe molto da fare.

Qui il maltempo batte il record ma spero che la Brighton irlandese[2] si comporti meglio. Le notizie che ci pervengono dall'America continuano ad essere poco allegre. Ebbi una lettera dalla Weaver. Essa ti vuol bene anche se si esprima male.

Mamma ed io stiamo abbastanza bene. Il famoso gatto, diventato randagio, fa il giro di tutti gli appartamenti e si fa mantenere da tutti con un cinismo quasi nobile. Ti abbraccio   BABBO

giovedì
li non so quanto maggio.[3]

[1] (Translation)
'Dear Lucia: Since the banks will be closed tomorrow and it might be too long to wait till Monday I am sending you two pounds with this.
   Excuse the brevity of this note. I hope you are keeping well.
   I sent you another story of Tolstoy: Meeting with a friend from Moscow in the Caucasus: which I hope you will like. It is a remarkable story. I think his name in Russian means 'great'. He deserves as much.
   I am afraid the Irish Customs will charge a high duty on the medicine sent to you. But never mind if it does you good. I embrace you   Babbo'
[2] Bray is meant.
[3] (Translation)
'Dear Lucia: I have heard nothing from you about the two books nor about the two sums of money, amounting to four pounds together. I hope your silence is not due to poor health. I enclose two more pounds anyway. I would appreciate two lines in reply.
   The reason Curran didn't go to see you is that his mother died a few days ago and he has had a great deal to do.
   The bad weather here is beating the record but I hope the Brighton of Ireland is behaving better. The news that reaches us from America continues to be not so cheerful. I had a letter from Miss Weaver. She is fond of you though she expresses herself badly.
   Mama and I are fairly well. The famous cat which went astray is now making a tour of all the flats and lives on everybody with an almost noble cynicism. I embrace you
                                                                                Babbo
Thursday I don't know what day of May.'

To LUCIA JOYCE   MS. National Library

15 May 1935   *7 rue Edmond Valentin, Paris 7ᵉ*

Cara Lucia: Ti ho spedito ieri un altro pacco di Hämostial ma non in fiaschi come volevi perchè costa giusto il doppio, cioè 200 franchi e c'è anche il rischio di rottura. Ti prego di seguire accuratamente le istruzioni mediche e di non esagerare le dosi. Spero che questa distillazione insieme coll'aria salubre del mare di Moyle ti faranno del bene. Le tue lettere sono sempre benvenute. Forse un incontro colla signora Bailly non ti nuocerebbe. La povera donna ha sofferto anche ma il suo temperamento continua ad essere quello che i musicisti chiamano 'vivace molto'.

Ieri la sorella[1] della Monnier ha aperto un esposizione. Mamma ci andò e le fu detto che qualche settimane fa hai mandato tre pezzetti di ricamo alla mia ex-editrice.[2] Ma perchè mandare vasi a Samo?

Non abbiamo altre notizie dall'America ma forse ne avremo stasera perchè il *Bremen* è arrivato. Anzi i giornali dicevano che Giovanni conte MacCormack doveva arrivare anche. Mamma andò alla stazione per incontrarlo o piuttosto per avere notizie di Giorgio. Ma quel cigno canoro aveva spiccato il volo altrove. E non posso biasimarlo perciò. Qui il tempo continua ad essere incredibilamente brutto. Ma a Bray, pare, il sole splende e splende ancora. Hai fiutato bene, birichina! Batto le mani! Ti abbraccio   BABBO[3]

---

[1] Marie Monnier Bécat.

[2] Sylvia Beach, who was a close friend of Mme Bécat.

[3] (Translation)

'Dear Lucia: I sent you yesterday another packet of Hämostial but not in bottles as you wanted because the cost is precisely double, that is, 200 francs and there is also the risk of breakage. I beg you to follow the medical instructions carefully and not to overdo the doses. I hope this distillation together with the invigorating air of the sea of Moyle will do you good. Your letters are always welcome. Perhaps a meeting with Mrs Bailly would not hurt you. The poor woman has suffered also but her temperament continues to be that which musicians call "vivace molto".

Yesterday Miss Monnier's sister opened an exhibition. Mama went to it and was told that some weeks ago you sent three pieces of embroidery to my ex-publisher. But why send vases to Samos?

We have not received any further news from America but perhaps we shall have some this evening because the *Bremen* has arrived. The papers even said that John count MacCormack should arrive too. Mama went to the station to meet him or rather to have news of Giorgio. But that melodious swan had taken flight elsewhere. And I cannot blame him. Here the weather continues to be incredibly vile. But at Bray, it seems, the sun shines and shines again. You have chosen well, little minx! Congratulations! I embrace you   Babbo'

To LUCIA JOYCE   MS. National Library

29 May 1935   *7 rue Edmond Valentin, Paris 7ᵉ*

Cara Lucia: Il proverbio inglese dice: No news, good news: e spero che questo sia il tuo caso. Ad ogni modo eccoti 2 lire sterline. Si dice che il mese di maggio sia il mese dei fiori ma questo maggio a Parrigi [sic] non è neanche il mese dei cavolfiori. Qui non c'è nulla di nuovo. Il conte Edgardo Carducci si è fatto vivo. Stava per divorziarsi ma poi ha cambiato parere. È sempre pieno d'idealismo ed ama le paste e la musica. Insomma, un buonissimo italiano. Le notizie dall'America sono migliori. Giorgio sembra amare abbastanza l'ambiente. Non sapevo che mio figlio avesse uno stomaco così forte. Più si vive e più s'impara. La signora Bailly ha cambiato domicilio ed ora abita nella casa di qualche arcivesco o monsignore. Beato lui! La signora Giedeon era qui per qualchi giorni e ti manda affettuosi saluti. È una brava donna anche se un pochino isterica.

Ti credi in Irlanda ma sei anche in Norvegia. I norvegesi fondarano la città di Wicklow che significa: Wick, un insenatura del mare, e low, un farro [sic].

Mamma ed io pensiamo spesso di te ma pare che in certi casi l'assenza e la forma più alta della presenza.

Non oso domandarti se canti qualche volta perchè mi fu detto recentemente che trovi le nuvole più belle che le pentoline. Forse Antoinette aveva la stessa opinione perchè non ho mai sentito una donna di servizio fare tanto baccano in cucina come lei.

Sta bene, godi la vita e dormi. Ti abbraccio   BABBO[1]

---

[1] (Translation)
'Dear Lucia: The English proverb says, No news, good news, and I hope that this is so in your case. Anyway here are 2 pounds for you. The month of May is said to be the month of flowers but this May in Paris is not even the month of cauliflowers. There is nothing new here. Count Edgardo Carducci has come to life. He was going to get a divorce but has now changed his mind. He is always full of ideals and he likes pastry and music. In short, a very good Italian. The news from America is better. Giorgio seems to like his surroundings well enough. I did not know my son had such a strong stomach. One lives and learns. Mrs Bailly has moved and now lives in the house of some archbishop or prelate. What luck for him! Mrs Giedion was here for some days and sends you affectionate greetings. She is a nice woman even if a little hysterical.

I believe you to be in Ireland but you are also in Norway. The Norwegians founded the town of Wicklow which means: Wick, little harbour, and low, lighthouse.

Mama and I are always thinking of you but it seems that in certain cases absence is the highest form of presence.

I dare not ask whether you sometimes sing because I heard recently that you find clouds more beautiful than pots and pans. Perhaps Antoinette was of the same opinion for I have never known a servant make so much noise in the kitchen as she did.

Keep well, enjoy life and sleep. I embrace you   Babbo'

To George Joyce   MS. Kastor

3 June 1935   *7 rue Edmond Valentin, Parigi 7*

Caro Giorgio: Ho ricevuto i due scenari[1] e ti ringrazio della tua prontezza. Non so quale destino l'avvenire loro riserbi. Il conte Carducci è venuto qui e vuol assolutamente metterli in musica. Agisce insieme con una dama o forse damigella che si chiama Pallustre. Essa è piena d'entusiasmo per la mia opera della quale però non ha letto una sola riga.

Dunque esiste negli Stati Uniti un essere che ignora la mia grandezza e crede che tu sei francese. Non poteva fare un piacere più puro a me nè un complimento più delicato a te. Benedetto sia lui fra tutti i Sullivans.[2] Ho letto con gaudio che hai innalzato la tua voce in favore della più fulgida e gloriosa ugola di tenore ch'io abbia mai sentito.[3] Non approderà a nulla, suppongo, ma deve essere un immenso sollievo per te di essere accolto così e ti domando infinite scuse per aver fatto parlare di me. Ma accetta le cose con calma filosofica. Quella gente farebbe altrettanto strepito per il figlio di qualche assassino balcanico. Ed a proposito di quell'odiato nome una sera al ristorante dei due Trianons, dove, del resto, ho lasciato patrimonio e matrimonio[,] Mamma disse al cantante in questione: Ieri sera, Signor Sullivan, avete cantato come un dio. Questo non credo perchè l'ultima volta che il Vecchio Signore ha parlato con me aveva una voce di basso degna di ogni lode. Come un arcangelo forse. Ad ogni modo quel mascalzone, quel maleducato, quell'ignobile individuo che osa persino scaracciare in presenza di femmine e che non fa alcun appello al sesso gentile, che non soltanto non paga i propri debiti ma non paga niente per nessuno rispose brutalmente: Signora, accanto al vostro marito io sono un insetto. Fia ver? Ma allora che ronzìo!

Cercherò una fotografia di Mamma ma essa dice che sono tutte cattive. Quando incontro una donna che è contenta della sua imagine dipinta manderò un mazzo di fiori al papa.

Leggiamo con piacere che tuo figlio diventa di più in più bello e di più in più attraente e vedo molta gioia paterna nella tua lettera. Conobbi anch'io quella gioia negli anni che furono. E prima di me tuo nonno. E prima di lui i tuoi avi che sono rinchiusi in una cantina della rue Cler[4] domandandosi con stupore che cosa diamine significhi quel trasloco e sperando e pregando di non finire nell'Asia Minore.

---

[1] For one of these two film scenarios of *Ulysses*, see p. 326, n. 4. Joyce may just mean two copies of this.

[2] Evidently a man named Sullivan had thought George Joyce was French.

[3] John Sullivan.   [4] That is, the portraits of his ancestors.

Vedo anche che la tua salute è più robusta ma sono arcicontento che i chirurghi non ti abbiano tagliato le quattro estremità. Mi dispiace che la Colm sia di nuovo malata perchè è una brava donna. E forse il consiglio che Colm ti ha dato è giusto perchè è un uomo retto al cospetto di Dio.

Mi scrivi che parti per le amene spiaggie [sic] di Long Beach. Mettendo insieme però la tua ultima lettera colla penultima non sarei troppo sorpreso se la prossima venisse dall'Alaska.

Ebbi ieri l'altro una lunga lettera da Lucia. È sempre a Bray e sembra essere sulla via della guarigione. Carducci mi disse a proposito che durante l'ultimo colloquio ch'ebbe con lei gli venne il sospetto ch'ella non fosse tutto ciò che una signorina per bene dovrebbe essere perchè quando le domandò perchè aveva abbandonato la musica essa additando il cielo: preferisco le nuvole alle pentoline. Ciò prova che lo spirito di Ponzio Pilato vaghi tuttora per il mondo e che la mela non cade lontano dall'albero.

Il proverbio: mai due senza tre. Ma spero che Helen non dovrà subire un'operazione alla gola.

I tuoi cari genitori stanno abbastanza bene. Mamma corre attorno come una lepre ed io continuo a scrivere regolarmente cinque parole al giorno. Ti mando un articolo apparso in un giornale londinese. Sembra dunque che per giudicare se un pezzo di prosa sia bello o meno bisogna metterlo su un gramofono e che, e per essere ben sicuri del talento o meno di uno scribacchino, bisogna ascoltare (con dovuta riverenza, si capisce) una conversazione tra un laureato della penna ed un ciambellano di stato. Ma non bisogna dimenticare che maggio è il mese dei ciucchi.

Soupault è andato in America a bordo di quel levriere oceanico che ha vinto per la misera Francia il record della velocità. Tutti hanno fretta oggidì. O furia come si dice a Trieste quando non si dice premura.

Adesso termino. Ho gli occhi stanchi. Da più di mezzo secolo scrutano nel nulla dove hanno trovato un bellissimo niente.

Domandi quali siano i nostri piani per l'estate. Bramo di andare in Danimarca perché i danesi hanno trucidato tante migliaia dei miei antenati. Gli Jolas partiranno presto per il mezzogiorno. I Gilbert pure. Mamma vorrebbe andare in Inghilterra per baciare re Giorgio, la regina come si chiama e gli altri membri della famiglia reale. E non dico di no, anche se resto qui. God save the King ed Iddio salvi Giorgio.

Tante belle cose a te, a Helen, ed al nipotino: e vi auguro buone vacanze. Dovrei fare un bagno anch'io ma sono troppo orgoglioso. O forse ho troppo rispetto per l'acqua.

'Sento le orme di passi spietati'.[1] È la domestica che mi porta un conto. Come la vita è quotidiana.[2] Ti abbraccio   BABBO[3]

[1] Joyce is quoting Giuseppe Verdi, *Un Ballo in maschera* (libretto by Antonio Somma). In Act II Renato warns Riccardo,

> Fuggi, fuggi: per l'orrida via
> Sento l'orma di passie spietati.

('Flee! flee! along the ghastly road / I hear the sound of merciless footsteps.')

[2] 'Ah! que la Vie est quotidienne . . .' Jules Laforgue, 'Complainte sur certains ennuis.'

[3] (Translation)

'Dear Giorgio: I received the two scenarios and thank you for your promptness. I don't know what fate the future has in store for them. Count Carducci came here and absolutely insists on setting them to music. He works with a lady or rather a ladykin named Pallustre. She is full of enthusiasm for my work of which however she has not read a single line.

So there exists in the United States a being who ignores my greatness and takes you to be French. He could not do me a greater favour or pay you a more delicate compliment. Blessed be he among all the Sullivans. I read with pleasure that you raised your voice in favour of the most splendid and glorious tenor throat I have ever heard. It won't do any good, I suppose, but it must be an immense relief for you to be welcomed like that and I apologize profusely for having made them talk about me. Take it all with philosophic calm. Those people would make as much to-do for the son of some Balkan murderer. And speaking of that hated name, one evening at the Deux Trianons restaurant where indeed I have left my patrimony and my matrimony, Mama said to the singer in question: Last night, Mr Sullivan, you sang like a god. This I do not believe since the last time that the Old Gentleman spoke with me he had a most praiseworthy bass voice. Like an angel perhaps. Anyway that rascal, that boor, that abominable fellow who even dares to spit in the presence of women and who makes no claim to be genteel, who not only fails to pay his own debts but pays nobody anything, replied brutally: Madame, next to your husband I am an insect. Can it be true? But if so, what a buzzing!

I will look for a photograph of Mama but she says they are all bad. When I find a lady who is content with her own picture I will send a bouquet to the Pope.

We read with pleasure that your son is becoming more and more handsome and more and more attractive and I see a lot of paternal pride in your letter. I too have known that joy in the years that were. And before me your grandfather. And before him your ancestors who are shut up in a cellar of the Rue Claire wondering what on earth this move means and hoping and praying not to end up in the Middle East.

I see also that your health is better but I am really glad the surgeons did not cut off your four limbs. Too bad that Mrs Colm is sick again for she is a good woman. And maybe the advice Colm gave you is good because he is an honest man before God.

You write that you are leaving for the pleasant shores of Long Beach. But putting your last two letters together with the one before I should not be too surprised if the next one came from Alaska.

The day before yesterday I had a long letter from Lucia. She is still in Bray and seems to be on the way to recovery. By the way, Carducci told me that during the last conversation he had with her he began to doubt that she was altogether a young lady for when he asked her why she had given up music she replied, pointing to the sky, I prefer the clouds to the pots. This proves that the spirit of Pontius Pilate is still wandering through the world and that the apple doesn't fall far from the tree.

The proverb: Never two without three. But I hope Helen will not have to undergo a throat operation.

Your dear parents are pretty well. Mama runs about like a hare and I continue to write regularly five words a day. I am sending you an article that appeared in a London newspaper. It seems that to judge whether a prose passage is beautiful or not it has to be put on a gramophone, and that, to be really sure of the talent of a scribbler, one must listen (with due reverence, of course) to a conversation between a laureate of the

To LUCIA JOYCE   MS. National Library

15 June 1935   *7 rue Edmond Valentin, Parigi 7*

Cara Lucia: Ieri sera venne un tuo dispaccio. Credo che il suo scopo fosse il denaro ma non son sicuro. Comunque sia stamane ne avrai ricevuto. In aspettativa più della tua risposta alla mia di venerdi mattina[1] ho alcune domande a farti.

Tre giorni fa ebbi una lunga lettera dalla tua cugina Boschenka.[2] Mi scrisse che da qualche tempo o tosse o sputa del sangue e che il suo medico affermò ch'ella era tisica. Se il caso è così (spero di no) credi tu che quello sia dal punto di vista dell'igiene un ambiente buono? Mi scrisse poi che tu eri partita dal bungalow dove stavi sotto la tutela della bungalowa, una certa Nicholls. In che circostanze e con quale scopo? 'She has got terribly fat' mi scrisse anche a proposito di te. Ordunque, mia cara balenetta, dimmi, ti prego, di quanto sei aumentata di peso e se sai perchè. Voglio dire il cibo, l'aria o forse qualche altra causa come le glandole, tiroide od altro, delle quali alcuno dei tuoi mille ed un medici parlò di quando in quando.

Ed insomma sei sempre contenta costì? Spero di si. Ma forse un cambiamento d'ambiente non totale, si capisce renderebbe la situazione meno pericolosa. E qui lascio la parola a te, cioè la risposta. Ti abbraccio

BABBO[3]

pen and a Lord Chamberlain. But we must not forget that May is the donkeys' month.

Soupault went to America on board that ocean greyhound that won the speed record for poor France. Everybody is in a hurry these days, in a fury as they say in Trieste when they do not say hurry.

Here I conclude. My eyes are tired. For over half a century, they have gazed into nullity where they have found a lovely nothing.

You ask about our summer plans. I yearn to go to Denmark because the Danes massacred so many thousands of my ancestors. The Jolases are leaving soon for the south. The Gilberts too. Mama would like to go to England to kiss King Giorgio, Queen what's-her-name and the other members of the royal family. I do not say no, even if I don't budge. God save the King and God save Giorgio.

Fond greetings to you, to Helen, and to the little grandson: and I wish you a pleasant holiday. I should take a bath too but I am too proud. Or perhaps I have too much respect for the water.

"I hear the sound of merciless footsteps." It is the maid bringing me a bill. How everydayish life is. I embrace you   Babbo'

[1] On 13 June Joyce sent his daughter two pounds but asked whether she had received money from him regularly, and why she did not write.

[2] Boschenka Schaurek, a daughter of Mrs Eileen Joyce Schaurek.

[3] (Translation)

'Dear Lucia: A telegram came from you yesterday. I think its purpose was money but I am not sure. Anyway you must have received some this morning. However while waiting for your reply to my letters of Friday morning I have several questions to put to you.

Three days ago I had a long letter from your cousin Boschenka. She wrote that for some time she has been coughing or spitting blood and that her doctor said she was

To MICHAEL HEALY   MS. Yale

[*? 15 June 1935*]   *7 rue Edmond Valentin, Paris 7ᵉ*

My dear Mr Healy: I think you ought to read the enclosed before you
visit Lucia. The writer is my niece Bosschenka Schaurek with whom
Lucia is staying and is the only news I have had for a month. From my
sister I heard last 3 months ago. When Lucia went to Bray she wrote me
she had found a *pension* at £1.5.0 a week and asked me to send her that
and pin money. I sent her regularly £4.0.0 a week since then in two
remittances of £2 each. I also wrote regularly and sent her books she
asked [for]. She answered fairly regularly but has not written for about
4 weeks though I wrote several times and asked her to reply by return. . . .

But apart from this the letter raises two points. Is it wise for Lucia to
remain in such close contact with her cousin who seems to be phthysical?
Have Bray and Ireland ceased to do her good and begun to do her harm
as it was at Nyon and at Küsnacht? In the form of mental or nervous
malady she is subject to, i.e. schizophrenia, the real trouble is not
violence or incendiarism or hysterics or simulated suicide. These are
hard to deal with but they prove that the person is still alive. The real
danger is torpor. The patient falls asleep, so to speak, and prefers to
live wholly in his or her inner world, losing more and more contact with
the outer world.

Disquieted by all this I wrote to Curran and asked his wife or
daughter to report to me.

In conclusion I have never met either of my nieces for years. They are
only 19 and 17, I think, and it may be merely a case of two young
persons struggling with a task too heavy for them.

With kindest regards and hopes that all is well with yourself and that
the visit to Dublin may be beneficial to Kathleen[1] believe me, my dear
Mr Healy, Sincerely yours   JAMES JOYCE

P.S. I don't think it would be right at present at least to go into the
financial part of this letter with Curran if you see him if time allows you

consumptive. If this is the case (I hope it isn't) do you think that place is good from the
point of view of hygiene? She then wrote that you had left the bungalow where you
were under the care of the bungalowess, a Mrs Nicholls. In what circumstances and
for what purpose? "She has got terribly fat," she wrote me also about you. Anyway,
my dear little whale, tell me please how much weight you have put on and why, if you
know. I mean: the food, the air or perhaps some other cause like the glands, thyroid
or another, of which some of your thousand and one doctors have sometimes spoken.
   Well, are you still glad to be there? I hope so. But maybe a change of atmosphere,
not a total one, would make the situation less dangerous. And here I leave the words
to you, the reply that is. I embrace you   Babbo'
[1] Nora Joyce's younger sister Kathleen (Mrs John Griffin) (d. 1963).

but you certainly [may] discuss all the rest. His mother died a few weeks ago and as he was a very good son he is naturally suffering from so recent a loss. Up to now I have managed to lead her through the wilderness with a rather unsteady hand and a somewhat stumbling foot it may be but nevertheless lead her a little.

We expect to be in London on Thursday night,[1] I am not quite sure of our address there so could you let me know where you expect to be on Tuesday and from Tuesday. I have just read in the *Irish Times* that all the hotels there are full up.   J.J.

To HELEN JOYCE   MS. Kastor

17 [June] 1935   *7 rue Edmond Valentin, Paris 7^e*

Dear Helen: I am sorry to have from you such bad news about your father. I had no idea he was so old or in such bad health. In these circumstances we find it quite natural you should stay with him. It would not be very human to do otherwise or for anybody to ask you to do so. I hope the case may not turn out to be so bad as the doctors say.

In spite of this care I hope you will pass a pleasant summer there.

Kind greetings from us both   BABBO

To HELEN JOYCE   MS. Kastor

25 June 1935   *Paris*

Dear Helen: Just to say I hope you are having a pleasant time and that Stevie is enjoying his holidays. And also that things in general may have taken a turn for the better.

There's no news beyond that in my letter to Giorgio.[2] Everybody just sitting around or walking about or lying down. As Lucia once remarked at dinner in a restaurant: Strange to think we are all sitting down and in a few hours we shall all be lying down.

I should like to know who keeps order in the servants room. A redskin? From the 30th we shall have not even the one we have as she is going on holiday to set us a good example.

A pair of shoes has just arrived and is being trained up and down the corridor. And my canaries are now cocoas. I had them dyed in response to general request.

I am sending some printed matter but will allow it to speak for itself.

With best wishes and hopes that the change and rest may benefit your father's health.   BABBO

---

[1] Joyce did not make this trip.   [2] This letter is in *Letters*, ed. Gilbert, p. 371.

To GEORGE JOYCE   MS. Kastor

10 July 1935   *7 rue Edmond Valentin, Paris*

Caro Giorgio: Grazie della tua breve lettera. Ora che il tuo sesto lustro
volge alla sua fine io apro l'abbaino della mia arca[1] e vedo che il mondo
terracqueo e le nostre sei vite in particolare sono in un tale brodo, per
non dire in tale broda, che non chiedo scusa a veruno dell'avere
cambiato il sesso della stagione dei sudori. Il mio testa è talmente piena
di cupe pensieri e di prosa bislacco che velament' noso più se solo
sulla segliola o si sonno sal sifi.[2]

Dunque. Dopo la lettera dello zio di mamma,[3] qualche giorno dopo,
venne un'altra nella quale mi disse che mi consigliava di cambiare
Lucia da Bray. Egli è molto buono ma 'vegliardo per antico pelo'[4] e
siccome c'erano parecchi punti oscuri sui quali volevo assolutamente
essere informato (la lettera è dalla Weaver perchè prima ho pensato a
lei come ambasciatrice) mandai la Jolas a Dublino. Essa partì il 6 luglio
e tornerà a Parigi l'undici. Ed allora saprò, spero, che cosa si deve fare.

Non abbiamo una domestica perchè non sappiamo ancora se sia
consigliabile di muovere o no ma abbiamo un lavorante che finge di
rinnovare l'impiantito nella cucina, mandatoci dal padrone di casa. Si
sede, si leva, scende le scale, monta le scale, parla con mamma, telefona
al padrone, va a desinare, torna dal desinare, misura, studia, lamenta,
comincia, smette. Ho pregato mama di suggerirgli il pianoforte come
consolazione.

Suppongo che tutti e tre siete già risplendenti d'una bella carnagione
di cioccolata con capelli biondi argentei come gli icon nelle chiese
greche. I veri sani che amano questa vera salute credono anche che
Victor Hugo è il re dei poeti e che fidarsi è bene ma non fidarsi è meglio.

Mama è molto contenta in questo appartamento e puoi dire a Helen
che ci sono cinque grandi specchi, anzi sei, e cinque più piccoli. Ci sono
anche grandi specchi su ogni pianerottolo e si può fermare l'ascensore a
tutti i piani di sotto.

Ti mando un giornale, un ritaglio, ed un libro. Forse ti divertiranno.
Ed a proposito potresti forse studiare un poco il pianoforte non per
diporto come il muratore di cui sopra.

Domenica otto S.[5] e sua moglie erano qui. Egli voleva farmi udire una
romanza dall'opera Il Duca d'Alba di Donizetti. Disse a sua moglie di

---

[1] Joyce was now developing this image in *Finnegans Wake*, II, iii.
[2] Intentional mistakes in Italian.   [3] Michael Healy.
[4] 'Un vecchio bianco per antico pelo,' Dante, *Inferno*, Canto 3, l. 83.
[5] John Sullivan.

accompagnarlo. Essa non aveva le lenti non vedeva, era troppo difficile. Egli canta, sbuffa, si ferma, ricomincia. Poi disse: 'Lève-toi, tu m'enerves'. Si sedette al piano e suonò l'accompagnamento da capo in fondo, cantando nel medesimo tempo a piena gola. È un peccato essere alla misericordia di un accompagnatore almeno per uso e consumo domestici.

Non trovo in nessun luogo quel libro-manoscritto di Chamber Music. Se l'ho dato in custodia alla Beach è ben scomparso. Essendo la prima edizione del mio primo libro deve avere per chi l'ha rubato un gran valore. E starebbe così bene nel nostro bel salotto.

Bailly è volato alla volta di Dublino anche ed è sceso oggi all'albergo Gresham dove è scesa pure la Jolas. Egli non sa dove si trovi sua moglie la quale lo cacciò dall'Irlanda tre settimane fa, dicendogli che non era degno di porre il piede sul suolo irlandese. Siamo stati con lui domenica a S. Leu-la-Forêt[1] per udire un concerto di musica antica inglese dato in un teatrino-giardino. Era molto bello. Ho l'impressione che quell'uomo comincia ad averne le tasche piene. It's a long branch that has no turning.

Marianna si concia per le feste, nel senso buono, ma quest'anno non avremo il 'ponte' e la piazzetta dove si danzerà è alquanto discosta.

Spero che il nubifragio d'ieri non sia passato vicino a voi. Mandaci qualche cartolina illustrata. Se fa troppo caldo scrivi soltanto T.C. Noto con piacere che Stevie è la stoffa di un nuotatore come suo padre.

Tantissime cose a lui, a Helen ed a te. Ti abbraccio   BABBO

P.S. Il brano citato da Eglinton[2] è di Newman non di Ruskin. Habent aures et non audient.[3]

P.S.

Risposte

1) L'editore inglese[4] cominciò a stampare *Ulisse* in settembre. Fino

[1] A commune in Seine-et-Oise.

[2] John Eglinton, in his essay, 'The Beginnings of Joyce,' included in *Irish Literary Portraits* (London, 1935), quotes the paragraph from the *Oxen of the Sun* episode of *Ulysses*, p. 552 (421), which begins, 'There are sins or (let us call them as the world calls them) evil memories which are hidden away by man in the darkest places of the heart but they abide there and wait. He may suffer their memory to grow dim, let them be as though they had not been and all but persuade himself that they were not or at least were otherwise. Yet a chance word will call them forth suddenly and they will rise up to confront him in the most various circumstances, a vision or a dream, or while timbrel and harp soothe his sense or amid the cool silver tranquillity of the evening or at the feast at midnight when he is now filled with wine. . . .' Eglinton guessed erroneously that the author parodied here is Ruskin.

[3] 'They have ears but they hear not.' Psalms 115: 5.

[4] John Lane The Bodley Head published the first English edition on 3 October 1936.

adesso hanno mantenuto un silenzio da sfinge. But they howpe to bwing it aht . . before Tibb's Eve (le calende greche)[1]

2) Soupault, pare, è andato alle isole Canarie. Quando tornerà cercherò di avere quell'istantanea. Frattanto si può avere un'altra.

3) Scenari.

a) A.L.P. Non appena ricevuto questo di ritorno telefonai a Carducci di venirlo a prendere. Rispose che sarebbe venuto il giorno dopo alle 5. Alle due mi telefonò ch'era a Fontainebleau e che sarebbe venuto il giorno dopo. Non venne e non telefonò. Io nemmeno[.] Sembra ch'io abbia accolto con troppa indifferenza le moine e le lusinghe d'una sua amica, una siora in capel che si vanta del nome di Palustre.

2) La proposta dell'amica della Beach andò a monte.

3) Cohen e Lieber. Chiesi informazioni. Ecco la risposta. Non troppo male. Rimandai i contratti suggerendo una modificazione in questo senso. Nessuna risposta. E nessuna risposta vuol dire visita di Lieber.

4) Zukofsky.[2] Gli scrivo oggi nello stesso senso. È inutile ch'io esamini in dettaglio il manoscritto prima. C'è molto lavoro dentro. Lo mostrai a Petitjean.[3] Ma ci sono anche grossi sbagli. Questi si possono cambiare. Ti prego di scusarmi presso questi giovani ma la mia mente era un pò altrove.

Domande

1) Sei sicuro che quel Chamber Music non sia in un tiretto in qualche tuo stipo? Non è tra i libri.

2) Ho detto alla Jolas d'esaminare il passaporto (ho fatto rinnovare qui la carta d'identità per lei) di Lucia. Se è rinnovabile c'è ora a Dublino il British High Commissioner per ciò. Se è scaduto questo funzionario probabilmente rilascerebbe un'altro. Ma non è sicuro poichè ella è sul luogo. Ma se ella per conto proprio o sotto l'influenza d'altri voleva un passaporto irlandese le autorità là forse domanderebbero le sue carte. Sono queste da te o da me?

3) Come stai ora di salute dopo l'operazione e come va la tua voce? Spero molto bene. Meno male che il tuo suocero non soffre tanto e sta meglio pure.

    Ora vado cambiare la pennetta di questo stylo.   B.

P.P.S.

Li 10 giugno,[4] mezzodì.

Nessun cenno dalla parte della Jolas nè a lui[5] nè a me. Ma ha molto da

[1] Tib's Eve, said to fall on the Greek Calends. These are proverbial expressions for 'never', since the English have no St Tib and the Greeks had no calends.
[2] See p. 326, n. 4.   [3] See p. 303.   [4] A slip for *luglio*.   [5] Eugene Jolas.

fare. Sarebbe una gran bella cosa se questa visita repentina ed inaspettata dovesse essere il punto decisivo e se una nuova vita si spianasse per quella povera e fiera anima che la tormenta ha si dura-mente assalita ma non vinta!¹   B.

¹ (Translation)

'Dear Giorgio: Thanks for your short letter. Now that your sixth lustrum is near its end I open the garret-window of my ark and see that the terraqueous world and our six lives in particular are in such a broth not to say dishwater that I don't feel like apologizing to anyone for changing the gender of the season of sweets. My haid is so full of grims thought and odd prose that I know not leally if I am on the chail or the sofi.

Well—After the letter of Mama's uncle, some days after, another one came in which he advised me to move Lucia away from Bray. He is very good but "an old man with ancient hair" and since there were several unclear points on which I wanted to be precisely informed (the letter is with Miss Weaver because I thought first of her as ambassadress) I sent Mrs Jolas to Dublin. She left on 6 July and will be back the 11th. And then I will know, I hope, what must be done.

We do not have a maid because we do not know if it is advisable to move or not, but we have a handyman, sent by the landlord, who pretends to resurface the kitchen floor. He sits, he stands up, goes downstairs, comes upstairs, speaks with Mama, telephones the landlord, goes out to dinner, comes back from dinner, measures, studies, complains, begins. I asked Mama to suggest the piano to him as a consolation.

I suppose all three of you have shining chocolate complexions with silver blond hair like the icons in Greek churches. The really healthy people who love real health also believe that Victor Hugo is the king of poets and that to trust others is good but to distrust them is better.

Mama is very pleased with the apartment and you can tell Helen there are five big mirrors, no six, and five smaller ones. There are also big mirrors on each landing and you can stop the elevator at every floor going down.

I am sending you a newspaper, a clipping and a book. Maybe they will amuse you. By the way you might study the piano a little not for pleasure like the above mentioned workman. Sunday 8th S[ullivan] and his wife were here. He wanted to let me hear a song from the opera, "Il Duca d'Alba," of Donizetti. He told his wife to accompany him at the piano. She did not have her glasses, so she could not see very well, it was too difficult. He sings, snorts, stops, starts again. Then he said: "Lève-toi, tu m'énerves." He sat down at the piano and played the accompaniment from beginning to end, singing with all his voice at the same time. It is a pity to be at the mercy of an accompanist, at least for domestic use and consumption.

I cannot find anywhere the manuscript-book of Chamber Music. If I intrusted it to Miss Beach it has certainly disappeared. Being the first edition of my first book it must be worth a good deal to whoever stole it. And it would look so well in our pretty sitting room.

Bailly flew to Dublin and went today to the Gresham Hotel where Mrs Jolas also stopped. He does not know where his wife is. She chased him out of Ireland three weeks ago, telling him he wasn't worthy to set foot on Irish soil. We were with him last Sunday at S. Leu-la-Forêt to hear a concert of old English music performed in a garden-theatre. It was very fine. I have the impression that that man is beginning to have a bellyful of it. It's a long branch that has no turning.

Marianna is dolling herself up for the holiday but this year we will not have the "bridge" and the little square where they will be dancing is rather far.

I hope yesterday's cloudburst did not come near you. Send us a few postcards. If it is too hot just write T.H. I note with pleasure that Stevie has the stuff to be a good swimmer like his father.

All the best to him, Helen and you. I embrace you   Babbo

P.S. The passage quoted by Eglinton is by Newman not Ruskin. Habent aures et non audient.   B

368 JULY 1935

To MICHAEL HEALY   MS. Yale

[13 July 1935]   *7 rue Edmond Valentin, Paris 7ᵉ*

My dear Mr Healy: Just a few lines for today. Our friend[1] returned
from Dublin. Her account was far worse than yours for she succeeded in
getting at the facts which you rightly suspected were being concealed
from you as they have been from me for four months. Yesterday I had
an air-message from M. Bailly saying Lucia had called on him and
asked him to have her placed in a nursing home. I had been arranging
for her removal to England but upon this I telephoned Curran and this
morning had a wire to say that she was now temporarily in a comfortable

(Translation continued)
P.S.
Replies
(1) The English publisher started printing *Ulysses* in September. So far they have
maintained a sphinxlike silence. But they howpe to bwing it aht . . before Tibb's Eve
(the Greek kalends)
(2) Soupault, it seems, has gone to the Canary Islands. When he comes back I will try
to obtain that snapshot. Meanwhile we can get another one.
(3) Scenarios.
  (a) A.L.P. As soon as I got this back I telephoned Carducci to come and take it. He
replied that he would come next day at five. At two he telephoned me that he was at
Fontainebleau and would come the day after. He neither came nor telephoned.
Neither did I. It seems that I received with too much indifference the grimaces and
cajoleries of a girlfriend of his, a would-be lady who brags of her name Palustre.
  (2) The proposal of Miss Beach's friend vanished in thin air.
  (3) Cohen and Lieber. I inquired about them. Here is the answer. Not too bad. I
sent back the contracts suggesting a modification thereof. No answer. And no answer
means a visit from Lieber.
  (4) Zukofsky. I am writing to him today on this matter. It is useless for me to
examine the manuscript in detail beforehand. A lot of work has gone into it. I showed
it to Petitjean. But there are also gross errors. These can be changed. Please make my
excuses to these young men but my mind has been elsewhere.

Questions
(1) Are you sure that *Chamber Music* is not in a drawer of some cabinet of yours? It
isn't among your books.
(2) I told Mrs Jolas to examine Lucia's passport (I had the identification card renewed
for her over there). If it is renewable there is now a British High Commissioner in
Dublin for that. If it has expired this official would probably issue another. But it is
not certain since she is there now. But if she on her own account or under the influence
of others wanted an Irish passport the authorities would probably ask for her documents. Do you or do I have them?
(3) How are you feeling now after your operation and how is your voice? I hope
very well. It's good that your father-in-law is not suffering much and is even getting
better.
  Now I am going to have the nib of this pen changed.   B.

P.P.S. 10 June [July], Noon.
  No word from Mrs Jolas either to him or to me. But she has a great deal to do. It
would be a fine thing if this sudden and unexpected visit [of Lucia to Ireland] were the
decisive point and if a new life opened up for that poor and proud soul, whom the
storm has so harshly assailed but not conquered!   B'
[1] Mrs Maria Jolas.

nursing-home. Apparently she is physically stronger and less unhappy. But I must think out some new plan for her.

I hope Kathleen's operation will soon be over and successfully. With very kind greetings sincerely yours   James Joyce

To George and Helen Joyce   MS. Kastor

16 July 1935   *7 rue Edmond Valentin, Paris 7ᵉ*

Dear Giorgio and Helen: We are both glad to hear your good news of general health, that Stevie is so attractive and that you admire the photograph.

Mrs Jolas came back on Thursday and her account was so much worse than Mr Healy's, tallying with an avion letter from Bailly and two requests from Lucia herself to go to a nursing-home that I had her placed in one temporarily on Saturday by telephone. On Monday (yesterday) came a very nice and affectionate letter from Lucia to her mother. I shall not tell you the details of Mrs Jolas's account unless requested to do so. You have troubles of your own, I understand, and are on holiday and may have a different point of view from mine. After Mr Healy's letter I was planning to remove her from Ireland by easy stages to within reach of us. On two points all agree 1) that she is much stronger, sturdier etc 2) less unhappy. My wife is of opinion that she should be left to have these two advantages at least. I am less keen on letting her [stay] with Miss Weaver as it turns out that the latter has been for months past in collusion with Eileen 'not to write this to Paris etc', keeping me in ignorance of all the sordid squalor of the case and of the warning of the authorities that their next step would be to commit her or intern her. I was told always 'she is getting on fine' and Miss Weaver, as with her other female charms, walked blue-eyed and prim-mouthed into my sister's booby-trap. I am not sending any of Lucia's letters. I expect a letter from Curran brought about the transfer. If so I may write again tomorrow as there is a second boat on the 18. Lucia is quite sunburnt, too, it seems.

Soupault still away. Any chance of having a good photo of Master Ringlets, dressed please. After which you may send a nudist group of all the household, including Blackaboots, arranged in the order of their lastification.[1]

And thanks for your cable on Independence, Dependence, and

---

[1] That is, the order of their birth (last born). A play on the book of essays, *Our Exagmination Round His Factification for Incamination of Work in Progress.*

Interdependence Day. And here is the N.Y.H. with Mrs Bailly's niece modestly beside the new Irish envoy.

Ay, I note you have moved from Boost and Worstworld Avenue to Booth and Wildwold Avenue and that you will autumn in Bleak and Wetwind Avenue before wintering in Block and Woolworth Avenues. My address is 7 Rapp, Bosquet, Pont Deloge, Dominique and Valentin Avenues, Paris (R.7)[1] Tantissime cose   BABBO

P.S. Just ran down to the hairdresser's to get shorn and ran up again. Don't jump to conclusions about Lucia: or reply that there is only one simple solution. Severe reclusion was tried in Nyon and, though it kept her out of harm's way, it was a calamitous failure. Total separation from her parents has been tried for the second time and you see the result.

I forgot to say that between Mrs Jolas's arrival and Bailly's mail I had a wire from Eileen and Lucia asking for 2000 francs at once. I telephoned Curran to find out and if Lucia was in difficulties to pay and notify me. She was not, luckily.

A few days ago Lucia sent me a song called *Dublin Bay*[2] about a certain Roy Neil who runs away with his bride from Dublin. They are wrecked and lost at sea, the bride singing 'O, why did we leave sweet Dublin Bay!' In replying to this I said (Giorgio will translate). Ho capito il latino.[3] E se fossi convinto che quello sarebbe per il tuo bene ma proprio bene malgrado tutto, ed a rischio di tutto . . . Ma ho sempre paura delle aringhe.[4]

Some days ago I bought a MS copy of *Pomes Penyeach* with her lettrines and sent it to Mr Healy to present to the Library of the University in Galway in my name. In her letter to her mother Lucia writes that some days ago she went to the Library of Dublin University (one of the 4 largest in the British Isles) and presented to it one of my

[1] Joyce was amused by the affluence of his son and daughter-in-law, and dressed up his own address, 7 rue Edmond Valentin, to sound as highflown as one of theirs. The rue Edmond Valentin lies between Avenue Rapp and Avenue Bosquet, intersects Rue Dupont-des-Loges, and is parallel to Rue Saint-Dominique. 'R.7' is Joyce's anglicization, imitating London postal zones, of the seventh arrondissement.

[2] Also known as 'O Bay of Dublin'. It can be found in Alfred Perceval Graves, *The Irish Song Book* (Dublin, 1895), and, like most of the songs named in these letters, is referred to several times in *Finnegans Wake*. See M. J. C. Hodgart and M. P. Worthington, *Song in the Works of James Joyce* (New York, 1959), p. 195.

[3] Lucia Joyce had a kind of secret mission in going to England and Ireland; she wished to smooth her father's ruffled relationship with Harriet Shaw Weaver, and to effect a similar reconciliation between him and Ireland. She had suggested he travel there.

[4] 'I have understood the Latin. And if I were convinced that it would do you good, really do you good, in spite of everything and at the risk of everything, perhaps, perhaps. . . . But I am always afraid of the herrings.'

letters to her which she had found particularly interesting. It will not be very amusing for Giorgio to hear this, less so for me, though behind the impulsive gesture there there [sic] is something I recognize.

And do not imagine anything bad has happened. Not yet and it won't now, I suppose.   B

To John Howley[1]   MS. University College, Galway

29 July 1935   *7 rue Edmond Valentin, Paris 7ᵉ*

Dear Sir: My uncle-in-law Mr Michael Healy has asked me to send you a prospectus concerning the facsimile MS edition of my booklet *Pomes Penyeach* (so brought out in Paris in 1932) which I had much pleasure in offering to your library and you the graciousness to accept. Two other European libraries possess copies, the Bibliothèque Nationale here and the British Museum in London. But I wished to offer a copy to your library not only because the designer of the *lettrines* is a grand-daughter of your city and the writer of the verses bears one of its tribal names but also as a small acknowledgement of a great debt of gratitude to Mr Healy himself for his kindness and courtesy during so many years.
Sincerely yours   JAMES JOYCE

To George Joyce   MS. Kastor

13 August 1935   [*Paris*]

Caro Giorgio. Se tu avessi veduto lo stato di Lucia dopo 7 mesi di reclusione a Nyon non mi daresti il consiglio di rimetterla in un istituto simile. Lo farò quando o se ogni altra via sarà chiusa. Niente di grave è successo in Irlanda. Tutti coloro che videro Lucia là sono d'accordo ch'era più forte e meno infelice. Ma viveva come una zingara nello squalore. Tutto ciò era noto ad Eileen e le altre due[2] ed alla Signorina Weaver e tutte di concerto me lo celarono! Meno male che il sig. Healy l'abbia vista. Egli, però, ha cambiato parere molto presto perchè da due anni a questa parte tanto lui che tua nonna scrivono sempre: Niente medici, niente sanatorio, niente esame di sangue! Ecc.

Lucia sta per ora colla Weaver (ho dovuto intervenire molto energica-mente ieri presso di quest'ultima per troncare un'altra corrispondenza con Eileen), ha avuto finora 10 iniezioni, e si è rimessa a disegnare

---

[1] John Howley (1866–1941), Professor of Philosophy and Librarian of University College, Galway.
[2] Mrs Schaurek's two daughters.

spontaneamente. Il medico afferma che guarirà. Avrà ricadute, dice, ma di più in più brevi e di più in più raramente. Indirizzo: 74 Gloucester Place, Londra, W.1.

So che il tuo consiglio è dettato dall'affezione per noi. Ma sento in me che la cosa va meglio ora. No, no. Tutto non è sciolto.[1] Tantissime cose a tuttitreissimi. Ti abbraccio   BABBO[2]

To HERBERT GORMAN (Express letter)   MS. S. Illinois (Croessmann)

14 August 1935   *7 rue Edmond Valentin, Paris 7ᵉ*
                                                   Tél: Inv. 50.38

Dear Gorman: I went to the American Express Office. The price with 20% rebate for return ticket Touquet–Paris, 7 days stay at Hotel Carlton, 19th to 26th inst is 600 frs per head plus hotel—bus fare Etaples–Le Touquet and back, thus made up:

Fare	120 frs
Board (full) & Room	420
Service	42
Taxe de sejour	?
	600 frs

The Carlton is a very good hotel but not *de luxe*.

We cannot go, however. On account of news from London last night it has been necessary for me to make, or rather, prepare other arrange-

[1] An allusion to Bellini's aria in *La Sonnambula* and to 'Tutto è sciolto' in *Pomes Penyeach.*

[2] (Translation)

'Dear Giorgio, If you had seen Lucia's condition after seven months of confinement at Nyon you would not advise me to put her back in such an institution. I shall do it when and if there is no other recourse. Nothing serious happened in Ireland. Everyone who saw Lucia there agreed that she was stronger and less unhappy. But she lived like a gipsy in squalor. All this was known to Eileen and the other two and to Miss Weaver and they all were in league to conceal it from me. It was a good thing that Mr Healy saw her. But he changed his mind very quickly for during the last two years he as well as your grandmother have been writing continually: No doctors, no sanatorium, no blood examination! etc.

Lucia is now staying with Miss Weaver (I had to intervene energetically with the latter to cut off another correspondence with Eileen), has had 10 injections up to now, and has taken up drawing again of her own accord. The doctor says that she will get well. She will have relapses, he says, but shorter and shorter ones and less and less frequently. Address: 74 Gloucester Place, London, W.1.

I know your advice is prompted by the affection you have for us. But I feel inwardly that the case is going better now. No, no. All is not undone. Best wishes to you superlative three. I embrace you   Babbo'

ments there. If you stop here on your way through I shall explain better.

I did not pay anything down to reserve until I heard from you. If you ring me tomorrow I can do so for you. The clerk says rooms will be free then but of course will telephone first Sincerely yours   JAMES JOYCE

To JOHN SULLIVAN   MS. Texas

28 August 1935   *7 rue Edmond Valentin, Paris 7*

Dear Mr Sullivan: Here is the page signed. It is not easy to sign on Indian paper. If you sign normally the ink spreads. I am late in returning it but the hook-on lens I use for writing was at the optician's being mended. I sent you also the disc and impressions of your namesake[1] as promised. I took him to see that film[2] of his native place and he was quite proud and pleased to learn, among other things, that every shebeen in Kerry had a telephone as far back as 1828 when Griffin[3] wrote *The Collegians.* I hope if this first Irish company screens *Maritana*[4] that the name part will be given to a bearded bull. Sincerely yours   JAMES JOYCE

To HERBERT GORMAN (Postcard)   MS. S. Illinois (Croessmann)

28 August 1935   [*Paris*]

Did Mrs Gorman lose a ring. We found one yesterday and it does not belong either to Mrs Sullivan or Mrs Shapiro the only two women who have been here since your visit. Plain ivory very small. Still here. News not good.   J.J.

To LUCIA JOYCE   MS. Private

29 September 1935   *Savoy Hotel, Fontainebleau*

Cara Lucia: Prendiamo congedo dell'uva e torniamo a Parigi.[5] Ti accludo alcune fotografie abbastanza miserabili ed, a questo proposito,

---

[1] Sean O'Sullivan (1906–1964), born in Kerry, Irish painter who was commissioned by C. P. Curran to paint Joyce's portrait.

[2] *The Lily of Killarney*, a film version of the opera by Sir Julius Benedict, which in turn was based upon Dion Boucicault's play *The Colleen Bawn*, itself an adaptation of Gerald Griffin's novel *The Collegians* (1829).

[3] Gerald Griffin (1803–40), Irish novelist and playwright.

[4] *Maritana*, an operetta by Vincent Wallace (1845).

[5] Joyce and his wife stayed in Fontainebleau during the month of September 1935. Herbert Gorman and his second wife, Claire, kept them company.

riceverai dalla signora Curran (a Londra in questo momento) un nuovo apparecchio che, spero, ti sarà utile e gradevole.

Siamo oltremodo contenti di avere avuto notizie del tuo progresso. Sono in fretta perchè il treno partirà senza di noi se non saremo pronti. Così fan treni.[1]

Eccoti la spiegazione degli acclusi.

Dopo la partenza dello zio[2] di Mamma da Dublino volevo fargli un piacere. Sapendo che egli non avrebbe mai accettato del denaro ho comperato uno degli ultimi esemplari che esistono adesso del *Pomes Penyeach* e l'ho presentato a nome nostro (cioè il tuo ed il mio) alla biblioteca dell'Università di Galway, siccome tu sei una nipote di quella città antica ed io discendente di una delle sue tribù. Hanno fatto fare un leggio speciale ed il bel libro si trova ora esposto nel centro della biblioteca. Il bibliotecario, il professore Howley, è venuto a Parigi durante la nostra assenza qui, come vedi dalla sua carta da visita acclusa, per ringraziarmi (e te) 'del dono squisito'.

Inoltre. Un pittore dublinese è venuto a Parigi per fare un disegno della mia testa per Curran. Mi ha fatto promettere di posare per lui quest'altro mese (8bre, voglio dire). Vuole che il mio ritratto sia definitivamente nella National Gallery a Dublino! Ora mi scrive che si sta preparando un banchetto là nel mio onore. Ed il sig. Bailly mi scrive lo stesso. E vuoi sapere come si chiama questo pittore. Si chiama (se non ti dispiace) John Sullivan.[3]

Casco dalle nuvole!

Ma ho ancora una buona nuova da darti. Però, basta per oggi. 'Una alla volta per carità'.[4]

Segue—come dicono i romanzi in appendice. Ti abbraccio BABBO[5]

[1] A play on Mozart's opera, *Così fan tutte* (1790).
[2] Michael Healy.
[3] That is, Sean O'Sullivan.
[4] An allusion to Gioacchino Rossini, *Il Barbiere di Siviglia* (libretto by Sterbini). In a famous aria in the first act, Figaro sings,

Tutti mi vogliono
Ahime che folla
Uno alla volta
per carità.

('Everyone wants me / Heavens, what a crowd! / One at a time / for pity's sake.')
[5] (Translation)

'Dear Lucia: We are taking leave of the grapes and going back to Paris. I enclose a few rather wretched photographs and, by the way, you will receive from Mrs Curran (just now in London) a new camera which, I hope, will prove useful and enjoyable.

We are extremely glad to have the news of your progress. I am in a hurry because the train will leave without us if we aren't ready. So trains behave.

Here is an explanation of the enclosures.

To FRANK BUDGEN   MS. Yale

8 October 1935   *7 rue Edmond Valentin, Paris 7ᵉ*

Dear Budgen: I am sorry to hear that Mrs Budgen is, or has been, ill
but hope she is all right by now. It so happens that I wanted to write to
her as perhaps she can help me with a line or two to some good furrier.
All Lucia's clothes were either lost or stolen or given away in Dublin—
two trunks full, including her fur cloak. Now I want to buy for her a
new one before the cold November long dreary weather starts. I thought
her (L's) doctor might give leave for her to come for one afternoon to
London and choose it with Mrs Budgen but, as that is impossible, a
letter to her former principal (?) might do.[1] If also an accommodation as
to payment could be arranged, *tant mieux*. If not, *tant pis*. Lucia's
address is

> c/o Miss H. Weaver
> Loveland's Cottage,
> Loveland's Lane
> Lower Kingswood,
> *Tadworth* (Surrey)[2]

The price of the cloak or terms of payment should not be discussed
either by letter or orally before Lucia or Miss Weaver, if, as is probable,
the latter comes to town as she would then offer to pay for it.

After the departure of Mama's uncle from Dublin I wanted to make him a present.
Knowing he would never accept money I bought one of the last copies of *Pomes
Penyeach* still extant and I presented it in our name (that is, yours and mine) to the
library of the University of Galway, as you are a grandchild of that ancient city and
I a descendant of one of its tribes. They had a special reading desk made and the
beautiful book is now on exhibit in the centre of the library. The librarian, Professor
Howley, came to Paris during our absence here, as you can see from the enclosed
visiting card, to thank me (and you) "for the exquisite gift".

Another thing. A Dublin painter has come to Paris to make a drawing of my head
for Curran. He made me promise to pose for him next month (October, that is). He
wants my portrait to go for sure into the National Gallery in Dublin! Now he writes
that he is organizing a banquet there in my honour. And Mr Bailly writes the same.
And would you like to know the name of this painter. His name is (if you don't mind)
John Sullivan.

I am thunderstruck!

But I have one other good piece of news for you. However, that is enough for today.
"One at a time, for pity's sake."

To be continued—as they say for serialized novels. I embrace you   Babbo'

[1] Mrs Budgen had worked in a fur shop.

[2] Dr W. G. Macdonald, a London surgeon associated with St Andrew's Hospital,
Northampton, attempted to cure Lucia's malady by glandular injections, during August
and September. When these were completed he suggested to Miss Weaver, who had been
taking care of Lucia in London, that the patient should convalesce in quieter surroundings. Accordingly Miss Weaver brought her to a bungalow near Reigate, with a trained
nurse to help.

My wife says she is writing you separately.

I hope this finds you both well and fixed for the winter. Sincerely
yours   JAMES JOYCE

To MRS HERBERT GORMAN (Postcard)   MS. S. Illinois (Croessmann)

9 October 1935   *Paris*

Dear Mrs Gorman: Will you please tell M Nadal[1] to do exactly as he
thinks best and send me the bill but not to write to me?

Many thanks and greetings sincerely yours   JAMES JOYCE

To LUCIA JOYCE   MS. Private

17 October 1935   *Parigi*

Cara Lucia: Abbiamo ricevuto le tue cartoline ed anche due fotografie
di te e della sig[na] Weaver. Grazie. La sig[na] Weaver è sempre quella e
quanto a te hai l'aria d'infischiarti sommamente del *globo terrestre*,
assorta nella tua lettura e facendo lo 'zittolo zottolo'.[2] Magari che tutti
gli abitanti della suddetta palla roteante fossero così pacifici!

Mi pare che il prossimo numero nel tuo programma di convalelescenza
dovrebbe essere un bel mantello di pelliccia. Cosa ti pare a te? Ho
scritto alla sigra Budgen che era per parecchi anni segretaria di una
ditta londinese che lavorava in questo articolo e quindi se n'intende.
Bisogna avere qualche consiglio di questo genere altrimenti si corre il
rischio di comprare—è proprio il caso di dirlo—un gatto in saccoccia.[3]

Il denaro che mandai alla sig[ra] Curran all'Euston mi rinvenne. Era
già via. Ma l'ho rimandato poi alla sig[na] Weaver e spero che adesso hai
la tua brava macchina fotografica.

Il proverbio dice che la penna è più potente della spada ma tu
certamente lo pensi diversamente, che la matita è più potente che la
penna e la spada e l'ombrello insieme. Voglio dire quando scrivi.
Purtroppo la mia lente d'ingrandimento rende quello che è scritto col
lapis ancora più vago e stinto.

Se la tua fotografia è un indice del tuo stato di salute devi stare molto,
ma molto meglio. Ed ora, cara Lucia, devi diventare ogni dì in ogni

[1] A bookbinder.
[2] Triestine dialect for 'swing'.
[3] 'Un gatto in saccoccia,' literally, 'a cat in the pocket,' is a humorous but slightly
confused translation of the German, 'eine Katze im Sack kaufen' ('to buy a cat in a bag').
The proverbial expression is not used in Italian but is common in German.

modo—insomma suona male in italiano ma è quello che predica il reverend-
issimo e sapientissimo dottore Coué.[1]

Il tuo amico Maurice Chevalier è rientrato a Parigi dove ha avuto un
gran successo imitando i suoi imitatori. Peccato che non ti abbia vista!
E se io mi mettessi ad imitare certi scribacchini?

La Jolas ha avuto anche delle cartoline tue. Sta adesso al numero 60
della stessa strada in una casa che ha, credo, 20 o 26 stanze, tutte sue.
Ci si può giocare a *mosca cieca*. La sua scuola conta ora 45 scolaretti e
scolarette.[2] Una volta tu usavi parlare dell'educazione o, più propri-
amente detto, dell'istruzione. Uno scolaro mio a Trieste era molto
pesante, stupido, calvo, lento e grasso. Però un dì mi raccontò questa
storiella a proposito dell'educazione' di una sua sorella che era probabilmente un tipo simile. Questa ragazza imparava alla scuola a fare la
calza ma niente le entrava in testa. La maestra cercò d'insegnarle come
farla. Così e così. Vedi adesso? Passa l'ago sotto, poi tira e così di
seguito. Infine le domandò se aveva una sorella maggiore. La ragazza
rispose di si. Allora, le disse la maestra, fa vedere il lavoro alla tua
sorella maggiore e domani riportati tutto in ordine. Capito? Si, siora
maestra.

L'indomani la ragazza arrivò a scuola ma il suo lavoro era peggiore
che prima. Come? disse la maestra. Non hai una sorella maggiore a
casa? Si, siora maestra. E non ti ho detto di domandarle come si fa? Si,
siora maestra. Ed hai domandato? Si, siora maestra. E cosa ti ha detto
tua sorella? La ga dito che vadi in malora lei e la calza.

Tanto per 'l'educazione'.

Se trovi questo abbastanza sciocco ti prego di biasimare il riscal-
dimento centrale che hanno cominciato oggi in casa nostra. Mi passano
questi ricordi ameni per la testa in piccole danze delle volte. Ma non fa
niente.

Salutami cordialmente la signorina Weaver e comprati una bella
pelliccia ed un calcio alla miseria. Ti abbraccio

Mamma ti scriverà fra qualche giorno anche. Intanto sta bene e
continua lo 'zittolo-zottolo'   BABBO[3]

---

[1] Emile Coué (1857–1926), French pharmacist who advocated auto-suggestion as a
cure for disease. His famous motto for the sick was, 'Day by day and in every way I am
growing better and better.'

[2] Mrs Eugene Jolas had organized her *École Bilingue* in Neuilly.

[3] (Translation)

'Dear Lucia: We received your post cards and the two photographs also, of you and
of Miss Weaver. Thank you. Miss Weaver is always the same and as for you, you look
as if you did not care in the least about the *terrestrial globe*, absorbed as you are in
your reading and swinging. If only all the inhabitants of the above mentioned rolling
ball were so peaceful!

To SIGNORA MARIA NEBBIA   MS. Bib. Municipale, Vichy

23 October 1935   *7 rue Edmond Valentin, Parigi 7*
Tél: Inv. 50.38

Gentile Signora, Tornato a Parigi giorni or sono ho sentito che Larbaud
era di nuovo ammalato e l'indomani quando andai alla rue Cardinal
Lemoine la portinaia mi disse che si trattava di un attacco acuto di
reumatismo. Vi lasciai la mia carta da visita e se trova il tempo o di
mandarci due righe o di telefonarci mia moglie ed io saremo molto grati.
Spero che Lei non considererà questa mia richiesta come un'intrusione.
Ad ogni modo La prego di dire a Larbaud che desidero molto avere le
sue notizie, che spero che la sua salute si rimetterà fra breve e definitiva-

I think the next number in your programme of convalescence should be a nice fur coat.
How does that strike you? I have written to Mrs Budgen who spent several years as
secretary of a London firm that dealt with these articles and is therefore an expert.
You must have good advice, otherwise you run the risk of buying, one might appro-
priately say, a *cat* in a poke.

The money I sent Mrs Curran at the Euston [Hotel] was returned to me. She had
already left. So I sent it again to Miss Weaver and I hope you now have your fine
camera.

The proverb says that the pen is mightier than the sword, but you have another idea,
that the pencil is more powerful than the pen and the sword and the umbrella all
together. I mean when you write. Unfortunately my magnifying glass makes pencil
writing even more vague and blurred.

If your picture is indicative of your state of health you must be much, much, better.
And now, dear Lucia, every day in every way you must get—well, it doesn't sound
right in Italian but it is what the most reverend and most wise Dr Coué preaches.

Your friend Maurice Chevalier has come back to Paris where he had a great success
imitating his imitators. Pity he hadn't seen you! What if I should begin to imitate
certain scribblers?

Mrs Jolas has also had postcards from you. She lives now at no. 60 of the same street
in a house with at least 20 or 25 rooms, all hers. You could play *blind man's buff* there.
Her school has now 45 boys and girls. Once you used to talk about education or, more
properly, instruction. One of my pupils in Trieste was very heavy, stupid, bald, slow
and fat. But one day he told me this little story a propos of the "education" of a sister
of his who must have been like him. This little girl was learning how to knit at school
but could get nothing into her head. The teacher tried to show her how to do it. Like
this, like this. Now do you see? Pass the needle under, then pull it through and so on.
At last she asked if the girl had an older sister. The girl replied she had. Then, said the
teacher, show her your work and tomorrow bring in everything done properly. Do
you understand? Yes, Miss.

The next day the girl came to school but the work was worse than before. How is
this? said the teacher, don't you have an older sister at home? Yes, Miss. And didn't
I tell you to ask her to show you? Yes, Miss. And what did your sister say? She said
that you and the knitting both should go to hell.

So much for "education"!

If you find this rather silly blame the central heating which went on today in our
place. These cheerful little memories dance through my head at times, but never mind.

Give my best regards to Miss Weaver and buy yourself a fine fur and give poverty
a kick. I embrace you   Babbo

Mama will write you in a few days. Meanwhile keep well and continue your swing.
Babbo'

mente e che sarò molto grato anche se egli mi permetterà di andarlo a visitare ed a stringere la mano che non ci siamo più veduti da secoli.

Gradisca, gentile signora, i miei ossequi amichevoli   JAMES JOYCE[1]

To GEORGE JOYCE   MS. Kastor

28 October 1935   *7 rue Edmond Valentin, Parigi 7*

Caro Giorgio: Tuo nonno, quando gli si narrava un incontro come quello tuo coll'impiegato della N.B.C., soleva pensare alle lagrime sparse nel grigiore dell'oliveto di Getsemani. Ma perchè proprio due persone eleganti come tu e la mia nuora vi ostinate a voler entrare nel palazzo del canto per la scala di servizio non mi è molto chiaro.

E non mi è molto chiaro come e cosa e quando devo scrivere. Secondo te a macchina o forse in istampato. Secondo Helen in inglese o forse in americano. Secondo mamma poco importa giacchè scrivo sempre 'all the wrong things'.

Aiutami dunque, O Musa, nitidissima Calligraphia!
Forbisci la forma e lo stil e frena lo stilo ribelle!
Mesci il limpido suon e distilla il liquido senso
E sulla rena riarsa, deh!, scuoti lungo il ramo!

Ho sentito una diffusione della *Forza del Destino* con Pinza.[2] Non c'è male, lui, voglio dire. Insomma al di sopra della media. La musica sarebbe ideale per un numero di prestidigitatore [sic] o piuttosto di orsacchiotti danzanti. Ho visto una pellicola irlandese *Lily of Killarney* basata sull'opera.[3] Sta a sentire. L'azione si svolge nel 1828. Ebbene i personaggi fumano sigarette, telefonano (in piena campagna irlandese) cantano *Father O'Flynn* (composta 60 anni più tardi da Villiers Stanford) il tenore canta la musica del baritono, i gendarmi sono vestiti alla foggia delle nuove guardie irlandesi. Roba da chiodi!

Quei due Zukovich (?)[4] e l'altro[5] mi propongono Laughton[6] per *Ulisse*

---

[1] (Translation)
  'Dear Madam: When I returned to Paris a few days ago I heard that Larbaud was ill again and the following day, when I went to rue Cardinal Lemoine, the concierge told me he had an acute attack of rheumatism. I left my visiting card and if you find time to write a note or to telephone us, my wife and I will be very grateful. I hope you will not consider this request an intrusion. In any case please tell Larbaud that I should like to have news about him and hope he will recover promptly and completely and that I shall be grateful if he will allow me to visit him and shake hands with him since we have not seen each other for ages. With kind regards,   James Joyce'
[2] Ezio Pinza.   [3] See p. 373.   [4] Louis Zukofsky.   [5] S. J. Reisman.
[6] Charles Laughton (1899–1962), English actor.

se approvo. Mi sembra troppo 'ariano'. Andrò a vedere Arliss[1] che fu, dicono, un buon Disraeli. E la tua voce che fa? E Stevie come sta. Di a Helen che siamo contenti ch'ella sta bene di nuovo e suo padre pure. Tante belle cose a tutti quanti. Ti abbraccio   BABBO[2]

To HERBERT GORMAN (Postcard)   MS. S. Illinois (Croessmann)

4 November 1935   *Paris*

Herbert Hughes is staying with Miss Painter at Crez (?)[3]-sur-Loing—Tel: 19 Crez (?). Athlone—Dublin R. N. will broadcast on Thursday 8 p.m. Act 1 of 'Shaun the Post' opera by Harold White and on Friday at 7.15 talk by Curran. What about my binder M. Nadal? Kind regards to you both.   J.J.

To W. B. YEATS   MS. Yeats

Postmark 20 November 1935   *7 rue Edmond Valentin, Paris 7ᵉ*

Dear Yeats: It was very kind of you to send me the signed copy of your collected poems.[4] I appreciate it very much for, though I have many friendly letters of yours, I have had no signed book of yours till now.

[1] George Arliss (1868–1946), English Jewish actor who played the title role in the film, *Disraeli* (1929).

[2] (Translation)

'Dear Giorgio: Your grandfather, when someone told him of a meeting like the one you had with that N.B.C. official, used to be reminded of the tears shed in the garden of olives of Gethsemane. But whyever two elegant people like you and my daughter-in-law persist in wanting to enter the palace of song by the service stairs is not altogether clear to me.

And how and what and when and how much I ought to write to you is not altogether clear to me either. According to you, on a typewriter or perhaps in print. According to Helen in English or perhaps in American. According to Mama it doesn't matter because I always write "all the wrong things".

> Aid me then, O Muse, resplendent Calligraphia!
> Supply the form and style, and curb the rebellious pen!
> Pour out limpid sound and distill the liquid sense.
> And over the parched sand, pray, extend your branch!

I heard a broadcast of the *Forza del Destino* with Pinza. Pretty good, I mean he was. On the whole, above average. The music would be ideal for a prestidigitator or for little dancing bears. I saw an Irish film in London *Lily of Killarney* based on the opera. Listen. The action takes place in 1828. Well, the characters smoke cigarettes, telephone (in the heart of the Irish countryside), sing *Father O'Flynn* (composed 60 years later by Villiers Stanford) the tenor sings the baritone role, the policemen are dressed after the style of the new Irish guards. Rubbish!

These two Zukovich (?) and the other are proposing Laughton for *Ulysses* if I think well. He seems too "Aryan" to me. I am going to see Arliss who was, they say, a good Disraeli. And how is your voice coming along? How is Stevie? Tell Helen we are glad she is well again and her father too. Good wishes to everybody. I embrace you
                                                            Babbo'

[3] Really Grez.

[4] Yeats wrote simply, 'Inscribed for James Joyce by W. B. Yeats, October 29, 1935.'

As a small return will you please accept a little book[1] I am sending you, also signed, a fragment of a book I am writing, published in Holland not long ago? The cover design is by my daughter.

I hope this letter and the book (for greater safety I am sending it, registered, through the Galignani Library here) will reach you safely at the only address I can find, that in Who's Who 1935. It seems that the other books I sent went astray and probably also the telegram sent you on your seventieth birthday,[2] sent to your former address in Merrion Square. With many good wishes sincerely yours   JAMES JOYCE

To ALFRED BERGAN   MS. N.Y. Public Library (Manuscript)

21 December 1935   *7 rue Edmond Valentin, Paris 7ᵉ*

Dear Mr Bergan: I hope this finds you hale and hearty and as I cannot easily manage to drink to both our good lucks at this distance perhaps the enclosed may solve the problem. These are such mad times in the world that it is probably the best thing to do.

I don't suppose there is any left now of my father's friends except you and Mr Devan. If you ever see him please remember me to him.

As you will see I have changed my address here and have been busy putting new frames round the portraits of Messieurs my ancestors. These worthy people are seeing quite a lot of Europe and they look at one another in a way that suggests: Where next?

I hope you will pass a very merry Christmas and that you will lift your glass to old times, as I shall do. And I wish you also good health and all happiness in the coming year. Sincerely yours   JAMES JOYCE

From STANISLAUS JOYCE[3]   TS. Private

12 April 1936   *Trieste, via Cesare Battisti 6*

Dear Jim, The latest is that an order has been issued for my expulsion from Italy.[4] It was communicated to me yesterday by the Vice Questore here, without notice, without warning, without explanation. I cannot understand it. At my lessons at the University and elsewhere I am very careful not to say anything that might be interpreted as a political allusion. I go nowhere, to no cafe, bar, or restaurant. I live a more retired life than you did here before the war. I see only my private pupils, who all come here—so the root of the evil must be there. I have a

---

[1] *The Mime of Mick Nick and the Maggies.*   [2] On 13 June 1935.
[3] From a copy.   [4] Stanislaus Joyce was a firm anti-fascist.

rather nicely furnished flat—the result of thirty years of incessant work
—and, though still in debt owing to the ruin of Schaurek's end, have
lived fairly comfortably, sometimes even taking a holiday. Now I feel my
feet cut from under me. I am doing what I can to have the order recinded.
I have written to Suvich,[1] who was my pupil, and some of the political
authorities here have promised to do the same. The Rector of the
University, who was greatly surprised and displeased, especially as the
authorities did not ask his opinion regarding me, has telegraphed to
the Ministero dell'Educazione Nazionale. I shall try to bring other influences to bear chiefly on Suvich, whose brother was a friend of mine
before the war (he was killed) but of course I cannot know with what
success. If all fails I shall be accompanied to the French frontier on
Saturday next.

I was ill a couple of weeks ago, fortunately not with another stone,
but with a consequence of the one that troubled me before. Now I am
all right again, and in any case I think pyelitis is not a serious thing. I
wanted to write to Helen and Giorgio and to send them a presnitz and
pinza, but I have mislaid Giorgio's letter and the only address I have:
Villa Scheffer, Paris, seems to me too vague. Besides I am informed I
could not have sent the cakes. Also I am too dreadfully upset.

I shall be very anxious to hear from you. Meanwhile tardy greeting to
you and Nora. I have not told Nelly anything yet not to spoil her
Easter. I shall tell her to-morrow.   STANNIE

From STANISLAUS JOYCE (Postcard)[2]   TS. Private

24 April 1936   [*Rome*]

Dear Jim, I have an appointment at the Foreign Office here this
afternoon. I still have hopes to right matters. I will certainly do my
utmost. But if I fail I shall have no choice but to come to Paris. Best
greetings also to Nora.   STANNIE

To MR and MRS FRANK BUDGEN (Postcard)   MS. Yale

27 April 1936   *Paris*

Congratulations[3] and long life to all the Budgens, from us both
                                                        JAMES JOYCE

---

[1] Fulvio Suvich (b. 1887), then Mussolini's Undersecretary of State.
[2] From a copy.
[3] On the birth of their daughter, Joan Budgen, 19 April 1936.

From STANISLAUS JOYCE[1]　　　　　　　　　　　　TS. Private

11 May 1936　　　　　　　　　　*Trieste, via Cesare Battisti 6*

Dear Jim,　As you know, I went to Rome where I had two interviews with Mr. S.[2] He received me very kindly, and did what he could for me. The matter, however, was not in his hands but in those of another personage.[3] The upshot is that I have been officially informed that the order against me has been suspended for an indefinite time. This is an unsatisfactory result. Meanwhile I have been relieved of my position at the University as a consequence of the first order against me. Now that it has been suspended, the authorities of the University will try to have me reinstated, a rather difficult matter in these times.[4] I have also been deprived by order of certain evening classes I used to have. Besides incurring the expense of a journey to Rome, I lost a month's lessons from the beginning of April to the beginning of May. From many other points of view the outlook is not bright. Moreover I am not disposed to eat humble pie for 68 L a month. I must look future possibilities in the face. What I want to know is, what are the prospects for an English teacher in Paris? I have been promised introductions from influential people—Greek acquaintances of yours, for example.[5] In fact I already have some letters. I have also a recommendation from the University. At the worst there is our old friend, the B. school.[6] If I could get a job in some school, French, English or American, I would not hesitate to scoot. It is not a brilliant end to twenty-seven years unbroken work in one city, four years internment in great part for my Italian sympathies, and fifteen years at the University. If I should be obliged to leave, I do not anticipate that I shall have any difficulty in obtaining permission to remain in France. At least so I am told here. Although I will do my utmost again to remain here, I should very much like to get an answer to the various questions in this letter. If it is too trying for you to write, perhaps Georgie would write for you. In any case please answer as soon as you can for I have been living in uncertainty from day to day for over a month. Remember me to Nora,　　　　　　　　　　　　　STANNIE

[1] From a copy.　　　　　　　　　　[2] Fulvio Suvich.
[3] Suvich referred the matter to Pietro Gerbore who, recognizing the name of Joyce, obtained Mussolini's permission to rescind the deportation order.
[4] They were successful, but with much delay, in reinstating Stanislaus Joyce.
[5] Sordina and Ralli are meant.　　　　　[6] Berlitz School.

To W. B. YEATS   MS. Yeats

18 May 1936   *7 rue Edmond Valentin, Paris 7ᵉ*

Dear Yeats: I was delighted to get your letter and to hear you are now much better. Long may you flourish!

Yes, I sent everything either to your Merrion Square address or c/o Abbey Theatre and am very sorry my telegram to you for your 70th birthday never reached you as I, of all people, would not have been wanting on that day. This telegram must have been delivered to somebody. Otherwise the French P.O. would have returned it to me.

If Mrs Yeats will unsew the first pages of your *Ulysses* and send them I shall sign them with great pleasure. I mean when you return to Dublin. Sincerely yours   JAMES JOYCE

To T. S. ELIOT   MS. Faber

3 June 1936   *7 rue Edmond Valentin, Paris 7ᵉ*

Dear Eliot: I shall be glad to see you again after such a long time but hope that you will do us the pleasure of dining with us instead.

I am in arrears with my correspondence. My daughter has been very ill indeed these last six months and four days ago my son too had to undergo an extremely delicate operation.[1] He is now getting on well.

Léon will undertake the work[2] of course but he says it is not the same thing now as it would have been in January when the text, with insertions and alignments, was quite fresh in his mind. Sincerely yours
                                                          JAMES JOYCE

To MARY M. COLUM   MS. N.Y. Public Library (Manuscript)

5 June 1936   *7 rue Edmond Valentin, Paris 7ᵉ*

Dear Mrs Colum: Thanks for your cable. By the next boat mail you will receive through my friend Léon a letter and a dozen or so prospectuses.[3] *Il s'agit d'un*[4] present and a surprise I am planning to make to Lucia for her next birthday 26 July. She is at present at the Maison

---

[1] A throat operation.
[2] Reading proofs of *Finnegans Wake*.
[3] Joyce had determined to publish Lucia's designs for *A Chaucer A. B. C.* for her birthday, 26 July. The prospectuses were to secure subscriptions.
[4] 'It is all a matter of a . . .'

de Santé Dr Delmas, 23 rue de la Mairie at Ivry, Paris.[1] She has been extremely and even dangerously low since last Xmas but I am still hoping and working, almost alone now I am afraid. I know you will do what you can to give her the poor pleasure I intend.

Giorgio was operated a week ago for his thyroid gland. The vocal chords seem to have been quite unaffected at any rate. He is making good progress and it is believed this will radically change his whole health.

How are you both? We hope for the best and that we may soon see you over here in spite of the disturbed conditions now abroad in the world.

It has been almost impossible for me to continue writing with such terrible anxiety night and day. Still I am doing what I can.

Our kindest remembrances to you both in which Giorgio, Helen and Stevie join. Sincerely yours   JAMES JOYCE

To HARRIET SHAW WEAVER   MS. British Museum

9 June 1936   *7 rue Edmond Valentin, Paris 7ᵉ*

Dear Miss Weaver: My brother, expelled from Italy, is due here on the 16 inst, with or without his wife and bulldog.[2] My son has to remain in bed or on a couch for 4 or 5 months after an operation on his throat.

I believe I can cover most of the expenses of publication of my daughter's alphabet.[3] My idea is not to persuade her that she is a Cézanne but that on her 29th birthday . . . she may see something to persuade her that her whole past has not been a failure. The reason I keep on trying by every means to find a solution for her case (which may come at any time as it did with my eyes) is that she may not think that she is left with a blank future as well. I am aware that I am blamed by everybody for sacrificing that precious metal money to such an extent for such a purpose when it would be done so cheaply and quietly by locking her up in an economical mental prison for the rest of her life.

I will not do so as long as I see a single chance of hope for her recovery, nor blame her or punish her for the great crime she has

[1] Lucia Joyce's behaviour had become so uncontrollable that Joyce reluctantly allowed her to be installed in a clinic in Le Vésinet in March 1936. There the doctors insisted she be withdrawn to a special institution, and in April Joyce had her transferred to Dr Achille Delmas's Maison de Santé at Ivry.

[2] In the end Stanislaus Joyce did not come to Paris, but he and his brother met in Switzerland in September 1936.

[3] *A Chaucer A. B. C.*, with initial letters by Lucia Joyce, was published with a preface by Louis Gillet in July 1936 by the Obelisk Press in Paris.

committed in being a victim to one of the most elusive diseases known to men and unknown to medicine. And I imagine that if you were where she is and felt as she must you would perhaps feel some hope if you felt that you were neither abandoned nor forgotten.

Some mysterious malady has been creeping on both my children (the doctors are inclined to trace it back to our residence in Switzerland during the war) and if they have not succeeded in doing anything for themselves it is to blame, not they. My daughter's case is far the worse of the two though how my son was able to do even as much as he did with his voice in the U.S. in such a state as he was (he could not lift a cup often from the table much less control his vocal chords) is also a mystery to me. . . . With kindest regards sincerely yours James Joyce

To Sean O'Faolain   MS. Ellmann

16 July 1936   *7 rue Edmond Valentin, Paris 7ᵉ*

Dear Sir: A bird alone—a pretty grey finch at present in a cage—flew into our flat through an open window yesterday morning. Perhaps he was scared and sought refuge from the air squadrons then over the city or perhaps he came from Wicklow to remind me that I had not acknowledged receipt of your book.[1] This I do now with thanks.

I am afraid, however, that I cannot be of any real service to you. I never write for any journal or periodical and I have not read a novel in any language for very many years so that my opinion is quite worthless. I buy them sometimes when [I] know the writer personally. Nevertheless, I shall take your book away with me when I go away on my holidays next month.

It was very kind of you to send me the book. Sincerely yours
                                                                    James Joyce

To Viscount Carlow[2]   MS. Yale

22 July 1936   *7 rue Edmond Valentin, Paris 7ᵉ*

Dear Lord Carlow: Would the piece in this issue of *transition*[3] with this initial suit you? You may keep the review in any case but I would ask

[1] Sean O'Faolain (b. 1900), the Irish novelist, short-story writer, and critic, had sent Joyce his new novel, *Bird Alone* (London and New York, 1936).

[2] George Lionel Seymour, Viscount Carlow (1907–44), published books under the imprint of the Corvinus Press, which he founded in March 1936.

[3] *transition* 23 (July 1935) 109–29 (*Finnegans Wake*, pp. 260–75, 304–308). Lord Carlow published this section under the title *Storiella as She Is Syung* (London, Corvinus Press, October 1937). He used one of Lucia Joyce's illuminated capitals at the beginning.

you to return me the *lettrine* if you decide that the piece is unsuitable for your purpose. I fear it is.

The copy I showed you of the Chaucer book[1] was an advance one and as the book itself will not be out till the 10 August I enclose a proof of Louis Gillet's preface which you may like to read. Sincerely yours

JAMES JOYCE

To MR and MRS CLAUD W. SYKES (Postcard)   MS. Yale

26 August 1936   [*Elsinore, Denmark*]

Greetings to the English Players from here in Elsinore

JAMES JOYCE, N JOYCE

To JOHN SULLIVAN (Postcard)   MS. Texas

26 August 1936   *Elsinore, Denmark*

Greetings from the place which inspired Ambroise Thomas[2]

JAMES JOYCE

To CAROLA GIEDION-WELCKER   MS. Giedion-Welcker

31 August 1936   *Copenhagen*

Dear Mrs Giedion: Do you or does Mr Giedion know anyone who has influence in Neuchatel? My brother Stanislaus has applied for a post there as professor of English in the Ecole Superieure de Commerce, director M. Vuillener. My brother has been a teacher of English all his life, is 48 and has held my post as professor of English in the University of Trieste since 1919. He is married to a Triestine Swiss, born Lichtensteiger.

On account of the British Italian friction he was dismissed from his post at the University of Trieste a few months ago and an order of expulsion was issued that he should leave Italy. But the then foreign Secretary Fulvio Suvich was our pupil from before the war and the

---

[1] *A Chaucer A. B. C.*
[2] The reference is to their standing joke that Ambroise Thomas's opera *Hamlet* (1868) had been Shakespeare's source for his play of the same name.

expulsion order was revoked or rather suspended. He was not reinstated in the university and finds the moral surroundings so intolerable that he has applied for this rather poorly paid post—6000 Sw. frs per annum. He has no children.

I am writing prof. Fleiner and Edmond Jaloux but perhaps you know somebody.

I hope you have got Lucia's book.

Friendly greetings to both

JAMES JOYCE

To VISCOUNT CARLOW   MS. Yale

1 September 1936   *Turist Hotel, København V*

Dear Lord Carlow: Please excuse my delay in answering but I have been travelling. I am very glad you like the two *lettrines*. Three things are lacking in the piece you have, a rubric for paragraph 2, a marginal insertion on the right of the second last page and a title. I shall attend to all this when we return to Paris in a week or so and then write to you. I have not the text here.

I hope this will reach you safely as I have forgotten the number of your house. But no doubt it will sincerely yours

JAMES JOYCE

To FRANK BUDGEN (Postcard)   MS. Yale

13 September 1936   *[Paris]*

Just back from Denmark[1] and can't find my stylo.[2] At Bonn I met my friend Prof Curtius who it seems never received the copy of your book I suggested should be sent him. Can I buy 4 more at the same price. Please reply by return. I hope the Budgens parents and daughter are flourishing. Salutations cordiales

J.J.

[1] Joyce finally realized in August 1936 his long ambition to go to Denmark. He and his wife stayed in Copenhagen into September, and on the return journey stopped at Bonn to see Professor Ernest Robert Curtius, the well-known German critic and literary historian, at the University there. Joyce wished to enlist Curtius's support, already given for *Ulysses*, for *Finnegans Wake* as well.

[2] 'Fountain pen.'

To B. W. HUEBSCH   MS. Buffalo

17 September 1936   *7 rue Edmond Valentin, Paris 7e*

Dear Huebsch: I regret we did not meet when I was up north, so near you. I got your Swedish address too late but in any case thank Mrs Huebsch and yourself for the kind invitation you extended to us.[1]

I hope you liked my daughter's *lettrines* for the Chaucer book.

Herewith I send you the T.L.S with an advertisement which Faber and Faber have put in. I also send you another copy of the book.[2] You will remember I gave you a copy of it in London already in 1931. Faber and Faber apparently bought over a good part of the Paris stock and re-bound it, I suppose. I think its issue in the U.S. would be also advisable as I told you then.

Ulysses should come out in London on 1 October.

I hope you had a pleasant holiday. sincerely yours   JAMES JOYCE

To JAMES STEPHENS[3]

18 September 1936   *Paris*

Dear Stephens: Have you time to read *Little Eyolf* which I am leaving for you and ring me up afterwards if and when you finish it. I should like to hear what you think of it. If you read it you should not interrupt any act of it.[4] Sincerely yours   JAMES JOYCE

From JAMES STEPHENS   MS. Buffalo

20 September 1936   *Campagne 1re 11. Paris*

My dear Joyce—There are two things about you which are unchange-able: you are the most subtil man, and the most continuously kind male creature I have ever known. All that merely apropos des bottes. I got the Ibsen book you left with my concierge—to think of you, with your poor sight, navigating the wilderness of Paris merely to give me a book, scandalises me, and makes me proud. I send you my love in return, but

---

[1] B. W. Huebsch had invited the Joyces to stay with his wife's family in Sweden.

[2] *Pomes Penyeach.* Joyce refers to the first English edition, printed in France, with Lucia Joyce's initial letters (Paris, Obelisk Press, and London, Desmond Harmsworth, October 1932), and to the Faber & Faber edition (London, March 1933). The Viking Press included it in *Collected Poems* (New York, 1937).

[3] From a typewritten copy.

[4] Joyce was eager to convert James Stephens to his own passion for Ibsen, and thought *Little Eyolf*, which Stephens admitted he had not read, would bring his friend around.

that is so easy to send by a postman that it is not worth signing a receipt for at the other end.

I take it that you sent me this book because of the remarks I made to you upon Ibsen. I will agree, with any man who cares to be agreed with, that Ibsen is a more than competent stage-manager. If a character of his sneezes in the first-act he will have a cold in the second-act, and will die of pneumonia in the third. My criticism (fault-finding) goes deeper than his handling of a selected matter in a first, a second and a third act. It is this: that of all those who have come to (deserved) eminence in drama, or, generally, in literature Ibsen is the most thorough-going liar, or falsifyer of the truth, that ever attained such eminence. His idealist in (was it?) The Wild Duck was no idealist,—He was a mere, uncomplicated, commonplace swindler. His Master-Builder man was, similarly, an ordinary, and exceedingly mere ass.

Now I have read, at your behest, his Little Eyolf—and, again, I take off all my hats to that exceedingly skilful presentation, and withdraw every demi-semi-quaver of my soul from his tale, and the truth of it. The catastrophe he so cogently engineers is everywhere unmerited: has not, by a single one of his characters, been worked for, or earned, or deserved. The man is a pestilent dramatist, and all his works are framed with the desire to make those pay who do not owe, and to make those suffer who have not merited it. If ever there was in literature a sadist such an one was Ibsen, and that anyone could ever have been taken in by him, critically or morally, remains for me as an inexplicable enigma. This play is, for me, an effect without a cause—which is ridiculous: and equally ill-founded, and as equally ridiculous are all his other triumphs. To hell with that dark man of the black north, for that is where he came from, and his literature is as nigh to hellish as the complete-bourgeois can possibly manage.

Mise agat-sa, do cara go deó[1]   JAMES STEPHENS

To WILHELM HERZ (WILLIAM H. HARTLEY)   MS. Hartley

21 September 1936   *7 rue Edmond Valentin, Paris 7ᵉ*

Dear Mr Hertz: Many thanks to you and your friend for copies of *Politiken*.[2] The letter to Lucia is just what I wanted. I have written to my German publisher about my book and if and when I get a copy you

[1] Irish for 'I am your friend forever'.
[2] A leading Copenhagen newspaper. Evidently Joyce's visit to Denmark had been noted in it.

will receive it. If not an English copy. Are the latter really not on sale in Cologne book shops. I mean, the Odyssey Press edition?

Giorgio and Helen are now back in Paris and are rather tired, at least Helen is. He is much stronger. We had a lovely day in Cologne thanks to Mrs Herz and yourself Sincerely yours   JAMES JOYCE

To CAROLA GIEDION-WELCKER (Postcard)   MS. Giedion-Welcker

22 September 1936   *Paris*

Dear Mrs Giedion, We are now back and I hear my brother lost that place by applying one week too late. Nevertheless if you hear of anything to suit him he wishes to get away from where he is at present, even at a low salary.

Kind greetings to both from both   JAMES JOYCE

To JAMES STEPHENS   MS. Stephens

25 September 1936   *7 rue Edmond Valentin, Paris*

Dear Stephens: Thanks for your letter. What you say is true but it is by no means all, in my opinion. Did you say you would be going back at the end of this week? Will you ask Mrs Stephens to ring me or us up so that we may arrange perhaps to meet again before you leave? Sincerely yours   JAMES JOYCE

To KATHLEEN BARNACLE   MS. Yale

30 September 1936   *7 rue Edmond Valentin, Paris 7ᵉ*

Dear Kathleen: I have received your letter from which I gather you want, or rather your mother wants, me to write in the first instance to my friend Mr Curran in Dublin.[1] He is due back in Dublin, I understand, on Thursday, 1st October. I shall therefore write to him fully on Sunday, 3rd October, unless I hear from you meanwhile that this is not what you want me to do.

I hope you can read my handwriting
Best greetings to you both   JIM

[1] Michael Healy died intestate on 7 November 1935, and Joyce asked Curran to look into the matter of disposition of the property. (*Letters*, ed. Gilbert, pp. 389–90)

From Stanislaus Joyce[1]   TS. Private

15 November 1936   *Trieste, via Cesare Battisti 6*

Dear Jim, On Friday last I sent you by registered book post 'Pebbles from a Brook'[2] and 'Il Fuoco'.[3] The house was turned upside down three times in three systematic searches for 'Michael Kramer'[4] and 'La Gioconda'.[5] They are not to be found. Instead of starting again to look for 'La Città Morta'[6] I have sent you 'Il Fuoco'. It should serve your purpose better than 'La Città Morta' as you mentioned it in 'The Day of the Rabblement'.

I have had no answer from Zugerberg as yet. I wrote twice and gave Prof Bernhard Fehr and others as references. But after all what can they say about me? In any case I must get out of Trieste. We are now in the middle of November, and I have an average of two and a half lessons. They used to begin, as you may remember, about the middle or end of September. Now, they begin—if this year they will begin at all— in December, and end in the middle of May. Six months ill-paid work in the year. It is clear to me that I shall not be able to hold out here during the coming summer and autumn. In one of the schools of the Dopo-lavoro[7] in which I have been teaching since it was founded, I was again offered my usual place this autumn, but the organizers could not get the permission of the political authorities. So that's off. Moreover, a great many pupils who would be willing to study privately with me are afraid to compromise themselves. This is not, as you will probably think, a hotheaded supposition of mine. Things English (and in this category they include things Joyce) are still taboo. Things Joyce doubly so. At one time I used to be able to have a 'par' inserted in one or other of the papers when something new cropped up regarding 'Ulysses' or its modest young author. This time both in the case of Lucia's book and the English edition of 'Ulysses' I have got promises but I am still waiting for them to materialize. Of course I shall not ask again. A southern Italian, D'Alesio, has been appointed English professor at I. R.[8] Università Commerciale di Trieste. He has also the chair in French. Two chairs, and plenty of cheek—one for each, in fact.

---

[1] From a typed copy. A few obvious typing errors are silently corrected here.

[2] John Eglinton, *Pebbles from a Brook* (Dublin, 1901), a book of essays.

[3] Gabriele D'Annunzio, *Il Fuoco* (1899).

[4] Gerhart Hauptmann, *Michael Kramer* (1900).

[5] D'Annunzio, *La Gioconda* (1899).   [6] D'Annunzio, *La Città Morta* (1898).

[7] Opera Nazionale Dopolavoro, an organization set up by the Fascist party to control various kinds of special education, trips, sports, and the like.

[8] Imperiale Regia ('Imperial Royal'), an Austro-Hungarian abbreviation and hence a sarcastic reference to hysterical Italian nationalism.

It seems to me that you are unable to realize how things are here, and I am unable to tell you.   STANNIE

To CAROLA GIEDION-WELCKER   MS. Giedion-Welcker

18 November 1936   *Paris*

Dear Mrs Giedion: I have sent on your letter to my brother. I enclose a letter just received from him. It is clear that his one desire is to leave Trieste and Italy as soon as possible, at practically any cost to himself and for good. Therefore perhaps you could make your suggested motor run to the school at Zug?[1] In fact, any school whatever which can pay a small monthly [salary]. It is useful to reflect that my brother who now wishes to leave Italy as he finds life intolerable there was imprisoned for 4 years by the Austrians because of his rabid pro-Italian sympathies! I never took much interest in his politics and don't understand the allusions in his letter to 'anti-Joyce'. But if it is so, it is so. *Und das ist mir ganz egal.*[2] Friendly greetings to you both. Friendly greetings to you both sincerely yours   JAMES JOYCE

To CAROLA GIEDION-WELCKER   MS. Giedion-Welcker

1 December 1936   *Paris*

Dear Mrs Giedion: My wife asks me to say she cashed your cheque and thanks you. A few days ago a letter came for you from Lucia. I can't find it. Anyhow it was nothing much. However if you care to send her a few lines, perhaps about her book[3] *et la pluie et le beau temps*[4] and seeing her again in Z'ch *when* she is better as you hear she is making progress I shall forward it.

Look out for the next issue of *Transition*.[5] I have something in it and it is chiefly or in great part about—Gideon. (Book of Judges, chap 6, verse 36 et seq.)[6]

Kind greetings to you both. Sincerely yours   JAMES JOYCE

---

[1] Stanislaus Joyce met his brother in Zurich in late August or early September. There was a position at a school at Zug, on the top of the Zugerberg. He did not reject it, but was not enthusiastic for so isolated a spot. This letter indicates he still had it in mind.

[2] 'And it is all the same to me.'   [3] *A Chaucer A. B. C.*

[4] 'And the rain and the good weather.'

[5] *transition* 26 (February 1937) 35–52 (*Finnegans Wake*, pp. 309–31).

[6] Joyce was punning on the name Giedion (which he habitually misspelt Gideon). In the passage in Judges 6: 36–40, Gideon asked God to manifest his power by not allowing the dew to come upon a fleece. 'And God did so that night: for it was dry upon the fleece only, and there was dew on all the ground.' This is paraphrased in *transition*

To VISCOUNT CARLOW   MS. Yale

18 February 1937   *7 rue Edmond Valentin, Paris 7ᵉ*

Dear Lord Carlow: The proofs have been corrected for several days. I
did not send them to Munich [?] as I thought you would be in
London between the 15 and 18? Where shall I send them now? I hope
wherever you may be that you are both well in spite of this hideous
weather. My piece about the Norwegian captain and the tailor[1] was
swamped out in the Ohio floods (*transition* this time being printed in
Cincinnati) but it has been reset and I believe they have now given a
second *bon à tirer*.[2] Sincerely yours   JAMES JOYCE

To FRANK BUDGEN (Postcard)   MS. Yale

27 February 1937   *Paris*

Many happy returns of S. David's Day.[3] The latest fragment of W i P
printed in Cincinnati was washed off by Anna Ohio out of pure jealousy.
It is now reset and you will have it shortly. Best wishes also to Mrs and
Miss Budgen   J.J.

To T. G. KEOHLER[4]

9 March 1937   *7 rue Edmond Valentin, Paris 7ᵉ*

Dear Keohler: It was very kind of you to send me a copy of your little
book[5] and I thank you for your kind remembrance. As I have been
carrying your other little book of poems[6] for so many years round
Europe perhaps you will do me the pleasure of inscribing it also? I
enclose it in any case and thank you in advance.

I hope you are well and weathering with your old amiable serenity
these somewhat gusty times and indeed I thank you for your kind words
about myself and reciprocate all your friendly remembrances Sincerely
yours   JAMES JOYCE

(p. 51): 'And Dub did glow that night. And it was dim upon the floods only and there
was day on all the ground.' In *Finnegans Wake* the first sentence is on p. 329, the second
on p. 330.
    [1] Joyce retells in *Finnegans Wake* (pp. 309–31) his father's story about a hunchbacked
Norwegian captain who ordered a suit from a Dublin tailor named Kerse. When it was
made, the captain complained that it did not fit, and the tailor said no one could make a
suit that would fit him. These pages were in *transition* 26 (February 1937) 35–52.
    [2] 'Ready to print.'   [3] 1 March, Frank Budgen's birthday.
    [4] From a photostatic copy.   [5] A privately printed volume of verse.
    [6] *Songs of a Devotee* (Dublin, Maunsel, 1906).

To STEPHEN JOYCE (Postcard)   MS. Kastor

6 April 1937   [*Zurich*]

Caro nipotino:[1] These are the 3 monskeyteers of Zurich.[2] Their names
are Athos, Porthos and Aramis. Porthos is in the middle and he makes
the most noise with his songs. Athos is on the right and he can put away
2 spoonfuls to the others' one. But Aramis on the left says soup is for
saps and what he wants is not singenò [?] *di coco.*[3]
        Such are monskeyteers   NONNO[4]

To WILHELM HERZ (WILLIAM H. HARTLEY)   MS. Hartley

8 April 1937   *Carlton Elite Hotel, Zurich*

Dear Mr Hertz: Perhaps before I come you may be able to find out if
there are vacancies in any schools of S. Gallen and whether, in general,
a permit of residence in the canton can be had for this type of work
anyhow. My brother was in correspondence with some school there. He
has a certain claim of preference, I think, in case there is. His wife is
from S. Gallen. The family name is Wirler Lichtensteiger and her father
who was born there comes of an old S. Gallen family. Her uncle Paul
Birnenstibel lives there still, I believe.
        Looking forward to the pleasure of seeing you and with thanks in
advance sincerely yours   JAMES JOYCE

To GEORGE JOYCE   MS. Kastor

11 April 1937 Sunday   *Carlton Elite Hotel, Zurich*

Caro Giorgio: Ho visto Vogt finalmente. Trovò la mia vista molto
migliorata il foro che praticò nell'occhio sinistro aggrandito. S'allar-
gherà, dice, ancora e fra due anni propone di fare un altro taglio.
Vorrei vedere meglio. Mi ha cambiato le lenti (3 punti diottrici e vuol
tenermi in osservazione per saper se m'abituo bene ai nuovi occhiali. Li
ho messi oggi. È un po' strano ma vedo già meglio. L'occhio destro—
nichtsehtum,[5] un po' peggiorato in durezza della cristallina verso il naso.
Si ma minacciava una di quelle brevi vampate che mi vengono di
quando in quando. Il clima qui è matto da legare. Infatti la vampata ci
fù un'ora dopo aver visto Vogt. Ma presi aspirina, e feci delle compresse

---

[1] 'Dear little grandson.'
[2] The postcard bore a picture of three chimpanzees at the Zurich zoo.
[3] 'A simiana [?] of cocoanut.'   [4] 'Grandpa.'
[5] A play on 'nichts zu tun' ('it can't be helped') and 'nicht sehen' ('not to see'),
meaning, 'No sight—and nothing to be done about it.'

calde ed oggi va molto meglio. Così non potevo andare a S. Gallen ieri.
Ma i cugini vennero qui invece ed abbiamo passato il dopopranzo e la
sera assieme, al Dolder, al Teatro (io, l'occhio bandato) ed alla Kronenhalle poi. Faceva un tempo siberiano dopo un venerdì molto caldo. Oggi
però sto molto meglio. V. voleva ch'io rimassi 10 giorni, ma gli chiese di
sollecitare la mia partenza e forse potremo partire verso la fine della
settimana.

Telefona a Lévi. Mi secca scrivere 2 volte.

In questo momento però è venuto un dispaccio da Stannie e Nellie
dai pressi di Verona. Sono già in viaggio ed arrivano a Zurigo stasera
alle 9. Ho trovato o quasi un posto per loro (essa pure ma dovrebbero
stare nel collegio convitto stesso) e questa brusca partenza può
significare tante cose. Ad ogni modo tutti sono d'accordo che S. non
troverà mai un posto qui senza prima presentarsi in persona. Credo
anche di aver superato le grandissime difficoltà di un permesso di
soggiorno. Ma vedremo.

Spero che state tutti bene. Ti abbraccio   BABBO[1]

To VISCOUNT CARLOW   MS. Yale

9 May 1937   *7 rue Edmond Valentin, Paris 7e*

Dear Lord Carlow: What is the name of your friend at the B.B.C. and
of what department is he chief? Perhaps you could give me a note to
him so that my son Giorgio could have an audition in London. He could

---

[1] (Translation)

'Dear Giorgio: I have seen Vogt at last. He found my sight much improved. The
hole he made in my left eye is enlarged. He says it will become even larger and two
years from now he proposes to make another cut. I should like to see better. He
changed my lenses (3 dioptical points) and wants to keep me under observation to find
out if I can get accustomed to new glasses. I put them on today. They feel a bit strange
but I see better already. The right eye—non-sight—a little deteriorated because of
hardening of the crystalline near the nose. Yes but he threatened me [with] one of those
brief burning flashes once in a while. The climate here is really crazy. In fact a burning
flash came an hour after I had seen Vogt. But I took aspirin and made hot compresses
and today it's much better. So I could not go to S. Gallen yesterday. But the cousins
came here and we spent the afternoon and evening together, on the Dolder, at the
theatre (I with my eye bandaged) and at the Kronenhalle afterwards. The weather was
Siberian after a very warm Friday. Today however I feel much better. V. wanted me to
stay 10 days but I asked him to hurry my departure and perhaps we will be able to
leave at the end of the week.

Telephone Lévi. It is annoying to have to write twice.

At this very moment a letter has come from Stannie and Nellie from near Verona.
They are on the way and will arrive in Zurich this evening at 9. I have more or less
found a place for them (although they are supposed to stay in the boarding school
itself) and this sudden departure may mean anything. Anyway everyone is sure that
S. won't find a job here without coming in person. I also think I've overcome the
serious difficulties of obtaining a residence permit. But we'll see.

I hope all goes well. I embrace you   Babbo'

go over about the end of June probably when and if life becomes a little more normal.

Also my friend Louis Gillet (who wrote the preface to the Chaucer A.B.C.) is in London till about the 19 inst. He is a great admirer of T. E. Lawrence and would like to see your press and your books. Perhaps you could manage to meet him. He is at the Savoy.

And finally. Faber and Faber have sent me a bundle of proofs of 'Work in Progress' and as their printer is nearing Miss Storiella could you send to my friend T. S. Eliot of that firm a list of the few corrections and additions to the text they have being very careful not to forget that marvellous marginal monosyllable 'Sic'.[1]

As I do not know your new address I am sending this to the old address. *transition* is still swimming bravely across the seven seas, a wave a week. Sincerely yours   JAMES JOYCE

To CAROLA GIEDION-WELCKER   MS. Giedion-Welcker

[18? May 1937]   *7 rue Edmond Valentin, Paris*

Dear Mrs Giedion: Thanks for your signed book and I was glad to see my old friend from Carnac in it.[2] Also for the typed certificates of my brother. I sent copies of these to Dr Steinberg,[3] Dr Speck[4] and Prof. Fleiner. The latter wrote he could do nothing about the Fremdenpolizei until Dr Steinberg or some other employer took the first step. I have now received a letter from my brother, the sense of which I have just communicated to Dr Speck. If you ring her up she will tell you how the case now stands. In a word my brother has a quasi-certainty of obtaining permission for Zurich if an application is made for him by his employer. You will see by the Paris Italian paper I send that the Paris Italian colony has just been fêting me. It is opportune (and quite right) that this should happen just now. Nevertheless the horizon looks to me so dark that I would be very glad to hear that my brother has definitely settled in Switzerland.

We have had a wretched Whitsuntide![5] Thank the Lord it is over!

Kind regards to you both sincerely yours   JAMES JOYCE

[1] *Finnegans Wake*, p. 260.
[2] Joyce was interested in the Druidic stones at Carnac.
[3] Dr S. D. Steinberg, a newspaper editor in Zurich.
[4] Dr Else Speck-Heinz, a pediatrician.
[5] Whitsunday in 1937 was 16 May, and suggests the approximate date of this letter.

To C. P. CURRAN[1]   MS. Curran

19 May 1937   *7 rue Edmond Valentin, Paris 7ᵉ*

Dear Curran: Herbert Gorman whom you met at Fontainebleau[2] is leaving for Dublin where he will stay a couple of weeks, at the Royal Hibernian Hotel, Dawson Street. As you know he is writing a life of me. He has letters from certain writers there but I am giving him this one to you. Perhaps you can show him some places, Chapelizod, Howth (if the rhododendrums are in bloom)[3] and Clongowes Wood: that is to say if you still have your car. If not, perhaps he could go by bus. I am sure you will help him.

Curiously enough, another friend of mine (who, I think is also doing a book about me) has gone to Dublin. In fact just as I sat down to write this a wire came from him to say he had arrived in Dublin two days before he had planned to get there. He has just delivered a lecture about me before the Italian Club here and he is giving two lectures in Dublin at one or other of the universities. He is Louis Gillet. He wrote the preface for Lucia's book. He is a son-in-law of René Doumic, editor of the *Revue des Deux Mondes* and perpetual secretary of the Academy, brother-in-law of the late Henri de Regnier and nephew of the late, the more than late José-Maria Heredia. I think he is staying at the French Legation in Dublin.

To return to Gorman. He also wants to be present at the first (and last?) performance of my first (and last?) play in Dublin.[4] It has already made spectral appearances on the boards at Munich, Milan, Berlin, New York and London. A child appears in the last act about 10.30 and I am not sure whether this will be allowed. Anyhow please present the bouquets to the two actresses whoever they are.

(Gorman asked me where my sister lives or rather my sisters. I told him that I don't know. And I might have said more. I have not told him any details of my daughter's sojourn in Ireland. The poor girl still speaks of it as if she had been in Tir-nan-Ogue.[5] But this is not due to any mistrust on my part but rather because after five or six years I find it useless to try to explain the case to anybody any more. From what I can discern everybody has one way or another made up his or her mind. Those who are not mystified are bored and those who are not bored are

---

[1] From a typewritten copy.

[2] The Joyces and Gormans were at Fontainebleau in August and September, 1935.

[3] The final pages of *Ulysses* describe a scene among the rhododendrons on Howth Head.

[4] According to Slocum and Cahoon, *Exiles* was not produced in Dublin until 1948.

[5] In Irish legend, this is the Land of the Ever Young or Fairyland.

more pleased than sorry. I think that if the mysterious malady which
has attacked her youth has not laid her out before now and if the green
isle of Erin let her escape alive I still hope.)

Our friendly regards to Mrs Curran and your daughter sincerely
yours   JAMES JOYCE.

To ALFRED BERGAN   MS. N.Y. Public Library (Manuscript)

25 May 1937   *7 rue Edmond Valentin, Paris 7ᵉ*

Dear Mr Bergan: I am so sorry to hear your bad news that our old
friend Mr Devin is gone. Only on Wednesday last I gave his name to a
young American writer who is doing my biography and has gone to
Dublin, Mr Herbert Gorman. I told him to see you and Mr Devin as
you were the only people still left (as I thought) who could remember all
the pleasant nights we used to have singing. Mr Devin's song was 'O
boys, keep away from the girls I say'. The moral of it fell on deaf ears in
my case and I dont think it meant very much to him either. He used to
play the *Intermezzo* from *Cavalleria Rusticana*—a version of his own
and would have been a fine pianist if he had studied as he had a very
agreeable touch on the keys. He used to collapse with laughter after a
preliminary scream in a high tone at certain sallies of my father's. He
must have been a fine looking fellow when he was young and he had
charming manners. He comes into Ulysses under the name of 'Mr
Power' and also into 'Dubliners'. I regret that my friend (who, by the
way, is staying quite close to you at the Royal Hibernian Hotel) did
not meet him and talk with him. He has letters to and from a number of
literary people in Dublin. Many of them are very fair written too and
one or two more than that but they never meant much to me personally
and mean less now.

The Lord knows whether you will be able to pick the Kersse-McCann
story[1] out of my crazy tale. It was a great story of my fathers and I'm
sure if they get a copy of *transition* in the shades his comment will be
'Well, he can't tell that story as I used to and that's one sure five!'

I hope you are well and send you all good and friendly greetings
sincerely yours   JAMES JOYCE

To STANISLAUS JOYCE (Postcard)   MS. Cornell

[? June 1937]   *7 rue Edmond Valentin, Paris 7ᵉ*

Dear Stannie: What news about your position in Switzerland. Here is

---

[1] The story of the Norwegian captain and the tailor. See p. 394. Philip McCann,
Joyce's godfather, was evidently the source of the story.

all I have. My play *Exiles* was not given in Dublin. Postponed from
3 May to 24 May and then to 1 Nov. Actor ill. Hope you are both well.
Saluti   JIM

To C. P. CURRAN[1]   MS. Curran
10 June 1937   *Paris*

Dear Curran: From my solicitors' letter today it looks as if they had
sent you 10/- instead of 10gns. If this is so please send me a police
constable and I shall reply by a medical officer for the difference.

I forgot to say that M. Jolas left with my concierge for my perusal a
copy of *A Page of Irish History*,[2] a book about U.C.[3] On p 338 I read
that in 1897 I opposed Skeffington for the auditorship of the L.&H.
Society.[4] This is incorrect. In 1897 I was still in the Senior Grade at
Belvedere. I never opposed Skeffington. My contest was some years
later against Kennedy.[5] He won by ca 22 to 16 all the U.C. staff voting
for him.[6]   J.J.

To MR and MRS MYRON C. NUTTING   MS. Northwestern
30 June 1937   *7 rue Edmond Valentin, Paris 7ᵉ*

Dear Mr and Mrs Nutting: Mrs Prost called yesterday and gave us
your address and your news after almost nine years I believe. I send you
a copy of *transition* and am hurrying myself with this note to catch the
boat train at S. Lazare. Dear Mrs Nutting, we are very sorry to hear
you have been in bad health and hope you are recovering. It seems
Nutting is well. *Tant mieux.* Lucia has been terribly ill for over five
years. She was given up and still we hoped on. Now it seems that she is
at last on the road to recovery. Giorgio is married and we have a
grandson Stevie aged 5½. Mrs Wallace is in London. I think she stays
with the Mackenzies and is a face *masseuse.* We have not been to Les
Trianons for years as we always go to Fouquet's. Giorgio had great
trouble with his thyroid gland but is now quite cured. Friendliest
remembrances from us both   JAMES JOYCE

[1] From a typewritten copy.
[2] *A Page of Irish History, 1883–1909*, compiled by the Fathers of the Society of Jesus
(Dublin and Cork, 1930).
[3] University College, Dublin.   [4] Literary and Historical Society.
[5] Hugh Boyle Kennedy (1879–1936), later the first Chief Justice of the Supreme Court
of the Irish Free State.
[6] Professor Felix E. Hackett, in *Centenary History of the Literary and Historical
Society of University College Dublin 1855–1955*, ed. James Meenan (Tralee, 1955?),
says the vote was 15 to 9 against Joyce (p. 61). The same figures are given on p. 327.

To HELEN JOYCE   MS. Kastor

25 July 1937   *Paris*

Dear Helen: . . . I hope Stevie is all right by now. Call at the hotel for the presents sent to Giorgio. We rang up your cook's clinic. She was operated and is well (4 p m today). Perhaps she may be visited by my wife tomorrow. Rang up the villa today. No answer. I think the other girl is gone. So I can't find the dog's address. Looked all over the *armoire* but can't imagine which of all the vets is yours? Let me know and will keep you posted. Unless Bertie your cook can tell us. . . .

    Glad you have got a house. Have a rest, *tout le monde*. . . .   BABBO

To HELEN JOYCE (Postcard)   MS. Kastor

2 August 1937   *Paris*

Just a scribbled line to say we got your letter. Will write tomorrow. A friend of Bertie's rang up yesterday to say she, B. was going yesterday not to her sister but to the flat of some friend, who would nurse her as she is not yet over strong. She will 'phone us later. Rang up the dog's home. S. all right. Going to Versailles 'un de ces jours' Saluti a tutti   B

To DAVID FLEISCHMAN   MS. Fleischman

8 August 1937   *7 rue Edmond Valentin, Paris 7ᵉ*

Dear David: If your mother has had more quieting news from New York and if you can find an evening hour in this blistering heat cooled off by *imber serotinus*[1] I should be much obliged if you could do me a favour.

    I have sent you registered a book[2] you certainly will have read as a young boy, probably more than once. I need to know something about it. I never read it and have nobody to read it to me and it takes too much time with all I am doing. Could you perhaps refresh your memory by a hasty glance through and then dictate to your mother (who, I hope, will buy me a bunch of new ribbons to spry up—her typewriter) an account of the plot in general as if it were a new book the tale of which

---

    [1] 'Evening rain,' a phrase from the Vulgate, Deuteronomy 11.14.
    [2] Mark Twain, *Huckleberry Finn*. There are scattered references to this book in *Finnegans Wake*. See Glasheen, *A Census of Finnegans Wake*, p. 38, and the *Finnegans Wake* holograph notebook VI. B.46 at Buffalo which contains material based on David Fleischman's work.

you had to narrate in a book review. After that I should like you to
mark with blue pencil in the margin the most important passages of the
plot itself and in red pencil here and there wherever the words or
dialogue seem to call for the special attention of a European. Don't
care about spoiling the book. It is a cheap edition. If you can then
return it to me soon I shall try to use whatever bears upon what I am
doing.

Many thanks in advance but if for any reason you cannot do this it
will be no great loss.

The heat is abominable. I hope you all, especially Stevie,[1] keep out of
the sight of that monotonous old gasometer,[2] the sun. Sincerely yours

JAMES JOYCE

To FRANK BUDGEN   MS. Yale

9 August 1937   *Paris*

Dear Budgen: If you are all right in this heat wave could you make for
me a *précis* of the plot of the book[3] I sent you, marking the margins
wherever you like in *blue* when the marked passage is noteworthy and
bears on the plot as you sent it red [sic] and in *red* when there is some
special attraction in the style or better in the dialogue? In this way I
can get an idea of the book in an hour or so. Terribly overworked on
proofs of W i P. which I should finish by end of year.

Hope Mrs Budgen and Joan are thriving also yourself sincerely yours

JAMES JOYCE

To GEORGE JOYCE (Postcard)   MS. Kastor

9 August 1937   *Paris*

My wife went up to see the cook and brought her fruit. She's all right
and gets up tomorrow. I hope the old bowler is too for these are his days.
Sending you a book about basques which you may read in the shade.[4]
Hope you have better news from N.Y. The heat is disgusting Saluti a
tutti   B.

[1] Stephen James Joyce.   [2] *Finnegans Wake*, pp. 95, 131.
[3] J. Sheridan Le Fanu, *The House by the Churchyard* (1863). See p. 301.
[4] Possibly an answer to a remark about 'basking in the sun', though it also reflects
Joyce's study at this time of Basque words.

To C. P. CURRAN[1]   MS. Curran

Postmark 17 August 1937   [*Basel*]

P.S. to my former letter.[2] I forgot to thank you for sending the teapot
to Galway[3] and Mrs Curran especially. It arrived all right. I hope they
put on the kettle and live happily.[4] (Also forgot to say that D-J Reddin[5]
arrived here as envoy of the Irish Pen Club. I, having been selected by
the French Committee, as one of the five guests of honour had the
additional honour of receiving him at my table—by no means for the
first time, may I add very dryly! He mentioned my sister who, he says, is
crazy.) I see one of your neighbours Mr Lennon[6] has also reached the
bench. Another to whom I had the honour of being host and to whom I
presented at his request, a signed copy of *Ulysses* after which, in an
article in the *Catholic World* U.S.A. he informed the Teagues that I had
acquired my 'abundant means' by selling to the British authorities in
Rome during the war everything I knew about the Austria which had
released me on *parole*. (I was in Switzerland during the war and for 4[7]
years in a lawsuit against the British Consulate in Zurich, a suit I won)
So much for Ireland's hearts and hands.

But most of all what I also want are the following numbers of the
Weekly Irish Times.

1933	Jan 7	1934	Jan 26
	Jan 21	1936	Aug 1 (4 copies)
	Feb 25		Aug 29
	Oct 14		July 18

With kind regards   J.J.

To MRS JOHN SULLIVAN   MS. S. Illinois (Feinberg)

27 August 1937   *Carlton Elite Hotel, Zurich*

Chère Madame Sullivan: Nous vous remercions beaucoup de votre
aimable lettre et des bonnes nouvelles qu'elle contient. Vous seriez bien
aimable aussi d'affranchiser la lettre ci-incluse (65c) et la mettre à Paris
comme si elle avait été envoyée par moi comme d'habitude.[8] J'espère
qu'à votre prochaine visite vous trouverez ma fille également bien. Et

---

[1] From a typewritten copy.   [2] Of 6 August 1937 (*Letters*, ed. Gilbert, pp. 394–95).
[3] That is, to Nora Joyce's sister Kathleen and her husband, John Griffin, who were
just married.
[4] Traditional ending of oral tale, much used in *Finnegans Wake*.
[5] Kenneth Shiels Reddin, Irish District Justice since 1922.
[6] See p. 235, n. 7.
[7] Hyperbole for two years.
[8] Joyce knew his absence from Paris disturbed Lucia, so when he went to Zurich he
had his letters to her posted as if from Paris.

comment va la volière ?[1] Il me semble que vous avez pas mal de charges de notre part. Le temps ici n'est pas fameux et je crois qu'on va bientôt rentrer on France. En tout cas vous pouvez toujours envoyer une carte à cette adresse.

Nous espérons que tout va bien chez vous et que Jacques[2] commence déjà casser les vitres à la manière de . . . votre bien devoué

JAMES JOYCE[3]

To FRANK BUDGEN   MS. Yale

28 August 1937   *Z'ch*

Thanks for the photo of yourself and daughter which is certainly she and you. Our compliments to the mother as well.

If you publish any articles on any subject tell me where I can see them.[4] I hope you will be able to do that for me but if you feel you cannot do so soon please send it back registered so that I may try elsewhere.

This copy of a Dublin 'throwaway' is a highly entertaining document to John Joyce's son. Whence comes this phantom ship and why ?[5]   J.J.

PS. By the way what of my mariner[6] in last *transition* ?

[1] Mrs Sullivan was taking care of the Joyces' canaries while they were in Zurich.
[2] The Sullivans' son.
[3] (Translation)
    'Dear Mrs Sullivan: We thank you very much for your kind letter and for the good news contained in it. Please be so kind as to stamp the letter enclosed (65 centimes) and post it in Paris as if it had been sent by me in the ordinary way. I hope that you will find my daughter just as well when you next go to see her. And how is the aviary? I am afraid you have taken on quite a few responsibilities on our behalf. The weather here is nothing much and I think we will come back to France soon. In any case you can always send a postcard to this address.
    We hope you are all well and that Jacques is beginning to break windows just like . . .
your very devoted   James Joyce'
[4] Joyce hoped Budgen might write an article praising Lucia's designs.
[5] Someone had sent Joyce a throwaway which said, 'Dublin Tenders Limited / 3 hour coastal cruise on board / pleasure steamer / J O H N   J O Y C E / sailing from Victoria Wharf, Dun Laoghaire / (weather and other circumstances permitting).' It fascinated Joyce (see *Letters*, ed. Gilbert, pp. 396–97), but neither he nor Budgen was able to find out the history of this ship. T. St. John Barry, of Independent Television News Ltd, London, informs me that the *John Joyce* was originally a River Mersey ferry boat, owned by the corporation of the County of Wallasey. Its original name was the 'Bluebell', then the 'Heatherbell', both of which names were refused by the Ferries Committee. At last it was decided to name her after the chairman of the committee, John Joyce. The *John Joyce* operated on the Mersey for twenty-six years, then was purchased in November 1936 by Messrs Palgrave, Murphy and Co. of Dublin, then in 1946 was bought by the Cork Harbour Commissioners who used her as a tender to meet the liners at Cobh harbour and after some time renamed her the 'Shandon'. In 1952 the 'Shandon' was sold and broken up at Passage.
[6] The Norwegian captain.

To ADOLPH KASTOR[1]   MS. Mrs Isaiah Rubin
30 August 1937   *Carlton Elite Hotel, Zurich*

Dear Mr Kastor: My wife and I have waited for some time before
venturing to convey to you our deep sympathy with you in the all but
tragic event which has taken place in your family. It now seems as if the
worst were really no longer to be dreaded and therefore I am writing to
say that we hope in spite of what has happened that eventually some
good may come of it. It is a terrible affliction to be cast upon you at your
age and it is a terrible trial for your poor son for whom everybody I
know that knows him has esteem and affection. We ourselves for the
past six years have undergone a dreadful strain on account of our
daughter Lucia whose happy and promising youth has been blighted by
another but perhaps even more incurable form of mental or moral
derangement. I have used the word 'incurable' because it was used so
often by doctors to me but it is entirely false. After that long ordeal to
herself and to us she is, in the opinion of everyone, slowly coming round
again. The famous Russian ballet dancer Nijinsky has been pronounced
also 'incurable' for the past eighteen years. Yet according to Dr
Binswamer[2] here (whose brother has him in charge at Kreuzlingen) he
also is on the road to recovery in consequence of an insulin or glandular
treatment. Your son's case cannot be nearly so bad as his (in spite of
what has happened) and very possibly the awful shock to himself may
have the effect of restoring the balance of his mind and bringing the
will to live and be happy again to the sufferer in spite of the malady's
workings. I sincerely trust that this may be so. The actual physical
disfigurement might be much worse as a result of a train or a machinery
accident and it may prove to be only a tribute which he had to pay in
order to buy off a demoniac possession.

I hope therefore to hear from Helen that time as it goes on will heal
not only the physical but the spiritual wounds and that you yourself
will soon find some solace in the certitude that an irreparable loss has
been averted. Sincerely yours   JAMES JOYCE

To WILHELM HERZ (WILLIAM H. HARTLEY)   MS. Hartley
30 August 1937   *Carlton Elite Hotel, Zurich*

Dear Mr Hertz: Will you please fill in the address on the enclosed letter
for me (I don't know it) and forward it to Helen's father? Many thanks.

[1] Helen Joyce's father.
[2] Dr Ludwig Binswanger (b. 1881), Medical Superintendent of Sanatorium Bellevue
at Kreuzlingen.

We are here but perhaps we shall leave for France on tomorrow or on Wednesday. We did not care to ring you up yesterday it being your first Sunday at home since you got back from holidays. Of course we should be delighted to see you but I fancy only your weekends are free.

There is something which I am very curious to find out. Have you a doctor in St Gallen or anybody else who knows the doctors (Binswamer etc) in the Kreuzlingen Sanatorium (about 30 Km off) where the famous Russian dancer Nijinsky has been for the past 18 years. He was supposed to be an absolutely hopeless case of *dementia praecox* and yet according to sensational reports a week ago in the press he is now miraculously cured as a result of insulin treatment. My reason for being curious is that only a fortnight ago it was proposed to me in Paris to submit Lucia to this identical treatment. There is no doubt about it that she is better as a result of glandular treatment during the past 18 months and I shall hesitate to have recourse to any more drastic method. Still since I am here on the spot I should very much like to know if this cure is authentic. If it is I believe it will or ought to revolutionise the treatment of mental-moral maladies which are also clearly physical.

Our friendly regards to Mrs Herz and yourself sincerely yours

JAMES JOYCE

To VISCOUNT CARLOW   MS. Yale

31 August 1937   *Carlton Elite Hotel, Zurich*

Dear Lord Carlow: I hope Lady Carlow and yourself enjoyed your trip round the North. I have been (unsuccessfully) dodging thunderstorms along the Rhine valley. We return to France tomorrow and to Paris in a week or so. Should I still be away when you come please ring up my friend Paul Léon. Mr Louis Golding did not call me up or write.

I forget whether it is mentioned on the title page that the *lettrine* is by my daughter? Is it?[1]

I have been working altogether too much at my book, now in its final stages. I wish it were in its final-final.

I have been trying to spin out the days until the first performance here of your operatic namesake, Verdi's *Don Carlo* but it is still ten days off. And we have had our fill of thunder-laden, lightning-furrowed Mitteleuropa's schöne Sommerzeit.[2] Sincerely yours   JAMES JOYCE

---

[1] When *Storiella as She Is Syung* was published in October 1937, the colophon explicitly stated: 'The illuminated capital letter at the beginning is the work of Lucia Joyce the author's daughter.'
[2] 'Central Europe's lovely summertime.'

To VISCOUNT CARLOW   MS. Yale

14 September 1937   [*Dieppe*]

Dear Lord Carlow: Just a line to say I got your letter here and it will be
all right if you put that information in the colophon (but I should like
to see the proof, if you can send it, because it should also say that the
piece is 'opening and closing pages of'.[1] Do you not think so?

I am sorry I did not overhear your talk with the Viking. Sincerely
yours   JAMES JOYCE

To MRS JOHN SULLIVAN   MS. S. Illinois (Feinberg)

24 September 1937   *Paris*

Chère Madame: Voulez-vous bien donner ces deux petits paquets à ma
fille si vous allez la voir dimanche. Le Docteur Achille Delmas est de
retour mais il ne semble pas très enthousiaste. Il m'a dit au téléphone
qu'il trouve son état stationnaire. Demandez-lui (à Lucia) si elle a reçu
la lettre de Sullivan en réponse de la sienne car autrement il faut que je
me charge de lui offrir des billets pour l'infirmiére à son insu, naturellement. Ma femme le trouve étrange quand méme qu'elle n'accuse pas
réception des chargements etc. par un petit mot. Et à propos j'ai oublié
de lui écrire que c'est sa belle-sœur qui lui a envoyé la ceinture. En
somme si vous pouvez nous donner un coup de téléphone après nous
l'apprécierons. J'espère qu'elle fait toujours un peu de musique.
Remerciements d'avance votre bien devoué   JAMES JOYCE[2]

To FRANK BUDGEN (Postcard)   MS. Yale

13 October 1937   *Paris*

Hope you are all well. If you have had time to mark that book[3] I should
like to have it back soon to see the passages. Am working very hard at
W i P and may finish it in some near time. Greetings   J.J.

---

[1] 'This book comprises the opening and closing pages of Part II: Section II: of "Work
in Progress".' From the colophon of *Storiella as She Is Syung.*

[2] (Translation)

'Dear Madame: Would you be so good as to take these two little packages to my
daughter if you go to see her on Sunday. Dr Achille Delmas is back but he does not
seem very enthusiastic. He told me on the telephone that he considers her condition to
be stationary. Ask her (Lucia) if she received Sullivan's letter answering hers for
otherwise I must take it upon myself to offer her the tickets for the nurse, of course
without her knowledge. My wife thinks it strange none the less that she has not
acknowledged receipt of the packages etc. by a note. And touching this subject, I
forgot to write to her that it was her sister-in-law who sent her the belt. In short if you
can ring us up afterwards we shall be grateful. I hope she keeps up her music somewhat. Thanks in advance your devoted friend   James Joyce'

[3] Le Fanu's *The House by the Churchyard.*

To EZRA POUND   MS. Pound

28 October 1937   *7 rue Edmond Valentin, Paris 7ᵉ*

Dear Pound: Your letter was delayed in transit. I have now rung up
Mrs Dyer (whom I know personally) but find she is in London and is
not expected back till the middle of next week. I shall ring her up again
on Wednesday or Thursday next and let you know.

Thanks for kind messages. I hope Mrs Pound, yourself and the boy
are all well. We are, I hope. Lucia has been ill but is now much better,
I am glad to say.

As a matter of fact I thought of going your way a few months ago
when, being in Zurich and wishing to go to the coast, I found that
Genoa (to my surprise) was only 9 hours away

That is a fine likeness of you in the corner of your notepaper. Tante
belle cose da noi tutti Una stretta di mano[1]   JAMES JOYCE

To VISCOUNT CARLOW   MS. Yale

1 November 1937 All Saints   *Paris*

Dear Lord Carlow: Thanks for the copies of Lewis's drawing.[2] If it is
not as good as others of his the sitter is at fault. We are sorry to hear
you had such a stormy homegoing. The last part is amusing, but in
retrospect only. I wish you better air luck.

The Librairie Rouge et Cie of Lausanne would like to have a
prospectus of the book. They bought the *A.B.C.*[3] The name is is [sic]
really Rouge. I mean it is not a symbol of any kind.

I shall add in a postscript the address of W K Magee ('John Eglinton')
if I can find it. He told me when I wrote to him some years ago that he
believed he could get for me the music of *Follow me up to Carlow* about
which—and *The Lord in His Mercy be Kind to Belfast*—about which I
had written to him. The tune is alluded to twice, I think, in *W i P.*[4]
sincerely yours   JAMES JOYCE

PS 21 Carberry Avenue
    West Southbourne
    Bournemouth

[1] 'All good wishes from us all. A handshake'
[2] One of several drawings which Wyndham Lewis made of Joyce.
[3] *A Chaucer A.B.C.*
[4] 'Follow Me Up to Carlow' appears seven times in *Finnegans Wake*. Hodgart and
Worthington, *Song in the Works of James Joyce*, p. 183.

To CAROLA GIEDION-WELCKER   MS. Giedion-Welcker

5 December 1937   *Paris*

Dear Mrs Giedion: If you have finished reading Dr Berman's book will
you please send it back as another person has asked me for it. I hope
that your daughter is better but one must have patience. Lucia had a
set-back some weeks ago but is now getting slowly better. These cases
always have their ups and downs. I suppose you are going up in the
Himalayas Helvétiques for Xmas. Do you happen to know anybody who
is coming soon to Paris because I should like him to bring me 10 (or
more?) Brissago cigars (*not* the 'Blaubart' mark). He can bring 10
without paying duty and they are all ready made up in a carton in every
Z'ch shop. Of course I'll pay and if . . he brings more, *tant mieux*.

Friendly greetings to you both   J.J.

From PAUL LÉON to HARRIET SHAW WEAVER TS. British Museum

18 December 1937   [*Paris*]

Dear Miss Weaver, Mr Joyce has given me a considerable amount of
autograph pages which are destined for you. They are additional pages
of corrections and enlargements for Part II of WIP. May I know
whether I can send them to your usual address as I remember that in
one of your last letters you were contemplating to move from there.

I am seeing Mr. Joyce rather rarely now and then only for work. My
part of it seems to be done but it takes some five or six other people
to check the corrections, verify the additions and read the proofs.
Himself, he does the composing part quite alone and from what I hear
of Mr. Joyce, he works daily to about five in the morning.

Mrs. Léon joins me in sending you our best Christmas wishes.

With kind regards. Sincerely yours.   PAUL LÉON.

To ALFRED BERGAN   MS. N.Y. Public Library (Manuscript)

21 December 1937   *7 rue Edmond Valentin, Paris 7ᵉ*

Dear Mr Bergan: The enclosed small offering in the name of our festive
past. I hope you are well and in good spirits for the Christmas and send
you many friendly remembrances. I hope you will lift your glass to me as
I shall do to you. Your old friend   JAMES JOYCE

To CAROLA GIEDION-WELCKER   MS. Giedion-Welcker

31 December 1937 New Year's Eve   *Paris*

Dear Mrs Giedion, Here is Dr Berman's[1] reply to my letter from Z'ch!!!

I hope the news of your daughter is better. I was with Lucia all Xmas afternoon. She is better but my opinion is she is not yet in a stable state. However, she is hopeful herself. Perhaps this year will cure her.

Giorgio and Helen have to leave for New York at practically a moment's notice as her father is gravely ill—operation to take place on Monday. We passed a bad Xmas and look as if we were going to have a worse S. Sylvester Night![2]

Nevertheless, good luck to you both for '38. *transition* held up. At the last moment I decided to collaborate! I hope to finish W.i.P. for 2 Feb. Sincerely yours   JAMES JOYCE

To CAROLA GIEDION-WELCKER (Postcard)   MS. Giedion-Welcker

Postmark 2 January 1938   *[Paris]*

Dear Mrs Giedion: Many thanks for the Brissagos which E.J.[3] brought and congratulations to Prof. Giedion on his Harvard nomination.[4] We are glad to hear your daughter is so much better. Lucia unfortunately continues to have a disconcerting and persistent relapse. We are thinking of going to Z'ch for a couple of weeks after my birthday (Maria Lichtmesse)[5] if all goes well. My son and family are in N.Y. I am working night and day and the last thing I shall publish in serial form will be in the coming *transition*.

Kind regards to you both sincerely yours   JAMES JOYCE

To GEORGE and HELEN JOYCE   MS. Kastor

12 January 1938 noon   *Paris*

Dear Giorgio and Helen: Your N.Y. cable came this morning. We are glad to hear you are all well and hope you had not a bad crossing.[6] No specially bad weather was announced in the press. We hope, Helen, you found your father in better state and on the way to a recovery which

---

[1] Joyce wrote to Berman, a gland specialist, to see what he would recommend for the Giedions' daughter.

[2] 31 December.   [3] Eugene Jolas.

[4] As Charles Eliot Norton Professor.   [5] Candlemas.

[6] George and Helen Joyce went to the United States, because of her father's illness, at the end of December 1937. They returned on 26 April 1938.

will render an operation unnecessary. Your first letter, however, will give us fuller news and we hope better news though today's is not bad.

Nino Frank dined with us on Sunday. According to him the Luxembourg people[1] would like to engage Giorgio's voice definitely, that is, for a certain number of broadcasts each month. So he seems to have made an excellent impression. I have sent them a reminder this morning that I am still waiting for the disc. Lord Carlow was here yesterday with the sheets for me to sign.[2] He got Giorgio's letter. I gave him the N. Y. Herald for the B.B.C. people and sent it also to Dulanty and the Luxembourg station. Mrs Jolas came back on Sunday. Jolas is in Zurich. I hope the winter is not too severe over there. I have not much news. I am rather tired as I worked very late but will add a postscript when I come back before this is mailed. We are going to the hospital to see Beckett.[3] I send you two bundles of papers.

P.S. 2 pm. Siamo tornati dall'ospedale. Oramai egli è fuori di pericolo. La stilettata era al di sopra del cuore. Questo è illeso, i polmoni anche ma c'è una perforazione della pleura, l'involucro circondante la pleura. La casa mia il giorno dopo la tua partenza era come la borsa, telefonate da ogni dove. Si saprà più di quest'affare quando sarà portato al tribunale. La polizia arrestò l'aggreditore ieri l'altro. La ferita non lascerà tracce pregiudiziali, dice il dott. Farvert che rimpiazza la Fontaine in quell'ospedale. Beckett l'ha scappata bella. Non avevo torto dunque d'allarmarmi quando appresi che aveva fatto una nottata fuori dell'albergo. Sua madre e suo fratello giunsero qui tre giorni fa col velivolo. Ho visto lui ma non lei. Insomma di quei due spromessi sposi[4] ambedue, cioè ed Enzo e Lucia, sono ora all'ospedale. Buona fortuna costì Ti abbraccio   BABBO[5]

---

[1] Radio Luxembourg.

[2] The first 25 copies of *Storiella as She Is Syung* were signed by Joyce in the colophon. The whole edition consisted of 175 copies.

[3] Samuel Beckett was gratuitously stabbed in Paris, and refused to prosecute his assailant.

[4] A play on the Italian classic novel, Alessandro Manzoni, *I Promessi Sposi* (1825–26), and on the fact that the young woman in the book is named Lucia. The young man is Renzo.

[5] (Translation)

'P.S. 2 p.m. We are back from the hospital, he is now out of danger. The stab was above the heart; that is uninjured, and the lungs also, but there is a perforation of the pleura, the layer of tissue surrounding the pleura. My house on the day after your departure was like the stock exchange, telephone calls from everywhere. We will know more about the affair when it goes to court. The police arrested the assailant the day before yesterday. The wound will not leave any harmful aftereffects, according to Dr Farvert who took Dr Fontaine's place at the hospital. Beckett has had a lucky escape. I had good reason to be alarmed when I heard he had spent the night away from his hotel. His mother and brother arrived here three days ago by airplane. I have seen him but not her. So, as for these two unbetrothed lovers, both, to wit Enzo and Lucia, are now in the hospital. Good luck there I embrace you   Babbo'

To HELEN JOYCE   MS. Kastor

20 January 1938   *Parigi*

Dear Helen: I hope you found your father and brother better than you
had expected and that we shall have good news when a letter comes from
N.Y. So far we had just the note Giorgio wrote on board which seemed
all right. The boat carrying this was harbour-bound yesterday. You
just got over before a terrific ocean storm. Not much news here. I rang
up your villa about a dozen times at different hours to find out if there
was any news and also to see had the case of S. Patrice[1] arrived. No
answer. Please thank the Turners[2] for the Xmas card from the ends of
the earth. It came yesterday. I am writing this in bed on a sloping book
so it is not over legible, as I [am] a bit fatigued. But I have finished the
piece for *Transition.* I hope you are all well.

Caro Giorgio: Col medesimo corriere ti mando una fotografia della
figlia di Dulanty (veramente non è una bellezza) che andò sposa l'altro
giorno ad uno degli ufficiali superiori della B.B.C. Nino Frank ci disse
che la Stazione L.. ma mi pare di avere già scritto ciò. Insomma vorr-
ebbero darti qualche specie d'impiego fisso. La famiglia di Beckett
riparte oggi col velivolo. La Fontaine[3] dice ch'egli dovrà restare
all'ospedale ancora qualche settimana. Era esaminato radiograficamente
ieri. C'è sempre una suffusione sanguigna nella pleura ma non compor-
terà gravi consequenze. Sembra che l'aggressore sia piuttosto uno
squilibrato anzichè delinquente. Così affermò ieri sua sorella Caprinosa
alla prim'udienza dinanzi al giudice istruttore. N. Frank e G. Pellorson
[sic][4] però asseriscono che il Beckett quando è alticcio è alquanto
accattabrighe e si lascia andare facilmente a vie di fatti. Avrò il tuo
disco fra qualche giorno. Spero che avrai l'occasione di cantare costì.
Siete partiti col vento in poppa. Invece da parecchi giorni un libeccio
violentissimo infuria sull'oceano. Meno male per Stevie specialmente.
Ti abbraccio   BABBO[5]

[1] A wine Joyce favoured. See p. 178.

[2] George Turner (b. 1896), and his wife, Rose Kurzman Turner (1891–1940). Turner,
an English businessman living in Paris, subsequently became an American citizen.

[3] Dr Thérèse Bertrand-Fontaine, Joyce's doctor in Paris, who was treating Beckett's
wound.

[4] Georges Pelorson.

[5] (Translation)

'Dear Giorgio: I am sending you by the same post a photograph of Dulanty's
daughter (obviously no beauty) who got married the other day to one of the top officials
of the B.B.C. Nino Frank tells us that Station L.. but it occurs to me I have already
written about that. Anyway they would like to give you some kind of regular position.
Beckett's family goes off today by airplane. Dr Fontaine says he will have to stay at
the hospital for several more weeks. He was given an X-ray examination yesterday.

To FRANK BUDGEN (Postcard)   MS. Yale

27 January 1938[1]   [*Paris*]

Dear Budgen: Can't write much as I have a slight attack in right eye (episcleritis). Sending you Fr. version of impressions of *S.* Have finished and sent to F. F. Pt III of W i P.[2] Can you send me 4 copies of your book. On receipt of invoice will remit amount. Write or have publisher write direct to Galignani and Miss Beach Kindest regards to both   J.J.

From PAUL LÉON to FRANK BUDGEN   TS. Budgen
(Largely dictated by Joyce)

?29 January 1938   *Paris*

Late spring three years ago J.J. coming back from Z'ch after a second visit to Vogt—sight may be a little better.

Concert of Volpi heard. Also much talk about a performance of William Tell with Volpi in the part of Arnold. Conversations with Sullivan establish that Volpi had the entire score cut by some half of it and the key lowered by a half note. This Volpi performance is narrated with all sorts of compliments in the N.Y. Herald (Paris edition) by their official musical critic (M. Louis Schneider). Immediately a letter is written to him containing a wager by Sullivan to let him and Volpi sing both the part of Arnold in the original score in any concert hall—the arbiter to be Mr. Schneider—and the stakes to be a copy of the original full score nicely bound. Naturally no reply from either Schneider or Volpi (considering Schneider had written that nobody at present could sing the part of Arnold as had been done by Volpi).

A week later—performance of Guillaume Tell with Sullivan. Sitting in the fifth row right aisle next to the passage your obedient servant next to him J.J. next to him, Mrs. Léon and next to her Mrs. J—somewhere in the stalls an Irish Miss correspondent of some paper, and a gentleman correspondent of the Neue Züricher Zeitung.

There are still traces of blood in the pleura but it will have no serious consequences. The attacker seems to have been unbalanced rather than delinquent. So his sister Caprinosa insisted yesterday at the first hearing before the examining magistrate. N. Frank and G. Pelorson assert however that Beckett, when he has drunk a bit, is rather quarrelsome and is easily impelled to blows. I will have your disc in a few days. I hope you will get a chance to sing there. You left with the wind in the poop. But for days now a violent southwest wind has been raging on the ocean. Just as well for Stevie especially. I embrace you   Babbo'
[1] Joyce dates the card 1936 but the postmark is clear.
[2] To Faber & Faber Part III of *Work in Progress* (*Finnegans Wake*, pp. 403–590),

First and second act pass with great applause, J.J. being greatly enthused. Third act where there is no Sullivan on the stage spent in the buffet.

Fourth Act after the Aria 'Asile héréditaire' sung with great brio and real feeling by S. applause interminable. J.J. excited to the extreme shouts 'Bravo Sullivan—Merde pour Lauri Volpi'. The abonnés (this being I believe a Friday) rather astonished, one of them saying: Il va un peu fort celui-là.

Half an hour later: at the Café de la Paix. Great conversation in which S. joins after he has changed clothes. At the moment of parting the Neue Züricher Zeitung correspondent having been talked to all evening about music approaches J.J. with the following words:

The Correspondent: Thank you so much for the delightful evening. I have some pull with my paper and should you wish I could arrange for an article or two by you to appear there about your Paris impressions:
J.J: Many thanks but I never write for the newspapers.
The Correspondent: Oh! I see you are simply a musical critic.

Next day article in the press. M. J.J. returned from Z'ch after a successful operation goes with friends to the Opera to hear his compatriot S. sing William Tell. Sitting in a box. After the fourth act aria he takes off his spectacles and is heard saying 'Thank God I have recovered my eyesight'.[1]

To GEORGE and HELEN JOYCE (Postcard)   MS. Kastor

7 February 1938   *Hotel de la Paix, Lausanne*

We called to see Ponisovsky.[2] His morale seems very good and Léon saw the doctor today who is quite satisfied but will not give his final opinion till after an examination on Thursday. He is very brave and cheerful. A bad fog here. We stay a day or two as I want to rest before seeing Vogt. My sight is much easier (100% better according to Collinson). I had no inflammation or redness just fatigue. Am sending this off in a hurry. Forgot to say Soupault and Curran's daughter[3] were at my party too

---

[1] Joyce was telescoping two incidents: (1) his taking off his bandages and crying out that he had recovered his sight; and (2) his shouting 'Bravo Sullivan—Merde pour Lauri Volpi'. By this time he apparently wished the former to be considered a journalistic invention, but his correspondence in 1930 indicates it was a carefully planned manoeuvre. See p. 199.

[2] Alexander Ponisovsky.

[3] Elizabeth Curran.

and Mlle Suzy, the hatter, sent a message to the *maître* (i.e. J.J.) saying *Ulysse* had opened up a new world for her. A.P.[1] sends greetings Tante belle cose a tutti

BABBO

To EZRA POUND   MS. Pound

9 February 1938   *Carlton Elite Hotel, Zurich*

Dear Pound: Retinal congestion suddenly developed in my left (the only one really left) eye in consequence of months of day and (literally) allnight work in finishing W i P. and I had to leave Paris and come here to see Prof. Vogt. All writing and reading were stopped but it was only strain and righted itself with a few weeks rest and I am now allowed 2 or 3 hours a day work. So I am writing to Hauptmann[2] by the next post both to explain and to thank him

I think I can now also send on your different enclosures to la Dyer ?[3]
I don't think I ever worked so hard even at *Ulysses*.
Galeotto è il libro e chi lo scrive.[4] Tante belle cose sincerely yours

JAMES JOYCE

To WILHELM HERZ (WILLIAM H. HARTLEY)   MS. Hartley

22 February 1938   *Carlton Elite Hotel, Zurich*

Dear Mr and Mrs Hertz: We hope you got home all right in the dark. Here is the come-all-you about the turkey.[5] You may copy it if you wish but please return it as I have no other myself. I have just had tea with your aunt and we got on very well together, I think, as I tried my clearest tenor tones. Greetings to you both sincerely yours

JAMES JOYCE

[1] Arthur Power.
[2] Joyce was aware that Ezra Pound and Gerhart Hauptmann lived near each other in Rapallo. In a letter of 12 November 1937 (*Letters*, ed. Gilbert, p. 398) he asked Pound to help him obtain Hauptmann's signature on a copy of *Michael Kramer*, one of the two plays by Hauptmann that he had attempted to translate in his youth. Pound agreed on 8 December 1937, 'Send the bloody book *here*, and when his nibs gets here I will lay it on the café table before him and say the grreat Jayzus James the Joyce in excelsis, rejoice in excelsis, wants the Xmas angels to sign it.' *Letters of Ezra Pound*, ed. Paige, p. 300.
[3] Pound was eager to have some of Jenkins's music performed, and Joyce thought Mrs Dyer would be interested.
[4] 'Galeotto fu il libro e chi lo scrisse.' Dante, *Inferno*, V, l. 137. 'Galeotto was the book and he that wrote it.' Galeotto was the pander who brought Lancelot and Guinevere together; the book about these three was the one that made Paolo and Francesca fall in love. Joyce alters the past tense to the present and uses the word 'Galeotto' to mean something like maledetto (cursed).
[5] For text of this 'Come-all-you', written for a Thanksgiving Day party at the Jolases', see *Pastimes of James Joyce* (New York, 1941) pp. 6-7.

To HERBERT GORMAN   MS. S. Illinois (Croessmann)
(Postcard)

22 February 1938   *Z'ch*

> 'Je ne suis pas *où* que l'on pense,
> Je ne suis pas où que l'on dit'[1]   J.J·

From PAUL LÉON to   TS. Giedion-Welcker
CAROLA GIEDION-WELCKER

9 March 1938   *Paris, as from 7 rue Edmond Valentin*

Dear Mrs Giedion, The books arrived safely and I am taking her copy
out to Miss Joyce to-morrow in order to find out also how she really is
as the reports are quite conflicting. Thanks also for the telegram, letters,
papers and photos. He says you can reproduce anyone but he prefers
the ones with his back turned. In fact if you could send him 4 or 5 of
these he would be thankful. He also got the Urban prospectus and will
wire here if returning to Zürich.

He thanks you for having run down the hall so quickly with the 300
frs the morning he left; evidently you have more trust in him, he says,
than the cashier of the Elite[2] who on Saturday afternoon last August
refused to cash a check—a draft of Lloyd's Bank London, on the
Kredit Anstalt next door—until it had been honoured. Of course it was
honoured the first thing on Monday morning, but in the meantime he
was left for the week-end with a couple of francs in his pocket—all his
Zürich friends being on vacation and even the concierge Phillipe having
a day off. It is this same cashier or receptionist who refused to remove
him for one night to quiet rooms in the hotel until he heard that they
had engaged rooms by telephone at the Hotel Neuer Schlop, and
finally tried to charge him double or treble prices for the two very
frugal meals he took in his room. As he has been going there for a dozen
years and has sometimes made stays of 3 and 7 months in the hotel
besides bringing friends there (one night I believe he entertained the
whole staff with a champagne supper which lasted till morning) besides
being extremely liberal with his gratuities such treatment is really
unexampled in his experience of hotels.

---

[1] Probably, as Stuart Gilbert suggests, Joyce's variant on the old *devinette*:

> Je ne suis pas ce que je suis,
> Car si j'étais ce que je suis
> Je ne serais pas ce que je suis.

('I am not what I follow, For if I were what I follow, I would not be what I am.')

[2] The Carlton Elite Hotel in Zurich, where Joyce usually stayed.

Now with regard to his eyes, I am enclosing a short typewritten report which you can perhaps leave with Fräulein Finker. From it you will see that what happened was exactly what he felt was coming on, and though it is impossible to be sure in these cases, he thinks it might have been avoided had he stayed on a few days more.

He hopes you are well. I am enclosing a 50 frs note to cover telegraph and postal expenses on his behalf—as you have also to send back to him the set of proofs and galleys. He hopes the Nizam[1] took the little New Yorker with him up to Davos. He will write to you about your article as soon as he is able to write, in the meantime he thanks you for your kindness. With kindest regards Sincerely yours   PAUL LÉON

P.S. If after having read the report Vogt has anything to say you might perhaps kindly ring up his secretary and find out what it is.

P.P.S. Soeben erhalte ich Ihren Brief—Die Elite hat sich nochmals unangenehm bewiesen—Sie konnten sogar nicht sie verteidigen [?]! Danke sehr für den Brief.[2]

From PAUL LÉON to   MS. Giedion-Welcker
CAROLA GIEDION-WELCKER (Postcard)

10 March 1938   [*Paris*]

Dear Mrs Giedion, Thanks again for your letter. I forgot to say that Mr J. will be glad if you personally will see that the volume of his poems and paper-jacket are returned to Dr Schoeck.[3] He thinks it likely that some of the verses will please him for musical setting. He says the hotel people have a cyclist chasseur and a telephone, but they would not use either though they knew how anxious he was about the arrival of the book. Incredible as it may seem he assures me that during all his many residences in the hotel besides paying his bill with his 10 or 15% service he has as regularly as the clock paid no less than 1000 french francs in tips beginning with 50 Swiss francs per month to the concierge and so on down to the chasseur. He suggests that the 1939 Ausstellung give the hotel a diploma as the 'Gemeinste Kneip[4] in Swindlerland'. Sincerely yours   PAUL LÉON

[1] A joking reference to Sigfried Giedion.
[2] 'I have just now received your letter—The Elite has behaved badly once again—even you could not excuse them. Thank you for the letter.'
[3] Othmar Schoeck (1886–1957), the composer, whose music for fourteen songs by Gottfried Keller, *Lebendig Begraben*, pleased Joyce very much.
[4] 'Meanest dive.'

To CAROLA GIEDION-WELCKER   MS. Giedion-Welcker

28 March 1938   *Paris*

Dear Mrs Giedion: Excuse this scribble. I am still ill—not eyes but
grip [sic]. In fact have been ill since I left Z'ch. Transition, of course, is
not yet out. I send you a copy of *Verve*.[1] There are several mistakes in
my text—misprints. But I am so tired I can't correct them. It's a pity
you didn't quote the sentences about Sihl and Limmat in your article on
me? They are in *Anna Livia Plurabelle*.[2] Also I got *Zur*,[3] thanks and if
you could send me 2 others, 1 for Giorgio 1 for Lucia. She has to be
radiographed in the morning as it is thought she may have some local
infection in teeth, none in any fool glands. All I can say about the
future in Z'ch is I hope whoever has it will respect Villa Giedion,
Othmar Schoeck, Vogt's clinic and the Kronenhalle.[4] But he can hang
all the staff of the Elite Hotel in comfortable sacks out of their own
windows for all I care and meanwhile Heaven help the poor jews who
fall into the hands of Mr Prager's[5] cashier.

Yes, I would like 4 or 5 of the photos in which my back is turned. This
is my favorite portrait of myself. Thanks, dear Mrs Giedion. At last a
view of myself which I can look at with some pleasure.

I hope Giedion is getting on well with his *Little New Yorker*.

I have no idea whether my son intends to return now as planned on
the 20 April. They seem to be very nervous No wonder.

I hope your daughter is getting on well. She has youth on her side and
will live down whatever she has wrong with her.

Friendly greetings from us both sincerely yours   JAMES JOYCE

To HELEN JOYCE   MS. Kastor

6 April 1938   *Paris*

Dear Helen: I am glad to hear you are so far improved that you are
going to the theatre as we see by your letter or rather Giorgio's which
also says you have booked on the *Queen Mary*. I shall arrange as you
wish with the Turners. Apparently they are not to be back today as

[1] 'A Phoenix Park Nocturne,' *Verve* (Paris) I.2 (March–June 1938) 26 (*Finnegans Wake*, pp. 244–46).
[2] The Sihl and Limmat are two rivers that meet at Zurich. See *Finnegans Wake*: 'legging a jig or so on the sihl to show them how to shake their benders' (p. 200), 'Yssel that the limmat!' (p. 198).
[3] Probably the *Neue Zürcher Zeitung*.
[4] A favourite restaurant of Joyce in Zurich.
[5] Prager was manager of the Carlton Elite Hotel in Zurich.

their concierge said since you give date of their arrival as 10 circ.
Anyhow I'll ring them up. By the same boat I had a long letter from
David[1] chiefly about Russian literature and his work. He wants to be a
jazz critic, I gather. We went to Gurievich's[2] concert. It was in a small
club hall, see enclosed. Paul Valéry was to have spoken but someone of
his family died and he sent a letter. Fernand Gregh[3] the poet spoke. He
was a friend of D'Annunzio's and in fact I think *L'Innocente* is dedicated
to him.[4] There was quite a pleasant atmosphere. G. played very well but
he then spoiled our hearing of the readings by walking about the hall.
Not knowing it was he I told him over my shoulder in French to sit down
in the name of God. He was quite unconscious. I didn't see Zecchi[5] there.
Perhaps I found his address too late. We went with Nino Frank. The
music of Pizzetti and Debussy was very charming. There was nothing
political or fashionable about it but one came away with a pleasant
taste in one's ears. He wanted to do a Franz concert for May. In view of
Giorgio's statement that he needs to gargle a few weeks first I shall say
nothing encouraging and leave the whole thing in the air till you arrive.

I really know nothing about Mrs K-F[6] except the two versions of her
children's death (neither of which seems to trouble her overmuch) and
the fact that she asked the pleasure of our company at dinner, which I
could hardly get out of being there in Lausanne. I will not say anything
to anybody about the letter you mention. It is rather curious that the
two men[7] in whom poor Lucia tried to see whatever she or any other
woman or girl is looking for should now be going around with two sisters.
After having got up, each of them, from a hospital bed. And that I
should have gone from one bed to the other.

Tonight we are to dine at the Gormans as it is her birthday and she
told me Beckett and Miss Curran are to be there. The Gorman child
scalded all the skin off both her legs and was in bed a month. I have not
seen Beckett for some weeks. I have had no time to see anybody as I had
a lot of interviewing and telephoning to do about this new doctor's idea.[8]

The Turners or Returners will be back at 10 p m but can't meet them
as we are going out to dine. So sent them flowers.

All right. We won't go to Cherbourg.[9] Instead I am chartering an

[1] David Fleischman.
[2] Gregoire Gourevitch (b. 1895), Russian-American pianist.
[3] Fernand Gregh (1873–1960), French poet and critic.
[4] Gabriele D'Annunzio, *L'Innocente* (Naples, 1892).
[5] Adone Zecchi (b. 1904), Italian composer.
[6] Unidentified.   [7] Samuel Beckett and Alexander Ponisovsky.
[8] A doctor had proposed an operation for Lucia Joyce.
[9] Joyce had threatened to meet Giorgio and Helen Joyce when they docked at
Cherbourg.

aeroplane and will meet you and escort you on from the Azores. Keep a
good look out for me, Stevie, up in the air. The name of the plane is
Dedalus 56[1]

Tante belle cose a tutti   BABBO

To HELEN JOYCE   MS. Kastor

20 April 1938   *Paris*

Dear Helen: I hope you had a very pleasant musical birthday, and that
you will all have a pleasant crossing. I hired an 8-lamp Philco and
Hamm's man fixed up an antenna on the balcony out of an old walking
stick Lucia gave me after we came back from Salzburg. We got the two
Italian songs better (very well) but Haendel used [*sic,* for 'seemed'] to
fade off and come back.[2] One would think on some notes he was in the
next room. The voice sounded very pastosa[3] we thought and also easy
and extended. A couple of notes (one certainly) were very slightly off
tune, at least as heard by me. The diction is a great personal satisfaction
to me. I told only the Jolases and the Luxembourg people about it. I did
not tell the Turners as she seemed so jaded when I last spoke to her. But
today she rang up to ask us to dine on Friday at 7.30! (6.30 pm real
time) I am going to say I have to go to the Greek church—perfectly true
it is their Good Friday—and can't get out till 8 at least so I am coming
at 8.15 at least.

Chialiapine had an imposing funeral. All traffic held up in the centre.
Ceremony lasting 5 hours. I was at the Opera when a requiem was sung
in the open air with Léon's two sisters. My wife went to the Russian
church.

I hope your father is now quite hale and hearty again, also the other
members of your family. Give him our congratulations on his rapid and
I hope lasting recovery.

I believe you are to have a smooth passage as the *lune rousse* and the
tâches au soleil[4] are to finish out in five or six days more, so they tell me.

I spent all Easter Day with Lucia, teaching her some Latin, eating
panettoni di Milano[5] and fooling generally. More in letter or rather note
to Giorgio.

I hope Stevie makes good use of the Zeiss glasses on the way back.

Arrivederci tutti ben presto e buon viaggio[6]   BABBO

---

[1] Joyce was fifty-six years old.
[2] George Joyce sang twice on the Columbia Broadcasting System in New York.
[3] 'Mellow.'   [4] 'Russet moon' and the 'sun spots', auguries of bad weather.
[5] Sweet cakes.   [6] 'We will see you soon. Have a good crossing.'

To MR and MRS HERBERT GORMAN (Postcard)

MS. S. Illinois (Croessmann)

11 May 1938   *Paris*

Dear Gorman and Mrs Gorman: Glad to hear you are enjoying your
rest. I wish to the Lord some carpet from the Arabian Nights would fly
me to the Vosges away from W.i.P. Giorgio and Helen are back and
blooming.

Greetings from both   J.J.

To FERDINAND PRIOR[1]   MS. Budtz-Jørgensen

29 May 1938[2]   *7 rue Edmond Valentin, Paris 7*[e]

Bedste Herre: Jeg har modtaget Deres venlige Brev af 17de denne
Maaned samt ved den uventede Gave 'Danske in Paris'. Bogen er
yderst smukke og meget interessant for mig. Som de vistnok ved allerede
er mit Fødselssted Dublin en norsk By og vi har haft et Danske komplette
Hus i vor Hovedstad gennem flere Aarhundreder endog efter Klontarfs-
slaget.[3] Vore Dublinerne ere temmelig naesevise og betragter også idag
Danskerne og Normaendene blot som Barbarer, Klosterplynderer o. s. v.,
men de 'sorthårige Fremmede' (som vi naevner dem 'Dubhgall') have
grundlaeggede den første Byencivilisation i den grønne ø.

Jeg har uheldigvis gjort kun et korte Besøg i Danmark to eller tre
Åre siden, når jeg var, som synger min Ven Kai Friis Møller 'i Lysets
Land kun seldvinbuden Gaest'.[4] Tvivlets vilde De finde mit 'Dansk' lidt
traettende og måske umulig at forstå. Jeg beder om Onskyld. Jeg
kjender Sproget, men har i alle Tilfaelde intet Øvelse deri her i Paris.
Modtag de hjaerteligste Hilsener og med aerbødigste Tak end al mere
for Deres Godhed jeg har den Aere at tegne mig Deres hengivne

JAMES JOYCE[5]

[1] Ferdinand Prior (1868–1948) was Danish Consul-General in Paris from 1919 to 1933.
A banker, he translated Kierkegaard into French.

[2] The texts of this letter and the following one are taken from an article by Jørgen
Budtz-Jørgensen, 'To Breve paa Dansk fra James Joyce,' in the Copenhagen newspaper,
Nationaltidende (12 May 1953) 8, with slight corrections based on photostatic copies of
the letters. Joyce's Danish is imperfect but comprehensible.

[3] Christ Church Cathedral, much remodelled since the Danes founded it.

[4] Kai Friis Møller, *Indskrifter* (Copenhagen, 1920), p. 9. The line quoted is also the
poem's title.

[5] (Translation by Jens Nyholm)
    'Dear Sir: I have received your kind letter of the 17th of this month, together with
the unexpected gift, *The Danes in Paris*. The book is extremely handsome and
interests me very much. Perhaps you are aware that my birthplace, Dublin, is a
Norwegian city and that we have had a complete Danish house in our capital for

To FERDINAND PRIOR   MS. Budtz-Jørgensen
30 May 1938   *Paris*

P.S. Jeg har skrevet så hurtig igår iaftes at jeg har glemt at sige at jeg
har bedt Fru Jolas at hun skulde sende Dem en Exemplar af *transition*
(det toogtyvende jeg tro)[1] hvori findes et Kapitel af min nuvaerende
Vaerk (Helten er en Vikingkjaempe), hertil naevnte 'Work in Progress'
fordi det indeholder den viderunderlige Eventyr af Skraederen fra
Dublin og Sømanden fra Norge. Men Fanden alene ved hvis De vilde
kunne forstå hvad Fortaellingen mener eller overhovedet hvad betyder
dette hele Ordspindelvaev!

Engang igien mange Tak   J.J.[2]

To VISCOUNT CARLOW   MS. Yale
Postmark 3 June 1938   *7 rue Edmond Valentin, Paris 7ᵉ*

Dear Lord Carlow: What must you not think of me? Well, I am nearly
exhausted, working literally night and day but I am going to take three
or four days of rest if I can switch my addled mind off that accursed
book of mine.

I received the copies of S.a.s.i.S[3] and they have been greatly admired
by all who have seen them. I heard last night that there was a very good
notice in the London *Star*. If you have seen it and know the date please
let me know and I shall order two copies. Louis Golding was over here
and we had lunch together. I liked him and was sorry he was not free to
dine for, as you know, I do not like luncheons.

The several accounts you have sent me of your 'pleasure cruise'

several centuries, that is, since the battle of Clontarf. Our Dubliners are rather impertinent and even today they consider the Danes and Norwegians to be just barbarians,
plunderers of monasteries, etc., but the "black-haired foreigners" (as we call them,
"Dubhgalls") founded the first city civilization on the green island. I have unfortunately made only one brief visit to Denmark two or three years ago, when I was, as my
friend Kai Friis Møller sings, "a self-invited guest in the land of light." Doubtless you
will find my "Danish" a bit tiring and perhaps impossible to comprehend. Please
excuse it. I know the language but have had no practice in it here in Paris. Please
accept my cordial greetings and my respectful thanks for your kindness. I have the
honour to sign myself Sincerely yours   James Joyce'

[1] A slip for *transition* 26 (February 1937) 109–29 (*Finnegans Wake*, pp. 309–31).

[2] (Translation)

    'P.S. I wrote so hurriedly last night that I forgot to tell you I had asked Mrs Jolas
to send you a copy of *transition* (22 I think), which contains a chapter from my
present work (the hero is a Viking giant), up to now entitled *Work in Progress*,
because it contains the wonderful story of the tailor from Dublin and the sailor from
Norway. But the devil knows whether you will be able to understand what the story
means or what this entire wordspiderweb is about.

    Once more, many thanks   J.J.'

[3] *Storiella as She Is Syung.*

reconcile me to my quiet life in *le vieux Paname*[1] here. My son returned from New York a few days ago. He sang a few times over Columbia Station[2] during his short stay and, in fact, I had a new wireless set rigged up for the occasion with the aid of an antenna on the balcony made out of one of my many walking sticks—not the ambassadorial Irish blackthorn—and we heard him singing across the ocean as clearly as if he had been in the next room.

I am asking my friend Eugene Jolas to send you a copy of the last issue of *transition* which contains a fragment of *W i P.*[3] I am offering prizes of 5/- 2/6 and 1/3 for the three best solutions but am not competing myself as I do not think I am at present capable of winning even the fourth prize of 7½d.

Since you are now one of my publishers I shall ask Paul Léon to send you a copy of *Europe.*[4] There is a long article on me in it which I have not read but I learn that the last ten pages on W i P are very intelligent. *Gott sei Dank!*[5]

My daughter was very delighted with the book too and we both thank you for having given us such a charming thing to have and to hold.

With kind regards to Lady Carlow and yourself from us both Sincerely yours   JAMES JOYCE

To VISCOUNT CARLOW   MS. Yale

6 June 1938   *7 rue Edmond Valentin, Paris 7*^e

Dear Lord Carlow: I am sending this to your former address because your last letter is put away with other correspondence and I omitted to write the new address in my notebook. I think it is 67 Westminster Gardens?

I hope you received the proofs and understood all my scrawls.

My son thanks you as do I for your good offices and for those proferred of Mr Gielgud.[6] His (my son's) experience of broadcasting in the U.S.A. (he sang for Columbia, the National Broadcasting Corporation and another one before the glandular trouble from which he has now made an astonishing recovery cut short his vocal career temporarily) is

---

[1] 'Old Paname' [Paris].
[2] Columbia Broadcasting System.
[3] *transition* 27 (April–May 1938) 59–78 (*Finnegans Wake*, pp. 338–55).
[4] The article, 'James Joyce,' was written by Jacques Mercanton (b. 1910), a Swiss critic, and appeared in *Europe* (15 April 1938). It is reprinted in his *Poètes de l'univers* (Paris, 1947), pp. 13–56.
[5] 'Thank God.'   [6] John Gielgud (b. 1904), the English actor.

that these Radio Companies are all in watertight compartments and that the director who has charge of the singing almost resents even a friendly introduction from the director, say, who controls the sports programme. In this concrete case is it possible to find out who has charge of the singers or the vocal part of the musical programme and get into relation with him directly? I will send further details about my son (or he can send them himself) if we can get this information. As you already know, I think, he was born in Italy and has lived 17 years in Paris. He sings German also and of course English. He studied singing for about 5 years with Lujol of the Opéra and Cunelli, a retired Greek tenor of the Italian school. His voice is light bass (basse chantante).

Paris is so full of international celebrities and will be for many months that it is hardly advisable for him to give a concert here at present. If he gets an audition in London I think he ought to get an engagement out of it. Voices seem to become rarer and rarer in that country.

Thanks very much in any case but I should like to hear from you about this before I make any plans. Sincerely yours   James Joyce

To Daniel Brody   MS. Brody

16 June 1938 Bloomsday   *Paris*

Dear Mr Bródy: Thanks for your good wishes on this day which you never forget. My book—on which I am working all day and all night as well—is to be published by Faber and Faber (London) and the Viking Press (New York). I am glad to know you are safe and well. Glad also to be able to tell in an anniversary message that last evening my friend in the French F.O. rang up to say that permission for H. Broch[1] to enter France had been telegraphed to the French C.G. in Vienna. I am trying to get two other people into America and hope I shall succeed.

With best wishes to Mrs Brody and yourself sincerely yours

James Joyce

To Viscount Carlow   MS. Yale

Postmark 17 June 1938   *Paris*

Dear Lord Carlow: Thanks for the *Star*. It was really scarcely worth troubling you about. I hope *S a S i S*[2] is meeting with success.

---

[1] Hermann Broch (1886–1951), Austrian novelist and critic. He was author of *James Joyce und die Gegenwart* (Vienna, Leipzig, Zurich, 1936). Broch and Daniel Brody were both obliged to emigrate because of being Jewish.

[2] *Storiella as She Is Syung.*

The accompanying copy of the Dublin *Times* ought to interest you. I am sure that if you care to write personally to Dr T. J. Kiernan,[1] director of Broadcasting at Radio Eireann [sic], G.P.O. Dublin and tell him who are you he will get into touch with these musicians and obtain the words and air of that fine old song[2] for you. I have been trying vainly, as you know, to get them for about 40 years. Dr Kiernan knows me. In fact he arranged a broadcast about me for my birthday this year.

I am still on night and day labour sincerely yours   JAMES JOYCE

To HELEN JOYCE   MS. Kastor

4 July 1938   [*Paris*]

Dear daughter-in-law: This being Independence Day please cheer up[3] for the love of Giorgio and accept these delightful blooms as a present from the garden where the pretties grow.[4]   BABBO

To HELEN JOYCE   MS. Kastor

17 July 1938   *Paris*

Dear Helen: Wake up!
            Stir up!
            Sit up!
            Get up!
            Buck up
            and
            Cheer up   BABBO

To GEORGE and HELEN JOYCE   MS. Kastor

6 August 1938   *Paris*

Caro Giorgio: Grazie della tua lettera. Eccoti il bollettino d'abbonamento per il N. Y. H. Tutto andrà bene e presto. Se non l'hai già fatto scrivi al segretario generale Radio P.T.T. Faceva un tempo insopportabile quà da tre giorni e perdura. Ti abbraccio   BABBO[5]

Dear Helen: Glad to have good news of you. All will go well. Lucky you

---

[1] Thomas Joseph Kiernan (b. 1897), Irish diplomat, later Ambassador to the United States.
[2] 'Follow Me Up to Carlow.'   [3] Helen Joyce was ill and depressed.
[4] 'The Garden where the Praties Grow,' a song.
[5] (Translation)
'Dear Giorgio: Thanks for your letter. Here is the New York Herald subscription for you. Everything will be well, and soon. If you have not already done so write the Secretary General of Radio P.T.T. The weather has been unendurable here for three days and still continues. I embrace you   Babbo'

got off on Wednesday as on Thursday we had a dreadful storm just at that hour. David[1] is coming to tea and after we work till dinner. Tomorrow he and his friend —[2] are to dine with us. I can't find any other paper or envelopes so here goes this. Huebsch dined with us last night and asked kindly for both of you. Invitations keep pouring in from all kinds of *emplâtres*.[3] Jolas seems to have gone off somewhere, I suppose for the weekend. He didn't even dine with us the night you all left. Stevie, I hear flourishes. Be good   BABBO

To HELEN JOYCE (Postcard)   MS. Kastor

17 August 1938   *Paris*

Dear Helen: The girl has just found this[4] in a chair under a cushion. David must have forgotten it and he may not have a copy and the one he sent to *Stories* at E.J's[5] suggestion may not be returned so will you please send it on to him as I have not heard from him since he left and don't know his address.

   Glad to hear you are beginning to go out into society again.
   Keep it up, Keep it up! Tante cose!   BABBO

To HERBERT GORMAN (Postcard)   MS. S. Illinois (Croessmann)

Postmark 21 August 1938   *Hotel de la Paix, Lausanne*

Giorgio who is in Montreux will return you the rest of the MS[6] tomorrow if he has not done so. If you have any more ready you may send it here. Thank heaven, the summer is nearly over. I hope Colum wrote to you but Mrs C has had another accident. Greetings to you both   J.J.

To HERBERT GORMAN (Postcard)   MS. S. Illinois (Croessmann)

23 August 1938   *Lausanne*

I saw Giorgio yesterday. He thinks that Devries's[7] real name should not be mentioned (an initial not D or any other name instead) as he belongs to a very well known Amsterdam family and has also, it seems, 'made good' at last. I agree. I don't know how it escaped me.   J.J.

---

[1] David Fleischman.   [2] Joyce left out the name.   [3] 'Louts.'
[4] A story by David Fleischman.   [5] Eugene Jolas.
[6] Gorman had virtually completed his biography of Joyce and was submitting it for approval. Joyce, besides reading it himself, had his son read it.
[7] In Gorman's *James Joyce*, p. 243, Juda De Vries appears under the name of 'Joe Martin'. De Vries was an errant acquaintance of Joyce in Zurich; he later became a respected dentist in Brussels. His letters to Joyce are at Cornell.

To Maurice James Craig[1]   MS. Yale

24 August 1938   *Hotel de la Paix, Lausanne*

Dear Mr Craig: Many thanks for your letter and friendly offices and
please convey to Professor Ogilvie[2] my son's and my thanks in advance.

You must have had an inspiring influence on my friend Eugene Jolas
for the day after it he suddenly guessed the title of my book which
nobody has succeeded in doing for the past sixteen years, thereby
winning a wager of 1000 frs which I had rashly made. He is now on the
top of one of his French Maritime Alps, Ubelle, with his secret and
perhaps I should ask Loki to make a hedge of fire round the foot until
I have written the final full stop. (There is none).

The name of the song is, I think 'The Lord in His mercy be kind (not
good) to Belfast'. I have been trying for many years to get the air and
words of it and also of 'Follow me up to Carlow'. With thanks once more
sincerely yours   JAMES JOYCE

To Viscount Carlow   MS. Yale

8 September 1938   *Hotel de la Paix, Lausanne*

Dear Lord Carlow: Many thanks for your letters and the welcome
enclosures. I am glad that you rejoice to have an heir to follow you up[3]
and also that my longsought song turned up so opportunely after so
many years. I sent the music on to my son as it needs a deep strong
voice, not my *tenore di grazia*,[4] to bassoon the close. You, however, as
titular chief of that region are the one who should sing it and with that
ambassadorial wand of office brandished high in your right hand. The
allusions so far in my book to Portarlington and Carlow have been of
such a drearily commestible kind—scallions, meat and so on—that I
shall have to find a place to suggest this ferocious and exciting song.[5]

I hope all your little storiellas have been safely disposed of by now and
are off the market for their mighty mother is now at last making ready to
take her slide into the unsuspecting sea. I am making a brief holiday
here but return to Paris in a few days to hammer on the last plates

---

[1] Maurice James Craig (b. 1919), Irish man of letters and an authority on architectural
history.

[2] Sir Frederick Ogilvie (1893–1949), Director of the British Broadcasting Company in
1938–42. Joyce had asked Craig to bring George Joyce's talent as a singer to Ogilvie's
attention.

[3] An allusion to the song, 'Follow Me Up to Carlow.'   [4] A light tenor.

[5] He did. See p. 408, n. 4.

and paint her title before the skippereeen father[1] gives her his blessing.

I do not know who Mr Barzun[2] is but have asked my friend E Jolas about him. And I wonder is the Mrs Betty Byrne alluded to in your letter a namesake only of the Betty Byrne alluded to on the first page of *A Portrait of the Artist as a Young Man*. That worthy lady herself would be about 140 years of age now. I thank her good sense for she introduced me to sweets for which, contradictory as it may seem, I have almost as fervent a feeling as I have for the delightful white wine of this and the next cantons. Sincerely yours   James Joyce

From Jacques Mercanton to Maurice James Craig   TS. Yale

9 September 1938   *Lausanne*

Monsieur, Avant de quitter Lausanne, où il a pris quelques jours de vacances, M. Joyce me prie de vous faire parvenir le texte de cette chanson 'Follow me up to Carlow', qu'il a reçu de Lord Carlow au moment même où il recevait votre lettre. Le texte était accompagné de la musique, que M. Joyce a envoyé à son fils. Il pense que peut-être, à l'occasion de la semaine du jubilé de Belfast, vous avez réussi à découvrir l'autre chanson dont il vous avait parlé.

Veuillez agréer, Monsieur, avec les meilleurs messages de M. Joyce et ses remerciements pour votre lettre, l'expression de mes sentiments distingués.   Jacques Mercanton[3]

FOLLOW ME UP TO CARLOW
by P. J. M'Call[4]

Lift, MacCahir Oge, your face,
Brooding o'er the old disgrace,

---

[1] The father of little boats, from *sgib* (Irish for 'boat') and *in* (diminutive ending), with a play on 'skipper' and on Skibbereen, County Cork, generally regarded as the looniest town in Ireland.

[2] Jacques Barzun (b. 1907), a professor of history and dean at Columbia University, well-known for his writings in intellectual history and music.

[3] (Translation)
'Dear Sir, Before departing from Lausanne, where he has spent a few days on holiday, Mr Joyce asks me to forward to you the words of that song, "Follow Me Up to Carlow," which he received from Lord Carlow at the very moment that your letter came. The words were accompanied by the music, which Mr Joyce sent on to his son. He thinks that maybe, during the week of the Belfast jubilee, you have succeeded in discovering the other song which he mentioned to you.
With kindest regards from Mr Joyce and his thanks for your letter, Sincerely yours,
                                              Jacques Mercanton'

[4] Patrick Joseph McCall (1861–1919), Dublin song writer. 'The Marching Song of Feagh MacHugh or Follow Me Up to Carlow' was included in his *Songs of Erinn* (London, 1899) and *Irish Fireside Songs* (Dublin, 1911). It is a tradition that this air, 'Follow me up to Carlow,' was first performed by the pipers of Fiach MacHugh O'Byrne

That black Fitzwilliam stormed your place
    And drove you to the fern!
Grey said victory was sure—
Soon the Firebrand he'd secure;
Until he met at Glenmalure
    Feagh MacHugh O'Byrne![1]

Chorus

Curse and swear, Lord Kildare![2]
Feagh will do what Feagh will dare;
Now, Fitzwilliam, have a care—
    Fallen is your star, low!
Up with halbert, out with sword,
On we go; for by the Lord!
Feagh MacHugh has given the word:
Follow me up to Carlow!

See the swords of Glen Imayle[3]
Flashing o'er the English Pale!
See all the children of the Gael
    Beneath O'Byrne's banners!
Rooster of a fighting stock,
Would you let a Saxon cock
Crow out upon an Irish rock?
    Fly up and teach him manners!

From Tassagart to Glonmore
Flows a stream of Saxon gore!
Och, great is Rory Oge O'More
    At sending loons to Hades!
White is sick and Lane is fled![4]
Now for black Fitzwilliam's head—
We'll send it over dripping red
    To 'Liza and her ladies!

as he marched to attack Carlow after his victory over the forces of the English Deputy,
Lord Grey de Wilton, at Glenmalure in 1580.
  [1] MacCahir Ogue was Brian MacCahir Cavanagh whom Sir William Fitzwilliam,
Lord Deputy and Lord Justice of Ireland from 1560 to 1594, had driven out of his
possessions. The Firebrand of the Mountains was Fiach MacHugh O'Byrne.
  [2] Henry, Twelfth Earl of Kildare (1562–97), known as Henry na tuagh or Henry of
the Battleaxes.
  [3] Glen Imaal, a glen in West Wicklow, supplied many of the fighting Irishmen in
1580 and again in 1798.
  [4] Rory Ogue O'More. White was Sir Nicholas White, Master of the Rolls, a well-
known rebel hunter. Lane was probably Ralph Lane, also active against rebels.

To Paul Ruggiero[1]   MS. Ruggiero

[*September 1938*]   [*Paris*]

Caro Ruggiero: L'altro giorno ho inteso alla radio un cantante
francese cantare molto bene la sua canzone: 'Epigha monós eis tin akro
thalassiá' in francese però. Vorrei comprare il disco, anzi due, uno per me
e uno per Lei. Andai da Durand (il Hüni[2] di Parigi) però senza il titolo
non si puo averlo. Comè si chiama la canzone? È greca o francese
tradotta in greco? Mi faccia sapere il titolo in greco o in francese con o
senza il nome del compositore. L'accompagnamento è molto bello ed il
cantante canta con squisito gusto. Bei tempi del passato. Saluti
cordiali   James Joyce[3]

To B. W. Huebsch   MS. Buffalo

20 September 1938   *Paris*

Dear Huebsch: Many thanks for your kind and prompt reply. I have
sent it on to Brauchbar.[4] I think I have placed his niece here and my
German publisher[5] writes from the Hague that he is doing all he can
about Holland. I hope I can get the others into Ireland.

I may go tomorrow to Dieppe for a few days and if so will send a line
from there if I do. I don't think any time should be lost.

Many thanks again sincerely yours   James Joyce

To Jacques Mercanton   MS. Mercanton

21 September 1938   *Hotel du Rhin et de Newhaven, Dieppe*

Cher Monsieur Mercanton: Pour l'amour du ciel expédiez cette carte
postale tout de suite.[6] Je l'ai oublié!

---

[1] From a typewritten copy.   [2] A music shop in Zurich.

[3] (Translation)

'Dear Ruggiero: The other day I heard a French singer on the radio singing your
song very well, 'I walked out all alone on the strand,' but in French. I want to buy the
disc, or rather two of them, one for me and one for you. I went to Durand's (the Hüni
of Paris) but without the title could not get it. What is the name of the song? Is it
Greek or French translated into Greek? Let me know the title in Greek or French with
or without the composer's name. The accompaniment is lovely and the singer sings
with exquisite taste. Auld lang syne. Cordial greetings   James Joyce'

[4] Edmund Brauchbar (1872–1952), a Zurich businessman who studied English with
Joyce during the first World War, and subsequently moved to New York. He was
attempting to aid Jewish refugees, including some of his relations, to establish themselves
in other countries. Joyce was happy to assist in this work, and asked Huebsch's help
with a young man named Alfred Perles, a nephew of Brauchbar.

[5] Daniel Brody.

[6] Joyce was in Lausanne in late August and early September 1937. When he went
with his wife to Dieppe, he wished Lucia to think he was still in Switzerland, and so
asked Mercanton to forward a postcard as if from there.

Aussi, je n'avais pas le temps avant de quitter Paris de lire votre lettre qui est restée sur mon bureau. Pourriez-vous m'en repéter le [sic] teneur par lettre écrite à la machine. Mon appartement est fermé car nous avons passé des journées très inquiètes.

Même ici nous ne savons jamais si d'un moment à l'autre nous ne devons pas rentrer à Paris pour repartir avec notre fille pour La Baule où tout l'asyl se transférerait le cas échéant. Ma femme voulait quelques jours de 'repos' après la soi-disante détente et nous voilà ici. Cordialement votre   JAMES JOYCE[1]

To HERBERT GORMAN (Postcard)   MS. S. Illinois (Croessmann)

21 September 1938   *Hotel du Rhin, Dieppe*

Here we are and it is very rainy indeed. Plan to stay 5–8 days if allowed. Friendly greetings to you both   J.J.

To MAURICE JAMES CRAIG (Postcard)   MS. Yale

23 September 1938   *Hotel du Rhin* [*Dieppe*]

Many thanks for the words of the song, Curiously enough I had just asked my friend, M. Mercanton of Lausanne to send it on to you. I hope the Belfast national anthem[2] will also announce itself to me suddenly. We are spending a weekend at the sea before returning to Paris after a not very restful vacation Sincerely yours   JAMES JOYCE

To DANIEL BRODY   MS. Brody

5 October 1938   *7 rue Edmond Valentin, Paris 7ᵉ*

Dear Mr Brody: We came back the day before yesterday—Lord knows for how long![3] Many thanks for your kind letter which I have forwarded to Mr Brauchbar.

I have just received the enclosed letter from Dr Goyert in which he

[1] (Translation)
'Dear Mr Mercanton: For heaven's sake mail this postcard at once. I forgot about it.
Also, I had no time before I left Paris to read your letter which is still on my desk. Could you repeat the gist of it in a typed letter. My flat is closed up, for we have had some very uneasy days.
Even here we never know from one moment to the next if we ought not to go back to Paris to set off again with our daughter for La Baule where the whole asylum is to be transferred if need be. My wife wanted a few days of "rest" after the so-called lessening of tension and so here we are. Cordially yours   James Joyce'
[2] See p. 408.   [3] Joyce was greatly alarmed by the threat of war.

asks about you. Will you please send it back as I wish to reply to it. I should like to see the articles he speaks of but have no idea how or where they can be obtained.

We stayed in La Baule a week. I chose it because the Maison de Santé at Ivry (near Paris, 6 K) where unfortunately my daughter still is had made all arrangements with the military government here to evacuate their premises *en masse* (105 patients and 60 staff) and transfer to the Hotel Edelweiss, La Baule, a big, disused hotel on the Avenue de Paris in a park. We passed a very anxious time. Did you ever see her illuminated work in Chaucer's *A B C*—a poem to the Madonna with a preface by Louis Gillet?

It is very kind of you to take such trouble for my friend.[1] I have had a more or less favorable reply from Dublin and think I can place two more of his Abrahamesque family there.

We spent a whole month in the Hague, my wife, my daughter and myself in the happy years gone by, Hotel Victoria, I think.[2] The best potatoes I ever ate since I left Ireland.

I have come back to put the finishing touches to *Work in Progress* and in what an atmosphere!

Friendly greetings from my wife also to Mrs Brody and yourself sincerely yours   JAMES JOYCE

To GEORG GOYERT   MS. S. Illinois (Croessmann)

11 October 1938   *7 rue Edmond Valentin, Paris 7ᵉ*

Geehrter und lieber Herr Goyert: Es ist eine grosse Freude—für mir— und welche angenehme Uberraschung!—einen Brief von Ihnen zu bekommen. Hoffentlich geht es Ihnen immer und ihre werte Familie recht gut. Uns geht es nicht so schlecht aber meine Tochter ist leider immer sehr krank aber wir glauben dass ihre lange Krankheit wird bald vorüber sein.

Besten Dank für Ihre freundliche Mitteilungen. Was die Universität Bonn betrifft könnte ich an Prof. Curtius schreiben um die betreffende Abhandlung zu haben—wenn das noch möglich ist—aber leider habe ich keine 'Relationen' mit Marburg. Wäre es Ihnen möglich die zweite Abhandlung[3] von welcher Sie schreiben durch einstmaligen Freund oder Bekannten in literarische Kreise zu haben?

Prof. H. Zimmer (der Sohn des berühmte keltischen Philologen[4] und

---

[1] Edmund Brauchbar.   [2] In May–June 1927.
[3] Untraced.   [4] Heinrich Zimmer (1851–1910).

jetzige Professor der Sanskrit in Heidelberg) ist mir in der letzen
Zeit sehr hilflich gewesen. Ich möchte ihn aber nicht stören in diese
Angelegenheit denn ich kenne ihn persönlich nicht.

Work in Progress—pfui!—ist beinahe geendet. Ich auch. Seit letzen
Oktober arbeite ich daran wie ein Maultier den ganzen Tag durch und
fast die ganze Nacht.

Je commence à en avoir marre—et comment!

Wann kommen wir wieder zusammen wie damals in Trianons
Restaurant? Der Himmel weiss was für ein Schicksal die Kritik für
meinem Buch reservirt. Das ist mir aber schlussegal[1]—um etwas unver-
blümtes nicht zu sagen—aber vielleicht habe ich noch eine Zukunft als
Strassensänger—hinter mich.

Eine freundlicher Händedruck   JAMES JOYCE[2]

To EDOUARD DUJARDIN   MS. Texas

5 December 1938   *Paris*

Cher maître: Je viens de recevoir 'We'll to the Woods No More'.[3] Je
trouve l'édition tout-à-fait charmante et la traduction très réussie.
J'espère que cette publication, si longtemps retardée, vous fera grand
plaisir.

Permettez-moi de vous en féliciter et de réitérer l'expression de ma
profonde reconnaissance envers l'artiste des *evergreen* 'Lauriers'.

[1] The usual German word is *scheissegal*, meaning indifferent (to it) as to shit, but
Joyce changes it to *schlussegal*, indifferent to the end.

[2] (Translation)

'My dear friend Mr Goyert, It is a great pleasure for me—and what an agreeable
surprise!—to receive a letter from you. I hope you and your fine family are keeping
well. We are not so bad, but my daughter, unfortunately, is always very ill; we
believe however that her illness will soon be over.

Many thanks for your friendly information. As far as the University of Bonn is
concerned I could write to Professor Curtius to obtain that article—if it is still possible
to do so—but unfortunately I have no contact with Marburg. Would it be possible
for you to obtain the second article you mentioned through some old friend or acquaintance of yours in literary circles?

Professor H. Zimmer (son of the famous Celtic philologist and presently Professor
of Sanskrit at Heidelberg) has lately been of great help to me. But I should not like
to bother him in this matter because I do not know him personally.

Work in Progress—pfui!—is almost finished. So am I. Since last October I have been
working like a mule at it all day long and almost all night long too.

I begin to have enough of it—and how!

When will we meet again as in those days at the Restaurant des Trianons? Heaven
knows what fate the critics have reserved for my book. But I don't give a hoot—to say
it mildly—and anyway perhaps I still have a future as a streetsinger—behind me.

A friendly handshake   James Joyce'

[3] Dujardin's *Les Lauriers sont coupés*, translated by Stuart Gilbert (Norwalk, Connecticut, New Directions, 1938).

Présentez, je vous prie, mes hommages à Madame et croyez-moi, cher maître, très cordialement votre   JAMES JOYCE[1]

To PAUL RUGGIERO[2]   MS. Ruggiero

9 December 1938   *Paris*

Caro Ruggiero: Le scrivo questa dal letto, essendo da circa una settimana poco bene. Dunque mi scusi. Grazie mille della sua pronta risposta. Ho cantato la canzone[3] ma il successo è stato piuttosto contrastato. Semberebbe che la canzone sia stata in origine una canzone francese tradotta poi in greco. Riveste tutto un'altro carattere in greco, non le pare? Ha ricevuto il disco? Le piace? Io sono molto debole e stanco. Ho ancora delle bozze a correggere. Magari fosse tutto finito.

Grazie, caro Ruggiero ed una stretta di mano   JAMES JOYCE[4]

To GEORG GOYERT (Postcard)   MS. S. Illinois (Croessmann)

23 December 1938   *Paris*

Pour vous souhaiter joyeux Noel. La revue de laquelle vous m'avez parlé ne m'est jamais parvenue. Par contre, avez-vous reçu un article qui est paru dans une revue de Lausanne?[5] Votre bien dévoué

JAMES JOYCE[6]

[1] (Translation)
'Dear maître: I have just received "We'll to the Woods No More". I think the edition is charming and the translation very successful. I hope that this publication, so long delayed, will give you great pleasure.
Allow me to congratulate you upon it and to reiterate the expression of my profound gratitude to the artist of the evergreen 'Laurels'.
Please convey my respects to Madame and believe me, dear maître, very cordially yours   James Joyce'
[2] From a typewritten copy.
[3] Joyce sang what he thought was a Greek love song at a Thanksgiving party given by Maria Jolas. He had first heard it from Ruggiero and obtained the words from him. (*Letters*, ed. Gilbert, p. 403)
[4] (Translation)
'Dear Ruggiero: I am writing this in bed, where I have been ailing for about a week. So please excuse me. Many thanks for your prompt reply. I sang the song but the effect was rather mixed. It appears that the song was originally French and then translated into Greek. It takes on quite a different character in Greek, don't you think? Did you get the disc? Do you like it? I am very weak and tired. I still have proofs to correct. If it were only all finished.
Thanks, dear Ruggiero, and a handshake   James Joyce'
[5] Jacques Mercanton, 'L'Esthétique de Joyce,' *Etudes de Lettres* (Lausanne) 13.1 (10 October 1938) 20–46.
[6] (Translation)
'To wish you a merry Christmas. The review you mentioned has never reached me. Have you, for your part, received an article which appeared in a Lausanne review? Faithfully yours   James Joyce'

To LIVIA SVEVO[1]   MS. Texas

[1 January 1939] 1938–39   *Parigi*

Gentile Signora: Finalmente ho finito di finire il mio libro. Sono già tre lustri che pettino e ripettino la chioma di Anna Livia. E ora che s'avanzi alla ribalta. Spero che Berenice intercederà per la sua piccola consorella affinchè trovi in questo vasto mondo, per la grazia delle dee, 'almeno un Deo Gratias qualunque'.[2]

Buon Natale e Buon Anno a Lei ed ai Suoi   JAMES JOYCE[3]

To VISCOUNT CARLOW (Express letter)   MS. Yale

28 January 1939   *7 rue Edmond Valentin, Paris 7ᵉ*

Dear Lord Carlow: Is it quite certain that you will be in Paris on Thursday morning next[4] and will you be passing the night of the same day, Candlemas, here? Because, if so, and if Lady Carlow is with you my daughter-in-law who is giving a dinner party in my honour and to celebrate the publication of my book asks me to say that you will be very welcome both. It is at my son's place this year 17 Villa Scheffer, Paris XVIᵉ.

There is another point. My book[5] is to be sent over on Wednesday by air express but unfortunately the delivery of these parcels is never certain because they pass through the *Douane* to collect a minimal duty and, of course, the *douanier* can have no idea that I shall be waiting for the wretched parcel. It might arrive at the last moment after a day of exhaustive waiting and even that would be too late to allow of my showing it to my daughter (who lives outside Paris) in the early afternoon. Or it might just arrive the morning after the 2nd in which case I should feel inclined to throw it out of the window. In sum, I should like to be sure of having it on that morning. It was only after you had rung off that I thought of this. Of course, I don't want to interfere in any way

---

[1] Signora Schmitz had changed her name legally to Svevo.
[2] The last words of Italo Svevo's *Senilità*.
[3] (Translation)

'Dear Signora: I have at last finished finishing my book. For three lustra I have been combing and recombing the locks of Anna Livia. It is now time that she tread the boards. I hope that Berenice will intercede for her little sister so that she may find in this vast world, thanks to the gods, "at least one solitary Deo Gratias".

Merry Christmas and Happy New Year to you and your family.   James Joyce'

[4] Joyce's fifty-seventh birthday, 2 February 1939.
[5] *Finnegans Wake*. It was not officially published until 4 May 1939, but Faber & Faber managed to have ready an unbound copy (really a set of final proofs) from the printer, R. MacLehose and Company, in time for Joyce's birthday.

with your plans but as you told them to me they seemed to fit in with my idea.

If you are not already in the country or at air work somewhere perhaps you could ring up Faber and Faber. The person who is [in] charge of the book there is Mr de la Mare.[1] The book is to be sent from the Glasgow printers or binders on Monday. Anyhow a telegram from you one way or another would relieve my mind.

I am still very exhausted but I shall try to be better by Thursday though I am afraid the traditional *pas seul* with high kicking effects associated with that birthday feast will be beyond my powers this year of grace.[2]

Incidentally you will discover the title of the book which my wife has kept secret for seventeen years, being the only one who knew it. I think I can see some lofty thinkers and noble livers turning away from it with a look of pained displeasure Sincerely yours   JAMES JOYCE

To EDMUND BRAUCHBAR   MS. Brauchbar

23 February 1939   [*Paris*]

Dear Mr Brauchbar: Thanks for your letter and good wishes. I am glad to hear from you and hope your stay in Valmont will soon put you all right again. For the moment we are not going to Switzerland. Perhaps later on. I had a visit from Mr Rich. Ofner (widower of the late Charlotte Sauermann,[3] soprano at the Z'ch Stadttheater) whose son, a dentist's *Tekniker* [sic],[4] I am trying to get into U.S.A. You remember him? Good luck sincerely yours   JAMES JOYCE

To JOAN BUDGEN   MS. Joan Budgen

27 February 1939   *Paris*

Dear Miss Joan: Will you please wish your father from me a happy birthday and many happy returns of the day. I hope you will all have a nice time together. Also give our kind regards to your mother and I hope some day to meet you yourself. introductorily yours

JAMES JOYCE

[1] Richard de la Mare (b. 1901), then a director and now Chairman of Faber & Faber.
[2] On his birthday Joyce customarily performed a dance, which consisted mostly of remarkably high kicks.
[3] Charlotte Sauermann, a soprano, was a neighbour and close friend of the Joyces during 1918 and 1919.
[4] Technician.

To Daniel Brody   MS. Brody

5 March 1939   *7 rue Edmond Valentin, Paris 7ᵉ*

Dear Mr Brody: Thanks for your card and Goyert's address. Some
time ago he sent me a work in German about Ulysses which you may
wish to see.[1] I shall send it on and shall be glad if you will return it when
you have looked at it.

As regards *F.W.* (no longer W.i.P.) I have just received some leaflets
and send you one. In my opinion the price is altogether too high but it
does not depend on me.[2] Sincerely yours   JAMES JOYCE

To Carola Giedion-Welcker   MS. Giedion-Welcker

5 March 1939   *Paris*

Dear Mrs Giedion: Thanks for your letter and kind proposal which we
can talk about if, as I hope, we see you on your way through here.
17 March is S. Patrick's Day and we expect to be here in Paris.

I enclose a leaflet about *F.W.* I find the price of the ordinary edition
too high but can do nothing about it.

Who has Prof. Fehr's place as Professor of English[3] at Z'ch University
now? Can you find out?

A bientôt from us both. Sincerely yours   JAMES JOYCE

To Mary M. Colum   MS. N.Y. Public Library (Manuscript)

29 March 1939   *7 rue Edmond Valentin*
after 15 April 1939
34 rue des Vignes, Passy, Paris
Tél: Aut 37–73

Dear Mrs Colum: Thanks for your letter and am glad to hear you are
both well. I wonder how are the Gormans. Never had a line from them
since they left. Hope they are not ill. You have curiously misunderstood
my letter. I am changing flat not city, so far as one can see, and of course
Lucia is still in Ivry and I visit her every Sunday.

[1] Perhaps Hermann Broch, *James Joyce und die Gegenwart* (1936).

[2] The limited edition of *Finnegans Wake*, which comprised 425 copies, was priced at
£5 5s. in Great Britain and at $25 in the United States; the regular edition, published
simultaneously, was priced at 25s. in Great Britain and at $5 in the United States.

[3] Professor Heinrich Straumann, whom Joyce came to know in Zurich late in 1940,
succeeded Bernhard Fehr as professor of English at the University of Zurich in 1938.

Herewith is the picture and explanatory letter from the unknown painter. No, I did not receive any notice from the Yeats family.[1] I do not know any member of the family. I met his very loquacious father once for a few minutes on Northumberland Road.[2]

There is no use now in going into the matter of the American publication of my book. So far it has been a hopeless bungle. As for the date every week we hear something different. The book, printed and bound, has been lying on my table for the past two months but the sheets for Mr Huebsch's limited edition have not yet left England.

It is a great bore having to move but we are lucky if we have not to move much farther and more hastily.

I was invited to New York by the Pen Club for next May but wrote to them, thanking and declining. I hope you will both come over in the summer as you say. Let us know sometime ahead when and for how long.

Kindest regards to you both sincerely yours   JAMES JOYCE

To STANISLAUS JOYCE (Postcard)   MS. Cornell

26 April 1939   *34 rue de Vignes, Paris XVI*

Dear Stannie, This is our new address. I hope you are both well. Lucia is still very ill and Helen has had a bad nervous breakdown. Giorgio's career as a singer is again held up.

My book *Finnegans Wake* will be published May 4. It is very expensive for these times. 25/- (Faber & Faber, London.) Only 14 copies (press) are available for European critics. I should like to send 2 to Italy. Can you suggest 2 Italian critics who would be likely to review it. I thought of Emilio Cecchi as one. Let me know please by return. Or should I send one to Benco? Will you also please tell my old pupil Marcello Rogers[3] I got his letter and have today written to his friend Giorgio. I don't know whether I can do much but shall try.   JIM

P.S. Six copies are for here, 5 for Germany and 2 for Denmark, 1 each Norway and Holland.

[1] When Yeats died on 28 January 1939, Joyce sent a wreath to the grave at Roquebrune in southern France. It arrived after the funeral, and Mrs Yeats was not informed of it until later, when she wrote Joyce to thank him.

[2] For a description of this meeting see Oliver St John Gogarty, *It Isn't This Time of Year at All* (London, 1954), pp. 69–70.

[3] Marcello Rogers was one of two sons of an English dentist resident in Trieste.

To Livia Svevo   MS. Texas

[1 May 1939] Calendimaggio[1]   *34 rue des Vignes, Paris, XVI*

Gentile signora: Ho ricevuto la lettera acclusa inviatami dal sig.
Scarpelli.[2] C'è un equivoco. Non avevo affatto l'intenzione di criticare
l'opera letteraria dell'autore ma bensì l'opera del suo legatore. Infatti i
fogli volanti (è proprio il termine) del libercolo si staccavano ad uno ad
uno dopo la lettura di ogni pagina. Forse il mio esemplare è eccezionale.
Ma in simili circostanze come non pensare alla commedia giacosiana[3] ed
alla caducità delle cose terrestri ? Non ho fatto che chiamare carta carta
e colla colla. La prego di rassicurarne lo scrittore. Pare che si senta
offeso. Non lo è e non lo era. Ma . . . Oibo! (per non dire Uibaldo!)[4]
Endove ze andado finir el morbin famoso dei terriestini ?[5] No ghe ze
gnente de mal, benedeto de Dio! Go ciolto un poco de zeroto da Smolars[6]
e adeso el se tien insieme pulido. E diga al sior Scarpelli che no stia
bazilar, che mi no go dito gnente de mal e per amirare quel bravo omo
che iera Italo Svevo semo in due, lu e mi.

Giovedì sarà pubblicado el mio libro a Londra e in Amerigo. Ze anca
la festa de Santa Moniga[7] se mi ricordo ben, al quatro. Moniga[8] son
stado mi forse (La mi scusi, siora) che go messo disdoto ani dela mia
vita a finir quel mostro de libro. Ma cossa La vol ? Se nasse cussì. E,
corpo de bigoli, ne go bastanza. Co ghe digo mi!

Con doverosi ossequi mi segno devmo   James Joyce

P.S. Lingua sciolta, nevvero, signora![9]

---

[1] 'Kalends of May.'
[2] Ubaldo Scarpelli, author of a pamphlet on Schmitz. Joyce complained that it needed
glue. (*Letters*, ed. Gilbert, p. 404).
[3] Joyce alludes to Giuseppe Giacosa's comedy, *Come le foglie* ('Like the leaves'), the
pun being on *foglie* ('leaves') and *fogli* ('pages').
[4] The rest of the letter is in Triestine dialect.
[5] A humorous echo of a song which was sung in Trieste in the mid-nineteenth century
by a Slovene streetsinger named Sonz: 'Viva Terjeste, Viva anche terjestini, Viva
l'zardin publico, Viva anca bela zatà.' ('Long live Trieste, Long live the Triestines too,
Long live the public garden, Long live also the beautiful city.') Joyce was acquainted
with the song.
[6] A well-known stationery store in Trieste.
[7] Saint Monica is celebrated in fact on May 4.
[8] An allusion to a local anecdote involving a complicated play on 'monica', which in
Triestine means 'nun' but is also a slightly euphemistic variation on 'mona', meaning
'vagina' and 'stupid person'.
[9] The following translation is taken, with slight changes, from 'Carteggio . . . Svevo–
Joyce', ed. Harry Levin, *Inventario* II.1 (Spring 1949) 136–37. The translator points

To SIGNORA MARIA NEBBIA   MS. Bib. Municipale, Vichy

4 May 1939   *34 rue des Vignes, Paris XVI*ᵉ
                                                       Tél: Aut 79.01

Gentile signora: Oggi questo mio libro si pubblica a Londra ed a Nuova York.¹ La prego di volere rimettere l'esemplare che accompagna la presente al mio buon amico Valery Larbaud.

Vorremmo molto parlare con Lei, signora. E vorrei sapere anche se non potrei eventualmente fare una visita al Larbaud. Sarebbe troppo pregarla di farcelo sapere o con una telefonata con una lettera? Potrebbe Lei, per esempio, venire da noi qualche pomeriggio per prendere il tè insieme?

Spero che le cose non vadano troppo male. È tutto che si può pretendere oggi in questo lurido mondo, mi pare.

Gradisca, gentile signora, i sensi dei miei più doverosi ossequi

JAMES JOYCE²

out the special Triestine expressions, *morbin* in the sense of *buon omore*, *bazilar* in the sense of *essere preoccupato*. The spelling is also dialectal.

'Dear Signora: I have received the enclosed letter sent me by Signor Scarpelli. There has been a misunderstanding. I did not at all intend to criticize the literary work of the author, but the work of his bindery. As a matter of fact the fly leaves (that is the word) of the pamphlet came out one by one as I read each page. Perhaps my copy is an exception. But under the circumstances how could one not think of Giacosa's comedy and of the transitoriness of all earthly things? I have only called paper paper and glue glue. I beg you to reassure the writer. It appears that he feels offended. He is not and never was. But . . . Alas! (Not to say alack!) What has become of the famous laughing spirit of the Terriestines? No harm was meant, God wot! I got a little tape at Smolars and now the thing holds together in fine shape. And tell Signor Scarpelli not to be upset, that I have spoken no evil and that he and I make two who admire the splendid man that Italo Svevo was.

Thursday my book will be published in London and in America. It is also Saint Monica's day, if I remember rightly, on the fourth. But it is I who am perhaps an ass (forgive me, Signora), to have devoted eighteen years of my life to completing that monster of a book. But what is one to do? One is born that way. Yet, by God, I have had enough. And that's that!

With due respect, I am your devoted   James Joyce

P.S.—This is free language, isn't it, Signora?'

¹ *Finnegans Wake* was published by Faber & Faber in London and by The Viking Press in New York, in a regular and a limited signed edition.

² (Translation)

'Dear Madame: Today this book of mine is published in London and in New York. Would you please send the copy which accompanies this letter to my good friend Valery Larbaud?

We would so much like to talk to you, Madame. And I would like to know if I could possibly pay a visit to Larbaud. Would it be an imposition to ask you to let us know by means of a telephone call or a letter? Could you for instance come and have tea with us one afternoon?

I hope things are not too bad. It is all one can hope for in this murky world, I think. Very sincerely yours,   James Joyce'

To JACQUES MERCANTON[1] (Postcard)   MS. Mercanton

7 May 1939   *34 rue des Vignes, Paris XVI*

Cher Monsieur Mercanton Si vous allez entendre *Guillaume Tell* le 9,
le 11 ou le 14 ou même (comme moi je le ferais) tous les soirs je voudrais
bien en avoir vos impressions, surtout de ce ténor Sullivan. J'espère
qu'il pourra le chanter, le rôle d'Arnold, sans coupures. J'ai beaucoup
entendu parler de lui.[2] Pendant le 3ième acte, sortez et fumez votre pipe
et rentrez pour *l'asile héréditaire* du 4ième. Surtout ne manquez pas le
terzetto du 2ième. J'ai entendu *les autres chanteurs* a la radio. Ils sont
tous bons mais c'est un diable de rôle pour le ténor. Envoyez-moi aussi,
s v p, les critiques de la presse. Je voudrais bien être là. Peutêtre sera-t-il
radiodiffusé cordialement votre   JAMES JOYCE[3]

To SIGNORA MARIA NEBBIA   MS. Bib. Municipale, Vichy

12 May 1939   *34 rue des Vignes, Paris XVI*

Gentile signora: Vorrebbe avere la bontà di farmi sapere se lunedì o
martedì venturo Le converrà, diciamo verso le 5½ pom? Saremo
lietissimi di rivedere i nostri buoni vecchi amici. Sono oltremodo
contento di sapere che Larbaud va ora da bene in meglio. Vento in
poppa!
  Gradisca, gentile signora, i sensi dei miei più doverosi ossequi
                                                      JAMES JOYCE[4]

---

[1] Mercanton was then in Florence.
[2] Joyce did not wish to sway Mercanton by owning his friendship with Sullivan.
[3] (Translation)
  'Dear Mr Mercanton If you are going to hear *Guillaume Tell* on the 9th, 11th or
14th or even (as I should do myself) all three evenings I should be glad to have your
impressions, especially of this tenor Sullivan. I hope they will let him sing the role of
Arnold without cuts. I have heard a good deal about him. During the third act go out
and smoke your pipe and come back for "*L'Asile héréditaire*" in the fourth. Above
everything, do not miss the trio in the second . . . I have listened to *the other singers* on
the radio. They are all good but it is a devil of a role for the tenor. Send me also,
please, the press notices. I should like to be there. Perhaps it will be broadcasted.
Cordially yours   James Joyce'
[4] (Translation)
  'Dear Signora: Would you kindly let me know if Tuesday or Wednesday afternoon
would suit, say about 5:30? We shall be most pleased to see our good old friends again.
I am extremely glad to learn that Larbaud is now getting better and better. The wind's
in the sail! Very sincerely yours   James Joyce'

To SEAN O'CASEY[1]   MS. O'Casey

Postmark 26 May 1939   *34 rue des Vignes, Paris*

Dear Mr O'Casey: I wonder whether you have seen already the Dublin paper[2] I sent you with its curious misprint—if it is a misprint. I hope it may be prophetical and that we may some day meet. When my wife recovers from an attack of influenza we are going to see your play[3] at the Theatre de l'Oeuvre and if I find that it is attributed to me I shall certainly send you on the programme. Anyhow I hope you will take the printer's error, as I do, for a happy and amusing omen.

    With all good wishes sincerely yours   JAMES JOYCE

From SEAN O'CASEY   MS. Buffalo

30 May 1939   *tingrith, station road, totnes devon. England*

My dear James Joyce: I was very glad to get a letter from you, and to find that you weren't annoyed at 'Finnegan's Wake' being put against my name. My mind is still far away from the power of writing such a book. I wish I could say that such a power is mine. I am reading it now, and, though I meet many allusions, the book is very high over my head. A friend here (a painter) and I often read it (or try to) together; and I, it is fair to say, am better than he, and lead him into many a laugh and into the midst of wander and wonderland. It is an amazing book; and hardly to be understood in a year, much less in a day. I've had constant contact with you in 'Dubliners'; in 'Portrait of the Artist', and in 'Ulysses'—that great and amazing work. As you see, we are now living in Devon—meself and herself, two kids and another coming, so I don't suppose you'll ever be near here. But God is good, and we may meet one day. I sincerely hope so.

    I don't think the reference was a misprint. I know many of Dublin's Literary Clique dislike me, and they hate you (why, God only knows), so that 'misprint' was a bit of a joke. Well, Oxford's going to hand the colored gown of a D.Litt. over the shoulders of Wodehouse, whom, Belloc says is the greatest living writer of English. So Finnegan's Wake will, I fear, be a wake in earnest.

---

    [1] From a copy made by David Krause.
    [2] The *Irish Times*, by inadvertence or design, announced the publication of *Finnegans Wake* by Sean O'Casey. The editor, R. M. Smyllie, visited Joyce in Paris to assure him it was an accidental misprint. Joyce, like O'Casey, was not fully persuaded.
    [3] *Juno and the Paycock.*

Them and their Academy of Litters—all in all, and in spite of all,
a deep bow to James Joyce. Yours very sincerely   SEAN O'CASEY

I do hope your wife is allright or much better by now.

To GEORGE ROGERS[1]   MS. Rogers
5 June 1939   *Parigi*

Caro signor Rogers: Mio figlio Giorgio partirà probabilmente domani
martedì. Scenderà per qualche notte, essendo accompagnato da un
amico, al Park Lane Hotel, Piccadilly. In seguito, sceglierà per sè un
albergo meno costoso. Egli La prega di fargli il piacere di pranzare con
lui alla 1 pom l'indomani del suo arrivo costì onde poter discutere sul da
farsi. Spera che l'ora ed il giorno Le converranno. Se ci saranno degli
impreveduti Le farò sapere. Altrimenti favorisca passare all'albergo
suddetto mercoledì al tocco. Saluti distinti   JAMES JOYCE[2]

From PAUL LÉON to   TS. S. Illinois (Croessmann)
HERBERT GORMAN (Dictated by James Joyce[3])

6 June 1939   *Paris*

Dear Mr. Gorman, Mr Joyce asks me to confirm his personal cable to
you in which he stated that he could not authorise the publication of
your biography of him without having in his possession for perusal and
comparison the entire set of the typescript and of course the subsequent
proofs and requesting the immediate dispatch of the other chapters
namely those which he has heard in non-consecutive order at intervals
during the last several years and those which he has not heard yet. His
reason for cabling you was, as he stated, that the exposition of two
points in chapters II and IV was incorrect and misleading on two vital
points. In fact as he expresses it the latter chapter read almost as if it
had been inspired by Mr Michael Lennon's article in the 'Catholic
World' of some years ago. Mr Joyce is definitely of opinion that his
friends did him a singular disservice in not drawing his attention to this

---

[1] George Rogers (b. 1911), Professor of the Royal Academy of Music, had offered to
introduce George Joyce to officials of the British Broadcasting Corporation.
[2] (Translation)
'Dear Mr Rogers: My son Giorgio will probably leave tomorrow Tuesday. He will
stay for a few nights at the Park Lane Hotel, Piccadilly, since he is accompanied by a
friend. Later on he will choose a less expensive hotel for himself. He asks you to be
good enough to lunch with him at 1 p.m. the day following his arrival so as to talk
over what is to be done. He hopes that the day and the time will suit you. If there
should be any unexpected complications I will let you know. Otherwise kindly call at
his hotel Wednesday on the hour. Kindest regards   James Joyce'
[3] Joyce's authorship of this letter is explicitly confirmed, p. 447.

article at the time; it was highly libellous and defamatory both to his father and to himself and in fact there is little doubt that the fact of its publication having gone without legal challenge had an extremely harmful effect on the artistic career of his son in the U.S.A.

The two points in question are the relations of Mr Joyce and his late father and the question of his marriage in 1904 which subsequently and for testamentary reasons was supplemented by retroactive civil marriage according to English law in 1931. The accounts you give to the public are, as above stated, incorrect and misleading. On the first point your account is so hopelessly wide off [sic] the mark that he despairs of even attempting to rectify it by this extremely tardy correspondence and consequently suggests that you cancel completely the pages dealing with his father in these chapters.[1] The second point is a very complicated legal problem which has already caused Mr Joyce heavy expenditure in the matter of legal opinions involving as it did the marriage laws of three different countries.[2] It would be necessary to devote an entire chapter of your book to its elucidation and I doubt whether his solicitors in London would advise him to place the dossier concerning it at your disposal. For the purpose of your book the only way now is to obliterate this passage and any subsequent reference of the same tenor confining yourself to a formal statement.

It is, he finds, incomprehensible that it should be necessary to write this letter now in response to a summary communication of yours after you had been engaged on the book for ten years, had resided in Paris for several years and after no communication on your part of some 8 or 9 months, on the eve of what you announce as a publication of a limited edition de luxe the sense of which completely mystifies him. In this connection I am enclosing a very emphatic denial by G.B.S. of another piece of gossip which is retailed in your pages.[3] There is so much

---

[1] Herbert Gorman had represented John Stanislaus Joyce too flamboyantly for his son's taste. James Joyce removed some of the references to financial irresponsibility, and inserted several remarks in Gorman's book on the close ties between himself and his father.

[2] Gorman had written that Joyce could not live 'in sin' with Nora Barnacle in Dublin in 1904 and that for this and other reasons he had left Ireland. Joyce made him remove this passage and others implying that he and Nora Barnacle were not married. In the end Gorman left the matrimonial question bewilderingly unresolved.

[3] Bernard Shaw, in a letter to the editor of *Picture Post*, 3 June 1939, wrote:

'In your issue of the 13th, Mr. Geoffrey Grigson, in an interesting article on James Joyce, states that I was "disgusted by the unsqueamish realism of *Ulysses*, and burnt my copy in the grate."

'Somebody has humbugged Mr. Grigson. The story is not true. I picked up *Ulysses* in scraps from the American *Little Review*, and for years did not know that it was the history of a single day in Dublin. But having passed between seven and eight thousand single days in Dublin I missed neither the realism of the book nor its poetry. I did not

conscientious work and artistic understanding in the rest of your work
that it would be lamentable from every point of view that it should be
disfigured by passages such as these.

Mr Joyce who has always been willing to give you all assistance in
his power has made a number of rectifications on many pages of the
typescript in his possession and these will be returned to you promptly
on receipt of the rest. Incidentally may I ask you to number your pages
so as to facilitate this work. Mr Joyce would also do what he can to
help you out with your publishers in the matter of additional photographs, but in his opinion the idea of printing on the cover the arms of
Dublin or those of the Joyce family had better be abandoned at once.
As to the colour of the binding he is more or less indifferent. With kind
regards to Mrs Gorman and yourself sincerely yours   PAUL LÉON

To HARRIET SHAW WEAVER (Postcard)   MS. British Museum

7 June 1939   *34 rue des Vignes, Paris, XVIᵉ*

Dear Miss Weaver: Have you a copy of the Epilogue to Ibsen's
Ghosts?[1] If so, can you send me a typed copy. Have you two versions?
If so, send the longer of the two. My own is unfindable.

Also if you are in London at present till what date will you be there?

I am having a share of trouble over Gorman's biography which they
are trying to rush for publication in N.Y. in July. I have cabled that I
shall refuse to authorise its publication unless I am given an opportunity
of seeing the proofs.

I think I sent you the Epilogue from Z'ch a few years ago.[2]

With thanks in advance and kindest regards sincerely yours
                                                         JAMES JOYCE

To GEORGE ROGERS (Postcard)   MS. Rogers

Postmark 10 June 1939   *[Paris]*

Ahì! Il protestantesimo e quel benedetto vescovo![3] Meno male che mi
sono bene informato prima. La persona alla quale pensavo di rivolgermi

burn it; and I was not disgusted. If Mr. Joyce should ever desire a testimonial as the
author of a literary masterpiece from me, it shall be given with all possible emphasis
and with sincere enthusiasm.
                              G. Bernard Shaw,
                              Ayot St. Lawrence, Welwyn, Herts'
[1] This ironical poem is included in *Critical Writings*, pp. 271–73.   [2] In April 1934.
[3] Rogers asked an English bishop who had confirmed him to suggest an Anglican
priest in Paris. He was informed that, since he was neither a refugee nor a Jew, the bishop
could do nothing for him.

non sarebbe affatto per Lei. Ebbi una risposta alquanto secca da una persona simile in un caso analogo. Però ho pensato ad un altro, un triestino da molti anni a Londra. Prima però bisogna che m'accerti se sia tuttora in questo lurido mondo. Scrivo a una sua amica. Pazienza.

J.J.[1]

To SIGNORA MARIA NEBBIA   MS. Bib. Municipale, Vichy

12 June 1939 Monday   *34 rue des Vignes, Paris XVI*ᵉ

Gentile signora: Mi dispiace seccarla ma se la fotografia del Larbaud[2] deve apparire nella mia biografia dovrebbe essere fra le mani del mio segretario, il sig. Paul Léon, domani per essere mandata a Nuova York colla *Queen Mary* che salpa per l'America l'indomani. Non prevedevo affatto questa fretta. M'aspettavo una pubblicazione nell'autunno. Ma ho ricevuto un dispaccio inatteso l'altro giorno. Così sono gli Americani.

Dunque, il Léon passerà dalla vostra portinaia domattina verso le 11. Se possiede una buona fotografia di V.L. la lasci là per lui. Altrimenti un Suo biglietto al fotografo autorizzandoci a ritirare una fotografia— contro pagamento, s'intende—che sarà la stessa cosa.

Vorrei che la fotografia del collega e dell'amico che tanto fece per un ignoto isolano all'epoca critica della mia vita non mancasse in questo libro.

Propongo di fargli una visitina ancora quest'altra settimana, se Lei me lo concede. Nel frattempo spero che il vino svizzero gli sia piaciuto.

Con dovuti ossequi mi segno, gentile Signora, di Lei devmo

JAMES JOYCE[3]

---

[1] (Translation)
   'Ahi! Protestantism and that bl—essed bishop! Lucky that I made proper inquiries beforehand. The person I had in mind to turn to would have been unsuitable for you. I once had a curt reply from someone in a similar situation. But I have thought of someone else, a Triestine who has lived for many years in London. First however I must make sure that he is still alive in this filthy world. I am writing now to a woman friend of his. Be patient.   J.J.'

[2] Joyce insisted that Gorman include a photograph of Larbaud in the book.

[3] (Translation)
   'Dear Madam: I am sorry to disturb you but if the photograph of Larbaud is to appear in my biography it should be in the hands of my secretary Mr Paul Léon by tomorrow so as to be shipped to New York on the *Queen Mary* which sails for America the day after. I had not foreseen this rush. I expected the book to be published in Autumn. But I suddenly received a cable the day before yesterday. The Americans are like that.
   So Léon will call on your concierge tomorrow morning about 11 o'clock. If you have

To HARRIET SHAW WEAVER   MS. British Museum

19 June 1939   *Paris*

Dear Miss Weaver: Thanks for copies of Epilogue. If you have finished please return the batch of clippings to Gilbert: 7 rue Jean du Bellay, Ile S. Louis, Paris. And please look through these and return them to Beckett, 6 rue des Favorites, Paris XV as soon as convenient. They are for his friend Alfred Perron[1] who is to talk on *F.W.* from Paris P.T.T. next week. Also please send on to me any other English clippings you may have in hand.

. . . If I can find it I shall put into this letter a copy of the last letter I sent Gorman, following up three very long cables I also found it necessary to send. The letter was dictated to P.L.[2] The allusion to Giorgio is he found when in the U.S. that the Irish-American element or catholic Irish element regarded him as the son of a British Government secret agent who had amassed much money during the war and in fact when Ireland was having a war with Britain all to herself. (See the *Catholic World* whatever date it was).[3] With kindest regards sincerely yours   JAMES JOYCE

To MRS VICTOR A. SAX (Postcard)   MS. Sax

3 July 1939   *Paris*

Dear Mrs Sax: My wife and your sister spent all Saturday afternoon together. She was in good spirits and talks of going to La Baule. Strange to say, we are going there too if anything happens as my daughter's *Maison de Santé* will be transferred there. She asks me to thank you for the nice box of chocolates. I shall report to you again. With best wishes for your reposeful progress sincerely yours

JAMES JOYCE

a good photo of V.L. please leave it with him. Otherwise your note to the photographer authorizing us to get a photograph, at my expense of course, would do equally well.

I should like the photograph of the colleague and friend who did so much for an unknown islander at the critical time of my life not to be missing from this book.

I intend to pay him a visit next week if you will permit me. In the meantime I hope he liked the Swiss wine. With due respect I sign myself, dear Madam, your devoted

James Joyce'

[1] A slip for Péron.   [2] Paul Léon.   [3] See p. 403.

To Georg Goyert   MS. S. Illinois (Croessmann)

8 July 1939   *34 rue des Vignes, Paris XVI*

Sehr geehrter Herr Goyert: Vielmals habe [ich] Sie wegen des hochwohl-
gestorbenen[1] Johannes Jeep ('Von der Sirenen Listigkeit, Thun die
Poeten Dichten')[2] ausgefragt. Er hat tatsächlich existiert, wie Sie sehen.[3]
Wenigstens so schreibt die Amerikanische 'Encyclopaedia of Music'

Und wie geht's unserem Freund Finnegan,[4] da wir vom Scheintod[5]
reden?

Freundliche Grüsse   James Joyce[6]

To Viscount Carlow   MS. Yale

15 July 1939   *34 rue des Vignes, Paris*

Dear Lord Carlow: Has Ibsen's Ghost[7] gone astray or have you not my
address. There is a label on the back of this note. And, by the way, I see
there is a typist's blunder in line 4 of stanza 3 which should read:

'When the wise sire knows which is which' and not 'When the wise
child etc'[8]

If you can't send a copy I would like to read the sheets which I would
return. Sincerely yours   James Joyce

[1] A pun on 'hochwohlgeboren', a pleonastic expression meaning 'high and well born'
which Joyce alters to 'high and well died'.

[2] Quoted by Stephen Dedalus to Bloom in the *Eumaeus* episode, *Ulysses*, p. 773 (663).

[3] Enclosed was a typed slip which identified 'Johann Jeppe' as a German composer,
1582–1650.

[4] That is, what reception was being given *Finnegans Wake* in Germany?

[5] Finnegan revives at his wake. Joyce was continuing the play on life and death in
'hochwohlgestorbenen'.

[6] (Translation)

'My dear Mr Goyert: I have often plied you with questions concerning the dead
highborn Johannes Jeep ("About the Sirens' wiles, the poets sing"). He actually
existed, as you see. At least that is what the American Encyclopaedia of Music says.

And how is our friend Finnegan, since we are on the subject of suspended anima-
tion? Kind regards   James Joyce'

[7] Carlow was publishing at his Corvinus Press a parody, *Ibsen's Ghosts*, by J. M.
Barrie.

[8] The stanza in Joyce's 'An Epilogue to Ibsen's *Ghosts*' reads:
My spouse bore me a blighted boy,
Our slavey pupped a bouncing bitch.
Paternity, thy name is joy
When the wise sire knows which is which.

To Frank Budgen   MS. Yale

22 July 1939   *Golf Hotels, Étretat*

Dear Budgen: Thanks for article and format received. I shall write you
about it when I get back to Paris, that is, after Lucia's birthday, the
26th. So far, I have received over 400 press notices and I think I may
send a dozen picked which perhaps you ought to see. These I should
want returned of course.

It seems to me an excellent article but I am sure you can amplify it at
at least three points with advantage to it and to yourself materially as
the *Fortnightly* pays per page. I am almost sure they will take it if
you write a letter on the lines I suggested. The fact that he was in the
rival *19th Century* doesn't mean much for they don't cover the same
ground.[1]

I see you had more B.A. workers in Britain yesterday. Sunny summer
seems to have become a misnomer. It's not hot here. My gracious is it
expensive. My daughter-in-law is in Switzerland.

I hope that Money bags knows what Ireland expects that every man
this day will do Very friendly regards sincerely yours

JAMES JOYCE

To C. P. Curran[2]   MS. Curran

Postmark 23 July 1939   *Golf Hotels, Étretat, Seine-Inférieure*

P.S.[3]

If you are not coming to the continent you could send the book by
someone else who is unless you have lent it in which case the problem is
solved for neither you nor I will ever see it again.

Some friend of yours, I suppose, in the Irish Tourist Association has
sent me a copy of the official Guide to Dublin in which I am mentioned.
Will you please thank him from me for his courtesy. As regards the
music section of it while the compilers may be correct, in the French
sense, in not claiming Dowland for Dalkey it seems to me Field and
Balfe should be mentioned.[4]

---

[1] Alex. Glendinning, 'Commentary: *Finnegans Wake*,' *Nineteenth Century* CXXVI
(July 1939), 73–82.

[2] From a typed copy.

[3] The postscript is to Joyce's letter of 22 July 1939 (*Letters*, ed. Gilbert, p. 405), in
which he offered to sign Curran's copy of *Finnegans Wake*.

[4] Dalkey people hold that the composer John Dowland (1563?–1626?) was born in
Dalkey, but the Dictionary of National Biography says Westminster. Both conjectures
have only tenuous support. Michael William Balfe (1808–70) and John Field (1782–
1837) were both born in Dublin, the first off Grafton Street, the second in Golden Lane.

I see too that our old dean of studies has gone. He was a well
meaning peacemaker and I hope he is blessed.[1] sincerely yours

                                                   JAMES JOYCE

To MRS VICTOR A. SAX   MS. Sax

28 July 1939   *Parigi*

Dear Mrs Sax: We rang up your sister when we came back and found
that she was not feeling too well physically so got her to see our physician
Dr Fontaine who says there is nothing the matter with her except
fatigue and gave her a tonic to take. She seems to have caught a summer
cold. Anyhow my wife saw her yesterday and I am to tell you there is
absolutely no need for you to worry. She hopes to begin her holiday next
week. We *may* go to Berne then too but it is not sure. The case of wine
has now come. Many thanks to Mr Sax but he is on no account to send
me any more of anything. My wife is not here at present and I cannot
make out your address on the picture postcard so I send this to Z'ch.
Thank heaven one of the summer months is almost over! I wish it would
snow.

   Friendly greetings from us to you both sincerely yours

                                                   JAMES JOYCE

To GEORGE ROGERS   MS. Rogers

Postmark 3 August 1939   *34 rue des Vignes, Paris XVI*

Caro signor Rogers: Dunque. Giorgio è stato bocciato ingloriosamente
dalla giuria invisibile della B.B.C.[2] Quell'alto consesso promulgò il suo
verdetto, vale a dire, che la sua voce era ben al disotto del livello
richiesto e che no vedeva nemmeno perchè il suo nome dovrebbe essere
aggiunto alla loro lista per un avvenire più o meno eventuale.

   Siccome Giorgio si mostra molto taciturno, mi rivolgo a Lei. Cosa
diamine è successa a quell' nazione? Si accorse Lei di qualche cosa
nell'ambiente, una stiza, un'ostilità, fretta, impreparazione ecc. Od il
timor panico distrusse la sua voce totalmente o cantò davvero in modo
da meritar l'opprobriosa sentenza. 'Al di sotto del livello della Gran-
bretagna in fatto di arte canora!' Per l'ugola celeste di Santa Cecilia,

---

[1] See II, p. 391, n. 2.

[2] Professor Rogers says that George Joyce sang very well and was grossly undervalued.

per quanto affirochito sia diventato il mio proprio ruggito, non m'aspettavo mai questo calcio di ciucco! Ed il guaio è ch'egli è sempre disposto ad accettare la condamna. Sarei molto grato di un Suo breve cenno in merito. SalutandoLa cordialmente devmo

JAMES JOYCE[1]

To MRS VICTOR A. SAX (Postcard)   MS. Sax

5 August 1939   *Paris*

Dear Mrs Sax: My wife saw your sister twice this week. She, your sister, said the tonic Dr Fontaine gave her did her great good. By the way our doctor is a woman and a very clever one too. In fact *Lui* is a *Lei* as in that libretto.[2] Your sister asked me for the name of a good hotel at Montreux. I advised the Monnet where we stayed some years ago. She left the other night, so far as I know, but we could not go to the station as here, in Passy, there was thunder overhead and when there's an *orage* my place is under the mattress.

We have not left for Berne. We hardly know where we are going or when. We might end up in Tasmania. I hate the summer and the storms and the heat and the crowds and the long days and all the nationals out for all the nature they can find. If we move I will let you know. Tanti saluti a Lei ed a Lui.

JAMES JOYCE

[1] (Translation)
'Dear Mr Rogers: So. Giorgio has been ingloriously failed by the invisible jury of the B.B.C. That high court issued its verdict, to wit, that his voice was well below the required standard and that no one saw reason to include his name on their list for some future date.
Since Giorgio is so reticent I turn to you. What the deuce did happen at that audition? Did you feel something in the atmosphere, a row, some hostility, haste, unprepared-ness etc. Or stage fright completely destroyed his voice and he really sang in a way to deserve the offensive sentence. "Below the level of Great Britain in the art of singing!" In the name of St Cecilia's heavenly ugola, even if my own lion's roar is half spent, I never expected this donkey's kick! And the trouble is that Giorgio is always inclined to accept condemnation. I should be very grateful for a short note from you about it all. With cordial greetings yours sincerely   James Joyce'
[2] Mrs Sax read the libretto of an Italian opera to Joyce once when his eyesight was bad, and she confused the pronunciation of 'Lui' and 'Lei'. The slip remained a standing joke between them.

To Cecil ffrench Salkeld[1]   MS. Northwestern

10 August 1939   *Hotel de la Paix, Lausanne*

Dear Mr Salkeld: My friend, Mr Samuel Beckett, has forwarded me
your letter. I thank you very much for your courteous invitation and for
the kind terms in which it is couched. I have not written any verse for
many years now and regret therefore that I am unable to contribute to
your venture to which, however, I wish all success.

I read your postscript with great interest and I hope that distinguished officer, your grandfather, did not lament too lyrically his
purchase of my book but that it afforded him some moments of
entertainment at least. Sincerely yours   James Joyce

To Georg Goyert   MS. S. Illinois (Croessmann)

12 August 1939   *Hotel de la Paix, Lausanne*

Lieber Herr Goyert: Leider ist Ihrer Brief und die Rezension der
D.A.Z.[2] sowohl andere Kritiken meines Buches verlierer gegangen.
Glücklicherweise habe ich sie zuerst gelesen. Wäre es möglich für Ihnen
mir ein anderes Exemplar dieser Zeitung zu verschaffen? Erinnern Sie
sich des Datums? Ich weiss nicht ob andere Rezensionen in Deutsch-
land erscheinen. Prof. Curtius enthielt eine Press-Kopie und auch Prof.
Zimmer (Heidelberg). Bis jetzt habe ich etwa 500 gehabt, kann sie aber
nicht schicken da ich nur diese Kopien besitze. Ich finde den Preis
meines Buches ganz verrückt 25 Schilling bei solchen Zeiten! Tadeln
Sie mich nicht, ich bin für nichts darin. Im Gegenteil!

Sie schreiben am besten an meine Pariser Adresse da wir fahren nach
Bern ubermorgen und dann nach Zurich. Freundliche Grüsse an Sie
und an Ihre Familie   James Joyce[3]

---

[1] Cecil ffrench Salkeld, Irish painter.
[2] *Deutsche Allgemeine Zeitung*, a Berlin newspaper.
[3] (Translation)

'Dear Mr Goyert: Unfortunately your letter and the review in the D.A.Z. as well as
other reviews of my book have been lost. Fortunately I had read them first. Would it
be possible for you to obtain another copy of this newspaper for me? Do you remember
the date? I do not know if other reviews have appeared in Germany. Prof. Curtius has
received a press copy, and also Prof. Zimmer (Heidelberg). So far I have had about
500, but I cannot send them since I have only these copies. I find the price of my book
completely crazy 25 shillings in times like these! Don't blame me, it's not my doing.
Just the opposite!

It would be best to write me at my Paris address since we go to Bern the day after
tomorrow and then to Zurich. Friendly greetings to you and your family

James Joyce'

To Mr and Mrs George Turner (Postcard)   MS. Ellmann

12 August 1939   [*Grand Hotel de la Paix*[1] *Lausanne*]

Here we are at Le Touquet with Vittel at the other side of the road and all surrounded by Beaugency, Spa and the half dozen other places we said we were going to. Greetings to you both from this synthetic pleasure resort   JAMES JOYCE

To Viscount Carlow   MS. Yale

Postmark 12 August 1939   *Hotel de la Paix, Lausanne*

Dear Lord Carlow: Thanks for the sheets of Barrie's *Ibsen's Ghosts* and for leave to keep them. It is an amusing burlesque which would have made old Henrik laugh. I saw J. L. Toole[2] act twice and he must have been droll and completely improbable in the part. As my *Epilogue* will be printed in H. Gorman's biography of me I thought of letting him see the sheets. There is a certain limit. J.M.B. in his preface alludes to Ibsen as 'the greatest dramatist of our age'. I would go much further. But I note there are only 16 copies not for sale of this as yet unpublished 'work' and perhaps you may not wish me to send this to the U.S.A. even as a brief temporary loan. It is by no means necessary that I should do so. ? Sincerely yours   JAMES JOYCE

To Paul Léon   MS. Private

2 September 1939   *Hotel Saint Christophe, La Baule*

Dear Léon: We moved into this cheap hotel today. I understood Ivry would leave when general mobilisation was proclaimed. Therefore went to Hotel Edelweiss into which it is supposed to move. The caretaker had never heard of any Dr Delmas or Maison de Santé. Was not expecting anyone. Mrs Delmas has no telephone. The Delmas villa is about 2 miles outside La Baule. There are no vehicles of any kind today. Walked there and found she knew nothing. He is supposed to be in pourparlers with the Banque Nationale in Paris. . . . 30,000 persons are supposed to arrive here on Sunday and Monday. A huge hotel (120 rooms) is not likely to be left vacant. Can you find out whether he has taken it or not, whether he has these famous cars which were to be ready to transport his

[1] The hotel is pictured on the other side of the postcard.
[2] John Lawrence Toole (1830–1906), English comic actor and theatre-manager.

maison and what he is waiting for since everyone is being urged to leave
Paris unless he knows the whole business is a farce.

You have troubles enough of your own but if you can find this out by
telephone so much the better. Nothing else is of much importance for
the moment. I suppose your idea of staying in Paris is to show your zeal
and readiness. Perhaps you are not there now.

I hope the rest of the family are all right. Helen wrote me to say they
would go to stay in the country house if war came. She is on way in
Etretat and says my concierge has forwarded three letters for me. Why?
With best wishes cordialement votre   JAMES JOYCE

To GEORGE JOYCE (Telegram)   TS. Private

3 September 1939   *La Baule*

ABSOLUMENT AUCUNE PROVISION FAITE ICI POUR
RECEVOIR MAISON SANTE STOP DELMAS PENSE POUVOIR
ARRANGER EVENTUELLEMENT D'ICI HUIT A QUINZE
JOURS STOP EN ATTENDANT LUCIA ABANDONNEE SEULE
IVRY MALGRE TOUS MES PREPARATIFS STOP ESSAYE
TE METTRE EN RAPPORT AVEC PERSONNEL MAISON
NOUS SOMMES HOTELSAINT CRISTOPHE ICI TELEPHONE
21-30 COURAGE BONNE CHANCE   BABBO[1]

To JACQUES MERCANTON (Postcard)   MS. Mercanton

8 September 1939 Fête de Marion Bloom[2]   *Hotel Saint Christophe,*
                                                  La Baule (Loire Infer.)

Cher Monsieur Mercanton: Nous voilà donc ici où depuis bien douze
jours nous attendons l'arrivée de ma fille. Je ne sais pas qu'est-ce que ce
medecin psychiâtre[3] attend pour transporter sa maison de santé de
Paris à la Baule comme c'était convenu et nous sommes dans tous nos
ébats. Depuis trois semaines toute personne qui peut le faire et n'a pas
d'affaires à Paris le quitte et il reste là-bas toujours avec ses malades. Il

---

[1] (Translation)
'Absolutely no provision made here to receive *maison de santé*. Delmas thinks he can
arrange eventually in a week or fortnight. Meanwhile Lucia is abandoned alone Ivry
in spite of all my arrangements. Try to get in touch with the staff of *maison*. We are at
Hotel St Cristophe here telephone 21-30. Courage good luck   Babbo'
[2] The feastday of the nativity of the Virgin. A year before this letter was written, Joyce
inscribed a copy of *Ulysses* to Mercanton on 7 September 1938, with the note, 'Veille de la
Fête de Madonna Bloom' ('Eve of the Feastday of Madonna Bloom').
[3] Dr Achille Delmas.

croît, parait-il, que les alertes de nuit font du bien pour la santé des gens nerveux. C'est inouï!

Il y a un long article sur moi dans la *Revue de Paris*, du Septembre.[1] Rien dans la *N.R.F.* je veux dire votre deuxième article.[2] Le numéro est dédié à la mémoire de Charles du Bos que je connaissais.

J'espère que vous allez bien malgré les évènements cordialement

JAMES JOYCE[3]

To SELSKAR MICHAEL GUNN[4]   MS. Harvard

15 September 1939   *La Baule*

Dear Gunn: As you kindly suggested I am sending a written message for M. Paul Léon (he will not trouble you much more for he is conscribed as from Tuesday next), namely, that I have now received the complete proofs of my biography and have written the N.Y. publisher that I shall deal with them directly.[5]

In this connection perhaps it may amuse you to look over the illustrations so I am leaving them and shall pick them up tomorrow from your hall porter if you will be good enough to leave them with him for me.

Many thanks in advance sincerely yours   JAMES JOYCE

---

[1] Georges Pelorson, 'Finnegans Wake de James Joyce ou le livre de l'homme,' *Revue de Paris* 46.17 (1 September 1939), 227–35.

[2] Mercanton published an article, 'Finnegans Wake,' in the *Nouvelle Revue Française* 27.308 (1 May 1939) 858–64. Joyce evidently expected another to follow.

[3] (Translation)
'Dear Mr Mercanton: We are in this place where for a good twelve days we have been awaiting the arrival of my daughter. I do not know what this psychiatrist is waiting for in order to move his institution from Paris to La Baule as it was arranged, and here we are frolicking away. Since three weeks ago everybody who could leave Paris and had no business there has been doing so, yet he is still there with his patients. He believes, it seems, that the night alerts improve the health of nervous people. It is incredible!
There is a long article on me in the *Revue de Paris* of September. Nothing in the N.R.F., I mean your second article. The issue is dedicated to the memory of Charles du Bos, whom I knew.
I hope you are well in spite of the events cordially   James Joyce'

[4] Selskar Michael Gunn (1883–1944), an authority on public health, was Vice-President of the Rockefeller Foundation and in charge of its Paris office, which had been moved to La Baule. He was the son of Michael Gunn, who built and operated the Gaiety Theatre in Dublin, and he had known Joyce during their early days in Dublin as well as during the late nineteen-thirties in Paris. The name 'Gunn' is played upon perhaps a dozen times in *Finnegans Wake*.

[5] A coolness was developing between Léon and Joyce because of tension between George and Helen Joyce. Léon was inclined to be sympathetic to Helen Joyce while Joyce naturally took his son's part.

To Valery Larbaud (Postcard)   MS. Bib. Municipale, Vichy

18 September 1939   *Hotel Saint Christophe, La Baule, L.I.*

Cher Larbaud: Deux lignes pour vous donner notre adresse. Nous sommes ici auprès de notre fille malade. Elle est à Pornichet, à 3 km. Aussi pour vous dire qu'il y a un article dans la *Revue de Paris* (le 1er pas le 15e septembre) sur mon livre qui vous interessera sans doute si vous ne l'avez pas déjà vu.

J'espère que le progrès se maintient chez vous. Esperons toujours. Mes hommages à Madame Larbaud cordialement votre James Joyce[1]

To Frank Budgen (Postcard)   MS. Yale

18 September 1939   *Hotel Saint Christophe, La Baule (L.I.)*

Dear Budgen: The above is our address. We are here near Lucia. Glad to know Mrs Budgen and Joan are in Berks and hope you are too by now. But probably you are not. Sorry the *Fortnightly* declined your article[2] no sense of business the *Nineteenth Century* had one 6 months before. I suppose you have tried another review—there is an article in the *Revue de Paris* (1 Sept) which your public library [should have]. You seem still surprised about the *Sunday Times*. Léon heard a long time ago that this paper had declared its intention to ignore the book on publication as 'irrelevant to literature'. A little coaxing may change that, however. With friendly greetings cordialement votre

James Joyce

To Farrar & Rinehart   TS. Holt, Rinehart and Winston
(Cablegram)

21 September 1939   *Hotel Saint Christophe, La Baule*

Proposal[3] inacceptable wait arrival corrections numerous inaccuracies final chapters sent today   James Joyce

---

[1] (Translation)
   'Dear Larbaud: Two lines to give you our address. We are here near our sick daughter. She is at Pornichet, three kilometers away. Also to tell you that there is an article in the *Revue de Paris* (the 1st not the 15th September) of my book which will doubtless be of interest to you if you have not already seen it.
   I hope you continue to make progress. We must always hope. My regards to Madame Larbaud cordially yours   James Joyce'

[2] Frank Budgen's article, 'Joyce's Chapters of Going Forth by Day,' was published in *Horizon* IV.21 (September 1941) 172–91.

[3] Regarding the publication of Herbert Gorman's biography of Joyce, which the publishers wished to hurry.

To John Farrar[1]   MS. Holt, Rinehart and Winston

21 September 1939   *Hotel Saint Christophe, La Baule*
(Loire-Inférieure), France

Dear Mr Farrar: I cabled you to stay your publication of my biography
till the arrival of the enclosed corrections and suggestions for Chapters
X and XI, which please pass on to Mr Gorman.

I shall now look at the revised proofs of the preceding chapters (where
I take it his corrections have already been made) and write you again in
a few days. Sincerely yours   James Joyce

To Farrar & Rinehart   TS. Holt, Rinehart and Winston
(Cablegram)

3 October 1939   *La Baule*

Final corrections sent in two registered letters please await acknowledge
arrival cable   James Joyce

To Viscount Carlow   MS. Yale

4 November 1939   *Hotel Lutétia, 43 Boulevard Raspail, Paris*

Dear Lord Carlow: I am glad to hear from you and to know you are
well and cheerful. We had to come up here in a hurry from La Baule
owing to a very serious illness of my daughter-in-law and are stopping
in this hotel as all the flats in our house are unoccupied and of course
unheated. I don't know when we shall be able to return so if you run
over here please ring me up.

I did not send the Barrie book to the U.S. after all.

With thanks for your good wishes in these tiresome times and with
my own good wishes to you and your family sincerely yours
                                                             James Joyce

To Mr and Mrs Victor A. Sax   MS. Sax

6 November 1939   *Hotel Lutétia, 43 Boulevard Raspail, Paris*

Chers amis: Merci de votre gentille pensée. Vous semblez être presque
les seules personnes en ce moment qui pensent à nous. Nous avons dû
quitter La Baule en hâte à cause de la grave maladie de ma bru et n'y

[1] John Farrar (b. 1896), American publisher and writer.

rentrerons que d'ici quelques semaines. Elle est maintenant dans une maison de santé à Suresnes, près de Paris, et son frère arrive ici demain de New York et il tâchera de l'emmener avec lui en Amérique.[1] L'enfant a été placé dans une école près de Vichy.[2] Une histoire lamentable et qui a semé le désastre à droite et à gauche. Mon fils et moi avons passé trois semaines angoissées pour ne pas parler de ma femme. Ma fille me croît souffrant et toujours à La Baule. Il [ne] nous manquait que cela vraiment. Nous sommes à l'hotel parce que l'appartement n'est pas chauffé.

En somme, du courage!

Très cordialement à Lui et à Lei[3]   JAMES JOYCE[4]

To STANISLAUS JOYCE (Note on scrap of paper)   MS. Cornell

Postmark 16 December 1939   [*Paris*]

Please have this[5] inserted in 'Il Piccolo' if you see no reason against it

JIM

[1] Helen Joyce returned to the United States with her brother on 2 May 1940.

[2] The Ecole Bilingue of Maria Jolas, which had been moved from Paris to Saint-Gérand-le-Puy.

[3] See p. 451, n. 2.

[4] (Translation)

'Dear friends: Thanks for your kind thought. You seem to be almost the only ones at the moment who do think of us. We have had to leave La Baule abruptly because of the serious illness of my daughter-in-law and we have been back here only a few weeks. She is now in a *maison de santé* at Suresnes, near Paris, and her brother is arriving tomorrow from New York and will try to take her back to the United States with him. The child has been placed in a school near Vichy. A lamentable business and one which has sown disaster right and left. My son and I have spent three anguishing weeks, not to mention my wife. My daughter believes I am ill and still at La Baule. Really this was all we needed. We are staying at the hotel because the flat has no heat.

In short, be brave!

Very cordially to him and to her   James Joyce'

[5] Enclosed was a clipping from a German newspaper stating that Joseph Prescott, of the Department of English at the University of Connecticut, was seeking manuscripts and other material relating to *Ulysses*, which he would carefully return to the owners. Professor Prescott is now at Wayne State University in Detroit.

Part V

SAINT-GÉRAND-LE-PUY, ZURICH

1939-41

Saint-Gérand-le-Puy, Zurich (1939-41)

The great chords of *Finnegans Wake* had been struck, even if few people heard them. Joyce's life now moved through dislocation and illness towards its end. Having resided in one city or another for fifty-seven years, he found the village life of St Gérand dull and more dull. The lack of distraction rendered more anguishing his growing recognition that even the life of his own family was out of control. His son's marriage had collapsed, and his daughter-in-law, shaken in mind for the last two years, was taken back to the United States. George Joyce stayed on in Paris, leaving his parents uncertain of his address. Lucia was off in Pornichet, too far away to visit. Only Stephen was close by at Mrs Jolas's school, and this was likely to be closed before long.

Joyce and Nora lived disconsolately at St Gérand for almost a year, from the day before Christmas 1939 until 14 December 1940, except for two months (mid-April to mid-June of 1940) when they went to nearby Vichy, which was less dreary. Any hope of waiting out the second World War as they had waited out the first waned rapidly. In May the Germans swarmed demonically into western Europe. After the fall of Paris on 14 June, a group of refugees appeared at St Gérand, including George, Samuel Beckett, and the Léons. The Germans passed through the village a few days later, but shortly withdrew and left the semblance of control of Unoccupied France to Pétain's government.

The presence of Léon pleased Joyce; he took the opportunity to check *Finnegans Wake* with him for misprints, and they made a list together. But in August and September it became clear that no one was planning to stay in St Gérand. Léon left in that month, and so did Maria Jolas at her husband's urging. Joyce had put off coming to any decision, but it seemed likely that George would be conscripted if they remained much longer, and the Vichy government was less than eager to entertain British subjects in its territory.

At the beginning of September Joyce still hesitated about where to go, but he began writing letters to Swiss mental asylums to see if he could find one suitable for Lucia. His preference for the continent over the United States focused his thoughts inevitably upon Switzerland. At first the Swiss were singularly unflattered by this decision, probably because the local officials had no notion who Joyce was. They rejected his first application on 30 September 1940. Then the most influential men in Zurich interceded on his behalf, friends offered financial guarantees, and on 29 November the Swiss relented and informed Joyce that he and his family would be admitted. With Stephen Joyce in their care, they left St Gérand on 14 December 1940 at 3 o'clock in the morning, and made their way slowly but without incident to Zurich, where they arrived on 17 December.

In Zurich Joyce stayed at a pension and lived quietly. He walked about with his grandson and told him stories; he made a few notes which unfortunately do not indicate with what sort of book he would next have boarded English literature. Depressed as he found himself, he could as always be enlivened in the evening with friends present. He wrote some letters thanking people for helping him to reach Switzerland, and his last written communication was a postcard to Stanislaus Joyce naming some people who might assist him if his wartime situation in Italy became untenable. The list, which included people in Switzerland, possibly suggests that he had begun to despair of much further communication with his brother, and perhaps of longer life.

His health had evidently been impaired at St Gérand because of an undiagnosed duodenal ulcer. He and his wife and son assumed that the sporadic pains he sometimes experienced came from nerves, as a doctor in Paris had assured them several years earlier. So at first no one was greatly concerned by the intense stomach pains he began to complain of on Friday night, 10 January 1941. But the morphine administered by a doctor who lived nearby did not alleviate them, and in the early morning Joyce was brought to a Zurich hospital. There, a perforated ulcer being suspected, an operation was performed that morning. At first it seemed to have been successful, but the next day his strength flagged and he lost consciousness. On 13 January, at 2.15 in the morning, Joyce died. He was buried two days later, after a small ceremony, in the Fluntern cemetery that overlooks the city of Zurich.

To Jacques Mercanton   MS. Mercanton

9 January 1940   *Hotel de la Paix, S. Gérand-le-Puy (Allier)*[1]

Cher Monsieur Mercanton: Voila les causes de mon long silence. Ma
bru, à son tour . . . a été internée d'office. . . . Mon fils, totalement
désorienté, se trouve à Paris avec les amis. Il cherche à s'occuper. J'ai
dû prendre l'enfant à mes charges. Il est ici dans une école et je fais
un partage entre ici, Paris et La Baule où ma fille est toujours.

Vous me parlez d'un certain 'roman' que j'ai écrit. Ici personne n'a
soufflé mot de son existence. J'ai reçu encore des critiques parmi
lesquelles une 'contribution' bien bizarre vient de Helsinki où, pour de bon
et comme le prophète le previt, le Finn again wakes.[2] Il y avait une aussi
dans la revue romaine *Panorama* du 12 novembre. Puisque le livre entier
est fondé sur l'œuvre d'un penseur italien . . .?[3] En somme, un 'fiasco'
total quant à la critique européenne jusqu'ici. Et je n'arrive pas même
à toucher mes tantièmes à cause des lois sur l'exportation du Kapital.

J'écrirai à Francini quand je retrouverai sa lettre. Va-t-il publier sa
brochure[4] dans une edition de luxe, sur Japon?

Si vous m'écrivez tapez à la machine. Si vous allez à Lausanne buvez
3 litres de Villeneuve à mes trois intentions. Cordialement votre

JAMES JOYCE[5]

[1] The Joyces went to stay at Saint-Gérand-le-Puy on 24 December 1939, chiefly to be
near their grandson at Mrs Jolas's school there.

[2] Joyce saw the Russo-Finnish war as a confirmation of his book's title.

[3] Giambattista Vico is meant.

[4] Alessandro Francini Bruni evidently had in mind republishing his lecture on Joyce,
Joyce intimo spogliato in piazza.

[5] (Translation)

'Dear M. Mercanton: Here are the reasons for my long silence. My daughter-in-law,
in her turn . . . has been interned. . . . My son, entirely disoriented, is now in Paris with
friends. He is trying to keep busy. I have had to take over the responsibility of the
child. He is at a school here and I divide myself among here, Paris, and La Baule
where my daughter still is.

You talk of a certain "novel" I wrote. Here no one has breathed a word of its
existence. I have received some more reviews among which is one very odd "contribution" from Helsinki where, happily and as the prophet foresaw, the Finn again wakes.
There was one also in the Roman review *Panorama* of 12 November. Seeing that the
whole book is founded on the work of an Italian thinker . . . ? In short, a complete
fiasco up to the present as far as European criticism is concerned. And I cannot even
get hold of my royalties because of the laws about the exportation of capital.

I will write to Francini when I find his letter again. Is he going to publish his
pamphlet in a de luxe edition, on Japan paper?

If you write me use a typewriter. If you go to Lausanne drink three litres of
Villeneuve to my three intentions. Cordially yours   James Joyce'

To Frank Budgen (Postcard)   MS. Yale

9 January 1940   *Hotel de la Paix, S. Gérand-le-Puy (Allier)*

Dear Budgen: I forgot to say Louis Gillet told me last week he had
bought a copy of your book marked: 4th impression. Is this worth
looking into? Was there any but a first edition which was remaindered
(Léon has been trying to get a copy for private use) or is this a ruse of
the publishing firm to give a false idea of sales or is an edition out
without your knowledge? If you reply to this write only about it in your
letter so that I can forward it to him (better type it) or wire yourself to
him direct, 17 rue Bonaparte, Paris 7e. He is an academician.[1] Sincerely
yours   James Joyce

To Daniel Brody (Postcard)   MS. Brody

10 January 1940   *Hotel de la Paix, S. Gérand-le-Puy (Allier)*

Dear Mr Brody: Thank you for your Christmas greetings. I hope you
and all your family are well. Another misfortune has fallen on mine. My
daughter-in-law has had a dreadful mental breakdown and is interned.
I have had to take over the child who is in a boarding school here. My
son's entire family life seems to be ruined. As if the affairs of my poor
daughter were not enough!

I hear today that the Italian version of *Anna Livia* is to be published
shortly in a review in Rome. Do you think it would be possible to
publish the version you have in Holland?[2] After all it is only about
rivers and washerwomen. I wonder whether that Dutch critic whose
address you sent me—I must look for his name—ever found his way
through my book. He wrote a very remarkable essay as [far as] it goes.
I have had several more reviews in Spanish, Italian, a very long one by a
Harvard professor, a Russian[3] (the best so far) and—naturally, I
suppose—the most curious of all, a symbolical commentary sent me
from Helsinki where, as predicted, the 'Finn again wakes'. The Dutch
critic's name is G. B. van der Vat (c/o Dr Zandwoort, The Hague
(English Studies).[4]

Greetings to Mrs Brody and yourself from us both sincerely yours

                                                      James Joyce

[1] That is, a member of the French Academy.

[2] Georg Goyert's translation of *Anna Livia Plurabelle* into German was published
much later, in *Die Fähre* (Munich) I.6 (1946) 337–40.

[3] Harry Levin (b. 1912), the critic, actually a native American, is meant. See p. 468,
n. 2.

[4] D. G. Van der Vat, 'Paternity in *Ulysses*,' *English Studies* XIX (August 1937)
145–58.

To VALERY LARBAUD (Postcard)   MS. Bib. Municipale, Vichy

[? *19 January 1940*][1]   *Hotel du Commerce, S. Gérand-le-Puy*

Mon cher Larbaud: Que je suis bête! Oui, ma biographie a été publiée en Amérique le 10 novembre et votre photographie agrandie occupe une page entière. Je n'ai pas encore reçu mon exemplaire. On m'a trouvé jadis de l'esprit. Oui, . . . mais de l'eschalier [sic]. Una stretta di mano

J.J.[2]

To C. P. CURRAN[3]   MS. Curran

11 February 1940   *Hotel de la Paix, S. Gérand-le-Puy (Allier)*

Dear Curran: This is to tell you your photograph appears in Gorman's life of me the first copies of which have now reached Paris, and I suppose, London from New York. The publishers are Farrar and Rinehart.[4]

I hope you and your family are well. Mine has been stricken by a new disaster. My unfortunate daughter-in-law has lost her reason and is at present internée d'office which is provisional certificate of lunacy. I had to rush up from La Baule where I was with Lucia (who is still ill but quieter) to Paris four months ago and we have had a dreadful time. . . . The flat in Villa Scheffer and the country house she intended to call Shillelagh are vacant and Giorgio is living with Léon's brother-in-law. They say she may recover as the attack was so sudden and violent and slow cases are worse. She staged a marvellous banquet for my last birthday and read the closing pages on the passing-out of Anna Livia— to a seemingly much affected audience. Alas, if you ever read them you will see that they were unconsciously prophetical! I am and have been much affected by all this [word omitted]. While I am writing the little golden book with the title and date and names she had made for that day attached to my fountainpen keeps on tinkling. (Giorgio has had a hard experience. He had practically to kidnap the child *en pleine rue*.[5] I have had to take him in charge and put him in Mme Jolas's school here.—We are staying here for the moment Giorgio and Becket are

---

[1] This date is written on the postcard in another hand. The postmark is blurred.

[2] (Translation)

'My dear Larbaud: How stupid of me! Yes, my biography has been out in America since 10 November and your photograph, enlarged, fills a whole page. I have not received my copy yet. People used to find me thoughtful. Yes, . . . or rather after-thoughtful. A handshake   J.J.'

Joyce plays here on the words *'esprit'* (wit), and *'esprit de l'escalier'* (the faculty of thinking up good ideas too late).

[3] From a typewritten copy, with a few obvious mistranscriptions corrected. A shorter version is in *Letters*, ed. Gilbert, p. 408.

[4] Regularly misspelt by Joyce as Reinhardt, a slip corrected in this book.

[5] 'In public.'

coming down for the boy's birthday—15th—. I wrote to Lucia explaining the whole case. She said we could stay here and go back to her later on.) Ahime![1]

I have received a number of foreign notices of my book, Italian, Spanish, American. The best is by a Russian American—a professor at Harvard—and the most curious comes from Helsinki where, as was predicted, the Finn again wakes.

Mrs J. F. Byrne writes to me from N.Y. asking me to approach publishers about a book (she says it is an epoch-making work) he has written.[2] I asked you if you had noticed anything about him the last time he was in Europe. I wonder if your daughter met him when she was in the U.S. I feel there is something not all right there. All the same I will do what I can, not very much.

With kind remembrances to Mrs and Miss Curran and yourself sincerely yours   JAMES JOYCE

To VALERY LARBAUD (Postcard)   MS. Bib. Municipale, Vichy

11 February 1940   *Hotel de la Paix, S. Gérand-le-Puy*

Cher Larbaud: Deux mots pour vous dire que nous sommes de nouveau vos voisins et que j'ai reçu ce matin ma biographie publiée à New York avec votre portrait agrandi. Le drôle qui l'a publiée n'a pas même pensé à m'envoyer un exemplaire et j'ai dû me l'acheter à Paris. Je vous la porterai un de ces jours, vers la fin de la semaine
    Mes hommages à Madame cordialement votre   JAMES JOYCE[3]

To DARIO DE TUONI[4]   MS. de Tuoni

20 February 1940   *Hotel de la Paix, S. Gérand-le-Puy, Allier, France*

Egregio signor de Tuoni: Dopo un buon—o piuttosto—un cattivo quarto di secolo Le sarà certo una sorpresa ricevere questa mia lettera.

---

[1] 'Alas.'
[2] Probably a book on cryptography, rather than Byrne's memoir, *Silent Years*.
[3] (Translation)
    'Dear Larbaud: Just a word to tell you that we are again neighbours of yours and that I received this morning my biography published in New York with your portrait enlarged. The silly fellow who published it didn't even think of sending me a copy and I have had to buy one in Paris. I will bring it to you some day soon, near the end of the week.
    My regards to Madame cordially yours   James Joyce'
[4] Dario de Tuoni (b. 1892 in Innsbruck), a Triestine poet whom Joyce had met before the first World War. They were introduced by Alessandro Francini Bruni. The text of this letter is taken from Dario de Tuoni, 'James Joyce nella Vecchia Trieste,' *Fiera Letteraria* (Rome) XVI.9 (26 February 1961) 5, where most of it is reproduced photographically.

Fatto sta che lessi qualche tempo addietro un Suo articolo su Morand e
Valery Larbaud e venerdì scorso, essendo a Vichy (20 chilometri di quà)
andai a rivedere il mio amico Larbaud al quale avevo a suo tempo
inviato l'articolo. Egli m'incarica di ringraziar La della Sua critica
amichevole. Gli ho spiegato che noi ci conoscevamo 'in illo tempore'[1] a
Trieste. La signora Larbaud[2] è genovese. Egli è stato molto ammalato
da parecchi anni ma secondo me ora va per la buona strada.

Spero che Lei stia bene malgrado questo tempo che corre quando non
zoppica. Mio fratello è sempre in Trieste, professore all'università. Io
sono nonno di un nipotino che ha festeggiato il suo ottavo compleanno
il 15 di questo mese. Ebbi recentemente una lettera di Francini il quale
è tornato al suo vecchio mestiere, l'insegnamento. È maestro alla
scuola dei padri 'Scalopi' a Firenze. E Tullio Silvestri? Dov'è e che cosa
è diventato? Ho sempre quattro o cinque dei suoi quadri nel mio
appartamento a Parigi. Era un buon pittore e anche una 'bela macia'[3]
come si soleva dire.

Mando questa lettera per tramite del giornale[4] nel quale lessi il Suo
articolo e così spero che, se Dio vuole, La giungerà finalmente. Me lo
faccia sapere, se vuole, con un Suo cenno in riscontro all'indirizzo qui
sopra.

SalutandoLa distintamente mi segno di Lei devo   JAMES JOYCE[5]

---

[1] This Latin phrase, meaning 'At that time', is inserted before the reading of any
gospel in Catholic churches.
[2] Signora Maria Nebbia.
[3] A Triestine expression, meaning approximately, 'Some character.'
[4] De Tuoni's article appeared in the *Meridiano di Roma*.
[5] (Translation)
'Dear Mr de Tuoni: After a good—or rather—a bad quarter of a century this letter
from me will certainly be a surprise for you. The fact is that I read some time ago an
article of yours on Morand and Valery Larbaud and last Friday, being at Vichy
(20 kilometers from here) I went to see my old friend Larbaud to whom I had previously
sent your article. He charged me to thank you for your friendly criticism. I explained
to him that we had known each other in that far-off time in Trieste. Signora Larbaud
is Genoese. He has been very ill for several years but I believe he is now getting better.
I hope you are well in spite of time, which runs when it doesn't limp. My brother is
still in Trieste, a professor at the university. I am the grandfather of a little grandson
who celebrated his eighth birthday the 15th of this month. I had a letter recently from
Francini, who has gone back to his old profession of teaching. He is an instructor at
the school of the Scalopi fathers in Florence. And Tullio Silvestri? Where is he and
what has become of him? I still have four or five of his paintings in my Paris flat. He
was a good painter and also quite a character, as people used to say.
I am sending this letter by way of the newspaper in which I read your article, so I
hope that, God willing, it will reach you sometime. Let me know, please, by acknowledging it to the above address.
With kind greetings I sign myself your devoted   James Joyce'

To James Laughlin[1] (Postcard)   MS. Harvard

21 February 1940   *Hotel de la Paix, S. Gérand-le-Puy*

Dear Mr Laughlin,   Many thanks for having sent me the book with
Prof. Levin's article.[2] Please convey to the writer my thanks also for his
friendly and painstaking study of my book. In the opinion of all those to
whom I have shown it his article, beginning with the title, is the most
striking one that has appeared so far. An Italian and a Dutch review
which I have read (Panorama, Rome, 12 November   Rotterdamsche
Courant, 3 February) might perhaps interest your critic but he would
certainly be more intrigued by an elaborate communication I received
from Helsinki so that my title too must be judged appropriate and
prophetical. Sincerely yours   James Joyce

To Frank Budgen (Postcard)   MS. Yale

Postmark 26 February 1940   *[S. Gérand-le-Puy]*

Dear Budgen: If this reaches you by S. David's Day this is to wish you
many happy returns. I have just read a long article by Mr K. Blistra in
the Rotterdamsche Courant (eng. edition) 3 Feb. 'Woorden aan den
Rekstok' ('Words on the Rack') about my book. If Mrs Budgen is from
that city maybe she knows him. The article is not very favourable but it
is sincere and intelligent. Perhaps he could have your article put into
Dutch and published in some Dutch review. It would not pay as well as
the *Fortnightly* but since that is paying nothing?
     Anyhow, I hope you will have lots of fun at.[3] Sincerely yours
                                                      James Joyce

To Nino Frank[4] (Postcard)

Postmark 13 March 1940   *Hotel de la Paix, S. Gérand-le-Puy (Allier)*

Caro Nino Frank: *Prospettive*, una rivista romana diretta da Curzio
Malaparte,[5] pubblicò li 15 febbraio la traduzione nostra di *Anna Livia*
con parecchi articoli su me e su *Finnegans Wake*.[6] Il Settanni mi scrive

---

[1] James Laughlin (b. 1914), American writer and publisher.

[2] Harry Levin, 'On First Looking into *Finnegans Wake*,' *New Directions in Prose and
Poetry*, 1939, pp. 253–87, ed. James Laughlin IV (Norfolk, Connecticut).

[3] Joyce had introduced Budgen already to the refrain of the ballad of 'Finnegan's
Wake', 'Lots of fun at Finnegan's Wake,' and he applied it also to his own book.

[4] The text of this letter is taken from a photostat now at Northwestern University.

[5] Curzio Malaparte (1898–1957), Italian writer and editor.

[6] 'Anna Livia Plurabella,' *Prospettive* IV.2 (15 February 1940) 13–15. The translation
is attributed to James Joyce and Ettore Settanni, though Settanni later acknowledged
Nino Frank's part in it and admitted that his own role was perfunctory.

da Capri che ha creduto bene raddolcirne certi passaggi. La prego di
procurarsela [sic] la rivista e di notare in margine le varianti. Vorrei
avere così il nostro testo. Il Settanni mi scrive che il Suo nome non
appare per ragioni che Lei capirà sul momento.[1] Ma non sarà sempre
celato, spero!

Giorgio e Beckett vengono qui per le vacanze pasquali. Provi di
vedere l'uno o l'altro forse prima. Il telefono di Giorgio è Inv. 52.63.

E come va il mio libro.[2] L'avrà presto finito? Insomma, diciamo, per
la fine del mese. Me lo faccia sapere ma *non* me lo mandi colla posta.

Un altro favore. Se mi scrive scriva piuttosto alla macchina causa la
mia vista. Una stretta di mano   JAMES JOYCE[3]

To FRANK BUDGEN   MS. Yale

13 March 1940   *Hotel de la Paix, S. Gérand-le-Puy, Allier, France*

Dear Budgen: I sent on your letter to Louis Gillet. He says his copy is
marked '4th impression'. I hope those publishers give you royalties on
these editions and that you didn't sell the rights off.

My biography by Gorman is published by Farrar and Rinehart of
New York at 3$50. I believe, if you had a good agent, you could dispose
of the U.S. rights of your book just now.

I enclose the Dutch article. Please send it back when read as I want
it for the files.

The Roman review *Prospettive* has just published my Italian version
of *Anna Livia* with articles on the writer and his latest book. Ettore
Settanni writes me that it is causing 'un gran scompiglio nel mondo
letterario'. (Great uproar)

I did not wish to inflict temporal art on a spatialist in asking you to

---

[1] Frank's name and work were officially unmentionable in Italy because of his
antifascist activity.

[2] *Finnegans Wake*, a copy of which Joyce had lent to Frank.

[3] (Translation)

'Dear Nino Frank: *Prospettive*, a Roman review edited by Curzio Malaparte,
published on 15 February our translation of *Anna Livia* with several articles on me
and on *Finnegans Wake*. Settanni writes me from Capri that he thought it as well to
soften certain passages. Please obtain a copy of the review and note the variants in the
margin. In that way I will have our original text. Settanni writes me that your name
does not appear for reasons you will understand at once. But it will not always be
kept hidden, I trust.

Giorgio and Beckett are coming here for the Easter holidays. Try to see one or the
other before if possible. Giorgio's telephone number is Inv. 52.63.

How is my book going? Will you have finished it soon? Say by the end of the
month. Let me know but do not send it by post.

One further favour. If you write me do so on a typewriter because of my sight.
A handshake   James Joyce'

go to the concert. I was struck by the similarity of the two 39 Belsizes and being a superstitious Cornishman felt I had to do something about it.[1]

I am sorry your wall humptydumptied like that. Possibly you had flung your copy of Finn again his Wake onto the top of it. However it is pleasing to know you are working for A L P,[2] that is, if I read aright.

Alas, my daughter-in-law is in a very bad way. Everything is in confusion. I am arranging to transfer Lucia here to Moulins in the vicinity.

Why despair of placing your very good article somewhere and getting paid for it? It is a pity the unimaginative Curtius sailed past you in the *Fortnightly*.[3] But there are others. Greetings to you both sincerely yours   JAMES JOYCE

To CAROLA GIEDION-WELCKER (Postcard)   MS. Giedion-Welcker

14 March 1940   *Hotel de la Paix, S. Gérand-le-Puy, Allier, France*

Dear Mrs Giedion: I hope you are well. Perhaps my letter did not reach you. I asked you for the name of the successor of Prof. Fehr and of a critic in Berne who writes for the Bund, if I remember rightly. These names are for my publishers.

A propos, there is a lot about Zurich in my biography by Herbert Gorman (*Farrar and Rinehart, New York*) which is now on sale in Europe.

Greetings from us both sincerely yours   JAMES JOYCE

To JACQUES MERCANTON (Postcard)   MS. Mercanton

14 March 1940   *S. Gérand-le-Puy (Allier), France*

Cher Monsieur Mercanton: Merci de votre lettre et de vos bonnes paroles. Envoyez-moi, je vous prie, l'adresse de Francini dont je ne trouve plus la lettre. Je suppose que vous serez chez vous pour les Rameaux. Vous ai-je dit qu'il y a un article sur moi dans 'Panorama' (Rome) 12 nov? Le '*Prospettive*' (Rome, 44 via Gregoriana) vient de publier (15 fév) deux articles et ma version italienne d'Anna Livia. Autre chose ma biographie par Herbert Gorman (Farrar et Rinehart, N. York) vient de paraître et est en vente. Puis, il y a un article très long et remarquable que je vous ai déja signalé publié dans *New*

[1] Joyce noticed that Humphrey Searle, a programme of whose works was being performed, lived at 39 Belsize Park Gardens while Budgen lived at 39 Belsize Square.
[2] Budgen was working in Air Raid Protection, ARP rather than ALP.
[3] No such article appeared at this time.

Directions (Norfolk, Connecticut). Peutêtre votre presque voisine Mme MacPherson l'avra et pourra vous le prêter si vous aurez le désir de vous adresser à elle.

J'espère que vous passerez des bonnes vacances et que vous n'oublierez pas d'aller à Montreux et à boire le Villeneuve dans la brasserie (pas le restaurant où nous avons mangé) Cordialement votre   JAMES JOYCE

P.S. Je fais des recherches pour vous à la *Nouvelle Revue Française.*[1]

To VICTOR A. SAX (Postcard)   MS. Sax

14 March 1940   *Hotel de la Paix, S. Gérand-le-Puy, Allier, France*

My dear pupil: You will find yourself alluded to a few times in the text and notes of my biography by Herbert Gorman (Farrar and Rinehart, New York) which is now on sale in Europe. There is a long chapter on Zurich. Also in a Roman review *Prospettive* (15 February) there appears an Italian version I made with 'E. Settanni' of the river piece in *Finnegans Wake* (a prophetic title) which is also reviewed there.

I hope Mrs Sax and your sister-in-law are well and you yourself. My daughter-in-law is extremely ill and my daughter not yet better. Sincerely yours   JAMES JOYCE

To FRITZ VANDERPYL   MS. S. Illinois (Croessmann)

14 March 1940   *Hotel de la Paix, S. Gérand-le-Puy, Allier*

Cher Vanderpyl: Madame Vanderpyl m'a rendu un grand service en m'envoyant ces bouquins,[2] mais le prix n'est pas indiqué. Faites-me-le savoir, je vous prie, afin que je puisse vous rembourser la somme due.

---

[1] (Translation)
'Dear Mr Mercanton: Thanks for your letter and for your good words. Please send me Francini's address since I cannot find his letter. I suppose you will be back home for Palm Sunday. Did I tell you that there is an article about me in *Panorama* (Rome) of 12 November? *Prospettive* (Rome, 44 via Gregoriana) has just published (15 February) two articles and my Italian version of *Anna Livia*. Also my biography by Herbert Gorman (Farrar and Rinehart, New York) has just appeared and is on sale. Then there is a very long and remarkable article which I already told you of in *New Directions* (Norfolk, Connecticut). Perhaps your almost neighbour Mme MacPherson has it and would lend it to you if you wish to ask her.
I hope you will have a good holiday and that you will not forget to go to Montreux and drink Villeneuve in the brasserie (not the restaurant where we ate) Cordially yours
James Joyce

P.S. I am doing some research for you in the *Nouvelle Revue Française.*'
[2] Mme Vanderpyl, a speech therapist, had been asked by Joyce to send him some books on the subject.

Je suppose que l'un des auteurs Edmond Pichon est le grand grammairien qui vient de mourir. L'autre, une dame, est Madame Buel-Maisonnay. J'ai trouvé son adresse et son numéro de téléphone: 10 rue de l'Armée (Litt. 23.31). Il s'agit de mon petit-fils, Stephen James, âgé de 8 ans. La directrice de l'école (évacuée) ou il est à présent près d'ici se rend à Paris dimanche et elle sera à l'Hotel Lutétia lundi et mardi. Elle s'appelle Mme Eugène Jolas et est la femme du directeur de *transition* que vous connaissez. Elle va se mettre en rapport avec Mme Maisonnay à propos du côté pratique du traitement qui n'est pas trop bien expliqué dans le bouquin. Si Mme Vanderpyl connaît cette dame— ce qui est fort probable—peutêtre pourait-elle[1] la rappeler par téléphone et lui dire un petit mot? Je sais que le téléphone est très mal vu par Vanderpyl lui-même!

Je vous envoie ci-inclus une critique que je viens de recevoir de votre pays natal. Est-ce que vous lisez encore le hollandais. Si je dois croire le guide égaré, non. En tout cas la voilà. Je l'ai lue. Elle n'est pas trop favorable mais l'hostilité est loyale et même intelligente. Je vous prie de vouloir bien me la renvoyer car je n'ai pas d'autre.

Et à ce propos il est bien singulier comment après la publication de mon livre (dont le titre signifie à la fois la veille mortuaire et le reveil du Finn, c-à-d, notre héros legendaire celto-nordique) la Finlande, jusqu'à alors terra incognita occupe tout-à-coup le centre de la scène d'abord par le fait que le prix Nobel de littérature a été décerné a un écrivain finnois et après à la suite du conflit russo-finnois. J'ai reçu, juste avant l'ouverture des hostilités, un commentaire bizarre de Helsinki à ce sujet. Votre bien dévoué   JAMES JOYCE[2]

[1] Joyce usually though not invariably spelled future and conditional forms of *pouvoir* with one *r*. Where this error occurs it has been preserved in transcription.

[2] (Translation)
'Dear Vanderpyl: Madame Vanderpyl has done me a great favour in sending me these booklets, but their price is not marked. Tell me what it is, please, so I can reimburse the sum due you.

I suppose that one of the authors, Edmond Pichon, is the great grammarian who has just died. The other, a lady, is Madame Buel-Maisonnay. I have found her address and telephone number: 10 rue de l'Armée (Litt. 23.31). The case is that of my grandson, Stephen James, age eight. The directress of the school (evacuated) where he is now is returning to Paris on Sunday and will be at the Hotel Lutétia Monday and Tuesday. Her name is Mme Eugene Jolas and she is the wife of the editor of *transition* whom you know. She is going to get in touch with Mme Maisonnay with regard to the practical side of the treatment which does not become altogether clear in the booklet. If Mme Vanderpyl knows this lady—as is likely—perhaps she would be able to ring her up and say a word to her? I know that the telephone is very poorly regarded by Vanderpyl himself!

I enclose a review that I have just received from your native land. Do you still read Dutch? If I am to believe the wandering guide, no. Anyway here it is. I have read it. It is not too favourable but the hostility is loyal and even intelligent. Please return it to me as I have no other.

To FRITZ VANDERPYL (Postcard)   MS. S. Illinois (Croessmann)

[? 20 March 1940]   *Hotel de la Paix, S. Gérand-le-Puy*

Je trouve que l'autre auteur n'est pas grammarien mais médecin. Quand même ma lettre tient car il est sans doute mobilisé et une entrevue est préférable en ce cas particulier. Si Mme ne la connaît pas cela ne fait rien. Merci quand même.   JAMES JOYCE[1]

To ETTORE SETTANNI[2]   MS. Settanni

26 March 1940   *Hotel de la Paix, S. Gérand-le-Puy*

Caro Settanni, La sua cartolina nonché il fascicolo di 'Prospettive' mi sono arrivati giorni fa dopo aver fatto una piccola odissea per conto proprio, ma spero che queste mie righe piuttosto frettolose le giungeranno più sollecitamente, malgrado la ambiguità dell'indirizzo preciso— Villa Castiglione, o Villa Castello? Un po' di poesia, Sant'Antonio, ma non troppa![3]

—È stato per me un gran piacere apprendere che la mia piccola donnicciuola, quella di Dublino, ha compiuto il suo pellegrinaggio ed ha fatto con tanto garbo il suo modesto inchino all'augusto Zio Tevere. Si è divertito almeno un poco il colendissimo vegliardo ad ascoltar quell'insolito chiacchierio insulso e bislacco? Il mio nuovo appartamento a Parigi (54, rue des Vignes, XVI) è chiuso, dimodochè quando lei tornerà a Parigi sarà meglio scrivermi all'indirizzo in testa al presente. Anche se sloggio, la sua lettera mi perverrà così più rapidamente. Frattanto la prego di porgere al direttore della rivista, Curzio Malaparte, i miei sentiti ringraziamenti (al Linati che conosco da molti anni invierò una cartolina anche) per la cortese accoglienza fattami nelle sue pagine. Grazie soprattutto a lei e una stretta di mano.   JAMES JOYCE[4]

And in this connection it is certainly singular that after the publication of my book (the title of which signifies at once the wake and the awakening of Finn, that is, of our legendary Celto-Nordic hero) Finland, up to then an unknown country, suddenly occupies the centre of the stage first by the fact that the Nobel Prize for Literature has been awarded to a Finnish writer and following close on that the Russo-Finnish war. I received just before the outbreak of hostilities a strange commentary from Helsinki on this subject. Very sincerely yours   James Joyce'
[1] (Translation)
'I find that the other author is not a grammarian but a doctor. My letter still holds good because he is undoubtedly mobilised and an interview is preferable in this special case. If Madame [Vanderpyl] does not know her that is all right. Thank you in any event.   James Joyce'
[2] Ettore Settanni, Italian journalist.   [3] See p. 166.
[4] (Translation)
'Dear Settanni, Your postcard as well as the February issue of *Prospettive* came to

To Mrs VICTOR A. SAX (Postcard)   MS. Sax

9 April 1940   *Hotel Beaujolais, Vichy, France*

Dear Mrs Sax: If you have returned from San Remo to San Romolo[1] there is something you could do for me. The name of the review which published my fragmentary translation of Anna Livia is Prospettive, the editor is Curzio Malaparte, the date is 15 February and the price is 3 lire. I have no copy myself as I gave mine away I cannot find a copy in the only two Italian bookshops I know in Paris. So if you could get through a bookshop a copy of the 15th February and also of the 15 March and send them to me I should be glad. If you tell me of some book you may want from here I would send it in exchange as one cannot easily send money. The news about your sister does not seem too bad. The two cases in our family continue with everything else to make our outlook anything but cheerful. We are glad to hear you are both well. Please send the review to me at my former address: Hotel de la Paix S Gerand-Le Puy/Allier.

Kind remembrances to you both from us both   J.J.

To NINO FRANK (Postcard)   MS. Northwestern

Postmark 9 April? 1940   *Hotel Beaujolais, Vichy*

Cher ami: 1°. D'abord j'espère que vous allez bien et Mme Frank aussi. 2°. Si vous avez bien reçu la revue avec la traduction d'Anna Livia que j'ai envoyé recommandée chez *Pour Vous*) pouvez-vous la prêter pour quelques semaines à Mlle A. Monnier, 7 rue de l'Odéon, puisqu'elle a été la première personne à l'imprimer dans sa revue *Navire d'Argent*? Vous pourriez lui téléphoner d'abord: Danton 07–47. Le numéro de mars contient une photographie du ministre de l'instruction publique

me some days ago after having made a little Odyssey by their own account, but I hope that these hasty lines of mine will reach you more promptly, in spite of the vagueness of your address. (Villa Castiglione or Villa Castle? A little poetry, Saint Anthony, but not too much!)

I have had much pleasure in learning that my little ladykin, the Dublin one, has completed her pilgrimage and has so tactfully made her modest curtsy before her august uncle Tiber. Did it amuse that very reverend greybeard at least a little to hear her unaccustomed silly and extravagant chatter? My new flat in Paris (54, rue des Vignes, XVI) is closed, so that when you go back to Paris it will be better to write me at the above address. Also if I move, your letter will reach me more quickly. In the meantime please present my sincere thanks to the editor of the review, Curzio Malaparte (I am sending a postcard also to Linati whom I have known for many years) for the courteous reception given me in his pages. Thanks above all to you and a handshake
James Joyce'

[1] That is, to Rome.

prise après lecture. Il a les yeux fermés et se plaint mélancoliquement de la migraine. Le numéro d'avril publie une lettre que j'écris a Settanni. Le texte les pronoms de la 3ième personne singuliere ont été changés en des prenoms de la 2ième pluriel![1] A propos de rien en particulier est-ce que je vous ai jamais prêté un livre *At Swim Two Birds* par F. O'Brien ?[2] Ce n'est pas une accusation : c'est une demande. Cordialement votre

JAMES JOYCE[3]

To CAROLA GIEDION-WELCKER (Postcard)   MS. Giedion-Welcker

17 April 1940   *Hotel Beaujolais, Vichy, Allier, France*

Dear Mrs Giedion: Ruggiero tells me you wrote me several times. I got one letter about ten days ago in reply to several cards. Many thanks. I have had a copy of my book sent to Prof. Diet but not to the other. I think the name of the critic in Berne is Riechner. An Italian review, *Prospettive* (Rome) published on 15 February an incomplete translation of Anna Livia together with several appreciative articles. Your news of your daughter does not seem so bad. I am glad to know you yourself are well and also that Prof. Vogt is flourishing and long may you both do so. My family is in pieces and in several places. As for me I cogitate therefore I exist. Kind greetings from us both sincerely yours

JAMES JOYCE

---

[1] The use of the second person plural pronoun *voi* instead of *Lei* was made obligatory under Fascism. For Settanni's revision of Joyce's letter, see *Prospettive* IV.4 (15 April 1940) 11.

[2] Flann O'Brien, *At Swim Two Birds* (London, 1939) was one of the few works by Irish contemporaries that pleased Joyce.

[3] (Translation)

'Dear friend: 1. First of all I hope you are well and Mme Frank too. 2. If you have received the review with the translation of *Anna Livia* which I sent registered to you at *Pour Vous* could you lend it for a few weeks to Mlle A. Monnier, 7 rue de l'Odéon, since she was the first person to print it in her review *Navire d'Argent*? You could telephone her first: Danton 07–47. The March issue contains a photograph of the minister of public instruction taken after reading. He has his eyes shut and complains sadly of migraine. The April issue is publishing a letter I wrote to Settanni. The text shows that the third person singular pronouns have been changed to second person plural pronouns! By the bye, did I ever lend you *At Swim Two Birds* by F. O'Brien? I am only asking, not accusing you. Cordially yours   James Joyce'

To NINO FRANK   MS. Northwestern

18 April 1940   *Hotel Beaujolais, Vichy, Allier*

Caro Signor Frank: Ecco la cartolina del Settanni. Egli dovrebbe essere oramai a Parigi. La libreria italiana 75 (?) Bd S. Germaine saprebbe forse il suo indirizzo. Ha ricevuto Lei la mia lettera colla quale le dissi che *Prospettive* (Roma, 15 febbraio) ha pubblicato la nostra versione di Anna Livia? Ha riveduto il Beckett e come va il sig. Finnegan e 'chi legge'? Saluti cordiali   JAMES JOYCE

P.S. Non so veramente dove mio figlio stia di casa—Telefoni Invalides 52–63 (27 rue Casimir-Perier)[1] e domandi se abiti là. Il Beckett sta, 6 rue des Favorites, ma non ha il telefono. Come si chiama la scrittrice che scrisse *La Moglie del Sardo?*[2] Larbaud me ne parlava l'altro giorno ma non poteva ricordarsi.   J.J.[3]

To MRS VICTOR A. SAX   MS. Sax

28 April 1940   *Hotel Beaujolais, Vichy, Allier*

Dear Mrs Sax: Many thanks for having so promptly sent all the numbers of *Prospettive* I asked for. The photograph of the minister is rather amusing and shows that he must have a sense of humour.[4] So much the better. When he was governor of Rome some years ago he invited me to be present as a guest at some literary function there. I can't remember exactly. I wrote thanking for the honour implied but declining. With my poor sight and general insipidity I am out of place

---

[1] Paul Léon's flat.
[2] Joyce referred to Grazia Deledda (1875–1936), Italian novelist born in Sardinia, who received the Nobel prize for literature in 1926.
[3] (Translation)
  'Dear Mr Frank: Here is Settanni's postcard. He should be in Paris by now. The Italian bookshop at 75 (?) Boulevard S. Germaine might know his address. Did you receive my letter telling you that *Prospettive* (Rome, 15 February) has published our version of *Anna Livia*? Have you seen Beckett again and how goes good Mr Finnegan and "who is reading"? Cordial greetings   James Joyce
  P.S. I really don't know where my son is staying. Telephone Invalides 52–63 (27 rue Casimir-Perier) and ask if he is living there. Beckett lives at 6 rue des Favorites, but he has no phone. What is the name of the woman writer who wrote *The Wife of Sardo?* Larbaud was talking to me about her the other day but I could not remember.   J.J.'
[4] In *Prospettive*, 15 March 1940, the issue following the one that contained *Anna Livia Plurabella*, there was a large photograph of Giuseppe Bottai, Minister of Education, said to have been taken after his reading of the Joyce chapter. 'He has his hand to his forehead,' Joyce wrote Miss Weaver (*Letters*, ed. Gilbert, p. 413) 'and there is an expression of pained bewilderment on his face. He has written an exclamation of humourous despair at the side.'

at such reunions. I wonder whether my poor *Anna Livia* gave Mr Sax and you a headache also?

As I said it is hard to remit money anywhere at present. So, as I suggested, I am sending you a book about Rome.[1] It was written by my friend Valery Larbaud and I hope you will like it with its purple and yellow sack. I would ask him to sign it but the poor man is paralyzed on the right side and cannot use his right hand. He lives here where there is a street named after him or perhaps it is after the *source* or *sources* of the family.[2]

I also received an envelope from you but there was nothing in it. So either you forgot to put the letter in [or] it got out *en route*.

We came here for a few weeks. My family troubles are just as they were. We hope your sister's condition is still not unfavourable. My daughter-in-law is reported to be slightly better but I am afraid the damage done cannot be remedied. I am still trying to bring Lucia (my daughter) to a place near here so that we may not be so scattered. But nothing is easy now.

With renewed thanks and our friendly greetings to you both sincerely yours   JAMES JOYCE

To NINO FRANK (Postcard)   MS. Northwestern

[*July 1940*]   *Hotel du Commerce, S. Gérand-le-Puy (Allier)*

Très content de vous savoir sains et saufs tous les deux. Avez-vous reçu la version italienne d'Anna Livia dans la revue romaine *Prospettive* que je vous ai envoyé sans être raccomandé et l'avez-vous passée à Mlle Monnier? Si non, où est-elle? Nous sommes ici sans ma fille qui est à La Baule. Cordialement votre   JAMES JOYCE[3]

[1] Valery Larbaud, *Aux Couleurs de Rome* (Paris, 1938).
[2] Larbaud's family had become wealthy from a mineral spring.
[3] (Translation)
  'Very glad to know you are both safe and sound. Have you received the Italian version of *Anna Livia* in the Roman review *Prospettive* which I sent to you without registering it and have you passed it on to Mlle Monnier? If not, where is it? We are here without my daughter, who is at La Baule. Cordially yours   James Joyce'

To NINO FRANK (Postcard)   MS. Northwestern

28 July 1940   *Hotel du Commerce, S. Gérand-le-Puy (Allier)*

Cher ami: Evidemment vous n'avez pas reçu ma 2ième lettre à Paris.
Quand vous y rentrerez je vous prie de téléphoner a Mlle Monnier, 7 rue
de l'Odéon, Dant. 07–47 lui offrant la lecture de la traduction italienne
d'Anna Livia—à titre de curiosité cela devra l'intéresser puisque c'est
elle qui l'a publiée la première. Ne me l'envoyez pas ici en tout cas et
faites-moi avoir de vos nouvelles

    L'adresse de Beckett est Villa S. George, 135 Boul. de la Plage,
Arcachon Cordialement votre   JAMES JOYCE[1]

To EDMUND BRAUCHBAR   MS. Brauchbar

30 July 1940   *Hotel du Commerce, S. Gérand-le-Puy, Allier, France*

Cher Monsieur Brauchbar: Merci de votre lettre du 21 mars et j'espère
que vous allez toujours bien. Je vous avais déjà écrit à Toronto en vous
envoyant une lettre que j'avais reçu de votre neveu à Dublin—la seule
personne, soit dit en passant, parmi les douze ou treize que j'avais
réussi à placer quelque part qui s'est dérangé jusqu'à maintenant pour
savoir si j'étais même vivant.

    Puisque vous me demandez de mes nouvelles nous en voilà. Ma
malheureuse bru après avoir répandu autour d'elle et en pleine guerre
une ruine materielle et morale indescriptible a été internée d'office par
les autorités françaises comme dangereuse pour elle-même et pour les
autres. Puis finalement elle a été transportée à New York par deux
médecins et deux infirmières et se trouve actuellement dans une
maison de santé à Connecticut. Cela s'est passé quelques jours à peine
avant la debâcle ici. Ma fille se trouve avec sa maison de santé près de
S. Nazaire, donc en plein zone occupée sur la côte dangereuse—et cela
malgré tout ce que j'avais essayé de faire d'avance pour assurer sa
tranquillité. Nous sommes ici, ma femme et moi avec notre fils et notre

---

[1] (Translation)
    'Dear friend: Evidently you did not receive my second letter to Paris. When you go
back there please telephone to Mlle Monnier, 7 rue de l'Odéon, Dant. 07–47 offering
to let her read the Italian translation of *Anna Livia*—it should interest her as a curiosity
since it was she who published it first. Do not send it to me here in any case and let
me have news of you
    Beckett's address is Villa S. George, 135 Boul. de la Plage, Arcachon Cordially yours
                                           James Joyce'

petit-fils et à la suite des 'évenements' je me trouve complètement isolé, coupé de mes ressources à Londres par les autorités britanniques et de mes ressources en banque ici par les autorités francaises, double blocus.

Si vous avez lu ma biographie vous avez certainement ri en lisant ce qu'écrit M. Gorman (qui, du reste, ne m'avait pas même signalé la publication ni son éditeur non plus) que l'astronome de l'Uraniaturm s'appelait . . . Siegmund Feilbogen![1]

Je ne sais pas ce qui est devenu mon appartement à Paris, mes livres et mes tableaux.

J'espère que notre 'tale of woes' n'est pas trop embêtant et que votre famille immédiate (puisque vos parents semblent être comme les feuilles de la forêt) se trouve, saine et sauve, autour de l'arbre maître et . . . utilisable.

Je vous serre la main cordialement   JAMES JOYCE[2]

[1] Siegmund Feilbogen, a bearded messianic professor from Vienna, came to Zurich during the first World War to edit his *International Review*, which appeared in both English and German. It was intended to help reconcile the two sides by persuading them that the atrocity stories of both were groundless. Joyce did some translating for the review.

[2] (Translation)

'Dear Mr Brauchbar: Thanks for your letter of 21 March and I hope you are keeping well. I had already written to Toronto sending you a letter that I had received from your nephew in Dublin—the only person, be it said in passing, among the twelve or thirteen whom I have managed to place somewhere who up to now has troubled to find out if I were still alive.

Since you ask me for my news, here we are. My unfortunate daughter-in-law after having spread around herself in the midst of war an indescribable ruin both material and moral was interned by the French authorities as dangerous to herself and others. Then finally she was taken back to New York by two doctors and two nurses and is now in a private asylum in Connecticut. That all happened hardly more than a few days before the debacle here. My daughter is with her *maison de santé* near S. Nazaire, hence deep in the occupied zone on the dangerous coast—and this in spite of everything I had tried to do in advance to assure her tranquillity. We are here, my wife and I with our son and our grandson and following the "events" I find myself entirely isolated, cut off from my resources in London by the British authorities and from my banked resources here by the French authorities, a double blockade.

If you have read my biography you have certainly laughed to read what Mr Gorman (who, indeed, did not even announce the publication to me, nor did his publisher either) writes, that the astronomer of the Uraniaturm was named . . . Siegmund Feilbogen!

I do not know what has happened to my flat in Paris, to my books and pictures.

I hope that our "tale of woe" is not too tiresome and that your immediate family (for your other relations seem to be like leaves in the forest) is clustered, safe and sound, around the paternal and . . . utilisable tree. I clasp your hand cordially   James Joyce'

To Jacques Mercanton   MS. Mercanton

5 August 1940   *Hotel du Commerce, S. Gérand-le-Puy, Allier, France*

Cher Monsieur Mercanton: Est-ce que la librairie de votre frère
pourait commander pour moi un livre qu'on m'a signalé: The Life and
Writings of Giambattista Vico (Londres, 1935 ou 1936)[1] prix 5 shillings?
Je ne peux vous donner que l'adresse du librairie qui le vend et qui me
l'a signalé. La voilà: 12 ou 14 Troy Street, Londres, W.1. Quand et si il
l'aura reçu faites-le-moi savoir avant de me l'envoyer.

Nous sommes ici en zone non occupée. Ma fille est près de S. Nazaire
en zone occupée avec toute la maison de santé. Je voudrais bien la
transférer—avec la permission des autorités allemandes, françaises et
suisses—en votre pays et même l'accompagner. J'ai écrit à ce propos à
la Légation Suisse à Lyon, quai du Général Sanais. Jusqu'ici je n'ai pas
eu de réponse. Une telle démarche coûterait bien cher mais je crois que
c'est peut-être préférable de la tenter.

J'espére que vous allez bien et qu'on se reverra. Mes salutations très
spéciales aux vignobles de Villeneuve.[2] Votre bien devoué

                                                        JAMES JOYCE[3]

To Jacques Mercanton   MS. Mercanton

Postmark 13 August 1940   *Hotel du Commerce, S. Gérand-le-Puy,*
                                                    Allier, France

Cher Monsieur Mercanton: Comme vous verrez par la lettre ci-avec
nous sommes en train de demander la permission d'entrer en Suisse—

---

[1] Henry P. Adams, *The Life and Writings of Giambattista Vico* (London, 1935).
[2] An allusion to Joyce's liking for white Vaudois wine, especially that of Villeneuve,
the grapes for which are gathered at the extremity of Lake Geneva.
[3] (Translation)
    'Dear Mr Mercanton: Could your brother's bookstore order a book that someone
mentioned to me: *The Life and Writings of Giambattista Vico* (London, 1935 or 1936)
price 5 shillings? I can give you only the address of the bookstore which is selling it
and announced it to me. It is: 12 or 14 Troy Street, London W.1. When and if he
receives it please tell me before you send it.
    We are here in the unoccupied zone. My daughter is near S. Nazaire in the occupied
zone with her whole maison de santé. I should like to move her—with the permission
of the German, French, and Swiss authorities—to your country and even to go with
her. I have written to this effect to the Swiss Legation at Lyons, quai du General
Sanais. Up to now I have had no reply. Such a step would cost a great deal but I
think it is worth trying.
    I hope you are well and that we will see each other. My particular greetings to the
vineyards of Villeneuve. Sincerely yours   James Joyce'

James Joyce in the late 1930s.

Nora Joyce on the same afternoon. (*Photographs by David Fleischman.*)

Joyce's grandson, Stephen Joyce.

Helen, Stephen, George, and James Joyce.

Joyce with Nora, Helen, George, and Stephen, photographed by
Robert Kastor with a home movie camera in the late 1930s.

Herbert Gorman with Joyce and Nora in the 1930s.

Throwaway about a pleasure steamer bearing the name of Joyce's father (p. 404).

Nora Joyce (right) with two friends in Beaugency, 1930s.

Joyce's Zurich publisher, Daniel Brody (at left), with
Hermann Broch.

Joyce with Carola Giedion-Welcker, 1935.

Joyce's funeral in Zurich, 15 January 1941.

James Joyce's grave in the Fluntern Cemetery, Zurich.

Nora Joyce's grave.

Death mask of James Joyce.

nous, c'est, mon fils avec son fils (agé de 8 ans), moi et ma femme et ma fille. Vous pouvez m'être très utile en me fournissant certains renseignements.

Mon petit fils irait, selon nos plans, à Lausanne avec son père, la mère étant malheureusement toujours internée d'office. Il voudrait avoir les prospectus des quelques pensionnats pour garçonnets à ou près de Lausanne. Le garçon parle couramment le français et l'anglais. Il est actuellement à l'Ecole Bilingue, Chateau de la Chapelle, près d'ici. Le prix de sa pension est de 1500 frs par mois, c'à'd, à l'échange actuelle, 100 frs suisses.

Ma fille est actuellement à la Clinique des Charmettes, Pornichet (L.I.) a 12 Km. de S. Nazaire, chez le Dr Achille Delmas, qui la soigne depuis cinq ans. Le prix de sa pension est 90 frs par jour, c'à'd, 6 frs suisses. Pour son transfert, qui conditionne le notre, il faudra un tas de choses. Les permissions collectives des autorités allemandes (de la zone occupée), françaises et suisses, l'escort de deux infirmiers (mâle et femelle) de Pornichet jusqu'à la frontière franco-suisse, les moyens de transport. J'ai demandé le prix de pension à Kilchberg, près de Zurich, car selon notre premier plan nous irions à Zurich. On me demande 15 frs suisses (225 frs français) par jour, plus un double versement à l'Etat et à l'Institut. Pour les versements ça va encore: la pension, non. J'ai demandé le prix à Burghölzli, Zurich, où elle a déjà été et aussi si l'on pouvait la rencontrer à la frontière (elle voyagerait par Nantes–Lyon–Genève) et la conduire ensuite à Genève. En y pensant pourtant nous sommes d'avis que cela serait moins couteux si nous étions tous à ou près Lausanne. C'est pourquoi je vous prie de vous mettre en communication avec la seule maison de santé de la Suisse française qui semble (si je me rappelle bien) avoir des prix a la portée de ma bourse actuelle. J'ai oublié le nom et l'adresse[1] mais elle est près de Vallorbe (si l'on vient de Paris) et de Collonges? (si l'on vient de Lausanne). Si vous y téléphonez vous pouvez dire que c'est Mme Fernandez (dont la fille Yva[2] y est une patiente) et le Dr Baruk de Paris qui vous ont donné l'adresse. Je veux savoir si l'on l'accepterait et si l'on pourait la rencontrer à la frontière quand et si elle y arrivera. Son cas est: cyclothimie qui date de $7\frac{1}{2}$ ans. Elle a auprès de 33 ans, parle couramment le francais. Elle est du caractère gai, doux et moqueur, mais elle a des crises soudaines de colère à propos de rien

---

[1] This was Le Pré Carré, at Corcelles near Chavarnay (Vaud). Joyce went to arrange matters there on 16 December 1940, just after crossing the Swiss border.

[2] Yva Fernandez was one of the three translators of *Dubliners* into French (*Gens de Dublin*, Paris, 1926).

quand il est necessaire de lui passer le maillet. Ces crises ne sont pas très fréquentes maintenant mais elles sont imprédictibles.

Repondez-moi, je vous [prie] (qu'on m'envoie les prospectus de la maison de santé et des pensionnats) le plus vite possible. Merci. Cordialement votre   JAMES JOYCE[1]

---

[1] (Translation)

'Dear Mr Mercanton: As you will see from the enclosed letter we are in process of asking permission to enter Switzerland—we, that is, my son with his son (age eight), I and my wife and my daughter. You can be very helpful to me if you will furnish certain information.

My grandson would go, according to our plan, to Lausanne with his father, his mother being unfortunately still interned. He would like to have the prospectuses of several boarding schools for boys at or near Lausanne. The boy speaks French and English fluently. He is now at the Ecole Bilingue, Chateau de la Chapelle, near here. The price of his board is from 1500 francs a month, that is, by present exchange, 100 Swiss francs.

My daughter is now at the Clinique des Charmettes, Pornichet (L.I.), 12 kilometers away from Saint Nazaire, in the care of Dr Achille Delmas who has looked after her for five years. The price of her board is 90 francs a day, that is, 6 Swiss francs. For her move, which conditions ours, a lot of things will be needed. The collective permissions of the German authorities of the occupied zone, of the French and of the Swiss, two nurses (male and female) to escort her from Pornichet to the French-Swiss border, the facilities to move her. I asked the price of pension at Kilabbey, near Zurich, for according to our first plan we would go to Zurich. They are asking me 15 Swiss francs (225 French francs) a day, besides a double payment to the State and the Institute. The payments would be all right, the pension, no. I asked the price at Burghölzli, Zurich, where she has once been and also if she could be met at the frontier (she would travel by Nantes–Lyons–Geneva) and be conducted then to Geneva. In thinking it over however we feel it would be less expensive if we were all at or near Lausanne. That is why I ask you to communicate with the only maison de santé in French Switzerland which seems (if I remember rightly) to have prices within the range of my present means. I have forgotten the name and address but it is near Vallorbe (when one is coming from Paris) and Collonges (if one is coming from Lausanne). If you telephone there you can say that it is Mme Fernandez (whose daughter Yva is a patient there) and Dr Baruk of Paris who have given you the address. I want to know if they would take her and if they could meet her at the frontier when and if she gets there. Her case is: cyclothimia dating from the age of seven and a half. She is about thirty-three, speaks French fluently. Her character is gay, sweet and ironic, but she has sudden bursts of anger over nothing when she has to be confined in a straitjacket. These crises are not frequent now but they are unpredictable.

Please reply (have them send me the prospectuses of the clinics and the boarding-schools) as soon as possible. Thank you Cordially yours   James Joyce'

To SIGNORA MARIA NEBBIA   MS. Bib. Municipale, Vichy

19 August 1940   *Hotel du Commerce, S. Gérand-le-Puy, Allier*

Gentile signora: Avevo incaricato la tintoria Duranton, 9 rue de Paris
a Vichy di prendere a casa Sua la mia pellicceria e il pastrano che Lei
ebbe la gentilezza di ospitare. La tintoria mi telefona che il Suo
appartamento è chiuso. Vorrei sapere se questi indumenti si trovano a
Vichy o se Loro pensano restare in campagna. Noi facciamo dei 'piani'
per partir verso il sud e vorrei collocare quegli due oggetti per farli
nettare e conservare fino all'inverno. Spero che l'assegno del Beckett sia
ben passato?[1] Io mi trovo fra l'incudine ed il martello. Credito bloccato
in Inghilterra ed in Francia anche! Mondo cane!
     Mi saluti l'amico Larbaud e mi creda di Lei Dev^mo   JAMES JOYCE[2]

To NINO FRANK (Postcard)   MS. Northwestern

Postmark 29 August 1940   *Hotel du Commerce, S. Gérand-le-Puy, Allier*

Cher ami: Merci de votre carte et excusez mon retard. J'ai été
souffrant. Savez-vous où Louis Gillet se trouve? Je lui ai écrit chez
Paris-Soir'. Pas de reponse. A ce propos dans le numéro du 7 aout de
Candide il y eut un long article de Marcel Roland sur le Perce-Oreille.
Le connaissez-vous? Y-a-t-il moyen de savoir qui il est, s'il a écrit
d'autres choses sur cet insecte? Si je lui écris chez le journal il ne
recevra jamais ma lettre. Sans doute serait-il interessé à savoir que j'ai
écrit un long bouquin dont le héros est précisément un certain Persse-
Oreilly[3] Earwigger. Louis Gillet qui a deux exemplaires pourrait bien
lui en préter un. Il sembre être entomologiste. La fable de l'Ondt and
the Gracehoper l'amuserait, je pense.
     Quels sont vos plans? Cordialement votre   JAMES JOYCE[4]

[1] Samuel Beckett needed to cash a check on an Irish bank and at Joyce's request
Larbaud cashed it.
[2] (Translation)
     'Dear Signora: I had instructed Duranton Dyers, 9 rue de Paris at Vichy to pick
up at your place my fur coat and overcoat that you kindly kept for me. The dyers
phoned to tell me your flat is closed. I wonder if these garments are in Vichy or if you
intend to stay in the country. We are making "plans" to leave for the south and I
should like to dispose of these two things by having them cleaned and stored until
winter. I hope the check to Beckett was accepted all right. I find myself between the
anvil and the hammer. My credit is blocked in England and in France too! Wretched
world!
     Greet friend Larbaud for me and believe me Devotedly yours   James Joyce
[3] *Perce-oreille*, French for 'earwig'.
[4] (Translation)
     'Dear friend: Thank you for your postcard and excuse my late reply. I have not
been well. Do you know where Louis Gillet is now? I wrote him in care of *Paris-Soir*.

To Carola Giedion-Welcker (Postcard)   MS. Giedion-Welcker

30 August 1940   *Hotel du Commerce, S. Gérand-le-Puy, Allier, France*

Chère Madame Giedion: Merci pour votre lettre. J'ai reçu—mais beaucoup plus tard—le prospectus de Kilchberg. Trop cher. Je ne peux plus payer 15 frs par jour. J'écris ensuite à Burghölzli qui me répondit, demandant 25 francs. J'ai trouvé une maison de santé près de Vallorbe à 8.50. Ça irait. Lucia est en zone occupée mais les autorités occupantes m'ont donné la permission de la sortir. Il s'agit de son transport et des fonds que j'attends. Le consulat suisse à Lyon m'a envoyé les feuilles à remplir. Il s'agit aussi d'obtenir des permissions de sortir pour nous autres. Je vous tiendrai au courant. Nous sommes seuls. Mrs Jolas et ses filles sont parties pour N. York. Je regrette que les nouvelles de votre fille ne sont pas très bonnes. Mais en tout cas dans ces maladies-là il n'y a guère de règles. Un bon souvenir   James Joyce[1]

To Jacques Mercanton (Postcard)   MS. Mercanton

Postmark 11 September 1940   *Hotel du Commerce, S. Gérand-le-Puy,*
                                           Allier, France

Cher Mercanton: Merci pour votre lettre. J'ai reçu une lettre du Pré Carré ce matin. On pourra tout arranger m'écrit-on pour recevoir ma fille à Chalon. Mais je ne peux rien arranger si vite que cela car depuis 10 semaines je suis sans nouvelles de ma fille. La poste ne marchait plus et maintenant on ne peut écrire que quelques mots de salutations. Je ne sais pas si notre demande d'entrée en Suisse va être accordée ni même notre sortie d'ici. Voulez-vous téléphoner à la maison de santé à

No answer. In this connection, the 7 August issue of *Candide* had a long article by Marcel Roland on the Earwig. Do you know him? Is there any way to find out who he is and whether he has written other things about this insect? If I wrote him in care of the newspaper he would never receive my letter. He would no doubt be interested to know that I have written a big book with a hero whose name is actually Persse-Oreilly Earwigger. Louis Gillet who has two copies could easily lend him one of them. He appears to be an entomologist. The fable of the Ondt and the Gracehoper would amuse him, I should think.

     What are your plans? Cordially yours   James Joyce'
   [1] (Translation)

     'Dear Mrs Giedion: Thanks for your letter. I received—but long after—the Kilchberg prospectus. Too expensive. I no longer can pay 15 francs a day. I wrote next to Burghölzli which replied asking 25 francs. I have found a maison de santé near Vallorbe at 8 francs 50. That would do. Lucia is in the occupied zone but the occupying authorities have given me permission to take her out. The question is one of transporting her and also of money I am expecting. The Swiss Consulate at Lyons has sent me forms to fill out. We also have to obtain permission for the rest of us to leave. I will keep you informed. We are alone. Mrs Jolas and her daughters have left for New York. I am sorry that the news of your daughter is not very good. But in any event these diseases do not abide by rules. Best wishes   James Joyce'

laquelle j'écrirai lundi ou mardi. Quant à l'enfant si vous serez absent de Lausanne du 18 sept. au 1 nov. pouvez-vous laisser les prospectus des écoles chez votre frère le libraire (quel est son adresse?) en le priant de me les envoyer. On a payé jusqu'ici 1500 frs mensuel mais on pourrait payer jusqu'à 2000 ou 2500. Il n'est pas dit que l'école doit être à Lausanne mais préférablement dans le canton de Vaud. Merci. Cordialement votre   JAMES JOYCE[1]

To JACQUES MERCANTON   MS. Mercanton

14 September 1940   Hotel du Commerce, S. Gérand-le-Puy, Allier, France

Cher Mercanton (c'est plus vite que 'Monsieur'.) Voilà où nous en sommes. Les autorités allemandes m'ont fait savoir verbalement qu'elles accorderaient libre sortie de la zone occupée à ma fille: et j'ai demandé l'entrée en Suisse pour elle. En même temps je l'ai demandée pour ma femme et moi-même et pour mon fils et son enfant. Reste à voir si c'est accordée. Reste à voir aussi si la sortie de la zone non occupée que nous avons aussi demandé en même temps aux autorités françaises nous sera accordée et quand. Reste alors à voir s'il me réussit d'avoir de l'Amérique mes fonds pour payer notre voyage à Nantes, le voyage de ma fille accompagnée de Pornichet–Nantes–Paris et de Paris à la frontière suisse et aussi les 3½ mois de pension arriérés que je dois. De l'Angleterre je ne pourrai pas avoir un sou de mon argent pendant que je suis en France. Et de l'Amérique c'est difficile.

Je viens de recevoir une letter de la maison de santé de Corcelles (Le Pré Carré: Tel: 5419). Pouvez-vous vous mettre en communication avec le secretaire M. Tschantz-Chevalier et lui dire que je viens de recevoir sa letter du 7 courant et les prospectus et suis d'accord sur le prix. Il semble ignorer pourtant ce que le consulat suisse à Lyon vient de m'avertir que le train Paris–Suisse ne passe plus par Vallorbe (où les ponts sont sautés, il parait) mais fait un détour par Aix–Annemasse. Si

[1] (Translation)

'Dear Mercanton: Thanks for your letter. I received a letter from the Pré Carré this morning. They can arrange everything, they say, to receive my daughter at Chalon. But I can arrange nothing so quickly as that for I have been without any news of my daughter for the last ten weeks. Mail has been cut off and now one can only write a few words of greeting. I do not know whether our request for entry into Switzerland will be granted or even our exit permit from here. Would you telephone to the maison de santé to which I shall be writing on Monday or Tuesday. As for the child, if you will be away from Lausanne from 18 September to 1 November could you leave the school prospectuses with your brother the bookseller (what is his address?) and ask him to send them on to me. We have been paying up to 1500 francs a month but we could pay up to 2000 or 2500. The school does not necessarily have to be in Lausanne but preferably in the canton of Vaud. Thank you. Cordially yours

James Joyce'

vous pouvez le voir ou à Lausanne par rendez-vous, ou en y allant avec votre petite reine[1] ce serait préférable. J'aimerais bien en tout cas avoir un mot de votre part par télégramme me disant que de toute façon la rencontre de ma fille sera faisable *si* tout le reste s'arrangera. Connaissez-vous quelqu'un à Berne en rapport avec le Bureau des Etrangers, Ministère des Affaires Etrangères, qui pourrait pistonner une demande d'entrée. Aussitôt en Suisse, nous, mon fils et moi, pourrons avoir au moins notre argent.

Cette lettre sera postée à Génève par un ami qui part d'ici en ce moment et cela pour gagner du temps Cordialement votre

JAMES JOYCE[2]

To GUSTAV ZUMSTEG[3] (Dictated letter)[4]   TS. Zumsteg

16 September 1940   *Hotel du Commerce, S. Gérand-le-Puy, Allier*
                                        Tél: S. Gérand-le-Puy, N° 9

Dear Mr Zumsteg,   Many thanks indeed for your kind and prompt action. I received this morning your letter of the 14th inst. with copy of

[1] Mercanton's bicycle, which amused Joyce.

[2] (Translation)

'Dear Mercanton (this is quicker than "Mr"): Here is where we are. The German authorities have given me to understand verbally that they would grant my daughter permission to leave the occupied zone: and I have requested entry into Switzerland for her. I have asked for it at the same time for my wife and myself and my son and his child. Whether it will be granted remains to be seen. It remains to be seen also whether the exit permit from the unoccupied zone for which we have applied to the French authorities will be granted us and when. It then remains to be seen whether I will succeed in obtaining from America the necessary money to pay for our trip to Nantes, for the trip of my daughter with escort from Pornichet–Nantes–Paris and from Paris to the Swiss frontier and also the three and a half months' arrears of her pension which I owe. I will not be able to get a penny from England so long as I am in France. And from America it is also hard.

I have just received a letter from the maison de santé at Corcelles (The Pré Carré: Tel: 5419). Can you communicate with the secretary, Mr Tschantz-Chevalier, and tell him I have just received his letter of the 7th inst. and the prospectuses and that I agree to the price. He seems unaware however of what the Swiss Consulate at Lyons has just informed me, that the Paris–Switzerland train no longer passes by Vallorbe (where the bridges are blown up, I gather) but makes a detour by way of Aix-Annemasse. If you could see him either by meeting him in Lausanne or by going out there with your little queen, it would be better. In any case I should greatly like to have a word from you by telegram saying for sure that the meeting with my daughter is practicable *if* everything else can be arranged. Do you know somebody at Berne who is in touch with the Bureau of Foreigners, the Ministry of Foreign Affairs, who could push along an application for entry. As soon as we reach Switzerland, we, my son and I, can at least have our money.

This letter will be posted at Geneva by a friend who is leaving from here this very moment, so as to gain time Cordially yours   James Joyce'

[3] Gustav Zumsteg (b. 1915), the son of the proprietor of Joyce's favourite Zurich restaurant, the Kronenhalle, and himself a businessman. He was very helpful to Joyce in arranging the details of leaving France and entering Switzerland.

[4] A few obvious mistypings have been corrected.

your letter to M. Georges Haldenwang, to whom I wrote after telephoning you but without giving details. I shall send these to-morrow to him in a separate letter. However he knows the name and the number of applicants for entrance. Our demands for entrance should have been at the Swiss Consulate in Lyons on Sunday morning, and so I telegraphed you this morning asking you to verify this, and, if possible, speed up the application. Communications between here and Vichy, postal and otherwise, become more and more difficult, so if there is anything very urgent, you had better either wire me or telephone.

With regard to my daughter, can you let me know after enquiry where the railway line from Paris to Switzerland passes the line of demarcation, and how long is the railway journey across the unoccupied zone, and at what Swiss frontier station it enters Switzerland by present arrangements. I am in correspondence with the Maison de Santé Pré Carré, Corcelles, railway station Chavornay, line Lausanne–Yverdon, and they could have arranged to meet her at Vallorbe, as they wrote me, evidently not knowing that this station was out of action. The persons who accompany my daughter eventually will probably have permission to conduct her only as far as the line of demarcation, so I shall have to send details of this new complication to the Director of the Maison de Santé. As you see, everything is extremely difficult. Our applications, for exits from France that is, for myself, my wife, my son and grandson, passed through the sous-préfecture of this department this morning, whence they will be forwarded for consideration to the Minister of the Interior in Vichy. I shall inform you by telephone or telegram the moment I know the result. As regards your visit to Paris, can you let me know the date of this, the probable length of your stay in Paris, and your address there. It is most kind of you to offer to place funds at my disposal which, it seems to me, I might need at some unexpected moment. I gratefully accept this offer, and shall of course reimburse your father at the earliest opportunity. It would be well however, if you are leaving Lyons on short notice, to instruct some member of your staff so that, in case of your absence, I could telephone him and have the amount telegraphed here. As regards the financial guarantee for Switzerland, I have no relatives there, but, as soon as we arrive there, or very soon after both my son and myself will be financially independent, as you know. If my statement should need any corroboration from a Swiss source, I take it, that your Firm in Zürich would be able to guarantee the truth of my statement, so as to reassure the Federal authorities on this point. I shall therefore leave it to your own discretion to communicate on the matter with Mr. Rudolf Brauchbar, or M.

Georges Haldenwang, or both, so that this point may not cause a hitch in the procedure.

In haste and with renewed thanks and friendly remembrances Sincerely yours   JAMES JOYCE

To CAROLA GIEDION-WELCKER (Postcard)   MS. Giedion-Welcker

18 September 1940   Hotel du Commerce, S. Gérand-le-Puy, Allier, France

Chère Madame Giedion: Mon fils et moi nous avons fait la semaine dernière des demandes d'entrée en Suisse pour nous et pour nos familles respectives. Sur la feuille à remplir il y avait 'l'alinéa' 'References en Suisse'. J'ai donné les noms de Giedion, Vogt, Moser et Schoeck. Je suppose que l'on pourra répondre de ma desirabilité. Quant à un garanti materiel j'ai prié la maison de Brauchbar de le donner. Il n'est pas strictement necessaire car aussitôt arrivés là-bas un peu après nous serons indépendants tandis qu'ici tout contact financier avec l'Angleterre et presque tout avec l'Amérique nous est fermé. Nous avons fait en même temps une demande aux autorités françaises pour la sortie. Les autorités allemandes ont déjà accordé d'avance la permission de sortie pour ma fille de la zone occupée. Espérons que la permission arrive de Berne et le plus vite possible! Veuillez communiquer ceci a mon ami *Ruggiero au Creditanstalt* pour le tenir au courant comme je lui ai promis. Votre bien devoué   JAMES JOYCE[1]

To CAROLA GIEDION-WELCKER   MS. Giedion-Welcker

28 September 1940   Hotel du Commerce, S. Gérand-le-Puy, Allier, France

Dear Mrs Giedion: Thanks for your postcard and offers of help. This letter explains itself. I am replying instructing the lawyer, so as to simplify matters, to apply directly for a permit for Zurich. I am arranging

---

[1] (Translation)

'Dear Mrs Giedion: My son and I applied last week for entry into Switzerland for ourselves and for our respective families. On the form to be filled out there was the paragraph, "References in Switzerland." I gave the names of Giedion, Vogt, Moser and Schoeck. I assume they can answer to my desirability. As for a material guaranty I asked the Brauchbar firm to give it. It is not strictly necessary for as soon as we are in Switzerland we shall be almost at once financially independent while here every financial arrangement with England and almost every one with America is blocked for us. We have applied at the same time to the French authorities for exit permits. The German authorities have already granted in advance permission for my daughter to leave the occupied zone. Let us hope that permission will arrive from Berne and as quickly as possible! Would you communicate this to my friend *Ruggiero at the Creditanstalt* to keep him posted as I promised him to do. Sincerely yours

James Joyce'

for Lucia to be transported from occupied France (by permission of the German authorities) to:

> Clinique du Pré-Carré
> Corcelles,
> sur Chavornay,
> Vaud

but that can be done when we are in Z'ch. We want to find a French-speaking school (boarding school) for the boy. But that we can do from Zurich too. If you can hurry things up from Berne, so much the better. Of course we are still waiting for permission to leave France. Kind regards to both Sincerely yours   JAMES JOYCE

To CAROLA GIEDION-WELCKER (Postcard)   MS. Giedion-Welcker

13 October 1940   Maison Ponthenier, S. Gérand-le-Puy, Allier, France

Chère Madame Giedion: Merci de votre lettre du 9 courant que j'ai transmise à M. Georges Haldenwang, 6 rue du Rhône, Genève auquel j'avais confié notre cause sur l'avis de M. G. Zumsteg de la Dienst A.B.C. à Lyon. Je ne comprends pas pourquoi il y a tellement de difficultés pour avoir le permis de séjour à Zurich puisque Ruggiero m'avait écrit qu'il y a là très peu d'étrangers en ce moment. Nous irions d'abord dans le Vaud si cela satisfaira les autorités. Peut-être pourriez-vous vous mettre en rapport avec l'avocat surnommé. Salutations amicales   JAMES JOYCE[1]

To JACQUES MERCANTON (Postcard)   MS. Mercanton

Postmark 14 October 1940   [*S. Gérand-le-Puy*]

Cher Mercanton: J'ai écrit une très longue lettre au Pré Carré. Maintenant quant à l'entrée en Suisse. C'est l'avocat Georges Haldenwang à Génève qui appuie ma demande. D'abord j'avais pensé rester dans le Vaud pour y placer le petit et ma fille et ensuite m'établir à Zurich. Il m'a conseillé de choisir ou l'un ou l'autre: alors j'ai demandé

---

[1] (Translation)

'Dear Mrs Giedion: Thanks for your letter of the 9th inst. which I sent on to M. Georges Haldenwang, 6 rue du Rhône, Geneva, to whom I have entrusted our case on the recommendation of M. G. Zumsteg of the A.B.C. Company at Lyons. I do not understand why there is so much difficulty in securing permission to reside in Zurich since Ruggiero wrote me that very few foreigners are there just now. We should go first into Vaud if the authorities agree. Perhaps you could get in touch with the above named lawyer. Friendly greetings   James Joyce'

Zurich d'où je croyais placer ma fille et le petit dans le Vaud. J'apprends hier de Berne qu'il y aura beaucoup de difficultés pour Zurich. On me conseille de tout recommencer et de demander séjour dans le Vaud où il faut donner 4 ou 5 references, moi qui connais que vous là-bas! Quelle barbe! Si j'avais le permis d'entrée en Suisse il serait peut-être plus facile d'avoir le permis de sortie d'ici lequel du reste n'est pas du tout facile. J'ai pensé à Jaloux mais il n'est pas suisse et je ne sais pas où il se trouve. Connaissez-vous cet avocat? En somme avant de partir envoyez moi un petit mot. Salutations cordiales,   JAMES JOYCE[1]

To EDMUND BRAUCHBAR   MS. Brauchbar

17 October 1940   c/o *U.S.A. Embassy, Vichy*

Dear Mr Brauchbar I received on 28 ult your cable of 26 ult and replied: and on the 7 inst your letter of 26 ult with your short cable address. Today I received the letter overleaf dated 24 ult.[2] I have not received the letter of the 16 ult and I have not received any money from Marseilles or anywhere else or any other letter. I send you this letter without any comment. It does not need a reply.

I wrote three or four letters enclosing copies of yours of last month to your son at Zurich but had no reply from him. I also wrote to Zumsteg who gave me the address of a lawyer, Mr Georges Haldenwang, 6 rue du Rhone, Geneva who, he wrote, for a lawyer's fee of 200 frs Swiss would be able to get my request for entry through the Berne Department within a month. Otherwise it might take 3 or 4 months. He said the Federal authorities would ask for a collective guarantee of 50,000 frs Swiss. I made the request and wrote to the lawyer 5 weeks ago. There is no answer: but one of my Zurich references (I gave 5: Vogt, Schoeck, Prager, Moser, Giedion) writes that on enquiry at Berne it was learned that the leave to go to Zurich would not be easily obtained. It is also by

[1] (Translation)
'Dear Mercanton: I have written a very long letter to the Pré Carré. Now about the entry into Switzerland. The lawyer Georges Haldenwang at Geneva is the one who is supporting my application. I had planned to stay in Vaud first so as to place the little boy and my daughter and then to settle in Zurich. He advised me to choose one or the other: so I applied for Zurich from where I believe I can place my daughter and the little boy in the Vaud. I learned yesterday from Berne that there will be a great deal of difficulty about Zurich. They advise me to begin again and to apply for residence in Vaud where I will have to give four or five references, I who know nobody but you there! What a nuisance! If I had the entry permit for Switzerland it would perhaps be easier to have the exit permit from here, which otherwise is not at all simple. I thought of Jaloux but he is not Swiss and I do not know where he may be. Do you know this lawyer? Before you leave be sure to send me a word. Cordial greetings,   James Joyce'
[2] A copy of a letter from The Viking Press discussing a way of sending Joyce his American royalties.

no means sure that we shall obtain from the French authorities permission to leave. My daughter has the German permission but I have no funds to pay her doctor with (Dr Achille Delmas, 23 rue de la Mairie, Ivry s/Seine, Paris). I have a place for her to go near Lausanne. Mr Zumsteg said that if I got the permission for Switzerland and needed funds to travel he would advance these and I could repay his father at Zurich. I have written the U.S. Legation at Berne to find whether I shall have the same difficulties with the State Department if and when I reach Switzerland. Many thanks to you in any case.   JAMES JOYCE

To JACQUES MERCANTON (Postcard)   MS. Mercanton

29 October 1940   Maison Ponthenier, S. Gérand-le-Puy, Allier, France

Cher Mercanton: Je suppose que vous êtes de retour. Nous sommes toujours ici, car nous n'avons pas reçu de Berne le permis de sejour en Suisse demandé il y a six semaines. Les autorités allemandes donnèrent immédiatement le permis de sortie pour ma fille, les autorités françaises ont donné également le permis de sortie pour nous tous. Tous nos papiers sont timbrés et en règle depuis deux semaines mais la durée est limitée. Pour simplifier les choses j'ai demandé le permis de séjour à Lausanne pour pouvoir placer ma fille et mon petit-fils dans un sanatorium et dans une école. Mon avocat est M. G. Haldenwang, 6 rue du Rhône à Genève. Comme réferences dans le Vaud j'ai donné votre nom, celui du Dr Forel à Prangins, Dr Loy à Montreux. Mme Giedion est allé [sic] au bureau de la police des étrangers à Zurich où l'on semble croire que je suis . . . juif! Tonerre [sic] m'enlève! Voilà une fameuse découverte! Cordialement votre   JAMES JOYCE[1]

[1] (Translation)
'Dear Mercanton: I suppose you are back. We are still here, for we have not received from Berne the permit to reside in Switzerland which we applied for six weeks ago. The German authorities gave my daughter an exit permit immediately, the French authorities have similarly granted us all exit permits. All our papers have been stamped and in order for two weeks but they are good only for a limited time. To simplify matters I asked for a permit to reside in Lausanne so as to be able to place my daughter and my grandson in a sanatorium and in a school. My lawyer is Mr G. Haldenwang, 6 rue du Rhône in Geneva. As my references in the Vaud I gave your name, that of Dr Forel at Prangins, Dr Loy at Montreux. Mme Giedion went to the Aliens' Police at Zurich where they seemed to believe that I am . . . a Jew! I am thunderstruck! There's a remarkable discovery! Cordially yours   James Joyce'

To GUSTAV ZUMSTEG   MS. Zumsteg

29 October 1940   *Maison Ponthenier, S. Gérand-le-Puy, Allier*

Cher Monsieur Zumsteg: Si le Marquis de Terrier[1] n'a pas pu vous avoir au téléphone voilà la substance de ce que je l'avais prié de vous demander.

Pouvez-vous me faire savoir (ici on est en pleine campagne sans moyens de communication avec Vichy ou presque) quel train nous pouvons prendre de S. Germain des Fossés pour Lyon et ensuite pour Annecy–Annemasse? Je désire vous voir en passant par Lyon car il faut que j'arrange des choses avec vous avant de partir. Il n'est plus necessaire pour nous de nous arrêter à Lyon car l'Ambassade des U.S.A. a renouvelé nos passeports britanniques. Le Ministère de l'Intérieur a donné le permis de sortie pour nous tous. Depuis huit jours tous nos papiers sont timbrés et en règle, mais la durée est limitée. La legation des U.S.A. à Berne m'écrit que quand je serai en Suisse je pourrais recevoir mon argent de New York. Mme Giedion m'écrit qu'à la Fremden-polizei de Zurich où elle était allée pour savoir la raison de la non-arrivée du permis d'entrée on semblait croire que j'étais un juif! C'est le bouquet, vraiment. Comme vous me le proposez j'ai demandé donc d'aller à Lausanne et de placer ma fille à la maison de santé Pré Carré à Corcelles sur Chavornay, Vaud, et de placer mon petit-fils dans un collège dans le Vaud. Mais si cela traine encore après 6 ou 7 semaines notre permis de sortie sera perimé. J'ai reçu une autre lettre du M. Ed. Brauchbar à son fils à Zurich.[2] Avez-vous vu ce dernier pendant votre visite à Zurich. Il n'a jamais répondu à mes lettres. Je voudrais être fixé sur ce point avant de répondre à son père. A-t-il repondu à la lettre que vous lui avez écrit naguère?

Autre chose. Pouvez-vous vous tenir en rapport avec le consulat suisse à Lyon de façon que si le permis arrive vous pouvez payer pour moi ce qu'il y a à payer pour gagner du temps, somme que je vous rembourserai à l'époque de mon passage par Lyon.

Quant au garanti financier, puisque M. R. Brauchbar ne l'avait pas donné (au moins jusqu'au 27 octobre) mes amis Giedion l'ont donné.

J'espère que vous vous êtes remis de votre indisposition et m'excuse de vous déranger continuellment.

Envoyez-moi une dépêche aussitôt que vous saurez quelque chose de définitif. Votre bien dévoué   JAMES JOYCE[3]

---

[1] Evidently someone Joyce had met at S. Gérand-le-Puy.

[2] Rudolf Brauchbar (b. 1908) handled the family business in Switzerland.

[3] (Translation)

'Dear Mr Zumsteg: If the Marquis de Terrier has not been able to reach you by telephone here is the substance of what I asked him to speak to you about.

Can you inform me (here we are out in the country with no way, or almost none, of communicating with Vichy) what train we should take from S. Germain des Fossés

To GUSTAV ZUMSTEG   MS. Zumsteg

31 October 1940   *Maison Ponthenier, S. Gérand-le-Puy*

Cher Monsieur Zumsteg: Merci pour votre lettre du 30. L'avocat de
Génève m'écrit dans le même sens. Il veut tout de suite 200 frs suisses.
Je ne les ai pas. Il veut aussi un garanti de M. R. Brauchbar. Qu'il
l'obtienne. Il a demandé un permis de séjour, il parait, pour nous à
Génève. Je ne l'ai jamais autorisé à le faire. J'ai demandé un permis
dans la canton de Vaud pour ma fille malade puisque la maison de santé
est là. J'ai demandé de pouvoir rester un peu de temps là aussi pour la
caser et mon petit-fils aussi et puis d'aller nous établir à Zurich pour
laquelle je donnerais des références. Quand vous m'avez dit que Zurich
n'allait pas j'ai dit: Bon, nous irons tous à Lausanne. J'écris à l'avocat
et en ce sens, et je lui donnais cinq nouvelles références. Maintenant il
parait qu'il a changé tout cela et a demandé le permis pour Zurich-Ville
où, du reste, on ne me veut pas parce que je suis juif. Je trouve tout cela
parfaitement ridicule: et il contraste singulièrement avec les réponses
qui m'ont été données par les autorités françaises et par les autorités
allemandes de ce côté de la frontière.

Avec mes remerciements à vous en tout cas croyez-moi votre bien
dévoué   JAMES JOYCE[1]

for Lyons and then for Annecy–Annemasse. I want to see you when we pass through
Lyons for I must arrange matters with you before leaving. We no longer are obliged to
stop at Lyons for the Embassy of the U.S.A. has renewed our British passports. The
Ministry of the Interior has granted exit permits to all of us. Our papers have been
stamped and in order for eight days now, but they are good only for a limited time.
The Legation of the U.S.A. at Berne writes me that when I reach Switzerland I can
receive my money from New York. Mrs Giedion writes me that the Aliens' Police in
Zurich to whom she went to find out why my entry permit had not arrived seemed to
believe that I was a Jew! That caps it all, really. As you suggest I therefore applied
to go to Lausanne and to place my daughter in the Pré Carré maison de santé at
Corcelles near Chavornay, Vaud, and to place my grandson in a school in the Vaud.
But if this is still dragging on after six or seven weeks our exit permits will expire. I
received another letter from Mr Edmund Brauchbar to his son in Zurich. Have you
seen this latter during your visit to Zurich. He has never replied to my letters. I should
like to be certain on this point before answering his father. Has he replied at all to the
letter that you wrote to him?

Another point. Can you be in touch with the Swiss Consulate in such a way that if
the permit arrives you can pay on my behalf whatever is due so as to save time, and I
will reimburse you when I pass through Lyons.

As for the financial guaranty, since Mr R. Brauchbar had not given it (at least up
to 27 October) my friends the Giedions have given it.

I hope you have recovered from your indisposition and apologize for troubling you
so constantly.

Send me a telegram as soon as you know something definite. Sincerely yours
                                                    James Joyce'

[1] (Translation)
'Dear Mr Zumsteg: Thank you for your letter of the 30th. The Geneva lawyer
writes me to the same effect. He wants 200 Swiss francs at once. I do not have them.

To CAROLA GIEDION-WELCKER   MS. Giedion-Welcker

1 November 1940   Maison Ponthenier, S. Gérand-le-Puy, Allier, France

Chère Madame Giedion: Je viens de recevoir la depêche signée par
vous et Ruggiero. Merci. Mais si vous n'êtes qu'en correspondance
'epistolaire' avec New York notre visa de sortie sera perimée longtemps
avant l'arrivée de la réponse même si celle-ci est favorable. Dejà le
maire d'ici et la gendarmerie qui nous a fait deux visites pendant ces
derniers huit jours à propos d'un recensement des sujets britanniques
actuellement en France tout en étant parfaitement courtois exprimaient
une surprise, légitime du reste, que nous étions toujours sur place après
avoir demandé avec une telle insistance le permis de partir qui nous à
été donné par ordre du Ministère de l'Intérieur, il y a dejà quinze jours.
D'après vòtre carte postale de l'autre jour je croyais la question du
garanti financier reglée une fois pour toutes. En attendant l'avocat à
Génève qui n'est pas arrivé jusqu'ici à obtenir quoi que ce soit de qui
que ce soit demande un versement à 200 francs suisses, somme que je
lui paierai naturellement quand je les aurai, c'est-à-dire, quand je
serai et si je serai en Suisse. La légation américaine à Bern m'écrit
qu'une fois en Suisse je pourai recevoir mon argent de New York.
L'avocat demande aussi un garanti de la part de M. Rudolph
Brauchbar. Eh bien, qu'il l'obtienne. Ce dernier n'a jamais répondu à
ma correspondance. Mais peut-être y-a-t-il une explication. L'avocat
écrit 'le cas J.J. est toujours en suspens chez la police fédérale suisse'.
C'est charmant. En somme on soulève une difficulté après l'autre. Nous
sommes des étrangers, puis des juifs, puis des mendiants. Quòi encore.
Des cambrioleurs, des lépreux? Ou bien c'est une longue histoire à
propos des cantons. L'avocat a demandé le permis d'abord pour
Genève. Je ne l'ai jamais autorisé de le faire. J'ai demandé d'abord pour
le Vaud pour ma fille puisque la maison de santé est là. Et pour nous d'y
rester le temps de la caser et mon petit-fils dans une école. Et ensuite à
Zurich. Quand on m'a dit que Zurich n'allait pas, j'ai dit: Bon, nous

He also wants a guarantee from Mr R. Brauchbar. Let him obtain it. He has applied
for a residence permit for us at Geneva, it seems. I never authorized him to do that. I
asked for a permit for the canton of Vaud for my sick daughter because the maison
de santé is there. I asked to be able to stay briefly there too so as to settle her and my
grandson as well and then to go to settle in Zurich, for which I would give references.
When you told me Zurich was not working out I said: Good, then we will all go to
Lausanne. I wrote to the lawyer and to this effect, and I gave him five new references.
Now it seems that he has altered all that and has asked for a permit for Zurich-City
where, after all, they do not want me because I am a Jew. I find all this absolutely
ridiculous: and it contrasts remarkably with the replies which have been given to me
by the French authorities and by the German authorities on this side of the frontier.
    With my thanks to you in any case, sincerely yours   James Joyce'

irons tous à Lausanne. Maintenant il semble que l'avocat veut demander pour Zurich-Ville. Dans les circonstances actuelles du monde et les miennes en particulier cette mode d'agir est hors de plan et elle contraste singulièrement, je dois le dire, avec les réponses courtoises et favorables qui m'ont été données par les autorités allemandes et par les autorités françaises ici. Et voilà une lettre de la direction de la maison de santé. Bien entendu, je ne pouvais rien arranger car je n'avais pas le permis pour ma fille. Et à propos de garantis financiers si mon fils et moi proposons de payer pour l'enfant dans un collège vaudois et pour ma fille dans une maison de santé je suppose que nous ne pouvons pas être dépourvus de moyens d'existence.

Je vous remercie en tout cas, tous les deux, et Ruggiero aussi. Salutations amicales   JAMES JOYCE[1]

[1] (Translation)

'Dear Mrs Giedion: I have just received the telegram signed by you and Ruggiero. Thanks. But if you are only in "epistolary" communication with New York our exit permit will expire long before the arrival of the reply even if that should be favourable. Already the mayor of this place and the police who have paid us two visits during the last eight days in connection with a census of British subjects now in France, although they were perfectly courteous, expressed surprise, legitimate surprise, that we were still here after having so urgently applied for the exit permit which was granted us by order of the Ministry of the Interior all of fifteen days ago. In view of your postcard of the other day I began to believe the question of the financial guarantee was settled once and for all. During this wait the Geneva lawyer, who has not managed up to now to obtain anything from anyone demands a fee of 200 Swiss francs, a sum I shall of course pay when I have it, that is, when I am and if I am in Switzerland. The American Legation at Berne writes me that once I am in Switzerland I can receive my money from New York. The lawyer also asks a guarantee by Mr Rudolph Brauchbar. Well, let him secure it. The latter has never answered my correspondence. But perhaps there is some explanation. The lawyer writes "The J.J. case is still pending with the Swiss Federal Police." That's nice. So they are raising one difficulty after another. We are aliens, then Jews, then beggars. What next. Burglars, lepers? Or else they give us a long story about cantons. The lawyer applied for the permit for Geneva first. I never authorised him to do that. I applied first for the Vaud for my daughter since the maison de santé is there. And for us to stay there long enough to settle her and my grandson in a school. Then on to Zurich. When they said that Zurich was not working out I said: Very well, then we will all go to Lausanne. Now it develops that the lawyer wishes to apply for Zurich-City. In the present world situation and my own in particular this kind of behaviour is out of joint and it contrasts oddly, I must say, with the courteous and favourable replies which were accorded me by the German authorities and by the French authorities here. And here is a letter from the management of the maison de santé. Of course I could not arrange anything for I had no permit for my daughter. As for the financial guarantees, if my son and I propose to pay for the child in a school in Vaud and for my daughter in a maison de santé, I suppose we cannot be entirely destitute of the means to exist.

I thank you anyway, both of you, and Ruggiero too. Friendly greetings

James Joyce'

To EDMUND BRAUCHBAR   MS. Brauchbar

3 November 1940   c/o *U.S.A. Embassy, Vichy, France*

Dear Mr Brauchbar: In reply to my two appeals by air mail on 5 August
to my two N.Y. publishers for help I received on 28 October through
American Export Lines of Marseilles the equivalent of 260$ from one
publisher, Huebsch, stated to be the amount due to me on 30 March
last. From the other publisher nothing came. The U.S.A. Embassy at
Vichy has now reduced the monthly subsidy we live on by 1500 frs. It
seems that for one reason or another the subsidy may be further reduced
or discontinued in the future.

About my daughter I shall write a little later. Now about ourselves.
As I told you the German authorities gave me permission to remove my
daughter from occupied France. I had arranged for the reception at a
Swiss *maison de santé* in the Vaud, Pré Carré, Corcelles. I then applied
to the French Ministry of the Interior for permission for us, my wife,
son, grandson and myself to leave unoccupied France. This also was
granted by an order of the Minister some weeks ago. Our passports are
stamped for exit and our luggage all packed also for weeks past. The
Swiss authorities however refused to allow any or all of us to enter.
Since the end of July last I have been writing letter after letter to
different persons in Switzerland and in addition to formal application
through the Lyons Swiss consulate placed the matter in the hands of a
Geneva lawyer. Yesterday I had a letter from him asking for 200 frs
Swiss. The letter states that the case is still in suspense at the Federal
Police Offices. Two of my Zurich references Mr and Mrs Giedion trying
to find out what this meant went to the Fremdenpolizei[1] where it was
found that I was considered by the officials to be . . . a Jew! Nothing
was known there of any guarantee or affidavit by your son to whom I
sent several letters but had no reply. I have now had a telegram signed
by Giedion and Ruggiero, a Zurich friend of mine of a very modest
station of life who is a clerk at the Zurich Kreditanstalt. It reads:
'Permis sejour obtenable question financière encore en suspens nous
correspondons Edmund'.[2] While I am guessing at what this means and

---

[1] Aliens' Police.

[2] 'Residence permit obtainable financial question still pending we are writing Edmund
[Brauchbar].'

Brauchbar's son Rudolf hesitated to give a financial guaranty for Joyce without
explicit instruction from his father in New York. This was forthcoming and
eventually the two financial guarantees were provided by Rudolf Brauchbar and
Sigfried Giedion.

waiting for some new objection to be raised by the Federal authorities the time accorded me for leaving France is running out. The gendarmes who came to our lodgings twice last week as they are making a census of British subjects resident in France, while quite polite, expressed surprise that we who had been so insistent on our desire to leave and had obtained ministerial permission to do so were still here. You may be able to draw some conclusions from these facts.

If the Swiss should decide to let us in we have now enough to pay our journey to Lausanne or Zurich and our luggage and debts here and arrive in Switzerland with some thousands of French francs over to start with, perhaps 5 or 6. What we get for them in Swiss francs I do not rightly know. Some say 10%, some 7% and some 5%. But we haven't got them yet.

The U.S.A. legation at Berne to which I wrote informs me that when I have established residence in Switzerland by a sworn declaration before a U.S. consul I can receive money from the U.S.A., that is, if anybody sends it. I hope he is right.

I send off this letter as you are doubtless expecting one. You can tell Huebsch I got the 260$. When he sends the usual account of sales I shall send the usual formal acknowledgement.

With friendly greetings to your good self in any case sincerely yours

JAMES JOYCE

To PAUL RUGGIERO[1]   MS. Ruggiero

19 November 1940   [*S. Gérand-le-Puy*]

Cher Ruggiero: Voilà la declaration. J'ai téléphoné à la Légation Suisse à Vichy. On m'a dit de la faire sur papier timbré et de la faire légaliser ici. Il nous est interdit d'aller à Vichy. Le secrétaire de légation m'a promis de me télégraphier aussitôt qu'il aura nos visas. J'ai arrangé de lui envoyer les passeports à Vichy par un ami qui nous les reportera timbrés. Il faut donc que l'on avise Vichy et pas Lyon.

Notre permis de sortie n'est valable que pour 8 jours encore. Il a été écrit il y a 6 semaines. Nous tâcherons de la faire renouveler pour un bref délai. Je ne garantie pas de pouvoir y reussir. En tout cas il me faudra quelque pièce imprimée ou autre des autorités là-bas pour justifier ma demande, pour expliquer notre presence etc. Si ce document est en allemand il faudra envoyer la traduction avec.

[1] From a typewritten copy.

Je comprends de moins en moins ce qui se passe. Mais il est clair que les Giedions et vous vous donnez énormément de peine pour moi. Cordialement votre   JAMES JOYCE[1]

To CAROLA GIEDION-WELCKER   MS. Giedion-Welcker

20 November 1940   [*S. Gérand-le-Puy*]

Chère Madame Giedion: J'ai reçu cette lettre il y a quatre jours de M. Gia Augsbourg. Je lui ai répondu. Il est arrivé ici ce matin à l'improviste et repartit après quelques heures d'entretien d'abord pour Vichy et ensuite pour Lausanne, ou il compte rentrer vendredi. Son adresse est: Ville Elisol, Prèchy, Lausanne. Il m'a promis de voir à Vichy le ministre irlandais, Mr S. Murphy (qui, comme vous le rappellerez, intervenait avec succès auprès des autorités occupantes à Paris pour la sortie de ma fille) et aussi de parler au Ministre Suisse à Vichy, M. Struck.[2] Aussitôt rentré en Suisse il dit qu'il fera tout en son pouvoir. Nous avons causé de ma fille mais pour arranger cela il faudrait que je cause d'abord avec les gens de la maison de santé quand je m'arrête à Lausanne—si jamais j'y arrive.

J'ai envoyé à Ruggiero les 2 declarations voulues par lettre exprès mais j'ai oublié de mettre mon nom sur l'enveloppe comme envoyeur. Tant pis, j'espère que cela vous arrive. Faites-moi savoir, s.v.p.

Je ne peux pas commencer à vous remercier tous les deux de tout ce que vous faites pour nous, mais quelles complications et malentendus et retards et contradictions! En tout cas il faut faire vite car notre permis de sortie n'est valable que pour 8 jours encore. Le faire renouveler sera difficile et impossible sans quelques pièces en appui de là-bas expliquant le retard. Jusqu'ici je n'ai rien reçu après trois mois. Les lettres personnelles ne comptent pas.

Peut-être vaut-il la pensée de vous mettre en rapports avec

---

[1] (Translation)

'Dear Ruggiero: Here is the declaration. I telephoned the Swiss Legation at Vichy. They told me to make it out on paper with an official stamp and to have it legalised here. We are forbidden to go to Vichy. The secretary of the legation promised to telegraph me as soon as he had our visas. I have arranged to send the passports to him at Vichy by a friend who will bring them back stamped. So Vichy, not Lyons, must be notified.

Our exit permit is good for only eight days more. It was issued six weeks ago. We shall try to have it renewed for a short additional period. I do not guarantee that I will succeed. I will have to have in any event some formal paper or other from the authorities there to justify my application, to explain our presence etc. If this document is in German a translation must be sent with it.

I understand less and less what is happening. But it is clear that the Giedions and you have taken enormous trouble on my account. Cordially yours   James Joyce'

[2] Walter Stucki (1888–1963).

Augsbourg. J'envoie cette lettre par le courrier ordinaire car ma lettre à Ruggiero dans le même sens est parti exprès. Mais écrivez-moi seulement exprès ou télégraphiez car le temps presse. Salutations très cordiales   JAMES JOYCE[1]

To GUSTAV ZUMSTEG   MS. Zumsteg

22 November 1940   Maison Ponthenier, S. Gérand-le-Puy, Allier

Cher Monsieur Zumsteg: Merci bien pour tout ce que vous avez fait. En réponse à votre lettre et coup de téléphone de Lyon j'ai envoyé express mardi dernier à Z'ch la déclaration exigée. Je crains pourtant que si l'on ne me voulait là-bas parce que l'on me croyait juif (Intelligence Service, sans doute?) après lecture de ma declaration l'on me voudra de moins en moins en s'apercevant que je ne suis pas juif du tout.

En attendant je voudrais bien être fixé sur deux points. 1°. Est-il sûr que si le permis d'entrer dans la terre promise arrive le consulat de Lyon enverra ceci à la legation à Vichy. J'y ai écrit et j'y ai téléphoné à ce propos. Un ami influent est allé là aussi. J'ai peur d'une nouvelle confusion. Il y en a assez déjà entre Genève, Lausanne, Zurich et Berne sans que Lyon et Vichy s'y incluent. Je voudrais éviter une nuit à Lyon si possible. 2°. Serait-il possible et légalement permissible pour vous d'effectuer un paiement pour moi à Paris—contre remboursement ou ici ou à Zurich selon les circonstances. Je dois payer une somme au docteur Achille Delmas, 23 rue de la Mairie à Ivry s/Seine avant de

---

[1] (Translation)

'Dear Mrs Giedion: I received this letter four days ago from Mr Gia Augsbourg. I answered him. He arrived here this morning unexpectedly and left after several hours of discussion first for Vichy and then for Lausanne, where he intends to return Friday. His address is: Villa Elisol, Prèchy, Lausanne. He promised me to see the Irish Minister at Vichy, Mr S. Murphy (who, you will recall, intervened successfully with the occupying authorities in Paris for the departure of my daughter) and also to speak to the Swiss Minister to Vichy, Mr Struck. Once back in Switzerland he says he will do everything in his power. We talked about my daughter but to arrange that I will have to speak first with the people at the maison de santé when I stop at Lausanne —if I ever arrive there.

I sent Ruggiero the 2 desired declarations by express letter but I forgot to put my name on the envelope as the sender. A pity but I hope it will arrive. Let me know, please.

I cannot begin to thank you both for all you are doing for us, but what complications and misunderstandings and delays and contradictions! Anyway we must act quickly for our exit permit is good for only eight days more. Renewing it will be difficult and impossible without some supporting papers from there explaining the delay. Up to now I have received none after three months. Personal letters are no use.

The idea might be considered of your getting in touch with Augsbourg. I am sending this letter by ordinary post but my letter to Ruggiero with the same contents has gone express. But write me only express or wire for time presses. Very cordial greetings   James Joyce'

faire les arrangements pour le transport eventuel de ma fille à la
Clinique du Pré Carré, Corcelles, Vaud. Dr Delmas est le proprietaire-
directeur de la maison de santé où ma fille se trouve. Il s'agit de quelques
milliers de francs. J'ai trouvé l'escorte pour elle et j'ai le permis allemand.
Quant au permis suisse, elle attend. Et moi, j'attends.

En remerciant d'avance Votre bien dévoué et assez dégoûté

JAMES JOYCE[1]

To ARMAND PETITJEAN   MS. Petitjean

23 November 1940   Maison Ponthenier, S. Gérand-le-Puy, Allier, France

Cher Petitjean: J'ai promis de vous tenir au courant de 'l'affaire' J.J.
Donc je vous envoie ceci chez votre ami M. Recht, ignorant toujours
votre addresse.

Voilà où nous en sommes. La Suisse, ayant decouvert que je ne suis
point juif de Judée mais aryen d'Erin a demandé outre les dix references
données un depot bancaire et une garantie de 500,000 francs ensemble.
Le dépot a été fait a mon nom à une banque zurichoise (200,000 frs
français) et la garantie donnée. La Suisse a ensuite demandé ou plutot
exigé une declaration détaillée de ma fortune personelle avec pièces
d'appui. Je l'ai fait mais je crains que après lecture de ma déclaration
les Suisses verront trop clairement que je ne suis pas juif et me rebutera
à nouveau.

En attendant notre permis de séjour n'est valable que jusqu'à la fin
de ce mois. Je tacherai de le faire renouveler pour un bref delai.

[1] (Translation)

'Dear Mr Zumsteg: Many thanks for all you have done. In reply to your letter and
telephone call from Lyons I sent by express on Tuesday last to Zurich the declaration
that was needed. I fear however that if they did not want me there because they
believed me to be a Jew (Intelligence Service, no doubt?), after reading my declaration
they will want me less and less as they perceive that I am not a Jew at all.

While we are waiting I should like to know two things for sure. 1. Is it certain that
if the entry permit for the promised land arrives the consulate at Lyons will send
it to the legation at Vichy. I wrote and telephoned there with that in mind. An influential friend has gone there as well. I am afraid of a new confusion. There are enough
already among Geneva, Lausanne, Zurich and Berne leaving out Lyons and Vichy. I
should like to avoid a night at Lyons if possible. 2. Would it be possible and legally
permissible for you to make payment for me in Paris—against reimbursement either
here or in Zurich depending upon the circumstances. I must pay some money to Dr
Achille Delmas, 23 rue de la Mairie in Ivry s/Seine before making arrangements for
the eventual transfer of my daughter to the Clinic of the Pré Carré, Corcelles, Vaud.
Dr Delmas is the owner-director of the maison de santé where my daughter now is.
Several thousand francs are involved. I have found an escort for her and I have the
German permit. As to the Swiss permit, she is waiting for it. And I too am waiting.

With thanks in advance Faithfully and rather disgustedly   James Joyce'

J'avais tout arrangé pour le transfert de ma fille malade mais, bien entendu, tout est en l'air.

Vous me demanderez pourquoi je m'obstine à vouloir pénétrer un pays si hermétiquement helvétique. Simplement parce que, étant ici, je suis coupé de mes ressources et l'ambassade des U.S.A. nous a fait savoir que nous ne pouvons pas compter longtemps sur l'aide mensuel qu'elle nous passe.

Merci à vous en tout cas et je vous ferai savoir ce qui arrivera.

A suivre Cordialement votre   JAMES JOYCE[1]

To PAUL RUGGIERO (Telegram)   TS. Ruggiero

25 November 1940   *S. Gérand-le-Puy*

Legalised declaration sent by express Wednesday I shall renew tomorrow We shall ask for prolongation Amitiés.   JAMES JOYCE

To CAROLA GIEDION-WELCKER   MS. Giedion-Welcker

28 November 1940   *Maison Ponthenier, S. Gérand-le-Puy*

Chère Madame Giedion: Hier à 7 a.m. ma 2^{ieme} déclaration est partie d'ici. À 5 p.m. Ruggiero m'a telegraphié de Zurich que le permis etait accordé. Donc ma 1ere déclaration est arrivée entre lundi et hier car ma 2^{ieme} ne pouvait être alors à Zurich? Ou il y a une autre explication? Je suis toujours sans réponse de M. Augsbourg. Peut-être, est-il intervenu autrement? En tout cas j'ai demandé une prolongation de 15 jours. Reste à voir si l'on me l'accorde. Je l'espère mais les choses deviennent de plus en plus difficiles.

[1] (Translation)
'Dear Petitjean: I promised to keep you in touch with the J.J. "affair." So I send you this in care of your friend Mr Recht, as I still do not know your address.
    Here is where we are. Switzerland, having discovered that I am not a Jew from Judea but an Aryan from Erin has asked not only for the ten references already given but also for a bank deposit and a guaranty of 500,000 francs together. The deposit has been made in my name by a Zurich bank (200,000 French francs) and the guaranty given. Switzerland has next asked or rather required a detailed declaration of my personal fortune with supporting documents. I have made it but I fear that after reading my declaration the Swiss will see too clearly that I am not a Jew and will reject me again.
    During this wait our residence permit is good only to the end of this month. I shall try to have it renewed for a brief additional period.
    I had arranged everything for the transfer of my sick daughter but, as you will understand, everything is up in the air.
    You will ask why I persist in wishing to penetrate that country which is so hermetically helvetic. Simply because, living here, I am cut off from my resources and the Embassy of the U.S.A. has let us know that we will not be able to count for long on the monthly aid which it is giving us.
    Thanks to you in any case and I will let you know what happens.
    More to follow Cordially yours   James Joyce'

J'ai reçu ce matin les 2 lettres ci-avec. Voilà donc que les retards ont pour suite. Les allemands accordèrent il y a déjà *3 mois* le permis de sortie pour Lucia et pendant tout ce temps là et même avant je n'ai pas cessé d'écrire et de téléphoner et de télégraphier. Maintenant le permis arrive et le permis de sortie est revoqué! Sans doute s'agit-il d'un ordre général. D'abord j'étais si contrarié que j'ai voulu abandonner l'idée d'aller en Suisse. Puis j'ai pensé qu'ici je serais de plus en plus impuissant et qu'en Suisse je pourrai faire plus pour elle qu'ici. J'ai téléphoné à la legation d'Irlande et le *ministre* me donne *une lettre de presentation à M Sears Lester*[1] à Genève. Je crois qu'il pourait intervenir avec effet avec l'aide de la *croix-rouge* international. Après tout ma fille est malade et dans un lieu dangereux. Je ne trouve pas son adresse. Si vous le savez vous pouvez lui envoyer une de ces copies en lui expliquant le cas. Si vous pouvez me faire parvenir son adresse par dépêche avant que nous partions j'irai le voir avec la lettre du ministre quand je serai à Lausanne où il faut que je m'arrête 1 ou 2 nuits pour parler avec la direction de la maison de santé à Corcelles, près de là. Le nom du chargé d'affaires à la legation d'Irlande à Berne est M. Frank Cremmins.[2] Gardez les autres copies pour lui mais ne les envoyez pas pour le moment. L'autre, Lester, sera plus efficace, je crois. Il y a aussi outre le comte O'Kelly,[3] chargé d'affaires d'Irlande à Paris que je connais il y a aussi le Dr Patrick O'Brien[4] de la Fondation Rockefeller, 20 rue Labanne, Paris 8° qui pourait aussi intervenir. Mais d'ici je ne pourais rien faire. Espèrons que notre permis ne soit pas revoqué aussi! Remerciez, je vous prie, toutes les personnes qui se sont dérangés pour m'aider. Je le ferai personnellement un jour. Cette lettre concerne principalement Lucia que j'envoie à vous. Salutations cordiales

JAMES JOYCE[5]

[1] Sears Lester (1889–1959), Irish diplomat, was Deputy Secretary-General of the League of Nations, 1937–40, and Secretary-General, 1940–47.

[2] Francis Thomas Cremins (b. 1885), Irish diplomat, chargé d'affaires in Berne, 1940–1949.

[3] Count Gerald Edward O'Kelly (b. 1890), Irish diplomat.

[4] Daniel Patrick O'Brien (1894–1958), physician and an official in the Rockefeller Institute for Medical Research from 1927 until his retirement in 1947.

[5] (Translation)

'Dear Mrs Giedion: Yesterday at 7 a.m. my second declaration left here. At 5 p.m. Ruggiero wired me from Zurich that the permit had been granted. Then my first declaration arrived between Monday and yesterday for my second could not be at Zurich yet? Or is there some other explanation? I have still had no reply from Mr Augsbourg. Has he perhaps intervened in another way? Anyway I have asked for a prolongation of 15 days. It remains to be seen if they will grant it. I hope so but things are becoming more and more difficult.

I received this morning the two letters attached. Here then is what comes of delays. The Germans granted the exit permit for Lucia *three months* ago and during all this time and even before it I have not stopped writing or telephoning or telegraphing.

To ARMAND PETITJEAN[1]   MS. Petitjean

3 December 1940   Maison Ponthenier, S. Gérand-le-Puy, Allier, France

Cette lettre est pour M. Paul Recht si son ami est parti.

Cher Petitjean: Merci. J'ai bien reçu votre dépêche encourageante du 2 courant. Mon fils m'a dit qu'il vous a rencontré a Vichy et que vous espériez pouvoir nous télégraphier définitivement et probablement jeudi. Je n'ai rien reçu. J'apprécie—mais pas officiellement—que l'on soulève à nouveau la question—déjà reglée par un ordre du ministre de l'Intérieur en date du 18 octobre mais à laquelle tous nos visas à la date précisée du 1er décembre ont été émis—de la 'mobilisabilité' (mot qui ne se trouve pas même dans *Finnegans Wake*) de mon fils—Cette mobilisabilité n'existe pas ni en fait ni en loi. Né en Italie, irlandais, fils des parents tous les deux de l'Irlande du Sud, n'ayant jamais résidé et ne résidant pas ni en Grande Bretagne ni en Irlande du Nord il n'est visé par aucune loi sur le service militaire britannique. J'ai obtenu de la Suisse une courte prolongation de nos visas d'entrée. Mais nous devrons partir ensemble. J'arrangerai l'affaire de ma fille plus aisément une fois que je serai la. Si le visa suisse était arrivé trois jours ou deux jours plus tôt nous serions déjà à Lausanne. Assurément ce n'est pas votre faute. Mais la mienne, non plus. C'est un contretemps : mais pour-quoi en faire un contresens ?

Si vous pouvez arranger l'affaire je suis sûr que vous le ferez. Cordialement votre   JAMES JOYCE[2]

Now the permit arrives and the exit permit is revoked! No doubt some general order is involved. First I was so impeded that I wanted to give up the idea of going to Switzerland. Then I thought that here I would be more and more powerless and that in Switzerland I would be able to do more than here. I telephoned the Irish Legation and *the minister* is giving me *a letter of introduction to Mr Sears Lester* at Geneva. I think he could intervene effectively with the assistance of the International *Red Cross*. After all my daughter is sick and in a dangerous place. I do not find his address. If you know it you can send him one of these copies and explain the matter to him. If you can let me have his address by wire before we leave I shall go see him with the minister's letter when I am in Lausanne where I shall have to stop over one or two nights to speak with the management of the maison de santé at Corcelles, near there. The name of the chargé d'affaires at the Irish Legation at Berne is Mr Frank Cremins. Keep the other copies for him but do not send them on for the moment. The other man, Lester, will be more useful, I think. There is also Count O'Kelly, chargé d'affaires of Ireland in Paris whom I know; there is also Dr Patrick O'Brien of the Rockefeller Foundation, 20 rue Labanne, Paris 8°, who could also intervene. But from here I can do nothing. Let us hope that our permit will not be revoked too! Please thank all the people who have taken the trouble to help me. The letter I send you is principally concerned with Lucia. Cordial greetings   James Joyce'

[1] From a typewritten copy.

[2] (Translation)

'This letter is for Mr Paul Recht if his friend has left.

Dear Petitjean: Thank you. I have indeed received your encouraging telegram of 2 inst. My son told me that he met you in Vichy and that you were hoping to be able to wire

To Gustav Zumsteg   MS. Zumsteg

[? 5 December 1940]   *Maison Ponthenier, S. Gérand-le-Puy*

Cher Monsieur Zumsteg: Merci pour votre lettre du 4 courant. Et
voilà la réponse que vous me priez de vous faire savoir.

Voyage: Si nous devons arriver à Lyon ou à 17.55 ou à 21.40 en partant
soit à 2.10 ou à 6.50 et repartir le matin après soit à 6.30 soit à 8.50
comment pourrons nous faire timbrer nos quatre passeports britanniques
pour l'entrée en Suisse (si accordée) au consulat suisse de Lyon (et payer ce
qu'il y aura à payer) puisque le consulat sera fermé ? Sera-t-il possible pour
vous avant votre depart pour Zurich samedi (il ne semble pas probable que
nous pouvons partir avant) d'arranger avec le consulat que la somme en
question soit payée d'avance (je vous le rembourserai d'ici par mandat)
et qu'au lieu de nous arrêter une journée entière à Lyon que le consulat
nous fasse parvenir un papier timbré couvrant les quatre passeports si
une telle chose est reguliere ? Nos passeports sont déjà timbrés et nos
cartes d'identité aussi tant pour le sauf-conduit à la frontière que pour
la sortie mais ces timbres ne sont pas valables que pour une autre
quinzaine de jours. Après cela il me faudrait recommencer de nouveau
auprès les autorités françaises et leur expliquer pourquoi nous n'avons
pas utilisé les visas qu'on nous avait donnés. Il faut que tout ce qu'on
fait dorénavant soit fait télégraphiquement et pas par lettre. Nous ne
pouvons plus quitter ce village depuis la loi d'hier, même pour aller à
Vichy sans un permis spécial. En somme nous devons rester ici ou
partir en Suisse.

Haldenwang: Je laisse cela à votre jugement puisque vous le connaissez. Il me semble d'après sa lettre que s'il n'est pas payé il laissera
tout tomber et peut-être pire. S'il est payé, moi, je reconnais la dette.
Jusqu'à maintenant je ne vois aucun résultat mais il pourrait peut-être
faire quelque chose. Cela aussi il faudrait le faire télégraphiquement.

us definitely and probably Thursday. I have not received anything. I understand—but
not officially—that the matter is being raised again which was already determined by
an order of the Ministry of the Interior dated 18 October but the law according to
which all our visas of the specified date of 1 December have been issued—of the
"mobilisability" (a word which cannot be found even in *Finnegans Wake*) of my son
—This mobilisability exists neither in fact nor in law. Born in Italy, Irish, son of
parents both from southern Ireland, never having lived and not living either in Great
Britain or in Northern Ireland he is not touched by any law about British military
service. I have obtained from Switzerland a short prolongation of our entry visas. But
we must leave together. I will arrange the matter of my daughter more easily as soon
as I am there. If the Swiss visa had arrived three days or two days sooner we should be
already in Lausanne. Of course that is not your fault. But not mine either. It is a
misfortune: but why make it a misdirection?

   If you can arrange the matter I am sure you will do it. Cordially yours

                                                      James Joyce'

Garanti financier: Si vous n'y comprenez rien à cette question (et moi moins encore) vous comprendrez encore moins après la lecture de la dépêche (dont une copie ci-jointe) reçue de Zurich hier soir. Je ne peux rien faire à ce propos. La partie stable de mon argent est à Londres. Tant que je suis en France je ne pourai toucher même les interêts. En suisse je pourai, après certaines formalités, toucher les interêts mais pas le capital car le gouvernment britannique s'opposera à la sortie de sterling, surtout en grosses sommes.

Indicateur: Si nous devons absolument aller au consulat à Lyon pour le visa l'indicateur Chaix (25 October) indique deux autres trains de S. Germain des Fossés, l'un à 3.23 du matin arrivant à 7.15 et l'autre partant à 6.30 et arrivant vers midi. Est-ce que ces trains existent hors de l'imagination du poète qui a controlé l'indicateur, l'immortel choix? Et est-ce que nous pourrions combiner l'un ou l'autre de ces trains avec le train national Lyon–Genève?

Remerciez, je vous en prie, Madame votre mère. Je suis sur qu'elle fera tout ce qui est en son pouvoir. Salutations cordiales JAMES JOYCE

P.S. Boum! Voilà une autre dépêche qui arrive de Zurich en ce moment.[1]

---

[1] (Translation)

'Dear Mr Zumsteg: Thank you for your letter of the 4th inst. And here is the answer that you ask me to let you have.

Journey: If we are to arrive at Lyons either at 17.55 or at 21.40 by leaving either at 2.10 or at 6.50 and to depart again the next morning either at 6.30 or at 8.50 how will we be able to have our four British passports stamped for the entry into Switzerland (if granted) at the Swiss Consulate in Lyons (and to pay what will be owing) since the Consulate will be shut? Will it be possible for you before you leave for Zurich on Saturday (it does not seem likely we can leave earlier) to arrange with the Consulate that the sum in question be paid in advance (I will reimburse you from here by postal order) and also that instead of our stopping for an entire day at Lyons the consulate forward us a stamped paper covering the four passports if such a thing is regular? Our passports are already stamped and our identity cards too both for the safe-conduct to the frontier and for the exit but these stamps are good for only another two weeks. After that I will have to start all over again with the French authorities and explain to them why we have not made use of the visas which they gave us. Everything from now on must be done by wire and not by letter. We cannot leave this village any more since the law of yesterday, even to go to Vichy, without a special permit. So we must stay here or leave for Switzerland.

Haldenwang: I leave this to your judgment since you know him. It seems to me after his letter that if he is not paid he will drop everything and maybe do worse. If he is paid, I do acknowledge the debt. Up to now I have seen no results but he could perhaps do something. This also must be handled by wire.

Financial guarantee: If you do not understand anything of this matter (and I even less) you will understand still less after reading this telegram (a copy of which is attached) received from Zurich yesterday evening. I can do nothing about it. The stable portion of my money is in London. So long as I stay in France I cannot even touch the interest. In Switzerland I can, after certain formalities, touch the interest but not the capital for the British government will oppose the flight of sterling, especially in large amounts.

Timetable: If we absolutely must go to the consulate at Lyons for the visa, the Chaix timetable (25 October) indicates two other trains from S. Germain des Fossés, one

To PAUL RUGGIERO (Telegram)   TS. Ruggiero

13 December 1940   *S. Gérand-le-Puy*

Partirons demain matin trois heures amities James Joyce[1]

To EDMOND JALOUX   MS. Mercanton

17 December 1940   *Hotel de la Paix, Lausanne*

Cher Jaloux: Que c'est difficile de se trouver ici-bas. J'ai toute une odysée à vous raconter mais mon bon ami Jacques Mercanton sera ma porte-voix en vous tendant cette feuille de salut et de départ. Je compte être de retour à Lausanne d'ici peu car je veux transférer ma fille à Corcelles. Mais je tendre la parole à Mercanton   Cordialement votre

JAMES JOYCE[2]

To JACQUES MERCANTON (Postcard)   MS. Mercanton

1 January 1941   *Pension Delphin, 69 Muhlebachstrasse, Zurich*

C'est moi donc qui vous le signale: L'article de Gillet sur F.W. est dans la *Revue des Deux Mondes* du 15 décembre. J'espère que Jaloux vous a donné un reçu pour la biographie si lui qui en reçoit d'ordinaire l'a reçu[3] en effet de vous et à la revoir cette année que je vous souhaite bonne.

J.J.[4]

at 3.23 in the morning arriving at 7.15 and the other leaving at 6.30 and arriving towards noon. Do these trains exist outside the poetic imagination which has evolved the time-table, the immortal choice? And could we combine the one or the other of these trains with the national Lyons-Geneva train?

Please thank your mother for me. I am sure that she will do everything in her power. Cordial greetings   James Joyce

P.S. Fine! Here is another telegram arriving from Zurich just at this moment.'

[1] (Translation)

'We leave tomorrow morning at three o'clock regards James Joyce.'

[2] (Translation)

'Dear Jaloux: How hard it is for us to find each other here. I have a whole Odyssey to tell you but my good friend Jacques Mercanton will be my speaking-tube on bearing this note of safety and departure to you. I expect to be back in Lausanne shortly for I want to transfer my daughter to Corcelles. But I give the floor to Mercanton   Cordially yours   James Joyce'

[3] Joyce had heard of but not seen Gillet's article in the *Revue des Deux Mondes* when he passed through Lausanne on 15–17 December, 1940. He had lent Gorman's biography to Mercanton who passed it on to Jaloux. Mercanton returned it to Nora Joyce after her husband's death.

[4] (Translation)

'It is I then who notify you of it: Gillet's article on F.W. is in the *Revue des Deux Mondes* for 15 December. I hope Jaloux gave you a receipt for the biography if he who usually receives such things has really received it from you and may I see it again this year which I wish happy for you.   J.J.

To ERNST WERTHEIMER[1]   TS. Brauchbar
(Cablegram)

1 January 1941   *Zurich*

THANKING YOU FOR AGREEABLE BUSINESS RELATIONS[2]
DURING THE YEAR WHICH HAS PASSED WE BEG TO
EXTEND TO YOU OUR BEST WISHES FOR THE NEW YEAR
                                                    JAMES JOYCE

To STANISLAUS JOYCE[3] (Postcard)   MS. Cornell

4 January 1941   *Pension Delphin, Muhlebachstrasse 69, Zurich*

Caro fratello: Forse questi indirizzi ti saranno utili. Sono di persone
che potrebbero, credo, aiutarti. Ad ogni modo prova. A. Francini,
presso la Scuola dei Padri Scalopi costì, Ezra Pound, 5 via Marsala,
Rapallo, Carlo Linati, 20 San Vittore, Milano, Curzio Malaparte ed
Ettore Settanni, redazione di 'Prospettive' via Gregoriana 44, Roma, il
primo direttore, il secondo collaboratore che fece con me (o piuttosto
rivise) la traduzione di un brano di *Anna Livia* apparso nel fascicolo del
15 febbraio 1940 (q.v.). Saluti da tutti.   JIM[4]

[1] The cable was addressed to Wertheimer but intended for Brauchbar. Ernst Wertheimer (d. 1964) was the son-in-law of Edmund Brauchbar.

[2] A wartime circumlocution for Brauchbar's helpfulness in enabling the Joyce family to reach Switzerland.

[3] This postcard was Joyce's last written communication. His final illness is described in a letter of 14 January 1941 from Wilhelm Herz [William H. Hartley] to Helen Joyce's brother Robert Kastor, which says in part: 'Last Friday Grete [Mrs Herz] was in Zurich to see Stephen and just on that day the trouble started. Mr Joyce got the most terrible pains and could only be relieved by morphium. The doctors together with one of the best known surgeons held a consilium that same night and decided to take him over to the Red Cross Hospital. The condition not improving they decided to operate on him Saturday morning, January 11. They evidently found a hole in the stomach resulting from an ulcer which had as the doctors claim been there for at least seven years without being discovered, or to say the least without the correct diagnosis having been given in spite of the reiterated complaints of Mr Joyce. On Sunday, the day after the operation, the patient was very weak as was to be expected for the next 3–4 days; but during the night of Sunday to Monday the exitus was clear and Giorgio and his mother were called to the hospital. . . .' James Joyce died on 13 January 1941 and was buried two days later.

[4] (Translation)
'Dear brother: Possibly these addresses will be of use to you. They are of people who might, I think, help you. Try them anyway. A. Francini, c/o Scuola dei Padri Scalopi there, Ezra Pound, 5 via Marsala, Rapallo, Carlo Linati, 20 San Vittore, Milano, Curzio Malaparte and Ettore Settanni, editorial office of *"Prospettive"*, via Gregoriana 44, Rome. The former is the director, the latter a contributor who made with me (or rather revised) the translation of a passage from *Anna Livia* which appeared in the issue of 25 February 1940 (q.v.). Greetings from all of us.   Jim'

APPENDIX

The following letters have come to light too late to appear in their proper places in the volumes.

To Ezra Pound[1]

17 March 1915   *c/o Gioacchino Veneziani, Murano, Venice (Italy)*

My dear Mr Pound I am very glad to get your letter of 9 inst and hope that you have now quite recovered from your illness.

I have written to Mr Pinker and said that you will interview him. It is very kind of you to offer to do this for me and I shall be guided by you in the matter. The rest of the *Portrait of the Artist* had better be sent on to Grant Richards as soon as it is ready.

As regards rights Mr Grant Richards has the right of refusal of this novel. If he decides not to publish, or rather, if he decides not to conclude the open agreement about it I am quite willing to entrust the disposal of the rights to Mr Pinker. Mr Grant Richards promised last July that he would give a definite answer within three weeks after the completed MS was in his possession. At least it seems to me that he did so but I cannot now find his letter.

My comedy *Exiles* is now finished but I should prefer to hold it over until my novel has been published in book form though I am willing to dispose of it also in the best way.

I believe, however, that the letter you send may have a good effect on Grant Richards. If you see Mr Pinker (I mean, of course, as soon as your illness allows you to go out of doors) you will perhaps explain to him why I have delayed in answering his letter and why I am obliged to write in such a roundabout fashion.

I must say in conclusion that you are a very good correspondent for you always send me lively and good news. I hope you are living well in these bad times. I am still quite unmolested and hope to remain so but the situation is not very pleasant. I am glad also to hear that *The Egoist* still continues to appear and beg you to convey my kind

[1] From a typewritten copy, deposited with the Society of Authors.

508

regards to the editor whose letter I received and answered some time ago. Very sincerely yours JAMES JOYCE

TO EZRA POUND[1]

[*22 October 1917*]   *Pension Villa Rossa, Locarno, Switzerland*

Dear Pound: I came here a few days ago but was so busy looking after luggage etc that I could not write. It is useless to go into the subject of my physical and financial collapse in August. As regards the former what is done is done. I cannot see very well even yet but the sight gets better. About the latter I owe you and Miss Weaver very much for your prompt kindness.[2] But for you I should have been derelict. I notice that you blame yourself for having misled me. The stupidity, however, is at my end. I am glad *Ulysses* is to appear in both reviews[3] from March on and now that I can read and write again I shall get to work. I hope you will both like it. I send you a copy of *Marzocco* with an article by Mr Diego Angeli. The Manager of Messrs Cres and Co spoke to me about a French translation of my novel (to be published in the course of the present century) and Dostoyevsky's daughter was here yesterday. She has read Mr Angeli's article and wants a copy of the book.[4] She will have to print one for herself, I fear. My wife told me you are bringing out a book with an essay in it about the novel. It may interest therefore to hear that after the first edition had been sold out and the book reviewed in eight countries the printers wrote asking the writer to delete and alter passages in it and refused to print even the second edition. I believe Miss Weaver has found some printer in the country who will do it, he says. I am now correcting proofs of *Exiles*. Yeats wrote to me about it but he seems to have forgotten what it is about.[5] In any case he says his theatre is passing through a crisis. The actors he has now cannot even play low comedy. In the hope that things may have improved I am writing to him again about [it] rather pressingly. I am also going to write to Mr Martyn[6] though I do not know him. If their theatre has no actors to play it surely they could be trained. If not what are they doing on the stage? I shall write also to Mr Sturge Moore who, you said, liked it and to Mr Archer again and to Mr [word missing] and possibly to Mr Short,[7] Mr Barker[8] and Mr

---

[1] From a typewritten copy, deposited with the Society of Authors.
[2] They helped persuade Edward Marsh to pay for the eye operation.
[3] The *Little Review* and the *Egoist*, though publication in the latter was delayed.
[4] See II, p. 408.   [5] Yeats's letter is in II, p. 405.
[6] Edward Martyn.   [7] Probably Clement Shorter (1857–1926), the English critic.
[8] H. Granville Barker.

Symons. In fact, as usual, I shall write a great number of letters to a great number of people.

I got copies of *Little Review* with your amusing and highspirited lines.[1] The review looks more prosperous since you took over the European editorship.

I hope Mrs Pound and yourself are quite well. This letter, tardy as it is, is not very long or even complete but sometimes I find it difficult to keep my eyes open—like the readers of my masterpieces.

I have the impression that I am forgetting to tell you many things. No doubt I shall remember them five minutes after having posted this letter. I got Mr Eliot's verses[2] only this morning.

Accept my very sincere thanks however lamely expressed, for having helped me at such a difficult moment. Yours very gratefully

JAMES JOYCE

To T. S. ELIOT   MS. Harvard

15 August 1923   *Victoria Palace Hotel, 6 rue
                                              Blaise-Desgoffe, Paris*

Dear Eliot: We left London on Thursday and here we are (homeless, ragged and tanned)[3] running about in taxis, looking for a flat.

I was very sorry our picnic was put off. I hope Mrs Eliot is now definitely better. Please give her our best wishes. The right treatment, in my case, at least, was found it seems after a disastrous series of wrong diagnosis and wrong treatment.

I shall let you know when we get some way settled. I expect I shall soon be in London again as I have a great deal to do there still. I enjoyed my visit very much. With renewed good wishes sincerely yours

JAMES JOYCE

To T. S. ELIOT   MS. Harvard

2 July 1929   *Imperial Hotel, Torquay*

Dear Eliot: We are well installed here for a good month, I hope, and like it very much. I hope you got A.L.P. from Paris. Gilbert is staying here for a week or so and has sent you on the typescript—less two or three chapters which he is still at work on.[4] He says that Cape wanted to publish the book but his reader dissuaded him, saying there was no

---

[1] Ezra Pound, '*L'Homme moyen sensuel*,' *Little Review* IV.5 (September 1917) 8–16.
[2] T. S. Eliot, *Prufrock and Other Observations* (London, 1917).
[3] The Joyces had been in Bognor.   [4] Of *James Joyce's* Ulysses.

interest for *Ulysses* in England. I suppose he knows the situation but possibly such an interest can be created.

I hope Mrs Eliot is going on well and that we may have an occasion to meet when we go back to London Sincerely yours   JAMES JOYCE

From LUCIA JOYCE to ADRIENNE MONNIER   MS. Princeton

16 April [*1930*]   *Hotel Rose, Wiesbaden*

Chère Mademoiselle, En l'absence de Mlle Beach mon père vous prie de faire pour lui les envois suivants:

1. *Exag* grand format à Monsieur Georges Borach, 21 Bellerivestrasse Zurich.

2. *Exag* grand format à Monsieur Edmond Brauchbar, Hotel des Ambassadeurs, Bd Haussmann, Paris.

3. *Exag* grand format et un Ulysse allemand à Monsieur et Mme Victor Sax, 14 Dufourstrasse, Zollikon, by Zurich.

4. 2 expl. Ulysse allemand, 1 expl. chaque, à Monsieur Hitpold [sic] et à Mlle Fleischmann, 6 Culmarstrasse, Zurich.[1]

Les envois 3. et 4. doivent être accompagnés par une petite note en français disant que mon père signera ces livres à l'occasion de sa prochaine visite à Zurich.

Il vous prie de téléphoner à mon frère, chez nous ou bien Littré 72–87 d'arranger un rendez vous pour lui mercredi prochain avec le Docteur La Personne où le Docteur Poularde, préférablement l'après-midi mais si ce n'est pas possible, le matin: et aussi de téléphoner à Monsieur Paul Léon Littré 88–89 s'il est possible de changer encore le mot 'ships' en 'skivs' dans la phrase 'seamen. We segn your ships and wives'.[2] M. Léon donnera à Mlle Beach tous les renseignements au sujet du Prof. Vogt à Zurich. Ce matin le Prof. Pagenstecher d'ici a confirmé cette opinion. J'ai oublié de vous dire que mon frère doit prêter à M. Léon le petit cahier noir éléctrique contenant tout ce qui a paru jusqu'ici de W. in P. qui se trouve dans le placard à coté de son bureau. Avec remerciements d'avance et salutations de notre part

LUCIA JOYCE[3]

---

[1] Martha Fleischmann (II, pp. 426–31) lived with Rudolf Hiltpold at 6 Culmann-strasse.

[2] *Finnegans Wake*, p. 540.

[3] (Translation)
'Dear Mademoiselle, Miss Beach being away my father asks you to send off the following for him:
1. *Exagmination* thick paper to Mr George Borach, 21 Bellerivestrasse, Zurich.
2. *Exagmination* thick paper to Mr Edmond Brauchbar, Hotel des Ambassadeurs Bd Haussmann, Paris.

To SYLVIA BEACH (Postcard)   MS. Princeton

18 July 1930   *Grand Hotel, Llandudno*

Dear Miss Beach Very glad to hear the good news about you. Have a
good rest.

    I wrote this all MYSELF[1] Amitiés à A.M.   JAMES JOYCE

To HERBERT GORMAN   TS. Princeton

24 January 1931   *192 rue de Grenelle, Paris*

Dear Gorman, This note is to let you and your publisher understand
that you are the only person authorized by me to write a book describing
my personal life and career. So far as I know no other writer has started
such a work; but if one does you may rest assured that I shall refuse
him information or access to any personal documents I may possess. Of
course, critical studies concerning my work are another matter. Yours
sincerely,   [Unsigned]

To SYLVIA BEACH   MS. Princeton

[Mid-September 1931] *[28ᴮ Campden Grove, Kensington, London, W.8]*

Dear Miss Beach: Am not very well so am scribbling this lying down—
intestinal attack, and heaviness in eyes.

    Please send all Rheinverlag, Frankfurter Z Brody or Goll letters you
may still have bearing on case at once to Monro Saw & Co, 44 Queen
Victoria Street, London EC.[2] I also want 3 copies each of *C. Trib* and
Intrans,[3] copies of which shd also be sent to Borach, Brody Goll and

3. *Exagmination* thick paper and a Ulysses in German to Mr and Mrs Victor Sax,
14 Dufourstrasse, Zollikon, near Zurich.
4. 2 copies of Ulysses in German, 1 copy for each, to Mr Hitpold and to Miss
Fleischmann, 6 Culmarstrasse, Zurich.
    Packages 3 and 4 should include a little note in French saying that my father will
inscribe these books during his coming visit to Zurich.
    He asks that you telephone my brother, at our flat or else Littré 72–87, to make an
appointment for him for next Wednesday with Dr La Personne or Dr Poularde,
preferably in the afternoon but if that isn't possible, in the morning: and also to
telephone Mr Paul Léon Littré 88–89 if it is still possible to change the word "ships"
to "skivs" in the phrase "seamen. We segn your ships and wives." Mr Léon will give
Miss Beach all the information about Prof. Vogt in Zurich. This morning Prof.
Pagenstecher from here has confirmed that opinion. I forgot to tell you that my
brother should lend to Mr Léon the little electric black notebook containing all that
has been published up to now of W. in P. which is in the cupboard beside his desk.
With thanks in advance and greetings from us   Lucia Joyce'
[1] Joyce was recovering from the eye operation performed in Zurich.
[2] The erroneous attribution to Joyce of an article in the *Frankfurter Zeitung*.
[3] *Chicago Tribune* and *L'Intransigeant*.

Curtius. You may mention Faber & Faber since it is out and the Viking but do not give my solicitor names without their permission. At what price will you remainder *Exag* and how many copies have you?

Those Japs have been translating essays galore, it seems, without asking leave or paying, out of *Exag* and everywhere. So I had Hiteshi Ito's article on me translated into English today and it will probably appear in English in some review here. Ito will be paid, less Pinker's fee and cost of translation, but I want the assent of the two Japs in writing to this as a preliminary to negotiations over *Ulysses*.

Will write to L.G.[1] after I have seen G.M. on Sunday.

If the F.R[2] has not printed S.G.'s article yet telephone him to ask it back.

F & F[3] have asked me scores of times about Gorman, where he is, what he is doing, whether he has abandoned the book or not, if I had seen any of it and whether it has my sanction and if they could see some of it. I said I knew nothing, that he had collected some material, that I had never seen a page of the book itself and that I heard he had laid the book aside temporarily and I supposed, was going back to U.S.A.
Sincerely yours   J.J.

---

[1] Louis Gillet, whom Joyce was urging to translate a book of George Moore.
[2] *Fortnightly Review.* For Stuart Gilbert's article see p. 195, n. 2.
[3] Faber & Faber.

INDEX OF CORRESPONDENTS

Bold-face numbers refer to Volume III

INDEX OF RECIPIENTS

Bold-face numbers refer to Volume III

GENERAL INDEX

Bold-face numbers refer to Volume III

For Joyce's published works, see also the Chronology of his writings in Volume II, pp. lxiii–lxxii. For his residences and travels, see also the list of his addresses in Volume II, pp. lv–lxii.

gives message to, **302**; knows J's number, **310**; J's treatment of, **345, 351**; Lucia sends gift to, **356**

Béaslái, Piaras, copy of J's Italian article on Shaw sent to, 250 n

Beaverbrook, Lord, J's putative meeting with, **171**

Bécat, Marie Monnier (Mme Paul Bécat), doing illustrations for *Finnegans Wake*, **209**; gives dinner for J, **235**; has exhibition, **356**

Beckett, Samuel, friendship with J, **6**; at Déjeuner *Ulysse*, **191**; helps translate *Anna Livia Plurabelle*, **209** n; J finds talent in, **316**; Lucia goes to see, **344**; stabbing of, **411**; parallel with Ponis-ovsky, **419** n; clippings to go to, **447**; transmits Salkeld's letter, **452**; comes to Saint-Gérand, **461, 466, 469**; J sends address of to Frank, **476, 478**; Larbaud cashes cheque for, **483**

Beecham, Sir Thomas, persuaded by J to hear Sullivan, **203**; J's further plans for, **223**; writes letter for George, **329**

Belfast, J visits, 268; J met Reynolds there, 269; J wants *Exiles* produced in, 415

Bell, G. N. A., Gogarty's letters to regarding tower, 51 n

Bellini, Vincenzo, his *Norma* mentioned, **306** n; centenary of, **343**; J sends aria of, **346**

Belvedere College, J at, 3

Belvedere, Mary Countess of, J plans to write about, 193; answer to J's inquiry about, **49–50**

Belvederian, The, publishes verse by J, 207 n

Benco, Silvio, J sends newspapers to, **19**; greeted by J, **45**; attitude to *Ulysses* of, **58**; signs protest against *Ulysses* piracy, **149, 152**; J may send *Finnegans Wake* to, **438**

Bennett, Andrew Percy, J's quarrel with, 425–26, 437–38, 439–40; in Panama, 447; J's letter about, 460; J suspects of rumourmongering, 13

Bennett, Arnold, press copy of *Ulysses* to, **69**; complains of misrepresentation, **109–110**; signs protest against *Ulysses* piracy, **152**; attitude to *Finnegans Wake* of, **197**; J and Larbaud to dine with, **211**

Bennett, James Gordon, race in Dublin, 39 n

Benoist-Méchin, Jacques, translates passages from *Ulysses*, **53, 55** n; thanked by J, **63**; signs protest against *Ulysses* piracy, **152**

Benson, Dr Arthur Henry, prescribes eye-glasses for J and his sister May, 37 n; J tells mother to consult, 38

Beran, Felix, to dine with J, **255**

Bergan, Alfred, helps settle affairs of J's father, 252–53, 256–57, 258, 260, 262; consulted by J about ancestors, 264; greeted by J, **295, 333–34, 381, 399, 409**

Berkeley, George, J dissociates from Synge and Gregory, 456, 457 n

Berlitz, M. D., quoted ironically by J, 175

Berlitz School (London), J checks credentials of E. Gilford with, 54, their uncertain reply, 55; possible offer of job, 57

Berlitz School (Paris), J considers position in, 20 n; describes work, 21; mother's comment on, 22

Berlitz School (Pola), J sent to, 63; arrival at, 68; conditions at, 69; Eyers at, 73; J transferred from, 84

Berlitz School (Rome), J to look into for Stanislaus, 166

Berlitz School (Trieste), J transferred to, 63, 84; J stops teaching at, 64; J hopes to teach at, 67; described by J, 87; description of, 93–94; job open for Stanislaus in, 112–13; J describes work at, 131; atmosphere of, 145; compared with Roman bank, 157; Stanislaus not to use school stamp, 204; J wishes to return to, 214–16; Joseph Guy at, 216 n; J asks about, 262; Colesser at, **222**; Stanislaus explains becoming teacher there, **226**; Stanislaus contemplates return to, **383**

Berlitz School (Zurich), J's departure for, 5; no position open at, 63–67

Berman, Dr Louis, advises J on medical problems, 71 n; book on glands by, **409**; replies to J, **410**

Bernhardt, Sarah, J sees in *Andromaque*, 27; J's review of, 31

Bertelli, Giuseppe, sub-director of Berlitz School, Trieste, 68; as poetaster, 93; J wants news of, 161; fails to write, 186

Bertrand-Fontaine, Dr Thérèse, consulted by Gilbert, **235**, by J, **276–77**; tends Beckett's wound, **411, 412**; recommended to Mrs Sax, **450, 451**

Best, Richard Irvine, his admiration for Anatole France, 110; out of Dublin, 230; thinks J mistreated by Roberts, 314

Betrayal, theme in J's works, 64; J's sense of friends' falsehood to him, 89; Gogarty's treachery, 96; J plans to write about betrayers, 110

Bible, 130th Psalm, 140 n; 'light under a bushel' quoted, **130**; 115th Psalm quoted, **365**; Gideon in, **393–94 n**; Vulgate quoted, **401**

Biblioteca Vittorio Emanuele, J looks up Vatican Council in, 192–93

Bibliothèque Nationale, J reading at, 38

Bibliothèque Sainte-Geneviève, J reading at, 38

Billeter (Judge), and J vs. Carr, 421–22, 422–23 n

'Billy Byrne of Ballymanus,' Palmer's music reminds J of, 227; J can't find right version, 245

Binswanger, Dr Ludwig, on Nijinsky, **405, 406**

Bird, William, offers to publish *Ulysses*, 82; tells J of Pound's operation, **166**

Bird, William (composer), J on 'Woods So Wild', 138

Birrell, Augustine, J's 'open letter' sent to, 441; supports J, 447; lectures on J, **282**

Björnson, Björnstjerne, Synge's resemblance to, 212

Black-Roberts, Gwladys, role in *Exiles*, **136–37**

Blackwood, Sir John, cited as model by Price, 300; in *Ulysses*, 413

Blake, William, J reads Figgis's book on, **139**

Blanche, Jacques Emile, J poses for, **303**; on Lucia's work, **320**; J asks if portrait exhibited, **329**

Blarney Castle, Pound's questions about, **237**, J's answer, **239**

Blast, Pound's verse in, 365; J obtains copy of, **188**

Bleibtreu, Karl, theory of Shakespeare, 415 n

Bliss, Arthur, setting of 'Simples' by, **287**; J likes setting by, **338**

Blistra, K., review of *Finnegans Wake* by, **468**

Bliznakoff, Mrs, quoted on Bruno Veneziani, **219**

Bloch, Konrad, J's lawyer in Zurich, 421–422, 422–23 n, 425

Bloch-Savitsky, Ludmila, *see* Savitsky, Ludmila

Bloom, Leopold (character in *Ulysses*), wears hat from Plasto's, 40; attraction for J of, 346; Pound calls 'a great man', 423; J suggests Budgen paint, 465; J needs Hungarian word, 18 n; J writing about, 32; J's song about, 34; cursed by J, 46; J's game with Larbaud about, 56; Stanislaus on, **105**; J's dream about, **142–43 n**

Bloom, Marionne L., offers to be J's American agent, 398 n

Bloom, Molly (character in *Ulysses*), her sweetheart Mulvey, 72 n; source of her punctuation, 173 n; Mrs Santas a model for, 216 n; J writing about, 48; J's game with Larbaud about, **56**; songs of, **63**; father of, **76 n**; Livia Schmitz's fear of being portrayed as, **133 n**; J's dream about, **142–43 n**

Bloom, Ursula, on when to say yes, **182**

Bloomsday (16 June 1904), J's attachment to, 5; circumstances of, 42 n

'Boarding-House, The' (in *Dubliners*), J sends to Stanislaus, 92; J explains frigidities of, 98; Stanislaus comments on, 115; 'Two Gallants' to precede, 130; 'A Little Cloud' to follow, 131 n; J says boarding-house keeper would denounce, 134; J's defence of, 136–37; Richards states position on, 138 n; J replies to Richards, 177; 'bloody' retained in, 179; idea of from Woodman, 212; Roberts wants J to change, 315, 325; published in *Smart Set*, 329 n

Boccaccio, Giovanni, his story of Dante, **258 n**

Bodkin, Michael, used in 'The Dead', 300 n

Bödoker (pupil), J arranges lesson for, 282

Bognor, J's plan to visit, **76 n**

Bolaffio (pupil), handed over to Stanislaus, 262

Bollach, Lily, types *Finnegans Wake*, **81, 84–85, 91–92, 113, 118, 135, 140–41**; J to help friend of, **147**

Boni and Liveright, J considers as publisher, **97**

Bontempelli, Massimo, friend of Nino Frank, **183**

Bookseller, The, letter from, 108 n

Book (baritone), sings *Saul*, **332**

Boon, Charles, refuses *Dubliners*, 320–21

Borach, Georges, friend of J, 345, **197 n**; writes Irene Kafka for J, **228 n**; sends letter to Miss Weaver, **254**; helps Sullivan, **257**, mentioned by J, **262**, urges J to rest, **270**; death of, **303**

Borsch, Dr Louis, J's doctor in Paris, **66 n**; advises sphincterotomy, **67**; recommends Dr Colin, **68**; operates on J, **72, 73, 75, 76, 77**; away, **80**; tells J to limit work, **92**; J to see about operation, **96, 97**; examines J after operation, **99**; another operation by, **110, 112**; another operation in store, **113–14, 115**; takes place, **119 n**; says another operation needed, **121, 122, 132, 134**; operates on J, **135**; threatens to operate again, **186**

Borsieri, Mrs, J leaves desk with, 305, 307, 314

192; contract with Mathews for, 206; J returns proofs, 216; J's feeling about, 219; J wants poems set to music, 219; changes in, 220; second proofs returned, 221; Palmer's settings of, 223–24, 227–228; Clery's review of, 233, 234; genesis of poems explained, 237; J planned to give copy to Sheehys, 244; copy sent to Kettle, 248, 260; J copying on parchment for Nora, 258, 269; review of by Kettle, 248 n; J needs family crest for Nora's manuscript of, 262 n; three of poems in *Dublin Book of Irish Verse*, 269; J tells Stanislaus to burn all MSS of, 270; J's MS book to Nora, 277–78, 280; musical settings of, 284, 285; J asks Mathews about royalties on, 296; review in *Liverpool Courier*, 304; J's concern for MS of, 305; J sends notices of to Mills and Boon, 320; J orders copies of, 321–22; J wants Symons's review of, 322; press notices of, 332–33 n, 334; J asks Huebsch to publish, 350; J has published only one poem since, 352; described by Yeats, 354; American edition of, 394; no royalties on, 399; J wants no poems added to it, 418; copy to Martha Fleischmann, 427, 434 n; second edition of, 462; McCormack wants to see Palmer's settings of, **35**; settings sent to Pound, **47**; mentioned to Francini, **55**; poems in *Der Querschnitt*, **83 n**; Stanislaus alludes to, **103**, **104**; J's plan to have Palmer's settings printed in Paris, **167**; settings of evaluated by J, **338**; J can't find manuscript of, **365**, **366**

i. published in *The Belvederian*, 207; included in Tynan's *Wild Harp*, 323 n, 330–31

ii. sent to Archer, 10

iii. included in Tynan's *Wild Harp*, 323 n, 330–31; Palmer to send his setting of to McCormack, **35**

iv. sent to Stanislaus, 27–28

v. J wants Mann to set to music, 287

vi. printed in *Speaker* incorrectly, 69, 70; quoted by J, 249–50

vii. published in *Dana*, 73 n

ix. quoted on Nora's necklace, 246

xi. not published in *Dana*, 73 n; sent to *Harper's*, 77; not accepted, 80; Stanislaus wants to offer to *Nationist*, 117; J tried to music, 227

xii. published in *Venture*, 72 n; inspired by Mary Sheehy, 238 n

xv. inspired by Mary Sheehy, 238 n

xvii. likely origin of, 46; quoted, 46 n; in *Speaker*, 70 n; quoted by Cosgrave, 126

xx. offered by J to *Saturday Review* 100

xxi. title 'To Nora' omitted, 92; J's allusion to, 97

xxvi. published in *Venture*, 72 n; imagined subject of, 237

xxvii. J changes last line of, 92; quotes in relation to Gogarty, 148; changes in, 220

xxviii. quoted by Nora, 96; imagined subject of, 237; Palmer to send setting of to McCormack, **35**

xxxi. Mann's setting of, 287; Palmer to send setting of to McCormack, **35**

xxxiv. metre of, 181; quoted, 236

xxxv. sent to Byrne, 20–21; Yeats's comment on, 23–24; placement of, 181

xxxvi. influenced by Gregan, 10 n; sent to Stanislaus, 27–29; placement of, 181; included in Tynan's *Wild Harp*, 323 n, 330–31; praised by Pound, 328; misprint in, 331; praised by Yeats, 351, 356, 381 n, 405

Chandler (character in 'A Little Cloud'), his toast to Gallaher, 148 n

Chanel, *see* Clery, Arthur Edward

Chaplin, Charlie, J goes to *The Kid*, 53; Lucia writes article on, **88**

Charles, Uncle (character in *A Portrait*), model for, 151 n

Charpentier, Clément, lends J money, 7

Chaucer, Geoffrey, European influence on, 134; Lucia's lettrines for *A Chaucer A. B. C.*, **256, 264, 266, 272, 308, 311**; subscriptions to *A. B. C.*, **384–85, 387, 432**; publicity for, **392**; mention of, **389, 408**

Che Buono, *see* Bulfin, William

Chevalier, Maurice, Lucia's interest in, **377**

Chesterton, G. K., derided by J, 203

'Christmas Eve' (unfinished story), J writing another, 67, 69; wants to submit to *Irish Homestead*, 70; half written, 71

Churchill, Winston, Edward Marsh his secretary, 380 n, 384; subscribes to *Ulysses*, **45**

Cicotti (editor), joins staff of *Avanti!*, 183

Cinema, J's interest in, 217

Cinematograph Volta, *see* Volta

Ciolkowska, Mrs Muriel, Paris correspondent of *Egoist*, 369

Cippico, Antonio, Yeats's theatrical agent, 298; opinion of J's and Vidacovich's translation, **195**

Civil List, grant to J, 345, 382, 426

Clancy, Long John, Bergan worked for, **252 n**

Cromwell, Oliver, allusion to, **232**

Cropper, Rev. James, author of pamphlet on Giant's Grave, **161**

'Croppy Boy, The,' J sends words of to George, **334–35**; stanza left out of, **341**

Crosby, Caresse, publishes *Tales Told of Shem and Shaun*, **189, 193**; J asks for author's copies, **191**; proposes to publish *Pomes Penyeach*, **234, 236**

Crosby, Harry, publishes part of *Finnegans Wake*, **189**; suicide of, **196**

Crowninshield, Frank, sends questionnaire to J, **193**

Cunard, Lady (Maud), helps J with grant from Civil List, 380 n, **384**; copy of *A Portrait* to, **386**; may help Budgen to job, **42, 46**; possible patron of Joyce, **155 n**; hears Sullivan, **203**; may subscribe to *Pomes Penyeach*, **252**

Cunard, Nancy, may subscribe to *Pomes Penyeach*, **252**

'Curious History, A,' first sent by J, **324–325**; in *Egoist*, 328, 360, 361, 367, 395, 399, **32**; to be omitted from *Dubliners*, 329, 334; published by Huebsch, 399 n; sent to Jenny Serruys, **9**

Curjel, Dr Hans von, meets J, **329**; J to see for George, **338**

Curran, Constantine Peter, rejects 'The Holy Office', 46 n; asked to meet and help J, **50**; J meets in Paris, 66; J wants to read *Stephen Hero* chapters, 75; J to send copy of verses to, 76; J considers generous, 79; wonders about length of *Stephen Hero*, 82; thinks J should lead unusual life, 84; Stanislaus to show chapters to, 100; J borrows from, 101; to receive chapters, 104; annoys J by lending MS of *Stephen Hero*, 113–14; asks about J's stories, 117; praises Turgenev, 118–19; apologizes for lending J's MS, 120; compared to Roman banker, 203; receives copy of *Chamber Music*, 223; unfriendly to J in Dublin, 230; says Lidwell's letter unfavourable to J's interest, 306; copy of *A Portrait* to, 388; his comments on book, 391 n; copy of *Exiles* to, 412; asked to circulate J's 'Open Letter', 442; and Lucia, **349, 353**; alarmed by Lucia, **354, 355**; asked by J to report on Lucia, **362, 363**; puts Lucia in nursing home, **368–69**; to help send Lucia back, **369**; telephoned by J, **370**; his wife to bring Lucia a camera, **374**; money returned by Mrs Curran, **376**; talks on radio, **380**; J writing to, **391**; asked to help Gorman, **398**; J sends correction to, **400**; asked for copies of *Irish Times*, **403**;

daughter of at party, **414, 419**; photograph in Gorman of, **465**

Curti, Arthur, takes legal action against English Players, 452–53, 454

Curtis Brown, Spencer, J enlists to help Pound publish *Cantos*, **217, 218**

Curtis, O'Leary, meets J in Dublin, 231; recommends Volta electrician, 277

Curtius, Ernst Robert, plans German translation of *Ulysses*, **109**; signs protest against *Ulysses* piracy, **152**; mentioned by Gillet, **210**; J consults about *Frankfurter Zeitung*, **229**; visit by J to, **388**; J may write to, **433**; receives copy of *Finnegans Wake*, **452**

Cusack, Michael, has died, 210

Cuttin, Vittorio, editor of Triestine newspaper, 59

Cuzzi, Emma, sends J picture of Daedalus and Icarus, 369–70

Czarnowski, S., J recommends his *Le Culte des héros*, **140**

Dada, J rumoured to have started, **22**

Daedalus, Maurice (character in *Stephen Hero*), Stanislaus model for, 104 n

Daedalus, Stephen, name signed to 'The Sisters' by J, 46; J speaks of Daedalean spell, 73; J on his change of mind, 79; love scene with Emma Clery, 93; *see also* Dedalus, Stephen

Daily Express (Dublin), J's reviews for, 18 n; has sent review of Gwynn to, 25; J sends critique of Bernhardt to, 27; no news from, 29; still no news, 31; J's review in, 31 n; J's mother asks about, 32; Stanislaus told to ask for payment, 34; J sends two reviews to, 39; slow to publish J's review of Lady Gregory, 40, publishes it, 38 n; refuses to have J interview Caruso, 238

Daily Express (London), article on J to appear in, **62**

Daily Herald, article on J in, **62**

Daily Mail, J reads in Rome, 159; J mentions column in, 188; 'The Swelling of Jordan' in, 190; J dislikes book supplement of, 197; review of E. Temple Thurston's *The Realist*, 201; report of Abbey riots, 207–208; refuses to have J interview Caruso, 238

Daily Telegraph, publishes article on English Players, 465

Dana, J asks if *Chamber Music*, xi, in, 73; Stanislaus thinks not, 117

Daniel (character in *Stephen Hero*), David Sheehy a mode lfor, 79 n

Daniel, Arnaut, Pound translating, 414

Danish, J's imperfect knowledge of, 82; study of, 83; has learned fairly well, 93, will take lessons from Pedersen, 151; making progress, 152; compared with Norwegian, 183; J orders Berlitz book in, 201, 209; plans Danish lessons, 207; J has book, 213; J's knowledge of, 219; J greets McAlmon in, 85; in *Anna Livia*, 92; wants Berlitz book from Trieste, 178; J greets Budgen in, 184; J writes Prior in, 421–22

D'Annunzio, Gabriele, his *Francesca da Rimini*, 19; J plans article on *La Figlia di Iorio*, 76, 80; his *The Light under the Bushel* produced, 85, inspired by Michetti's painting, 169 n; Pound comments on, 470; J's mocking tribute to, 110; Stanislaus sends *Il Fuoco* to J, 392; Gregh a friend of, 419

Dante Alighieri, J compares self to, 432; quoted by Yeats, 258; quoted by J, 318, 364; J's allusion to Galeotto, 415

Dara, William, J plans to write about, 193

Darantière, Maurice, promises first copies of *Ulysses*, 57, 58 n, 242; Miss Weaver sends instructions to, 68; on legality of second printing of *Ulysses*, 69 n; and sixth printing of *Ulysses*, 126

Darlington, Rev. Joseph, J annoyed with, 28

Davidson, Rev. Harold Francis, J's allusion to, 246

Davidson, Jo, helps arrange New York production of *Exiles*, 80; promises help with flat, 81; helping with Sullivan, 196; conscripted for J's Sullivan campaign, 213, 214, 220; did bust of J, 220

Davidson, John Morrison, J orders book by, 78

Daviel, André, *see* Hébertôt

Davies, Hubert Henry, English Players give play by, 439

Davray, Henry, J hopes for review by, 418; thanked for review, 443–44; asked to publicise English Players, 461, and does so, 466; J promises to contribute to Davray's review, 466; asked by J to help with *Mercure de France*, 14

Dawes, Charles Gates, asked by J to help Sullivan, 213, 214, 220

'Day of the Rabblement, The,' J's essay, 4; Yeats's reply, 14; manner of publication, 28 n; Delany objects to, 153; reference to Bruno in, 217 n; *Il Fuoco* mentioned in, 392

'Dead, The' (in *Dubliners*), Mrs Callanan a model for Miss Morkan in, 51 n; Gabriel Conroy's letter based on one from J to Nora Barnacle, 56 n; J plans

in Rome, 63, writes in Trieste, 64; Nora's love for boy who died, 72; J buys galoshes (like Gabriel), 86; a source for, 166 n; dance in, 186 n; J plans to write, 209; delayed by *Playboy* riots, 212; and Anatole France, 212; Nora's involvement in, 239; J visits Oughterard graveyard, 300; Roberts suspicious of, 306; George Moore on, 380; and Thomas Moore's song, 348 n

De Amicis, Edmondo, J plans to read, 86

Deasy, Mr (character in *Ulysses*), modelled by Price, 286; revised speech of, 413

Debray, Dr, checks J's health, 270, 273, 276, 277, 285

Debussy, Claude, J likes music by, 419

Dedalus, Simon (character in *A Portrait*), on Archbishop Walsh, 151 n

Dedalus, Stephen, contrasted with Bloom, 346; bas-relief of Daedalus and Icarus, 369 n; J's limerick on, 387; and Mr Deasy, 413; compared by Pound to Bloom, 423; allusion to name of, 420; *see also* Daedalus, Stephen

de la Mare, Richard, Carlow to call, 436

de la Mare, Walter, Pound compares J to, 360

Delany, Rev. William, letters on coeducation, 153–54

Deledda, Grazia, J needs name of, 476

Delimata, Mrs Boschenka Schaurek, writes J about Lucia, 361, 362

Delmas, Dr Achille, Lucia under care of, 385; has little hope for Lucia, 407; clinic moves her to La Baule, 453; J's debt to, 491, 499–500

Denmark, J hopes to go to, 359, does so, 388; writes Prior about, 421–22

Denson, Alan, his *Letters from AE* cited, 11 n, 12 n

Deslys, Gaby, mentioned by Pound, 372

Desprès, Suzanne, to help produce *Exiles*, 24, 26

de Tuoni, Dario, J renews acquaintance with, 466–67

de Valera, Eamon, J's suggestion about eyesight of, 271

Devin, Thomas, sees J and Nora on mailboat, 66; borrows from J, 275; fails to repay, 279–80; still alive, 260; greeted by J, 381; death of, 399

Devitt, Rev. Matthew, in Rome, 160

De Vries, Juda, J deletes name of, 426

Dial, The, to publish Linati, 469, 470; notice of *Ulysses* in, 29; J suggests Boyd write for, 36; has published articles on J, 60, 83; wants to delete one third of *Shaun* section, 142, 144

538

Feilbogen, Siegmund, Gorman's error about, **479**

Feis Ceoil, J discusses Palmer's songs with secretary of, 245

Fels, Florent, wants to translate *A Portrait*, 450 n, **8 n, 12**

Femme en gris, La (Frau Sorge), by Hermann Sudermann, J's pawn ticket in, 25

Fendant de Sion, wine J would like to drink with Budgen, 465

Fénéon, Félix, signs contract with J, **47**

Fenollosa, Ernest, Pound working on his papers, 385–86

Fernandez, Yva, translates story from *Dubliners*, 26; Lucia likes brother of, **353**; a patient, **481**

Ferrero, Guglielmo, on moral code of soldier and gallant, 133; J wants news of, 152; J sends Stanislaus pictures of, 159; on Horace, 190; on kinds of emigrants, 190; on cakes, 191; admiration for Scandinavian cities, 201; gave J idea for 'Two Gallants', 212

Ferri, Enrico, splits with Labriola, 152; replaces editors of *Avanti!*, 183; J's estimate of, 188

Ferrieri, Enzo, Pound to meet, 469; may have Schmitz's lecture, **190**

Field, John, J insists on Dublin birthplace of, **449**

Field, William, J writes about foot and mouth disease to, 300, 301

Fiera Letteraria, invites J to Florence, 177; publishes 'A Painful Case', **240 n**

Figaro, Le, J reads in Rome, 159

Figgis, Darrell, J reads book on Blake by, **139**

'Final Peace, The,' J's poem, 10

Finn MacCumhal (MacCool), legend about, **348**; rising of, **472, 473 n**

Finnegans Wake, Buckley in, 87 n; cottage in, 97 n; J's plan for, 4–5; begun by J, **73, 79, 193**; progress of, 6; Roderick O'Conor fragment, **73 n, 79 n**; St Patrick in, **108 n**; first problems of book solved, 110; fifth chapter in *Criterion*, 114 n; Vico in, 117, 118 n; J's symbols for sections of, 145; giant's-grave piece of first chapter written for Miss Weaver, 144, 147, 148, 149; first page of, 146; J's defence of, 6, 146; Mrs Nutting likes *Earwicker*, 148; J's plan for James Stephens to finish book, 161; Miss Weaver tries to guess title, 161 n, **163**; attempt to avoid piracy of, 165; Miss Beach has first right to publish, **166**; corrections for, **168**; Friede publishes part of, 170; plan to publish in

U.S.A., **170–71, 172 n**; J writing Part II, Ch. I, 205; his hope to finish first draft of book by end of 1931, 209; Gillet's interest in, **211**; Stanislaus' distaste for, **216**; J's verse advertisements for Faber, **228**; first eight episodes pulled together, **232, 235**; J needs to consult MS of, **233**; Four Masters quoted by J to Pound, **239**; J busy on Book II, Ch. I, **259**; Budgen to paint scenes from, **271**; Old Catholics in, 284–85; *Filioque* clause in, 284–85; J eager to finish, **286**; Faber's rights to, **297, 300**; Petitjean's book on, **303**; J sends fragment of, **306**; mistakes in, **308**; oldest tree on Howth and, **309**; more MS to Miss Weaver, **311**; St Patrick and Druid in, **345**; St Brendan in, **351 n**; allusion to, **352 n**; new fragment (Book II, Ch. II) to appear, **354**; Noah's ark in, **364 n**; 'Dublin Bay' in, **370**; J wants Curtius's support for, **388 n**; Gideon in, **393–94 n**; Norwegian captain and tailor in, **394, 399, 404, 422**; Faber in course of printing, **397**; use of *Huckleberry Finn* in, **401 n**; J expects to finish, **402, 415, 432, 433**; gasometer in, **402 n**; oral tale ending in, **403 n**; 'Follow Me Up to Carlow' in, **408, 427 n, 428–29**; MSS sent to Miss Weaver, **409**; J's labour on, **410, 415, 425**; 'A Phoenix Park Nocturne' published in *Verve*, **418**; Scandinavian influence on, **421–22**; J jokes about new fragment, **423**; Lord Carlow to bring first copy, **435, 436**; J complains of price of, **437**, wants Italian critics to review, **438**; copy to Larbaud, **440**; O'Casey called author of, **442**; Pelorson's review, **455, 456**; disappointing response to, **461, 463**; events confirm book's title, **463, 466, 470–71, 472**; review in *Panorama*, **463**; other reviews, especially Levin's, **464**; banquet for, **465**; review in *Prospettive*, **468**; Budgen's copy of, **470**; earwigs in, **483**; a word not found in, **503**; Gillet's review **506**

Anna Livia Plurabelle (ALP): Stephens' praise of, **6, 169**; sent to Miss Weaver, **90**, to Larbaud, **91**; J quotes, **97**; complaints about, **131**; J still working on, **122**; J writes Miss Beach about, **122, 125**; printers refuse to set, **127, 128**; in *Navire d'argent*, **121, 128, 132**; use of Livia Schmitz's name for, **133**; Wilson's article on, **134**; revision of, **142, 163, 164, 165, 178**; J stakes everything on, **163**; Veruda's portrait of Livia Schmitz, **172–73**; published,

Grigson, Geoffrey, mistaken about Shaw and J, **444**

Gromen (baritone), may sing with Sullivan, **223**

Grosvenor House Hotel, uses J's name in advertisement, **188**

Gschwind, Frank, manager of English Players, 440

Guillermet, Fanny, J thanks for review of *A Portrait*, 416–17; J sends *Exiles* to, 417

Guinness, Richard, to hear Sullivan sing, **204**

Gunn, Michael, of Gaiety Theatre, **455 n**

Gunn, Selskar Michael, to see Gorman's biography, **455**

Gurievich *see* Gourevitch, Gregoire

Guy, Joseph, J hopes for loan from, 216

Guy Fawkes' Day, explained by J, **339**

Gwynn, Stephen, J reviews book of, 25–27 n; review quoted, 27–28; review mentioned, 31 n; supports Abbey Theatre, 211; reviews *Ulysses*, **74**

H. D., *see* Doolittle, Hilda

Hackett, E. Byrne, helping J find American publisher, 379; dispute with Quinn, 395 n

Hackett, Felix E., on college election, **400 n**

Haines (character in *Ulysses*), Trench a model for, 51

Haldenwang, Georges, J employs to help with Swiss visas, **487, 488, 489–90, 491, 493, 494, 495, 504**

Halévy, Jacques Fromental, J alludes to *La Juive*, **257, 319 n**

Hall, H. Fielding, J reviews book of, 31 n

'Hallow Eve,' *see* 'Clay'

Hamnett, Nina, J's apology to, **57**

Hamsun, Knut, Ibsen's allusion to, 201 n

Hand, Augustus, on *Ulysses*, **315**

Hand, Learned, on *Ulysses*, **315**

Hand, Robert (character in *Exiles*), Gogarty a model for, **148 n**

Handel, George Friderick, his *Saul* recommended to George, **332**; sung by George, **420**

Harding, Patrick, knocked off car, 244; funeral of, **256–57**

Hardy, Thomas, Victorian attitude to, 135; J plans to read, 186; J reading *Life's Little Ironies*, 198; J's criticism of stories, 199–200; his servant girls compared with Nora, 201; J gives up reading, 201; J plans to alternate with Mirbeau, 202; Pound compares J to, 359–60, 364, **9**; attitude of Eliot to,

155 n; J's letter to *Revue Nouvelle* about, **169–70**

Hariot, Monsieur, Sullivan to approach, **257**

Harmsworth, Desmond, J hopes he will publish Pound's *Cantos*, **220**; publishes *Pomes Penyeach*, **234, 261, 389**

Harrington, Timothy Charles, note on, 17 n; introduction of J, 17–18; bank manager asks about J's relation to, 145; and John Joyce's voter registration, 229

Harris, Morris, divorce suit of, 189, 194

Harrison, Mrs, typist of *Ulysses*, **40–41**

Harte, Bret, J to buy his *Gabriel Conroy*, 166 n

Hartley, William, *see* Herz, Wilhelm

Hartmann, Albert, book on *Odyssey* by, 187

Harvey, Rupert, role in *Exiles* of, **136–37**

Hassall, Christopher, biography of Marsh, 380 n, 407 n

Hauptmann, Gerhard, J's translations of *Before Dawn* and *Michael Kramer*, 58; *Elga* produced in Berlin, 85; J notes dream mechanism of *Elga*, 85; his *Hanneles Himmelfahrt*, 85 n; J admires political aptitude of, 86; J tempted to buy *Rosa Bernd*, 152; J comments favorably on plays of, 173; opera based on work by, **330**; J wants copy of *Michael Kramer*, **392**; J writing to, **415**

Haveth Childers Everywhere, see Finnegans Wake

Haynes, Battison, his 'Off to Philadelphia', **347, 348, 351 n**

Healey, George Harris, edition of Stanislaus J's diary, 182 n, **106**

Healy, Catherine, J wants will of, 87; possible reference to, 88

Healy, Michael, supports Barnacle family, 72; to help bring J over, 296 n; health of, 297; feeds J well, 300; J tells Stanislaus to write to, 301; J staying with, 302; J sends regards to, 308; helps J financially, 345, 353, 358–59; copy of *A Portrait* to, 386, 390; copy of *Exiles* to, 412; gifts to John Joyce from, **212**; asked to see Lucia, **362**; alarmed by Lucia, **364**; J replies to, **368–69**; transmits *Pomes Penyeach*, 370, **371**; death of, **391** n

Healy, Thomas, attitude towards Nora Barnacle, 73; death of, **127**

Heap, Jane, begins to publish *Ulysses*, 346, **242**; on *Exiles*, 423 n; J sends photograph to, 458; legal difficulties over *Ulysses*, **28**; possible copyright of *Ulysses* by, **155**

276; J savage about, 288–89, 319; asks
Yeats's help for literature of, 322; J's
attitude to Irish politics, 362; George
Moore on, 380–81; J thinks of finishing
Ulysses in, 468–69; J's sympathy for
MacSwiney's hunger strike, **16 n**, **17**;
plan for Irish concert in Zurich, **35 n**;
Nora's visit to, **63**; J not a part of Irish
literary movement, **77 n**; J declines to
represent, **177**; and ban on *Ulysses*, **233**;
Pound's poem about Irish censorship,
237–38; Lucia wishes to reconcile J
with, **330**; J sends map of to George,
341; Lucia urges J to make peace with,
370

Ireland's Eye, allusion to, 161
Irish Agricultural Organisation Society,
Irish Homestead its official organ, 43 n
Irish Catholic, The, J describes issue of,
153–54
Irish Homestead, The, J's stories for, 5;
Russell invites J to contribute to, 43;
his stories, 43 n; 'After the Race' in, 67;
J asks for copy again, 68; wants to
submit *Christmas Eve* to, 70; wants copy
of 'After the Race' in, 74–75; J sends
'Hallow Eve' to, 77, 83, wants decision
on 'Hallow Eve', 91
Irish Independent, J's dislike of, 77;
Kettle's election reported in, 147; on
Ibsen, 166
Irish Literary Theatre, J's attack on, 4;
J puzzled by mother's interest in, 39;
J's German translations submitted to,
58 n
Irish National Theatre Society, precedes
Abbey Theatre, 11; J expects Synge's
plays to be produced by, 35; J comments
on new season of, 189
Irish Republican Brotherhood, Joseph
Casey in, 36 n
Irish Theatre, produces Colum's plays, 208
Irish Times, J seeks to write for, 25;
reminds father of, 26; another reminder,
27; nothing done at, 31–32; more efforts
on J's behalf, 32; J's interview with
Fournier in, 39; refuses to have J inter-
view Caruso, 238; J sends copy to Miss
Beach, **106**; Gogarty's poem in, **313**;
praises work by J, **330**; J reading, **346**,
363; J needs copies of, **403**; J sends
Carlow copy of, **425**; confusion of
O'Casey and J in, **442**
Irish Voices, J wants news of, 77
Isabel (character in *Stephen Hero*),
immateriality of, 79
Italian, J's study of, 63; objects to phrases
in, 158; knowledge of, 219
Italy, J on Italian socialism, 152, 173–74;

183, 187–88; J comments on political
situation, 188; vulgarity of, 198; J sick
of, 201–202, 203; dislikes Italian men,
218; J wants to leave, 219
Iveagh House, John Joyce leaves, 317
'Ivy Day in the Committee-Room' (in
Dubliners), J sends to Stanislaus, 105,
checks details in, 109; Stanislaus's
answer, 114–15; J says a Dubliner
would denounce, 134; J's defence of,
136; alteration of, 136 n; 'bloody'
omitted from, 144, 179; J argues with
Richards over, 177; restoration of
'bloody', 203; Edward VII in, 288 n,
292–93, 298; Lidwell on, 306 n, 309; J
agrees to change passage, 314; Roberts
wants further change, 315; J to publish
in Italian, 329

Jackson, Holbrook, article on J, **47**
Jacobsen, Jens Peter, J reading his stories,
83
Jaloux, Edmond, sends suggestions to
McAlmon, **67**; reviews *Ulysses*, **74**;
signs protest against *Ulysses* piracy,
152; asked to help Stanislaus, **388**; J
hopes to see soon, **506**
James, Dr, J's ophthalmologist in London,
66, 68
James, Henry, J reading his *Madonna of
the Future*, 71, and likes it, 72; J
amused by essay on Baudelaire, 76; J
finds Stanislaus boring on, 81; J finds
Confidence uninteresting, 85, and boring,
87; view of Rome mocked by J, 198;
'teaslop' about Rome, 201; derided by J,
203; compared to J by Pound, 327,
359–60, 364, **9**
Jameson's, John & Son, J's favorite
whiskey, **161**
Japan, J on navy of, 188
Jarnach, Philipp, contributes to *The Joyce
Book*, **208**; delays it, **234**
Jeep, Johannes (Johann Jeppe), allusion
to in *Ulysses*, **447**
Jenkins, John, Pound wants performance
of music by, **415**
Jesuits, on Inquisition, 148; called by J
'the black lice', 160; Mirbeau on, 202;
J grateful for their discipline, 84; J's
pun on, **352**
Jesus Christ, J compares self to, 109, 110;
Stanislaus' estimate of, 117–18;
Gogarty on, 126–27; J says he is not a
literary Jesus Christ, 162; Ferrero
compares to Marx, 190; compared to
Nora, 273; J refers to Jewish birth of,
432, 433 n; *see also* Catholicism

Joyce, Florence (J's sister), as peacemaker, 33; first communion, 117; father's plans for, 290; meets Nora in Dublin, 296, 303; has no job, 317

Joyce, George Alfred (J's brother), J thinks George understood him, 39 n; calls Stanislaus 'Brother John', 81 n

Joyce, George (Giorgio) (J's son), birth of, 64, 100–102; J thinks of names for, 95; still unnamed, 105; described by J, 107–108; called by Stanislaus 'the nameless one', 119; his early sounds, 123; not baptized, 124; J babysits, 138; J's love for as stabilizing influence, 139; well-behaved on trip to Rome, 144; popular with Romans, 147; bonnet for, 149; behaviour in Rome, 152; struck by whip, 155; weather becoming too cool for, 159; whip mark gone, 160; has cold, 164, is better, 167; has bronchitis, 168, is better, 169; his appetite, 171; Nora on growth of, 173; cost of food of, 175; first words, 188; mentioned by Nora, 197; described by J, 206; weaned, 209; new clothes of, 213; J's fondness for, 215; will not starve, 219; grandfather wants picture of, 223, 228; to go to Dublin, 225–26, with Stanislaus, 226; in Dublin with J, 230; not going to Galway, 231; J's anxiety over, 232; to sleep in same room as Eva Joyce, 234, 244, 251; needs half ticket for return trip, 246, 247; J sends love to, 254; will always be foreigner in Ireland, 255; J regards as his image, 257; J greets in letter, 259; J wants to save from eviction, 265; Nora to find bed for, 276; J informs of return, 280, 282; sent book by Roberts, 287; grandfather wants to see, 291; with Maria Kirn at farm, 293–94; Yeats gives fruit to, 298; with J in Galway, 302–303; J sends love to, 308; May Joyce asks about, 383; does not remember Martha Fleischmann, 430; greets Stanislaus, 446; marriage of, 6, 208; to work in office, 8–9. 10, 17; birthday of, 12; coached by J in correspondence work, 22; given money by Dr Collins, 33; in Zurich, 45; with Hummel, 42, 46; McAlmon to give message to, 57; greeted by Stanislaus, 59; advises against flat, 78; J refers Miss Weaver to, 79; sings in concert, 82; citizenship of, 105; J obtains records for, 118–19, 120; portrait by Opffer of, 139; in Pyrenees, 178, 180; reads Budgen's article to J, 184; singing debut of, 189; at Déjeuner Ulysse, 191; grandfather to write to, 212; his marriage encourages

J to move, 215; helping J with Corti, 216, 219, 220; takes poems to printer, 236; with Kastors, 249 n; letter about Lucia sent to, 254–55; J sends poem to, 255, 256 n; alarmed by J's stomach pains, 276; wants to move to Vienna, 286; J pleased by singing of, 294; sails for U.S.A., 306; has sold his Rolls-Royce, 305; friendly with Jolas, 307; told not to cable Lucia, 309; sad letter to J from, 312; in New York, 313; J informs of Lucia's condition, 318, and of other matters, 320–21; encouraged by J, 326–27; urged to see Sanborn, 328; suggestions for repertoire of, 332, 334–36, 341, 342–43, 344, 345–46, 348; sings in New York, 333; J stores pictures and books of, 347; photographs of, 352; is well, 353; J pleads Lucia's case with, 370, 371; allusion by Stanislaus to, 382, 383; illness of, 384, 386; operation on, 385; is stronger, 391; J describes to Nutting, 400; J sends book to, 402; goes to New York, 410; and Radio Luxembourg, 411; informed about Beckett, 412; may not return as planned, 418; return of, 419, 421, 423; sings for CBS, 420, 423; difficulties of, 423–24; advised by J, 425; reads Gorman's MS, 426; J sends songs to, 427; Rogers to help, 443; attacks on in U.S.A., 447; has audition at BBC, 450; asked to find out Delmas's plans, 454; tension with Helen, 455 n; anguish over Helen, 458, 463; in Paris, 461; living with relative of Léon, 465; keeps Stephen, 465; coming to Saint-Gérand, 469; J unsure of address of, 476; taking Stephen to Lausanne, 481; not conscriptable for French army, 503; called to father's death bed, 507 n

Joyce, Helen Kastor Fleischman (Mrs George Joyce), married to George, 6, 208; greeted by J, 95, 322, 346, 359; at Déjeuner Ulysse, 191; pregnancy of, 240; sister of Robert Kastor, 241; first son of, 255 n; painting of by Marchand, 280; is well, 305; sails for U.S.A., 306; her cousin in Paris, 312; J's answer to, 315–16; still in New York, 333; her father better, 341, 347; flat of, 351; may need throat surgery, 359; illness of her father, 363; asks J to write in English, 379; is tired, 391; J writes about her flat to, 401; illness of her brother, 405; goes to New York, 410, 412; return of, 419, 420, 421; encouraged by J, 425; is better, 426; has breakdown, 7, 438; going to country, 454; tension with George,

Léger, Fernand, J at studio of, **304**; on Lucia's work, **320**

Lenehan (character in 'Two Gallants' and *Ulysses*), J compares to Ibsen's characters, 183

Lennon, Michael J., helps J with Sullivan, **207, 214**; attacks J in *Catholic World*, **235–36, 240, 403, 443**

Leo XIII, J's parody of his prayer, 210

Léon, Lucie (Mme Paul Léon) (Lucie Noël), friendship with J, **6**; at *William Tell* with J, **413–14**; at Saint-Gérand, **461**

Léon, Paul L., friendship with J, **6**; helps translate *Anna Livia Plurabelle*, **209** n; copy of *Four* to be returned to, **233**; J reports on eyesight to, **248–49**; discusses film of *Ulysses*, **262–63**; writes Miss Weaver about J's problems, **267–68, 269–71, 271–72, 276–78, 285–87**; strained relations with J's family, **278**; writes Budgen for J, **279–80**; writes Morley for J, **289**; writes Gorman about plan of *Ulysses*, **291, 296, 300**; with Eliot and J, **293**; J receives letters through, **302**; intercedes for Pinker, **308**; knows J's number, **310**; sends MSS to Miss Weaver, **311**; at Fouquet's, **312**; calls for *Ulysses* decision, **315**; suggests J cable to George, **318**; letters returned to, **320**; wires advice to J, **325**; cables Cerf, **328**; to read proofs of *Finnegans Wake*, **384**; Carlow to telephone to, **406**; not often with J, **409**; notes on Sullivan, **413–14**; reports J's mistreatment by Swiss hotel, **416–17**; J with sisters of, **420**; sending copy of *Europe*, **423**; writes Gorman for J, **443–44, 447**; asked to help with Delmas, **453–54**; J's coolness towards, **455** n; hears *Sunday Times* opposed to *Finnegans Wake*, **456**; corrects *Finnegans Wake* with J, **461**

Leonardo da Vinci, his way of writing notes, 194

Lepracaun, The, J disturbed by issue of, **91**; J receives copy of, **189**; J sends copy to Stanislaus, 195

Lermontov, Mikhail Yurevitch, on Rousseau, 106; *Hero of Our Days* compared with *Stephen Hero* by J, 111

Leslie, Shane, controversy with Gogarty, **70**

Lester, Sears, J telephones for help to, **502**

Letters of James Joyce (Vol. I), *see* Gilbert, Stuart, editor of

Leventhal, A. J., reviews *Ulysses*, 88

Lever, Charles, his 'The Man for Galway', 294

Levi, Simeone, limerick on, **406**; subscribes to *Egoist*, 417

Levin, Harry, edits Svevo-Joyce correspondence, **98** n, **136** n, **143** n, **172** n, **439** n; his review of *Finnegans Wake* the best, **464, 466, 468, 470**

Lewis, Wyndham, Pound sells pictures of, 385; painting in army, 414; annoyed by Pound's view of *Tarr*, 423; J tries to have *Tarr* reviewed, 437; compared to J by Pound, 471; attacks J in 1927, **5, 6**; describes first meeting with J, **14**; subsequent meetings, **17**; Budgen told to see, **42, 46, 50**; edits *Tyro*, **60**; press copy of *Ulysses* to, **69**; on *Ulysses*, **103**; J's idea about Lewis as part of Pound group, **118**; plans to publish some of *Finnegans Wake* in *The Enemy*, **142**; signs protest against *Ulysses* piracy, **153**; *Childermass* compared to *Ulysses*, **173**; attacks J in *Enemy*, **188** n; J asks price of *Apes of God*, **205**; J alludes to, **230**; J's comment on attacks by, **250**; may subscribe to *Pomes Penyeach*, **252**; J mentions politics of, **311**; drawing of J by, **408**

Lewisohn, Alice and Irene, produce *Exiles*, 80

Lewisohn, Ludwig, helps write protest against piracy of *Ulysses*, **151** n; signs it, **153**

Lichtensteiger, Nelly, *see* Joyce, Nelly L.

Lidwell, John G., J's solicitor in Dublin, **289**; helping J with Roberts, **301, 303, 304**; letter regarding *Dubliners* from, **306** n; legal advice of, **307**; another letter, **308, 309**; J in office of, **311** n; J badly treated, **312**; J's father makes new will because of death of, **457**

Liffey Press, J to publish *Dubliners* under this imprint, 317

Lily of Killarney, The (opera), film about, **373** n, **379**

Linati, Carlo, translates J, **437** n, **447**; J sends *Exiles* for translation to, **456–57, 459, 460, 462, 463**; J sends 'A Memory of the Players ...' to, **462**; Pound offers to publish work of, **469–70**; gets rooms for J, **8**; no news of, **75, 128**; may have Schmitz's lecture, **190**; translates Yeats, **195**; J writes to thank, **473**; J gives address of to Stanislaus, **507**

Lir, daughters of, mentioned by J, **339–40, 341** n

Litany of Loreto, quoted by J, 436

Literary and Historical Society, J reads paper at, 3–4

Literary World, The, J submits 'Clay' to, 100; receives no reply, 109

Senigaglia, Dr Gilberto, delivers Giorgio, 101

Serafin, Tullio, and John Sullivan, **200**

Sermini, Gentile, J reading, 212

Serpentine (Hyde Park), and Nora J's plight, 96

Serravallo family, Eileen Joyce working for, 295

Serruys, Jenny, *see* Bradley, Jenny Serruys

Servire Press, wishes to publish *A Chaucer A. B. C.*, **317**; J sends *lettrines* to, **325**

Settanni, Ettore, and translation of *Anna Livia*, **468, 469, 471**; thanked by J, **473**; J's letter to in next issue, **475, 476**; J gives address of to Stanislaus, **507**

Seven Arts, The, Pound suggests may publish J, 386, 387

Shakespeare, William, J on, 4; in J's history of English literature, 90; Stanislaus compares to J, 115; Dowland a friend of, 258; Bleibtreu's theory of, 415; J compares his age to age of, 432, 433 n; Shaw's *Dark Lady of the Sonnets*, 453 n; Larbaud compares Bloom and Falstaff, **39 n**; allusion by Stanislaus to, **58**; allusion to *Hamlet*, **111**; Lear related to Lir, **340**; mocking allusion to, **344**; joke about *Hamlet*, **387 n**

Shakespeare and Company, opened by Sylvia Beach, **12**; publishes *Ulysses*, **3, 242**; Miss Moschos in, **60 n**; Cecchi to send review to, **75**; publishing and printing, **85**; royalty to J, **93**; publishes *Pomes Penyeach* and *Exagmination*, **243**; Miss Weaver on, **299**

Sharp, Cecil James, J orders copy of his *Book of British Song for Home and School*, 21

Shaun (character in *Finnegans Wake*), compared to Charles Joyce by J, **107**

Shaun the Post, see Finnegans Wake

Shaw, Bernard, derided by J, 203; production at Abbey of *The Shewing-Up of Blanco Posnet*, 236; J to attend, 238; J's article on play, 240, 252; copy of article sent to, 250; changes mind about *Exiles*, 411 n, 460; English Players give plays by, 425, 439; J's 'Open Letter' sent to, 441; his rights infringed by English Players, 452–53, 454; comments on *Ulysses*, **50, 51, 58**; congratulated by J on Nobel Prize, 146; refuses to sign *Ulysses* protest, **150 n**; J explains not using name of, **228**; fails to answer Lucia, **250**; invites J to join Irish Academy, **258, 261, 265**; denies being disgusted by *Ulysses*, **444**

Shawe-Taylor, Captain John, in Galway election, 190

'She Weeps over Rahoon' (in *Pomes Penyeach*), apparent reference to, 309; published in *Poetry*, 403 n

Sheehan, Daniel T., at debate on Synge's *Playboy*, 211, 212; meets J in Dublin, 231

Sheehan, W., will sing J's songs, 271

Sheehy, David, not model for Fulham in *Stephen Hero*, 79; his daughter Margaret, 80 n; joins Sheehy-Skeffington in attacking 'God Save the King', 186; did not invite J, 238, 244; snubs J, 262

Sheehy, Kathleen, marries Cruise O'Brien, 238

Sheehy, Margaret, J asks if married, 80

Sheehy, Mary, marries Kettle, 238

Sheehy, Richard, anecdote of, 191; at debate on Synge's *Playboy*, 211; death of, **81–82**

Sheehy-Skeffington, Francis, J annoyed with, 28; invites J to teach French, 41; mocking reference to, 73; J asks about, 80; J is working him into *Stephen Hero*, 80; called impostor by J, 81; J says he will repay, 85; in a bad way, J thinks, 89; to receive 'The Holy Office', 91; thinks woman man's equal, 96; found insufferable by J, 97; Cosgrave to inform on Giorgio's birth, 103; called a brisk idiot by J, 107; wife not pregnant, 125; on *Dialogues of the Day*, 153; J misses *Dialogues of the Day*, 165; attacked as mountebank, 167; protests playing of 'God Save the King', 186; J on his sexual purity, 191; at debate on Synge's *Playboy*, 211; meets J in Dublin, 231; has son, 238; J sends news of, 300; J did not run against, **400**

Sheehy-Skeffington, Mrs Hanna, on J's appearance, 231

Shelley, Harriet, compared to Nora J, 96 n

Shelley, Percy Bysshe, Archer refers to, 10; in J's history of English literature, 90; J sees Roman house of, 144; J on sexual life of, 191; J sees granddaughter of, 194

Shem the Penman, see Finnegans Wake

Shine and Dark, J's early lyrics, 4

Ship (public house), J sends gloves from, 258

'Shule Aroon,' J sends words of to George, **336**

Sidler-Huguenin, Dr Ernst, operates on J, 405

'Silent, O Moyle,' explained by J, **339–40**

Silhouettes, J's early prose sketches, 3

belle, **209 n**; advises J on American publication of *Ulysses*, **232–33**; negotiating with Budgen, **296**; expelled from Germany, **319**; reports on George's affairs to J, **344**, **351**; off to U.S.A., **359**; in Canary Islands, **366**, **369**; at party, **414**

Speaker, The, Yeats offers to get J work on, 17; Yeats sees editor of, 19; Yeats fails to see editor, 23–24; J plans to write for, 25–26; editor asks review of Ibsen's *Catalina*, 26; J awaiting payment, 28; no news from, 29; proofs of *Catalina* review, 31; article not yet published, 34; Synge comments on, 35; J worried about article, 36; article still not published, 36; J waiting to be paid by, 38; review appears, 39; no news from, 40; prints *Chamber Music*, vi, 69; J wants copy of, 70, 71; J to spend cheque on teeth, 73; J's concern over payment from, 76, 78, 81, 82, 83; Stanislaus thinks J should write for, 117; J has written for, 219

Speck-Heinz, Dr Else, helping Stanislaus, **397**

Spectator, The, derided by Pound, 326

Spicer-Simson, Theodore, invitation to J, 284–85; J informs of expected publication of *Dubliners*, 284; wants to do portrait of J, **66**

Spielberg, Peter, allusion to his *James Joyce's Manuscripts . . .*, **245**

Spinoza, Baruch, Synge compares J's mind to, 35

Spitteler, Carl, wins Nobel Prize, **30**

Spoerri, James F., on best edition of *Ulysses*, **259**

Sporting Times, The, attack on *Ulysses* in, **74**

Squire, Sir John Collings, review of *Dubliners*, 336 n; invites J to write for *New Statesman*, 393; J thanks for review of *A Portrait*, 394; J's 'Open Letter' sent to, 441

Stack, William, role in *Exiles* of, **137**

Stage Society, Pound recommends to produce *Exiles*, 366; considers it, 374; rejects it, 392; uncertain about it, 394, 398 n; possibly to produce it, 411, 415, 418, 419; refuses, 447; J's summary of relations with, 460; to produce *Exiles*, **124, 126**

Stampa, La (Turin), refuses to review *A Portrait*, 397

Stanford, Villiers, songs by, **343**; 'Father O'Flynn' by, **379**

Starkey, James S. (Seumas O'Sullivan), asked to rescue J's belongings from

Martello Tower, 53; J asks for help to leave Ireland, 59; in George Russell's group, 78 n; J asks Stanislaus if *The Twilight People* is good, 86; poems in *Sinn Féin*, 170; J on verse of, 189; his imagined response to J's work in Rome, 199; poem in *Sinn Féin*, 209; signs protest against *Ulysses* piracy, **153**

Stein, Gertrude, on J's poverty, **55 n**; linked by Lewis with J, **188 n**; compared to J by Stanislaus, **216**; sponsored by Cerf, **351**

Steinberg, Dr S. D., helping Stanislaus, **397**

Steiner, Ignazio, J sends tweed samples to, 260, 261; no word from, 263–64, 267

Steinhardt, Dr, messmate of Sykes, 409 n

Stendhal (Marie Henri Beyle), Pound compares J to, 359, 364

Stephen Hero, J writes Chapters XII to XXIV, 63; reconstructed as *A Portrait of the Artist*, 64; J has finished Ch. XII, 67, 68–69; end of Ch. XI written in Zurich, 71; J's discontent with, 71; half of Ch. XIII written, 72; J reads Ch. XI to Nora, 73; Ch. XIII finished, 74; J to send chapters to Stanislaus, is working on Ch. XV, 75–76; writing Ch. XVI, 76; epiphanies copied into, 78; J replies to Stanislaus's criticism of, 79; writing Ch. XVI, 80; writing Ch. XVII, 81; writing Ch. XVIII, 82; J thinks of changing title of, 83; to end with exile, 84; has finished Ch. XVIII, 86; has finished Ch. XIX and XX, 87; has finished Ch. XXI, 88; writing Ch. XXII, 89; J wants chapters back, 90; J comments on title of, 90; has finished Ch. XXIV, 91; J likes love scene in, 93; Cosgrave's comments on, 103–104; J compares to Lermontov's *Hero of Our Days*, 111; J doesn't want Curran to lend MS, 113–14; Cosgrave unable to comment on, 125; 914 pages written, 132; Mrs Murray wants J to continue, 139; J hopes to finish in Rome, 140; J unable to complete, 177–78, 179–80; rewritten as *A Portrait*, 234 n; Emma Clery in, 238

Stephens, Edward, author (with David Greene), of Synge biography, 34 n

Stephens, James, J on two stories in *Sinn Féin* by, 260; another story, 261; Yeats compares to J, 361; asked by J to finish *Finnegans Wake*, **6**; slow to sign *Ulysses* protest, **150**; signs it, **153**; J's plan that Stephens finish *Finnegans Wake*, **161**, and Stephens's reply, **169**; J secures invitation for, **177**; J hopes to make disc

580 GENERAL INDEX

legal prospects of, **298, 300–301**; sales of, **302, 303**; Matisse to illustrate, **304, 317, 332**; J troubled about government appeal of decision, **308, 311, 313**; favourable decision, **314–15, 316, 318**; English edition, **318, 321, 341, 365, 368 n, 389**; possible appeal to Supreme Court, **320, 328**; English royalty on, **322–23**; filming of, **325**; Antheil's unwritten opera of, **344**; Sylvia Beach's rights to, **345**; price of first edition at auction, **351**; Cerf said to be neglecting, **351**; film scenario for, **358**; J to sign Yeats's copy, **384**; Odyssey Press edition, **391**; Stanislaus unable to publicize any more, **392**; Thomas Devin as 'Mr Power' in, **399**; copy of to Lennon, **403**; influences Mlle Suzy, **415**; J on labours at, **415**; praised by O'Casey, **442**; Shaw's attitude toward, **444**; article on, **464**; *see also* Bloomsday

Telemachus: 'Ballad of Joking Jesus' in, 126–27; Stephen's estimate of Mulligan, 187 n; Mulligan on Stephen's mother, 206 n; Stephen on free thought, 218 n; Pound comments on phrases in, 414; in Italian, **240**; Latin mass quoted in, **284**

Nestor: Price as model for Mr Deasy, 286, 300 n; Sir John Blackwood in, 300 n; changes in, 413, 415

Proteus: preparation for writing, 28 n; epiphany of Paris used in, 49 n; Joachim Abbas in, 148 n; Simon Dedalus mocks wife's relatives, 222 n; changes in, 416; Budgen to paint scene from, **193**

Lotus Eaters: Martha Clifford's letter, 268 n

Hades: a model for funeral in, 32 n

Aeolus: J records Taylor's speech in, **111 n, 118, 142 n**; allusion to, **262 n**

Lestrygonians: censored in New York, 448 n

Scylla and Charybdis: reference to J's review of Lady Gregory, 38 n; theory of paternity in, 108 n; Dr Best in, 110; Miss Weaver on, 436; censored in New York, 448 n; J offers to explain, **73**

Wandering Rocks: Thomas Devin in, 66; Conmee on Countess of Belvedere, 193; J sends to Pound, 436; Henry and James in, **68**

Sirens: Lidwell in, 301 n; reference to use of Greek e's in, 347, 431; J finishing, 436; delayed, 440; mentioned, **13**

Cyclops: J calls printer 'one-eyed', 133; Cusack model for 'Citizen' in, 210 n; J writing, 451, 452 n; sent to

Pound, 455; allusion to, **18**; changes in, **55**; Antheil's setting of, **131**; Bergan in, **252**

Nausikaa: and Martha Fleischmann, 428, 431; finished, **458**; *Little Review* confiscated because of, **27, 28, 29, 30, 33, 39**; underclothes in, **280**

Oxen of the Sun: J writing, 458, 459; completed, 464, 465, 466; J comments on, **16**; published, **33**; parody of Newman, not Ruskin, in, **365**

Circe: 'Ballad of Joking Jesus' in, 126–27; progressing, **9, 11, 24**; difficulties with, **15**; allusion to, **18**; written six times, **19**, five times, **21**; J writing final version, **26, 30, 31, 32, 35, 38, 43, 51**; new scene in, **53**; Stanislaus on, **104–105**

Eumaeus: completed, **38**; Johannes Jeep quoted in, **448 n**

Ithaca: Bloom's ideal home in, 97 n; orientation of Blooms in bed, 202 n; J writing, **39, 43, 45, 46, 48, 49, 51, 52**

Penelope: original of Mulvey in, 72 n; coprophilia, 274 n; J writing, **39**; sent to Budgen, **48**; sent to printers, **49, 51**; sent to Larbaud, **51**; sent to McAlmon, **57**; Jung on, **253**; rhododendrons in, **398 n**

'Ulysses' (story), first mentioned by J, 168; J thought of beginning, 190; J pleased with title, 193; hasn't written, 209

Unicorn Press, J's instructions about, 20; Stanislaus to write at once to, 35

United Irishman, J mocks over Maud Gonne MacBride, 85; notice of Gogarty's marriage in, 149–50; J speaks favourably of, 157–58; copy of to Stanislaus, 164; J sends copy to Stanislaus, 195

United States, George goes to, **306**, and again, **410**; may not return, **418**; George attacked in because of father, **447**; *see also* Americans

Università del Popolo (Trieste), J's lectures at, 220 n; needs testimonial from, 234; J meets Mazzoni at, 323 n

Università di Trieste, J invited to teach at, 446 n; back salary at, **10**; expulsion of Stanislaus from, **381–83, 387–88, 392**

University College, Dublin, Dean of studies at, 28; overture to J, 41; J writing about, 76; J expects to finish writing about, 89; made part of National University, 155 n; O'Brien in Debating Society, 205; Sheehan at, 211 n; J's degree not equivalent to Italian, 294 n; J's degree from, 354, 358

Unwin, T. Fisher, rejected *Chamber Music*, 107

'Upa-Upa,' music of by Pierre Loti, 30